Behavioral Genetics

Behavioral Genetics

SEVENTH EDITION

Valerie S. Knopik
Rhode Island Hospital and Brown University

Jenae M. Neiderhiser
Penn State University

John C. DeFries
University of Colorado, Boulder

Robert Plomin
Institute of Psychiatry, Psychology and Neuroscience, London

worth publishers
Macmillan Learning
New York

Vice President, Editorial, Sciences and Social Sciences: Charles Linsmeier
Senior Associate Editor: Sarah Berger
Editorial Assistant: Melissa Rostek
Senior Marketing Manager: Lindsay Johnson
Marketing Assistant: Morgan Ratner
Executive Media Editor: Noel Hohnstine
Media Editor: Jessica Lauffer
Director, Content Management Enhancement: Tracey Kuehn
Managing Editor, Sciences and Social Sciences: Lisa Kinne
Senior Project Editor: Elizabeth Geller
Media Producer: Joseph Tomasso
Senior Production Supervisor: Stacey Alexander
Photo Editor: Sheena Goldstein
Director of Design, Content Management: Diana Blume
Interior Design: Patrice Sheridan
Cover Design: Blake Logan
Art Manager: Matthew McAdams
Composition: Jouve North America
Printing and Binding: RR Donnelley
Cover Photo: ozgurdonmaz/Getty Images

Library of Congress Control Number: 2016943660

ISBN-13: 978-1-4641-7605-0
ISBN-10: 1-4641-7605-1

Worth Publishers
One New York Plaza
Suite 4500
New York, NY 10004-1562
www.macmillanlearning.com

Contents

About the Authors

VALERIE S. KNOPIK is Director of the Division of Behavioral Genetics at Rhode Island Hospital and a professor in the Departments of Psychiatry & Human Behavior and Behavioral & Social Sciences at the Warren Alpert School of Medicine at Brown University. She received her doctorate in psychology from the University of Colorado, Boulder, in 2000, where she worked with John DeFries and conducted research in the Colorado Learning Disabilities Research Center. She subsequently completed a fellowship in psychiatric genetics and genetic epidemiology at Washington University School of Medicine in St. Louis from 2000 to 2002 and continued as junior faculty for two years. She joined the faculty at Brown University in 2004 and holds an adjunct associate professor appointment at Washington University School of Medicine in St. Louis. Knopik's primary area of interest is the joint effect of genetic and environmental (specifically prenatal and early postnatal) risk factors on child and adolescent externalizing behavior, associated learning and cognitive deficits, and later substance use. She is currently conducting a family study, the Missouri Mothers and Their Children Study, that is designed to disentangle prenatal environmental effects from genetic effects on child and adolescent behavior. Her work has been recognized by the Research Society for Alcoholism; the NIDA Genetics Workgroup; and the Behavior Genetics Association, from whom she received the Fuller and Scott Early Career Award in 2007. She was the secretary of the Behavior Genetics Association (2013–2016), currently serves as an associate editor of *Behavior Genetics*, and is on the editorial board of *Psychological Medicine*.

JENAE M. NEIDERHISER is Liberal Arts Research Professor of Psychology at Penn State University. After receiving her PhD in Human Development and Family Studies from Penn State University in 1994, she joined the faculty of the Center for Family Research, Department of Psychiatry and Behavioral Science, at The George Washington University in Washington, DC, advancing from assistant research professor to professor from 1994 to 2007. In 2007 she joined the Department of Psychology at Penn State University, and she also holds the appointment of Professor of Human Development and Family Studies and is co-director of the Gene and Environment Research Initiative at Penn State University. Neiderhiser's work has focused on how genes and environments work together throughout the life span. She has had a particular focus on genotype-environment correlation and how individuals shape their own environments, especially within the family. In her pursuit of this question she has collaborated on developing a number of novel or underutilized research designs, including the extended children of twins design and an ongoing prospective adoption study, the Early Growth and Development Study. Neiderhiser is an associate editor for *Frontiers in Behavioral and Psychiatric Genetics* and is on the editorial board of several developmental psychology journals.

JOHN C. DEFRIES is a faculty fellow, Institute for Behavioral Genetics, and professor emeritus, Department of Psychology and Neuroscience, University of Colorado, Boulder. After receiving his doctorate in agriculture (with specialty training in quantitative genetics) from the University of Illinois in 1961, he remained on the faculty of the University of Illinois for six years. In 1962, he began research on mouse behavioral genetics, and the following year he was a research fellow in genetics at the University of California, Berkeley. After returning to Illinois in 1964, DeFries initiated an extensive genetic analysis of open-field behavior in laboratory mice. Three years later, he joined the Institute for Behavioral Genetics, and he served as its director from 1981 to 2001. DeFries and Steve G. Vandenberg founded the journal *Behavior Genetics* in 1970, and DeFries and Robert Plomin founded the Colorado Adoption Project in 1975. For over three decades, DeFries' major research interest has concerned the genetics of reading disabilities, and he founded the Colorado Learning Disabilities Research Center with Richard K. Olson in 1990. He served as president of the Behavior Genetics Association in 1982 and 1983, receiving the association's Th. Dobzhansky Award for Outstanding Research in 1992, and he became a fellow of the American Association for the Advancement of Science (Section J, Psychology) in 1994 and the Association for Psychological Science in 2009.

ROBERT PLOMIN is MRC Research Professor of Behavioral Genetics at the Social, Genetic and Developmental Psychiatry Centre at the Institute of Psychiatry, Psychology and Neuroscience in London. He received his doctorate in psychology from the University of Texas, Austin, in 1974, one of the few graduate programs in psychology that offered a specialty in behavioral genetics at that time. He then joined the faculty of the Institute for Behavioral Genetics at the University of Colorado, Boulder, where he began working with John DeFries. Together, they created the longitudinal Colorado Adoption Project of behavioral development, which has continued for more than 30 years. Plomin worked at Penn State University from 1986 until 1994, when he moved to the Institute of Psychiatry, Psychology and Neuroscience in London to help launch the Social, Genetic and Developmental Psychiatry Centre. The goal of his research is to bring together genetic and environmental research strategies to investigate behavioral development. Plomin launched a study of all twins born in England during 1994 to 1996, focusing on developmental delays in childhood. He served as secretary (1983–1986) and president (1989–1990) of the Behavior Genetics Association, and has received lifetime achievement awards from the Behavior Genetics Association (2002), American Psychological Society (2005), the Society for Research in Child Development (2005), and the International Society for Intelligence Research (2011).

Preface

S ome of the most important scientific accomplishments of the twentieth century occurred in the field of genetics, beginning with the rediscovery of Mendel's laws of heredity and ending with the first draft of the complete DNA sequence of the human genome. The pace of discoveries has continued to accelerate in the first part of the twenty-first century. One of the most dramatic developments in the behavioral sciences during the past few decades is the increasing recognition and appreciation of the important contribution of genetic factors to behavior. Genetics is not a neighbor chatting over the fence with some helpful hints—it is central to the behavioral sciences. In fact, genetics is central to all the life sciences and gives the behavioral sciences a place in the biological sciences. Genetic research includes diverse strategies, such as twin and adoption studies (called quantitative genetics), which investigate the influence of genetic and environmental factors, as well as strategies to identify specific genes (called molecular genetics). Behavioral geneticists apply these research strategies to the study of behavior in biopsychology, clinical psychology, cognitive psychology, developmental psychology, educational psychology, neuroscience, psychopharmacology, and social psychology, and increasingly in other areas of the social sciences such as behavioral economics and political science.

The goal of this book is to share with you our excitement about behavioral genetics, a field in which we believe some of the most important discoveries in the behavioral sciences have been made in recent years. This seventh edition continues to emphasize what we know about genetics in the behavioral sciences rather than how we know it. Its goal is not to train students to become behavioral geneticists but rather to introduce students in the behavioral, social, and life sciences to the field of behavioral genetics.

This seventh edition represents a passing of the baton to the next generation. Two new and younger authors (Knopik and Neiderhiser) have joined forces with two authors from the previous editions (Plomin and DeFries), which has brought new energy and ideas that help to capture developments in this fast-moving and highly interdisciplinary field. In addition to updating research with more than 600 new references, this edition represents a substantial reorganization. One feature of this edition is that it continues to highlight the value of behavioral genetics for understanding the environment (Chapter 7) and its interplay with genetics (Chapter 8). At first, chapters on the environment might seem odd in a textbook on genetics, but in fact the environment is crucial at every step in the pathways between genes, brain, and behavior. One of the oldest controversies in the behavioral sciences, the so-called nature (genetics) versus nurture (environment) controversy, has given way to a view that both nature and nurture are important for complex behavioral traits. Moreover, genetic research has made important discoveries about how the environment affects behavioral development.

We have also expanded our coverage of genomewide sequencing, gene expression, and especially epigenetics as pathways between genes and behavior (Chapter 10). Our review of cognitive abilities includes a new section on neurocognitive measures (Chapter 11). Coverage of psychopathology and substance abuse has been expanded (Chapters 13, 14, 15, and 17), a new section on obesity and the microbiome has been included (Chapter 18), and a new chapter on aging has been added (Chapter 19), reflecting the enormous growth of genetic research in these areas. We have also reorganized the presentation of the history of the field of behavioral genetics (Chapter 2).

We begin with an introductory chapter that will, we hope, whet your appetite for learning about genetics in the behavioral sciences. The next few chapters present historical perspectives, the basic rules of heredity, its DNA basis, and the methods used to find genetic influence and to identify specific genes. The rest of the book highlights what is known about genetics in the behavioral sciences. The areas about which the most is known are cognitive abilities and disabilities, psychopathology, personality, and substance abuse. We also consider areas of behavioral sciences that were introduced to genetics more recently, such as health psychology and aging. Throughout these chapters, quantitative genetics and molecular genetics are interwoven. One of the most exciting developments in behavioral genetics is the use of molecular genetics to assess the substantial genetic influence on behavioral traits. The final chapter looks to the future of behavioral genetics.

Because behavioral genetics is an interdisciplinary field that combines genetics and the behavioral sciences, it is complex. We have tried to write about it as simply as possible without sacrificing honesty of presentation. Although our coverage is representative, it is by no means exhaustive or encyclopedic. History and methodology are relegated to boxes and an appendix to keep the focus on what we now know about genetics and behavior. The appendix, by Shaun Purcell, presents an overview of statistics, quantitative genetic theory, and a type of quantitative genetic analysis called model fitting. In this edition we have retained an interactive website that brings the appendix to life with demonstrations: http://pngu.mgh.harvard.edu/purcell/bgim/. The website was designed and written by Shaun Purcell. A list of other useful websites, including those of relevant associations, databases, and other resources, is included after the appendix. Following the websites list is a glossary; the first time each glossary entry appears in the text it is shown in boldface type.

We thank the following individuals, who gave us their very helpful advice for this new edition: Avshalom Caspi, *Duke University;* Thalia Eley, *King's College London;* John McGeary, *Providence VA Medical Center;* Rohan Palmer, *Rhode Island Hospital and Brown University;* Nancy Pedersen, *Karolinska Institute;* Chandra Reynolds, *University of California, Riverside;* Helen Tam, *Pennsylvania State University.*

We also gratefully acknowledge the important contributions of the coauthors of the previous editions of this book: Gerald E. McClearn, Michael Rutter, and Peter McGuffin. We especially wish to thank Ashten Bartz, who helped us organize the revision and references and prepare the final manuscript. Finally, we thank our editors at Worth Publishers, Sarah Berger and Christine M. Cardone, our Worth editorial assistant, Melissa Rostek, and the Senior Project Editor, Liz Geller, who helped support our efforts in this new edition.

CHAPTER **ONE**

Overview

S ome of the most important recent discoveries about behavior involve genetics. For example, autism (Chapter 15) is a severe disorder beginning early in childhood in which children withdraw socially, not engaging in eye contact or physical contact, with marked communication deficits and stereotyped behavior. Until the 1980s, autism was thought to be environmentally caused by cold, rejecting parents or by brain damage. But genetic studies comparing the risk for identical twins, who are identical genetically (like clones), and fraternal twins, who are only 50 percent similar genetically, indicate substantial genetic influence. If one member of an identical twin pair is autistic, the risk that the other twin is also autistic is very high, about 60 percent. In contrast, for fraternal twins, the risk is low. Molecular genetic studies are attempting to identify the **genes*** that contribute to the genetic susceptibility to autism.

Later in childhood, a very common concern, especially in boys, is a cluster of attention-deficit and disruptive behavior problems called attention-deficit/ hyperactivity disorder (ADHD) (Chapter 15). Results obtained from numerous twin studies have shown that ADHD is highly heritable (genetically influenced). ADHD is one of the first behavioral areas in which specific genes have been identified. Although many other areas of childhood psychopathology show genetic influence, none are as heritable as autism and ADHD. Some behavior problems, such as childhood anxiety and depression, are only moderately heritable, and others, such as antisocial behavior in adolescence, show little genetic influence.

More relevant to college students are personality traits such as risk-taking (often called sensation seeking) (Chapter 16), drug use and abuse (Chapter 17), and learning abilities (Chapters 11). All these domains have consistently shown substantial genetic

* Boldface indicates the first appearance in the text of a word or phrase that is in the Glossary.

influence in twin studies and have recently begun to yield clues concerning individual genes that contribute to their **heritability**. These domains are also examples of an important general principle: Not only do genes contribute to disorders such as autism and ADHD, they also play an important role in normal variation. For example, you might be surprised to learn that differences in weight are almost as heritable as differences in height (Chapter 18). Even though we can control how much we eat and are free to go on crash diets, differences among us in weight are much more a matter of nature (genetics) than nurture (environment). Moreover, normal variation in weight is as highly heritable as overweight or obesity. The same story can be told for behavior. Genetic differences do not just make some of us abnormal; they contribute to differences among all of us in normal variation for mental health, personality, and cognitive abilities.

One of the greatest genetic success stories involves the most common behavioral disorder in later life, the terrible memory loss and confusion of Alzheimer disease, which strikes as many as one in five individuals in their eighties (Chapter 19). Although Alzheimer disease rarely occurs before the age of 65, some early-onset cases of dementia run in families in a simple manner that suggests the influence of single genes. Three genes have been found to be responsible for many of these rare early-onset cases.

These genes for early-onset Alzheimer disease are not responsible for the much more common form of Alzheimer disease that occurs after 65 years of age. Like most behavioral disorders, late-onset Alzheimer disease is not caused by just a few genes. Still, twin studies indicate genetic influence. If you have a twin who has late-onset Alzheimer disease, your risk of developing it is twice as great if you are an identical twin rather than a fraternal twin. These findings suggest genetic influence.

Even for complex disorders like late-onset Alzheimer disease, it is now possible to identify genes that contribute to the risk for the disorder. For example, a gene has been identified that predicts risk for late-onset Alzheimer disease far better than any other known risk factor. If you inherit one copy of a particular form (**allele**) of the gene, your risk for Alzheimer disease is about four times greater than if you have another allele. If you inherit two copies of this allele (one from each of your parents), your risk is much greater. Finding these genes for early-onset and late-onset Alzheimer disease has greatly increased our understanding of the brain processes that lead to dementia.

Another example of recent genetic discoveries involves intellectual disability (Chapter 12). The single most important cause of intellectual disability is the inheritance of an entire extra **chromosome** 21. (Our **DNA**, the basic hereditary molecule, is packaged as 23 pairs of chromosomes, as explained in Chapter 4.) Instead of inheriting only one pair of chromosomes 21, one from the mother and one from the father, an entire extra chromosome is inherited, usually from the mother. Often called Down syndrome, trisomy-21 is one of the major reasons why women worry about pregnancy later in life. Down syndrome occurs much more frequently when mothers are over 40 years old. The extra chromosome can be detected early in pregnancy by a variety of procedures, including **amniocentesis,** chorionic villus sampling, and newer noninvasive methods that examine fetal DNA in the maternal bloodstream (Wagner, Mitchell, & Tomita-Mitchell, 2014).

Another gene has been identified that is the second most common cause of intellectual disability, called *fragile X syndrome.* The gene that causes the disorder is on the X chromosome. Fragile X syndrome occurs nearly twice as often in males as in females because males have only one X chromosome. If a boy has the fragile X allele on his X chromosome, he will develop the disorder. Females have two X chromosomes, and it is necessary to inherit the fragile X allele on both X chromosomes in order to develop the disorder. However, females with one fragile X allele can also be affected to some extent. The fragile X gene is especially interesting because it involves a type of genetic defect in which a short sequence of DNA mistakenly repeats hundreds of times. This type of genetic defect is now also known to be responsible for several other previously puzzling diseases (Chapter 12).

Genetic research on behavior goes beyond just demonstrating the importance of genetics to the behavioral sciences and allows us to ask questions about how genes influence behavior. For example, does genetic influence change during development? Consider cognitive ability, for example; you might think that as time goes by we increasingly accumulate the effects of Shakespeare's "slings and arrows of outrageous fortune." That is, environmental differences might become increasingly important during one's life span, whereas genetic differences might become less important. However, genetic research shows just the opposite: Genetic influence on cognitive ability increases throughout the individual's life span, reaching levels later in life that are nearly as great as the genetic influence on height (Chapter 11). This finding is an example of developmental behavioral genetic research.

School achievement and the results of tests you took to apply to college are influenced almost as much by genetics as are the results of tests of cognitive abilities such as intelligence (IQ) tests (Chapter 11). Even more interesting, the substantial overlap between such achievement and the ability to perform well on tests is nearly all genetic in origin. This finding is an example of what is called **multivariate genetic analysis.**

Genetic research is also changing the way we think about environment (Chapters 7 and 8). For example, we used to think that growing up in the same family makes brothers and sisters similar psychologically. However, for most behavioral dimensions and disorders, it is genetics that accounts for similarity among siblings. Although the environment is important, environmental influences can make siblings growing up in the same family different, not similar. This genetic research has fostered environmental research looking for the environmental reasons why siblings in the same family are so different.

Recent genetic research has also shown a surprising result that emphasizes the need to take genetics into account when studying environment: Many environmental measures used in the behavioral sciences show genetic influence! For example, research in developmental psychology often involves measures of parenting that are, reasonably enough, assumed to be measures of the family environment. However, genetic research has convincingly shown genetic influence on parenting measures. How can this be? One way is that genetic differences among parents influence their behavior toward their children. Genetic differences among children can also make a contribution. For example, parents who have more books in their home have children who do better in school, but this **correlation** does not necessarily mean that having more books in the home is an environmental cause for children performing well in school. Genetic factors could affect parental traits that relate both to the number of books parents have in their home and to their children's achievement at school. Genetic involvement has also been found for many other ostensible measures of the environment, including childhood accidents, life events, and social support. To some extent, people create their own experiences for genetic reasons (Chapter 8).

These are examples of what you will learn about in this book. The simple message is that genetics plays a major role in behavior. Genetics integrates the behavioral sciences into the life sciences. Although research in behavioral genetics has been conducted for many years, the field-defining text was published only in 1960 (Fuller & Thompson, 1960). Since that date, discoveries in behavioral genetics have grown at a rate that few other fields in the behavioral sciences can match. This growth is accelerating following the sequencing of the human **genome,** that is, identifying each of the more than 3 billion steps in the spiral staircase that is DNA, leading to the identification of the DNA differences among us that are responsible for the heritability of normal and abnormal behavior.

Recognition of the importance of genetics is one of the most dramatic changes in the behavioral sciences during the past several decades. Over 80 years ago, Watson's (1930) behaviorism detached the behavioral sciences from their budding interest in heredity. A preoccupation with the environmental determinants of behavior continued until the 1970s, when a shift began toward the more balanced contemporary view that recognizes genetic as well as environmental influences. This shift toward genetics in the behavioral sciences can be seen in the increasing number of publications on behavioral genetics. As shown in Figure 1.1, the increase in human behavioral genetic publications has been meteoric, with the numbers of publications doubling on average every five years since the 1990s. During the last five years, more than 2000 papers were published each year.

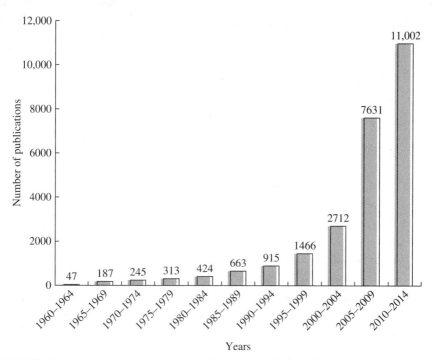

FIGURE 1.1 Numbers of human behavioral genetic papers published in five-year intervals since the field-defining textbook on behavioral genetics in 1960. Data from a resource of behavioral genetic papers (Ayorech et al., 2016).

CHAPTER TWO

Historical Perspective

Everyone can cite some examples in which some degree of talent, quality of temper, or other trait is characteristic of a family. Phrases like "a chip off the old block" and "it runs in the family" indicate a notion that behavioral traits, like physiological ones, can be inherited. The concept that "like begets like" has had great practical importance in the development of domesticated animals, which have been bred for behavioral as well as morphological characteristics (see Chapter 5). The notion of inheritance, including inheritance of behavioral traits, appeared in human thought tens of thousands of years ago, when the domestication of the dog began.

Biological thought during recorded history was dominated by Aristotle in the fourth century BC, and by the teachings of Galen, a Roman, concerning anatomy in the second century AD. Progress in understanding biological phenomena virtually halted during the Middle Ages from the fifth to the fifteenth century. Then came the Renaissance and Leonardo da Vinci's study of anatomy in connection with art. Leonardo's work characterized the far-ranging inquisitiveness of Renaissance scholars. However, it was the exhaustive work of Andreas Vesalius on human anatomy, published in 1543, and the discovery of the circulation of blood by William Harvey in 1628 that opened the doors to experimentation on the phenomena of life.

THE ERA OF DARWIN

After Harvey's discovery, the pace of biological research quickened and many fundamental developments in technique and theory ensued in the following century. One of the cornerstones of biology was laid by the Swede Karl von Linne (better known as Linneaus), who, in 1735, published *Systema Naturae,* in which he established a system of taxonomic classification of all known living things. In so doing, Linneaus emphasized the separateness and distinctness of species. As a result, the view that species were fixed and unchanging became the prevailing one. This was a view that fit the biblical account of creation. However, this was not the only perspective. For example, in the latter part of the eighteenth century the Englishman Erasmus Darwin suggested that plant and animal species appear capable of improvement, although he believed that God had so designed life. Another view was promoted by the Frenchman Jean Baptiste Lamarck, who argued that the deliberate efforts of an animal could result in modifications of the body parts involved, and that the modifications so acquired could be transmitted to the animal's offspring. Changes of this sort could accumulate, so that eventually the characteristics of the species would change. While Lamarck was not the first to assume that changes acquired in this manner could be transmitted to the next generation, he crystallized the notion. This view became known as Lamarckism, or the law of use and disuse. As we shall see, this is an incorrect view of evolution, but it was significant in that it questioned the prevailing view that species do not change.

Charles Darwin

One of the most influential books ever written, the 1859 *On the Origin of Species,* was authored by Erasmus Darwin's grandson, Charles Darwin (Figure 2.1). Darwin's famous 1831–1836 voyage around the world on the *Beagle* led him to observe the remarkable adaptations of species to their environments. For example, he made particularly compelling observations about 14 species of finches found in a small area on the Galápagos Islands. The principal differences among these finches were in their beaks, and each beak was exactly appropriate for the particular eating habits of the species (Figure 2.2).

FIGURE 2.1 Charles Darwin as a young man. (Fine Art / Corbis.)

FIGURE 2.2 The 14 species of finches in the Galápagos Islands and Cocos Island. (a) A woodpecker-like finch that uses a twig or cactus spine instead of its tongue to dislodge insects from tree-bark crevices. (b–e) Insect eaters. (f, g) Vegetarians. (h) The Cocos Island finch. (i–n) The birds on the ground eat seeds. Note the powerful beak of (i), which lives on hard seeds. (Reproduced with permission. Copyright © 1953 Scientific American, a division of Nature America, Inc. All rights reserved.)

Theology of the time proposed an "argument from design," which viewed the adaptation of animals and plants to the circumstances of their lives as evidence of the Creator's wisdom. Such exquisite design, so the argument went, implied a "Designer." Darwin was asked to serve as a naturalist on the surveying voyage of the *Beagle* in order to provide more examples for the "argument from design." However, during his voyage, Darwin began to realize that species, such as the Galápagos finches, were not designed once and for all. This realization led to his heretical theory that species evolve one from another: "Seeing this gradation and diversity of structure in one small, intimately related group of birds, one might really fancy that from an original paucity of birds in this archipelago, one species had been taken and modified for different ends" (Darwin, 1896, p. 380). For over 20 years after his voyage, Darwin gradually and systematically marshaled evidence for his theory of evolution.

Darwin's theory of evolution begins with variation within a population. Variation exists among individuals in a population due, at least in part, to heredity. If the likelihood of surviving to maturity and reproducing is influenced even to a slight degree by a particular trait, offspring of the survivors will show more of the trait than their parents' generation. In this way, generation after generation, the characteristics of a population can gradually change. Over a sufficiently long period, the cumulative changes can be so great that populations become different species, no longer capable of interbreeding successfully.

For example, the different species of finches that Darwin saw on the Galápagos Islands may have evolved because individuals in a progenitor species differed slightly in the size and shape of their beaks. Certain individuals with slightly more powerful beaks may have been more able to break open hard seeds. Such individuals could survive and reproduce when seeds were the main source of food. The beaks of other individuals may have been better at catching insects, and this shape gave those individuals a selective advantage at certain times. Generation after generation, these slight differences led to other differences, such as different habitats. For instance, seed eaters made their living on the ground and insect eaters lived in the trees. Eventually, the differences became so great that offspring of the seed eaters and insect eaters rarely interbred. Different species were born. A Pulitzer Prize–winning account of 25 years of repeated observations of Darwin's finches, *The Beak of the Finch* (Weiner, 1994), shows **natural selection** in action (see "Galapagos Finch Evolution": https://www.youtube.com/watch?v=mcM23M-CCog).

Although this is the way the story is usually told, another possibility is that behavioral differences in habitat preference led the way to the evolution of beaks rather than the other way around. That is, heritable individual differences in habitat preference may have existed that led some finches to prefer life on the ground and others to prefer life in the trees. The other differences, such as beak size and shape, may have been secondary to these habitat differences. Although this proposal may seem to be splitting hairs, this alternative story makes two points. First, it is difficult to know the mechanisms driving evolutionary change. Second, although behavior is not as well preserved as physical characteristics, it is likely that behavior is often at the cutting edge of natural selection. Artificial selection studies (Chapter 5) show that behavior can be changed through selection, as seen in the dramatic behavioral differences between breeds of dogs (see Figure 5.1), and that form often follows function.

Darwin's most notable contribution to the theory of evolution was his principle of natural selection:

> Owing to this struggle [for life], variations, however slight and from whatever cause proceeding, if they be in any degree profitable to the individuals of a species, in their infinitely complex relations to other organic beings and to their physical conditions of life, will tend to the preservation of such individuals, and will generally be inherited by the offspring. The offspring, also, will thus have a better chance of surviving, for, of the many individuals of any species which are periodically born, but a small number can survive. (Darwin, 1859, pp. 51–52)

Although Darwin used the phrase "survival of the fittest" to characterize this principle of natural selection, it could more appropriately be called reproduction of the fittest. Mere survival is necessary, but it is not sufficient. Most important is the relative number of surviving and reproducing offspring.

Darwin convinced the scientific world that species evolved by means of natural selection. *Origin of Species* is at the top of most scientists' lists of books of the millennium—his theory has changed how we think about all of the life sciences. Nonetheless, outside science, controversy continues (Pinker, 2002). For instance, in the United States, boards of education in several states have attempted to curtail the teaching of evolution in response to pressure from creationists who believe in a literal biblical interpretation of creation. Advocates of creationism have lost every major U.S. federal court case for the past 40 years (Berkman & Plutzer, 2010). Nevertheless, recent research investigating the evolution-creationism battle in state governments and classrooms has revealed the reluctance of teachers to teach evolutionary biology. In fact, 60 percent of teachers are strong advocates neither for evolution nor for nonscientific alternatives. Interestingly, much of this hesitancy appears to be due, at least in part, to a lack of confidence in their ability to defend evolution, perhaps because of their own lack of exposure to courses on evolution (Berkman & Plutzer, 2011). However, most people, but not everyone—see, for example, Dawkins (2006) versus Collins (2006)—accept the notion that science and religion occupy distinctly different realms, with science operating in the realm of verifiable facts and religion focused on purpose, meaning, and values. "Respectful noninterference" between science and religion is needed (Gould, 2011).

Scientifically, Darwin's theory of evolution had serious gaps, mainly because the mechanism for heredity, the gene, was not yet understood. Gregor Mendel's work on heredity was not published until seven years after the publication of the *Origin of Species,* and even then it was ignored until the turn of the century. Mendel provided the answer to the riddle of inheritance, which led to an understanding of how variability arises through mutations and how genetic variability is maintained generation after generation (Chapter 3). A rewrite of the *Origin of Species* points out how evolutionary theory and research have changed since Darwin and shows how pre-scient Darwin was (Jones, 1999).

Darwin considered behavioral traits to be just as subject to natural selection as physical ones. In the *Origin of Species,* an entire chapter is devoted to instinctive behavior patterns. In a later book, *The Descent of Man and Selection in Relation to Sex,* Darwin (1871) discussed intellectual and moral traits in animals and humans, concluding that the difference between the mind of a human being and the mind of an animal "is certainly one of degree and not of kind" (p. 101). Over 150 years after the publication of the *Origin of Species,* Darwin's influential theory is still highly relevant for the study of human behavior.

Francis Galton

Among the supporters and admirers of Darwin at this time was another one of Erasmus Darwin's grandsons, Francis Galton (see Box 2.1). By the time *The Origin of Species* was published, Galton had already established himself as an inventor and explorer; however, upon reading Darwin's work, Galton's curiosity and talents were directed to biological phenomena. He soon developed what was to be a central and abiding interest for the rest of his life: the inheritance of mental characteristics.

In 1865, two articles by Galton, jointly titled "Hereditary Talent and Character," were published in *MacMillan's Magazine.* Four years later a greatly expanded discussion was published under the title *Hereditary Genius: An Inquiry into Its Laws and Consequences.* The general argument presented in this work is that a greater number of extremely able individuals are found among the relatives of persons endowed with high mental ability than would be expected by chance. Further, Galton discovered that the closer the family relatedness, the higher the incidence of individuals with high mental ability.

In his work on mental characteristics, Galton realized the importance of proper assessment. In a prodigious program of research, he developed apparatus and procedures for measuring auditory thresholds, visual acuity, color vision, touch, smell, judgment of the vertical, judgment of length, weight discrimination, reaction time, and memory span. Of course, with all of these data, the problems of properly expressing and evaluating the data obtained were formidable, and Galton then turned his remarkable energies to statistics. He pioneered the development of the concepts of the median, percentiles, and correlation.

Galton introduced (1876) the use of twins to assess the roles of nature (inheritance) and nurture (environment). The essential question in his examination of twins was whether twins who were alike at birth became more dissimilar as a consequence of any dissimilarities in their nurture. Conversely, did twins who were unlike at birth become more similar as a consequence of similar nurture? Galton's work set the stage for the essence of the twin method, which was discovered 50 years later (Rende, Plomin, & Vandenberg, 1990) and is the topic of Chapter 6.

The ten years between *The Origin of Species* and *Hereditary Genius* had not been sufficient for Darwin's theory to be completely accepted. However, for those

BOX 2.1 Francis Galton

Francis Galton's life (1822–1911) as an inventor and explorer changed as he read the now-famous book on evolution written by Charles Darwin, his half cousin. Galton understood that evolution depends on heredity, and he began to ask whether heredity affects human behavior. He suggested the major methods of human behavioral genetics—family, twin, and adoption designs—and conducted the first systematic family studies showing that behavioral traits "run in families." Galton invented correlation, one of the fundamental statistics in all of science, in order to quantify degrees of resemblance among family members (Gillham, 2001).

One of Galton's studies on mental ability was reported in an 1869 book, *Hereditary Genius: An Enquiry into Its Laws and Consequences*. Because there was no satisfactory way at the time to measure mental ability, Galton had to rely on reputation as an index. By "reputation," he did not mean notoriety for a single act, nor mere social or official position, but "the reputation of a leader of opinion, or an originator, of a man to whom the world deliberately acknowledges itself largely indebted" (1869, p. 37). Galton identified approximately 1000 "eminent" men and found that they belonged to only 300 families, a finding indicating

(Mary Evans Picture Library/Alamy.)

that the tendency toward eminence is familial.

Taking the most eminent man in each family as a reference point, the other individuals who attained eminence were tabulated with respect to closeness of family relationship. As indicated in the diagram on the facing page, eminent status was more likely to appear in close relatives, with the likelihood of eminence decreasing as the degree of relationship became more remote.

who accepted Darwin's theory, Galton's work was a natural and logical extension: humans differ from animals most strikingly in mental ability; humans, like other animals, have evolved; evolution works by inheritance; mental traits are heritable. Galton's conclusion that "nature prevails enormously over nurture" (Galton, 1883, p. 241) set the stage for a needless battle by pitting nature against nurture. Nonetheless, his work was pivotal in documenting the range of variation in human behavior and in suggesting that heredity underlies behavioral variation.

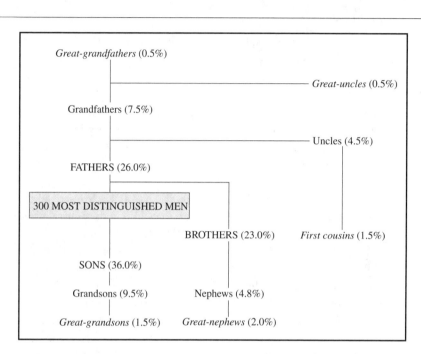

Galton was aware of the possible objection that relatives of eminent men share social, educational, and financial advantages. One of his counterarguments to this was that many men had risen to high rank from humble backgrounds. Nonetheless, such counterarguments do not today justify Galton's assertion that genius is solely a matter of nature (heredity) rather than nurture (environment). Family studies by themselves cannot disentangle genetic and environmental influences.

Galton famously argued that "there is no escape from the conclusion that nature prevails enormously over nurture" (Galton, 1883). This exaggerated claim launched a century-long controversy about nature versus nurture. Despite this needless controversy, Galton was a pioneer in documenting the wide range of behavioral differences between people and in proposing that heredity is responsible for these differences. For this reason, Galton can be considered the father of behavioral genetics.

Galton's work was neither completely in step nor completely out of step with his times. He lived during a period of great intellectual turmoil in biology. His work was both a product and a cause of the advances that were made. He was not the first to insist on the importance of heredity in traits of behavior nor was he the first to place his conclusions in an evolutionary context. But it was Galton who championed the idea of the inheritance of behavior and vigorously consolidated and extended it. In effect, we may regard Galton's efforts as the beginning of behavioral genetics.

PRE-MENDELIAN CONCEPTS OF HEREDITY AND VARIATION

Neither Darwin nor Galton understood the mechanism by which heredity works or how heritable variation is maintained.

Heredity

Long before Darwin and Galton, there had been substantial evidence of the importance of heredity, although its laws had proved extremely resistant to analysis. In particular, a vast amount of data had been accumulated from plant and animal breeding. Many offspring bore a closer resemblance to one parent than to the other. It was also common for the appearance of offspring to be intermediate between the two parents. But two offspring from the same parents could also be quite unlike. As J. L. Lush described the situation considerably later, the first rule of breeding is that "like produces like," while the second rule is that "like does not always produce like" (1951, p. 496).

The theory of heredity that seemed to explain most adequately the confusion of facts in Darwin's time was the "provisional hypothesis of pangenesis." In this view, the cells of the body, "besides having the power, as is generally admitted, of growing by self-division, throw off free and minute atoms of their contents, that is gemmules. These multiply and aggregate themselves into buds and the sexual elements" (Darwin, 1868, p. 481). Gemmules, miniature replicas of the parent cells, were presumably thrown off by each cell throughout its course of development. In embryogenesis and later development, gemmules from the parents, originally thrown off during various developmental periods, would come into play at the proper times, thus directing the development of a new organ like that of the parents. The theory of pangenesis was quite reasonable (although it was wrong). It was particularly compelling because it was compatible with Lamarck's notion of "use and disuse" as the source of variation in evolution.

Variation

The source of heritable variation was the most difficult component of the model of evolution for Darwin to explain. Without heritable variation in each generation, evolution could not continue. Because children often express some of the same characteristics of each of their parents, it was commonly accepted that characteristics of parents merged or blended in their offspring. The troublesome implication of such a "blending" hypothesis was that variation would be greatly reduced (in fact, roughly halved) each generation. For example, if one parent were tall and the other short, the offspring would be average height. Thus, the blending hypothesis implies that variability would rapidly diminish to a trivial level if it were not replenished in some manner. Although Darwin worried about this problem, he never resolved it. He suggested two ways in which variability might be induced, but both of these assumed that environmental factors altered the stuff of heredity. The theory of pangenesis suggested that gemmules could reflect changes in environment. Darwin vaguely concluded that changes in the conditions of life in some way altered gemmules in the reproductive systems of animals so that their offspring were more variable than they would have been under stable conditions. Ordinarily, this increment in variability would be random. Natural selection would then preserve the deviants that by chance happened to be better adapted as a consequence of their deviation.

Sometimes, however, an environmental condition might induce *systematic* change. Darwin hesitatingly accepted Lamarckian theory of use and disuse to suggest that acquired characteristics can be inherited. In *The Descent of Man,* Darwin speculated about the alleged longer legs and shorter arms of sailors as compared to soldiers: "Whether the several foregoing modifications would become hereditary, if the same habits of life were followed during many generations, is not known, but it is probable" (1871, p. 418). In some of his writings, Darwin seemed sure that variations in life experiences would increase genetic variability: "there can be no doubt that use in our domestic animals has strengthened and enlarged certain parts, and disuse diminished them; and that such modifications are inherited" (1859, p. 102). Likewise he stated, with respect to behavioral characteristics, that "some intelligent actions, after being performed during several generations, become converted into **instincts** and are inherited" (1871, p. 447). However, for the most part, Darwin was unsure of the source of variability: "Our ignorance of the laws of variation is profound. Not in one case out of a hundred can we pretend to assign any reason why this or that part has varied . . . Habit in producing constitutional peculiarities and use in strengthening and disuse in weakening and diminishing organs, appear in many cases to have been potent in their effects" (1859, p. 122).

While Darwin struggled with these issues, in his files was an unopened manuscript by an Augustinian monk, Gregor Mendel (Allen, 1975). As we will see in Chapter 3, Mendel's research on pea plants in the garden of a monastery at Brunn, Moravia, provided the answer to the riddle of inheritance.

Summary

The field of behavioral genetics is said to have a long past but a short history (Loehlin, 2009). While one cannot specify an exact date that behavioral genetics became a distinct scientific discipline, the notion of inheritance of behavioral traits appeared in ancient times with the domestication of dogs for behavioral as well as physical traits. The history of behavioral genetics really began with Darwin, Galton, and as we will see in Chapter 3, Mendel. Darwin's theory of natural selection as an explanation for the origin of species made a major impact on scientific thinking. Galton was the first to study the inheritance of mental characteristics and to suggest using twins and adoptees to study nature-nurture problems.

CHAPTER THREE

Mendel's Laws and Beyond

MENDEL'S LAWS

Huntington disease (HD) begins with personality changes, forgetfulness, and involuntary movements. It typically strikes in middle adulthood; during the next 15 to 20 years, it leads to complete loss of motor control and intellectual function. No treatment has been found to halt or delay the inexorable decline. This is the disease that killed the famous Depression-era folksinger Woody Guthrie. Although it affects only about 1 in 20,000 individuals, a quarter of a million people in the world today will eventually develop Huntington disease.

When the disease was traced through many generations, it showed a consistent pattern of heredity. Afflicted individuals had one parent who also had the disease, and approximately half the children of an affected parent developed the disease. (See Figure 3.1 for an explanation of symbols traditionally used to describe family trees, called *pedigrees*. Figure 3.2 shows an example of a Huntington disease pedigree.)

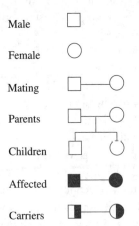

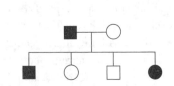

FIGURE 3.2 Huntington disease. HD individuals have one HD parent. About 50 percent of the offspring of HD parents will have HD.

FIGURE 3.1 Symbols used to describe family pedigrees.

What rules of heredity are at work? Why does this lethal condition persist in the population? We will answer these questions in the next section, but first, consider another inherited disorder.

In the 1930s, a Norwegian biochemist discovered an excess of phenylpyruvic acid in the urine of a pair of mentally disabled siblings and suspected that the condition was due to a disturbance in the metabolism of phenylalanine. Phenylalanine is one of the essential *amino acids*, which are the building blocks of proteins, and is present in many foods in the normal human diet. Other intellectually disabled individuals were soon found with this same excess. This type of mental disability came to be known as phenylketonuria (PKU).

Although the frequency of PKU is only about 1 in 10,000, PKU once accounted for about 1 percent of the mentally disabled institutionalized population. PKU has a pattern of inheritance very different from that of Huntington disease. PKU individuals do not usually have affected parents. Although this might make it seem at first glance as if PKU is not inherited, PKU does in fact "run in families." If one child in a family has PKU, the risk for siblings to develop it is about 25 percent, even though the parents themselves may not be affected (Figure 3.3). One more piece of the puzzle is the observation that when parents are genetically related ("blood" relatives), typically in marriages between cousins, they are more likely to have children with PKU. How does heredity work in this case?

Mendel's First Law of Heredity

Although Huntington disease and phenylketonuria, two examples of hereditary transmission of mental disorders, may seem complicated, they can be explained by a simple set of rules about heredity. The essence of these rules was worked out more than a century ago by Gregor Mendel (Mendel, 1866).

Mendel studied inheritance in pea plants in the garden of his monastery in what is now the Czech Republic (Box 3.1). On the basis of his many experiments, Mendel concluded that there are two "elements" of heredity for each trait in each individual and that these two elements separate, or segregate, during reproduction. Offspring receive one of the two elements from each parent. In addition, Mendel concluded that one of these elements can "dominate" the other, so that an individual with just one dominant element will display the trait. A nondominant, or *recessive,* element is expressed only if both elements are recessive. These conclusions are the essence of Mendel's first law, the *law of segregation.*

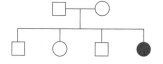

FIGURE 3.3 Phenylketonuria. PKU individuals do not typically have parents with PKU. If one child has PKU, the risk for other siblings is 25 percent. As explained later, parents in such cases are carriers for one allele of the PKU gene, but a child must have two alleles in order to be afflicted with recessive disorders such as PKU.

BOX 3.1 Gregor Mendel's Luck

Before Mendel (1822–1884), much of the research on heredity involved crossing plants of different species. But the offspring of these matings were usually sterile, which meant that succeeding generations could not be studied. Another problem with research before Mendel was that features of the plants investigated were complexly determined. Mendel's success can be attributed in large part to the absence of these problems.

Mendel crossed different varieties of pea plants of the same species; thus the offspring were fertile. In addition, he picked simple either-or traits, qualitative traits, that happened to be due to single genes. He was also lucky that in the traits he chose, one allele completely dominated the expression of the other allele, which is not always the case. However, one feature of Mendel's research was not due to luck. Over seven years, while raising over 28,000 pea plants, he counted all offspring rather than being content, as researchers before him had been, with a verbal summary of the typical results.

Mendel studied seven qualitative traits of the pea plant, such as whether the seed was smooth or wrinkled. He obtained 22 varieties of the pea plant that differed in these seven characteristics. All the varieties were *true-breeding plants:* those that always yield the same result when crossed with the same kind of plant. Mendel presented the results of eight years of research on the pea plant in his 1866 paper. This paper, "Experiments with Plant Hybrids," now forms the cornerstone of genetics and is one

Gregor Johann Mendel. A photograph taken at the time of his research. (Authenticated News/Getty Images.)

of the most influential publications in the history of science.

In one experiment, Mendel crossed true-breeding plants with smooth seeds and true-breeding plants with wrinkled seeds. Later in the summer, when he opened the pods containing their offspring (called the F_1, or first filial generation), he found that all of them had smooth seeds. This result indicated that the then-traditional view of blending inheritance was not correct. That is, the F_1 did not have seeds that were even moderately wrinkled. These F_1 plants were fertile, which allowed Mendel to take the next step of allowing plants of the F_1 generation to self-fertilize and then studying their offspring, F_2.

The results were striking: Of the 7324 seeds from the F_2, 5474 were smooth and 1850 were wrinkled. That is, 3/4 of the offspring had smooth seeds and 1/4 had wrinkled seeds. This result indicates that the factor responsible for wrinkled seeds had not been lost in the F_1 generation but had merely been dominated by the factor causing smooth seeds. The figure below summarizes Mendel's results.

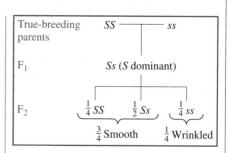

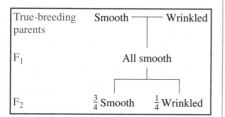

Given these observations, Mendel deduced a simple explanation involving two hypotheses. First, each individual has two hereditary "elements," now called alleles (alternate forms of a gene). For Mendel's pea plants, these alleles determined whether the seed was wrinkled or smooth. Thus, each parent has two alleles (either the same or different) but transmits only one of the alleles to each offspring. The second hypothesis is that, when an individual's alleles are different, one allele can dominate the other. These two hypotheses neatly explain the data (see the figure above right).

The true-breeding parent plant with smooth seeds has two alleles for smooth seeds (SS). The true-breeding parent plant with wrinkled seeds has two alleles for wrinkled seeds (ss). First-generation (F_1) offspring receive one allele from each parent and are therefore Ss. Because S dominates s, F_1 plants will have smooth seeds. The real test is the F_2 population. Mendel's theory predicts that when F_1 individuals are self-fertilized or crossed with other F_1 individuals, 1/4 of the F_2 should be SS, 1/2 Ss, and 1/4 ss. Assuming S dominates s, then Ss should have smooth seeds like the SS. Thus, 3/4 of the F_2 should have smooth seeds and 1/4 should have wrinkled, which is exactly what Mendel's data indicated. Mendel also discovered that the inheritance of one trait is not affected by the inheritance of another trait. Each trait is inherited in the expected 3:1 ratio.

Mendel was not so lucky in terms of acknowledgment of his work during his lifetime. When Mendel published the paper about his theory of inheritance in 1866, reprints were sent to scientists and libraries in Europe and the United States. However, for 35 years, Mendel's findings on the pea plant were ignored by most biologists, who were more interested in evolutionary processes that could account for change rather than continuity. Mendel died in 1884 without knowing the profound impact that his experiments would have during the twentieth century.

No one paid any attention to Mendel's law of heredity for over 30 years. Finally, in the early 1900s, several scientists recognized that Mendel's law is a general law of inheritance, not one peculiar to the pea plant. Mendel's "elements" are now known as *genes,* the basic units of heredity. Some genes may possibly have only one form within a population, for example, in all members of a variety of pea plants or all members of an **inbred strain** of mice (see Chapter 5). However, genetic analyses focus on genes that have different forms: differences that cause some pea seeds to be wrinkled or smooth, or that cause some people to have Huntington disease or PKU. The alternative forms of a gene are called *alleles.* An individual's combination of alleles is its *genotype,* whereas the observed traits are its *phenotype.* The fundamental issue of heredity in the behavioral sciences is the extent to which differences in genotype account for differences in phenotype, observed differences among individuals.

This chapter began with two very different examples of inherited disorders. How can Mendel's law of segregation explain both examples?

Huntington Disease   Figure 3.4 shows how Mendel's law explains the inheritance of Huntington disease. HD is caused by a dominant allele. Affected individuals have one dominant allele (*H*) and one recessive, normal allele (*h*). (It is rare that an HD individual has two *H* alleles, an event that would require both parents to have HD.) Unaffected individuals have two normal alleles.

As shown in Figure 3.4, a parent with HD whose genotype is *Hh* produces **gametes** (egg or sperm) with either the *H* or the *h* allele. The unaffected (*hh*) parent's gametes all have an *h* allele. The four possible combinations of these gametes from the mother and father result in the offspring genotypes shown at the bottom of Figure 3.4. Offspring will always inherit the normal *h* allele from the unaffected parent, but they have a 50 percent chance of inheriting the *H* allele from the HD parent. This pattern of inheritance explains why HD individuals always have a parent with HD and why 50 percent of the offspring of an HD parent develop the disease.

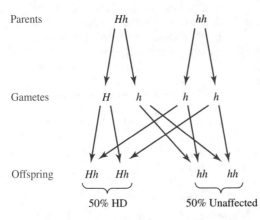

Parents   *Hh*   *hh*

Gametes   *H*   *h*   *h*   *h*

Offspring   *Hh*   *Hh*   *hh*   *hh*

50% HD   50% Unaffected

FIGURE 3.4 Huntington disease is due to a single gene, with the allele for HD dominant. *H* represents the dominant HD allele, and *h* is the normal recessive allele. Gametes are sex cells (eggs and sperm); each carries just one allele. The risk of HD in the offspring is 50 percent.

Why does this lethal condition persist in the population? If HD had its effect early in life, HD individuals would not live to reproduce. In one generation, HD would no longer exist because any individual with the HD allele would not live long enough to reproduce. The dominant allele for HD is maintained from one generation to the next because its lethal effect is not expressed until after the reproductive years.

A particularly traumatic feature of HD is that offspring of HD parents know they have a 50 percent chance of developing the disease and of passing on the HD gene. In 1983, **DNA markers** were used to show that the gene for HD is on chromosome 4, as will be discussed in Chapter 4. In 1993, the HD gene itself was identified. Now it is possible to determine for certain whether a person has the HD gene.

This genetic advance raises its own problems. If one of your parents had HD, you would be able to find out whether or not you have the HD allele. You would have a 50 percent chance of finding that you do not have the HD allele, but you would also have a 50 percent chance of finding that you do have the HD allele and will eventually die from it. In fact, most people at risk for HD decide *not* to take the test (Walker, 2007). Identifying the gene does, however, make it possible to determine whether a fetus has the HD allele and holds out the promise of future interventions that can correct the HD defect (Chapter 9).

Phenylketonuria Mendel's law also explains the inheritance of PKU. Unlike HD, PKU is due to the presence of two recessive alleles. For offspring to be affected, they must have two copies of the PKU allele. Those offspring with only one copy of the PKU allele are not afflicted with the disorder. They are called *carriers* because they carry the allele and can pass it on to their offspring. Figure 3.5 illustrates the inheritance of PKU from two unaffected carrier parents. Each parent has one PKU allele and one normal allele. Offspring have a 50 percent chance of inheriting the PKU allele from one parent and a 50 percent chance of inheriting the PKU allele from the other parent. The chance of both these things happening is 25 percent. If you flip a coin, the chance of heads is 50 percent. The chance of getting two heads in a row is 25 percent (i.e., 50 percent times 50 percent).

This pattern of inheritance explains why unaffected parents have children with PKU and why the risk of PKU in offspring is 25 percent when both parents are carriers. For PKU and other recessive disorders, identification of the genes makes it possible to determine whether potential parents are carriers. Identification of the PKU gene also makes it possible to determine whether a particular pregnancy involves an affected fetus. In fact, all newborns in most countries are screened for elevated phenylalanine levels in their blood, because early diagnosis of PKU can help parents prevent retardation by serving low-phenylalanine diets to their affected children.

Figure 3.5 also shows that 50 percent of children born of two carrier parents are likely to be carriers, and 25 percent will inherit the normal allele from both parents. If you understand how a recessive trait such as PKU is inherited, you should be able to work out the risk for PKU in offspring if one parent has PKU and the other parent is a carrier. (The risk is 50 percent.)

Parents

Gametes

Offspring

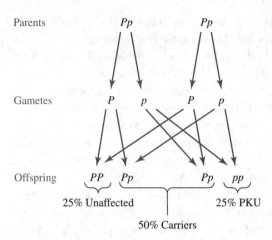

FIGURE 3.5 PKU is inherited as a single gene. The allele that causes PKU is recessive. *P* represents the normal dominant allele, and *p* is the recessive allele for PKU. When both parents are carriers, the risk of PKU for their children is 25 percent.

How does this explain why recessive traits like PKU are seen more often in off-spring whose parents are genetically related? Although PKU is rare (1 in 10,000), about 1 in 50 individuals are carriers of one PKU allele (Box 3.2). If you are a PKU carrier, your chance of marrying someone who is also a carrier is 2 percent. However, if you marry someone genetically related to you, the PKU allele must be in your family, so the chances are much greater than 2 percent that your spouse will also carry the PKU allele.

BOX 3.2 How Do We Know That 1 in 50 People Are Carriers for PKU?

f you randomly mate F_2 plants to obtain an F_3 generation, the frequencies of the *S* and *s* alleles will be the same as in the F_2 generation, as will the frequencies of the *SS, Ss,* and *ss* genotypes. Shortly after the rediscovery of Mendel's law in the early 1900s, this implication of Mendel's law was formalized and eventually called the **Hardy-Weinberg equilibrium:** The frequencies of alleles and genotypes do not change across generations unless forces such as natural selection or migration change them. This rule is the basis for a discipline called **population genetics,** whose practitioners study forces that change **allelic frequencies.**

Hardy-Weinberg equilibrium also makes it possible to estimate frequencies of alleles and genotypes. The frequencies of the dominant and recessive alleles are usually referred to as *p* and *q,* respectively. Eggs and sperm have just one allele for each gene. The chance that any particular egg or sperm has the dominant allele is *p*. Because sperm and egg unite at random, the chance that a sperm with the dominant allele fertilizes an egg with the dominant allele is the product of the two frequencies, $p \times p = p^2$. Thus, p^2 is the frequency of offspring with two dominant alleles (called the *homozygous dominant* genotype). In the same way, the *homozygous recessive* genotype has a frequency of q^2. As shown in the diagram, the frequency of offspring with one dominant allele and one recessive allele

It is very likely that we all carry at least one harmful recessive gene of some sort. However, the risk that our spouses are also carriers for the same disorder is small unless we are genetically related to them. In contrast, about half the children born to incestuous relationships between father and daughter show severe genetic abnormalities, often including childhood death or mental retardation (Wolf & Durham, 2005). This pattern of inheritance explains why most severe genetic disorders are recessive: Because carriers of recessive alleles do not show the disorder, they escape eradication by natural selection.

It should be noted that even single-gene disorders such as PKU are not so simple, because many hundreds of different **mutations** of the gene occur and these have different effects (Mitchell, Trakadis & Scriver, 2011). New PKU mutations emerge in individuals with no family history of the disorder. Some single-gene disorders are largely caused by new mutations. In addition, age of onset may vary for single-gene disorders, as it does in the case of HD.

Mendel's Second Law of Heredity

Not only do the alleles for Huntington disease segregate independently during gamete formation, they are also inherited independently from the alleles for PKU. This finding makes sense, because Huntington disease and PKU are caused by different genes; each of the two genes is inherited independently. Mendel experimented systematically with crosses between varieties of pea plants that differed in two or more

(called the heterozygous genotype) is $2pq$. In other words, if a population is in Hardy-Weinberg equilibrium, the frequency of the offspring genotypes is $p^2 + 2pq + q^2$. In populations with random mating, the expected **genotypic frequencies** are merely the product of $p + q$ for the mothers' alleles and $p + q$ for the fathers' alleles. That is, $(p + q)^2 = p^2 + 2pq + q^2$.

	Eggs	
Frequencies	p	q
Sperm $\quad p$	p^2	pq
$\quad\quad\quad q$	pq	q^2

For PKU, q^2, the frequency of PKU individuals (homozygous recessive) is 0.0001. If you know q^2, you can estimate the frequency of the PKU allele and PKU carriers, assuming Hardy-Weinberg equilibrium. The frequency of the PKU allele is q, which is the square root of q^2. The square root of 0.0001 is 0.01, so that 1 in 100 alleles in the population are the recessive PKU alleles. If there are only two alleles at the PKU **locus,** then the frequency of the dominant allele (p) is $1 - 0.01 = 0.99$. What is the frequency of carriers? Because carriers are heterozygous genotypes with one dominant allele and one recessive allele, the frequency of carriers of the PKU allele is 1 in 50 (that is, $2pq = 2 \times 0.99 \times 0.01 = 0.02$).

traits. He found that alleles for the two genes assort independently. In other words, the inheritance of one gene is not affected by the inheritance of another gene. This is Mendel's *law of independent assortment.*

KEY CONCEPTS

Gene: Basic unit of heredity. A sequence of DNA bases that codes for a particular product.

Allele: Alternative form of a gene.

Genotype: An individual's combination of alleles at a particular locus.

Phenotype: Observed or measured traits.

Dominant allele: An allele that produces the same phenotype in an individual regardless of whether one or two copies are present.

Recessive allele: An allele that produces its phenotype only when two copies are present.

Most important about Mendel's second law are its exceptions. We now know that genes are not just floating around in eggs and sperm. They are carried on chromosomes. The term *chromosome* literally means "colored body," because in certain laboratory preparations the staining characteristics of these structures are different from those of the rest of the **nucleus** of the cell. Genes are located at places called *loci* (singular, *locus,* from the Latin, meaning "place") on chromosomes. Eggs contain just one chromosome from each pair of the mother's set of chromosomes, and sperm contain just one from each pair of the father's set. An egg fertilized by a sperm thus has the full chromosome complement, which, in humans, is 23 pairs of chromosomes. Chromosomes are discussed in more detail in Chapter 4.

When Mendel studied the inheritance of two traits at the same time (let's call them A and B), he crossed true-breeding parents that showed the dominant trait for both A and B with parents that showed the recessive forms for A and B. He found second-generation (F_2) offspring of all four possible types: dominant for A and B, dominant for A and recessive for B, recessive for A and dominant for B, and recessive for A and B. The frequencies of the four types of offspring were as expected if A and B were inherited independently. Mendel's law is violated, however, when genes for two traits are close together on the same chromosome. If Mendel had studied the joint inheritance of two such traits, the results would have surprised him. The two traits would not have been inherited independently.

Figure 3.6 illustrates what would happen if the genes for traits A and B were very close together on the same chromosome. Instead of finding all four types of F_2 offspring, Mendel would have found only two types: dominant for both A and B and recessive for both A and B.

The reason why such violations of Mendel's second law are important is that they make it possible to map genes to chromosomes. If the inheritance of a particular pair of genes violates Mendel's second law, then it must mean that they tend to be

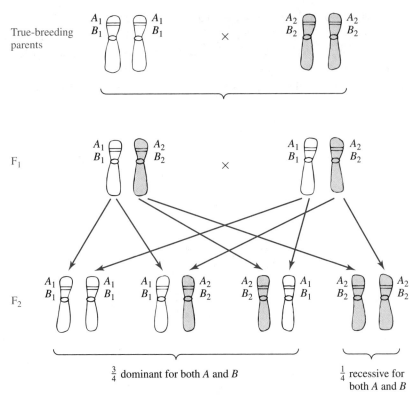

True-breeding parents

F_1

F_2

$\frac{3}{4}$ dominant for both A and B

$\frac{1}{4}$ recessive for both A and B

FIGURE 3.6 An exception to Mendel's second law occurs if two genes are closely linked on the same chromosome. The A_1 allele and the B_1 allele are dominant; the A_2 and B_2 alleles are recessive.

inherited together and thus reside on the same chromosome. This phenomenon is called **linkage.** However, it is actually not sufficient for two linked genes to be on the same chromosome; they must also be very close together on the chromosome. Unless genes are near each other on the same chromosome, they will recombine by a process in which chromosomes exchange parts. **Recombination** occurs during **meiosis** in the ovaries and testes, when gametes are produced.

Figure 3.7 illustrates recombination for three loci (A, C, B) on a single chromosome. The maternal chromosome, carrying the alleles A_1, C_1, and B_2, is represented in white; the paternal chromosome with alleles A_2, C_2, and B_1 is blue. During meiosis, each chromosome duplicates to form sister **chromatids** (Figure 3.7b). These sister chromatids may cross over one another, as shown in Figure 3.7c. This overlap happens an average of one time for each chromosome during meiosis. During this stage, the chromatids can break and rejoin (Figure 3.7d). Each of the chromatids will be transmitted to a different gamete (Figure 3.7e). Consider only the A and B loci for the moment. As shown in Figure 3.7e, one gamete will carry the genes A_1 and B_2, as in the mother, and one will carry A_2 and B_1, as in the father. The other two will carry

A_1 with B_1 and A_2 with B_2. For the latter two pairs, recombination has taken place—these combinations were not present on the parental chromosomes. The probability of recombination between two loci on the same chromosome is a function of the distance between them. In Figure 3.7, for example, the A and C loci have not recombined. All gametes are either $A_1 C_1$ or $A_2 C_2$, as in the parents, because the **crossover** did

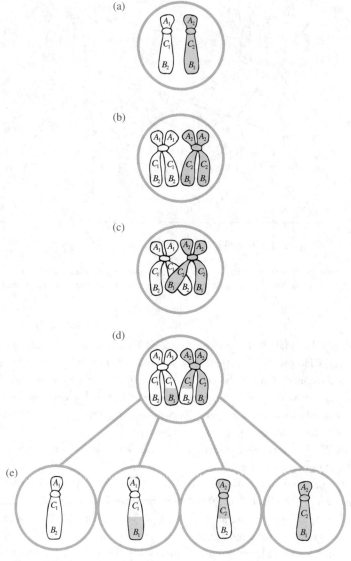

FIGURE 3.7 Illustration of recombination. The maternal chromosome, carrying the alleles A_1, C_1, and B_2, is represented in white; the paternal chromosome, with alleles A_2, C_2, and B_1, is blue. The right chromatid (the duplicated chromosome produced during meiosis) of the maternal chromosome crosses over (recombines) with the left chromatid of the paternal chromosome.

not occur between these loci. Crossover could occur between the *A* and *C* loci, but it would happen less frequently than between *A* and *B*.

These facts have been used to "map" genes on chromosomes. The distance between two loci can be estimated by the number of recombinations per 100 gametes. This distance is called a map unit or *centimorgan*, named after T. H. Morgan, who first identified linkage groups in the fruit fly *Drosophila* (Morgan, Sturtevant, Muller, & Bridges, 1915). If two loci are far apart, like the *A* and *B* loci, recombination will separate the two loci as often as if the loci were on different chromosomes, and they will not appear to be linked.

To identify the location of a gene on a particular chromosome, *linkage analysis* can be used. Linkage analysis refers to techniques that use information about violations of independent assortment to identify the chromosomal location of a gene. DNA markers serve as signposts on the chromosomes, as discussed in Chapter 9. Since 1980, the power of linkage analysis has greatly increased with the discovery of millions of these markers. Linkage analysis looks for a violation of independent assortment between a trait and a DNA marker. In other words, linkage analysis assesses whether the DNA marker and the trait co-assort in a family more often than expected by chance.

In 1983, the gene for Huntington disease was shown to be linked to a DNA marker near the tip of one of the larger chromosomes (chromosome 4; see Chapter 9) (Gusella et al., 1983). This was the first time that the new DNA markers had been used to demonstrate a linkage for a disorder for which no chemical mechanism was known. DNA markers that are closer to the Huntington gene have since been developed and have made it possible to pinpoint the gene. As noted earlier, the gene itself was finally located precisely in 1993.

KEY CONCEPTS

Chromosome: A threadlike structure that contains DNA and resides in the nucleus of cells. Humans have 23 pairs.

Locus (plural, loci): The site of a specific gene on a chromosome. Latin for "place."

Linkage: Loci that are close together on a chromosome and thus inherited together within families. Linkage is an exception to Mendel's second law of independent assortment.

Recombination: A process that occurs during meiosis in which chromosomes exchange parts.

Once a gene has been found, two things are possible. First, the DNA variation responsible for the disorder can be identified. This identification provides a DNA test that is directly associated with the disorder in individuals and is more than just a risk estimate calculated on the basis of Mendel's laws. That is, the DNA test can be used to diagnose the disorder in individuals regardless of information about other family members. Second, the protein coded by the gene can be studied; this investigation is a major step toward understanding how the gene has its effect and thus can possibly lead to a therapy. In the case of Huntington disease, the gene codes for a previously unknown protein, called *huntingtin*. This protein interacts with many other proteins, which has hampered efforts to develop drug therapies (Ross et al., 2014).

Although the disease process of the Huntington gene is not yet fully understood, Huntington disease, like fragile X syndrome (mentioned in Chapter 1 and discussed in detail in Chapter 12), also involves a type of genetic defect in which a short sequence of DNA is repeated many times. The defective gene product slowly has its effect over the life course by contributing to neural death in the cerebral cortex and basal ganglia. This leads to the motoric and cognitive problems characteristic of Huntington disease.

Finding the PKU gene was easier because its enzyme product was known. In 1984, the gene for PKU was found and shown to be on chromosome 12 (Lidsky et al., 1984). For decades, PKU infants have been identified by screening for the physiological effect of PKU — high blood phenylalanine levels — but this test is not highly accurate. Developing a DNA test for PKU has been hampered by the discovery that there are hundreds of different mutations at the PKU locus and that these mutations differ in the magnitude of their effects. This diversity contributes to the variation in blood phenylalanine levels among PKU individuals.

Of the several thousand single-gene disorders known (about half of which involve the nervous system), the precise chromosomal location has been identified for most of these genes (Rabbani, Mahdieh, Hosomichi, Nakaoka, & Inoue, 2012; Zhang, 2014). The gene sequence and the specific mutation have been found for at least half, and this number is increasing. One of the goals of the Human Genome Project was to sequence the whole genome and identify all genes. Now the challenge to scientists is to discover the genetic bases of human health and disease by deciphering the genome sequence, understanding how genes work, and eventually developing medicines targeted to an individual's genetic makeup (National Human Genome Research Institute, 2010). Rapid progress in these challenging areas holds the promise of identifying genes even for complex behaviors influenced by multiple genes as well as environmental factors.

BEYOND MENDEL'S LAWS

Complex Traits

Most psychological traits show patterns of inheritance that are much more complex than those of Huntington disease or PKU. Consider schizophrenia and general cognitive ability (intelligence).

Schizophrenia Schizophrenia (Chapter 13) is a severe mental condition characterized by thought disorders. Nearly 1 in 100 people throughout the world are afflicted by this disorder at some point in life, 100 times more than is the case with Huntington disease or PKU. Schizophrenia shows no simple pattern of inheritance like Huntington disease or

PKU, but it is familial (Figure 3.8). A special incidence figure used in genetic studies is called a *morbidity risk estimate* (also called the *lifetime expectancy*), which is the chance of being affected during an entire lifetime. The estimate is "age-corrected" for the fact that some as yet unaffected family members have not yet lived through the period of risk. If you have a **second-degree relative** (grandparent or aunt or uncle) who is schizophrenic, your risk for schizophrenia is about 4 percent, four times greater than the risk in the general population. If a **first-degree relative** (parent or sibling) is schizophrenic, your risk is about 9 percent. If several family members are affected, the risk is greater. If your fraternal twin has schizophrenia, your risk is higher than for other siblings, about 17 percent, even though fraternal twins are no more similar genetically than are other siblings. Most striking, the risk is about 48 percent for an identical twin whose co-twin is schizophrenic. Identical twins develop from one embryo, which in the first few days of life splits into two embryos, each with the same genetic material (Chapter 6).

Clearly, the risk of developing schizophrenia increases systematically as a function of the degree of genetic similarity that an individual has to another who is affected. Heredity appears to be implicated, but the pattern of affected individuals does not conform to Mendelian proportions. Are Mendel's laws of heredity at all applicable to such a complex outcome?

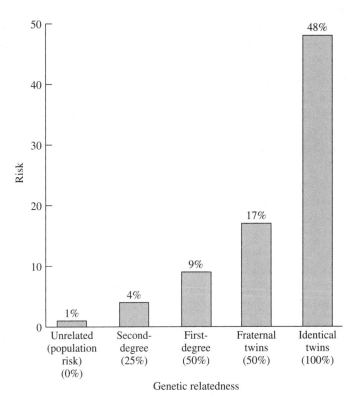

FIGURE 3.8 Risk for schizophrenia increases with genetic relatedness. (Data from Gottesman, 1991.)

General Cognitive Ability   Many psychological traits are **quantitative dimensions,** as are physical traits such as height and biomedical traits such as blood pressure. Quantitative dimensions are often continuously distributed in the familiar bell-shaped curve, with most people in the middle and fewer people toward the extremes. For example, an intelligence test score from a general test of intelligence is a composite of diverse tests of cognitive ability and is used to provide an index of general cognitive ability. Intelligence test scores are normally distributed for the most part. (See Chapter 11.)

Because general cognitive ability is a quantitative dimension, it is not possible to count "affected" individuals. Nonetheless, it is clear that general cognitive ability runs in families. For example, parents with high intelligence test scores tend to have children with higher than average scores. As with schizophrenia, transmission of general cognitive ability does not seem to follow simple Mendelian rules of heredity.

The statistics of quantitative traits are needed to describe family resemblance (see Appendix). Over a hundred years ago, Francis Galton, the father of behavioral genetics, tackled this problem of describing family resemblance for quantitative traits. He developed a statistic that he called *co-relation* and that has become the widely used correlation coefficient. More formally, it is called the Pearson product-moment correlation, named after Karl Pearson, Galton's colleague. The *correlation* is an index of resemblance that ranges from -1.0, indicating an inverse relationship; to 0.0, indicating no resemblance; to 1.0, indicating perfect positive resemblance.

Correlations for intelligence test scores show that the resemblance of family members depends on the closeness of the genetic relationship (Figure 3.9). The correlation of intelligence test scores for pairs of individuals taken at random from the population is 0.00. The correlation for cousins is about 0.15. For **half siblings,** who have just one parent in common, the correlation is about 0.30. For **full siblings,** who have both parents in common, the correlation is about 0.45; this correlation is similar to that between parents and offspring. Scores for fraternal twins correlate about 0.60, which is higher than the correlation of 0.45 for full siblings but lower than the correlation for identical twins, which is about 0.85. In addition, husbands and wives correlate about 0.40, a result that has implications for interpreting sibling and **twin correlations,** as discussed in Chapter 11.

How do Mendel's laws of heredity apply to continuous dimensions such as general cognitive ability?

Pea Size   Although pea plants might not seem relevant to schizophrenia or cognitive ability, they provide a good example of complex traits. A large part of Mendel's success in working out the laws of heredity came from choosing simple traits that are either-or qualitative traits. If Mendel had studied, for instance, the size of the pea seed as indexed by its diameter, he would have found very different results. First, pea seed size, like most traits, is continuously distributed. If he had taken plants with big seeds and crossed them with plants with small seeds, the seed size of their offspring would have been neither big nor small. In fact, the seeds would have varied in size from small to large, with most offspring seeds of average size.

Only ten years after Mendel's report, Francis Galton studied pea seed size and concluded that it is inherited. For example, parents with large seeds were likely to have

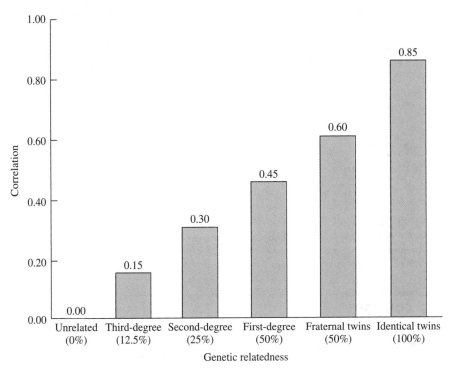

FIGURE 3.9 Resemblance for general cognitive ability increases with genetic relatedness. (Data from Bouchard & McGue, 1981, as modified by Loehlin, 1989.)

offspring with larger than average seeds. In fact, Galton developed the fundamental statistics of regression and correlation in order to describe the quantitative relationship between pea seed size in parents and offspring. He plotted parent and offspring seed sizes and drew the regression line that best fits the observed data (Figure 3.10). The slope of the regression line is 0.33. This means that, for the entire population, as parental size increases by one unit, the average offspring size increases one-third of one unit.

Galton also demonstrated that human height shows the same pattern of inheritance. Children's height correlates with the average height of their parents. Tall parents have taller than average children. Children with one tall and one short parent are likely to be of average height. Inheritance of this trait is quantitative rather than qualitative. Quantitative inheritance is the way in which nearly all complex behavioral as well as biological traits are inherited.

Does quantitative inheritance violate Mendel's laws? When Mendel's laws were rediscovered in the early 1900s, many scientists thought this must be the case. They thought that heredity must involve some sort of blending, because offspring resemble the average of their parents. Mendel's laws were dismissed as a peculiarity of pea plants or of abnormal conditions. However, recognizing that quantitative inheritance does *not* violate Mendel's laws is fundamental to an understanding of behavioral genetics, as explained in the following section.

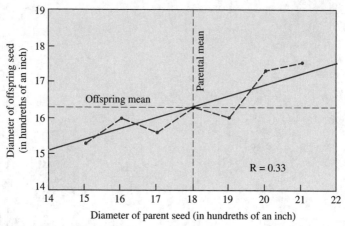

FIGURE 3.10 First regression line (solid blue line), drawn by Galton in 1877 to describe the quantitative relationship between pea seed size in parents and offspring. The dashed blue line connects actual data points. (Courtesy of the Galton Laboratory.)

KEY CONCEPTS

Morbidity risk estimate: The chance of being affected during an entire lifetime.
Correlation: An index of relationship between two variables.

Multiple-Gene Inheritance

The traits that Mendel studied, as well as Huntington disease and PKU, are examples in which a single gene is necessary and sufficient to cause the disorder. That is, you will have Huntington disease only if you have the *H* allele (necessary); if you have the *H* allele, you will have Huntington disease (sufficient). Other genes and environmental factors have little effect on its inheritance. In such cases, a dichotomous (either-or) disorder is found: You either have the specific allele, or not, and thus you have the disorder, or not. More than 3000 such single-gene disorders are known definitely and again as many are considered probable (Zhang, 2014).

In contrast, more than just one gene is likely to affect complex disorders such as schizophrenia and continuous dimensions such as general cognitive ability. When Mendel's laws were rediscovered in the early 1900s, a bitter battle was fought between so-called Mendelians and biometricians. Mendelians looked for single-gene effects, and biometricians argued that Mendel's laws could not apply to complex traits because they showed no simple pattern of inheritance. Mendel's laws seemed especially inapplicable to quantitative dimensions.

In fact, both sides were right and both were wrong. The Mendelians were correct in arguing that heredity works the way Mendel said it worked, but they were wrong in assuming that complex traits will show simple Mendelian patterns of inheritance. The biometricians were right in arguing that complex traits are distributed quantitatively, not qualitatively, but they were wrong in arguing that Mendel's laws of inheritance are particular to pea plants and do not apply to higher organisms.

The battle between the Mendelians and biometricians was resolved when biometricians realized that Mendel's laws of inheritance of single genes also apply to complex traits that are influenced by *several* genes. Such a complex trait is called a *polygenic trait*. Each of the influential genes is inherited according to Mendel's laws.

Figure 3.11 illustrates this important point. The top distribution shows the three genotypes of a single gene with two alleles that are equally frequent in the population. As discussed in Box 3.1, 25 percent of the genotypes are homozygous for the A_1 allele (A_1A_1), 50 percent are heterozygous (A_1A_2), and 25 percent are homozygous for the A_2 allele (A_2A_2). If the A_1 allele were dominant, individuals with the A_1A_2 genotype would look just like individuals with the A_1A_1 genotype. In this case, 75 percent of individuals would have the observed trait (phenotype) of the dominant allele. For example, as discussed in Box 3.1, in Mendel's crosses of pea plants with smooth or wrinkled seeds, he found that in the F_2 generation, 75 percent of the plants had smooth seeds and 25 percent had wrinkled seeds.

However, not all alleles operate in a completely dominant or recessive manner. Many alleles are additive in that they each contribute something to the phenotype. In Figure 3.11a, each A_2 allele contributes equally to the phenotype, so if you had two A_2 alleles, you would have a higher score than if you had just one A_2 allele. Figure 3.11b adds a second gene (B) that affects the trait. Again, each B_2 allele makes a contribution. Now there are nine genotypes and five phenotypes. Figure 3.11c adds a third gene (C), and there are 27 genotypes. Even if we assume that the alleles of the different genes equally affect the trait and that there is no environmental variation, there are still seven different phenotypes.

So, even with just three genes and two alleles for each gene, the phenotypes begin to approach a normal distribution in the population. When we consider environmental sources of variability and the fact that the effects of alleles are not likely to be equal, it is easy to see that the effects of even a few genes will lead to a quantitative distribution. Moreover, the complex traits that interest behavioral geneticists may be influenced by hundreds or even thousands of genes. Thus, it is not surprising to find continuous variation at the phenotypic level, even though each gene is inherited in accord with Mendel's laws.

Quantitative Genetics

The notion that multiple-gene effects lead to quantitative traits is the cornerstone of a branch of genetics called *quantitative genetics.*

Quantitative genetics was introduced in papers by R. A. Fisher (1918) and by Sewall Wright (1921). Their extension of Mendel's single-gene model to the multiple-gene model of quantitative genetics (Falconer & MacKay, 1996) is described in the Appendix. This multiple-gene model adequately accounts for the resemblance of relatives. If genetic factors affect a quantitative trait, phenotypic resemblance of relatives should

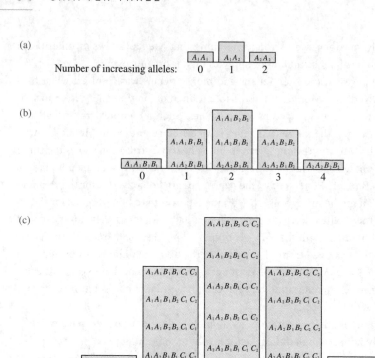

(a)

Number of increasing alleles:

(b)

(c)

(d)

FIGURE 3.11 Single-gene and multiple-gene distributions for traits with additive gene effects. (a) A single gene with two alleles yields three genotypes and three phenotypes. (b) Two genes, each with two alleles, yield nine genotypes and five phenotypes. (c) Three genes, each with two alleles, yield twenty-seven genotypes and seven phenotypes. (d) Normal bell-shaped curve of continuous variation.

increase with increasing degrees of **genetic relatedness.** First-degree relatives (parents / offspring, full siblings) are 50 percent similar genetically. The simplest way to think about this is that offspring inherit half their genetic material from each parent. If one sibling inherits a particular allele from a parent, the other sibling has a 50 percent chance of inheriting that same allele. Other relatives differ in their degree of genetic relatedness.

Figure 3.12 illustrates degrees of genetic relatedness for the most common types of relatives, using male relatives as examples. Relatives are listed in relation to an individual in the center, the **index case** (or **proband**). The illustration goes back three

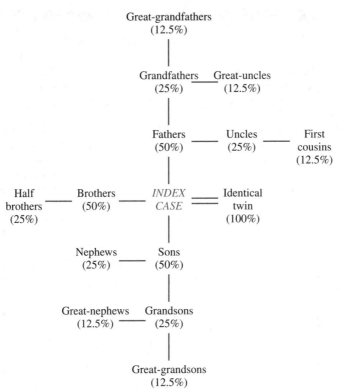

FIGURE 3.12 Genetic relatedness: Male relatives of male index case (proband), with degree of genetic relatedness in parentheses.

generations and forward three generations. First-degree relatives (e.g., fathers / sons), who are 50 percent similar genetically, are each one step removed from the index case. Second-degree relatives (e.g., uncles / nephews) are two steps removed and are only half as similar genetically (i.e., 25 percent) as first-degree relatives are. **Third-degree relatives** (e.g., cousins) are three steps removed and half as similar genetically (i.e., 12.5 percent) as second-degree relatives are. Identical twins are a special case, because they are the same person genetically.

For our two examples, schizophrenia and general cognitive ability, phenotypic resemblance of relatives increases with genetic relatedness (see Figures 3.8 and 3.9). How can there be a dichotomous disorder if many genes cause schizophrenia? One possible explanation is that genetic risk is normally distributed but that schizophrenia is not seen until a certain threshold is reached. Another explanation is that disorders are actually dimensions artificially established on the basis of a diagnosis. That is, there may be a continuum between what is normal and abnormal. These alternatives are described in Box 3.3.

These data for schizophrenia (Figure 3.8) and general cognitive ability (Figure 3.9) are consistent with the hypothesis of genetic influence, but they do not *prove* that genetic factors are important. It is possible that familial resemblance increases with

BOX 3.3 Liability-Threshold Model of Disorders

f complex disorders such as schizophrenia are influenced by many genes,
why are they diagnosed as **qualitative disorders** rather than assessed as
quantitative dimensions? Theoretically,
there should be a continuum of genetic
risk, from people having none of the
alleles that increase risk for schizophrenia to those having most of the

alleles that increase risk. Most people
should fall between these extremes,
with only a moderate susceptibility to
schizophrenia.

One model assumes that risk, or
liability, is distributed normally but that
the disorder occurs only when a certain
threshold of liability is exceeded, as
represented in the accompanying

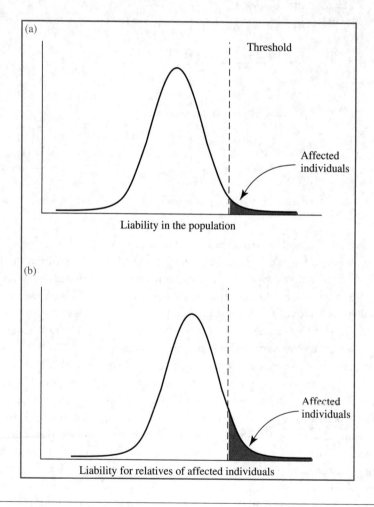

figure by the shaded area in (a). Relatives of an affected person have a greater liability; that is, their distribution of liability is shifted to the right, as in (b). For this reason, a greater proportion of the relatives of affected individuals exceed the threshold and manifest the disorder. If there is such a threshold, familial risk can be high only if genetic or shared environmental influence is substantial, because many of an affected individual's relatives will fall just below the threshold and not be affected.

Liability and threshold are hypothetical constructs. However, it is possible to use the **liability-threshold model** to estimate correlations from family risk data (Falconer, 1965; Smith, 1974). For example, the correlation estimated for first-degree relatives for schizophrenia is 0.45, an estimate based on a population base rate of 1 percent and risk to first-degree relatives of 9 percent.

Although correlations estimated from the liability-threshold model are widely reported for psychological disorders, it should be emphasized that this statistic refers to hypothetical constructs of a threshold and an underlying liability derived from diagnoses, not to the risk for the actual diagnosed disorder. In the previous example, the actual risk for schizophrenia for first-degree relatives is 9 percent, even though the liability-threshold correlation is 0.45.

Alternatively, a second model assumes that disorders are actually continuous phenotypically. That is, symptoms might increase continuously from the normal to the abnormal; a diagnosis occurs only when a certain level of symptom severity is reached. The implication is that common disorders are in fact quantitative traits (Plomin, Haworth, & Davis, 2009). A continuum from normal to abnormal seems likely for common disorders such as depression and alcoholism. For example, people vary in the frequency and severity of their depression. Some people rarely get the blues; for others, depression completely disrupts their lives. Individuals diagnosed as depressed might be extreme cases that differ quantitatively, not qualitatively, from the rest of the population. In such cases, it may be possible to assess the continuum directly, rather than assuming a continuum from dichotomous diagnoses using the liability-threshold model. Even for less common disorders like schizophrenia, there is increasing interest in the possibility that there may be no sharp threshold dividing the normal from the abnormal, but rather a continuum from normal to abnormal thought processes. A method called *DF extremes analysis* can be used to investigate the links between the normal and abnormal (see Chapter 12).

The relationship between dimensions and disorders is a key issue, as discussed in later chapters. The best evidence for genetic links between dimensions and disorders will come as specific genes are found for behavior. For example, will a gene associated with diagnosed depression also relate to differences in mood within the normal range?

genetic relatedness for environmental reasons. First-degree relatives might be more similar because they live together. Second-degree and third-degree relatives might be less similar because of less similarity of rearing.

Two experiments of nature are the workhorses of human behavioral genetics that help to disentangle genetic and environmental sources of family resemblance. One is the *twin study*, which compares the resemblance within pairs of identical twins, who are genetically identical, to the resemblance within pairs of fraternal twins, who, like other siblings, are 50 percent similar genetically. The second is the *adoption study*, which separates genetic and environmental influences. For example, when a child is placed for adoption at birth, any resemblance between the adopted child and the child's birth parents can be attributed to shared heredity rather than to shared environment if there is no selective placement. In addition, any resemblance between the adoptive parents and their adopted children can be attributed to shared environment rather than to shared heredity. The twin and adoption methods are discussed in Chapter 6.

KEY CONCEPTS

Polygenic: Influenced by multiple genes.

Genetic relatedness: The extent or degree to which relatives have genes in common. *First-degree relatives* of the **proband** (parents and siblings) are 50 percent similar genetically. *Second-degree relatives* of the proband (grandparents, aunts, and uncles) are 25 percent similar genetically. *Third-degree relatives* of the proband (first cousins) are 12.5 percent similar genetically.

Liability-threshold model: A model that assumes that dichotomous disorders are due to underlying genetic liabilities that are distributed normally. The disorder appears only when a threshold of liability is exceeded.

The X-chromosome: An Extension to Mendel's Laws

Color blindness is a complex trait (Deeb, 2006; Neitz & Neitz, 2011) that shows a pattern of inheritance that does not appear to conform to Mendel's laws. While there is quite a bit of variation in the color vision phenotype (Deeb, 2006), there are two major types of color blindness: those who have difficulty distinguishing between red and green, and those who have difficulty distinguishing between blue and yellow. In this section, we will focus on the most common color blindness, which involves difficulty in distinguishing red and green, a condition caused by a lack of certain color-absorbing pigments in the retina of the eye. It occurs more frequently in males than in females. More interesting, when the mother is color blind and the father is not, all of the sons but none of the daughters are color blind (Figure 3.13a). When the father is color blind and the mother is not, offspring are seldom affected (Figure 3.13b). But something remarkable happens to these apparently normal

(a)

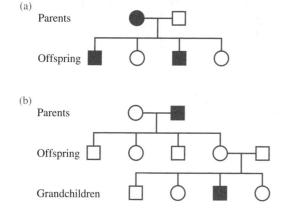

FIGURE 3.13 Inheritance of color
blindness. (a) A color-blind mother
and unaffected father have color-
blind sons but unaffected daughters. (b) An unaffected mother and
color-blind father have unaffected
offspring, but daughters have sons
with 50 percent risk for color blindness. (See Figure 3.1 for symbols
used to describe family pedigrees).

daughters of a color-blind father: Half of their sons are likely to be color blind. This is the well-known skip-a-generation phenomenon—fathers have it, their daughters do not, but some of the grandsons do. What could be going on here in terms of Mendel's laws of heredity?

Genes on the X Chromosome The 23 pairs of chromosomes mentioned earlier include one pair called the **sex chromosomes** because they differ for males and females. Females have two X chromosomes, and males have one X chromosome and a smaller chromosome called Y.

Color blindness, specifically red-green color blindness, is caused by a recessive allele on the X chromosome. But males have only one X chromosome; so, if they have one allele for color blindness (*c*) on their single X chromosome, they are color blind. For females to be color blind, they must inherit the *c* allele on both of their X chromosomes. For this reason, the hallmark of a sex-linked (meaning *X-linked*) recessive gene is a greater incidence in males. For example, if the frequency of an X-linked recessive allele (*q* in Box 3.2) for a disorder is 10 percent, then the expected frequency of the disorder in males would be 10 percent, but the frequency in females (q^2) would be only 1 percent (i.e., $0.10^2 = 0.01$).

Figure 3.14 illustrates the inheritance of the sex chromosomes. Both sons and daughters inherit one X chromosome from their mother. Daughters inherit their father's single X chromosome and sons inherit their father's Y chromosome. Sons cannot inherit an allele on the X chromosome from their father. For this reason, another sign of an X-linked recessive trait is that father-son resemblance is negligible. Daughters inherit an X-linked allele from their father, but they do not express a recessive trait unless they receive another such allele on the X chromosome from their mother.

Inheritance of color blindness is further explained in Figure 3.15. In the case of a color-blind mother and unaffected father (Figure 3.15a), the mother has the *c* allele on both of her X chromosomes and the father has the normal allele (*C*) on his single

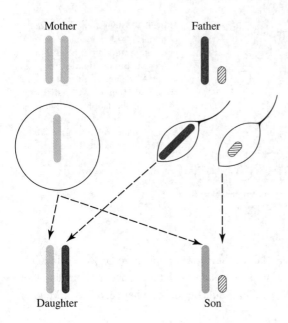

Mother   Father

FIGURE 3.14 Inheritance of X and Y chromosomes.

Daughter   Son

X chromosome. Thus, sons always inherit an X chromosome with the c allele from their mother and are color blind. Daughters carry one c allele from their mother but are not color blind because they have inherited a normal, dominant C allele from their father. They carry the c allele without showing the disorder, so they are called *carriers*, a status indicated by the two-toned circles in Figure 3.15.

In the second example (Figure 3.15b), the father is color blind but the mother is neither color blind nor a carrier of the c allele. None of the children are color blind, but the daughters are all carriers because they must inherit their father's X chromosome with the recessive c allele. You should now be able to predict the risk of color blindness for offspring of these carrier daughters. As shown in the bottom row of Figure 3.15b, when a carrier daughter (Cc) has children by an unaffected male (C), half of her sons but none of her daughters are likely to be color blind. Half of the daughters are carriers. This pattern of inheritance explains the skip-a-generation phenomenon. Color-blind fathers have no color-blind sons or daughters (assuming normal, noncarrier mothers), but their daughters are carriers of the c allele. The daughters' sons have a 50 percent chance of being color blind.

The sex chromosomes are inherited differently for males and females, so detecting X linkage is much easier than identifying a gene's location on other chromosomes. Color blindness was the first reported human X linkage. Over 1500 genes have been identified on the X chromosome, as well as a disproportionately high number of single-gene diseases (Ross et al., 2005). The Y chromosome has over 200 genes, including those for determining maleness, and the smallest number of genes associated with disease of any chromosome (Bellott et al., 2014; Cortez et al., 2014).

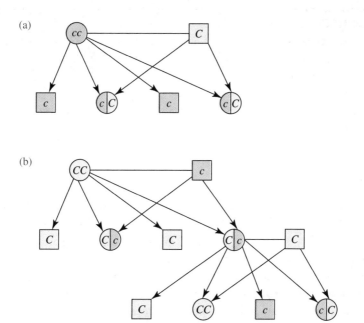

FIGURE 3.15 Color blindness is inherited as a recessive gene on the X chromosome. *c* refers to the recessive allele for color blindness, and *C* is the normal allele. (a) Color-blind mothers are homozygous recessive (*cc*). (b) Color-blind fathers have a *c* allele on their single X chromosome, which is transmitted to daughters but not to sons.

Several other genetic phenomena also do not appear to conform to Mendel's laws in the sense that they are not inherited in a simple way through the generations. The most common involve new, or *de novo*, mutations that do not affect the parent because they occur during the formation of the parent's eggs or sperm. But this situation is not really a violation of Mendel's laws, because the new mutations are then passed on to offspring according to Mendel's laws, even though affected individuals have unaffected parents. Many genetic diseases involve such spontaneous mutations, which are not inherited from the preceding generation. An example is Rett syndrome, an X-linked dominant disorder that has a prevalence of about 1 in 10,000 in girls. Although girls with Rett syndrome develop normally during the first year of life, they later regress and eventually become both mentally and physically disabled. Boys with this mutation on their single X chromosome die either before birth or in the first two years after birth. (See Chapter 12.)

In addition, DNA mutations frequently occur in cells other than those that produce eggs or sperm and are not passed on to the next generation. This mutation type is the cause of many cancers, for example. Although these mutations affect DNA, they are not heritable because they do not occur in the eggs or sperm. Other exceptions to Mendel's laws include chromosomal abnormalities (such as extra copies of chromosomes), repeat sequences of parts of chromosomes, and **genomic imprinting.** These will be discussed in later chapters.

KEY CONCEPTS

Sex-linked (X-linked): A phenotype influenced by a gene on the X chromosome. X-linked recessive diseases occur more frequently in males because they only have one X chromosome.

Carrier: An individual who is heterozygous at a given locus, carrying both a normal allele and a mutant recessive allele, and who appears normal phenotypically.

Summary

Huntington disease (HD) and phenylketonuria (PKU) are examples of dominant and recessive disorders, respectively. They follow the basic rules of heredity described by Mendel more than a century ago. A gene may exist in two or more different forms (alleles). One allele can dominate the expression of the other. The two alleles, one from each parent, separate (segregate) during gamete formation. This rule is Mendel's first law, the law of segregation.

Mendel's second law is the law of independent assortment: The inheritance of one gene is not affected by the inheritance of another gene. However, genes that are closely linked on the same chromosome can co-assort, thus violating Mendel's law of independent assortment. Such violations make it possible to map genes to chromosomes by using linkage analysis. For Huntington disease and PKU, linkage has been established and the genes responsible for the disorders have been identified.

Mendel's laws of heredity do not, however, explain all genetic phenomena. Genes on the X chromosome, such as the gene for red-green color blindness, require an extension of Mendel's laws. Further, most psychological dimensions and disorders show more complex patterns of inheritance than do single-gene disorders such as Huntington disease, PKU, or X-linked conditions such as red-green color blindness. Complex disorders such as schizophrenia and continuous dimensions such as cognitive ability are likely to be influenced by multiple genes as well as by multiple environmental factors. Quantitative genetic theory extends Mendel's single-gene rules to multiple-gene systems. The essence of the theory is that complex traits can be influenced by many genes, but each gene is inherited according to Mendel's laws. Quantitative genetic methods, especially adoption and twin studies, can detect genetic influence for complex traits.

CHAPTER **FOUR**

The Biological Basis of Heredity

M endel was able to deduce the laws of heredity even though he had no idea of how heredity works at the chemical or physiological level. Quantitative genetics, such as twin and adoption studies, depends on Mendel's laws of heredity but does not require knowledge of the biological basis of heredity. However, it is important to understand the biological mechanisms underlying heredity for two reasons. First, understanding the biological basis of heredity makes it clear that the processes by which genes affect behavior are not mystical. Second, this understanding is crucial for appreciating the exciting advances in attempts to identify genes associated with behavior. This chapter describes the biological basis of heredity. There are many excellent genetics texts that provide great detail about this subject (e.g., Hartwell, Goldberg, Fischer, Hood, & Aquadro, 2014). The biological basis of heredity includes the fact that genes are contained on structures called chromosomes. The linkage of genes that lie close together on a chromosome has made possible the **mapping** of the human genome. Moreover, abnormalities in chromosomes contribute importantly to behavioral disorders, especially intellectual disability.

DNA

Nearly a century after Mendel did his experiments, it became apparent that DNA (deoxyribonucleic acid) is the molecule responsible for heredity. In 1953, James Watson and Francis Crick proposed a molecular structure for DNA that could explain how genes are replicated and how DNA codes for proteins. As shown in Figure 4.1, the DNA molecule consists of two strands that are held apart by pairs of four bases: adenine, thymine, guanine, and cytosine. As a result of the structural properties of these bases, adenine always pairs with thymine and guanine always pairs with cytosine. The backbone of each strand consists of sugar and phosphate molecules. The strands coil around each other to form the famous double helix of DNA (Figure 4.2).

The specific pairing of bases in these two-stranded molecules allows DNA to carry out its two functions: to replicate itself and to direct the synthesis of proteins. Replication of DNA occurs during the process of cell division. The double helix of the DNA molecule unzips, separating the paired bases (Figure 4.3). The two strands unwind, and each strand attracts the appropriate bases to construct its complement. In this way, two complete double helices of DNA are created where there was previously only one. This process of replication is the essence of life, which began billions of years ago when the first cells replicated themselves. It is also the essence of each of our lives, beginning with a single cell and faithfully reproducing our DNA in trillions of cells.

The second major function of DNA is to direct the synthesis of proteins according to the genetic information that resides in the particular sequence of bases. DNA encodes the various sequences of the 20 amino acids making up the thousands of specific enzymes and other proteins that are the stuff of living organisms. Box 4.1 describes this process, the so-called central dogma of **molecular genetics.**

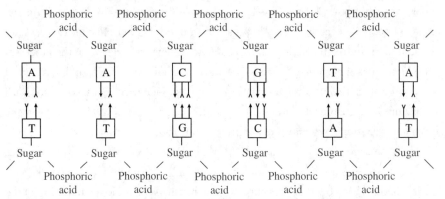

FIGURE 4.1 Flat representation of the four DNA bases in which adenine (A) always pairs with thymine (T) and guanine (G) always pairs with cytosine (C). (Information from *Heredity, Evolution, and Society* by I. M. Lerner. W. H. Freeman and Company. ©1968.)

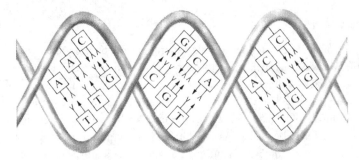

FIGURE 4.2 A three-dimensional view of a segment of DNA. (Information from *Heredity, Evolution, and Society* by I. M. Lerner. W. H. Freeman and Company. ©1968.)

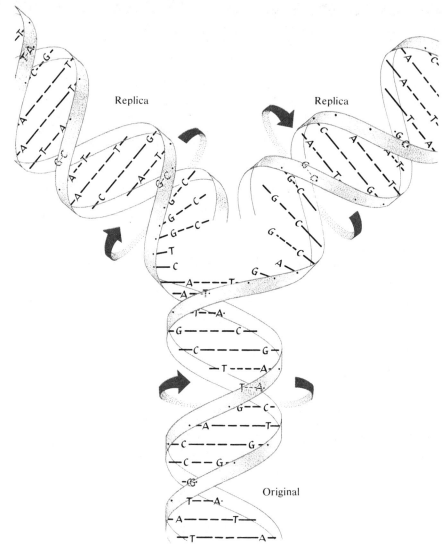

FIGURE 4.3 Replication of DNA. (Information from *Molecular Biology of Bacterial Viruses* by G. S. Stent. W. H. Freeman and Company. ©1963.)

What is the genetic code contained in the sequence of DNA bases, which is transcribed to **messenger RNA (mRNA**; see Box 4.1) and then translated into amino acid sequences? The code consists of various sequences of three bases, which are called *codons* (Table 4.1). For example, three adenines in a row (AAA) in the DNA molecule will be transcribed in mRNA as three uracils (UUU). This mRNA codon codes for the amino acid phenylalanine. Although there are 64 possible **triplet codons** ($4^3 = 64$), there are only 20 amino acids. Some amino acids are coded by as many as six codons. Any one of three particular codons signals the end of a transcribed sequence (stop signals).

BOX 4.1 The "Central Dogma" of Molecular Genetics

Genetic information flows from DNA to RNA to protein. These protein-coding genes are DNA segments that are a few thousand to several million DNA base pairs in length. The DNA molecule contains a linear message consisting of four bases (adenine, thymine, guanine,

and cytosine); in this two-stranded molecule, A always pairs with T and G always pairs with C. The message is decoded in two basic steps, shown in the figure: (a) **transcription** of DNA into a different sort of nucleic acid called ribonucleic acid, or RNA, and (b) **translation** of RNA into proteins.

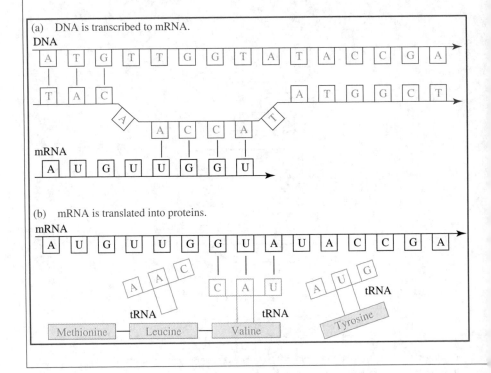

This same genetic code applies to all living organisms. Discovering this code was one of the great triumphs of molecular biology. The human set of **DNA sequences** (the genome) consists of about 3 billion **base pairs**, counting just one chromosome from each pair of chromosomes. The 3 billion base pairs contain about 20,000 protein-coding genes, which range in size from about 1000 bases to 2 million bases. The chromosomal locations of most genes are known. About a third of our protein-coding genes are expressed only in the brain; these are likely to be most important for behavior. The human genome sequence is like an encyclopedia of genes with 3 billion letters, equivalent in length to about 3000 books of 500 pages each. Continuing with this simile, the encyclopedia of genes is written in an alphabet consisting of 4 letters

In the transcription process, the sequence of bases in one strand of the DNA double helix is copied to RNA, specifically a type of RNA called *messenger RNA (mRNA)* because it relays the DNA code. mRNA is single stranded and is formed by a process of base pairing similar to the replication of DNA, except that uracil substitutes for thymine (so that A pairs with U instead of T). In the figure, one DNA strand is being transcribed—the DNA bases ACCA have just been copied as UGGU in mRNA. mRNA leaves the nucleus of the cell and enters the cell body (cytoplasm), where it connects with **ribosomes,** which are the factories where proteins are built.

The second step involves translation of the mRNA into amino acid sequences that form proteins. Another form of RNA, called **transfer RNA (tRNA),** transfers amino acids to the ribosomes. Each tRNA is specific to 1 of the 20 amino acids. The tRNA molecules, with their attached specific amino acids, pair up with the mRNA in a sequence dictated by the base sequence of the mRNA, as the ribosome moves along the mRNA strand. Each of the 20 amino acids found in proteins is specified by a codon made up of three sequential mRNA bases. In the figure, the mRNA code has begun to dictate a protein that includes the amino acid sequence methionine-leucine-valine-tyrosine. Valine has just been added to the chain that already includes methionine and leucine. The mRNA triplet code GUA attracts tRNA with the complementary code CAU. This tRNA transfers its attached amino acid valine, which is then bonded to the growing chain of amino acids. The next mRNA codon, UAC, is attracting tRNA with the complementary codon, AUG, for tyrosine. Although this process seems very complicated, amino acids are incorporated into chains at the incredible rate of about 100 per second. Proteins consist of particular sequences of about 100 to 1000 amino acids. The sequence of amino acids determines the shape and function of proteins. Protein shape is subsequently altered in other ways called **posttranslational modifications**. These changes affect its function and are not controlled by the genetic code.

Surprisingly, DNA that is transcribed and translated like this represents only about 2 percent of the genome. What is the other 98 percent doing? See Chapter 10 for an answer.

(A, T, G, C), with 3-letter words (codons) organized into 23 volumes (chromosomes). This simile, however, does not comfortably extend to the fact that each encyclopedia is different; millions of letters (about 1 in 1000) differ for any two people. There is no single human genome; we each have a different genome, except for identical twins. Most of the life sciences focus on the generalities of the genome, but the genetic causes of diseases and disorders lie in these variations in the genome. These variations on the human theme are the focus of behavioral genetics.

The twentieth century has been called the century of the gene. The century began with the re-discovery of Mendel's laws of heredity. The word *genetics* was first coined in 1905. Almost 50 years later, Crick and Watson described the double helix of DNA,

TABLE 4.1
The Genetic Code

Amino Acid*	DNA Code
Alanine	CGA, CGG, CGT, CGC
Arginine	GCA, GCG, GCT, GCC, TCT, TCC
Asparagine	TTA, TTG
Aspartic acid	CTA, CTG
Cysteine	ACA, ACG
Glutamic acid	CTT, CTC
Glutamine	GTT, GTC
Glycine	CCA, CCG, CCT, CCC
Histidine	GTA, GTG
Isoleucine	TAA, TAG, TAT
Leucine	AAT, AAC, GAA, GAG, GAT, GAC
Lysine	TTT, TTC
Methionine	TAC
Phenylalanine	AAA, AAG
Proline	GGA, GGG, GGT, GGC
Serine	AGA, AGG, AGT, AGC, TCA, TCG
Threonine	TGA, TGG, TGT, TGC
Tryptophan	ACC
Tyrosine	ATA, ATG
Valine	CAA, CAG, CAT, CAC
(Stop signals)	ATT, ATC, ACT

*The 20 amino acids are organic molecules that are linked together by peptide bonds to form polypeptides, which are the building blocks of enzymes and other proteins. The particular combination of amino acids determines the shape and function of the polypeptide.

the premier icon of science. The pace of discoveries accelerated greatly during the next 50 years, culminating at the turn of the twenty-first century with the sequencing of the human genome. Most of the human genome was sequenced by 2001 (International Human Genome Sequencing Consortium, 2001; Venter et al., 2001). Subsequent publications have presented the finished sequence for all chromosomes (e.g., Gregory et al., 2006).

Sequencing of the human genome and the technologies associated with it have led to an explosion of new findings in genetics. One of many examples was *alternative splicing,* in which mRNA is spliced to create different transcripts, which are then translated into different proteins (Brett, Pospisil, Valcárcel, Reich, & Bork, 2002). Alternative splicing has a crucial role in the generation of biological complexity, and its disruption can lead to a wide range of human diseases (Barash et al., 2010;

Matera & Wang, 2014). The speed of discovery in genetics is now so great that it would be impossible to predict what will happen in the next 5 years, let alone the next 50 years. Most geneticists would agree with Francis Collins (2010, 2015), the director of the U.S. National Institutes of Health and leader in the Human Genome Project, who expects that the entire genome of all newborns will soon be sequenced to screen for genetic problems and that eventually we will each possess an electronic flash drive containing our DNA sequence. Individual DNA sequences would herald a revolution in personalized medicine in which treatment could be individually tailored rather than dependent on our present one-size-fits-all approach. That is, DNA may allow us to predict problems and intervene to prevent them. In the near future, physicians can look forward to a medical landscape in which the pairing of affordable, efficient DNA sequencing and electronic health records could be used to inform a lifetime of health care strategies (Collins, 2015). This could involve genetic engineering that alters DNA; however, such efforts with regard to gene therapy in the human species have been historically difficult, even for single-gene disorders. Importantly, to prevent complex behavioral problems that are affected by many genes as well as many environmental factors, behavioral and environmental engineering will be needed.

We are now in a better position to understand DNA changes in health, behavior, and disease in ways that would not have been thought possible five years ago. There are detailed maps of genetic variation, and much is known about the function of genes and the effects of genetic variation. Thanks to decreasing costs of new sequencing technologies (see Chapter 9), researchers are examining genome changes that lead to both inherited rare and common diseases. Another new direction for research involves efforts to understand the *human microbiome* (Lepage et al., 2013), the genomes of the microbes that live in and on our bodies, as well as the *epigenome* (see Chapter 10), chemical marks on our DNA that regulate gene expression (Rivera & Ren, 2013). For behavioral genetics, the most important thing to understand about the DNA basis of heredity is that the process by which genes affect behavior is not mystical. Genes code for sequences of amino acids that form the thousands of proteins of which organisms are made. Proteins create the skeletal system, muscles, the endocrine system, the immune system, the digestive system, and, most important for behavior, the nervous system. Genes do not code for behavior directly, but DNA variations that create differences in these physiological systems can affect behavior. We will discuss DNA variations in Chapter 9.

KEY CONCEPTS

Codon: A sequence of three bases that codes for a particular amino acid or the end of a transcribed sequence.

Transcription: The synthesis of an RNA molecule from DNA in the cell nucleus.

Translation: Assembly of amino acids into peptide chains on the basis of information encoded in messenger RNA. Occurs on ribosomes in the cell cytoplasm.

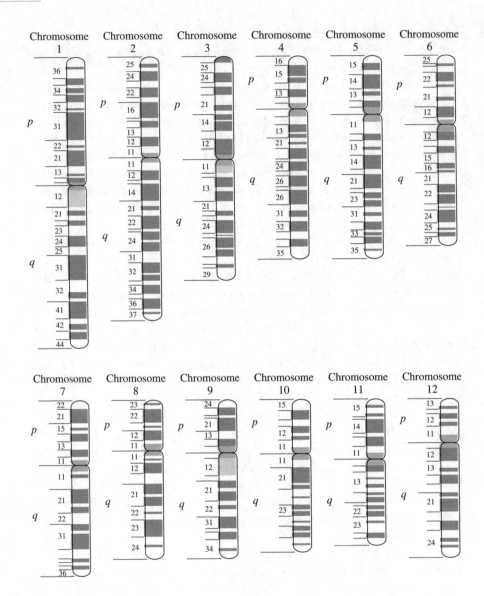

CHROMOSOMES

As discussed in Chapter 3, Mendel did not know that genes are grouped together on chromosomes, so he assumed that all genes are inherited independently. However, Mendel's second law of independent assortment is violated when two genes are close together on the same chromosome. In this case, the two genes are not inherited independently; and, on the basis of this nonindependent assortment, linkages between DNA markers have been identified and used to produce a map of the genome. With the same technique, mapped DNA markers are used to identify linkages with disorders and dimensions, including behavior, as described in Chapter 9.

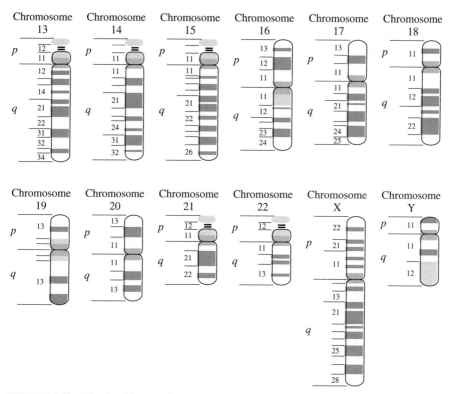

FIGURE 4.4 The 23 pairs of human chromosomes. The short arm above the centromere is called *p*, and the long arm below the centromere is called *q*. The bands, created by staining, are used to identify the chromosomes and to describe the location of genes. Chromosomal regions are referred to by chromosome number, arm of chromosome, and band. Thus, 1*p*36 refers to band 6 in region 3 of the *p* arm of chromosome 1. For more details about each chromosome and the locus of major genetic disorders, see http://www.ornl.gov/sci/techresources/Human_Genome /posters/chromosome/chooser.shtml

Our species has 23 pairs of chromosomes, for a total of 46 chromosomes. The number of chromosome pairs varies widely from species to species. Fruit flies have 4, mice have 20, dogs have 39, and butterflies have 190. Our chromosomes are very similar to those of the great apes (chimpanzee, gorilla, and orangutan). Although the great apes have 24 pairs, two of their short chromosomes have been fused to form one of our large chromosomes.

As noted in Chapter 3, one pair of our chromosomes is the *sex chromosomes* X and Y. Females are XX and males are XY. All the other chromosomes are called *autosomes*. As shown in Figure 4.4, chromosomes have characteristic banding patterns when stained with a particular chemical. The *bands*, whose function is not known, are used to identify the chromosomes. At some point in each chromosome, there is a *centromere*, a region of the chromosome without genes, where the chromosome is attached to its new copy when cells reproduce. The short arm of the chromosome above the centromere is called *p* and the long arm below the centromere is called *q*.

The location of genes is described in relation to the bands. For example, the gene for Huntington disease is at 4*p*16, which means the short arm of chromosome 4 at a particular band, number 6 in region 1 (Bobori, 2015).

In addition to providing the basis for **gene mapping,** chromosomes are important in behavioral genetics because mistakes in copying chromosomes during cell division affect behavior. There are two kinds of cell division. Normal cell division, called *mitosis,* occurs in all cells not involved in the production of gametes. These cells are called *somatic cells.* The sex cells produce eggs and sperm, the *gametes.* In mitosis, each chromosome in the somatic cell duplicates and divides to produce two identical cells. A special type of cell division called *meiosis* occurs in the sex cells of the ovaries and testes to produce eggs and sperm, both of which have only one member of each chromosome pair. Each egg and each sperm have 1 of over 8 million (2^{23}) possible combinations of the 23 pairs of chromosomes. Moreover, crossover (recombination) of members of each chromosome pair (see Figure 3.7) occurs about once per meiosis and creates even more genetic variability. When a sperm fertilizes an egg to produce a **zygote,** one chromosome of each pair comes from the mother's egg and the other from the father's sperm, thereby reconstituting the full complement of 23 pairs of chromosomes.

KEY CONCEPTS

Centromere: A chromosomal region without genes where the chromatids are held together during cell division.

Mitosis: Cell division that occurs in somatic cells in which a cell duplicates itself and its DNA.

Meiosis: Cell division that occurs during gamete formation and results in halving the number of chromosomes, so that each gamete contains only one member of each chromosome pair.

A common copying error for chromosomes is an uneven split of the pairs of chromosomes during meiosis, called *nondisjunction* (see Figure 4.5). The most common form of intellectual disability, Down syndrome, is caused by nondisjunction of one of the smallest chromosomes, chromosome 21. Many other chromosomal problems occur, such as breaks in chromosomes that lead to inversion, deletion, duplication, and translocation. About half of all fertilized human eggs have a chromosomal abnormality. Most of these abnormalities result in early spontaneous abortions (miscarriages). At birth, about 1 in 250 babies have an obvious chromosomal abnormality. Small abnormalities such as deletions have been difficult to detect but are being made much easier to detect by DNA **microarrays** and sequencing, which are described in Chapter 9. Although chromosomal abnormalities occur for all chromosomes, only fetuses with the least severe abnormalities survive to birth. Some of these babies die

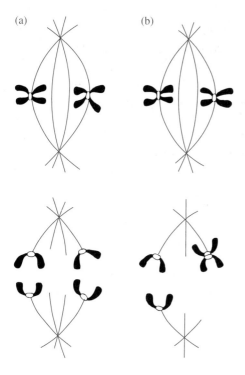

(a)   (b)

FIGURE 4.5 Nondisjunction of chromo-somes. (a) When eggs and sperm are formed, chromosomes for each pair line up and then split, and each new egg or sperm has just one member of each chromosome pair. (b) Sometimes this division does not occur properly, so one egg or sperm has both members of a chromosome pair and the other egg or sperm has neither.

soon after they are born. For example, most babies with three chromosomes (**trisomy**) of chromosome 13 die in the first month, and most of those with trisomy-18 die within the first year. Other chromosomal abnormalities are less lethal but result in behavioral and physical problems. Nearly all major chromosomal abnormalities influence cognitive ability, as expected if cognitive ability is affected by many genes. Because the behavioral effects of chromosomal abnormalities often involve intellectual disability, they are discussed in Chapter 12.

Missing a whole chromosome is lethal, except for the X and Y chromosomes. Having an entire extra chromosome is also lethal, except for the smallest chromosomes and the X chromosome, which is one of the largest. The reason why the X chromosome is the exception is also the reason why half of all chromosomal abnormalities that exist in newborns involve the sex chromosomes. In females, one of the two X chromosomes is inactivated, in the sense that most of its genes are not transcribed. In males and females with extra X chromosomes, the extra X chromosomes also are inactivated. For this reason, even though X is a large chromosome with many genes, having an extra X in males or females is not lethal. The most common sex chromosome abnormalities are XXY (males with an extra X), XXX (females with an extra X), and XYY (males with an extra Y), each with an incidence of about 1 in 1000. The incidence of XO (females with just one X) is lower, 1 in 2500 at birth, because 98 percent of such conceptuses abort spontaneously.

Summary

One of the most exciting advances in biology has been understanding Mendel's "elements" of heredity. The double helix structure of DNA relates to its dual functions of self-replication and protein synthesis. The genetic code consists of a sequence of three DNA bases that codes for amino acids. DNA is transcribed to mRNA, which is translated into amino acid sequences.

Genes are inherited on chromosomes. Linkage between DNA markers and behavior can be detected by looking for exceptions to Mendel's law of independent assortment, because a DNA marker and a gene for behavior are not inherited independently if they are close together on the same chromosome. Our species has 23 pairs of chromosomes. Mistakes in duplicating chromosomes often affect behavior directly. About 1 in 250 newborns has a major chromosomal abnormality, and about half of these abnormalities involve the sex chromosomes.

CHAPTER **FIVE**

Animal Models in Behavioral Genetics

B ehavioral genetic research includes both human and animal studies. In this chapter we will describe the different ways that animal research has been used to help us understand the roles of genes and environments in behavior. The first part of the chapter focuses on quantitative genetic designs, while the second describes how animal studies help to identify genes and clarify their function.

QUANTITATIVE GENETIC EXPERIMENTS TO INVESTIGATE ANIMAL BEHAVIOR

Dogs provide a dramatic yet familiar example of genetic variability within species (Figure 5.1). Despite their great variability in size and physical appearance—from a height of six inches for the Chihuahua to three feet for the Irish wolfhound—they are all members of the same species. Molecular genetic research suggests that dogs, which originated from wolves about 30,000 years ago as they were domesticated, may have enriched their supply of genetic variability by repeated intercrossing with wolves (vonHoldt et al., 2010). The genome of the domestic dog has been sequenced (Lindblad-Toh et al., 2005), which makes it possible to identify dog breeds on the basis of DNA alone and suggests that there are four basic genetic clusters of dogs: wolves and Asian dogs (the earliest domesticated dogs, such as Akitas and Lhasa Apsos), mastiff-type dogs (e.g., mastiffs and boxers), working dogs (e.g., collies and sheepdogs), and hunting dogs (e.g., hounds and terriers) (Parker et al., 2004). A surprising finding from molecular genetic research on dogs is that only a small number of major genes are involved in the high degree of diversity in dog species (Wayne & vonHoldt, 2012).

Dogs also illustrate genetic effects on behavior. Although physical differences between breeds are most obvious, dogs have been bred for centuries as much for

FIGURE 5.1 Dog breeds illustrate genetic diversity within species for behavior as well as physical appearance.

their behavior as for their looks. In 1576, the earliest English-language book on dogs classified breeds primarily on the basis of behavior. For example, terriers (from *terra,* which is Latin for "earth") were bred to creep into burrows to drive out small animals. Another book, published in 1686, described the behavior for which spaniels were originally selected. They were bred to creep up on birds and then spring to frighten the birds into the hunter's net, which is the origin of the *springer spaniel.* With the advent of the shotgun, different spaniels were bred to point rather than to spring. The author of the 1686 work was especially interested in temperament: "Spaniels by Nature are very loveing, surpassing all other Creatures, for in Heat and Cold, Wet and Dry, Day and Night, they will not forsake their Master" (cited by Scott & Fuller, 1965, p. 47). These temperamental characteristics led to the creation of spaniel breeds selected specifically to be pets, such as the King Charles spaniel, which is known for its loving and gentle temperament.

Behavioral classification of dogs continues today. Sheepdogs herd, retrievers retrieve, trackers track, pointers point, and guard dogs guard with minimal training. Breeds also differ strikingly in trainability and in temperamental traits such as emotionality, activity, and aggressiveness, although there is also substantial variation in these traits within each breed (Coren, 2005). The selection process can be quite fine-tuned. For example, in France, where dogs are used chiefly for farm work, there are 17 breeds of shepherd and stock dogs specializing in aspects of this work. In England, dogs have been bred primarily for hunting, and there are 26 recognized breeds of hunting dogs. Dogs are unusual in the extent to which different breeds have been intentionally bred to accentuate genetic differences in behavior. Studies have also examined the heritability of specific behaviors in dogs, especially for social behaviors. That is, although there are breed-specific behaviors, there is also substantial individual variation that is heritable (e.g., Persson, Roth, Johnsson, Wright, & Jensen, 2015), which helps to explain why we see a great deal of variation even within well-characterized dog breeds.

An extensive behavioral genetic research program on breeds of dogs was conducted over two decades by J. Paul Scott and John Fuller (1965). They studied the development of pure breeds and hybrids of the five breeds pictured in Figure 5.2: wire-haired fox terriers, cocker spaniels, basenjis, sheepdogs, and beagles. These breeds are all about the same size, but they differ markedly in behavior. Although considerable genetic variability remains within each breed, average behavioral differences among the breeds reflect their breeding history. For example, as their history would suggest, terriers are aggressive scrappers, while spaniels are nonaggressive and people-oriented. Unlike the other breeds, sheepdogs have been bred, not for hunting, but for performing complex tasks under close supervision from their masters. They are very responsive to training. In short, Scott and Fuller found behavioral breed differences just about everywhere they looked—in the development of social relationships, emotionality, and trainability, as well as many other behaviors. They also found evidence for interactions between breeds and training. For example, scolding that would be brushed off by a terrier could traumatize a sheepdog.

FIGURE 5.2 J. P. Scott with the five breeds of dogs used in his experiments with J. L. Fuller. Left to right: wire-haired fox terrier, American cocker spaniel, African basenji, Shetland sheepdog, and beagle. (From "Genetics and the Social Behavior of the Dog" by J. P. Scott & J. L. Fuller © 1965 by The University of Chicago Press. All rights reserved.)

Selection Studies

Laboratory experiments that select for behavior provide the clearest evidence for genetic influence on behavior. As dog breeders and other animal breeders have known for centuries, if a trait is heritable, you can breed selectively for it. Research in Russia aimed to understand how our human ancestors had domesticated dogs from wolves by selecting for tameness in foxes, which are notoriously wary of humans. Foxes that were the tamest when fed or handled were bred for more than 40 generations. The result of this selection study is a new breed of foxes that are like dogs in their friendliness and eagerness for human contact (Figure 5.3), so much so that these foxes have now become popular house pets in Russia (Kukekova et al., 2011; Trut, Oskina, & Kharlamova, 2009).

Laboratory experiments typically select high and low lines in addition to maintaining an unselected control line. For example, in one of the largest and longest selection studies of behavior (DeFries, Gervais, & Thomas, 1978), mice were selected for activity in a brightly lit box called an open field, a measure of fearfulness (Figure 5.4). In the open field, some animals become immobile, defecate, and urinate, whereas others actively explore it. Lower activity scores are presumed to index fearfulness.

FIGURE 5.3 Foxes are normally wary of humans and tend to bite. After selecting for tameness for 40 years, a program involving 45,000 foxes has developed animals that are not only tame but friendly. This one-month-old fox pup not only tolerates being held but is licking the woman's face. (Lyudmila N. Trut.)

FIGURE 5.4 Mouse in an open field. The holes near the floor transmit light beams that electronically record the mouse's activity. (Courtesy of E. A. Thomas.)

The most active mice were selected and mated with other high-active mice. The least active mice were also mated with each other. From the offspring of the high-active and low-active mice, the most and least active mice were again selected and mated in a similar manner. This selection process was repeated for 30 generations. (In mice, a generation takes only about three months.)

The results are shown in Figures 5.5 and 5.6 for replicated high, low, and control lines. Over the generations, selection was successful: The high lines became increasingly more active and the low lines less active (see Figure 5.5). Successful selection can occur only if heredity is important. After 30 generations of such **selective breeding**, a 30-fold average difference in activity had been achieved. There was no overlap between the activity of the low and high lines (see Figure 5.6). Mice from the high-active line

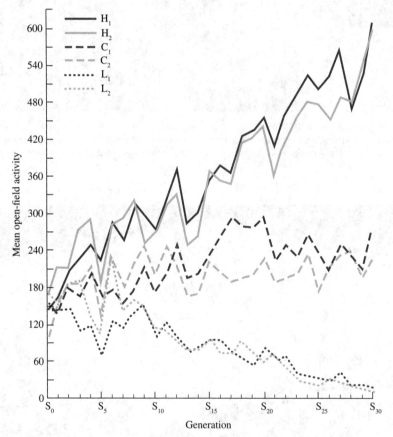

FIGURE 5.5 Results of a selection study of open-field activity. Two lines were selected for high open-field activity (H_1 and H_2), two lines were selected for low open-field activity (L_1 and L_2), and two lines were randomly mated within each line to serve as controls (C_1 and C_2).
(Data from "Response to 30 generations of selection for open-field activity in laboratory mice" by J. C. DeFries, M. C. Gervais, & E. A. Thomas. *Behavior Genetics, 8*, 3–13. ©1978 by Plenum Publishing Corporation. All rights reserved.)

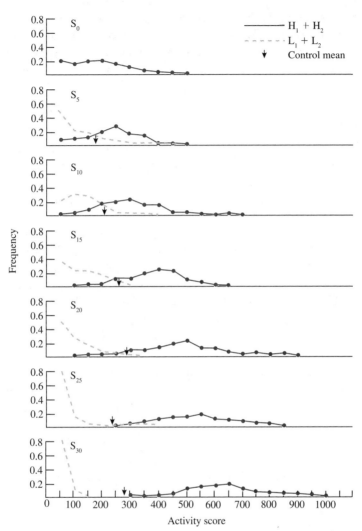

FIGURE 5.6 Distributions of activity scores of lines selected for high and low open-field activity for 30 generations (S_0 to S_{30}). Average activity of control lines in each generation is indicated by an arrow. (Data from "Response to 30 generations of selection for open-field activity in laboratory mice" by J. C. DeFries, M. C. Gervais, & E. A. Thomas. *Behavior Genetics, 8,* 3–13. ©1978 by Plenum Publishing Corporation. All rights reserved.)

boldly ran the equivalent total distance of the length of a football field during the six-minute test period, whereas the low-active mice quivered in the corners.

Another important finding is that the difference between the high and low lines steadily increases each generation. This outcome is a typical finding from selection studies of behavioral traits and strongly suggests that many genes contribute to variation in behavior. If just one or two genes were responsible for open-field activity, the two lines would separate after a few generations and would not diverge any further in later generations.

Despite the major investment required to conduct a selection study, the method continues to be used in behavioral genetics, in part because of the convincing evidence it provides for genetic influences on behavior and in part because it produces lines of animals that differ as much as possible genetically for a particular behavior (e.g., Zombeck, DeYoung, Brzezinska, & Rhodes, 2011).

Inbred Strain Studies

The other major quantitative genetic design for animal behavior compares *inbred strains*, in which brothers have been mated with sisters for at least 20 generations. This intensive **inbreeding** makes each animal within the inbred strain virtually a genetic clone of all other members of the strain. Because inbred strains differ genetically from one another, genetically influenced traits will show average differences between inbred strains reared in the same laboratory environment. Differences within strains are due to environmental influences. In animal behavioral genetic research, mice are most often studied (Beck et al., 2000). Some of the most frequently studied inbred strains are shown in Figure 5.7. A database cataloging differences between inbred mouse strains—including behavioral differences such as anxiety, learning and memory, and stress reactivity—can be found at: http://phenome.jax.org/, which includes data for over 3500 different measurements from more than 300 inbred strains (Grubb, Bult, & Bogue, 2014).

Inbred strain studies suggest that most mouse behaviors show genetic influence. For example, Figure 5.8 shows the average open-field activity scores of two inbred strains called BALB/c and C57BL/6. The C57BL/6 mice are much more active than the BALB/c mice, an observation suggesting that genetics contributes to open-field activity. The mean activity scores of several crosses are also shown: F_1, F_2, and F_3 crosses (explained in Box 2.1) between the inbred strains, the backcross between the F_1 and the BALB/c strain (B_1 in Figure 5.8), and the backcross between the F_1 and the C57BL/6 strain (B_2 in Figure 5.8). There is a strong relationship between the average open-field scores and the percentage of genes obtained from the C57BL/6 parental strain, which again points to genetic influence.

Rather than just crossing two inbred strains, the ***diallel design*** compares several inbred strains and all possible F_1 crosses between them. Figure 5.9 shows the open-field results of a diallel cross between BALB/c, C57BL/6, and two other inbred strains (C3H/2 and DBA/2). C3H/2 is even less active than BALB/c, and DBA/2 is almost as active as C57BL/6. The F_1 crosses tend to correspond to the average scores of their parents. For example, the F_1 cross between C3H/2 and BALB/c is intermediate to the two parents in open-field activity.

Studies of inbred strains are also useful for detecting environmental effects. First, because members of an inbred strain are genetically identical, individual differences within a strain must be due to environmental factors. Large differences within inbred strains are found for open-field activity and most other behaviors studied, reminding us of the importance of prenatal and postnatal nurture as well as nature.

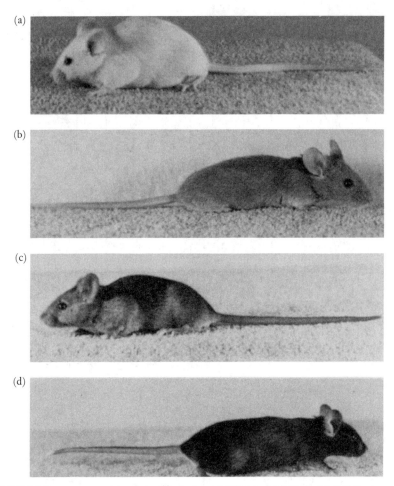

FIGURE 5.7 Four common inbred strains of mice: (a) BALB/c; (b) DBA/2; (c) C3H/2; (d) C57BL/6. (Courtesy of Professor Robert Plomin.)

Second, inbred strains can be used to assess the net effect of mothering by comparing F_1 crosses in which the mother is from either one strain or the other. For example, the F_1 cross between BALB/c mothers and C57BL/6 fathers can be compared to the genetically equivalent F_1 cross between C57BL/6 mothers and BALB/c fathers. In a diallel study like that shown in Figure 5.9, these two hybrids had nearly identical scores, as was the case for comparisons between the other crosses as well. This result suggests that prenatal and postnatal environmental effects of the mother do not importantly affect open-field activity. If maternal effects are found, it is possible to separate prenatal and postnatal effects by cross-fostering pups of one strain with mothers of the other strain.

Third, the environments of inbred strains can be manipulated in the laboratory to investigate interactions between genotype and environment, as discussed

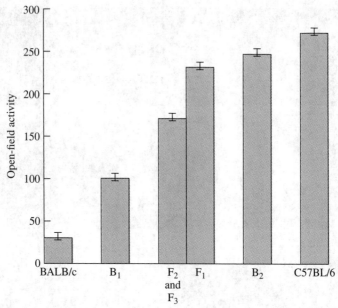

FIGURE 5.8 Mean open-field activity (± the standard error) of BALB/c and C57BL/6 mice and their derived F_1, backcross (B_1 and B_2), F_2, and F_3 generations. (Data from "Response to 30 generations of selection for open-field activity in laboratory mice" by J. C. DeFries, M. C. Gervais, & E. A. Thomas. *Behavior Genetics, 8,* 3–13. ©1978 by Plenum Publishing Corporation. All rights reserved.)

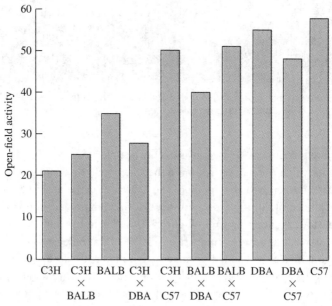

FIGURE 5.9 Diallel analysis of four inbred mouse strains for open-field activity. The F_1 strains are ordered according to the average open-field activity score of their parental inbred strains. (Data from Henderson, 1967.)

in Chapter 8. A type of **genotype-environment interaction** was reported in an influential paper in which genetic influences as assessed by inbred strains differed across laboratories for some behaviors, although the results for open-field activity were robust across laboratories (Crabbe, Wahlsten, & Dudek, 1999b). Subsequent studies indicated that the rank order between inbred strains for behaviors showing large strain differences is stable across laboratories (Wahlsten et al., 2003). For example, comparisons over 50 years of research on inbred strains for locomotor activity and ethanol preference yield rank-order correlations of 0.85 to 0.98 across strains (Wahlsten, Bachmanov, Finn, & Crabbe, 2006). Another study of more than 2000 outbred mice also showed few interactions between open-field activity and experimental variables, such as who tests the mice and order of testing (Valdar et al., 2006b). Nonetheless, there is value in multi-laboratory studies in terms of generalizability of inbred strain results (Kafkafi, Benjamini, Sakov, Elmer, & Golani, 2005). Inbred strains are also being used to test for gene-environment interactions more generally on a wide variety of behavioral phenotypes and environmental conditions. For example, mouse strains that mimic the genetics of autism spectrum disorders have been used as models to identify whether exposure to environmental toxicants are important in the development of autism spectrum and related disorders (Schwartzer, Koenig, & Berman, 2013).

More than 1000 behavioral investigations involving genetically defined mouse strains were published between 1922 and 1973 (Sprott & Staats, 1975), and the pace accelerated into the 1980s. Studies such as these played an important role in demonstrating that genetics contributes to most behaviors. Although inbred strain studies now tend to be overshadowed by more sophisticated genetic analyses, inbred strains still provide a simple and highly efficient test for the presence of genetic influence. For example, inbred strains have recently been used to screen for genetic mediation of associations between genomewide gene expression profiles and behavior (Letwin et al., 2006; Nadler et al., 2006), a topic to which we will return in Chapter 10.

KEY CONCEPTS

Selective breeding: Breeding for a phenotype over several generations by selecting parents with high scores on the phenotype, mating them, and assessing their offspring to determine the response to selection. Bidirectional selection studies also select in the other direction, that is, for low scores.

Inbred strain: A strain of animal (usually mice) that has been bred by sibling matings for at least 20 generations, resulting in individuals that are nearly genetically identical. Use of inbred strains allows genetic and environmental influences on behavior to be investigated.

ANIMAL STUDIES FOR IDENTIFYING GENES AND GENE FUNCTIONS

The first part of this chapter described how inbred strain and selection studies with animals provide direct experiments to investigate genetic influence. In contrast, as we will describe in Chapter 6, quantitative genetic research on human behavior is limited to less direct designs, primarily adoption, the experiment of nurture, and twinning, the experiment of nature. Similarly, animal models provide more powerful means to identify genes than are available for our species because genes and genotypes can be manipulated experimentally. Chapter 9 will describe methods for identifying genes in humans.

Long before DNA markers became available in the 1980s (see Box 9.1 for more information on DNA markers), associations were found between single genes and behavior. The first example was discovered in 1915 by A. H. Sturtevant, inventor of the chromosome map. He found that a single-gene mutation that alters eye color in the fruit fly *Drosophila* also affects their mating behavior. Another example involves the single recessive gene that causes albinism and also affects open-field activity in mice. Albino mice are less active in the open field. It turns out that this effect is largely due to the fact that albinos are more sensitive to the bright light of the open field. With a red light that reduces visual stimulation, albino mice are almost as active as pigmented mice. These relationships are examples of what is called *allelic association,* the association between a particular allele and a phenotype. Rather than using genes that are known by their phenotypic effect, like those for eye color and albinism, it is now possible to use millions of **polymorphisms** in DNA itself, either naturally occurring DNA polymorphisms, such as those determining eye color or albinism, or artificially created mutations.

Creating Mutations

In addition to studying naturally occurring genetic variation, geneticists have long used chemicals or X-irradiation to create mutations in the DNA in order to identify genes affecting complex traits, including behavior. This section focuses on the use of mutational screening to identify genes that affect behavior in animal models.

Hundreds of behavioral mutants have been created in organisms as diverse as bacteria, roundworms, fruit flies, zebrafish, and mice (Figure 5.10). Information about these and other animal models for genetic research is available from http://www.nih.gov/science/models. This work illustrates that most normal behavior is influenced by many genes. Although any one of many single-gene mutations can seriously disrupt behavior, normal development is orchestrated by many genes working together. An analogy is an automobile, which requires thousands of parts for its normal functioning. If any one part breaks down, the automobile may not run properly. In the same way, if the function of any gene breaks down through mutation, it is likely to affect many behaviors. In other words, mutations in single genes can drastically affect behavior

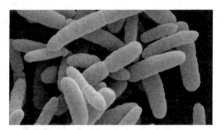

Bacteria

Zebrafish

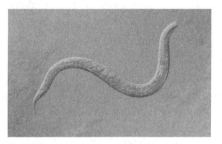

Roundworm

Fruit fly

Mouse

FIGURE 5.10 Behavioral mutants have been created in bacteria (shown magnified 25,000 times), roundworms (about 1 mm in length), fruit flies (about 2–4 mm), zebrafish (about 4 cm), and mice (about 9 cm without the tail). (Bacteria: Scimat Scimat/Science Source/Getty Images. Roundworm: Sinclair Stammers/Science Source. Fruit fly: Biosphoto/Bartomeu Borrell. Zebrafish: Mirko_Rosenau/iStock/Getty Images. Mouse: Redmond Durrell/Alamy.)

that is normally influenced by many genes. An important principle is *pleiotropy*, the effect of a single gene on many traits. The corollary is that any complex trait is likely to be *polygenic*, that is, influenced by many genes. Also, there is no necessary relationship between naturally occurring genetic variation and experimentally created genetic variation. That is, creating a mutation that affects a behavior does not imply that naturally occurring variation in that gene is associated with naturally occurring variation in the behavior.

Bacteria Although the behavior of bacteria is by no means attention-grabbing, they do behave. They move toward or away from many kinds of chemicals by rotating their propeller-like flagella. Since the first behavioral mutant in bacteria was isolated in

1966, the dozens of mutants that have been created emphasize the genetic complexity of an apparently simple behavior in a simple organism. For example, many genes are involved in rotating the flagella and controlling the duration of the rotation.

Roundworms Among the 20,000 species of nematode (roundworm), *Caenorhabditis elegans* is about 1 mm in length and spends its three-week life span in the soil, especially in rotting vegetation, where it feeds on microbes such as bacteria. Conveniently, it also thrives in laboratory Petri dishes. Once viewed as an uninteresting, featureless tube of cells, *C. elegans* is now studied by thousands of researchers. It has 959 cells, of which 302 are nerve cells, including neurons in a primitive brain system called a nerve ring. A valuable aspect of *C. elegans* is that all its cells are visible with a microscope through its transparent body. The development of its cells can be observed, and it develops quickly because of its short life span.

Its behavior is more complex than that of single-celled organisms like bacteria, and many behavioral mutants have been identified (Hobert, 2003). For example, investigators have identified mutations that affect locomotion, foraging behavior, learning, and memory (Ardiel & Rankin, 2010; Rankin, 2002). *C. elegans* is especially important for functional genetic analysis because the developmental fate of each of its cells and the wiring diagram of its 302 nerve cells are known. In addition, most of its 20,000 genes are known, although we have no idea what half of them do (http://www.wormbase.org/; Harris et al., 2010). About half of the genes are known to match human genes. *C. elegans* has the distinction of being the first animal to have its genome of 100 million base pairs (3 percent of the size of the human genome) completely sequenced (Wilson, 1999). Despite these huge advantages for the experimental analysis of behavior, it has been difficult to connect the dots between genes, brain, and behavior (Schafer, 2005), which is a lesson to which we will return in Chapter 10.

Fruit flies The fruit fly *Drosophila*, with about 2000 species, is the star organism in terms of behavioral mutants, with hundreds identified since the pioneering work of Seymour Benzer (Weiner, 1999). Its advantages include its small size (2–4 mm), the ease of growing it in a laboratory, its short generation time (about two weeks), and its high productivity (females can lay 500 eggs in ten days). Its genome was sequenced in 2000.

The earliest behavioral research involved responses to light (phototaxis) and to gravity (geotaxis). Normal *Drosophila* move toward light (positive phototaxis) and away from gravity (negative geotaxis). Many mutants that were either negatively phototaxic or positively geotaxic were created.

The hundreds of other behavioral mutants included *sluggish* (generally slow), *hyperkinetic* (generally fast), *easily shocked* (jarring produces a seizure), and *paralyzed* (collapses when the temperature goes above 28°C). A *drop dead* mutant walks and flies normally for a couple of days and then suddenly falls on its back and dies. More complex behaviors have also been studied, especially courtship and learning. Behavioral mutants for various aspects of courtship and copulation have been found. One male mutant, called *fruitless,* courts males as well as females and does not copulate. Another male mutant cannot disengage from the female after copulation and is given the dubious title *stuck.* The first learning behavior mutant was called *dunce* and could not learn to avoid an odor associated with shock even though it had normal sensory and motor behavior.

Drosophila also offer the possibility of creating *genetic mosaics,* individuals in which the mutant allele exists in some cells of the body but not in others (Hotta & Benzer, 1970). As individuals develop, the proportion and distribution of cells with the mutant gene vary across individuals. By comparing individuals with the mutant gene in a particular part of the body—detected by a cell marker gene that is inherited along with the mutant gene—it is possible to localize the site where a mutant gene has its effect on behavior.

The earliest mosaic mutant studies involved sexual behavior and the X chromosome (Benzer, 1973). *Drosophila* were made mosaic for the X chromosome: Some body parts have two X chromosomes and are female, and other body parts have only one X chromosome and are male. As long as a small region toward the back of the brain is male, courtship behavior is male. Of course, sex is not all in the head. Different parts of the nervous system are involved in aspects of courtship behavior such as tapping, "singing," and licking. Successful copulation also requires a male thorax (containing the fly's version of a spinal cord between the head and abdomen) and, of course, male genitals (Greenspan, 1995).

Many other gene mutations in *Drosophila* have been shown to affect behaviors (Sokolowski, 2001). The future importance of *Drosophila* in behavioral research is assured by its unparalleled genomic resources (often called *bioinformatics*) (Matthews, Kaufman, & Gelbart, 2005). For example, gene expression data in different tissues of *Drosophila* are available in a Web-based resource (http://flyatlas.org and http://flyatlas .gla.ac.uk; Robinson, Herzyk, Dow, & Leader, 2013).

Zebrafish Although invertebrates like *C. elegans* and *Drosophila* are useful in behavioral genetics, many forms and functions are new to vertebrates. The zebrafish, named after its horizontal stripes, is common in many aquaria, grows to about 4 cm, and can live for five years. It has become a key vertebrate for studying early development because the developing embryo can be observed directly—it is not hidden inside the mother as are mammalian embryos. In addition, the embryos themselves are translucent. Zebrafish have been useful for behavioral genetic research with studies on sensory and motor development (Guo, 2004), food and opiate preferences (Lau, Bretaud, Huang, Lin, & Guo, 2006), social behavior including aggression (Jones & Norton, 2015; Miller & Gerlai, 2007), associative learning (Sison & Gerlai, 2010), complex brain disorders (Kalueff, Echevarria, & Stewart, 2014), and alcohol consumption (Sterling, Karatayev, Chang, Algava, & Leibowitz, 2015). About 70 percent of human genes are similar to zebrafish genes (Howe et al., 2013).

Mice and rats The mouse is the main mammalian species used for mutational screening (Kile & Hilton, 2005). Hundreds of lines of mice with mutations that affect behavior have been created (Godinho & Nolan, 2006). Many of these are preserved in frozen embryos that can be "reconstituted" on order. Resources describing the behavioral and biological effects of the mutations are available (e.g., http://www .informatics.jax.org/). Major initiatives are under way to use chemical mutagenesis to screen mice for mutations on a broad battery of measures of complex traits (Kumar et al., 2011) and to understand the flow of biological information, from molecular to cellular to complex phenotype, and any steps in between, known as systems genetics (Civelek & Lusis, 2014). Behavioral screening is an important part of these initiatives because behavior can be an especially sensitive indicator of the effects of mutations (Crawley, 2003; Crawley, 2007).

After the human, the mouse was the next mammalian target for sequencing the entire genome, which was accomplished in 2001 (Venter et al., 2001). The rat, whose larger size makes it the favorite rodent for physiological and pharmacological research, is also coming on strong in genomics research (Jacob & Kwitek, 2002; Smits & Cuppen, 2006). The rat genome was sequenced in 2004 (Gibbs et al., 2004). The bioinformatics resources for rodents are growing rapidly with a genome database now also available for rats (http://rgd.mcw.edu/; Shimoyama et al., 2015).

Targeted mutations In addition to mutational screening, the mouse is also the main mammalian species used to create *targeted mutations* that knock out the expression of specific genes. A targeted mutation is a process by which a gene is changed in a specific way to alter its function (Capecchi, 1994). Most often, genes are "knocked out" by deleting key DNA sequences that prevent the gene from being transcribed. Many techniques produce more subtle changes that alter the gene's regulation; these changes lead to underexpression or overexpression of the gene rather than knocking it out altogether. In mice, the mutated gene is transferred to embryos (a technique called *transgenics* when the mutated gene is from another species). Once mice homozygous for the **knock-out** gene are bred, the effect of the knock-out gene on behavior can be investigated.

More than 20,000 knock-out mouse lines have been created, many of which affect behavior. For example, over 200 genes have been genetically engineered for their effect on alcohol responses (Crabbe, Phillips, & Belknap, 2010; Koscielny et al., 2014; also see http://www.mousephenotype.org/). Another example is aggressive behavior in the male mouse, for which genetically engineered genes show effects (Maxson, 2009). 250 knock-out mouse lines created as part of international consortium efforts were systematically screened for adult phenotypes replicating existing work and identifying many new phenotypes for known genes (White et al., 2013).

Gene-targeting strategies are not without their limitations (Crusio, 2004). One problem with knock-out mice is that the targeted gene is inactivated throughout the animal's life span. During development, the organism copes with the loss of the gene's function by compensating wherever possible. For example, deletion of a gene coding for a dopamine transporter protein (which is responsible for inactivating dopaminergic neurons by transferring the neurotransmitter back into the presynaptic terminal) results in a mouse that is hyperactive in novel environments (Giros, Jaber, Jones, Wightman, & Caron, 1996). These knock-out mutants exhibit complex compensations throughout the dopaminergic system that are not specifically due to the dopamine transporter itself (Jones et al., 1998). However, in most instances, compensations for the loss of gene function are invisible to the researcher, and caution must be taken to avoid attributing compensatory changes in the animals to the gene itself. These compensatory processes can be overcome by creating conditional knock-outs of regulatory elements; these conditional mutations make it possible to turn expression of the gene on or off at will at any time during the animal's life span, or the mutation can target specific areas of the brain (e.g., White et al., 2013).

Gene silencing In contrast to knock-out studies, which alter DNA, another method uses double-stranded RNA to "knock down" expression of the gene that shares its sequence (Hannon, 2002). The **gene-silencing** technique, which was discovered in 1997 and won the Nobel Prize in 2006 (Bernards, 2006), is called *RNA interference (RNAi)* or *small interfering RNA (siRNA),* because it degrades complementary RNA transcripts (http://www.ncats.nih.gov/rnai). siRNA kits are now available commercially that target nearly all the genes in the human and mouse genomes. More than 8000 papers on siRNA were published in 2010 alone, primarily about using cell cultures where delivery of the siRNA to the cells is not a problem. However, in vivo animal model research necessary for behavioral analysis has begun. Although delivery to the brain remains a problem (Gavrilov & Saltzman, 2012; Thakker, Hoyer, & Cryan, 2006), injecting siRNA in mouse brains has yielded knock-down results on behavior similar to results expected from knock-out studies (Salahpour, Medvedev, Beaulieu, Gainetdinov, & Caron, 2007). It is hoped that siRNA will soon have therapeutic applications (Kim & Rossi, 2007), for example, for prevention of infection by a respiratory virus (Yin et al., 2014).

CRISPR gene editing An exciting new approach to changing the sequence of specific genes uses what is called the *CRISPR/Cas9 system.* CRISPR/Cas (clustered regularly interspaced short palindromic repeats) and Cas9 (CRISPR-associated protein 9) is an enzyme system that works somewhat like RNAi to cut foreign DNA and insert itself in the invading DNA (Doudna & Charpentier, 2014). CRISPR/ Cas9 has become popular because it can cleave nearly any DNA sequence, which makes it relatively easy to use in order to add or delete base pairs for specific genes in any species (Haimovich, Muir & Isaacs, 2015). Concern has been raised because of research showing that it could be used to change the human germline (Lanphier, Urnov, Haecker, Werner, & Smolenski, 2015).

KEY CONCEPTS

Mutation: A heritable change in DNA base-pair sequences.

Targeted mutation: The changing of a gene in a specific way to alter its function, such as gene knock-outs.

Gene silencing: Suppressing expression of a gene.

Quantitative Trait Loci

Creating a mutation that has a major effect on behavior does not mean that this gene is specifically responsible for the behavior. Remember the automobile analogy in which any one of many parts can go wrong and prevent the automobile from running properly. Although the part that goes wrong has a big effect, that part is only one of many parts needed for normal functioning. Moreover, the genes changed by artificially created mutations are not necessarily responsible for the naturally occurring genetic variation detected in quantitative genetic research. Identifying genes responsible for naturally occurring genetic variation that affects behavior has only become possible in recent years. The difficulty is that, instead of looking for a single gene with a major effect, we are looking for many genes, each having a relatively small **effect size**—**quantitative trait loci** (QTLs), a term that has been used primarily in agricultural genetics (Wallace, Larsson, & Buckler, 2014).

Animal models have been particularly useful in the quest for QTLs because both genetics and environment can be manipulated and controlled in the laboratory. Animal model work on natural genetic variation and behavior has primarily studied the mouse and the fruit fly *Drosophila* (Kendler & Greenspan, 2006). Although this section emphasizes research on mice, similar methods have been used in *Drosophila* (Mackay & Anholt, 2006) and have been applied to many behaviors (Anholt & Mackay, 2004), such as aggressive behavior (Shorter et al., 2015), alcohol use (Grotewiel & Bettinger, 2015), avoidance behavior (Ghosh et al., 2015), mating behavior (Moehring & Mackay, 2004), odor-guided behavior (Sambandan, Yamamoto, Fanara, Mackay, & Anholt, 2006), and locomotor behavior (Jordan, Morgan, & Mackay, 2006). In addition, as mentioned in the previous section, behavioral genetic research on the rat is also increasing rapidly (Smits & Cuppen, 2006).

In animal models, linkage can be identified by using Mendelian crosses to trace the cotransmission of a marker whose chromosomal location is known and a single-gene trait, as illustrated in Figure 3.6. Linkage, which is also described in Chapter 9, is suggested when the results violate Mendel's second law of independent assortment. However, as emphasized in previous chapters, behavioral dimensions and disorders are likely to be influenced by many genes; consequently, any one gene is likely to have only a small effect. If many genes contribute to behavior, behavioral traits will be distributed quantitatively. The goal is to find some of the many genes (QTLs) that affect these quantitative traits.

F$_2$ crosses Although linkage techniques can be extended to investigate quantitative traits, most QTL analyses with animal models use allelic association, which is more powerful for detecting the small effect sizes expected for QTLs. *Allelic association* refers to the correlation or association between an allele and a trait. For example, the allelic frequency of DNA markers can be compared for groups of animals high or low on a quantitative trait. This approach has been applied to open-field activity in mice (Flint et al., 1995). F$_2$ mice were derived from a cross between high and low lines selected for open-field activity and subsequently inbred by using brother-sister matings for over 30 generations. Each F$_2$ mouse has a unique combination of alleles from the original parental strains because there is an average of one recombination in each chromosome inherited from the F$_1$ strain (see Figure 3.7). The most active and the least active F2 mice were examined for 84 DNA markers spread throughout the mouse chromosomes in an effort to identify chromosomal regions that are associated with open-field activity (Flint et al., 1995). The analysis simply compares the frequencies of marker alleles for the most active and least active groups. This method has been applied to other behaviors such as drug preference (Doyle et al., 2014).

Figure 5.11 shows that regions of chromosomes 1, 12, and 15 harbor QTLs for open-field activity. A QTL on chromosome 15 is related primarily to open-field activity and not to other measures of fearfulness, an observation suggesting the possibility of a gene specific to open-field activity. The QTL regions on chromosomes 1 and 12, on the other hand, are related to other measures of fearfulness, associations suggesting that these QTLs affect diverse measures of fearfulness. QTLs were subsequently mapped in two large (N = 815 and 821) F$_2$ crosses from the replicate inbred lines of mice initially selected for open-field activity (Turri, Henderson, DeFries, & Flint, 2001). Results of this study both confirmed and extended the previous findings reported by Flint et al. (1995). QTLs for open-field activity were replicated on chromosomes 1, 4, 12, and 15, and new evidence for additional QTLs on chromosome 7 and the X chromosome was also obtained. An exception is exploration in an enclosed arm of a maze (see Figure 5.11), which was included in the study as a control because other research suggests that this measure is not genetically correlated with measures of fearfulness. Several studies have also reported associations between markers on the distal end of chromosome 1 and quantitative measures of emotional behavior, although it has been difficult to identify the specific gene responsible for the association (Fullerton, 2006).

Heterogeneous stocks and commercial outbred strains Because the chromosomes of F$_2$ mice have an average of only one crossover between maternal and paternal chromosomes, the method has little resolving power to pinpoint a locus, although it has good power to identify the chromosome on which a QTL resides. That is, QTL associations found by using F$_2$ mice refer only to general "neighborhoods," not specific addresses. The QTL neighborhood is usually very large, about 10 million to 20 million base pairs of DNA, and thousands of genes could reside there. One way to

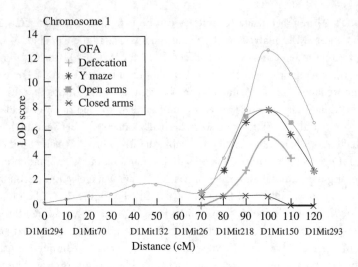

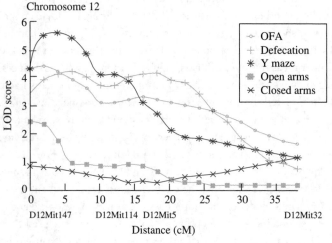

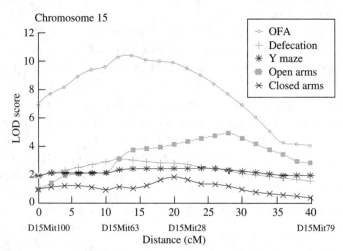

increase the resolving power is to use animals whose chromosomes are recombined to a greater extent, by breeding for many generations animals derived either from two inbred strains (an *advanced intercross*) (Darvasi, 1998) or from multiple inbred strains (*heterogeneous stocks*) (Valdar et al., 2006a). The latter approach was used to increase 30-fold the resolving power of the QTL study of fearfulness (Talbot et al., 1999). Mice in the top and bottom 20 percent of open-field activity scores were selected from 751 heterogeneous stock mice. The results confirmed the association between emotionality and markers on chromosome 1, although the association was closer to the 70-cM region than the 100-cM region of chromosome 1 found in the earlier study (see Figure 5.11). Some supporting evidence for a QTL on chromosome 12 was also found, but none was found for chromosome 15. Even greater mapping resolution is possible using commercially available outbred mice (Yalcin et al., 2010). For example, using commercial outbred strains, the chromosome 1 association with emotionality was mapped to an interval containing a single gene (Yalcin et al., 2004). Commercial outbreds are a resource for **genomewide association studies** in mice and have the potential to identify multiple genes involved in behavior. The advanced intercross has also been used in other species such as *Drosophila* (Long, Macdonald, & King, 2014), for example, to study aggressive behavior (Shorter et al., 2015).

Much QTL research in mice has been in the area of ***pharmacogenetics***, a field in which investigators study genetic effects on responses to drugs. Dozens of QTLs have been mapped for drug responses such as alcohol drinking, alcohol-induced loss of righting reflex, acute alcohol and pentobarbital withdrawal, cocaine seizures, and morphine preference and analgesia (Crabbe et al., 2010; Crabbe, Phillips, Buck, Cunningham, & Belknap, 1999a). In some instances, the location of a mapped QTL is close enough to a previously mapped gene of known function to make studies of that gene informative for human studies (Ehlers, Walter, Dick, Buck, & Crabbe, 2010). Pharmacogenetics QTL-mapping research also has been extended to rats (Spence et al., 2009).

Recombinant inbred strains Another method used to identify QTLs for behavior involves special inbred strains called **recombinant inbred (RI) strains.** RI strains are inbred strains derived from an F_2 cross between two inbred strains; this process leads

FIGURE 5.11 QTLs for open-field activity and other measures of fearfulness in an F_2 cross between high and low lines selected for open-field activity. The five measures are (1) open-field activity (OFA), (2) defecation in the open field, (3) activity in the Y maze, (4) entry in the open arms of the elevated plus maze, and (5) entry in the enclosed arms of the elevated plus maze, which is not a measure of fearfulness. LOD (logarithm to the base 10 of the odds) scores indicate the strength of the effect; a LOD score of 3 or greater is generally accepted as significant. Distance in centimorgans (cM) indicates position on the chromosome, with each centimorgan roughly corresponding to 1 million base pairs. Below the distance scale are listed the specific short-sequence repeat markers for which the mice were examined and mapped. (Reprinted with permission from "A simple genetic basis for a complex psychological trait in laboratory mice" by J. Flint et al. *Science, 269*, 1432–1435. ©1995 American Association for the Advancement of Science. All rights reserved.)

to recombination of parts of chromosomes from the parental strains (Figure 5.12). Thousands of DNA markers have been mapped in RI strains, thus enabling investigators to use these markers to identify QTLs associated with behavior without any additional genotyping (Plomin & McClearn, 1993). The special value of the RI QTL approach is that it enables all investigators to study essentially the same animals because the RI strains are extensively inbred. This feature of RI QTL analysis means that each RI strain needs to be genotyped only once and that genetic correlations can be assessed across measures, across studies, and across laboratories. The QTL analysis itself is much like the F_2 QTL analysis discussed earlier except that, instead of comparing individuals with recombined genotypes, the RI QTL approach compares means of recombinant inbred strains. RI QTL work has also focused on pharmacogenetics. For example, RI QTL research has confirmed some of the associations for responses to alcohol found using F_2 crosses (Buck, Rademacher, Metten, & Crabbe, 2002). Research combining RI and F_2 QTL approaches is also making progress toward identifying genes for alcohol-related behaviors (Bennett, Carosone-Link, Zahniser, & Johnson, 2006; Bennett et al., 2015).

An initial problem with the RI QTL method was that only a few dozen RI strains were available, which means that only associations of large effect size could be

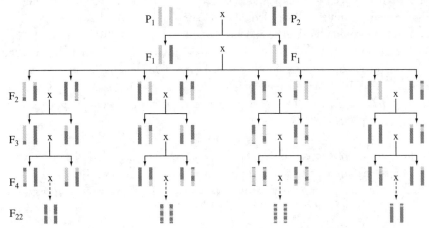

FIGURE 5.12 Construction of a set of recombinant inbred strains from the cross of two parental inbred strains. The F_1 is heterozygous at all loci that differ in the parental strains. Crossing F_1 mice produces an F_2 generation in which alleles from the parental strains segregate so that each individual is genetically unique. By inbreeding the F_2 with brother-sister matings for many generations, recombination continues until each RI strain is fixed homozygously at each gene for a single allele inherited from one or the other progenitor inbred strain. Unlike F_2 crosses, RI strains are genetically stable because each strain has been inbred. This means that a set of RI strains needs to be genotyped only once for DNA markers or phenotyped only once for behaviors and the data can be used in any other experiment using that set of RI strains. Similar to the F_2 cross, QTL association can be detected by comparing the quantitative trait scores of RI strains that differ genotypically for a particular DNA marker.

detected. Also, it has been difficult to locate the specific genes responsible for associations. A major new development is the creation of an RI series that includes as many as 1000 RI strains from crosses between eight inbred strains (Chesler et al., 2008). When eight inbred strains are crossed, the resulting RI strains will show greater recombination than seen in the two-strain RI example shown in Figure 5.12; they will also yield sufficient power to detect QTL associations of modest effect size. The Collaborative Cross, as the project is known, is now beginning to provide a valuable resource not only for the identification of genes associated with complex traits but also for integrative analyses of complex systems that include gene expression as well as neural, pharmacological, and behavioral data (Aylor et al., 2011; Buchner & Nadeau, 2015), as described in Chapter 10. Moreover, the collaborative cross mice have been intercrossed at various stages of inbreeding to create mice with varying degrees of relatedness (Svenson et al., 2012). The resulting diversity outcross population was designed to be complementary to the collaborative cross population to help increase the precision in mapping of QTLs and the correlation of behavioral phenotypes (Chesler, 2014).

A strategy similar to using RI strains that has been very useful in helping to clarify the genetics of complex traits in mice is the creation of **chromosome substitution strains (CSSs)**. CSSs are created by introducing individual chromosomes from a donor inbred strain into a host inbred strain background resulting in a panel of 22 mouse strains that vary on a single chromosome from two well-characterized inbred strains (Singer et al., 2004). CSSs have proven to be very powerful in identifying QTLs for traits like body weight and activity level (Buchner & Nadeau, 2015).

Synteny Homology

QTLs found in mice can be used as candidate QTLs for human research because nearly all mouse genes are similar to human genes. Moreover, chromosomal regions linked to behavior in mice can be used as candidate regions in human studies because parts of mouse chromosomes have the same genes in the same order as parts of human chromosomes, a relationship called *synteny homology*. It is as if about 200 chromosomal regions have been reshuffled onto different chromosomes from mouse to human. (See http://www.informatics.jax.org/ for details about synteny homology.) For example, the region of mouse chromosome 1 shown in Figure 5.11 to be linked with open-field activity has the same order of genes that happen to be part of the long arm of human chromosome 1, although syntenic regions are usually on different chromosomes in mouse and human. As a result of these findings, this region of human chromosome 1 has been considered as a candidate QTL region for human anxiety, and linkage with the syntenic region in human chromosome 1 has been reported in several large studies (e.g., Ashbrook, Williams, Lu, & Hager, 2015; Fullerton et al., 2003; Nash et al., 2004). QTLs in syntenic regions for mouse and human chromosomes have also been reported for alcohol use (Ehlers et al., 2010).

Summary

Quantitative genetic studies of animal behavior provide powerful tests of genetic influence. These studies include selection studies and studies of inbred strains; through their use we have learned a great deal about how genes and environments influence behavior. For example, studies of mice have helped to clarify how genes are involved in fearful and aggressive behavior, and there have been many studies of alcohol-related behaviors in mice. Studies of animal behavior have also been used to identify genes. Many behavioral mutants have been identified from studies of chemically induced mutations in organisms as diverse as single-celled organisms, roundworms, fruit flies, and mice. Associations between such single-gene mutations and behavior generally underline the point that disruption of a single gene can drastically affect behavior normally influenced by many genes. Experimental crosses of inbred strains are powerful tools for identifying linkages, even for complex quantitative traits for which many genes are involved. Such quantitative trait loci (QTLs) have been identified for several behaviors in mice, such as fearfulness and responses to drugs.

CHAPTER SIX

Nature, Nurture, and Human Behavior

Most behavioral traits are much more complex than single-gene disorders such as Huntington disease and PKU (see Chapter 3). Complex dimensions and disorders are influenced by heredity, but not by one gene alone. Multiple genes are usually involved, as well as multiple environmental influences. The purpose of this chapter is to describe ways in which we can study genetic effects on complex behavioral traits in humans. Chapter 5 described how complex behavioral traits are examined using animal models. The words *nature* and *nurture* have a rich and contentious history in the field, but they are used here simply as broad categories representing genetic and environmental influences, respectively. They are not distinct categories — Chapter 8 discusses the interplay between them, and the importance of gene-environment interplay is woven throughout this book.

The first question that needs to be asked about behavioral traits is whether heredity is at all important. For single-gene disorders, this is not an issue because it is usually obvious that heredity is important. For example, for dominant genes, such as the gene for Huntington disease, you do not need to be a geneticist to notice that every affected individual has an affected parent. Recessive gene transmission is not as easy to observe, but the expected pattern of inheritance is clear. For complex behavioral traits in the human species, an experiment of nature (twinning) and an experiment of nurture (adoption) are widely used to assess the net effect of genes and environments. The theory underlying these methods is called *quantitative genetics.* Quantitative genetics estimates the extent to which observed differences among individuals are due to genetic differences of any sort and to environmental differences of any sort without specifying what the specific genes or environmental factors are. When heredity is important — and it almost always is for complex traits like behavior — it is now possible to identify specific genes by using the methods of molecular genetics, the topic of Chapter 9. Behavioral genetics uses the methods of both quantitative genetics and molecular genetics to study behavior. Using genetically sensitive designs also facilitates the identification of specific environmental factors, which is the topic of Chapter 7.

INVESTIGATING THE GENETICS OF HUMAN BEHAVIOR

Quantitative genetic methods to study human behavior are not as powerful or direct as the animal approaches described in Chapter 5. Rather than using genetically defined populations such as inbred strains of mice or manipulating environments experimentally, human research is limited to studying naturally occurring genetic and environmental variation. Nonetheless, adoption and twinning provide experimental situations that can be used to test the relative influence of nature and nurture. As mentioned in Chapter 1, increasing recognition of the importance of genetics during the past three decades is one of the most dramatic shifts in the behavioral sciences. This shift is in large part due to the accumulation of adoption and twin research that consistently points to the important role played by genetics even for complex psychological traits.

Adoption Designs

Many behaviors "run in families," but family resemblance can be due either to nature or to nurture, or to some combination of both. The most direct way to disentangle genetic and environmental sources of family resemblance involves adoption. Adoption creates sets of genetically related individuals who do not share a common family environment because they were adopted apart. Their similarity estimates the contribution of genetics to family resemblance.

Adoption also produces adopted-together family members who share a common family environment but are not genetically related. Their resemblance estimates the contribution of the family environment to family resemblance. In this way, the effects of nature and nurture can be inferred from the adoption design. As mentioned earlier, quantitative genetic research does not in itself identify specific genes or environments. It is possible to incorporate direct measures of genes and environments into quantitative genetic designs, and a few such studies are under way (Chapter 7).

For example, consider parents and offspring. Parents in a **family study** are "genetic-plus-environmental" parents in that they share both heredity and environment with their offspring. The process of adoption results in "genetic" parents and "environmental" parents (Figure 6.1). "Genetic" parents are birth parents who place their child for adoption shortly after birth. Resemblance between birth parents and their adopted offspring directly assesses the genetic contribution to parent-offspring resemblance. "Environmental" parents are adoptive parents who adopt children genetically unrelated to them. When children are placed into adoptive families as infants, resemblance between adoptive parents and their adopted children directly assesses the postnatal environmental contributions to parent-offspring resemblance. Additional environmental influences on the adopted children come from the prenatal environment provided by their birth mothers. Genetic influences can also be

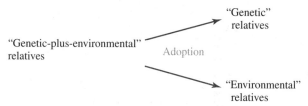

FIGURE 6.1 Adoption is an experiment of nurture that creates "genetic" relatives (biological parents and their adopted-away offspring; siblings adopted apart) and "environmental" relatives (adoptive parents and their adopted children; genetically unrelated children adopted into the same adoptive family). Resemblance for these "genetic" and "environmental" relatives can be used to test the extent to which resemblance between the usual "genetic-plus-environmental" relatives is due to either nature or nurture.

assessed by comparing "genetic-plus-environmental" families with adoptive families who share only family environment.

"Genetic" siblings and "environmental" siblings can also be studied. "Genetic" siblings are full siblings adopted apart early in life and reared in different homes. "Environmental" siblings are pairs of genetically unrelated children reared in the same home. This can be due to two children being adopted early in life by the same adoptive parents, to adopted children being reared with children who are biological to the adoptive parents, or to being part of a stepfamily where each parent brings a child from a previous marriage. As described in the Appendix, these adoption designs can be depicted more precisely as path models that are used in **model fitting** to test the fit of the model, to compare alternative models, and to estimate genetic and environmental influences (see the Appendix; Boker et al., 2011; Boker et al., 2012).

Adoption studies often yield evidence for genetic influence on behavioral traits, although results depend on the trait examined and the age of the adopted child. Specifically, studies of infants and toddlers examining behavioral outcomes find few main effects of genetics (e.g., Natsuaki et al., 2010), although there is evidence of gene-environment interplay (see Chapter 8). When children are examined later in childhood for traits like cognitive ability and other behavioral outcomes, genetic factors appear to be important (Plomin, Fulker, Corley, & DeFries, 1997).

Figure 6.2 summarizes adoption results for general cognitive ability (see Chapter 11 for details). "Genetic" parents and offspring and "genetic" siblings significantly resemble each other even though they are adopted apart and do not share family environment. You can see that genetics accounts for about half of the resemblance for "genetic-plus-environmental" parents and siblings. The other half of familial resemblance appears to be explained by shared family environment, assessed directly by the resemblance between adoptive parents and adopted children, and between **adoptive siblings.** Chapter 7 describes an important finding that the influence of shared environment on cognitive ability decreases dramatically from childhood to adolescence.

One of the most surprising results from genetic research is that, for many psychological traits, resemblance between relatives is accounted for by shared heredity

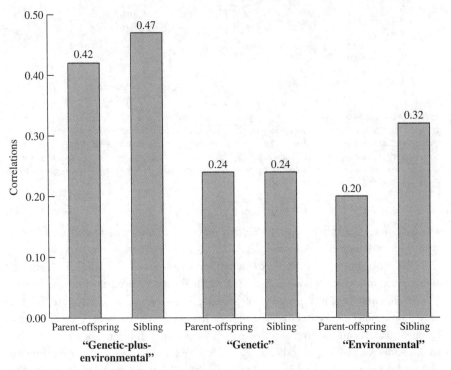

FIGURE 6.2 Adoption data indicate that family resemblance for cognitive ability is due both to genetic resemblance and to environmental resemblance. "Genetic" relatives refer to genetically related relatives adopted apart. "Environmental" relatives refer to genetically unrelated individuals adopted together. (Data from Loehlin, 1989.)

rather than by shared environment. For example, the risk of schizophrenia is just as great for offspring of schizophrenic parents whether they are reared by their biological parents or adopted at birth and reared by adoptive parents. This finding implies that sharing a family environment does not contribute importantly to family resemblance for these psychological traits. It does not mean that the environment generally or even the family environment is unimportant. As discussed in Chapter 7, quantitative genetic research, such as adoption studies, provides the best available evidence for the importance of environmental influences. The risk for first-degree relatives of schizophrenic probands who are 50 percent similar genetically is only about 10 percent, not 50 percent. Furthermore, although family environment does not contribute to the resemblance of family members for many traits, such factors could contribute to *differences* among family members, ***nonshared environmental influences*** (Chapter 7).

The first adoption study of schizophrenia, reported by Leonard Heston in 1966, is a classic study that was highly influential in turning the tide from assuming that schizophrenia was completely caused by early family experiences to recognizing the importance of genetics (Box 6.1). Box 6.2 considers some methodological issues in adoption studies.

BOX 6.1 The First Adoption Study of Schizophrenia

nvironmentalism, which assumes that we are what we learn, dominated the behavioral sciences until the 1960s, when a more balanced view emerged that recognized the importance of nature as well as nurture. One reason for this major shift was an adoption study of schizophrenia reported by Leonard Heston in 1966. Although twin studies had, for decades, suggested genetic influence, schizophrenia was generally assumed to be environmental in origin, caused by early interactions with parents. Heston interviewed 47 adult adopted offspring of hospitalized schizophrenic women. He compared their incidence of schizophrenia with that of matched adoptees whose birth parents had no known mental illness. Of the 47 adoptees whose birth mothers were schizophrenic, 5 had been hospitalized for schizophrenia. Three were chronic schizophrenics hospitalized for several years. None of the adoptees in the control group were schizophrenic.

The incidence of schizophrenia in these adopted offspring of schizophrenic birth mothers was 10 percent. This risk is similar to the risk for schizophrenia found when children are reared by their schizophrenic birth parents. Not only do these findings indicate that heredity makes a major contribution to schizophrenia, they

also suggest that rearing environment has little effect. When a birth parent is schizophrenic, the risk for schizophrenia is just as great for the offspring when they are adopted at birth as it is when the offspring are reared by their schizophrenic birth parents.

Several other adoption studies have confirmed the results of Heston's study. His study is an example of what is called the *adoptees' study method* because the incidence of schizophrenia was investigated in the adopted offspring of schizophrenic birth mothers. A second major strategy is called the *adoptees' family method.* Rather than beginning with parents, this method begins with adoptees who are affected (probands) and adoptees who are unaffected. The incidence of the disorder in the biological and adoptive families of the adoptees is assessed. Genetic influence is suggested if the incidence of the disorder is greater for the biological relatives of the affected adoptees than for the biological relatives of the unaffected control adoptees. Environmental influence is indicated if the incidence is greater for the adoptive relatives of the affected adoptees than for the adoptive relatives of the control adoptees.

These adoption methods and their results for schizophrenia are described in Chapter 13.

Twin Design

The other major method used to disentangle genetic from environmental sources of resemblance between relatives involves twins (Segal, 1999). Identical twins, also called ***monozygotic (MZ)*** twins because they derive from one fertilized egg (zygote), are genetically identical. If genetic factors are important for a trait, these genetically identical pairs of individuals must be more similar than first-degree relatives, who

BOX 6.2 Issues in Adoption Studies

The adoption design is like an experiment that untangles nature and nurture as causes of family resemblance. The first adoption study, which investigated IQ, was reported in 1924 (Theis, 1924). The first adoption study of schizophrenia was reported in 1966 (see Box 6.1). Adoption studies have become more difficult to conduct as the number of domestic adoptions has declined over the past 50 years. Domestic adoption has become less common as contraception and abortion have increased and as more unmarried mothers have decided to rear their infants. However, there has been an increase in international adoptions, with children typically being adopted at age 1 or older.

One issue about adoption studies is representativeness. If biological parents, adoptive parents, or adopted children are not representative of the rest of the population, the generalizability of adoption results could be affected. However, means are more likely to be affected than variances, and genetic estimates rely primarily on variance. In the population-based Colorado Adoption Project (Petrill, Plomin, DeFries, & Hewitt, 2003), for example, biological and adoptive parents appear to be quite representative of nonadoptive parents, and adopted children seem to be reasonably representative of nonadopted children. Similar findings of representativeness have been found for the Early Growth and Development Study (Leve et al., 2013b). Other adoption studies, however, have sometimes shown less representativeness. Restriction of range in the environments of adoptive families can also limit generalizations from adoption studies (Stoolmiller, 1999), although at least one study has found that even though there was some restriction of range, this did not have an impact on the children's development (McGue et al., 2007).

Another issue concerns prenatal environment. Because birth mothers provide the prenatal environment for the children they place for adoption, the resemblance between the birth mother and the adopted child might reflect prenatal environmental influences as well as genetic influences. A strength of adoption studies is that prenatal effects can be tested independently from postnatal environment by comparing correlations for birth mothers and birth fathers. Although it is more difficult to study birth fathers, results for small samples of birth fathers show results similar to those for birth mothers for a wide variety of behaviors including executive functioning and internalizing problems in young children (Leve et al., 2013a; Brooker et al., 2014) and educational attainment and substance use in adult adoptees (Björklund, Lindahl, & Plug, 2006; Kendler, Ohlsson, Sundquist, & Sundquist, 2015). Another approach to this issue is to compare adoptees' biological half siblings related through the mother (maternal half siblings) with those related through the father (paternal half siblings). For schizophrenia, paternal half siblings of schizophrenic adoptees show the same risk for schizophrenia as maternal half siblings do, an observation suggesting that prenatal factors may not be of great importance for the development of schizophrenia (Kety, 1987). Another strategy for disentangling the effects of genetic influences from prenatal environmental influences is to directly measure the prenatal environment, such as the birth mother's depressive symptoms during pregnancy. Findings from the Early Growth and Development Study have found that when prenatal environmental influences are included in the model, they can have an effect on child behavioral outcomes, although including genetic influences often decrease or eliminate these direct prenatal influences (Pemberton et al., 2010; Marceau et al., 2013; Leve et al., 2013a). In other words, what look like effects of the prenatal environment may be due instead to genetic influences.

For the past two decades, most domestic adoptions in the United States have been "open" to some extent. This means that the birth parents and the adoptive families know or share information about each other with the other party and the adopted child. Ongoing studies of domestic adoption have examined the extent to which openness in the adoption influences the functioning of the adoptive parents and the birth parents and found that, in general, more open adoptions were associated with better mental health (Ge et al., 2008). Openness in adoption raises some concerns about the extent to which the adopted child's rearing environment is truly independent of genetic influences from the birth parents. The majority of work in this area indicates that although there may

be contact among birth parents, adoptive parents, and adopted children, this contact is relatively infrequent, and when included as an additional variable in analyses, openness does not play an important role.

Finally, **selective placement** could cloud the separation of nature and nurture by placing adopted-apart "genetic" relatives into correlated environments. For example, selective placement would occur if the adopted children of the brightest biological parents are placed with the brightest adoptive parents. If selective placement matches biological and adoptive parents, genetic influences could inflate the correlation between adoptive parents and their adopted children, and environmental influences could inflate the correlation between biological parents and their adopted children. If data are available on biological parents as well as adoptive parents, selective placement can be assessed directly. If selective placement is found in an adoption study, its effects need to be considered in interpreting genetic and environmental results. Although some adoption studies show selective placement for IQ, other psychological dimensions and disorders show little evidence for selective placement. The Early Growth and Development Study examined selective placement effects and found that of 132 comparisons only 3 were significant suggesting that selective placement does not occur systematically in domestic adoptions in the United States (Leve et al., 2013b).

are only 50 percent similar genetically. Rather than comparing identical twins with nontwin siblings or other relatives, nature has provided a better comparison group: fraternal (*dizygotic,* or *DZ*) twins. Unlike identical twins, fraternal twins develop from separately fertilized eggs. They are first-degree relatives, 50 percent genetically related like other siblings. Half of fraternal twin pairs are same-sex pairs and half are opposite-sex pairs. Twin studies usually focus on same-sex fraternal twin pairs because they are a better comparison group for identical twin pairs, who are always same-sex pairs. If genetic factors are important for a trait, identical twins must be more similar than fraternal twins. (See Box 6.3 for more details about the twin method.)

How can you tell whether same-sex twins are identical or fraternal? DNA markers can tell. If a pair of twins differs for DNA markers (excluding laboratory error or new mutations, called *de novo mutations*), they must be fraternal because identical twins are nearly identical genetically. If many markers are examined and no differences are found, the twin pair has a high probability of being identical. Physical traits such as eye color, hair color, and hair texture can be used in a similar way to diagnose whether twins are identical or fraternal. Such traits are highly heritable and are affected by many genes. If members of a twin pair differ for one of these traits, they are likely to be fraternal; if they are the same for many such traits, they are probably identical. In most cases, it is not difficult to tell whether twins are identical or fraternal (Figure 6.3). In fact, a single question works pretty well because it sums up many such physical traits: When the twins were young, how difficult was it to tell them apart? To be mistaken for another person requires that many heritable physical characteristics be identical. Using physical similarity to determine whether twins are identical or fraternal is generally more than 95 percent accurate when compared with the results of DNA markers (e.g., Christiansen et al., 2003b; Gao et al., 2006).

If a trait is influenced genetically, identical twins must be more similar than fraternal twins. However, it is also possible that the greater similarity of MZ twins is caused environmentally rather than genetically because MZ twins are the same sex and age and they look alike. The *equal environments assumption* of the twin method assumes that environmentally caused similarity is roughly the same for both types of twins reared in the same family. If the assumption were violated because identical twins experience more similar environments than fraternal twins, this violation would inflate estimates of genetic influence. The equal environments assumption has been tested in several ways and appears reasonable for most traits (Bouchard & Propping, 1993; Derks, Dolan, & Boomsma, 2006).

Prenatally, identical twins may experience greater environmental *differences* than fraternal twins. For example, identical twins show greater birth weight differences than fraternal twins do. The difference may be due to greater prenatal competition, especially for the majority of identical twins who share the same *chorion* (see Box 6.3). To the extent that identical twins experience less similar environments, the twin method will underestimate heritability. Postnatally, the effect of labeling a twin pair as identical or fraternal has been studied by using twins who were misclassified by their parents or by themselves (e.g., Gunderson et al., 2006; Scarr & Carter-Saltzman, 1979). When

FIGURE 6.3 Twinning is an experiment of nature that produces identical twins, who are genetically identical, and fraternal twins, who are only 50 percent similar genetically. If genetic factors are important for a trait, identical twins must be more similar than fraternal twins. DNA markers can be used to test whether twins are identical or fraternal, although for most pairs it is easy to tell because identical twins (top photo) are usually much more similar physically than fraternal twins (bottom photo). (Courtesy of Professor Robert Plomin.)

BOX 6.3 The Twin Method

Francis Galton (1876) studied developmental changes in twins' similarity, but in one of the first real twin studies, conducted in 1924, identical and fraternal twins were compared in an attempt to estimate genetic influence (Merriman, 1924). This twin study assessed IQ and found that identical twins were markedly more similar than fraternal twins, a result suggesting genetic influence. Dozens of subsequent twin studies of IQ confirmed this finding. Twin studies have also been conducted for many other psychological dimensions and disorders; they provide the bulk of the evidence for the widespread influence of genetics on behavioral traits. Although most mammals have large litters, primates, including our species, tend to have single offspring. However, primates occasionally have multiple births. Human twins are more common than people usually realize—about 32 in 1000 deliveries in the United States are twins (i.e., 16 pairs of twins). Surprisingly, as many as 20 percent of fetuses are twins, but because of the hazards associated with twin pregnancies, often one member of the pair dies very early in pregnancy. Among live births, the numbers of identical and same-sex fraternal twins are approximately equal. That is, of all twin pairs, about one-third are identical twins, one-third are same-sex fraternal twins, and one-third are opposite-sex fraternal twins.

Identical twins result from a single fertilized egg (called a zygote) that splits for unknown reasons, producing two (or sometimes more) genetically identical individuals. For about a third of identical twins, the zygote splits during the first five days after fertilization as

parents think that twins are fraternal but they really are identical, these mislabeled twins are as similar behaviorally as correctly labeled identical twins.

Another way in which the equal environments assumption has been tested takes advantage of the fact that differences within pairs of identical twins can only be due to environmental influences. The equal environments assumption is supported if identical twins who are treated more individually than others do not behave more differently. This is what has been found for most tests of the assumption in research on behavioral disorders and dimensions (e.g., Kendler, Neale, Kessler, Heath, & Eaves, 1994; Mazzeo et al., 2010).

A subtle, but important, issue is that identical twins might have more similar experiences than fraternal twins because identical twins are more similar genetically. That is, some experiences may be driven genetically. Such differences between identical and fraternal twins in experience are not a violation of the equal environments assumption because the differences are not caused environmentally (Eaves, Foley, & Silberg, 2003). This topic is discussed in Chapter 8.

As in any experiment, generalizability is an issue for the twin method. Are twins representative of the general population? Two ways in which twins are different are that twins are often born three to four weeks prematurely and intrauterine environments it makes its way down to the womb. In this case, the identical twins have different sacs (called chorions) within the placenta. Two-thirds of the time, the zygote splits after it implants in the placenta and the twins share the same chorion. Identical twins who share the same chorion may be more similar for some psychological traits than identical twins who do not share the same chorion, although there is not much support for this in the literature (e.g., Hur & Shin, 2008, Marceau et al., 2016). When the zygote splits after about two weeks, the twins' bodies may be partially fused—conjoined twins. Fraternal twins occur when two eggs are separately fertilized; they have different chorions. Like other siblings, they are 50 percent similar genetically.

The rate of fraternal twinning differs across countries, increases with maternal age, and may be inherited in some families. Increased use of fertility drugs results in greater numbers of fraternal twins because these drugs make it likely that more than one egg will ovulate. The numbers of fraternal twins have also increased since the early 1980s because of in vitro fertilization, in which several fertilized eggs are implanted and two survive. The rate of identical twinning is not affected by any of these factors.

Identical twins are nearly identical for the sequence of DNA with the exception of *de novo* mutations. However, identical twins differ for the expression (transcription) of DNA, just as we differ from ourselves for gene expression from minute to minute. These expression differences within pairs of identical twins include epigenetic differences, discussed in Chapter 10.

can be adverse when twins share a womb (Phillips, 1993). Newborn twins are also about 30 percent lighter at birth than the average singleton newborn, a difference that disappears by middle childhood (MacGillivray, Campbell, & Thompson, 1988). There is also the suggestion that brain development differs in twins versus singleton children during early infancy (Knickmeyer et al., 2011). In childhood, language develops more slowly in twins, and twins also perform less well on tests of verbal ability and IQ (Ronalds, De Stavola, & Leon, 2005). These delays are similar for MZ and DZ twins and appear to be due to the postnatal environment rather than prematurity (Rutter & Redshaw, 1991). Most of this cognitive deficit is recovered in the early school years (Christensen et al., 2006a). Twins do not appear to be importantly different from singletons for personality (Johnson, Krueger, Bouchard, & McGue, 2002), for psychopathology (Robbers et al., 2011), or in motor development (Brouwer, van Beijsterveldt, Bartels, Hudziak, & Boomsma, 2006). In addition, a study of adolescent twins and siblings found no evidence of systematic differences between twin and nontwin siblings on a wide range of psychological outcomes (Reiss, Neiderhiser, Hetherington, & Plomin, 2000).

In summary, the twin method is a valuable tool for screening behavioral dimensions and disorders for genetic influences (Boomsma, Busjahn, & Peltonen, 2002;

Martin, Boomsma, & Machin, 1997). More than 20,000 papers on twins were published during the five years from 2010 to 2014, with more than half of these focused on behavior (Ayorech et al., 2016). The value of the twin method explains why most developed countries have twin registers (Hur & Craig, 2013). The assumptions underlying the twin method are different from those of the adoption method, yet both methods converge on the conclusion that genetics is important in the behavioral sciences. Recall that for schizophrenia, the risk for a fraternal twin whose co-twin is schizophrenic is about 15 percent; the risk is about 50 percent for identical twins (see Figure 3.8). For general cognitive ability, the correlation is about 0.60 for fraternal twins and 0.85 for identical twins (see Figure 3.9). The fact that identical twins are so much more similar than fraternal twins strongly suggests genetic influences. However, on a variety of behaviors fraternal twins are more similar than nontwin siblings, perhaps because twins shared the same uterus at the same time and are exactly the same age (Koeppen-Schomerus, Spinath, & Plomin, 2003; Reiss et al., 2000).

Combination

During the past two decades, behavioral geneticists have begun to use designs that combine the family, adoption, and twin methods in order to bring more power to bear on these analyses. For example, it is useful to include nontwin siblings in twin studies to test whether twins differ statistically from singletons and whether fraternal twins are more similar than nontwin siblings.

Two major combination designs bring the adoption design together with the family design and with the twin design. The adoption design comparing "genetic" and "environmental" relatives is made much more powerful by including the "genetic-plus-environmental" relatives of a family design. This is the design of two of the largest adoption studies of behavioral development, the Colorado Adoption Project (Rhea, Bricker, Wadsworth, & Corley, 2013), and the Early Growth and Development Study (Leve et al., 2013b). The Colorado Adoption Project, which has been following children from infancy to adulthood and is the longest ongoing adoption study, has found, for example, that genetic influences on general cognitive ability increase during infancy and childhood (Plomin et al., 1997).

The adoption-twin combination involves twins adopted apart and compares them with twins reared together. Two major studies of this type have been conducted, one in Minnesota (Bouchard, Lykken, McGue, Segal, & Tellegen, 1990; Lykken, 2006) and one in Sweden (Kato & Pedersen, 2005; Pedersen, McClearn, Plomin, & Nesselroade, 1992). These studies have found, for example, that identical twins reared apart from early in life are almost as similar in terms of general cognitive ability in adulthood as are identical twins reared together, an outcome suggesting strong genetic influence and little environmental influence caused by growing up together in the same family (shared family environmental influence).

An interesting combination of the twin and family methods comes from the study of families of twins, which has come to be known as the *families-of-twins method*

(Knopik, Jacob, Haber, Swenson, & Howell, 2009; Singh et al., 2011). When identical twins become adults and have their own children, interesting family relationships emerge. For example, in families of male identical twins, nephews are as related genetically to their twin uncle as they are to their own father. That is, in terms of their genetic relatedness, it is as if the first cousins have the same father. Furthermore, the cousins are as closely related to each other as half siblings are. Using this type of design, the effects of the rearing environment within the family can be disentangled from genetic influences for examining intergenerational transmission (McAdams et al., 2015). An extension of the families-of-twins method includes the combination of twins and their children (**children-of-twins design**) and a sample of children who are twins and their parents (Narusyte et al., 2008; Silberg, Maes, & Eaves, 2010). This **extended children-of-twins design** allows the effects of parents on children and of children on parents to be examined (see Chapter 8 for more discussion about what this means).

Although not as powerful as standard adoption or twin designs, a design that has been used by a few research groups takes advantage of the increasing number of stepfamilies created as a result of divorce and remarriage (Harris et al., 2009; Reiss et al., 2000). Half siblings typically occur in stepfamilies because a woman brings a child from a former marriage to her new marriage and then has another child with her new husband. These children have only one parent (the mother) in common and are 25 percent similar genetically, unlike full siblings, who have both parents in common and are 50 percent similar genetically. Half siblings can be compared with full siblings in stepfamilies to assess genetic influences. Full siblings in stepfamilies occur when a mother brings full siblings from her former marriage or when she and her new husband have more than one child together. A useful test of whether stepfamilies differ from never-divorced families is the comparison between full siblings in the two types of families. This type of design can also include stepsiblings who are genetically unrelated because each parent brought a child from a previous marriage. In the absence of **assortative mating** (Chapter 11) by the stepparents, the similarity of two stepsiblings tests the importance of shared environmental influences.

Summary

Quantitative genetic methods can detect genetic influence for complex traits. Adoption and twin studies are the workhorses for human quantitative genetics. They capitalize on the quasi-experimental situations caused by adoption and twinning to assess the relative contributions of nature and nurture. For schizophrenia and cognitive ability, for example, resemblance of relatives increases with genetic relatedness, an observation suggesting genetic influence. Adoption studies show family resemblance even when family members are adopted apart. Twin studies show that identical twins are more similar than fraternal twins. Results of family, adoption, and twin studies converge on the conclusion that genetic factors contribute substantially to complex human behavioral traits, among other traits.

There is a new wave of studies that combine designs, such as including the children of twins or nontwin sibling pairs. These combined and extended designs help to increase our ability to test different questions about the roles of genes and environment in behavior and also increase our confidence that the findings from such studies are generalizable beyond the special populations of twins and adoptees. In Chapters 7 and 8 the importance of such combination designs will be discussed in more detail.

CHAPTER **SEVEN**

Estimating Genetic and Environmental Influences

U p to this point, we have described different concepts and strategies involved in identifying genetic and environmental influences on behavior. Chapter 5 described animal research and Chapter 6 considered human research in this area. Although it is useful to be able to indicate that environmental and genetic factors contribute to behavior, quantifying those influences allows the relative importance of each to be considered. In this chapter, we will describe the techniques used to quantify genetic and environmental influences in human research using the designs presented in Chapter 6. As noted elsewhere in this book, and in more detail in Chapter 8, genes and environments work together to influence behavior, and their influences can and do change over time or depending upon circumstances. Therefore, although it is possible and useful to quantify relative genetic and environmental influences, it is also necessary to recognize that these values can change based on the population studied, the age of the sample, and many other factors.

HERITABILITY

For the complex traits that interest behavioral scientists, it is possible to ask not only whether genetic influences are important but also *how much* genetics contributes to the trait. The question about whether genetic influences are important involves *statistical significance*, the reliability of the effect. For example, we can ask whether the resemblance between "genetic" parents and their adopted offspring is significant or whether identical twins are significantly more similar than fraternal twins. Statistical significance depends on the size of the effect and the size of the sample. For example, a "genetic" parent-offspring correlation of 0.25 will be statistically significant if the adoption study includes at least 45 parent-offspring pairs. Such a result would indicate that it is highly likely (95 percent probability) that the true correlation is greater than zero.

The question about how much genetics contributes to a trait refers to *effect size*, the extent to which individual differences for the trait in the population can be accounted for by genetic differences among individuals. Effect size in this sense refers to individual differences for a trait in the entire population, not to certain individuals. For example, if PKU were left untreated, it would have a huge effect on the cognitive development of individuals homozygous for the recessive allele. However, because such individuals represent only 1 in 10,000 individuals in the population, this huge effect for these few individuals would have little effect overall on the variation in cognitive ability in the entire population. Thus, the size of the effect of PKU in the population is very small.

Many statistically significant environmental effects in the behavioral sciences involve very small effects in the population. For example, birth order is significantly related to intelligence test (IQ) scores (first-born children have higher IQs). This is a small effect in that the mean difference between first- and second-born siblings is less than two IQ points and their IQ distributions almost completely overlap. Birth order accounts for about 1 percent of the variance of IQ scores when other factors are controlled. In other words, if all you know about two siblings is their birth order, then you know practically nothing about their IQs.

In contrast, genetic effect sizes are often very large, among the largest effects found in the behavioral sciences, accounting for as much as half of the variance. The statistic that estimates the genetic effect size is called *heritability*. Heritability is the proportion of phenotypic variance that can be accounted for by genetic differences among individuals. As explained in the Appendix, heritability can be estimated from the correlations for relatives. For example, if the correlation for "genetic" (adopted-apart) relatives is zero, then heritability is zero. For first-degree "genetic" relatives, their correlation reflects half of the effect of genes because they are only 50 percent similar genetically. That is, if heritability is 100 percent, their correlation would be 0.50. In Figure 6.2, the correlation for "genetic" (adopted-apart) siblings is 0.24 for IQ scores. Doubling this correlation yields a heritability estimate of 48 percent, which suggests that about half of the variance in IQ scores can be explained by genetic differences among individuals.

Heritability estimates, like all statistics, include error of estimation, which is a function of the effect size and the sample size. In the case of the IQ correlation of 0.24 for adopted-apart siblings, the number of sibling pairs is 203. There is a 95 percent chance that the true correlation is between 0.10 and 0.38, which means that the true heritability is likely to be between 20 and 76 percent, a very wide range. For this reason, heritability estimates based on a single study need to be taken as very rough estimates surrounded by a large confidence interval unless the study is very large. For example, if the correlation of 0.24 were based on a sample of 2000 instead of 200, there would be a 95 percent chance that the true heritability is between 40 and 56 percent. Replication across studies and across designs also allows more precise estimates.

If identical and fraternal twin correlations are the same, heritability is estimated as zero. If identical twins correlate 1.0 and fraternal twins correlate 0.50, a heritability of 100 percent is implied. In other words, genetic differences among individuals completely account for their phenotypic differences. A rough estimate of heritability in a twin study can be made by doubling the difference between the identical and fraternal twin correlations [heritability = $2\ (r_{MZ} - r_{DZ})$]. As explained in the Appendix, because identical twins are identical genetically and fraternal twins are 50 percent similar genetically, the difference in their correlations reflects half of the genetic effect and is doubled to estimate heritability. For example, in Figure 3.9, IQ correlations for identical and fraternal twins are 0.85 and 0.60, respectively. Doubling the difference between these correlations results in a heritability estimate of 50 percent, which also suggests that about half of the variance of IQ scores can be accounted for by genetic factors. Because these studies include more than 10,000 pairs of twins, the error of estimation is small. There is a 95 percent chance that the true heritability is between 0.48 and 0.52.

Because disorders are diagnosed as either-or dichotomies, familial resemblance for disorders is assessed by **concordances** rather than by correlations. As explained in the Appendix, *concordance* is an index of risk. For example, if sibling concordance is 10 percent for a disorder, we say that siblings of probands have a 10 percent risk for the disorder. The use of concordance to estimate genetic risk for disorders is very common in medical genetics for the study of disorders like heart disease and cancer (Lichtenstein et al., 2000; Wu, Snieder, & de Geus, 2010) and in psychiatric genetics (see Chapters 13 and 14 for more information on behavioral genetic studies of psychiatric disorders).

If identical and fraternal twin concordances are the same, heritability must be zero. To the extent that identical twin concordances are greater than fraternal twin concordances, genetic influences are implied. For schizophrenia (see Figure 3.8), the identical twin concordance of 0.48 is much greater than the fraternal twin concordance of 0.17, a difference suggesting substantial heritability. The fact that in 52 percent of the cases identical twins are *dis*cordant for schizophrenia, even though they are genetically identical, implies that heritability is much less than 100 percent.

One way to estimate heritability for disorders is to use the liability-threshold model (see Box 3.3) to translate concordances into correlations on the assumption that a continuum of genetic risk underlies the dichotomous diagnosis. For schizophrenia, the identical and fraternal twin concordances of 0.48 and 0.17 translate into liability correlations of 0.86 and 0.57, respectively. Doubling the difference between these liability correlations suggests a heritability of about 60 percent. A meta-analysis of 12 published twin studies of schizophrenia found the heritability of liability to schizophrenia was 81 percent (Sullivan, Kendler, & Neale, 2003). As explained in Box 3.3, this statistic refers to a hypothetical construct of continuous liability as derived from a dichotomous diagnosis of schizophrenia rather than to the diagnosis of schizophrenia itself.

Modern genetic studies are typically analyzed by using an approach called *model fitting*. Model fitting tests the significance of the fit between a model of genetic and environmental relatedness against the observed data using **structural equation modeling (SEM)**. Different models can be compared, and the best-fitting model is used to estimate the effect size of genetic and environmental effects. Model fitting is described in the Appendix.

Quantitative genetic designs estimate heritability indirectly from familial resemblance. Their great strength is that they can estimate genetic influences regardless of the number of genes or magnitude or complexity of the genes' effects. As discussed in Chapter 9, DNA studies to date suggest that the heritability of behavioral disorders and dimensions is highly *polygenic*, that is, due to the relatively small effects of many genes. Consequently, it is difficult to identify the specific genes responsible for heritability. However, an exciting new approach estimates heritability directly from DNA differences between individuals even though we do not know which genes contribute to heritability. This approach estimates a type of heritability called *SNP heritability*, which is described in Box 7.1.

INTERPRETING HERITABILITY

Heritability refers to the genetic contribution to individual differences, *not* to the phenotype of a single individual. For a single individual, both genotype and environment are indispensable—a person would not exist without both genes and environment. As noted by Theodosius Dobzhansky (1964), the first president of the Behavior Genetics Association:

> The nature-nurture problem is nevertheless far from meaningless. Asking right questions is, in science, often a large step toward obtaining right answers. The question about the roles of genotype and the environment in human development must be posed thus: To what extent are the differences observed among people conditioned by the differences of their genotypes and by the differences between the environments in which people were born, grew and were brought up? (p. 55)

This issue is critical for the interpretation of heritability (Sesardic, 2005). For example, it is nonsensical to ask about the separate contributions of length and width to the area of a single rectangle because area is the product of length and width. Area does not exist without both length and width. However, if we ask not about a single rectangle but about a population of rectangles (Figure 7.1), the variance in areas could be due entirely to length (b), entirely to width (c), or to both (d). Obviously, there can be no behavior without both an organism and an environment. The scientifically useful question concerns the origins of differences among individuals.

For example, the heritability of height is about 90 percent, but this does not mean that you grew to 90 percent of your height for reasons of heredity and that the other inches were added by the environment. What it means is that most of the height

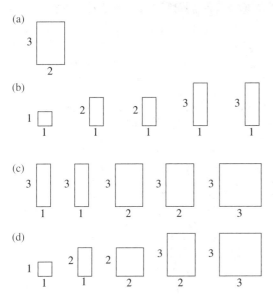

FIGURE 7.1 Individuals and individual differences. Genetic and environmental contributions to behavior do not refer to a single individual, just as the area of a single rectangle (a) cannot be attributed to the relative contributions of length and width, because area is the product of length and width. However, in a population of rectangles, the relative contribution of length and width to differences in area can be investigated. It is possible that length alone (b), width alone (c), or both (d) account for differences in area among rectangles.

differences among individuals are due to the genetic differences among them. Heritability is a statistic that describes the contribution of genetic differences to observed differences among individuals in a particular population at a particular time. In different populations or at different times, environmental or genetic influences might differ, and heritability estimates in such populations could differ.

A counterintuitive example concerns the effects of equalizing environments. If environments were made the same for everyone in a particular population, heritability would be high in that population because individual differences that remained in the population would be due exclusively to genetic differences. Using education as an example, if a society were able to give all children the same education, the heritability of educational achievement in that society would be high compared to societies in which educational opportunity differed.

A related issue concerns average differences between groups, such as average differences between males and females, between social classes, or between ethnic groups. It should be emphasized that the causes of individual differences within groups have no implications for the causes of average differences between groups. Specifically, heritability refers to the genetic contribution to differences among individuals within a group. High heritability within a group does not necessarily imply that average differences between groups are due to genetic differences between groups. The average differences between groups could be due solely to environmental differences even when heritability within the groups is very high.

This point extends beyond the politically sensitive issues of gender, social class, and ethnic differences. As discussed in Chapters 13 and 14, a key issue in psychopathology concerns the links between the normal and the abnormal. Finding heritability

BOX 7.1 Estimating Heritability Directly from DNA

An exciting new quantitative genetic technique estimates genetic influences directly from measured genotypes rather than indirectly from comparisons between groups that differ on average genetically, such as MZ and DZ twins (Yang, Lee, Goddard, & Visscher, 2011a). These estimates, sometimes called *SNP heritability,* require thousands of individuals who have been genotyped on hundreds of thousands of DNA markers called **single nucleotide polymorphisms (SNPs)**, as described in Chapter 9. Many samples meeting these requirements have been obtained thanks to SNP arrays that can genotype hundreds of thousands of SNPs quickly and inexpensively. Such studies were created to identify specific genes (see Chapter 9), but an important by-product is their ability to estimate heritability directly from DNA.

The **SNP heritability method** compares chance genetic similarity across hundreds of thousands of SNPs for each pair of individuals in a matrix of thousands of unrelated individuals. This chance genetic similarity is then used to predict phenotypic similarity for each pair of individuals, as illustrated below. That is, instead of comparing phenotypic resemblance for groups who differ in genetic relatedness such as MZ twins (100 percent) and DZ twins (~50 percent), SNP heritability uses chance genetic resemblance pair-by-pair for a large sample of individuals even though their overall genetic resemblance varies by only 1 or 2 percent, as shown in the distribution of chance genetic similarity (opposite page). Despite this minuscule variation in genetic resemblance, the large sample size makes it possible to estimate heritability directly from SNPs

	Genetic similarity $\longrightarrow$			Phenotypic similarity			
	S_1	S_2	S_3	S_4	S_1	S_2	S_3	S_4
S_1		+0.1%	−0.5%	+0.1%		++	−−	+
S_2			−0.2%	+0.5%			−	++
S_3				+0.2%				+
S_4								

Estimation of SNP heritability uses genetic similarity assessed on the basis of hundreds of thousands of SNPs to predict phenotypic resemblance for pairs of individuals in a matrix of thousands of unrelated individuals. This matrix illustrates for just four individuals their genetic similarity, which is used to predict their phenotypic similarity, shown here as minuses and pluses.

measured on the array. For example, a sample of 3000 individuals yields 4.5 million pair-by-pair comparisons. Analogous to quantitative genetic methods for estimating heritability, such as the twin method, SNP heritability estimates the extent to which phenotypic variance can be explained by genetic variance. The major advance of SNP estimates of heritability is that they come directly from measured SNP differences between individuals. Recently it has been shown that SNP heritability can also be estimated merely using association results for each SNP in a genomewide association study rather than using SNP data for individuals (Bulik-Sullivan et al., 2015). It should be noted that SNP heritability is a quantitative genetic method and does not identify which SNPs are responsible for the heritability of a trait.

SNP heritability has provided direct DNA tests of quantitative genetic estimates based on twin and adoption studies. One problem is that many thousands of individuals are required to provide reliable estimates. Another problem is that SNP heritability is limited to the specific SNPs on the SNP array, and these arrays have focused on common SNPs. As a result, SNP heritability estimates are generally about half the estimates from twin and adoption studies for physical traits (Yang et al., 2011b) and cognitive abilities (Davies et al., 2011; Plomin et al., 2013). The value of SNP heritability is that it does not require special samples such as twins or adoptees: In any large sample with DNA genotyped on SNP arrays, SNP heritability can be used to estimate genetic influence for behavioral traits. Multivariate extensions of SNP heritability (Bulik-Sullivan et al., 2015; S. H. Lee et al., 2012) can be used to estimate genetic overlap between traits or across age.

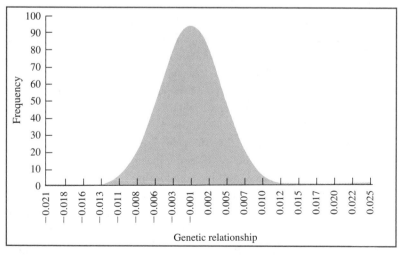

Distribution of chance genetic similarity for pairs of individuals across hundreds of thousands of SNPs (from Davies et al., 2011, Supplementary Figure 8). The SNP heritability method estimates genetic influence by predicting phenotypic resemblance from genetic resemblance. (Data from Macmillan Publishers, Ltd: *Molecular Psychiatry,* 16, 996–1005, © 2011.)

for individual differences within the normal range of variation does not necessarily imply that the average difference between an extreme group and the rest of the population is also due to genetic factors. For example, if individual differences in depressive symptoms for an unselected sample are heritable, this finding does not necessarily imply that severe depression is also due to genetic factors. This point is worth repeating: The causes of average differences between groups are not necessarily related to the causes of individual differences within groups.

A related point is that heritability describes *what is* in a particular population at a particular time rather than *what could be*. That is, if either genetic influences change (e.g., changes due to migration) or environmental influences change (e.g., changes in educational opportunity), then the relative impact of genes and environment will change. Even for a highly heritable trait such as height, changes in the environment *could* make a big difference, for example, if an epidemic struck or if children's diets were altered. Indeed, the huge increase in children's heights during the past century is likely to be a consequence of improved diet. Conversely, a trait that is largely influenced by environmental factors *could* show a big genetic effect. For example, genetic engineering can knock out a gene or insert a new gene that greatly alters the trait's development, something that can now be done in laboratory animals, as discussed in Chapter 5.

Although it is useful to think about what could be, it is important to begin with what is—the genetic and environmental sources of variance in existing populations. Knowledge about what is can sometimes help guide research concerning what could be, as in the example of PKU, where the effects of this single-gene disorder can be blocked by a diet low in phenylalanine (Chapter 3). Most important, heritability has nothing to say about *what should be*. Evidence of genetic influence for a behavior is compatible with a wide range of social and political views, most of which depend on values, not facts. For example, no policies necessarily follow from finding genetic influences or even specific genes for cognitive abilities. It does not mean, for example, that we ought to put all our resources into educating the brightest children. Depending on our values, we might worry more about children falling off the low end of the bell curve in an increasingly technological society and decide to devote more public resources to those who are in danger of being left behind. For example, we might decide that all citizens need to reach basic levels of literacy and numeracy to be empowered to participate in society.

A related point is that heritability does not imply genetic determinism. Just because a trait shows genetic influences does not mean that nothing can be done to change it. Environmental change is possible even for single-gene disorders. For example, when PKU was found to be a single-gene cause of intellectual disability, it was not treated by means of eugenic (breeding) intervention or genetic engineering. An environmental intervention was successful in bypassing the genetic problem of high blood levels of phenylalanine: Administer a diet low in phenylalanine. This important environmental intervention was made possible by recognition of the genetic basis for this type of intellectual disability.

For behavioral disorders and dimensions, the links between specific genes and behavior are weaker because behavioral traits are generally influenced by multiple genes and environmental factors. For this reason, genetic influences on behavior involve probabilistic propensities rather than predetermined programming. In other words, the complexity of most behavioral systems means that genes are not destiny. Although specific genes that contribute to complex disorders such as late-onset Alzheimer disease are beginning to be identified, these genes only represent genetic risk factors in that they increase the probability of occurrence of the disorder but do not guarantee that the disorder will occur. An important corollary of the point that heritability does not imply genetic determinism is that heritability does not constrain environmental interventions such as psychotherapy.

We hasten to note that finding a gene that is associated with a disorder does not mean that the gene is "bad" and should be eliminated. For example, a gene associated with novelty seeking (Chapter 16) may be a risk factor for antisocial behavior, but it could also predispose individuals to scientific creativity. The gene that causes the flushing response to alcohol in Asian individuals protects them against becoming alcoholics (Chapter 17). The classic evolutionary example is a gene that causes sickle-cell anemia in the recessive condition but protects carriers against malaria in heterozygotes. As we will see, most complex traits are influenced by multiple genes, so we are all likely to be carrying many genes that contribute to risk for some disorders.

Finally, finding genetic influences on complex traits does not mean that the environment is unimportant. For single-gene disorders, environmental factors may have little effect. In contrast, for complex traits, environmental influences are usually as important as, or in some cases more important than, genetic influences. When one member of an identical twin pair is schizophrenic, for example, the other twin is not schizophrenic in about half the cases, even though members of identical twin pairs are identical genetically. Such differences within pairs of identical twins can only be caused by nongenetic factors. Despite its name, behavioral genetics is as useful in the study of environment as it is in the study of genetics. In providing a "bottom line" estimate of all genetic influences on behavior, genetic research also provides a "bottom line" estimate of environmental influences. Indeed, genetic research provides the best available evidence for the importance of the environment. Moreover, genetic research has made some of the most important discoveries in recent years about how the environment works in psychological development (Chapter 8).

KEY CONCEPTS

Heritability: Proportion of phenotypic variance that can be accounted for by genetic differences among individuals.

Effect size: The size of the estimate or effect in the population.

Twin correlation: Correlation of twin 1 with twin 2. Typically computed separately for MZ and DZ twins. Used to estimate genetic and environmental influences.

Concordance: The presence of the same trait in both members of a twin pair. Used to estimate risk for disorder.

Model fitting: A statistical strategy for testing the significance of the fit between a model of genetic and environmental relatedness against the observed data.

Structural equation modeling (SEM): A statistical method for testing a conceptual or theoretical model. In behavioral genetics this method is used to estimate heritability and environmentality based on the similarity and differences among family members.

SNP heritability: Heritability estimated directly from DNA differences between individuals.

ENVIRONMENTALITY

From Freud onward, most theories about how the environment works in behavioral development have implicitly assumed that offspring resemble their parents because parents provide the family environment for their offspring and that siblings resemble each other because they share that family environment. Twin and adoption research during the past three decades has dramatically altered this view. In fact, genetic designs, such as twin and adoption methods, were devised specifically to address the possibility that some of this widespread familial resemblance may be due to shared heredity rather than to **shared environmental influences.**

As with heritability, we can estimate *how much* environmental influences contribute to individual differences in complex behaviors. The twin, adoption, sibling, and combination designs described in Chapter 6 help to clarify environmental influences as much as they help to estimate genetic influences. We can compute the statistical significance of such **environmentality** in the same way as we compute the significance of genetic influences.

Shared Environment

Shared environmental influences refer to all nongenetic influences that make family members similar to one another. This can include a wide range of factors, including neighborhood, parental education, and family factors such as parenting or the amount of conflict or chaos in the household. These factors will be shared environmental influences only if they result in greater similarity among individuals living in the same household and if they do not vary as a function of genetic relatedness. In other words, if fraternal twins are as similar as identical twins, and this similarity is not negligible, then shared environmental influences are important. Similarly, if "environmental" siblings are as alike as "genetic" siblings, then shared environmental influences are indicated. The Appendix provides more detail about how shared environmental influences are estimated in twin, sibling, and combination designs.

There has been confusion about shared environmental influences. As will be described in Chapters 11 through 19, there is little evidence of shared environmental influences on many commonly studied behaviors such as personality and cognitive abilities, especially after adolescence. The shared environmental influences that have been found are often significant only during childhood and adolescence (Plomin, 2011; Plomin & Daniels, 1987), especially for certain types of behavior problems (Burt, 2009b). In other words, residing in the same household does increase the similarity of family members, although these effects do not appear to persist once children have moved out of the home.

Nonshared Environment

Nonshared environmental influences are all nongenetic influences that are independent (or uncorrelated) for family members, including error of measurement. Because identical twins living in the same household share all of their genes and share their environment, the only thing that can account for differences within pairs of identical twins is nonshared environmental influences. Sources of nonshared environmental influences include differences in their family experience, such as different treatment by parents, or differential experiences outside the family, such as having different friends.

Quantitative genetic designs provide an essential starting point in the quantification of the net effect of genetic and environmental influences in the populations studied. If the net effect of genetic factors is substantial, there will be value in seeking to identify the specific genes responsible for that genetic effect. Similarly, if environmental influences are largely nonshared rather than shared, this finding should deter researchers from relying solely on family-wide risk factors that pay no attention to the ways in which these influences impinge differentially on different children in the same family. Current research is trying to identify specific sources of nonshared environment and to investigate associations between nonshared environment and behavioral traits, as discussed later.

Estimating Shared and Nonshared Environmental Influences

How do genetic designs estimate the net effects of shared and nonshared environment? Heritability is estimated, for example, by comparing identical and fraternal twin resemblance or by using adoption designs. In quantitative genetics, environmental variance is variance not explained by genetics. Shared environment is estimated as family resemblance not explained by genetics. Nonshared environment is the rest of the variance: variance not explained by genetics or by shared environment. The conclusion that environmental variance in adult behavior is largely nonshared refers to this residual component of variance, usually estimated by model-fitting analyses. However, more direct tests of shared and nonshared environments make it easier to understand how they can be estimated.

A direct test of shared environment is resemblance among adoptive relatives. Why do genetically unrelated adoptive siblings correlate about 0.25 for general cognitive ability in childhood? In the absence of selective placement, the answer must be shared environment because adoptive siblings are unrelated genetically. This result fits with the conclusion in Chapter 11 that about one-quarter of the variance of general cognitive ability in childhood is due to shared environment. By adolescence, the correlation for adoptive siblings plummets to zero and is the basis for the conclusion that shared environment has negligible impact in the long run. For personality and some measures of psychopathology in adults, adoptive siblings correlate near zero, a value implying that shared environment is unimportant and that environmental influences, which are substantial, are of the nonshared variety. For some measures of behavior problems in children and adolescents, adoptive siblings correlate significantly greater than zero, indicating that shared environmental influences are present (Burt, 2009b).

Just as genetically unrelated adoptive siblings provide a direct test of shared environment, identical twins reared together provide a direct test of nonshared environment. Because they are essentially identical genetically, differences within pairs of identical twins can only be due to nonshared environment. For example, for self-report personality questionnaires, identical twins typically correlate about 0.45. This value means that about 55 percent of the variance is due to nonshared environment plus error of measurement. Identical twin resemblance is also only moderate for most mental disorders, an observation implying that nonshared environmental influences play a major role.

Differences within pairs of identical twins provide a conservative estimate of nonshared environment because twins often share special environments that increase their resemblance but do not contribute to similarity among "normal" siblings. For example, for general cognitive ability, identical twins correlate about 0.85, a result that does not seem to leave much room for nonshared environment (i.e., $1 - 0.85 = 0.15$). However, fraternal twins correlate about 0.60 and nontwin siblings correlate about 0.40, implying that twins have a special shared twin environment that accounts for as much as 20 percent of the variance (Koeppen-Schomerus, Spinath, & Plomin, 2003). For this reason, the identical twin correlation of 0.85 may be inflated by 0.20 because of this special shared twin environment. However, a different study that included twins and nontwin siblings in different families found no systematic indication of a special shared twin environment for a wide range of adolescent adjustment measures (Reiss, Neiderhiser, Hetherington, & Plomin, 2000).

Identifying Specific Nonshared Environment

The next step in research on nonshared environment is to identify specific factors that make children growing up in the same family so different. To identify nonshared environmental factors, it is necessary to begin by assessing aspects of the environment specific to each child, rather than aspects shared by siblings. Many measures of the environment used in studies of behavioral development are general to a family rather than specific to a child. For example, whether or not their parents have been divorced is the same for two children in the family. Assessed in this family-general way, divorce cannot be a source of differences in siblings' outcomes because it does not differ for two children in the same family. However, research on divorce has shown that divorce affects children in a family differently (Hetherington & Clingempeel, 1992). If the divorce is assessed in a child-specific way (e.g., by assessing the children's perceptions about the stress caused by the divorce, which may, in fact, differ among siblings), divorce could well be a source of differential sibling outcome.

Some family structure variables, such as birth order and sibling age spacing, are, by definition, nonshared environmental factors. However, these factors have generally been found to account for only a small portion of variance in behavioral outcomes. Research on more dynamic aspects of nonshared environment has found that children growing up in the same family lead surprisingly separate lives (Dunn & Plomin, 1990). Siblings perceive their parents' treatment of themselves and the other siblings as quite different, although parents generally perceive that they treat their children similarly, depending on the method of assessment. Observational studies tend to back up the children's perspective.

Table 7.1 shows sibling correlations for measures of family environment in a study focused on these issues, called the Nonshared Environment and Adolescent Development (NEAD) project (Reiss et al., 2000). During two 2-hour visits to 720 families with two siblings ranging from 10 to 18 years of age, a large battery of questionnaire and interview measures of the family environment was administered to both parents and both siblings. Parent-child interactions were videotaped during a session when problems in family relationships were discussed. Sibling correlations for children's reports of their family interactions (e.g., children's reports of their parents' negativity) were modest; they were also modest for observational ratings of child-to-parent interactions and parent-to-child interactions. This finding suggests that these

TABLE 7.1
Sibling Correlations for Measures of Family Environment

Type of Data	Sibling Correlation
Child reports	
Parenting	0.25
Sibling relationship	0.40
Parent reports	
Parenting	0.70
Sibling relationship	0.80
Observational data	
Child to parent	0.20
Parent to child	0.30

SOURCE: *Data from Reiss et al. (2000).*

experiences are largely nonshared. In contrast, parent reports yielded high sibling correlations, for example, when parents reported on their own negativity toward each of the children. Although this may be due to a "rater" effect, in that the parent rates both children, the high sibling correlations indicate that parent reports of children's environments are not good sources of candidate variables for assessing nonshared environmental factors.

As mentioned earlier, nonshared environment is not limited to measures of the family environment. Indeed, experiences outside the family, as siblings make their own way in the world, are even more likely candidates for nonshared environmental influences (Harris, 1998). For example, how similarly do siblings experience peers, social support, and life events? The answer is "only to a limited extent"; with shared environmental influences accounting for only modest or none of the variance while the majority of the variance is due to genetic and nonshared environmental effects (Plomin, 1994; Horwitz & Neiderhiser, 2015). It is also possible that nonsystematic factors, such as accidents and illnesses, initiate differences between siblings. Compounded over time, small differences in experience might lead to large differences in outcome.

Identifying Specific Nonshared Environment That Predicts Behavioral Outcomes

Once child-specific factors are identified, the next question is whether these nonshared experiences relate to behavioral outcomes. For example, to what extent do differences in parental treatment account for the nonshared environmental variance known to be important for personality and psychopathology? Some success has been achieved in predicting differences in adjustment from sibling differences in their experiences. The NEAD project mentioned earlier provides an example in that negative parental behavior directed specifically to one adolescent sibling (controlling for parental treatment of the other sibling) relates strongly to that child's antisocial behavior and, to a lesser extent, to that child's depression (Reiss et al., 2000). Most of these associations involve negative aspects of parenting, such as conflict, and negative outcomes, such as antisocial behavior. Associations are generally weaker for positive parenting, such as affection.

A meta-analysis of 43 papers that addressed associations between nonshared experiences and siblings' differential outcomes concluded that "measured nonshared environmental variables do not account for a substantial portion of the nonshared variability" (Turkheimer & Waldron, 2000, p. 78). Looking at the same studies, however, an optimist could conclude that this research is off to a good start (Plomin, Asbury, & Dunn, 2001). The proportion of total variance accounted for in adjustment, personality, and cognitive outcomes was 0.01 for family constellation (e.g., birth order), 0.02 for differential parental behavior, 0.02 for differential sibling interaction, and 0.05 for differential peer or teacher interaction. Moreover, these effects are largely independent because they add up in predicting the outcomes—incorporating all of these measures of differential environment accounts for about 13 percent of the total variance of the outcome measures. If nonshared environment accounts for 40 percent of the variance in these domains, we could say the cup is already more than one-quarter full.

When associations are found between nonshared environment and outcome, the question of the direction of effects is raised. That is, is differential parental negativity the cause or the effect of sibling differences in antisocial behavior? Genetic research is beginning to suggest that most differential parental treatment of siblings is in fact the effect rather than the cause of sibling differences. One of the reasons why siblings differ is genetics. Siblings are 50 percent similar genetically, but this statement implies that siblings are also 50 percent different. Research on nonshared environment needs to be embedded in genetically sensitive designs in order to distinguish true nonshared environmental effects from sibling differences due to genetics. For this reason, the NEAD project included identical and fraternal twins, full siblings, half siblings, and genetically unrelated siblings. Multivariate genetic analysis of associations between parental negativity and adolescent adjustment yielded an unexpected finding: Most of these associations were mediated by genetic factors, although some nonshared environmental influence was also found (Pike, McGuire, Hetherington, Reiss, & Plomin, 1996a). This finding and similar research (Burt, McGue, Krueger, & Iacono, 2005; Moberg, Lichtenstein, Forsman, & Larsson, 2011) implies that differential parental treatment of siblings to a substantial extent reflects genetically influenced differences between the siblings, such as differences in personality. The role of genetics in environmental influences is given detailed consideration in the next chapter.

Because MZ twins are identical genetically, they provide an excellent test of nonshared environmental influences. Nonshared environmental influence is implicated if MZ differences in experience correlate with MZ differences in outcome. In the NEAD project, analyses of MZ differences confirmed the results of the full multivariate genetic analysis mentioned above (Pike et al., 1996a) in showing that MZ differences in experiences of parental negativity correlated modestly with MZ differences in adjustment outcomes (Pike, Reiss, Hetherington, & Plomin, 1996b). Other studies of MZ differences have also identified nonshared environmental factors free of genetic confound (e.g., Barclay, Eley, Buysse, Maughan, & Gregory, 2011; Hou et al., 2013; Viding, Fontaine, Oliver, & Plomin, 2009). A longitudinal study of MZ differences that extended from infancy to middle childhood found that MZ differences in birth weight and family environment during infancy related to their differences in behavior problems and academic achievement as assessed by their teachers at age 7 (Asbury, Dunn, & Plomin, 2006). Another longitudinal study of MZ differences suggested a pernicious downward spiral of the interplay of nonshared environmental influence between negative parenting and children's behavior problems (Burt et al., 2005). A different study also using the MZ twin difference method found that more differences in friends' aggression in kindergarten were linked with increased differences in twin aggression in first grade (Vitaro et al., 2011).

Support for the hypothesis that chance plays an important role in nonshared environment comes from longitudinal genetic analyses of age-to-age change and continuity. Longitudinal genetic research indicates that nonshared environmental influences are age-specific for psychopathology (Kendler, Neale, Kessler, Heath, & Eaves, 1993; Van den Oord & Rowe, 1997), personality (Loehlin, Horn, & Willerman, 1990; McGue, Bacon, & Lykken, 1993a), and cognitive abilities (Cherny, Fulker, & Hewitt, 1997). That is, nonshared environmental influences at one age are largely different from nonshared environmental influences at another age. In an effort to understand if nonshared environmental influences are more stable over short periods of time, one study examined stability in behavioral affect over seven days and in observer-rated warmth and control over seven minutes. Genetic and shared environmental influences were highly stable over both time spans, while the nonshared environmental influences were not (Burt, Klahr, & Klump, 2015). It is difficult to imagine environmental processes, other than chance, that could explain these results. Nonetheless, our view is that chance is the null hypothesis—systematic sources of nonshared environment need to be thoroughly examined before we conclude that chance factors are responsible for nonshared environment.

MULTIVARIATE ANALYSIS

The estimation of genetic and environmental influences is not limited to examining the variance of a single behavior. The same model can be applied to investigating genetic and environmental influences on the covariance between two or more traits, which is one of the most important advances in quantitative genetics in the past few decades (Martin & Eaves, 1977). Just as univariate genetic analyses estimate the relative contributions of genetic and environmental factors to the variance of a trait, multivariate genetic analyses estimate the relative contributions of genetic and environmental factors to the covariance between traits. In other words, multivariate genetic analysis estimates the extent to which the same genetic and environmental factors affect different traits. An important developmental application of multivariate genetic analysis is to examine genetic and environmental contributions to stability and change longitudinally in the same individuals from age to age.

As explained in the Appendix, the essence of multivariate genetic analysis is the analysis of cross-covariance in relatives. That is, instead of asking whether trait X in one twin covaries with trait X in the co-twin, *cross-covariance* refers to the covariance between trait X in one twin and a different trait, trait Y, in the co-twin. Two new statistical constructs in multivariate genetic analysis are the correlation between genetic influences on X and Y, and the corresponding correlation between environmental influences on the two traits. Focusing on the genetic contribution to the covariance between trait X and trait Y, the ***genetic correlation*** estimates the extent to which genetic deviations that affect X literally correlate with genetic deviations that affect Y. The genetic correlation is independent of heritability. That is, traits X and Y could be highly heritable but their genetic correlation could be zero. Or traits X and Y could be only slightly heritable yet their genetic correlation could be 1.0. A genetic correlation of zero would indicate that the genetic influences on trait X are not associated with those on trait Y. In contrast, a genetic correlation of 1.0 would mean that all genetic influences on trait X also influence trait Y. Another useful statistic from multivariate genetic analysis is *bivariate heritability*, which estimates the contribution of genetic influences to the phenotypic correlation between the two traits.

Multivariate genetic analysis will be featured in many subsequent chapters. The most interesting result occurs when the genetic structure between traits differs from the phenotypic structure. For example, as explained in Chapter 14, multivariate genetic analysis has shown that the genetic structure of psychopathology differs from phenotypic diagnoses in that many aspects of psychopathology are correlated genetically. The same pattern of general effects of genes is found for specific cognitive abilities (Chapter 11). A surprising example is that measures that are ostensibly environmental measures often correlate genetically with behavioral measures (Chapter 8). Another example is that multivariate genetic analyses across age typically find substantial age-to-age genetic correlations, suggesting that genetic factors contribute largely to stability from age to age; environmental factors contribute largely to change.

KEY CONCEPTS

Environmentality: Proportion of phenotypic variance that can be accounted for by environmental influences.

Shared environmental influences: Nongenetic influences that make family members similar.

Nonshared environmental influences: Nongenetic influences that are uncorrelated for family members.

Genetic correlation: A statistic indexing the extent to which genetic influences on one trait are correlated with genetic influences on another trait independent of the heritabilities of the traits.

Summary

Quantitative genetic methods can detect genetic influences for complex traits. These genetic influences are quantified by heritability, a statistic that describes the contribution of genetic differences to observed differences in a particular population at a particular time. For most behavioral dimensions and disorders, including cognitive ability and schizophrenia, genetic influences are not only detectable but also substantial, often accounting for as much as half of the variance in the population. Genetic influence in the behavioral sciences has been controversial in part because of misunderstandings about heritability.

Genetic influence on behavior is just that—an influence or contributing factor, not something that is preprogrammed and deterministic. Environmental influences are usually as important as genetic influences; they are quantified as shared environmental influences and nonshared environmental influences. Behavioral genetics focuses on why people differ, that is, the genetic and environmental origins of individual differences that exist at a particular time in a particular population. Behavioral genetic research has helped to increase our understanding of how environmental factors influence behavioral outcomes. A major example is that behavioral genetic research finds modest evidence for shared environmental influences and often large nonshared environmental influences. Understanding how genetic and environmental influences can make family members similar and different can help to guide work aimed at improving developmental outcomes for individuals. The following chapter continues this discussion about how genes and environments work together.

CHAPTER **EIGHT**

The Interplay between Genes and Environment

Previous chapters described how genetic and environmental influences can be assessed and the various designs that are typically used in human and animal behavioral genetic research. As described in Chapter 7, behavioral genetic research has helped to advance not just our understanding of how genes influence behavior but also of how environments influence behavior. Although much remains to be learned about the specific mechanisms involved in the pathways between genes and behavior, we know much more about genes than we do about the environment. We know that genes are located on chromosomes in the nucleus of cells, how their information is stored in the four nucleotide bases of DNA, and how they are transcribed and then translated using the triplet code. In contrast, we don't yet know where environmental influences are expressed in the brain, how they change in development, and how they cause individual differences in behavior. Given these differences in levels of understanding, genetic influences on behavior may be construed as easier to study than environmental influences.

One thing we know for sure about the environment is that it is important. Quantitative genetic research, reviewed in Chapters 11 to 19, provides the best available evidence that the environment is an important source of individual differences throughout the domain of behavior. Moreover, quantitative genetic research is changing the way we think about the environment. Three of the most important discoveries from genetic research in the behavioral sciences are about nurture rather than nature. The first discovery is that nonshared environmental influences are surprisingly large and important in explaining individual differences. The second discovery is equally surprising: Many environmental measures widely used in the behavioral sciences show genetic influence. This research suggests that people create their own experiences, in part for genetic reasons. This topic has been called the *nature of nurture,* although in genetics it is known as *genotype-environment correlation* because it refers to experiences that are correlated with genetic propensities. The third discovery at the interface between nature and nurture is that the effects of the environment can depend on genetics and that the effects of genetics can depend on the environment. This topic is called *genotype-environment interaction,* genetic sensitivity to environments.

Genotype-environment correlation and genotype-environment interaction—often referred to collectively as gene-environment interplay—are the topics of this chapter. The goal of this chapter is to show that some of the most important questions in genetic research involve the environment, and some of the most important questions for environmental research involve genetics. Genetic research will profit if it includes sophisticated measures of the environment, environmental research will benefit from the use of genetic designs, and behavioral science will be advanced by collaboration between geneticists and environmentalists. These are some of the ways in which behavioral scientists are bringing nature and nurture together in the study of development to understand the processes by which genotypes eventuate in phenotypes (Rutter, Moffitt, & Caspi, 2006).

Three reminders about the environment are warranted. First, as noted above, genetic research provides the best available evidence for the importance of environmental factors. The surprise from genetic research has been the discovery that genetic factors are so important throughout the behavioral sciences, often accounting for as much as half of the variance. However, the excitement about this discovery should not overshadow the fact that environmental factors are at least as important. Heritability rarely exceeds 50 percent and thus environmentality is rarely less than 50 percent.

Second, in quantitative genetic theory, the word *environment* includes all influences other than inheritance, a much broader use of the word than is usual in the behavioral sciences. By this definition, environment includes, for instance, prenatal events and biological events such as nutrition and illness, not just family socialization factors.

Third, as explained in Chapter 7, genetic research describes *what is* rather than predicts *what could be.* For example, high heritability for height means that height differences among individuals are largely due to genetic differences, given the genetic and environmental influences that exist in a particular population at a particular time (*what is*). Even for a highly heritable trait such as height, an environmental intervention such as improving children's diet or preventing illness could affect height (*what could be*). Such environmental factors are thought to be responsible for the average increase in height across generations, for example, even though individual differences in height are highly heritable in each generation.

BEYOND HERITABILITY

As mentioned in Chapter 1, one of the most dramatic shifts in the behavioral sciences during the past few decades has been toward a balanced view that recognizes the importance of both nature and nurture in the development of individual differences in behavior. Behavioral genetic research has found genetic influence nearly everywhere it has looked. Indeed, it is difficult to find any behavioral dimension or disorder that reliably shows no genetic influence. On the other hand, behavioral genetic research also provides some of the strongest available evidence for the importance of environmental influences for the simple reason that heritabilities are seldom greater than 50 percent. This means that environmental factors are also important. This message of the importance of both nature and nurture is repeated throughout the following chapters. It is a message that seems to have gotten through to the public as well as academics. For example, a survey of parents and teachers of young children found that over 90 percent believed that genetics is at least as important as environment for mental illness, learning difficulties, intelligence, and personality (Walker & Plomin, 2005).

As a result of the increasing acceptance of genetic influence on behavior, most behavioral genetic research reviewed in the rest of the book goes beyond merely estimating heritability. Estimating whether and how much genetics influences behavior are important first steps in understanding the origins of individual differences. But these are only first steps. As illustrated throughout this book, quantitative genetic research goes beyond heritability in three ways. First, instead of estimating genetic and environmental influence on the variance of one behavior at a time, multivariate genetic analysis investigates the origins of the covariance between behaviors. Some of the most important advances in behavioral genetics have come from multivariate genetic analyses. A second way in which behavioral genetic research goes beyond heritability is to investigate the origins of continuity and change in development. This is why so much recent behavioral genetic research is developmental, as reflected throughout Chapters 11 to 19, most notably in Chapter 15, which addresses developmental psychopathology. Third, behavioral genetics considers the interface between nature and nurture, which is the topic of this chapter. Moreover, the rapid advances in our ability to identify genes (Chapter 9) and to link genes to behaviors via molecular genetics have revolutionized our ability to integrate genetic and social science research. It is possible to address multivariate, developmental, and gene-environment interplay with much greater precision and ease; as described in Chapter 10, we are also making advances in understanding the pathways between genes and behavior. In fact, these many advances have resulted in research cutting across multiple and diverse areas, including genetics, sociology, family relations, and prevention science, to name just a few. The rest of this chapter will focus on how genes and environments work together, that is, gene-environment interplay.

GENOTYPE-ENVIRONMENT CORRELATION

As illustrated in Chapter 7, behavioral genetic research helps to clarify both genetic and environmental influences. Genetic research is also changing the way we think about the environment by showing that we create our experiences in part for genetic reasons. That is, genetic propensities are correlated with individual differences in experiences, an example of a phenomenon known as genotype-environment correlation. In other words, what seem to be environmental effects can reflect genetic influence because these experiences are influenced by genetic differences among individuals. This is just what genetic research during the past decade has found: When environmental measures are examined as phenotypes in twin and adoption studies, the results consistently point to some genetic influence, as discussed later. For this reason, genotype-environment correlation has been described as genetic control of exposure to the environment (Kendler & Eaves, 1986).

Genotype-environment correlation adds to phenotypic variance for a trait (see Appendix), but it is difficult to detect the overall extent to which phenotypic variance is due to the correlation between genetic and environmental effects (Plomin, DeFries, & Loehlin, 1977b). Therefore, the following discussion focuses on detection of specific genotype-environment correlations rather than on estimating their overall contribution to phenotypic variation.

The Nature of Nurture

The first research on this topic was published over two decades ago, with several dozen studies using various genetic designs and measures converging on the conclusion that measures of the environment show genetic influence (Plomin & Bergeman, 1991). After providing some examples of this research, we will consider how it is possible for measures of the environment to show genetic influences.

A widely used measure of the home environment that combines observations and interviews is the Home Observation for Measurement of the Environment (HOME; Caldwell & Bradley, 1984; Caldwell & Bradley, 2003). HOME assesses aspects of the home environment such as parental responsivity, encouragement of developmental advance, and provision of toys. In an adoption study, HOME correlations for nonadoptive and adoptive siblings were compared when each child was 1 year old and again when each child was 2 years old (Braungart, Fulker, & Plomin, 1992a). HOME scores were more similar for nonadoptive siblings than for adoptive siblings at both 1 and 2 years (0.58 versus 0.35 at 1 year and 0.57 versus 0.40 at 2 years), results suggesting genetic influence on HOME scores. Genetic factors were estimated to account for about 40 percent of the variance of HOME scores.

Other observational studies have found evidence of genetic influences on parent-child interactions during infancy, childhood, and adolescence using a variety of genetic designs (see Klahr & Burt, 2014 for a recent meta-analysis). These other studies suggest that genetic effects on family interactions are not solely in the eye of the beholder. Most genetic research on the nature of nurture has used questionnaires rather than observations. Questionnaires add another source of possible genetic influence: the subjective processes involved in perceptions of the family environment. The pioneering research in this area included two twin studies of adolescents' perceptions of their family environment (Rowe, 1981; Rowe, 1983). Both studies found substantial genetic influence on adolescents' perceptions of their parents' acceptance and no genetic influence on perceptions of parents' control.

The Nonshared Environment in Adolescent Development (NEAD) project, mentioned in Chapter 7, was designed in part to investigate genetic contributions to diverse measures of family environment. As shown in Table 8.1, significant genetic influence was found for adolescents' ratings of composite variables of their parents' positivity and negativity (Plomin, Reiss, Hetherington, & Howe, 1994). The highest heritability of the 12 scales that contributed to these composites was for a measure of closeness (e.g., intimacy, supportiveness), which yielded heritabilities of about 50 percent for both mothers' closeness and fathers' closeness as rated by the adolescents. As found in Rowe's original studies and in several other studies (Bulik, Sullivan, Wade, & Kendler, 2000), measures of parental control showed lower heritability than measures of closeness (Kendler & Baker, 2007). The NEAD project also assessed parents' perceptions of their parenting behavior toward the adolescents (lower half of Table 8.1). Parents' ratings of their own behavior yielded heritability estimates similar to those for the adolescents' ratings of their parents' behavior. Because the twins were children in these studies, genetic influence on parenting comes from parents' response to genetically influenced characteristics of their children. In contrast, when the twins are parents, genetic influence on parenting can come from other sources, such as the parents' personality. Nonetheless, studies of twins as parents have generally yielded similar results that show widespread genetic influence (Neiderhiser et al., 2004; Klahr & Burt, 2014).

More than two dozen other studies of twins and adoptees have reported genetic influence on family environment (Plomin, 1994). A recent meta-analysis of results from twin, sibling, and adoption studies of parenting found evidence for genetic influence of both parents and children on parental warmth, control, and negativity (Avinun & Knafo, 2013; Klahr & Burt, 2014). In addition, there is evidence that shared environmental influence on parenting decreases and nonshared environmental

TABLE 8.1
Heritability Estimates for Questionnaire Assessments of Parenting

Rater	Ratee	Measure	Heritability
Adolescent	Mother	Positivity	0.30
		Negativity	0.40
Adolescent	Father	Positivity	0.56
		Negativity	0.23
Mother	Mother	Positivity	0.38
		Negativity	0.53
Father	Father	Positivity	0.22
		Negativity	0.30

Plomin et al. (1994).

influence increases from childhood to adolescence while genetic influence is consistent across child age. Multivariate genetic research suggests that genetic influence on perceptions of family environment is mediated in part by personality (Horwitz et al., 2011; Krueger, Markon, & Bouchard, 2003) and that genetic influence on personality can also explain covariation among different aspects of family relations, such as marital quality and parenting (Ganiban et al., 2009b).

Genetic influence on environmental measures also extends beyond the family environment. For example, several studies have found genetic influence on measures of life events and stress, especially life events over which we have some control, such as problems with relationships and financial disruptions (e.g., Federenko et al., 2006; Plomin, Lichtenstein, Pedersen, McClearn & Nesselroade, 1990b; Thapar & McGuffin, 1996). As is the case for genetic influence on perceptions of family environment, genetic influence on life events and stress is also mediated in part by personality (Kendler, Gardner, & Prescott, 2003a; Saudino, Pedersen, Lichtenstein, McClearn, & Plomin, 1997).

Genetic influence has also been found for characteristics of children's friends and peer groups (e.g., Brendgen et al., 2009; Iervolino et al., 2002) as well as adults' friends (Rushton & Bons, 2005), with genetic influence increasing during adolescence and young adulthood as children leave their homes and create their own social worlds (Kendler et al., 2007a). Several studies have found genetic influences on the tendency to be bullied during middle and late childhood and adolescence (e.g., Ball et al., 2008; Brendgen et al., 2011) and also on the likelihood of repeatedly being victimized (Beaver, Boutwell, Barnes, & Cooper, 2009). It is important to note that in the studies of bullying and peer victimization, heritabilities were somewhat less when peer nominations were used (Brendgen et al., 2008; Brendgen et al., 2011) as compared to parent and self-reports (Ball et al., 2008; Beaver et al., 2009; Bowes, Maughan, Caspi, Moffitt, & Arseneault, 2010).

The school environment also shows genetic influences. For example, genetic influences have been found in children's perceptions of their classroom environment (Walker & Plomin, 2006), in the amount of effort teachers report investing in their adolescent students (Houts, Caspi, Pianta, Arseneault, & Moffitt, 2010), and in the peer learning environment (Haworth et al., 2013). Other environmental measures that have shown genetic influence include television viewing (Plomin, et al., 1990b), school connectedness (Jacobson & Rowe, 1999), work environments (Hershberger, Lichtenstein, & Knox, 1994), social support (Agrawal, Jacobson, Prescott, & Kendler, 2002; Bergeman, Plomin, Pedersen, McClearn, & Nesselroade, 1990), accidents in childhood (Phillips & Matheny, 1995), the propensity to marry (Johnson, McGue, Krueger, & Bouchard, 2004), marital quality (Spotts, Prescott, & Kendler, 2006), divorce (McGue & Lykken, 1992), exposure to drugs (Tsuang et al., 1992), and exposure to trauma (Lyons et al., 1993). In fact, there are few measures of experience examined in genetically sensitive designs that *do not* show genetic influence. It has been suggested that other fields, such as demography, also need to consider the impact of genotype-environment correlation (Hobcraft, 2006).

In summary, diverse genetic designs and measures converge on the conclusion that genetic factors contribute to experience. A review of 55 independent genetic studies using environmental measures found an average heritability of 0.27 across 35 different environmental measures (Kendler & Baker, 2007). The large number of different environmental measures that have been found to show genetic influences demonstrates the key role that genetic influences play in the environments that individuals experience. A key direction for research on the interplay between genes and environment is to investigate the causes and consequences of genetic influence on measures of the environment.

Three Types of Genotype-Environment Correlation

What are the processes by which genetic factors contribute to variations in environments that we experience? There are three types of genotype-environment correlation: passive, evocative, and active (Plomin et al., 1977b). *Passive genotype-environment correlation* occurs when children passively inherit from their parents family environments that are correlated with their genetic propensities. *Evocative,* or reactive, *genotype-environment correlation* occurs when individuals, on the basis of their genetic propensities, evoke reactions from other people. *Active genotype-environment correlation* occurs when individuals select, modify, construct, or reconstruct experiences that are correlated with their genetic propensities (Table 8.2).

For example, consider musical ability. If musical ability is heritable, musically gifted children are likely to have musically gifted parents who provide them with both genes and an environment conducive to the development of musical ability (passive genotype-environment correlation). Musically talented children might also be picked out at school and given special opportunities (evocative genotype-environment

TABLE 8.2
Three Types of Genotype-Environment Correlation

Type	Description	Source of Environmental Influence
Passive	Children receive genotypes correlated with their family environment	Parents and siblings
Evocative	Individuals are reacted to on the basis of their genetic propensities	Anybody
Active	Individuals seek or create environments correlated with their genetic proclivities	Anybody or anything

Reprinted with permission of Robert Plomin, Institute for Behavioral Genetics, University of Colorado.

correlation). Even if no one does anything about their musical talent, gifted children might seek out their own musical environments by selecting musical friends or otherwise creating musical experiences (active genotype-environment correlation).

Passive genotype-environment correlation requires interactions between genetically related individuals. The evocative type can be induced by anyone who reacts to individuals on the basis of their genetic proclivities. The active type can involve anybody or anything in the environment. We tend to think of positive genotype-environment correlation, such as providing a musical environment, as being positively correlated with children's musical propensities, but genotype-environment correlation can also be negative. As an example of negative genotype-environment correlation, slow learners might be given special attention to boost their performance.

Three Methods to Detect Genotype-Environment Correlation

Three methods are available to investigate the contribution of genetic factors to the correlation between an environmental measure and a behavioral trait. These methods differ in the type of genotype-environment correlation they can detect. The first method is limited to detecting the passive type. The second method detects the evocative and active types. The third method detects all three types. All three methods can also provide evidence for environmental influence free of genotype-environment correlation.

The first method compares correlations between environmental measures and traits in nonadoptive and adoptive families (Figure 8.1). In nonadoptive families, a correlation between a measure of family environment and a behavioral trait of children could be environmental in origin, as is usually assumed. However, genetic factors might also contribute to the correlation. Genetic mediation would occur if genetically influenced traits of parents are correlated with the environmental measure and with the children's trait. For example, a correlation between HOME scores and children's cognitive abilities could be mediated by genetic factors that affect both the cognitive abilities of parents and their scores on the HOME. In contrast, in adoptive families,

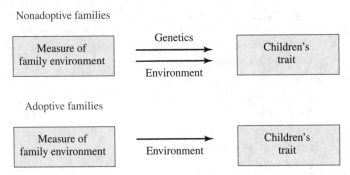

FIGURE 8.1 Passive genotype-environment correlation can be detected by comparing correlations between family environment and children's traits in nonadoptive and adoptive families.

this indirect genetic path between family environment and children's traits is not present because adoptive parents are not genetically related to their adopted children. For this reason, a genetic contribution to the covariation between family environment and children's traits is implied if the correlation is greater in nonadoptive families than in adoptive families. The genetic contribution reflects passive genotype-environment correlation because children in nonadoptive families passively inherit from their parents both genes and environment that are correlated with the trait. In both nonadoptive and adoptive families, the environmental measure might be the consequence rather than the cause of the children's traits, which could involve genetic influence of the evocative or active type of genotype-environment correlation. However, this source of genetic influence would contribute equally to environment-outcome correlations in nonadoptive and adoptive families. Increased correlations in nonadoptive families would occur only in the presence of passive genotype-environment correlation. This method uncovered significant genetic contributions to associations between family environment and children's behavioral development in the Colorado Adoption Project. For example, the correlation between HOME scores and the cognitive development of 2-year-olds is higher in nonadoptive families than in adoptive families (Plomin, Loehlin, & DeFries, 1985). The same pattern of results was found for correlations between HOME scores and language development.

The children-of-twins (COT) method can be used to address similar questions (McAdams et al., 2014). As described in Chapter 6, the COT approach provides a powerful pseudo-adoption design that allows for control of genetic risk of parental variables, such as family conflict and parental substance use, in order to examine whether measures of the family environment have a direct effect on child outcomes or are mediated genetically. For example, a COT analysis looking at a general measure of family functioning that included family conflict, marital quality, and agreement about parenting found that family conflict had both a direct and genetically mediated association with adolescents' internalizing and externalizing problems (Schermerhorn et al., 2011). Other efforts using the COT design have focused on parental substance use, including drug use during pregnancy, and have found that the association between maternal alcohol use and child attention-deficit/hyperactivity disorder (ADHD) is genetically influenced (Knopik et al., 2006), while the association between paternal alcohol use and child ADHD is more likely to be indirect and a result of multiple pathways (Knopik, Jacob, Haber, Swenson, & Howell, 2009b). Other maternal variables, such as substance use during pregnancy, appeared to have genetically mediated as well as direct environmental effects on child ADHD (Knopik et al., 2006; Knopik et al., 2009b).

Evocative and active genotype-environment correlations are assumed to affect both adopted and nonadopted children and would not be detected using this first method. The second method for finding specific genotype-environment correlations involves correlations between birth parents' traits and adoptive families' environment (Figure 8.2). This method addresses the other two types of genotype-environment correlation, evocative and active. Traits of birth parents can be used as an index of

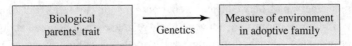

FIGURE 8.2 Evocative and active genotype-environment correlation can be detected by the correlation between birth parents' traits (as an index of adopted children's genotype) and the environment of adoptive families.

adopted children's genotype, and can be correlated with any measure of the adopted children's environment. Although birth parents' traits are a relatively weak index of their adopted children's genotype, finding that birth parents' traits correlate with the environment of their adopted children suggests that the environmental measure reflects genetically influenced characteristics of the adopted children. That is, adopted children's genetic propensities evoke reactions from adoptive parents. Attempts to use this method in the Colorado Adoption Project yielded only meager evidence for evocative and active genotype-environment correlation (Plomin, 1994), although this strategy has proven more successful in recent research from the Early Growth and Development Study (Leve et al., 2013b). For example, evidence for evocative genotype-environment correlation has been found for parenting (Fearon et al., 2014; Harold et al., 2013) and problems with peers (Elam et al., 2014) during early and middle childhood.

The third method to detect genotype-environment correlation involves multivariate genetic analysis of the correlation between an environmental measure and a trait (Figure 8.3). This method is the most general in the sense that it detects genotype-environment correlation of any kind—passive, evocative, or active. As explained in the Appendix, multivariate genetic analysis estimates the extent to which genetic effects on one measure overlap with genetic effects on another measure. In this case, genotype-environment correlation is implied if genetic effects on an environmental measure overlap with genetic effects on a trait measure.

Multivariate genetic analysis can be used with any genetic design and with any type of environmental measure, not just with measures of the family environment. However, because all genetic analyses are analyses of individual differences, the environmental measure must be specific to each individual. For example, an environmental measure that is the same for all family members, such as the family's socioeconomic status, could not be used in these analyses. However, a child-specific measure, such as children's perceptions of their family's socioeconomic status, could be analyzed in this way. One of the first studies of this type used the sibling adoption design to

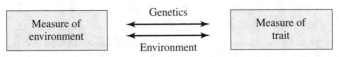

FIGURE 8.3 Passive, evocative, and active genotype-environment correlation can be detected by using multivariate genetic analysis of the correlation between environmental measures and traits.

compare cross-correlations between one sibling's HOME score (a child-specific rather than family-general measure of the environment) and the other sibling's general cognitive ability for nonadoptive and adoptive siblings at 2 years of age in the Colorado Adoption Project (Braungart et al., 1992a). Multivariate genetic model fitting indicated that about half of the phenotypic correlation between HOME scores and children's cognitive ability is mediated genetically. Similar findings have been reported for parenting and child prosocial and problem behaviors during childhood and adolescence (e.g., Knafo & Plomin, 2006; Reiss, Neiderhiser, Hetherington, & Plomin, 2000; Burt, Krueger, McGue, & Iacono, 2003). For each of these correlations, more than half of the correlation is mediated genetically. There is also evidence that genetic influences account for the associations among peer characteristics and adolescent drinking (Loehlin, 2010) and young adult smoking (Harakeh et al., 2008). Evidence for genetic mediation has also been found in adulthood for a wide variety of environmental measures with adult mental and physical health (e.g., Boardman, Alexander, & Stallings, 2011; Bergeman, Plomin, Pedersen, & McClearn, 1991; Spotts et al., 2005; Lichtenstein, Harris, Pedersen, & McClearn, 1992; Carmelli, Swan, & Cardon, 1995).

Multivariate genetic analysis can be combined with longitudinal analysis to disentangle cause and effect in the relationship between environmental measures and behavioral measures. For example, if negative parenting at one age is related to children's antisocial behavior at a later age, it would seem reasonable to assume that the negative parenting caused the children's antisocial behavior. However, the first twin study of this type found that this pathway is primarily mediated genetically (Neiderhiser, Reiss, Hetherington, & Plomin, 1999), a finding supported in subsequent studies using different samples (Burt, McGue, Krueger, Iacono, 2005; Moberg, Lichtenstein, Forsman, & Larsson, 2011). In contrast, a longitudinal study of twins concerned with the effects of childhood adversity on antisocial behavior in adolescence and young adulthood found that although passive genotype-environment correlation was significant, the majority of the variance was due to the direct environmental effects of childhood adversity (Eaves, Prom, & Silberg, 2010).

Recent studies have attempted to clarify whether associations between parenting and child adjustment are due to evocative genotype-environment correlation, passive genotype-environment correlation, or direct environmental effects of parenting on child adjustment. These different mechanisms can be disentangled by combining a multivariate genetic analysis of parenting and child adjustment with a combination of children-of-twins and parents-of-twins designs, referred to as extended children-of-twins (ECOT; Narusyte et al., 2008). Studies that have used the ECOT design have found evidence for evocative genotype-environment correlation for parental negativity and child internalizing and externalizing behavior (Marceau et al., 2013; Narusyte et al., 2008; Narusyte et al., 2011). In other words, adolescents' behavior evoked a particular type of response from their parents for genetically influenced reasons. In contrast, two reports have found evidence for direct environmental influences but no genotype-environment correlation between parental criticism and adolescent somatic symptoms

(Horwitz et al., 2015) and between parental monitoring and adolescent externalizing behavior (Marceau et al., 2015b). These findings highlight how multiple strategies can be combined to yield novel information about how genes and environments work together and also help to illustrate the nuances of environmental influences.

Research on the interplay between genes and environment will be greatly facilitated by identifying some of the genes responsible for the heritability of behavior (Jaffee & Price, 2007). The conclusion from research reviewed in this section is that we may be able to identify genes associated with environmental measures because these are heritable. For example, recent research using SNP-based heritability as well as polygenic scores has found significant genetic influence on the socioeconomic status (SES) of children's families and on the association between family SES and children's educational achievement (Krapohl & Plomin, 2015; Plomin, 2014). Of course, environments per se are not inherited; genetic influence comes into the picture because these environmental measures involve behavior. For example, many life events and stressors are not things that happen to us passively — to some extent, we contribute to these experiences.

Implications

Research using diverse genetic designs and measures leads to the conclusion that genetic factors often contribute substantially to measures of the environment. The most important implication of finding genetic contributions to measures of the environment is that the correlation between an environmental measure and a behavioral trait does not necessarily imply exclusively environmental causation. Genetic research often shows that genetic factors are substantially involved in correlations between environmental measures and behavioral traits. In other words, what appears to be an environmental risk might actually reflect genetic factors. Conversely, of course, what appears to be a genetic risk might actually reflect environmental factors.

This research does not mean that experience is entirely driven by genes. Widely used environmental measures show significant genetic influence, but most of the variance in these measures is not genetic. Nonetheless, environmental measures cannot be assumed to be entirely environmental just because they are called environmental. Indeed, research to date suggests that it is safer to assume that measures of the environment include some genetic effects. Especially in families of genetically related individuals, associations between measures of the family environment and children's developmental outcomes cannot be assumed to be purely environmental in origin. Taking this argument to the extreme, two books have concluded that socialization research is fundamentally flawed because it has not considered the role of genetics (Harris, 1998; Rowe, 1994).

These findings support a current shift from thinking about passive models of how the environment affects individuals toward models that recognize the active role we play in selecting, modifying, and creating our own environments. Progress in this field will be fostered by developing measures of the environment that reflect the active role we play in constructing our experience.

KEY CONCEPTS

Passive genotype-environment correlation: A correlation between genetic and environmental influences that occurs when children inherit genes with effects that covary with their family's environment.

Evocative genotype-environment correlation: A correlation between genetic and environmental influences that occurs when individuals evoke environmental effects that covary with their genetic propensities.

Active genotype-environment correlation: A correlation between genetic and environmental influences that occurs when individuals select or construct environments with effects that covary with their genetic propensities.

Children-of-twins design: A study that includes parents who are twins and the children of each twin.

Extended children-of-twins design: A study that combines a children-of-twins design and a comparable sample of twins who are children and the twins' parents.

GENOTYPE-ENVIRONMENT INTERACTION

The previous section focused on correlations between genotype and environment. Genotype-environment correlation refers to the role of genetics in exposure to environments. In contrast, genotype-environment interaction involves genetic sensitivity, or susceptibility, to environments. There are many ways of thinking about genotype-environment interaction (Rutter, 2006; Reiss, Leve, & Neiderhiser, 2013), but in quantitative genetics the term generally means that the effect of the environment on a phenotype depends on genotype or, conversely, that the effect of the genotype on a phenotype depends on the environment (Kendler & Eaves, 1986; Plomin, DeFries, & Loehlin, 1977a). As discussed in Chapter 7, this is quite different from saying that genetic and environmental effects cannot be disentangled because they "interact." When considering the variance of a phenotype, genes can affect the phenotype independent of environmental effects, and environments can affect the phenotype independent of genetic effects. In addition, genes and environments can interact to affect the phenotype beyond the independent prediction of genes and environments.

This point can be seen in Figure 8.4, in which scores on a trait are plotted against low- versus high-risk genotypes for individuals reared in low- versus high-risk environments. Genetic risks can be assessed using animal models, adoption designs, or DNA, as discussed below. The figure shows examples in which (a) genes have an effect with no environmental effect, (b) environment has an effect with no genetic effect, (c) both genes and environment have effects, and (d) both genes and environment have effects *and* there is also an interaction between genetics and environment. In the last case, the interaction involves a greater effect of genetic risk in a high-risk environment. In psychiatric genetics, this type of interaction is called the

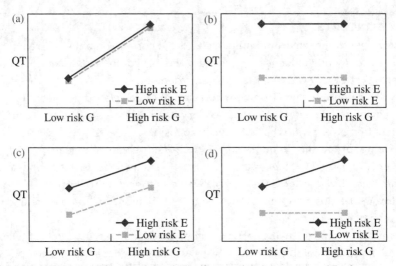

FIGURE 8.4 Genetic (G) and environmental (E) effects and their interaction. QT refers to a phenotypic quantitative trait. (a) G can have an effect without an effect of E, (b) E can have an effect without G, (c) both G and E can have an effect, and (d) both G and E can have an effect and there can also be an interaction between G and E.

diathesis-stress model (Gottesman, 1991; Paris, 1999). That is, individuals at genetic risk for psychopathology (diathesis, or predisposition) are especially sensitive to the effects of stressful environments. Although there is evidence for genotype-environment interactions of this sort, some studies show greater genetic influence in permissive, low-risk environments (Kendler, 2001).

As was the case for genotype-environment correlation, genotype-environment interaction adds to phenotypic variance for a trait (see Appendix), but it is difficult to detect the overall extent to which phenotypic variance is due to the interaction between genetic and environmental effects (Jinks & Fulker, 1970; Plomin et al., 1977b; van der Sluis, Dolan, Neale, Boomsma, & Posthuma, 2006). For this reason, the following discussion focuses on detection of specific genotype-environment interactions rather than on estimating their overall contribution to phenotypic variation.

Animal Models

Genotype-environment interaction is easier to study in laboratory animals because both genotype and environment can be manipulated. Chapter 11 describes one of the best-known examples of genotype-environment interaction. Maze-bright and maze-dull selected lines of rats responded differently to "enriched" and "restricted" rearing environments when compared to maze-bright and maze-dull rats reared in a standard laboratory environment (Cooper & Zubek, 1958). The enriched condition had no effect on the maze-bright selected line, but it improved the maze-running performance of the maze-dull rats. The restricted environment was detrimental to the performance of the maze-bright rats but had little effect on the maze-dull rats. This result is an interaction in that the effect of restricted versus enriched environments depends on the genotype of the animals. Other examples from animal research in which environmental effects on behavior differ as a function of genotype have also been found (Erlenmeyer-Kimling, 1972; Fuller & Thompson, 1978; Mather & Jinks, 1982). However, a series of learning studies in mice failed to find replicable genotype-environment interactions (Henderson, 1972).

As mentioned in Chapter 5, an influential paper reported genotype-environment interaction in which genotype was assessed using inbred strains of mice and environment was indexed by different laboratories (Crabbe, Wahlsten, & Dudek, 1999b). However, subsequent studies found much less evidence for genotype-environment interaction of this particular type (Valdar et al., 2006a; Wahlsten et al., 2003; Wahlsten, Bachmanov, Finn, & Crabbe, 2006). Despite the power of animal model research to manipulate genotype and environment, there is surprisingly little systematic research on genotype-environment interaction. (Animal model research in the laboratory is less suited to the study of genotype-environment correlation because such research requires that animals be free to select and modify their environment, which rarely happens in laboratory experiments.)

Adoption Studies

Although genes and environment cannot be manipulated experimentally in the human species as in animal model research, the adoption design can explore genotype-environment interaction, as illustrated in Figure 8.4. Chapter 16 describes an example of genotype-environment interaction for criminal behavior found in two adoption studies (Bohman, 1996; Brennan, Mednick, & Jacobsen, 1996). Adoptees whose birth parents had criminal convictions had an increased risk of criminal behavior, suggesting genetic influence; adoptees whose adoptive parents had criminal convictions also had an increased risk of criminal behavior, suggesting environmental influence. However, genotype-environment interaction was also indicated because criminal convictions of adoptive parents led to increased criminal convictions of their adopted children mainly when the adoptees' birth parents also had criminal convictions.

Another example of a similar type of genotype-environment interaction has been reported for adolescent conduct disorder (Cadoret, Yates, Troughton, Woodworth, & Stewart, 1995b). Genetic risk was indexed by birth parents' antisocial personality diagnosis or drug abuse, and environmental risk was assessed by marital, legal, or psychiatric problems in the adoptive family. Adoptees at high genetic risk were more sensitive to the environmental effects of stress in the adoptive family. Adoptees at low genetic risk were unaffected by stress in the adoptive family. This result confirms previous research that also showed interactions between genetic risk and family environment in the development of adolescent antisocial behavior (Cadoret, Cain, & Crowe, 1983; Crowe, 1974).

The Early Growth and Development Study (EGDS; Leve et al., 2013b) is a longitudinal adoption study that follows adopted children, their adoptive parents, and their birth mothers and birth fathers. A surprising number of genotype-environment interactions have emerged from the EGDS for child behaviors from infancy to middle childhood. For example, for children whose birth parents had more psychopathology symptoms (depressive and anxiety symptoms, antisocial behaviors, drug and alcohol use), adoptive mothers' use of more structured parenting when the adopted child was 18 months old was associated with significantly fewer child behavior problems than when less structured parenting was used (Leve et al., 2009). Genotype-environment interactions were also found for children's behavioral inhibition (Natsuaki et al., 2013), internalizing problems (Brooker et al., 2014), externalizing problems (Lipscomb et al., 2014), and social competence (Van Ryzin et al., 2015).

There are, however, examples in which genotype-environment interaction could not be found, especially for cognitive development. For example, using data from the classic adoption study of Skodak and Skeels (1949), researchers compared general cognitive ability scores for adopted children whose birth parents were high or low in level of education (as an index of genotype) and whose adoptive parents were high or low in level of education (as an index of environment) (Plomin et al., 1977b). Although the level of education of the birth parents showed a significant effect on the adopted children's general cognitive ability, no environmental effect was found for adoptive parents' education and no genotype-environment interaction was found. A similar adoption analysis using more extreme groups found both genetic and environmental effects but, again, no evidence for genotype-environment interaction (Capron & Duyme, 1989; Capron & Duyme, 1996; Duyme, Dumaret, & Tomkiewicz, 1999). Other attempts that used adoption analyses to find genotype-environment interaction for cognitive ability in infancy and childhood have not been successful (Plomin, DeFries, & Fulker, 1988).

Twin Studies

The twin method has also been used to identify genotype-environment interaction. One twin's phenotype can be used as an index of the co-twin's genetic risk in an attempt to explore interactions with measured environments. Using this method, researchers found that the effect of stressful life events on depression was greater for individuals at genetic risk for depression (Kendler et al., 1995). Another study found that the effect of physical maltreatment on conduct problems was greater for children with high genetic risk (Jaffee et al., 2005). The approach is stronger when twins reared apart are studied, an approach that has also yielded some evidence for genotype-environment interaction (Bergeman, Plomin, McClearn, Pedersen, & Friberg, 1988).

The most common use of the twin method in studying genotype-environment interaction simply involves asking whether heritability differs in two environments. Large samples are needed to detect this type of genotype-environment interaction. About 1000 pairs of each type of twin are needed to detect a heritability difference of 60 percent versus 40 percent. For example, Chapter 17 mentions several examples in which the heritability of alcohol use and abuse is greater in more permissive environments. Analyses of differences in heritability as a function of the environment can treat the environment as a continuous variable rather than dichotomizing it (Purcell, 2002; Purcell & Koenen, 2005; van der Sluis, 2012). In fact, there has been an explosion of studies examining moderation of heritability and environmentality (e.g., Brendgen et al., 2009; Feinberg, Button, Neiderhiser, Reiss, & Hetherington, 2007; Tuvblad, Grann, & Lichtenstein, 2006).

One analysis of this type showed that heritability of general cognitive ability is significantly greater in families with more highly educated parents (74 percent) than in families with less well-educated parents (26 percent) (Rowe, Jacobson, & van den Oord, 1999). Subsequent studies have produced apparently inconsistent results for parental education and socioeconomic status, but a recent meta-analysis found such effects primarily in U.S. studies but not in studies outside the United States. This suggests the intriguing possibility that the genotype-environment interaction may not be found in countries where access to high-quality education may be more uniform than in the United States (Tucker-Drob & Bates, 2016).

In addition, several twin studies indicate that heritability of behavior problems in children is moderated by the social environment, such as parenting (Alexandra Burt, Klahr, Neale, & Klump, 2013; Lemery-Chalfant, Kao, Swann, & Goldsmith, 2013; Samek et al., 2015), peer rejection (Brendgen et al., 2009), and a positive relationship with a teacher (Brendgen et al., 2011). As the appropriate data for use in genotype-environment interaction analyses continue to become available we will continue to uncover the nuances of how genes and environments work together to influence behavioral outcomes. These processes are also likely to change over time and with the age of the child (Marceau et al., 2015a), although longitudinal examinations of genotype-environment interactions are just beginning (Burt & Klump, 2014).

DNA

DNA studies of gene-environment interaction have yielded exciting results in two of the most highly cited papers in behavioral genetics. The first study involved adult antisocial behavior, childhood maltreatment, and a functional polymorphism in the gene for monoamine oxidase A (*MAOA*), which is widely involved in metabolizing a broad range of neurotransmitters (Caspi et al., 2002). As shown in Figure 8.5, childhood maltreatment was associated with adult antisocial behavior, as has been known for decades. *MAOA* was not related to antisocial behavior for most individuals who experienced no childhood maltreatment—that is, there was no difference in antisocial behavior between children with low and high *MAOA* genotypes. However, *MAOA* was strongly associated with antisocial behavior in individuals who suffered severe childhood maltreatment, which suggests a genotype-environment interaction of the diathesis-stress type. The rarer form of the gene, which lowers MAOA levels, made individuals especially vulnerable to the effects of childhood maltreatment. Although attempts to replicate this finding have been mixed, it is supported by a meta-analysis of all extant studies (Byrd & Manuck, 2014).

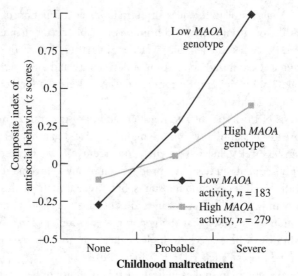

FIGURE 8.5 Gene-environment interaction: The effect of a polymorphism in the *MAOA* gene on antisocial behavior depends on childhood maltreatment. (Data from Caspi et al., 2002.)

The second study involved depression, stressful life events, and a functional polymorphism in the promoter region of the serotonin transporter gene (*5-HTTLPR*) (Caspi et al., 2003). As shown in Figure 8.6, there was no association between the gene and depressive symptoms in individuals reporting few stressful life events. An association appeared with increasing number of life events, which is another example of

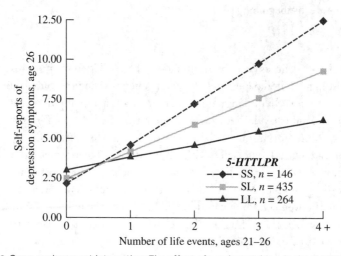

FIGURE 8.6 Gene-environment interaction: The effect of a polymorphism in the *5-HTTLPR* gene on depression depends on the number of life events. The short (S) allele is associated with lower transcriptional efficiency of the promoter region of the *5-HTTLPR* gene compared with the long (L) allele. (Data from Caspi et al., 2003.)

the diathesis-stress model of genotype-environment interaction. This interaction has been replicated in several studies (e.g., Vrshek-Schallhorn et al., 2013). This finding has also received support from mouse and nonhuman primate research in which the serotonin transporter gene was found to be involved in emotional reactions to environmental threats (Caspi, Hariri, Holmes, Uher, & Moffitt, 2010). There have been a series of meta-analyses and debates in the literature about the interaction between stressful life events and the serotonin transporter gene. Two meta-analyses reported in 2009 found that the evidence for such interactions was due to chance (Munafo, Durrant, Lewis, & Flint, 2009) or simply not present (Risch et al., 2009). Two more recent meta-analyses, however, found evidence for an interaction between stress and the serotonin transporter gene in risk for depression (Karg, Burmeister, Shedden, & Sen, 2011; Sharpley, Palanisamy, Glyde, Dillingham, & Agnew, 2014). Research continues on this topic and the conditions in which the interaction occurs (McGuffin & Rivera, 2015; Dick et al., 2015).

To date, many studies have reported genotype-environment interactions, most focusing on the genes involved in these first studies. There is a need for caution when considering the findings of studies examining **candidate gene-by-environment interactions,** however. One report examined all published studies of candidate gene-by-environment interactions — 103 studies published from 2000 to 2009 — and found that 96 percent of novel reports were significant, while only 27 percent of replication attempts were significant (Duncan & Keller, 2011). A recent report reviews the candidate gene-by-environment interaction literature and outlines a set of recommendations for continued research in this area (Dick et al., 2015).

Genomewide approaches, which utilize DNA variation across the genome, have also begun to be applied in the search for **genomewide gene-by-environment interaction** (Aschard et al., 2012; Thomas, Lewinger, Murcray, & Gauderman, 2012). Systematic strategies that can be used in mining data from genomewide association studies in examining genotype-environment interaction have been proposed (Thomas, 2010) and include experimental intervention as a way of manipulating the environment (van Ijzendoorn et al., 2011).

KEY CONCEPTS

Genotype-environment interaction: Genetic sensitivity or susceptibility to environments. Genotype-environment interaction is usually limited to statistical interactions, such as genetic effects that differ in different environments. The most common use of the twin method in studying genotype-environment interaction involves testing whether heritability differs in different environments.

Diathesis-stress: A type of genotype-environment interaction in which individuals at genetic risk for a disorder (diathesis) are especially sensitive to the effects of risky (stress) environments.

Candidate gene-by-environment interaction: Genotype-environment interaction in which an association between a particular (candidate) gene and a phenotype differs in different environments.

Genomewide gene-by-environment interaction: A method for searching for genotype-environment interaction that assesses DNA variation throughout the genome.

Summary

The interplay between genes and environment has been the subject of a vast amount of research, especially over the past decade. There are two main foci of this work: genotype-environment correlation and genotype-environment interaction. What is clear from this research is that genes and environment operate together to influence behavior through genotype-environment correlations and interactions.

One of the most surprising findings in genetic research was that our experiences are influenced in part by genetic factors. This finding is the topic of genotype-environment correlation. Dozens of studies using various genetic designs and measures of the environment converge on the conclusion that genetic factors contribute to the variance of measures of the environment. Genotype-environment correlations are of three types: passive, evocative, and active. Several different methods are available to assess specific genotype-environment correlations between behavioral traits and measures of the environment. These methods have identified several examples of genotype-environment correlation and have helped to clarify how genotype-environment correlations may change over time.

Genotype-environment interaction is the second way that genes and environments work together. Animal studies, in which both genotype and environment can be controlled, have yielded examples in which environmental effects on behavior differ as a function of genotype. Examples of genotype-environment interaction for human behavior have also been found in adoption and twin studies and in molecular genetic studies using functional polymorphisms in **candidate genes.** The general form of these interactions is that stressful environments primarily have their effect on individuals who are genetically at risk, a diathesis-stress type of genotype-environment interaction.

The recognition through behavioral genetic research of genotype-environment correlations and interactions emphasizes the power of genetic research to elucidate environmental risk mechanisms. Understanding how nature and nurture correlate and interact will be greatly facilitated as more genes are identified that are associated with behavior and with experience.

CHAPTER **NINE**

Identifying Genes

M uch more quantitative genetic research of the kind described in Chapters 6, 7, and 8 is needed to identify the most heritable components and constellations of behavior, to investigate developmental change and continuity, and to explore the interplay between nature and nurture. However, one of the most exciting directions for research in behavioral genetics is the coming together of quantitative genetics and molecular genetics in attempts to identify specific genes responsible for genetic influence on behavior, even for complex behaviors for which many genes as well as many environmental factors are at work.

Quantitative genetics and molecular genetics both began around the beginning of the twentieth century. The two groups, biometricians (Galtonians) and Mendelians, quickly came into contention, as described in Chapter 2. Their ideas and research grew apart as quantitative geneticists focused on naturally occurring genetic variation and complex quantitative traits, and molecular geneticists analyzed single-gene mutations, often those created artificially by chemicals or X-irradiation (described in Chapter 5). Since the 1980s, however, quantitative genetics and molecular genetics have begun to come together again to identify genes for complex, quantitative traits. Such a gene in multiple-gene systems is called a *quantitative trait locus* (*QTL*). Unlike single-gene effects that are necessary and sufficient for the development of a disorder, QTLs contribute like probabilistic risk factors, creating quantitative traits rather than qualitative disorders. QTLs are inherited in the same Mendelian manner as single-gene effects; however, if there are many genes that affect a trait, then each gene is likely to have a relatively small effect (see Chapter 3).

In addition to producing indisputable evidence of genetic influence, the identification of specific genes will revolutionize behavioral genetics by providing measured genotypes for investigating, with greater precision, the multivariate, developmental, and gene-environment interplay issues that have become the focus of quantitative genetic research. In Chapter 5, we briefly presented various ways of identifying genes in animal models. We now turn our attention to identifying genes associated with human behavior. Once a gene, or a set of genes, is identified, it is possible to begin to explore the pathways between genes and behavior, which is the topic of Chapter 10.

MUTATIONS

Behavioral genetics asks why people are different behaviorally—for example, why people differ in cognitive abilities and disabilities, psychopathology, and personality. For this reason, it focuses on genetic and environmental differences that can account for these observed differences among people. New DNA differences occur when mistakes, called mutations, are made in copying DNA. These mutations result in different alleles (called polymorphisms), such as the alleles responsible for the variations that Mendel found in pea plants, for Huntington disease and PKU, and for complex behavioral traits such as schizophrenia and cognitive abilities. Mutations that occur in the creation of eggs and sperm will be transmitted faithfully unless natural selection intervenes (Chapter 2). The effects that count in terms of natural selection are effects on survival and reproduction. Because evolution has so finely tuned the genetic system, most new mutations in regions of DNA that are translated into amino acid sequences have deleterious effects. However, sometimes such mutations are neutral overall, and once in a great while a mutation will make the system function a bit better. In evolutionary terms, this outcome means that individuals with the mutation are more likely to survive and reproduce.

A single-base mutation can result in the insertion of a different amino acid into a protein. Such a mutation can alter the function of the protein. For example, in the figure in Box 4.1, if the first DNA codon TAC is miscopied as TCC, the amino acid arginine will be substituted for methionine. (Table 4.1 indicates that TAC codes for methionine and TCC codes for arginine.) This single amino acid substitution in the hundreds of amino acids that make up a protein might have no noticeable effect on the protein's functioning; then again, it might have a small effect or it might have a major, even lethal, effect. A mutation that leads to the loss of a single base is likely to be more damaging than a mutation causing a substitution because the loss of a base shifts the reading frame of the triplet code. For example, if the second base in the box figure were deleted, TAC-AAC-CAT becomes TCA-ACC-AT. Instead of the amino acid chain containing methionine (TAC) and leucine (AAC), the mutation would result in a chain containing serine (TCA) and tryptophan (ACC).

Expanded Triplet Repeats

Mutations are often not so simple. For example, a particular gene can have mutations at several locations. As an extreme example, hundreds of different mutations have been found in the gene responsible for PKU, and some of these different mutations have different effects (Scriver, 2007). Another example involves *repeat sequences* of DNA. Although we do not know why, some very short segments of DNA—two, three, or four nucleotide bases of DNA (Chapter 4)—repeat a few times or up to a few dozen times. Different repeat sequences can be found in more than 50,000 places in the human genome. Each repeat sequence has several, often a dozen or more, alleles that consist of various numbers of the same repeat sequence; these alleles are usually inherited from generation to generation according to Mendel's laws. For this reason, and because there are so many of them, repeat sequences are widely used as DNA markers in linkage studies, as we will see later in this chapter.

Most cases of Huntington disease (Chapter 3) are caused by three repeating bases (CAG). Normal alleles have from 11 to 34 CAG repeats in a gene that codes for a protein found throughout the brain. For individuals with Huntington disease, the number of CAG repeats varies from 37 to more than 100. The expanded number of triplet repeats is unstable and can increase in subsequent generations. This phenomenon explains a previously mysterious non-Mendelian process called *genetic anticipation,* in which symptoms appear at an earlier age and with greater severity in successive generations. For Huntington disease, longer expansions lead to earlier onset of the disorder and greater severity. Because triplet repeats involve three bases, the presence of any number of repeats does not shift the reading frame of transcription. However, the **expanded triplet repeat** (CAG) responsible for Huntington disease is transcribed into mRNA and translated into protein, which means that multiple repeats of an amino acid are inserted into the protein. Which amino acid? CAG is the mRNA code, so the DNA code is GTC. Table 4.1 shows that GTC codes for the amino acid glutamine. Having a protein encumbered with many extra copies of glutamine reduces the protein's normal activity; therefore, the lengthened protein would show loss of function. However, although Huntington disease is a dominant disorder, the other allele should be operating normally, producing enough of the normal protein to avoid trouble. This possibility suggests that the Huntington allele, which adds dozens of glutamines to the protein, might confer a new property (such as a gain of function) that creates the problems of Huntington disease.

Fragile X syndrome, the most common cause of intellectual disability after Down syndrome, is also caused by an expanded triplet repeat. Although this type of intellectual disability is known to occur almost twice as often in males as in females, its pattern of inheritance does not conform to sex linkage because it is caused by an unstable expanded repeat. As explained in Chapter 12, the expanded triplet repeat makes the X chromosome fragile in a certain laboratory preparation, which is how fragile X received its name. Parents who inherit X chromosomes with a normal number of repeats (5 to 40 repeats) at a particular locus sometimes produce eggs or sperm with an expanded number of repeats (up to 200 repeats), called a *premutation.* This premutation does not cause disability in the offspring, but it is unstable and often leads to more expansions (200 or more repeats) in the next generation, which do cause disability (Figure 9.1). Unlike the expanded repeat responsible for Huntington

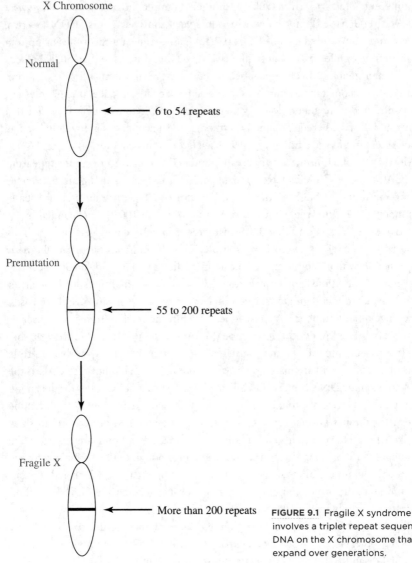

FIGURE 9.1 Fragile X syndrome involves a triplet repeat sequence of DNA on the X chromosome that can expand over generations.

disease, the expanded repeat sequence (CGG) for fragile X syndrome interferes with transcription of the DNA into messenger RNA (Bassell & Warren, 2008; see Chapter 12).

Many of our 3 billion base pairs differ among individuals, and over 2 million differ for at least 1 percent of the population. As described in the following section, these DNA polymorphisms have made it possible to identify genes responsible for the heritability of traits, including complex behavioral traits.

DETECTING POLYMORPHISMS

Much of the success of molecular genetics comes from the availability of millions of DNA polymorphisms. Previously, genetic markers were limited to the products of single genes, such as the red blood cell proteins that define the blood groups. In 1980, new genetic markers that are the actual polymorphisms in the DNA were discovered. Because millions of DNA base sequences are polymorphic, these DNA polymorphisms can be used in genomewide linkage studies to determine the chromosomal location of single-gene disorders, described later in this chapter. In 1983, such DNA markers were first used to localize the gene for Huntington disease at the tip of the short arm of chromosome 4. Technology has advanced to the point where we can now use millions of DNA markers to conduct genomewide association studies to identify genes associated with complex disorders, including behavioral disorders (Hirschhorn & Daly, 2005).

We are also able to detect every single DNA polymorphism by sequencing each individual's entire genome, called **whole-genome sequencing** (Lander, 2011). The race is on to determine how to sequence all 3 billion bases of DNA of an individual for less than $1000 (Hayden, 2014). There has been some success in this effort to reduce costs, but only for very high-throughput studies (Illumina, 2015; see Sadava, Hillis, Heller, & Berenbaum, 2010 and http://bit.ly/1YvWlX5 for animation of high throughput sequencing). The evolution of whole-genome sequencing will allow researchers to focus not just on the 2 percent of DNA involved in coding genes but also on any DNA sequence variation that might contribute to heritability. The 1000 Genomes Project, launched in 2008, aims to characterize human genetic variation across the world (Altshuler et al., 2010a; 1000 Genomes Project Consortium, 2012). More recently, the 10,000 Genomes Project was started with the goal of identifying even rarer DNA variants (http://www.uk10k.org/). As mentioned in Chapter 4, with the move toward affordable whole-genome sequencing, there is the very real possibility that the entire genome of all newborns could be sequenced to screen for genetic problems and that eventually we will each have the opportunity to know our own DNA sequence (Collins, 2010). Until whole-genome sequencing becomes affordable, sequencing the 2 percent of the genome that contains protein-coding information has become widely used, especially for discovering rare alleles for unsolved Mendelian disorders (Bamshad et al., 2011).

Although it is possible that rare alleles of large effect explain some of the heritability of complex traits, two types of common DNA polymorphisms can be genotyped affordably in the large samples needed to detect associations of small effect size: *microsatellite markers,* which have many alleles, and single nucleotide polymorphisms (SNPs), which have just two alleles (Weir, Anderson, & Hepler, 2006). Box 9.1 describes how microsatellite markers and SNPs are detected and explains the technique of **polymerase chain reaction (PCR)**. This is fundamental for detection of all DNA markers because PCR makes millions of copies of a small stretch of DNA. The triplet repeats mentioned in relation to Huntington disease are an example of a

BOX 9.1 DNA Markers

Microsatellite repeats and SNPs are genetic polymorphisms in DNA. They are called DNA markers rather than genetic markers because they can be identified directly in the DNA itself rather than being attributed to a gene product, such as the red blood cell proteins responsible for blood types. Investigations of both of these DNA markers are made possible by a technique called *polymerase chain reaction (PCR)*. In a few hours, millions of copies of a particular small sequence of DNA a few hundred to two thousand base pairs in length can be created. To do this copying, the sequence of DNA surrounding the DNA marker must be known. From this DNA sequence, 20 bases on both sides of the polymorphism are synthesized. These 20-base DNA sequences, called **primers,** are unique in the genome and identify the precise location of the polymorphism.

Polymerase is an enzyme that begins the process of copying DNA. It begins to do so on each strand of DNA at the point of the primer. One strand is copied from the primer on the left in the right direction and the other strand is copied from the primer on the right in the left direction. In this way, PCR results in a copy of the DNA between the two primers. When this process is repeated many times, even the copies are copied and millions of copies of the double-stranded DNA between the two primers are produced (for an animation, see http://www.dnalc.org/resources/animations/pcr.html).

The simplest way to identify a polymorphism from the PCR-amplified DNA fragment is to sequence the fragment. Sequencing would indicate how many repeats are present for microsatellite markers and which allele is present for SNPs. Because we have two alleles for each SNP, we can have two different alleles (heterozygous) or two copies of the same allele (homozygous). For microsatellite markers, a more cost-effective approach that sorts DNA fragments by length is used; this indicates the number of repeats. For SNPs, the DNA fragments can be made single-stranded and allowed to find their match (hybridize) to a single-stranded probe for one or the other SNP allele. For example, in the figure in this box, the target probe is ATCATG, with a SNP at the third nucleotide base. The PCR-amplified DNA fragment TAGTAC has hybridized successfully with the probe. In high-throughput approaches, a fluorescent molecule is attached to the DNA fragments so that the fragments light up if they successfully hybridize with the probe. (The TATTAC allele is unable to hybridize with the probe.)

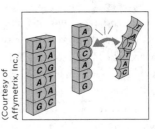

(Courtesy of Affymetrix, Inc.)

microsatellite marker, which can involve two, three, or four base pairs that are repeated up to a hundred times and which have been found at as many as 50,000 loci throughout the genome. The number of repeats at each locus differs among individuals and is inherited in a Mendelian manner. For example, a microsatellite marker might have three alleles, in which the two-base sequence C-G repeats 14, 15, or 16 times.

SNPs (called "snips") are by far the most common type of DNA polymorphisms. As their name suggests, a SNP involves a mutation in a single nucleotide. As mentioned earlier, a mutation that changes the first codon in Box 4.1 from TAC to TCC will substitute arginine for methionine when the gene is transcribed and translated into a protein. SNPs like this that involve a change in an amino acid sequence are called *nonsynonymous* and are thus likely to be functional: The resulting protein will contain a different amino acid. Most SNPs in **coding regions** are *synonymous:* They do not involve a change in amino acid sequence because the SNP involves one of the alternate DNA codes for the same amino acid (see Table 4.1). Although nonsynonymous SNPs are more likely to be functional because they change the amino acid sequence of the protein, it is possible that synonymous SNPs might have an effect by changing the rate at which mRNA is translated into proteins. The field is just coming to grips with the functional effects of other SNPs throughout the genome, such as SNPs in **non-coding RNA (ncRNA)** regions of the genome (see Chapter 10). More than 38 million SNPs have been reported in populations around the world (1000 Genomes Project Consortium, 2012), and most of these have been validated (http://www.ncbi.nlm.nih.gov/SNP/). This work is being systematized by the International HapMap Consortium (http://hapmap.ncbi.nlm.nih.gov/), which initially genotyped more than 3 million SNPs for 270 individuals from four ethnic groups (Frazer et al., 2007); more recently, the International Hapmap 3 Consortium genotyped 1.6 million common SNPs in 1184 individuals from 11 populations and sequenced specific regions in 692 of these individuals (Altshuler et al., 2010b). The project is called HapMap because its aim is to create a map of correlated SNPs throughout the genome. SNPs close together on a chromosome are unlikely to be separated by recombination, but recombination does not occur evenly throughout the genome. There are blocks of SNPs that are very highly correlated with one another and are separated by so-called *recombinatorial hotspots*. These blocks are called *haplotype blocks*. (In contrast to *genotype*, which refers to a pair of chromosomes, the DNA sequence on one chromosome is called a *haploid genotype*, which has been shortened to *haplotype*.) By identifying a few SNPs that tag a haplotype block, it is necessary to genotype only half a million SNPs rather than many millions in order to scan the entire genome for associations with phenotypes.

Until recently, only common DNA variants, such as SNPs, occurring at relatively high frequency in the population, were well-studied. However, rarer SNPs no doubt also contribute to genetic risk for common diseases; many SNPs occur in just one person (Manolio et al., 2009). Other types of rare polymorphisms have attracted considerable attention. One example is *copy number variants (CNVs)*, which involve duplication or deletion of long stretches of DNA, often encompassing protein-coding genes as well as non-coding genes (Conrad et al., 2010; Redon et al., 2006). Recent reports suggest a role for rare CNVs in the risk for a range of common diseases, such as autism spectrum disorder (Pinto et al., 2014) and schizophrenia (Malhotra & Sebat, 2012). Many CNVs, like other mutations, are not inherited and appear uniquely in an individual (*de novo*). However, a comprehensive map of 11,700 CNVs suggests that 4.8 percent of the genome involves CNVs and that 80 to 90 percent of CNVs appear at a frequency of at least 5 percent in the population (Zarrei, MacDonald, Merico, & Scherer, 2015). Whole-genome sequencing is greatly adding to the number of rare variations found in DNA sequence. These advances concerning genetic variation in populations will undoubtedly help to answer questions about the role of genetics in human disease and behavior.

KEY CONCEPTS

Quantitative trait loci (QTLs): Genes of various effect sizes in multiple-gene systems that contribute to quantitative (continuous) variation in a phenotype.

Polymorphism: A locus with two or more alleles; Greek for "multiple forms."

Microsatellite markers: Two, three, or four DNA base pairs that are repeated up to a hundred times. Unlike SNPs, which generally have just two alleles, microsatellite markers often have many alleles that are inherited in a Mendelian manner.

Single nucleotide polymorphism (SNP): The most common type of DNA polymorphism, which involves a mutation in a single nucleotide. SNPs (pronounced "snips") can produce a change in an amino acid sequence (called nonsynonymous, i.e., not synonymous).

Polymerase chain reaction (PCR): method to amplify a particular DNA sequence.

Primer: A short (usually 20-base) DNA sequence that marks the starting point for DNA replication. Primers on either side of a polymorphism mark the boundaries of a DNA sequence that is to be amplified by polymerase chain reaction (PCR).

Recombinatorial hotspot: Chromosomal location subject to much recombination; often marks the boundaries of haplotype blocks.

Haploid genotype (haplotype): The DNA sequence on one chromosome. In contrast to *genotype,* which refers to a pair of chromosomes, the DNA sequence on one chromosome is called a *haploid genotype,* which has been shortened to *haplotype.*

Haplotype block: A series of SNPs that are very highly correlated (i.e., seldom separated by recombination). The HapMap project is systematizing haplotype blocks for several ethnic groups (http://hapmap.ncbi.nlm.nih.gov).

Copy number variants (CNVs): A polymorphism that involves duplication or deletion of long stretches of DNA, often encompassing protein-coding genes as well as non-coding genes. Frequently used more broadly to refer to all structural variations in DNA, including insertions and deletions.

HUMAN BEHAVIOR

In studying our species, we cannot manipulate genes or genotypes as in knock-out studies or minimize environmental variation in a laboratory. Although this prohibition makes it more difficult to identify genes associated with behavior, this cloud has the silver lining of forcing us to deal with naturally occurring genetic and environmental variation. The silver lining is that results of human research will generalize to the world outside the laboratory and are more likely to translate to clinically relevant advances in diagnosis and treatment.

As described in Chapter 3, linkage has been extremely successful in locating the chromosomal neighborhood of single-gene disorders. For many decades, the actual residence of a single-gene disorder could be pinpointed when a physical marker for the disorder was available, as was the case for PKU (high phenylalanine levels), which led to identification of the culprit gene in 1984. With the discovery of DNA markers in the 1980s, screening the genome for linkage became possible for any single-gene disorder, which in 1993 led to the identification of the gene that causes Huntington disease (Bates, 2005).

During the past decade, attempts to identify genes responsible for the heritability of complex traits have moved quickly from traditional linkage studies to **QTL linkage analysis** to candidate gene association to genomewide association studies. Most recently, researchers are using whole-genome sequencing to identify all variants in the genome as it became apparent that genetic influence on complex traits is caused by many more genes of much smaller effect size than anticipated. This fast-moving journey is briefly described in this section.

Linkage: Single-Gene Disorders

For single-gene disorders, linkage can be identified by using a few large family pedigrees, in which cotransmission of a DNA marker allele and a disorder can be traced. Because recombination occurs an average of only once per chromosome in the formation of gametes passed from parent to offspring, a marker allele and an allele for a disorder on the same chromosome will usually be inherited together within a family. In 1984, the first DNA marker linkage was found for Huntington disease in a single five-generation pedigree shown in Figure 9.2. In this family, the allele for Huntington disease is linked to the allele labeled C. All but one person with Huntington disease has inherited a chromosome that happens to have the C allele in this family. This marker is not the Huntington gene itself, because a recombination was found between the marker

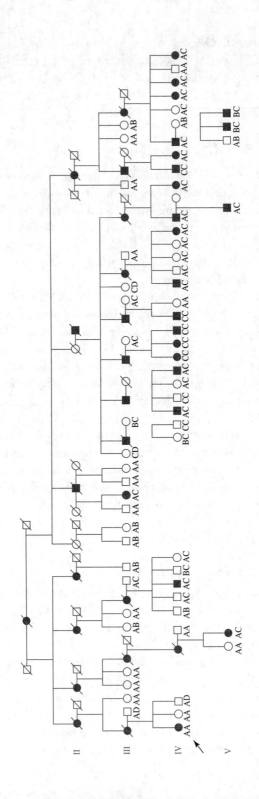

allele and Huntington disease for one individual; the leftmost woman with an arrow in generation IV had Huntington disease but did not inherit the C allele for the marker. That is, this woman received that part of her affected mother's chromosome carrying the gene for Huntington disease, which is normally linked in this family with the C allele, but in this woman it is recombined with the A allele from the mother's other chromosome. The farther the marker is from the disease gene, the more recombinations will be found within a family. Markers even closer to the Huntington gene were later found. Finally, in 1993, a genetic defect was identified as the CAG repeat sequence associated with most cases of Huntington disease, as described above. A similar approach was used to locate the genes responsible for thousands of other single-gene disorders, such as PKU on chromosome 12 and fragile X syndrome on the X chromosome.

Linkage: Complex Disorders

Although linkage analysis of large pedigrees has been very effective for locating genes for single-gene disorders, it is less powerful when several genes are involved. Another linkage approach has greater power to detect genes of smaller effect size and can be extended to quantitative traits. Rather than studying a few families with many relatives as in traditional linkage, this method studies many families with a small number of relatives, usually siblings. The simplest method examines *allele sharing* for pairs of affected siblings in many different families, as explained in Box 9.2.

Linkage based on allele sharing can also be investigated for quantitative traits by correlating allele sharing for DNA markers with sibling differences on a quantitative trait. That is, a marker linked to a quantitative trait will show greater than expected allele sharing for siblings who are more similar for the trait. The sib-pair QTL linkage design was first used to identify and replicate a linkage for reading disability on chromosome 6 (6p21; Cardon et al., 1994), a QTL linkage that has been replicated in several other studies (see Chapter 12). As seen in the following chapters, many genomewide linkage studies have been reported. However, replication of linkage results has generally not been as clear as in the case of reading disability, as seen, for example, in a review of 101 linkage studies of 31 human diseases (Altmuller, Palmer, Fischer, Scherb, & Wjst, 2001).

Association: Candidate Genes

A great strength of linkage approaches is that they systematically scan the genome with just a few hundred DNA markers looking for violations of Mendel's law of independent assortment between a disorder and a marker. However, a weakness of linkage approaches

FIGURE 9.2 Linkage between the Huntington disease gene and a DNA marker at the tip of the short arm of chromosome 4. In this pedigree, Huntington disease occurs in individuals who inherit a chromosome bearing the C allele for the DNA marker. A single individual shows a recombination (marked with an arrow) in which Huntington disease occurred in the absence of the C allele. (Information from "DNA markers for nervous-system diseases" by J. F. Gusella et al. *Science*, 225, 1320–1326. © 1984.)

BOX 9.2 Affected Sib-Pair Linkage Design

The most widely used linkage design in quantitative genetics includes families in which two siblings are affected. *Affected* could mean that both siblings meet criteria for a diagnosis or that both siblings have extreme scores on a measure of a quantitative trait. The **affected sib-pair linkage design** is based on allele sharing—whether affected sibling pairs share 0, 1, or 2 alleles for a DNA marker (see the figure). For simplicity, assume that we can distinguish all four parental alleles for a particular marker. Linkage analyses require the use of markers with many alleles so that, ideally, all four parental alleles can be distinguished. The father is shown as having alleles A and B, and the mother has alleles C and D. There are four possibilities for sib-pair allele sharing: They can share no parental alleles, they can share one allele from the father or one allele from the mother, or they can share two parental alleles. When a marker is not linked to the gene for the disorder, each of these possibilities has a probability of 25 percent. In other words, the probability is 25 percent that sibling pairs share no alleles, 50 percent that they share one allele, and 25 percent that they share two alleles. Deviations from this expected pattern of allele sharing indicate linkage. That is, if a marker is linked to a gene that influences the disorder, more than 25 percent of the affected sibling pairs will share two alleles for the marker. Several examples of affected sib-pair linkage analyses are mentioned in later chapters.

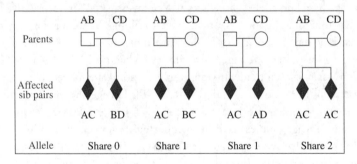

is that they cannot detect linkage for genes of small effect size expected for most complex disorders (Risch, 2000; Risch & Merikangas, 1996). Using linkage is like using a telescope to scan the horizon systematically for distant mountains (large QTL effects). However, the telescope goes out of focus when trying to detect nearby hills (small QTL effects).

In contrast to linkage, which is systematic but not powerful, allelic association is powerful but, until recently, not systematic. Association is powerful because, rather than relying on recombination within families as in linkage, it simply compares allelic frequencies for groups such as individuals with the disorder (cases) versus controls, or low-scoring versus high-scoring individuals on a quantitative trait (Sham, Cherny, Purcell, & Hewitt, 2000). For example, a particular allele of a gene (so-called allele 4 for *apolipoprotein E* on chromosome 19) involved in cholesterol transport is associated with late-onset Alzheimer disease (Corder et al., 1993). In dozens of association studies, the frequency of allele 4 was found to be about 40 percent in individuals with Alzheimer disease and about 15 percent in controls. In recent years, allelic associations have been reported for all domains of behavior, as discussed in later chapters, although none have nearly as large an effect as the association between *apolipoprotein E* and Alzheimer disease.

The weakness of allelic association is that an association can only be detected if a DNA marker is itself the functional gene (called **direct association**) or very close to it (called **indirect association** or **linkage disequilibrium**). If linkage is a telescope, association is a microscope. As a result, hundreds of thousands of DNA markers need to be genotyped to scan the genome thoroughly. For this reason, until very recently, allelic association has been used primarily to investigate associations with genes thought to be candidates for association. For example, because the drug most commonly used to treat hyperactivity, methylphenidate, acts on the dopamine system, genes related to dopamine, such as the dopamine transporter and dopamine receptors, have been the target of candidate gene association studies of hyperactivity. Evidence for QTL associations with hyperactivity involving the D_4 dopamine receptor (*DRD4*) and other dopamine genes is growing (Banaschewski, Becker, Scherag, Franke, & Coghill, 2010; Sharp, McQuillin, & Gurling, 2009). For example, a meta-analysis of 27 studies found that the *DRD4* 7-repeat (*DRD4-7r*) allele increases the risk for attention-deficit/hyperactivity disorder (ADHD; Smith, 2010). Specifically, the frequency of the *DRD4* allele associated with hyperactivity is about 25 percent for children with hyperactivity and about 15 percent in controls. The problem with the candidate gene approach is that we often do not have strong hypotheses as to which genes are candidate genes. Indeed, as discussed in Chapter 5, pleiotropy makes it possible that any of the thousands of genes expressed in the brain could be considered as candidate genes. Moreover, candidate gene studies are limited to the 2 percent of the DNA that lies in coding regions.

The biggest problem is that reports of candidate gene associations have been difficult to replicate (Tabor, Risch, & Myers, 2002). This is a general problem for all complex traits, not just for behavioral traits (Ioannidis, Ntzani, Trikalinos, & Contopoulos-Ioannidis, 2001). For example, in a review of 600 reported associations with common medical diseases, only six have been consistently replicated (Hirschhorn, Lohmueller, Byrne, & Hirschhorn, 2002), although a follow-up meta-analysis indicated greater replication for larger studies (Lohmueller, Pearce, Pike, Lander, & Hirschhorn, 2003). Essentially, as explained in the next section, the failure to replicate is due to the fact that the largest effect sizes are much smaller than expected. In other words, these candidate gene studies were underpowered to detect such effects. Few candidate gene associations have been replicated in genomewide association studies (Siontis, Patsopoulos, & Ioannidis, 2010).

Association: Genomewide

In summary, linkage is systematic but not powerful, and candidate gene allelic association is powerful but not systematic. Allelic association can be made more systematic by using a dense map of markers. Historically, the problem with using a dense map of markers for a genome scan has been the amount of genotyping required and its expense. For example, 750,000 well-chosen SNPs genotyped for 1000 individuals (500 cases and 500 controls) would require 750 million genotypings. Until recently, such an effort would have cost tens of millions of dollars. This is why, in the past, most association studies have been limited to considering a few candidate genes.

Technological advances have made genomewide association investigations possible (Hirschhorn & Daly, 2005). Microarrays can be used to genotype millions of SNPs on a "chip" the size of a postage stamp (Box 9.3). With microarrays, the

BOX 9.3 SNP Microarrays

Microarrays have made it possible to study the entire genome (DNA), the entire **transcriptome** (RNA) (Plomin & Schalkwyk, 2007), the entire *methylome* (**methylation** sites across the genome, discussed in Chapter 10), and the entire exome (or coding regions), covering variation seen in as little as 0.1 percent of the population. A *microarray* is a glass slide the size of a postage stamp dotted with short DNA sequences called probes. Microarrays were first used to assess gene expression, which will be discussed in Chapter 10. In 2000, microarrays were developed to genotype SNPs. Microarrays detect SNPs using the same hybridization method described in Box 9.1. The difference is that microarrays probe for millions of SNPs on a platform the size of a postage stamp. This miniaturization requires little DNA and makes the method fast and inexpensive. This is an advantage in the interim as we wait for whole-genome sequencing to become widely available.

Several types of microarrays are available commercially; the figure shows one example of a microarray manufactured by Illumina called BeadChip®. As shown in the figure, many copies of a certain target nucleotide base sequence surrounding and including a SNP are used to probe reliably for each allele of the SNP. An individual's DNA is cut with **restriction enzymes** into tiny fragments, which are then all amplified by PCR (see Box 9.1). Using a single PCR to chop up and amplify the entire genome, called *whole-genome amplification,* was the crucial trick that made microarrays possible. The PCR-amplified DNA fragments are made single-stranded and washed over the probes on the microarrays so that the individual's DNA fragments will hybridize to the probes if they find exact matches. The microarray includes probes for both SNP alleles to indicate whether an individual is homozygous or heterozygous.

Microarrays make it possible to conduct genomewide association studies with millions of SNPs. However, any DNA probes can be selected for genotyping on a microarray. As mentioned above, microarrays can include rare SNPs rather than common SNPs or can include probes for CNVs (mentioned earlier in this chapter). Microarrays are also being custom-ized for certain diseases, such as specialized microarrays now available for all DNA variants related to cardio-vascular (CardioChip) and immuno-logical (ImmunoChip) function and dysfunction, as well as for psychiatric cost of the experiment described above is less than half a million dollars instead of tens of millions. As a result of microarrays, genomewide association analysis began to dominate attempts to identify genes for complex traits in recent years. However, genomewide studies have found that the largest effects are much smaller than originally expected, and evidence suggests that genome scans of 500,000 or more SNPs are needed on very large samples (tens of thousands of people) to identify replicable associations. As of 2016, 2414 genomewide association studies with a total of 16,696 unique SNP-trait associations have been published (http://www.ebi.ac.uk/gwas/;

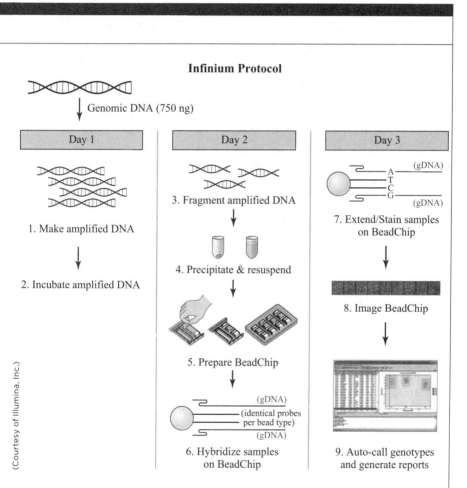

Infinium Protocol

Genomic DNA (750 ng)

| Day 1 | Day 2 | Day 3 |

1. Make amplified DNA

2. Incubate amplified DNA

3. Fragment amplified DNA

4. Precipitate & resuspend

5. Prepare BeadChip

(gDNA)
(identical probes per bead type)
(gDNA)

6. Hybridize samples on BeadChip

7. Extend/Stain samples on BeadChip

8. Image BeadChip

9. Auto-call genotypes and generate reports

(Courtesy of Illumina, Inc.)

disorders (PsychChip). The cost of microarrays is steadily declining; however, it can still be quite expensive to conduct studies with the many thousands of subjects needed to detect associations of small effect size.

Welter et al., 2014). Reports suggest that combining all known SNP associations for any trait explains a small proportion of heritability, ranging from about 1 percent (Manolio et al., 2009) to, at most, 20 percent of the known heritability (Park et al., 2010). This gap between the genomewide identified associations and heritability has become known as the *missing heritability* problem (Maher, 2008; See Chapter 7).

What good will come from identifying genes if they have such small effect sizes? One answer is that we can study pathways between each gene and behavior. Even for genes with a very small effect on behavior, the road signs are clearly marked in a bottom-up analysis that begins with **gene expression,** although the pathways quickly divide and become more difficult to follow to higher levels of analysis such as the brain and behavior. However, even if there are hundreds or thousands of genes that have small effects on a particular behavior, this set of genes will be useful in top-down analyses that begin with behavior; proceed to investigate multivariate, developmental, and genotype-environment interface issues, and then translate these findings into gene-based diagnosis and treatment as well as prediction and prevention of disorders. These issues about pathways between genes and behavior are the topic of Chapter 10. With DNA microarrays, it would not matter for top-down analyses if there were hundreds or thousands of genes that predict a particular trait. Indeed, for each trait, we can imagine DNA microarrays with thousands of genes that include all the genes relevant to that trait's multivariate heterogeneity and **comorbidity,** its developmental changes, and its interactions and correlations with the environment. However, whole-genome sequencing will eliminate the need for such microarrays because it identifies all DNA sequence variation throughout the genome.

Recent efforts have considered the possibility of aggregating the small effects of many DNA variants associated with a trait (Wray et al., 2014). These composite polygenic scores have typically focused on common DNA variants and have been called *polygenic susceptibility scores* (Pharoah et al., 2002), *genomic profiles* (Khoury, Yang, Gwinn, Little, & Flanders, 2004), *SNP sets* (Harlaar et al., 2005a), and *aggregate risk scores* (Purcell et al., 2009). With the advent of rare variant genotyping, new approaches combine the effects of rare and common variants, including variants that are risk-inducing as well as protective (Neale et al., 2011, Ionita-Laza et al., 2013). It is possible that these polygenic composites can aid in explaining more of the genetic variance. Moreover, they could also be useful for identifying groups of individuals at high and low genetic risk in certain areas of research, such as neuroimaging, where large sample sizes are difficult to study. Polygenic scores are often referred to as polygenic *risk* scores because their constituent associations were derived from case-control studies comparing a group of individuals diagnosed with a disorder and controls. However, it is important to keep in mind that, because these polygenic scores are distributed normally, their distribution has a positive tail as well as a negative tail. This opens up opportunities for considering *positive genetics*—how children flourish rather than flounder and about resilience rather than vulnerability (Plomin, Haworth, & Davis, 2009; Plomin, DeFries, Knopik, & Neiderhiser, 2016). Finally, the inability of association studies to account for most of the reported heritability has also led to a renewed interest in the use of the family design, suggesting that the rare variant approach and whole-genome sequencing will improve the power of family-based approaches (Ott, Kamatani, & Lathrop, 2011; Perdry, Müller-Myhsok, & Clerget-Darpoux, 2012).

Although there is currently no definitive answer to the missing heritability problem, the speed at which the field of behavioral genetics is advancing suggests that the gap between known DNA associations and heritability will narrow. Whole-genome sequencing, with its ability to sequence an individual's entire genome, offers new hope for gene identification. However, the significance of the information gained by determining the entire genomic sequence is unknown. Each individual genome contains millions of genetic variants that are then compared to a reference human genome sequence (such as HapMap individuals, described above) in order to find where there are differences. Some of these differences might not affect health or behavior, while others might be clinically significant. The challenge for researchers is how to analyze, interpret, and manage the large amounts of data generated by whole-genome sequencing techniques. Ultimately, understanding how the individual causal variants discovered by whole-genome sequencing affect health and behavior will facilitate diagnosis as well as an understanding of the pathways between genes and behavior (Dewey et al., 2014).

KEY CONCEPTS

Linkage analysis: A technique that detects linkage between DNA markers and traits, used to map genes to chromosomes.

Allelic association: An association between allelic frequencies and a phenotype.

Candidate gene: A gene whose function suggests that it might be associated with a trait. For example, dopamine genes are considered as candidate genes for hyperactivity because the drug most commonly used to treat hyperactivity, methylphenidate, acts on the dopamine system.

Linkage disequilibrium: A violation of Mendel's law of independent assortment. It is most frequently used to describe how close together DNA markers are on a chromosome; linkage disequilibrium of 1.0 means that the alleles of the DNA markers are perfectly correlated; 0.0 means that there is no correlation.

Genomewide association study: A study that assesses the association between individual differences in a quantitative character and DNA variation throughout the genome.

Missing heritability: The difference between results obtained from genomewide-identified associations and heritability estimates from quantitative genetic studies, such as twin and family designs.

Microarray: Commonly known as gene chips, microarrays are slides the size of a postage stamp with hundreds of thousands of DNA sequences that serve as probes to detect gene expression (RNA microarrays) or single nucleotide polymorphisms (DNA microarrays).

Whole-genome amplification: The use of a few restriction enzymes in polymerase chain reactions (PCRs) to chop up and amplify the entire genome; this makes microarrays possible.

Summary

Although much more quantitative genetic research is needed, one of the most exciting directions for genetic research in the behavioral sciences involves harnessing the power of molecular genetics to identify specific genes responsible for the widespread influence of genetics on behavior.

The two major strategies for identifying genes for human behavioral traits are allelic association and linkage. Allelic association is simply a correlation between an allele and a trait for individuals in a population. Linkage is like an association within families, tracing the co-inheritance of a DNA marker and a disorder within families. Linkage is systematic but not powerful for detecting genes of small effect size; association is more powerful but until recently was not systematic and was restricted to candidate genes. SNP microarrays have made possible genomewide association studies using millions of SNPs and incorporating common as well as rare variation.

For complex human behaviors, many associations and linkages have been reported. Ongoing genomewide association studies using SNP microarrays with large samples identify genes of small effect size associated with behavior. The results of genomewide association have yielded genes accounting for much less of the genetic variance than once expected, leaving us with the missing heritability problem. New technologies such as whole-genome sequencing may begin to shed light on this issue; however, in the interim, combining the effects of multiple genes of small effect may aid in accounting for more of the genetic influence on behavior.

As discussed in the next chapter, the goal is not only finding genes associated with behavior but also understanding the pathways between genes and behavior, that is, the mechanisms by which genes affect behavior, sometimes called *functional genomics.*

CHAPTER **TEN**

Pathways between Genes and Behavior

Quantitative genetic research consistently shows that genetics contributes importantly to individual differences in nearly all behaviors, such as learning abilities and disabilities, psychopathology, and personality. You will see in later chapters that quantitative genetics and molecular genetics are coming together in the study of complex traits and common disorders. Molecular genetic research, which attempts to identify the specific genes responsible for the heritability of these behaviors, has begun to identify such genes, although, as noted in Chapter 9, research using genomewide association scans with large samples suggests that the heritabilities of complex traits and common disorders are due to many genes of small effect. Nonetheless, the bottom line for behavioral genetics is this: Heritability means that DNA variation creates behavioral variation, and we need to find these DNA sequences to understand the mechanisms by which genes affect behavior.

The goal is not only finding genes associated with behavior but also understanding the pathways between genes and behavior, that is, the mechanisms by which genes affect behavior, sometimes called *functional genomics* (Figure 10.1). This chapter

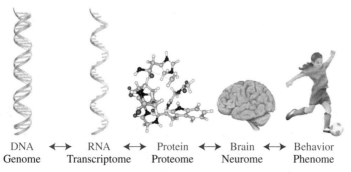

DNA ↔ RNA ↔ Protein ↔ Brain ↔ Behavior
Genome   Transcriptome   Proteome   Neurome   Phenome

FIGURE 10.1 Functional genomics includes all levels of analysis from genome (DNA) to phenome (behavior).

considers ways in which researchers are attempting to connect the dots between genes and behavior. (See Box 10.1 for a discussion of some relevant philosophical issues.) We begin with a description of gene expression, including how **epigenetics** relates to expression, and then expand our discussion to consider expression of all the genes in the genome, called the *transcriptome*. The next step along the pathways from genes to behavior is all the proteins coded by the transcriptome, called the *proteome*. Next is the brain, which, continuing the *–omics* theme, has been referred to as the *neurome*. This chapter stops at the brain level of analysis because the mind (cognition and emotion) and behavior—sometimes called the *phenome*—will be the focus of Chapters 11 to 19.

It should be reiterated that this chapter is about connecting the dots between genes and behavior through the epigenome, the transcriptome, the proteome, and the brain. It is not meant to describe each of these areas *per se*, four of the most active areas of research in all of the life sciences. Although our focus here is on the links between genes and behavior, it should also be kept in mind that the environment plays a crucial role at each step in the pathways between genes and behavior (Chapter 8).

KEY CONCEPTS

Functional genomics: The study of how genes work by tracing pathways among genes, brain, and behavior. It usually implies a bottom-up approach that begins with molecules in a cell, in contrast to *behavioral genomics.*

Behavioral genomics: The study of how genes throughout the genome function at the behavioral level of analysis. In contrast to *functional genomics,* behavioral genomics is a top-down approach to understanding how genes work in terms of the behavior of the whole organism.

Genome: All the DNA sequences of an organism. The human genome contains about 3 billion DNA base pairs.

Epigenome: Epigenetic events throughout the genome that influence gene expression.

Transcriptome: RNA transcribed from all genomic DNA.

Proteome: All the proteins translated from RNA (transcriptome).

Neurome: Effects of the genome throughout the brain.

GENE EXPRESSION AND THE ROLE OF EPIGENETICS

Genes do not blindly pump out their protein products. As explained in Box 4.1, genetic information flows from DNA to messenger RNA (mRNA) to protein. When the gene product is needed, many copies of its mRNA will be present, but otherwise

BOX 10.1 Levels of Analysis

The relationship between brain and "mind" (mental constructs) has been a central issue in philosophy for four centuries, since Descartes advocated for a mind-body dualism in which the mind was nonphysical. Because this dualism of mind and body is now generally rejected (see Bolton & Hill, 2004; Kendler, 2005), we will simply assert the view that all behavior is biological in the general sense that behavior depends on physical processes. Does this mean that behavior can be reduced to biology (Bickle, 2003)? Because all behavior is biological, it would seem that the answer must logically be "yes." However, saying that all behavior is biological is similar to saying that all behavior is genetic (because without DNA there can be no behavior) or that all behavior is environmental (because without the environment there can be no behavior).

Behavioral genetics' way out of this philosophical conundrum is to focus empirically on individual differences in behavior and to investigate the extent to which genetic and environmental differences can account for these differences in behavior (see Chapter 7). The point of this chapter is to consider some of the levels of analysis that lie between genes and behavior. The ultimate goal of behavioral genetics is to understand the links between genes and behavior at all levels of analysis.

Different levels of analysis are more or less useful for addressing different questions, such as questions about causes and questions about cures (Bolton & Hill, 2004). Functional genomics generally assumes a bottom-up approach that begins at the level of cells and molecular biology. The phrase **behavioral genomics** has been proposed as an antidote emphasizing the value of a top-down approach that attempts to understand how genes work at the level of the behavior of the whole organism (Plomin & Crabbe, 2000). Behavioral genomics may be more fruitful than other levels of analysis in terms of predicting, diagnosing, intervening in, and preventing behavioral disorders.

Finally, relationships between levels of analysis should be considered correlational until proven causal, which is why the connections between levels in Figure 10.1 are double-headed arrows. For example, associations between brain differences and behavioral differences are not necessarily caused by the brain differences: Behavior can cause changes in brain structure and function. A striking example is that the posterior hippocampus, a part of the brain that stores spatial representations of the environment, is significantly larger in London taxi drivers (Maguire et al., 2000); the size is correlated with the number of years spent driving a taxi (Maguire, Woollett, & Spiers, 2006). Similarly, correlations between gene expression and behavior are not necessarily causal because behavior can change gene expression. A crucial point is that the only exception to this rule is DNA: Correlations between differences in DNA sequence and differences in behavior are causal in the sense that behavior does not change the nucleotide sequence of DNA. In this sense, DNA is in a causal class of its own.

very few copies of the mRNA are transcribed. In fact, you are changing the rates of transcription of genes for neurotransmitters by reading this sentence. Because mRNA exists for only a few minutes and then is no longer translated into protein, changes in the rate of transcription of mRNA are used to control the rate at which genes produce proteins. This is what is meant by *gene expression*.

RNA is no longer thought of as merely the messenger that translates the DNA code into proteins. In terms of evolution, RNA was the original genetic code, and it still is the genetic code for most viruses. Double-stranded DNA presumably had a selective advantage over RNA because the single strand of RNA left it vulnerable to predatory enzymes. DNA became the faithful genetic code that is the same in all cells, at all ages, and at all times. In contrast, RNA, which degrades quickly, is tissue-specific, age-specific, and state-specific. For these reasons, RNA can respond to environmental changes by regulating the transcription and translation of protein-coding DNA. This is the basis for the process of gene expression.

An area relevant to gene expression that has seen rapid growth over the past few decades is *epigenetics*. Epigenetics is focused on understanding a type of slow-motion, developmentally stable change in certain mechanisms of gene expression that do not alter DNA sequence and can be passed on from one cell to its daughter cells (Bird, 2007). The prefix *epi-* means "above." You can think about the epigenome as the cellular material that sits on top, or outside, of the genome. It is these epigenetic marks that tell your genes to switch on or off, to scream or whisper. It may be through epigenetic marks that environmental factors like diet, stress, and prenatal nutrition can change gene expression from one cell to its daughter cells and, in some cases, from one generation to the next, called **imprinting** (see Chapter 12).

There are excellent epigenetics texts that provide great detail about these modes of action (e.g., Allis, Caparros, Jenuwein, Reinberg, & Lachlan, 2015). We will focus briefly on the most widely studied mechanism of epigenetic regulation of gene expression: **DNA methylation** (Bird, 2007). A methyl group is a basic unit in organic chemistry: one carbon atom attached to three hydrogen atoms. When a methyl group attaches to a specific DNA sequence in a gene's promoter region—a process called *DNA methylation*—it silences the gene's expression by preventing the gene's transcription. Conversely, when a gene's promoter is not methylated, that gene will not be silenced (Maccani & Marsit, 2009).

There is some evidence to suggest that direct exposure to toxins, such as drug use or pollution, is associated with changes in methylation patterns (Zhou, Enoch, & Goldman, 2014; Yang & Schwartz, 2012); however, there remains considerable debate as to whether epigenetic effects can indeed be transmitted across multiple generations. Although intergenerational effects (such as effects of maternal exposure to toxins during pregnancy) certainly occur in mammals, the degree to which epigenetic effects can be transmitted across generations remains unclear (Heard & Martienssen, 2014). Thus, as one example, if a mother smoked during her pregnancy, she is exposing the developing embryo and its germline (which will eventually produce grandchildren). A transgenerational epigenetic effect would need to be seen in the great-grandchildren who were not exposed to any smoking during pregnancy (Daxinger & Whitelaw, 2012). To date, we have not seen robust evidence in support of this phenomenon in humans.

Unlike epigenetic marks that effect long-term developmental changes in gene expression, many changes in gene expression are short term, providing quick reactions to changes in the environment. One such recently discovered mechanism of gene regulation is called *non-coding RNA*. As mentioned in Box 4.1, only about 2 percent of the genome involves protein-coding DNA as described by the central dogma. What is the other 98 percent doing? It had been thought that it is "junk" that has just hitched a ride evolutionarily. However, we now know that most human DNA is transcribed into RNA that is not the mRNA translated into amino acid sequences. This so-called non-coding RNA instead plays an important role in regulating the expression of protein-coding DNA, especially in humans.

One type of non-coding RNA has been known for almost 40 years. Embedded in protein-coding genes are DNA sequences, called *introns,* that are transcribed into RNA but are spliced out before the RNA leaves the nucleus. The remaining parts of the RNA are spliced back together, exit the nucleus, and are then translated into amino acid sequences. The DNA sequences in protein-coding genes that are transcribed into mRNA and translated into amino acid sequences are called *exons.* Exons usually consist of only a few hundred base pairs, but introns vary widely in length, from 50 to 20,000 base pairs. Only exons are translated into amino acid sequences that make up proteins. However, introns are not "junk." In many cases they regulate the transcription of the gene in which they reside, and in some cases they also regulate other genes.

Introns account for about one quarter of the human genome. A further quarter of the human genome produces non-coding RNA anywhere in the genome, not just near protein-coding genes. One class of such non-coding RNA that has attracted much attention is called **microRNA,** small RNAs 21 to 25 nucleotides in length capable of posttranscriptionally regulating genes. Even though they are tiny, microRNAs play a big role in gene regulation and exhibit tissue-specific expression and function. MicroRNAs have also been shown to be responsive to environmental exposures, such as cigarette smoke (Maccani & Knopik, 2012). The human genome is thought to encode close to 2000 microRNAs, capable of regulating up to 60 percent of protein-coding genes by binding to (and thus posttranscriptionally silencing) target mRNA (Nair, Pritchard, Tewari, & Ionnidis, 2014). Moreover, microRNAs appear to be just the tip of the iceberg of non-coding RNA effects on gene regulation. The list of novel mechanisms by which non-coding RNA can regulate gene expression is growing rapidly (Cech & Steitz, 2014).

Epigenetics and non-coding RNA are recently discovered mechanisms that regulate gene expression. Figure 10.2 shows how regulation works more generally for classical protein-coding genes. Many of these genes include regulatory sequences that normally block the gene from being transcribed. If a particular molecule binds with the regulatory sequence, it will free the gene for transcription. Figure 10.2 also illustrates epigenetic regulation. Most gene regulation involves several mechanisms that act like a committee voting on increases or decreases in transcription. That is, several transcription factors act together to regulate the rate of specific mRNA transcription. Non-coding RNA transcripts can regulate the expression of other genes without being translated into proteins. Non-coding RNA primarily regulates gene expression by altering the rate of transcription, but other factors include changes in the RNA transcript itself and the way the RNA transcript interacts with its regulatory targets, which are often messenger RNA transcripts.

Rather than just looking at the expression of a few genes, researchers can now use microarrays to assess the degree of expression of all genes in the genome simultaneously including non-coding RNA (the *transcriptome*), and profiles of DNA methylation of all coding genes in the genome (called the *methylome* or *epigenome*), as described in the following section. The importance of microarrays for gene expression and methylome profiling for behavioral genetics lies in the fact that the epigenome and the transcriptome are the first steps in the correlation between genes and behavior. Because gene expression and methylation (which affects gene expression) are sensitive to the environment, the transcriptome and epigenome could be useful as biomarkers of environmental change (Heard & Martienssen, 2014), including prenatal experiences (Zhang & Meaney, 2010; Hochberg et al., 2010) and mother-infant interactions (Champagne & Curley, 2009; Meaney, 2010).

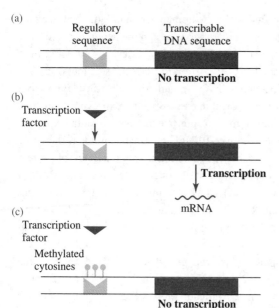

FIGURE 10.2 Transcription factors can regulate protein-coding genes by controlling mRNA transcription. (a) A regulatory sequence normally shuts down transcription of its gene; (b) but when a particular transcription factor binds to the regulatory sequence, the gene is freed for transcription. (c) One type of epigenetic regulation involves DNA methylation of cytosine residues in the gene's promoter region; this can regulate transcription by altering the microenvironment so that the transcription factor cannot bind its regulatory sequence, thereby reducing or halting transcription.

THE TRANSCRIPTOME: GENE EXPRESSION THROUGHOUT THE GENOME

As just outlined, gene expression is the first step on any pathway from genes to behavior: A polymorphism in DNA can have an effect only when the gene is expressed. Some genes, called *housekeeping genes*, are expressed at a steady rate in most of our cells. Other genes are expressed as their product is needed in response to the environment. For protein-coding genes, expression is most affected by altering the rate of transcription initiation, but other factors that affect expression include alteration of the RNA transcript, passage of the messenger RNA through the nuclear membrane, protection or degradation of the RNA transcript in the cytoplasm, the rate of translation, and posttranslational modification of the protein.

Gene Expression Profiles: RNA Microarrays and Sequence-Based Approaches

For both protein-coding and non-protein-coding DNA, gene expression can be indexed by the number of RNA transcripts, which is the end result of the various processes mentioned, not just the initial transcription process. In contrast to DNA, which faithfully preserves the genetic code in all cells, at all ages, and at all times, RNA degrades quickly and is tissue-specific, age-specific, and state-specific, as noted above. Two of the key aims of "transcriptomics" are to catalog all types of transcripts, including mRNA, non-coding RNA, and small RNAs, and to quantify their changing expression levels during development and under different conditions (Wang, Gerstein, & Snyder, 2009). Various techniques have been developed to examine the transcriptome or, in other words, to assess the expression of all genes in the genome simultaneously, called *gene expression profiling.*

Specialized gene expression (RNA) microarrays have been designed that are the same as the DNA microarrays described in Box 9.3 except that the probes in RNA microarrays detect a particular sequence of RNA, rather than identifying a particular SNP allele in a DNA sequence. In addition, the goal of using RNA microarrays is to detect the quantity of each of the RNA transcripts; for this reason, each probe is represented with many copies. In contrast, SNP probes detect the presence or absence of SNP alleles; multiple probes for each allele are used only in order to increase the accuracy of genotyping. RNA microarrays were originally limited to probes for exons that assessed transcription of the 2 percent of the genome that involves protein-coding genes. One of the most important developments in the recent history of genetics is the ability to sequence an individual's entire genome (Chapter 9). This development has also provided a new method for quantifying the transcriptome by sequencing RNA (Wang et al., 2009). RNA sequencing has resulted in, and will undoubtedly continue to drive, many exciting discoveries within the next few years (McGettigan, 2013). For example, RNA exome sequencing, which involves sequencing only RNA transcribed from exomes, is being widely used to identify rare mutations of large effect in the coding regions of genes (Bamshad et al., 2011). However, similar to whole-genome sequencing (Chapter 9), the cost of RNA sequencing in individuals remains quite high. Thus, until the costs decrease, a combination of approaches is likely to be used, such as using sequencing data that have detected all possible polymorphisms in DNA and RNA to guide the creation of custom microarrays that are much less expensive than sequencing.

Transcriptomics, including RNA microarrays and sequencing, makes it possible to take snapshots of gene expression throughout the genome at different times (e.g., during development, or before and after interventions) and in different tissues (e.g., in different brain regions). Scores of studies have investigated changes in gene expression profiling in response to drugs (Zhang et al., 2015) and between groups such as psychiatric cases and controls (Torkamani, Dean, Schork, & Thomas, 2010; Mistry, Gillis, & Pavlidis, 2013). Gene expression profiling of the brain is like structural genetic neuroimaging in that it can create an atlas of localized patterns of gene expression throughout the brain. Because genetic neuroimaging requires brain tissue, its use in the human species is limited to postmortem brains (Kleinman et al., 2011), which raises questions about lack of control concerning gene expression at the time of death (Konradi, 2005), and to tissue samples removed during surgery, such as tumors (Yamasaki et al., 2005). For this reason, structural genetic neuroimaging research has historically been conducted in mice rather than humans. Structural brain maps of gene expression are fundamental because genes can only function if they are expressed. A comprehensive atlas of expression profiles of 20,000 genes in the adult mouse brain is publicly accessible via the Allen Brain Atlas (Lein et al., 2007; http://mouse.brain-map.org/). Additional brain atlases are available for the adult human brain (Hawrylycz et al., 2012; http://human.brain-map.org/) and the prenatal human brain (Miller et al., 2014; www.brainspan.org). These are rich resources for understanding abnormal and normal human brain function and development. Further efforts involve functional genetic neuroimaging—studying changes in gene expression in the brain during development, following interventions such as drugs or cognitive tasks or following exposures such as sleep deprivation (Havekes, Meerlo, & Abel, 2015). In 2011, BrainCloud was announced as the result of efforts to gain a global molecular perspective on the role of the human genome in brain development, function, and aging. Researchers used an extensive series of postmortem brains from fetal development through aging to examine the timing and genetic control of transcription in the human prefrontal cortex and discovered a wave of gene expression changes occurring during fetal development that are reversed in early postnatal life (Colantuoni et al., 2011, http://braincloud.jhmi.edu/). An extension of the BrainCloud application characterizes methylation changes that happen over the course of development (BrainCloudMethyl; Numata et al., 2012) and results show, as described above, that DNA methylation is strongly correlated with gene expression, including genes involved in brain development.

Because of the practical and scientific limitations of using postmortem brain tissue, RNA microarrays will be much more widely applicable to human research if easily available tissue such as blood can be used for gene expression profiling. Some similarities between expression in blood and brain have been reported (e.g., Tian et al., 2009). Although gene expression profiling in blood cannot be used to localize patterns of gene expression in the brain, blood could be used to address some important questions, most notably, gene expression profile differences as a function of development or interventions. Rather than studying the expression of each gene in isolation, researchers can use RNA microarrays and sequencing to study profiles of gene expression across the transcriptome, which leads to understanding the coordination of gene expression throughout the genome (Ghazalpour et al., 2006; Schadt, 2006).

Gene Expression and Genetics

So far, we have discussed gene expression from a normative perspective rather than considering individual differences. The field of gene expression has also considered individual differences as well as their causes and consequences (Cobb et al., 2005; Rockman & Kruglyak, 2006). Much research has been directed toward treating gene expression as a phenotypic trait and finding loci (called *expression QTLs* or *eQTLs*) associated with gene expression in mice (Schadt, 2006; Williams, 2006) and humans (Morley et al., 2004). These links have become explicit because research using DNA microarrays (see Chapter 9) can scan the genome for SNP associations with genomewide gene expression assessed on RNA microarrays (Skelly, Ronald, & Akey, 2009; Powell et al., 2013).

Research on genomewide gene expression in rodents has profited from the availability of inbred lines and especially recombinant inbred lines, which facilitate both quantitative genetic and molecular genetic research (Chesler et al., 2005; Letwin et al., 2006; Peirce et al., 2006) and provide access to brain tissue. However, for rodent research as well as human research, although many eQTL associations have been reported, most suffer from low power and few have been replicated (Skelly et al., 2009). This is a repeat of the story told in Chapter 9 in which genetic effects on complex traits, including individual differences in gene expression, appear to be caused by many QTLs of small effect size. As a result, very large samples will be needed to attain adequate statistical power to detect reliable associations with gene expression traits.

Gene Expression as a Biological Basis for Environmental Influence

To what extent are individual differences in gene expression genetic in origin? It cannot be assumed that individual differences in gene expression are highly heritable because gene expression has evolved to be responsive to intracellular and extracellular environmental variation. Indeed, quantitative genetic studies of human RNA transcript levels suggest that heritabilities appear to be modest on average across the genome, which implies that most of the variability in transcript levels is due to environmental factors (Cheung et al., 2003; Correa & Cheung, 2004; McRae et al., 2007; Monks et al., 2004; Sharma et al., 2005). Members of identical twin pairs become increasingly different in gene expression profiles throughout the life span (Fraga et al., 2005; Petronis, 2006;

Zwijnenburg, Meijers-Heijboer, & Boomsma, 2010). Environmental factors involved in gene expression are part of a rapidly expanding area of research. However, it should be noted that gene expression is a phenotype; individual differences in expression itself or in epigenetic processes that lead to individual differences in expression may be due to genetic differences (Richards, 2006; Numata et al., 2012) or environmental differences. The transcriptome and methylome (or epigenome) could serve as important biomarkers of environmental change because they evolved to be sensitive to the environment. Examples of such environments include, but are not limited to, prenatal experiences, mother-infant interaction, and exposure to trauma. This perspective could provide a biological foundation upon which to build an understanding of more complex levels of environmental analysis typically studied in behavioral research. It could also have far-reaching impact on translational research by providing biomarkers for differential diagnosis and providing a biological basis for monitoring environmental interventions such as drugs and other therapies (Li, Breitling, & Jansen, 2008).

As noted at the outset of this chapter, we cannot hope to provide a review of all that is known about gene expression or the role of epigenetics in gene expression. Of special interest in terms of pathways between genes and behavior is the extent to which DNA associations with behavior are mediated by individual differences in gene expression. In the following section, we will continue along the pathways between genes and behavior by considering the next level of analysis, the proteome.

KEY CONCEPTS

Gene expression: Transcription of DNA into mRNA.

Epigenetics: DNA modifications that affect gene expression without changing the DNA sequence; involved in long-term developmental changes in gene expression.

DNA methylation: An epigenetic process by which gene expression is inactivated by the addition of a methyl group.

Non-coding RNA: RNA that is not translated into amino acid sequences.

Intron: DNA sequence within a gene that is transcribed into messenger RNA but spliced out before the translation into protein. (Compare with *exon*.)

Exon: DNA sequence transcribed into messenger RNA and translated into protein. (Compare with *intron*.)

MicroRNA: A class of non-coding RNA involving 21 to 25 nucleotides that can degrade or silence gene expression by binding with messenger RNA.

Gene expression profiling: Using microarrays to assess the expression of all genes in the genome simultaneously.

Expression QTL (eQTL): When treating gene expression as a phenotype, QTLs can be identified that account for genetic influence on individual differences in gene expression.

THE PROTEOME: PROTEINS CODED THROUGHOUT THE TRANSCRIPTOME

The proteome, which refers to the entire complement of proteins, brings an increase in complexity for three reasons. First, there are many more proteins than genes, in part because alternative splicing of genes can produce different messenger RNA transcripts (Brett et al., 2002). Second, after amino acid sequences are translated from messenger RNA, they undergo modifications, called *posttranslational modifications,* that change their structure and thus change their function. Third, proteins do not work in isolation; their function is affected by their interactions with other proteins as they form protein complexes.

The proteome can be identified using gels in an electrical field (*electrophoresis*) to separate proteins in one dimension on the basis of their charge and in a second dimension on the basis of their molecular weight, called *two-dimensional gel electrophoresis.* The precision of identifying proteins has been greatly improved by the use of *mass spectrometry,* which analyzes mass and charge at an atomic level (Aebersold & Mann, 2003). Based on these techniques, a proteome atlas of nearly 5000 proteins and 5000 protein complexes is available for the fruit fly (Giot et al., 2003); similar resources are available for the hippocampus of the mouse (Pollak, John, Hoeger, & Lubec, 2006a) and the hippocampus of the rat (Fountoulakis, Tsangaris, Maris, & Lubec, 2005). As the mass spectrometry techniques have been further refined for higher resolution and high-throughput characterization of proteomic samples, there are now draft maps of the human proteome (Kim et al., 2014, http://humanproteomemap.org/; Wilhelm et al., 2014).

In addition to mass and charge, the relative quantity of each protein can also be estimated. Individual differences in the quantity of a protein in a particular tissue represent a protein trait that is analogous to the RNA transcript traits discussed in the previous section. As with the transcriptome, the proteome needs to be considered as a phenotype that can be attributed to genetic and environmental factors. Such protein traits can be related to individual differences in behavior. For example, human studies using cerebrospinal fluid have yielded hundreds of differences in protein levels and protein modifications in psychiatric disorders (Fountoulakis & Kossida, 2006); neurodegenerative disorders, such as Parkinson disease (Kroksveen, Opsahl, Aye, Ulvik, & Berven, 2011); and rheumatic disorders (Cretu, Diamandis, & Chandran, 2013). Sophisticated approaches to proteomic characterization of specific brain regions implicated in schizophrenia have also suggested differences that may influence behavior (Matsumoto et al., 2011; Wesseling et al., 2013).

Historically, the transcriptome has been and still is the target of much more genetic research than the proteome; however, the interest in the proteome is gaining momentum. Just as the Human Genome Project revolutionized how biologically driven research is performed, there is now a systematic effort under way to characterize the protein products of the human genome — the Human Proteome Project (http://www.thehpp.org; Legrain et al., 2011). The mission of this project is to provide a resource to help elucidate biological and molecular function and advance diagnosis and treatment of diseases.

As in research on the transcriptome, the mouse has historically been the focus of proteomic work because of the availability of brain tissue. A pioneering study that examined 8767 proteins from the mouse brain as well as other tissues found that 1324 of these proteins showed reliable differences in quantity as well as structure and function of the proteins in a large backcross (see Chapter 5) (Klose et al., 2002). Of these proteins, 466 were mapped to chromosomal locations. Although such linkages need to be replicated, the genetic results are interesting for two reasons: Most proteins showed linkage to several regions, and the chromosomal positions often differed from those of the genes that code for the proteins. These results suggest that multiple genes affect protein traits. Another study on protein expression in the hippocampus yielded similar results (Pollak, John, Schneider, Hoeger, & Lubec, 2006b). As methods have become more efficient, they have been applied to human studies of psychiatric and behavioral phenotypes (Benoit, Rowe, Menard, Sarret, & Quirion, 2011; Filiou, Turck, & Martins-de-Souza, 2011; Patel, 2012; Schutzer, 2014).

The Brain

Each step along the pathways from genome to transcriptome to proteome involves huge increases in complexity, but these pale in comparison to the complexity of the brain. The brain has trillions of junctions between neurons (*synapses*) instead of billions of DNA base pairs, and hundreds of neurotransmitters, not just the four bases of DNA. Although the three-dimensional structure of proteins and their interaction in protein complexes contribute to the complexity of the proteome, this complexity is nothing compared to the complexity of the three-dimensional structure and interactions among neurons in the brain.

Neuroscience, the study of brain structure and function, is another extremely active area of research. This section provides an overview of neurogenetics as it relates to behavior. Because the brain is so central in the pathways between genes and behavior, brain phenotypes are sometimes referred to as *endophenotypes*, as discussed in Box 10.2.

As mentioned earlier in this chapter, research on the transcriptome and proteome has begun to build bridges to the brain by creating atlases of gene and protein expression throughout the brain. Most of this research involves animal models because of the access to brain tissue in nonhuman animals. A huge advantage for neurogenetic research in the human species is the availability of neuroimaging, which, as discussed later, makes it possible to assess the structure and function of the human brain. However, in the section that follows, we describe one major area of neurogenetic research on behavior that focuses on animal models, particularly the fruit fly *Drosophila* and the mouse: learning and memory. The advantage of neurogenetic research with animal models is the ability to use both natural and induced genetic mutations to dissect pathways between neurons and behavior.

BOX 10.2 Endophenotypes

The goal of behavioral genetics is to understand pathways between genes and behavior at all levels of analysis. In addition, each level of analysis warrants attention in its own right (see Box 10.1). Using the brain level of analysis as an example, there is much to learn about the brain itself regardless of the brain's relationship to genes or to behavior. However, the focus of behavioral genetics, and this chapter, is on the brain as a pathway between genes and behavior.

Levels of analysis lower than behavior itself are sometimes called endophenotypes, where *endo* means "inside." The term *intermediate phenotype* has also been used as a synonym for endophenotype. It has been suggested that these lower levels of analysis, such as the brain level, might be more amenable to genetic analysis than behavior (Bearden & Freimer, 2006; Gottesman & Gould, 2003). In addition, lower-level processes, such as neurotransmitter levels in the brain, can be modeled more closely in animals and humans than can behavior itself (Gould & Gottesman, 2006). Specifically, it is hoped that genes will have larger effects on lower levels of analysis and will thus be easier to identify. Recent genetic research on the brain neuroimaging of phenotypes supports this hypothesis (see text), for example, in research on alcoholism (Hill, 2010). However, caution is warranted until these DNA associations are replicated because genetic influences are likely to be pleiotropic and polygenic for brain traits as well as behavioral traits (Kovas & Plomin, 2006). Moreover, a meta-analysis of genetic associations reported for endophenotypes concluded that genetic effect sizes are no greater for endophenotypes than for other phenotypes (Flint & Munafo, 2007). In addition, recent work suggests that careful attention should be paid to claims of causality, measurement error, and environmental factors that can influence both the endophenotype and the final outcome (Kendler & Neale, 2010).

Although less complex than behavioral traits, brain traits are nonetheless very complex, and complex traits are generally influenced by many genes of small effect (see Chapter 9). Indeed, the most basic level of analysis, gene expression, appears to show influence by many genes of small effect as well as substantial influence by the environment. One might think that lower levels of analysis are more heritable, but this does not seem to be the case. Using gene expression again as an example because it is the most basic level of analysis, individual differences in transcript levels across the genome do not appear to be highly heritable.

Another issue is that the goal of behavioral genetics is to understand pathways among genes, brain, and behavior. Genes found to be associated with brain phenotypes are important in terms of the brain level of analysis, but their usefulness for behavioral genetics depends on their relationship with behavior (Rasetti & Weinberger, 2011; Glahn et al., 2014). In other words, when genes are found to be associated with brain traits, the extent to which the genes are associated with behavioral traits needs to be assessed rather than assumed.

KEY CONCEPTS

Posttranslational modification: Chemical change to polypeptides (amino acid sequences) after they have been translated from mRNA.

Electrophoresis: A method used to separate DNA fragments or proteins by size. When an electrical charge is applied to DNA fragments or proteins in a gel, smaller fragments travel farther.

Endophenotype: An 'inside' or intermediate phenotype that is causally related to overt behavior.

Synapse: A junction between two nerve cells through which impulses pass by diffusion of a neurotransmitter, such as dopamine or serotonin.

Learning and Memory

One important area of neurogenetic research has considered learning and memory, key functions of the brain. Much of this research involves the fruit fly *Drosophila*. *Drosophila* can indeed learn and remember, abilities that have been studied primarily in relation to spatial learning and olfactory learning (Moressis, Friedrich, Pavlopoulos, Davis, & Skoulakis, 2009; Skoulakis & Grammenoudi, 2006). Learning and memory in *Drosophila* constitute one of the first areas to connect the dots among genes, brain, and behavior (Davis, 2011; Margulies, Tully, & Dubnau, 2005; McGuire, Deshazer, & Davis, 2005). For example, in studies of chemically created mutations in *Drosophila melanogaster,* investigators have identified dozens of genes that, when mutated, disrupt learning (Waddell & Quinn, 2001). A model of memory has been built by using these mutations to dissect memory processes. Beginning with dozens of mutations that affect overall learning and memory, investigators found, on closer examination, that some mutations (such as *dunce* and *rutabaga*) disrupt early memory processing, called *short-term memory (STM)*. In humans, this is the memory storage system you use when you want to remember a telephone number temporarily. Although STM is diminished in these mutant flies, later phases of memory consolidation, such as long-term memory (LTM), are normal. Other mutations affect LTM but do not affect STM.

Neurogenetic research is now attempting to identify the brain mechanisms by which these genes have their effect. Several of the mutations from mutational screening were found to affect a fundamental signaling pathway in the cell involving cyclic AMP (cAMP). *Dunce,* for example, blocks an early step in the learning process by degrading cAMP prematurely. Normally, cAMP stimulates a cascade of neuronal changes including production of a protein kinase that regulates a gene called *cAMP-responsive element* (*CRE*). CRE is thought to be involved in stabilizing memory by changing the expression of a system of genes that can alter the strength of the synaptic connection between neurons, called *synaptic plasticity,* which has been the focus of research in mice (see below). In terms of brain regions, a major target for research in *Drosophila* has been a type of neuron, called a *mushroom body neuron,* that appears to be the major site of olfactory learning in insects (Busto, Cervantes-Sandoval, & Davis, 2010; Heisenberg, 2003), although many other neurons are also involved (Davis, 2011). Pairing shock with olfactory cues triggers a complex series of signals that results in a cascade of expression of different genes. These changes in gene expression produce long-lasting functional and structural changes in the synapse (Liu & Davis, 2006).

Learning and memory also constitute an intense area of research activity in the mouse. However, rather than relying on randomly created mutations, neurogenetic research on learning and memory in the mouse uses targeted mutations. It also focuses on one area of the brain called the hippocampus, which has been shown in studies of human brain damage to be crucially involved in memory. In 1992, one of the first gene targeting experiments for behavior was reported (Silva, Paylor, Wehner, & Tonegwa, 1992). Investigators knocked out a gene (*a-CaMKII*) that normally codes for the protein a-Ca^{2+}-calmodulin kinase II, which is expressed postnatally in the hippocampus and other forebrain areas critical for learning and memory. Mutant mice homozygous for the knock-out gene learned a spatial task significantly more poorly than control mice did, although otherwise their behavior seemed normal.

In the 1990s, there was an explosion of research using targeted mutations in the mouse to study learning and memory (Mayford & Kandel, 1999), with 22 knock-out mutations shown to affect learning and memory in mice (Wahlsten, 1999). Many of these targeted mutations involve changes in the strength of connections across the synapse and have been the topic of numerous papers focused on the genetics of synaptic plasticity. Memories are made of long-term synaptic changes, called *long-term potentiation* (Lynch, 2004). The idea that information is stored in neural circuits by changing synaptic links between neurons was first proposed in 1949 (Hebb, 1949).

Although genes drive long-term potentiation, understanding how this occurs is not going to be easy because each synapse is affected by more than a thousand protein components. The *a-CaMKII* gene, mentioned earlier in relation to the first reported knock-out study of learning and memory, activates *CRE*-encoded expression of a protein called *CRE-binding protein (CREB)*, which affects long-term but not short-term memory (Silva, Kogan, Frankland, & Kida, 1998). CREB expression is a critical step in cellular changes in the mouse synapse, as it is in *Drosophila*. In *Drosophila*, another gene that activates CREB was the target of a *conditional* knock-out that can be turned on and off as a function of temperature. These changes in CREB expression were shown to correspond to changes in long-term memory (Yin, Del Vecchio, Zhou, & Tully, 1995). A complete knock-out of CREB in mice is lethal, but deletions that substantially reduce CREB have also been shown to impair long-term memory (Mayford & Kandel, 1999).

A receptor involved in neurotransmission via the basic excitatory neurotransmitter glutamate plays an important role in long-term potentiation and other behaviors in mice as well as humans (Newcomer & Krystal, 2001). The N-methyl-D-aspartate

(NMDA) receptor serves as a switch for memory formation by detecting coincident firing of different neurons; it affects the cAMP system among others. Overexpressing one particular *NMDA* gene (*NMDA receptor 2B*) enhanced learning and memory in various tasks in mice (Tang et al., 1999). A conditional knock-out was used to limit the mutation to a particular area of the brain—in this case, the forebrain. Normally, expression of this gene has slowed down by adulthood; this pattern of expression may contribute to decreased memory in adults. In this research, the gene was altered so that it continued to be expressed in adulthood, resulting in enhanced learning and memory. However, this particular *NMDA* gene is part of a protein complex (*N-methyl-D-aspartate receptor complex*) that involves 185 proteins; mutations in many of the genes responsible for this protein complex are associated with behavior in mice and humans (Grant, Marshall, Page, Cumiskey, & Armstrong, 2005).

Targeted mutations indicate the complexity of brain systems for learning and memory. For example, none of the genes and signaling molecules in flies and mice found to be involved in learning and memory are specific to learning processes. They are involved in many basic cell functions, a finding that raises the question of whether they merely modulate the cellular background in which memories are encoded (Mayford & Kandel, 1999). It seems likely that learning involves a network of interacting brain systems.

Neuroimaging

In humans, the structure and function of brain regions can be assessed using noninvasive neuroimaging techniques. There are many ways to scan the brain, each with a different pattern of strengths and weaknesses. As one example, brain structures can be seen clearly using magnetic resonance imaging (MRI) (Figure 10.3). Functional MRI

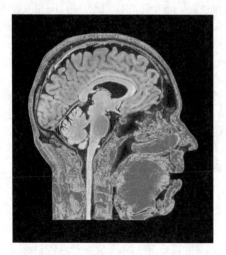

FIGURE 10.3 Magnetic resonance imaging (MRI) scan of the human brain. (DU CANE MEDICAL IMAGING LTD/SCIENCE PHOTO LIBRARY/Getty Images.)

(fMRI) is able to visualize changing blood flow in the brain, which is associated with neural activity. The spatial resolution of fMRI is good, about two millimeters, but its temporal resolution is limited to events that take place over several seconds. *Electroencephalography (EEG)*, using electrodes placed on the scalp, measures voltage differences across the brain that index electrical activity. It provides excellent temporal resolution (less than one millisecond), but its spatial resolution is poor because it averages activity across adjacent regions on the brain's surface. It is possible to combine the spatial strength of fMRI and the temporal strength of EEG (Debener, Ullsperger, Siegel, & Engel, 2006), which can be accomplished using a different technology, *magnetoencephalography* (MEG; Ioannides, 2006).

Neuroimaging is now often used in genetic research. For example, the IMAGEN study was announced as the first multicenter genetic neuroimaging study aimed at identifying the genetic and neurobiological basis of individual variability in impulsivity, reinforcer sensitivity, and emotional reactivity, and how these affect the development of psychiatric disorders (Schumann et al., 2010). Several twin studies using structural neuroimaging have shown that individual differences in the volume of many brain regions are highly heritable and correlated with general cognitive ability (Posthuma et al., 2002; Thompson et al., 2001; Wallace et al., 2006) and vulnerability for psychopathic traits (Rijsdijsk et al., 2010). Twin data have recently been used to develop the first brain atlas of human cortical surface area based solely on genetically informative data (Chen et al., 2012). This atlas, shown in Figure 10.4, was created, in part, by using genetic correlations estimated from twin data between different points on the cortical surface.

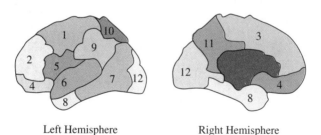

Left Hemisphere   Right Hemisphere

FIGURE 10.4 Brain atlas of human cortical surface area (left and right hemispheres) based solely on genetically informative data. (Adapted from Chen et al., 2012.) Map of twelve genetic clusters of the human cortical surface: 1, motor-premotor cortex; 2, dorsolateral prefrontal cortex; 3, dorsomedial frontal cortex; 4, orbitofrontal cortex; 5, pars opercularis and subcentral region; 6, superior temporal cortex; 7, posterolateral temporal cortex; 8, anteromedial temporal cortex; 9, inferior parietal cortex; 10, superior parietal cortex; 11, precuneus; and 12, occipital cortex. These genetic clusters tend to correspond to traditional cortical structures. (Republished with permission of AAAS, from Chen et al. (2012), "Hierarchical genetic organization of human cortical surface area," 335, 1634-1636; permission conveyed through Copyright Clearance Center, Inc.)

Summary

As genes associated with behavior are identified, genetic research will switch from finding genes to using genes to understand the pathways from genes to behavior, that is, the mechanisms by which genes affect behavior. Three general levels of analysis between genes and behavior are the transcriptome (gene expression throughout the genome), the proteome (protein expression throughout the transcriptome), and the brain. RNA sequencing and RNA microarrays make it possible to study the expression of all genes in the genome across the brain, across development, across states, and across individuals. All pathways between genes and behavior travel through the brain, as can be glimpsed in neurogenetic research on learning and memory.

CHAPTER **ELEVEN**

Cognitive Abilities

*C*ognitive abilities, individual differences in performance on tests such as reasoning and memory, is one of the oldest and most studied areas of behavioral genetics. In part, interest in cognitive abilities is driven by their importance in our increasingly knowledge-based society in which "intellectual capital" is key (Neisser et al., 1996). In addition, cognitive tests predict major social outcomes such as educational and occupational success far better than any other trait (Gottfredson, 1997; Strenze, 2007); they also predict health and longevity (Deary, 2013).

Genetic research is based on a model in which cognitive abilities are organized hierarchically (Carroll, 1993; Carroll, 1997), from individual tests to specific cognitive abilities to general cognitive ability (Figure 11.1). There are hundreds of tests of diverse cognitive abilities. These tests measure several specific cognitive abilities such as verbal ability, spatial ability, memory, and speed of processing. These specific cognitive abilities intercorrelate modestly. *General cognitive ability (g)*, that which is in common among specific cognitive abilities, was discovered by Charles Spearman over a century ago, the

General cognitive
ability (*g*)

Specific cognitive
abilities

Tests

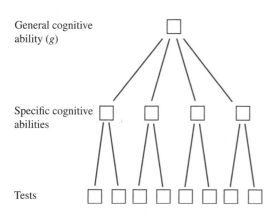

FIGURE 11.1 Hierarchical model of cognitive abilities.

same time that Mendel's laws of inheritance were rediscovered (Spearman, 1904). The phrase *general cognitive ability* is better than the word *intelligence* because the latter has so many different meanings in psychology and in society (Jensen, 1998). General texts on *g* are available (Hunt, 2011; see Deary, 2012, for an overview of other books).

Most people are familiar with intelligence tests, often called *IQ tests* (intelligence quotient tests). These tests typically assess several cognitive abilities and yield total scores that are reasonable indices of *g*. For example, the Wechsler tests of intelligence, widely used clinically, include ten subtests such as vocabulary, picture completion (indicating what is missing in a picture), analogies, and block design (using colored blocks to produce a design that matches a picture). In research contexts, *g* is usually derived by using a technique called *factor analysis* that weights tests differently, according to how much they contribute to *g*. This weight can be thought of as the average of a test's correlations with every other test. This is not merely a statistical abstraction—one can simply look at a matrix of correlations among such measures and see that all the tests intercorrelate positively and that some measures (such as spatial and verbal ability) intercorrelate more highly than do other measures (such as nonverbal memory tests). A test's contribution to *g* is related to the complexity of the cognitive operations it assesses. More complex cognitive processes such as abstract reasoning are better indices of *g* than less complex cognitive processes such as simple sensory discriminations.

Although *g* explains about 40 percent of the variance among such tests, most of the variance of specific tests is independent of *g*. Clearly there is more to cognitive abilities than *g*, which is why we will consider specific cognitive abilities and educationally relevant cognitive skills. Also, there is much more to achievement than cognitive abilities. Personality, mental health, and motivation, all play a part in how well someone does in life.

In this chapter, we summarize behavioral genetic research on cognitive abilities, beginning with a brief overview of animal research.

ANIMAL RESEARCH

Although much animal research has focused on learning, most of this research has not considered individual differences in performance, which is the starting point for genetic research. In this section, we will describe two classic genetic studies of cognitive abilities in rats. One of the earliest studies, a 20-year study begun in 1924, used the selection design to breed rats for their performance in learning to navigate a maze in order to find food. As shown in Figure 11.2, after only a few generations of selective breeding, there was practically no overlap between the maze-bright lines (few errors) and maze-dull lines (many errors); all rats in the maze-bright line were able to learn to run through a maze with fewer errors than any of the rats in the maze-dull line.

Maze-bright and maze-dull selected rats were used in one of the best-known psychological studies of genotype-environment interaction (Cooper & Zubek, 1958). Rats from the two selected lines were reared under one of two conditions. One condition was "enriched," in that the cages were large and contained many movable toys. For the second condition, called "restricted," small gray cages without movable objects were used. Rats reared under the two conditions were compared to maze-bright and maze-dull rats reared in a standard laboratory environment.

The results of testing the maze-bright and maze-dull rats reared in these conditions are shown in Figure 11.3. Not surprisingly, in the normal environment in which the rats had been selected, there was a large difference between the two selected lines. A clear genotype-environment interaction emerged for the enriched and restricted

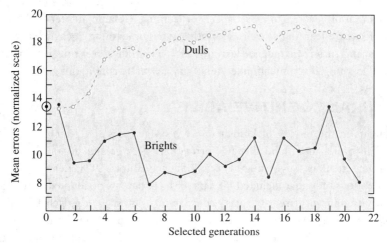

FIGURE 11.2 The results of selective breeding for maze brightness and maze dullness in rats. (Data from "The inheritance of behavior" by G. E. McClearn. In L. J. Postman (Ed.), *Psychology in the Making.* © 1963.)

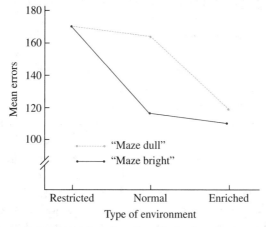

FIGURE 11.3 Genotype-environment interaction. The effects of rearing in a restricted, normal, or enriched environment on maze-learning errors differ for maze-bright and maze-dull selected rats. (Data from Cooper & Zubek, 1958.)

environments. The enriched condition had no effect on the maze-bright rats, but it greatly improved the performance of the maze-dull rats. On the other hand, the restricted environment was detrimental to the maze-bright rats but had little effect on the maze-dull ones. In other words, there is no simple answer concerning the effect of restricted and enriched environments in this study. It depends on the genotype of the animals. This example illustrates genotype-environment interaction, the differential response of genotypes to environments, as discussed in Chapter 8. Despite this persuasive example, other systematic research on learning generally failed to find clear-cut evidence of genotype-environment interaction (Henderson, 1972).

In the 1950s and 1960s, studies of inbred strains of mice showed the important contribution of genetics to most aspects of learning. Genetic differences have been shown for maze learning as well as for other types of learning, such as active avoidance learning, passive avoidance learning, escape learning, lever pressing for reward, reversal learning, discrimination learning, and heart rate conditioning (Bovet, 1977).

GENERAL COGNITIVE ABILITY

Highlights in the history of human research on genetics and *g* include two early adoption studies that found that IQ correlations were greater in nonadoptive than in adoptive families, suggesting genetic influence (Burks, 1928; Leahy, 1935). The first adoption study that included IQ data for birth parents of adopted offspring also showed a significant parent-offspring correlation, again suggesting genetic influence (Skodak & Skeels, 1949). Begun in the early 1960s, the Louisville Twin Study was the first major longitudinal twin study of IQ that charted the developmental course of genetic and environmental influences (Wilson, 1983).

In 1963, a review of genetic research on *g* was influential in showing the convergence of evidence pointing to genetic influence (Erlenmeyer-Kimling & Jarvik, 1963). In 1966, Cyril Burt summarized his decades of research on MZ twins reared apart, which added the dramatic evidence that MZ twins reared apart are nearly as similar as MZ twins reared together. After his death in 1973, Burt's work was attacked, with allegations that some of his data were fraudulent (Hearnshaw, 1979). Two subsequent books reopened the case (Fletcher, 1990; Joynson, 1989). Although the jury is still out on some of the charges (Mackintosh, 1995; Rushton, 2002), it appears that at least some of Burt's data are dubious.

During the 1960s, environmentalism, which had been rampant until then in American psychology, was beginning to wane, and the stage was set for increased acceptance of genetic influence on *g*. Then, in 1969, a monograph on the genetics of intelligence by Arthur Jensen almost brought the field to a halt because a few pages in this lengthy monograph suggested that ethnic differences in IQ might involve genetic differences. Twenty-five years later, this issue was resurrected in *The Bell Curve* (Herrnstein & Murray, 1994) and caused a similar uproar. As we emphasized in Chapter 7, the causes of average differences between groups need not be related to the causes of individual differences within groups. The former question is much more difficult to investigate than the latter, which is the focus of the vast majority of genetic research on IQ. The storm raised by Jensen's monograph led to intense criticism of all behavioral genetic research, especially in the area of cognitive abilities (e.g., Kamin, 1974). These criticisms of older studies had the positive effect of generating bigger and better behavioral genetic studies that used family, adoption, and twin designs. These new projects produced much more data on the genetics of *g* than had been obtained in the previous 50 years. The new data contributed in part to a dramatic shift that occurred in the 1980s in psychology toward acceptance of the conclusion that genetic differences among individuals are significantly associated with differences in *g* (Snyderman & Rothman, 1988).

In the early 1980s, a review of genetic research on *g* was published that summarized results from dozens of studies (Bouchard & McGue, 1981). Figure 11.4 is an expanded version of the summary of the review presented earlier in Chapter 3 (see Figure 3.9).

First-degree relatives living together are moderately correlated for *g* (about 0.45). This resemblance could be due to genetic or to environmental influences because such

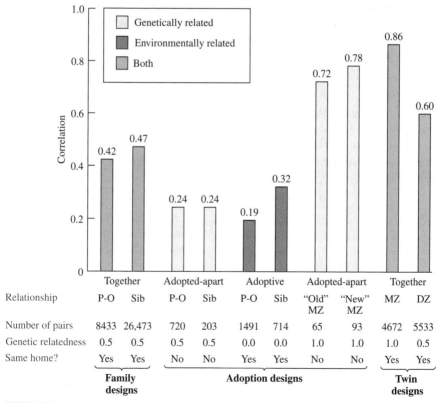

FIGURE 11.4 Average IQ correlations for family, adoption, and twin designs. P-O = Parent-Offspring. Based on reviews by Bouchard and McGue (1981), as amended by Loehlin (1989). "New" data for adopted-apart MZ twins include Bouchard et al. (1990) and Pedersen et al. (1992).

relatives share both. Adoption designs disentangle these genetic and environmental sources of resemblance. Because birth parents and their offspring who are separated by adoption, as well as siblings who are adopted by different families, share heredity but not family environment, their similarity indicates that resemblance among family members is due in part to genetic factors. For g, the correlation between adopted children and their genetic parents is 0.24. The correlation between genetically related siblings reared apart is also 0.24. Because first-degree relatives are only 50 percent similar genetically, doubling these correlations gives a rough estimate of heritability of 48 percent. As discussed in Chapter 7, this outcome means that about half of the variance in IQ scores in the populations sampled in these studies can be accounted for by genetic differences among individuals.

The twin method supports this conclusion. Identical twins are nearly as similar as the same person tested twice. (Test-retest correlations for g are generally between 0.80 and 0.90.) The average twin correlations are 0.86 for identical twins and 0.60 for fraternal twins. Doubling the difference between MZ and DZ correlations estimates heritability as 52 percent. The most dramatic adoption design involves MZ twins who were reared apart. Their correlation provides a direct estimate of heritability. For obvious reasons, the number of such twin pairs is small. For several small studies published before 1981, the average correlation for MZ twins reared apart is 0.72 (excluding the suspect data of Cyril Burt). This outcome suggests higher heritability (72 percent) than do the other designs. This high heritability estimate has been confirmed in two other studies of twins reared apart (Bouchard et al., 1990; Pedersen et al., 1992). Although the small sample sizes warrant caution in interpreting this higher heritability estimate for adopted-apart MZ twins, a possible explanation is discussed later in a section on developmental changes in heritability.

Model-fitting analyses that simultaneously analyze all the family, adoption, and twin data summarized in Figure 11.4 yield heritability estimates of about 50 percent (Chipuer, Rovine, & Plomin, 1990; Loehlin, 1989). It is noteworthy that genetics can account for half of the variance of a trait as complex as general cognitive ability. In addition, the total variance includes error of measurement. Corrected for unreliability of measurement, heritability estimates would be higher. Regardless of the precise estimate of heritability, the point is that genetic influence on g is not only statistically significant, it is also substantial.

SNP-based heritability estimates also find evidence for genetic influence on g. As explained in Chapter 7, SNP heritability uses hundreds of thousands of SNPs genotyped on large samples to estimate heritability directly from DNA. It does not specify which SNPs are associated with a phenotype. Instead, it relates chance genetic similarity on SNPs to phenotypic similarity pair by pair in a large sample of conventionally unrelated individuals. SNP heritability estimates are generally about half the estimates from twin studies for g as well as other behavioral traits (Plomin et al., 2013). For example, SNP heritability of g was recently estimated as 28 percent in two samples totaling 12,000 individuals (Davies et al., 2015).

Although heritability could differ in different cultures, it appears that the level of heritability of *g* also applies to populations outside North America and Western Europe, where most studies have been conducted. Similar heritabilities have been found in twin studies in Russia (Malykh, Iskoldsky, & Gindina, 2005) and in the former East Germany (Weiss, 1982), as well as in rural India, urban India, and Japan (Jensen, 1998).

If half of the variance of *g* can be accounted for by heredity, the other half can be attributed to environment (plus errors of measurement). Some of this environmental influence appears to be shared by family members, making them similar to one another. Direct estimates of the importance of shared environmental influence come from correlations for adoptive parents and children and for adoptive siblings. Particularly impressive is the correlation of 0.32 for adoptive siblings (see Figure 11.4). Because they are unrelated genetically, what makes adoptive siblings similar is shared rearing—having the same parents and the same diet, attending the same schools, and so on. The adoptive sibling correlation of 0.32 suggests that about a third of the total variance can be explained by shared environmental influences. The correlation for adoptive parents and their adopted children is lower ($r = 0.19$) than that for adoptive siblings, a result suggesting that shared environment for less resemblance between parents and offspring than between siblings.

Shared environmental effects are also suggested because correlations for relatives living together are greater than correlations for adopted-apart relatives. Twin studies also suggest shared environmental influence. In addition, shared environmental effects appear to contribute more to the resemblance of twins than to that of nontwin siblings because the correlation of 0.60 for DZ twins exceeds the correlation of 0.47 for nontwin siblings. Twins may be more similar than other siblings because they shared the same womb and are exactly the same age. Because they are the same age, twins also tend to be in the same school, sometimes the same class, and share many of the same peers (Koeppen-Schomerus et al., 2003).

Model-fitting estimates of the role of shared environment for *g* based on the data in Figure 11.4 are about 20 percent for parents and offspring, about 25 percent for siblings, and about 40 percent for twins (Chipuer et al., 1990). The rest of the environmental variance is attributed to nonshared environment and errors of measurement. However, when these data are examined developmentally, a different picture emerges, as discussed later in this chapter.

SPECIFIC COGNITIVE ABILITIES

Specific cognitive abilities generally yield genetic results similar to *g*, although much less research has focused on specific cognitive abilities (Plomin & DeFries, 1998). The largest family study of specific cognitive abilities, called the Hawaii Family Study of Cognition, included more than a thousand families (DeFries et al., 1979). Like other work in this area, this study used a technique called factor analysis to identify the tightest clusters of intercorrelated tests. Four group factors were derived from

15 tests: verbal (including vocabulary and fluency), spatial (visualizing and rotating objects in two- and three-dimensional space), perceptual speed (simple arithmetic and number comparisons), and visual memory (short-term and longer-term recognition of line drawings). All factors showed substantial parent-offspring resemblance, although the verbal and spatial factors showed somewhat more familial resemblance than the perceptual speed and memory factors.

The results of dozens of early twin studies of specific cognitive abilities are summarized in Figure 11.5 (Nichols, 1978; see also DeFries, Vandenberg, & McClearn, 1976). When we double the difference between the correlations for identical and fraternal twins to estimate heritability (see Chapter 6), these results suggest that specific cognitive abilities show slightly less genetic influence than general cognitive ability. Memory and verbal fluency show lower heritability, about 30 percent; the other abilities yield heritabilities of 40 to 50 percent. Verbal and spatial abilities generally show greater heritability than do perceptual speed and, especially, memory abilities (Plomin, 1988).

Similar to the results for g, the twin correlations in Figure 11.5 also imply moderate influence of shared environment for specific cognitive abilities; however, adoption designs show little influence of shared environment. For example, the correlations for adoptive siblings are only about 0.10, suggesting that only 10 percent of the variance of verbal and spatial abilities is due to shared environmental factors. The results for family, twin, and adoption studies of verbal and spatial ability are summarized in Figure 11.6. The results converge on the conclusion that both verbal and spatial ability show substantial genetic influence but only modest influence of shared environment.

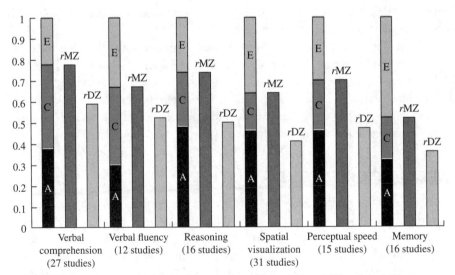

FIGURE 11.5 Average twin correlations for tests of specific cognitive abilities. A = additive genetic influence; C = shared environmental influence; E = nonshared (unique) environmental influence; r = correlation; MZ = monozygotic; DZ = dizygotic. (Data from Nichols, 1978.)

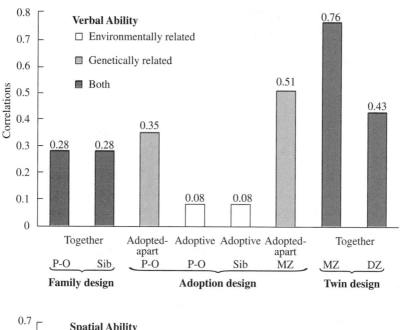

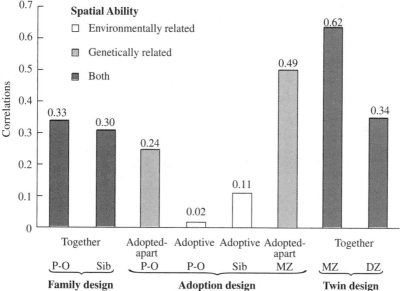

FIGURE 11.6 Family, twin, and adoption results for verbal and spatial abilities. The family study results are from the nearly 1000 Caucasian families in the Hawaii Family Study of Cognition, with parent-offspring (P-O) correlations averaged for mothers and fathers (DeFries et al., 1979). The adoption data are from the Colorado Adoption Project, with parent-offspring correlations shown when the adopted children were 16 years old and adoptive sibling correlations averaged across 9 to 12 years (Plomin et al., 1997). The adopted-apart MZ twin data are averaged from the 95 pairs reported by Bouchard et al. (1990) and Pedersen et al. (1992). The twin study correlations are based on more than 1500 pairs of wide age ranges in seven studies from four countries (Plomin, 1988). (Data from "Human behavioral genetics of cognitive abilities and disabilities" by R. Plomin & I. W. Craig. *BioEssays*, *19*, 1117–1124. © 1997.)

NEUROCOGNITIVE MEASURES OF COGNITIVE ABILITIES

Much research has used laboratory tasks developed by cognitive psychologists to assess how information is processed, often using reaction time to measure information-processing speed (Deary, 2000). These measures and models have developed separately from the hierarchical model of cognitive abilities but they have evolved in a similar direction. The most widely cited model, called the *working memory model,* assumes a central executive system that regulates other subsystems involved in attention, short-term and long-term memory, and other processes (Baddeley, 2007). Although individual differences in these processes are not often the focus of neurocognitive research (Miyake & Friedman, 2012), twin studies suggest that measures of executive function and working memory are highly heritable (Blokland et al., 2011; Friedman et al., 2008; Panizzon et al., 2011). Specific tests of these cognitive processes are only moderately correlated with g (Ackerman, Beier, & Boyle, 2005; Friedman et al., 2006), but composite measures correlate substantially with g (Colom, Rebollo, Abad, & Shih, 2006). One study reported a genetic correlation of 0.57 between a general executive function factor and IQ (Friedman et al., 2008). (As explained in Chapter 7, a genetic correlation estimates the extent to which genetic differences that affect one trait correlate with genetic effects on the other trait.)

Some genetic research has systematically explored elementary information-processing tasks assessed using reaction time measures (T. Lee et al., 2012; Neubauer, Spinath, Riemann, Borkenau, & Angleitner, 2000; Petrill, Thompson & Detterman, 1995; Singer, MacGregor, Cherkas, & Spector, 2006; Vinkhuyzen, van der Sluis, Boomsma, de Geus, & Posthuma, 2010). These studies generally find that more complex tasks are more heritable and more correlated genetically with g (Plomin & Spinath, 2002).

Attempts to investigate even more basic neurocognitive processes have led to studies of speed of nerve conduction and brain wave (EEG) measures of event-related potentials. However, the genetic as well as phenotypic correlations are low between cognitive abilities and peripheral nerve conduction (Rijsdijk & Boomsma, 1997) and these EEG measures (Posthuma, Neale, Boomsma, & de Geus, 2001b; van Baal, Boomsma, & de Geus, 2001).

Magnetic resonance imaging (MRI) and other brain imaging techniques provide greater resolution of brain regions and stronger correlations with cognitive abilities. Combining such brain imaging techniques with genetics has led to a new field called *imaging genetics* (Thompson, Martin, & Wright, 2010). Imaging genetics research began with brain structure, which can be assessed more reliably than brain function. One of the most robust findings is that total brain volume, as well as the volume of most brain regions, correlate moderately (~0.40) with cognitive abilities (Deary, Penke, & Johnson, 2010). Twin studies have found strong genetic influences on individual differences in the size of many brain regions (Blokland, de Zubicaray, McMahon, &

Wright, 2012; Pennington et al., 2000; Thompson et al., 2001). Multivariate genetic twin analyses indicate that the correlation between these measures of brain structure and cognitive ability is largely genetic in origin (Betjemann et al., 2010; Hulshoff Pol et al., 2006; Peper, Brouwer, Boomsma, Kahn, & Hulshoff Pol, 2007; Posthuma et al., 2002) and that most of these genetic effects are explained by total brain volume rather than by the volume of specific brain regions (Schmitt et al., 2010). Twin studies have recently mapped the surface and thickness of areas of cortical brain regions in terms of the genetic correlations among the regions (Chen et al., 2011; Eyler et al., 2011; Rimol et al., 2010). Other more specific measures of brain structure are beginning to be explored. For example, individual differences in the degree of thinning of the cerebral cortex during adolescence are highly heritable (Joshi et al., 2011; van Soelen et al., 2012) and are related to cognitive abilities (Shaw et al., 2006). Structural measures of connectivity also show high heritability and strong correlations with cognitive abilities (Chiang et al., 2009).

Functional imaging studies identify regions of brain activation in response to tasks. A surprising finding is that high cognitive ability is associated with *less* brain activation, presumably because these brains are more efficient (Neubauer & Fink, 2009). Similar to structural imaging results, functional imaging research suggests that activation occurs across diverse brain regions rather than being restricted to a single brain region (Deary et al., 2010). Twin studies are beginning to untangle genetic and environmental sources of these effects. For example, twin studies using functional MRI (fMRI) have found moderate heritability for individual differences in activation of several brain regions during cognitive tasks (Blokland et al., 2011; Koten et al., 2009). fMRI twin studies of functional connectivity between regions of the brain also indicate moderate heritability (Posthuma et al., 2005). Multivariate genetic analysis is beginning to be used to map genetically driven patterns of activity across brain regions (Park, Shedden, & Polk, 2012). The goal is to understand the genetic and environmental etiologies of individual differences in brain structure and function as they relate to cognitive abilities (Karlsgodt, Bachman, Winkler, Bearden, & Glahn, 2011).

SCHOOL ACHIEVEMENT

At first glance, tests of school achievement seem quite different from tests of specific cognitive abilities. School achievement tests focus on performance in specific subjects taught at school, such as literacy (reading), numeracy (mathematics), and science. Although some subjects, such as history, might seem to largely involve memorizing facts, doing well in such subjects requires cognitive skills such as extracting complex information and reasoning. Other subjects, such as reading, mathematics, and science, seem more similar to cognitive abilities because they clearly involve general cognitive processes beyond specific content. In the case of reading, most children quickly progress in the early school years from learning to read to reading to learn, that is, to using reading to absorb information. One difference is that the fundamentals of reading and mathematics are taught in school, whereas the cognitive abilities discussed earlier—*g* and its verbal, spatial, memory, and perceptual speed components—are not taught explicitly. Nonetheless, as we shall see, multivariate genetic research finds considerable genetic overlap between domains of school achievement and cognitive abilities.

The word *achievement* itself implies that school achievement is due to dint of effort, assumed to be an environmental influence, in contrast to *ability*, for which genetic influence seems more reasonable. For the past half-century, the focus of educational research has been on environmental factors, such as characteristics of schools, neighborhoods, and parents. Hardly any attention has been given to the possibility that genetic influences on the characteristics of children affect learning in school (Asbury & Plomin, 2013; Wooldridge, 1994).

The present discussion considers the normal range of individual differences in school achievement; reading and mathematics disabilities and other cognitive disabilities are discussed in Chapter 12. The most well-studied area by far is reading ability (Olson, 2007). As shown in Figure 11.7, a meta-analysis of a dozen twin studies indicates that reading-related processes such as word recognition, spelling, and reading comprehension show substantial genetic influence, with all average heritability estimates within the narrow range of 0.54 to 0.63 (Harlaar, 2006). An interesting analysis across countries suggests that heritability of reading ability in first grade is similar in Australia, Scandinavian countries, and the United States (Samuelsson et al., 2008). General reading composites from such tests yield an average heritability estimate of 0.64. Similar results have been reported for a twin study in China, despite the different orthography of Chinese (Chow, Ho, Wong, Waye, & Bishop, 2011).

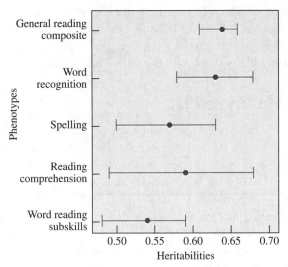

FIGURE 11.7 Meta-analysis of heritabilities of reading-related processes. The circles indicate the average heritability, and the lines around the circles indicate the 95 percent confidence intervals. (Data from Harlaar, 2006.)

Although it would be reasonable to expect that learning to read (e.g., word recognition) might be less heritable than reading to learn (e.g., reading comprehension), reading ability in the early school years is also highly heritable (Harlaar, Hayiou-Thomas, & Plomin, 2005b; Petrill et al., 2007). Even pre-reading skills such as phonological awareness, rapid naming, and verbal memory show substantial genetic influence (Hensler, Schatschneider, Taylor, & Wagner, 2010; Samuelsson et al., 2007). Another interesting finding concerns genotype-environment interaction. Twin studies of genotype-environment interaction reported lower heritability of reading ability for families in low-income neighborhoods (Taylor & Schatschneider, 2010b) and greater heritability of reading ability for students with better teachers (Taylor, Roehrig, Hensler, Connor, & Schatschneider, 2010a).

What about academic subjects other than reading? Early twin studies indicated substantial heritability and moderate shared environmental influence for all subjects (Husén, 1959; Loehlin & Nichols, 1976). Similar results have been obtained in the Netherlands (Bartels, Rietveld, van Baal, & Boomsma, 2002), Australia (Wainwright, Wright, Luciano, Geffen, & Martin, 2005), and the United Kingdom (Kovas, Haworth, Dale & Plomin, 2007). In the latter study, twin results for English, mathematics, and science assessed using criteria based on the UK National Curriculum were remarkably consistent across subjects and across ages, suggesting heritabilities of about 0.60 and shared environment of only about 0.20, despite the fact that the twins grew up in the same family, attended the same school, and were often taught by the same teacher in the same classroom. Similar results have also recently been reported for UK nationwide tests of educational achievement at the end of compulsory education at age 16 (Shakeshaft et al., 2013).

THREE SPECIAL GENETIC FINDINGS ABOUT COGNITIVE ABILITIES

As you will see in the rest of this book, these results for cognitive ability showing moderate genetic influence and little influence of shared environment are typical of most behavioral traits. However, there are three genetic findings that are special about cognitive abilities.

Heritability Increases During Development

Try asking people this question: As you go through life, do you think the effects of heredity become more important or less important? Most people will usually guess "less important" for two reasons. First, it seems obvious that life events such as accidents and illnesses, education and occupation, and other experiences accumulate during a lifetime. This fact implies that environmental differences increasingly contribute to phenotypic differences, so heritability necessarily decreases. Second, most people mistakenly believe that genetic effects never change from the moment of conception.

Because it is so reasonable to assume that genetic differences become less impor- tant as experiences accumulate during the course of life, one of the most interesting findings about cognitive abilities is that the opposite is closer to the truth. Genetic factors become increasingly important throughout an individual's life span.

For example, a longitudinal adoption study called the Colorado Adoption Project (Plomin et al., 1997) provides parent-offspring correlations for general cognitive ability from infancy through adolescence. As illustrated in Figure 11.8, correlations between parents and children from control (nonadoptive) families increase from less than 0.20 in infancy to about 0.20 in middle childhood and to about 0.30 in adolescence. The corre- lations between birth mothers and their adopted-away children follow a similar pattern, thus indicating that parent-offspring resemblance for g is due to genetic factors. Parent- offspring correlations for adoptive parents and their adopted children hover around zero, which suggests that family environment shared by parents and offspring does not contribute importantly to parent-offspring resemblance for g. These parent-offspring correlations for adoptive parents and their adopted children are slightly lower than those reported in other adoption studies (see Figure 11.6), possibly because selective placement was negligible in the Colorado Adoption Project (Plomin & DeFries, 1985).

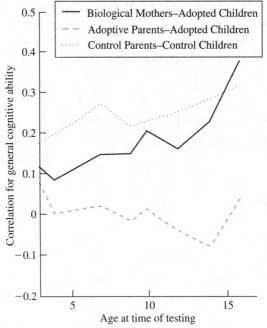

FIGURE 11.8 Parent-offspring correlations between parents' g scores and children's g scores for adoptive, birth, and control parents and their children at 3, 4, 7, 9, 10, 12, 14, and 16 years. Parent- offspring correlations are weighted averages for mothers and fathers to simplify the presenta- tion. (Data from "Nature, nurture and cognitive development from 1 to 16 years: A parent-offspring adoption study" by R. Plomin, D. W. Fulker, R. Corley, & J. C. DeFries. *Psychological Science, 8,* 442–447. © 1997.)

Twin studies also show increases in heritability from childhood to adulthood (McCartney, Harris, & Bernieri, 1990; McGue, Bouchard, Iacono, & Lykken, 1993b; Plomin, 1986). A recent report on a sample of 11,000 pairs of twins, a larger sample than that in all previous studies combined, showed for the first time that the heritability of general cognitive ability increases significantly from about 40 percent in childhood (age 9) to 55 percent in adolescence (age 12) and to 65 percent in young adulthood (age 17) (Haworth et al., 2010), as shown in Figure 11.9. A meta-analysis of results from longitudinal twin and adoption studies also found increases in heritability from infancy through adolescence (Briley & Tucker-Drob, 2013). This increase in heritability is even more remarkable because most traits show a slight *decrease* in heritability across the life span (Polderman et al., 2015).

Although the trend of increasing heritability appears to continue throughout adulthood to about 80 percent at age 65 (McGue & Christensen, 2013; Panizzon et al., 2014), some research suggests that heritability declines in later life (Reynolds & Finkel, 2015). The increase in heritability from childhood to adulthood could explain the higher heritability estimate for adopted-apart MZ twins, mentioned earlier: The adopted-apart MZ twins were much older than subjects in the other twin and adoption studies summarized in Figure 11.4.

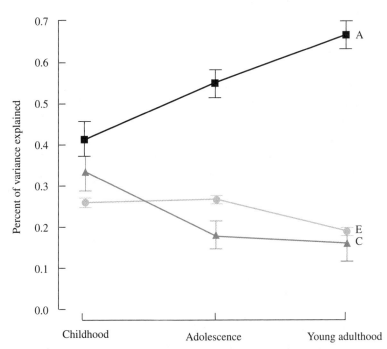

FIGURE 11.9 Twin studies show increasing heritability and decreasing shared environmental influence for general cognitive ability from childhood to adulthood. A = additive genetic; C = common or shared environment; E = nonshared environment. (Data from Haworth et al., 2010.)

Why does heritability increase during the life course? Perhaps completely new genes come to affect *g* in adulthood. However, for cognitive abilities as well as most behavioral traits, longitudinal genetic studies suggest that the same genes largely affect traits across age, contributing to age-to-age continuity, whereas age-to-age change is primarily due to environmental factors (Briley & Tucker-Drob, 2013). This finding creates an apparent paradox: How can the heritability of *g* increase so substantially throughout development if genetic effects are mostly stable from age to age? The most plausible possibility is that genetic nudges early in development are magnified as time goes by, with the same genetic factors creating larger and larger phenotypic effects, a process that has been called *genetic amplification* (Plomin & DeFries, 1985). This amplification model has recently been supported in a meta-analysis of 11,500 twin and sibling pairs with longitudinal data on intelligence, which found that a genetic amplification model fit the data better than a model in which new genetic influences arise across time (Briley & Tucker-Drob, 2013). Genotype-environment correlation seems the most likely explanation in which small genetic differences are amplified as children select, modify, and create environments correlated with their genetic propensities, as described in Chapter 8.

A related developmental finding is that the effects of shared environment appear to decrease. Twin study estimates of shared environment are weak because shared environment is estimated indirectly by the twin method; that is, shared environment is estimated as twin resemblance that cannot be explained by genetics. Nonetheless, the twin study illustrated in Figure 11.9 also found that shared environment effects for *g* decline from adolescence to adulthood.

The most direct evidence comes from the resemblance of adoptive siblings, pairs of genetically unrelated children adopted into the same adoptive families. Figure 11.4 indicates an average IQ correlation of 0.32 for adoptive siblings. However, these studies assessed adoptive siblings when they were children. In 1978, the first study of older adoptive siblings yielded a strikingly different result: The IQ correlation was essentially zero (−0.03) for adoptive siblings who were 16 to 22 years of age (Scarr & Weinberg, 1978b). Other studies of older adoptive siblings have found similarly low IQ correlations. The most impressive evidence comes from a ten-year longitudinal follow-up study of adoptive siblings. At the average age of 8, the IQ correlation was 0.26. Ten years later, the IQ correlation was near zero (Loehlin, Horn, & Willerman, 1989). Figure 11.10 shows the results of studies of adoptive siblings in childhood and in adulthood (McGue et al., 1993b). In childhood, the average adoptive sibling correlation is 0.25; but in adulthood, the correlation for adoptive siblings is near zero.

These results represent a dramatic example of the importance of genetic research for understanding the environment. Shared environment is an important factor for *g* during childhood, when children are living at home. However, its importance fades in adulthood as influences outside the family become more salient. In summary, from childhood to adulthood, the heritability of *g* increases and the importance of shared environment decreases (Figure 11.11). Although there is much less developmental research on specific cognitive abilities, results seem to be similar (Plomin et al., 1997). However, as mentioned earlier, school achievement such as literacy and numeracy is highly heritable (about 60 percent) in the early school years and remains high throughout schooling. In contrast, the heritability of g increases during childhood; as a result, school achievement is more highly heritable than g in the early school years (Kovas et al., 2013; Figure 11.12).

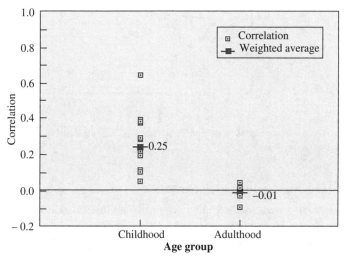

FIGURE 11.10 The correlation for adoptive siblings provides a direct estimate of the importance of shared environment. For g, the correlation is 0.25 in childhood and –0.01 in adulthood, a difference suggesting that shared environment becomes less important after childhood. (Data from McGue et al., 1993b, p. 67.)

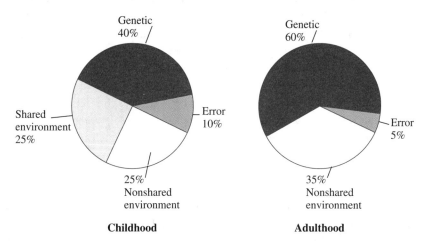

FIGURE 11.11 From childhood to adulthood, heritability of g increases and shared environment declines in importance.

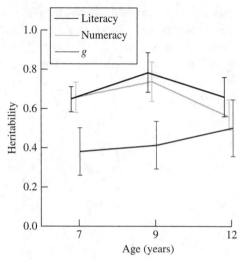

FIGURE 11.12 Heritabilities of literacy, numeracy, and general cognitive ability from 7 to 12 years of age. (Data from Kovas et al., 2013).

Assortative Mating Is Substantial

A second special genetic finding about cognitive abilities is that *assortative mating*, the phenotypic correlation between spouses, is greater for cognitive abilities than for other traits. Assortative mating is about 0.10 for personality (Vandenberg, 1972), 0.20 for height (Keller et al., 2013) and for weight (Whitaker, Jarvis, Beeken, Boniface, & Wardle, 2010), and about 0.40 for g (Jensen, 1978). This finding has some real-world significance in that when you choose a spouse, your choice is based much more on similarity in cognitive ability than similarity in personality or height and weight. Moreover, verbal intelligence shows greater assortative mating (~0.50) than nonverbal intelligence (~0.30), perhaps because it is easier to gauge someone's verbal ability such as vocabulary than their nonverbal intelligence such as spatial ability. Assortative mating for g is caused by initial selection of a mate (assortment) rather than by couples becoming more similar to each other after living together (convergence) (Vinkhuyzen, van der Sluis, Maes, & Posthuma, 2012b). In part, spouses select each other for cognitive ability on the basis of education—spouses correlate about 0.60 for years of education (Jensen, 1998)—which correlates about 0.45 with g (Mackintosh, 2011). Assortative mating may be greater for a few other traits such as social attitudes, smoking, and drinking, although these traits might be affected by convergence.

Assortative mating has important implications for the genetic architecture of cognitive abilities because it increases **additive genetic variance.** *Additive genetic variance* refers to the independent effects of alleles or loci that "add up," in contrast to nonadditive effects of **dominance** within a locus, and *epistasis* across loci in which the effects of alleles or loci interact, as mentioned in Chapter 3 and discussed in the Appendix. Assortative mating of parents increases additive genetic variance in their offspring because offspring receive a random sampling of half of each parent's genes and resemble their parents to the extent that each allele shared with their parents has an average additive effect. Because offspring inherit only one of each of the parents' pairs of alleles, offspring do not resemble their parents for nonadditive interactions.

For example, if spouses mated randomly in relation to g, highly intelligent women would be just as likely to mate with men of low as high intelligence. Offspring of the matings of women of high intelligence and men of low intelligence would generally be of average intelligence. However, because there is strong positive assortative mating, children with highly intelligent mothers are also likely to have highly intelligent fathers, and the offspring themselves are likely to be more intelligent than average. The same thing happens for less intelligent parents. In this way, assortative mating increases additive genetic variance in that the offspring differ more from the average than they would if mating were random. The increase in additive genetic variance can be substantial because its effects accumulate generation after generation until an equilibrium is reached. For example, if the heritability of g with random mating were 0.40, the additive genetic variance of g would increase by one-quarter at equilibrium given assortative mating of 0.40 (Falconer & MacKay, 1996).

The extra additive genetic variance for g induced by assortative mating is important for three genetic reasons. First, parents share only additive genetic variance with their offspring, so that genetic predictions from parent to offspring ought to be greater for cognitive abilities. Second, because SNP heritability is limited to detecting additive genetic variance, SNP heritability should be greater for g than for traits that show less assortative mating, such as personality. Some evidence supports this prediction in that SNP heritability estimates for personality appear to be much lower (about 0.15; Genetics of Personality Consortium et al., 2015) than for g (about 0.30; Davies et al., 2015). Moreover, SNP heritability estimates are greater, although not significantly so, for verbal than for nonverbal cognitive abilities (Davies et al., 2011; Plomin et al., 2013), which is consistent with the greater assortative mating for verbal than for nonverbal ability. Third, because genomewide association (GWA) is also limited to detecting additive genetic variance, the substantial additive genetic influence on cognitive abilities makes them a good target for GWA studies, as discussed later in this chapter.

Assortative mating is also important because it affects estimates of heritability. For example, it increases correlations for first-degree relatives. If assortative mating were not taken into account, it could inflate heritability estimates obtained from studies of parent-offspring (e.g., birth parents and their adopted-apart offspring) or sibling resemblance. For the twin method, however, assortative mating could result in underestimates of heritability. Assortative mating does not affect MZ correlations because MZ twins are identical genetically, but it raises DZ correlations because DZ twins are first-degree relatives. In this way, assortative mating lessens the difference between MZ and DZ correlations; it is this difference that provides estimates of heritability in the twin method. The model-fitting analyses described above took assortative mating into account in estimating the heritability of g to be about 50 percent. If assortative mating had not been taken into account, its effects would have been attributed to shared environment.

Finally, assortative mating for cognitive abilities and years of education might contribute to the third special genetic finding, which is discussed in the following section.

The Same Genes Affect Diverse Cognitive and Learning Abilities

Another special genetic feature of cognitive abilities is that to a large extent the same genes affect cognitive abilities as diverse as, for example, spatial ability, vocabulary, processing speed, executive function, and memory. Most of the genetic action lies with these general (highly pleiotropic) effects rather than effects specific to each ability, leading to a Generalist Genes Hypothesis (Plomin & Kovas, 2005). This is a surprising finding because very different neurocognitive processes appear to be involved in such cognitive abilities (Deary et al., 2010). Although these genetic correlations put g at the pinnacle of the hierarchical model of cognitive abilities, there is also genetic specificity that builds the genetic architecture for the rest of the hierarchical structure of group factors and specific tests (Figure 11.1). In a meta-analysis of 322 studies, the average correlation among individual diverse cognitive tests is about 0.30 (Carroll, 1993). The surprising finding is how high the genetic correlations are among diverse cognitive abilities such as verbal, spatial, and memory. On average, genetic correlations exceed 0.50 in childhood (Alarcón, Plomin, Fulker, Corley, & DeFries, 1999; Cardon, Fulker, DeFries, & Plomin, 1992; LaBuda, DeFries, & Fulker, 1987; Luo, Petrill, & Thompson, 1994; Petrill, Luo, Thompson, & Detterman, 1996; Thompson, Detterman, & Plomin, 1991), adolescence (Calvin et al., 2012; Luciano et al., 2003; Rijsdijk, Vernon, & Boomsma, 2002), adulthood (Finkel & Pedersen, 2000; Martin & Eaves, 1977; Pedersen, Plomin, & McClearn, 1994; Tambs, Sundet, & Magnus, 1986), and old age (Petrill et al., 1998). These genetic correlations of 0.50 or greater provide strong support for genetic g, but they also indicate that there are some genetic effects specific to each of the specific cognitive abilities because the genetic correlations are far less than 1.0.

These general genetic effects permeate not only cognitive abilities such as spatial ability and vocabulary that are used as part of the assessment of intelligence but also extend to education-related learning abilities such as reading and mathematics. Figure 11.13 shows the results of a multivariate genetic analysis of 14 tests that comprise four distinct test batteries—intelligence, reading, mathematics, and language—for more than 5000 pairs of 12-year-old twins (Davis, Haworth & Plomin, 2009). The genetic correlations between intelligence and learning abilities are uniformly high: 0.88 with reading, 0.86 with mathematics, and 0.91 with language. Weighting these genetic correlations by the heritabilities of the latent factors, it can be shown that about two-thirds of the phenotypic correlations between the factors can be explained genetically. One advantage of using such latent factors is that they exclude uncorrelated measurement error. As a result, these genetic correlations are higher than those found when uncorrected composite scores rather than latent factors are analyzed: 0.66 for reading, 0.73 for mathematics, and 0.80 for language (Trzaskowski et al., 2013). A review of a dozen such studies found average genetic correlations of about

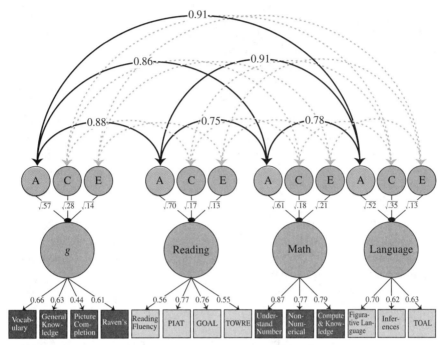

FIGURE 11.13 Genetic correlations among learning abilities and *g*. A = additive genetic effects; C = shared (common) environmental effects; E = nonshared environmental effects. Squares represent measured traits; circles represent latent factors. Multiple tests are used to index "latent" factors of *g*, reading, mathematics, and language. The lower tier of arrows represents factor loadings of the tests on the latent factor. The second tier of coefficients represents the square roots of the genetic and environmental components of the variance of the latent variables. The curved arrows at the top represent correlations between genetic influences. (From "Learning abilities and disabilities: Generalist genes in early adolescence" by O. S. P. Davis, C. M. A. Haworth, & R. Plomin. *Cognitive Neuropsychiatry*, Vol. 14, 4–5 (2009), pp. 312–331; www.tandfonline.com, http://www.tandfonline.com/doi/full/10.1080/13546800902797106).

0.70 between school achievement measures and about 0.60 between these measures and *g* (Plomin & Kovas, 2005).

Bivariate SNP-based analyses support the hypothesis of general genetic effects on broad cognitive and learning ability-related differences. The SNP estimates of genetic correlation between intelligence and learning abilities are highly similar to the twin study estimates just mentioned for composite scores uncorrected for error: 0.89 for reading, 0.74 for mathematics, and 0.81 for language, estimated from unrelated individuals from the same sample (Trzaskowski et al., 2013). An important feature of bivariate SNP-based analysis is that it yields genetic correlations similar to genetic correlations estimated from the twin method, even though SNP-based heritabilities are lower than twin heritabilities. The reason is that estimates of genetic correlations are functions of both genetic variances and covariances (see the Appendix). Because SNP-based estimates of genetic variances and covariances are underestimated to the same extent, these effects cancel out, and the resulting SNP-based estimates of genetic correlation are unbiased (Trzaskowski et al., 2013).

This finding of strong genomewide pleiotropy across diverse cognitive and learning abilities, indexed by *g*, is a major finding about the origins of individual differences in cognitive abilities. This *Generalist Genes Hypothesis* is compatible with various neurocognitive models of causal pathways. The modularity model of cognitive neuroscience might suggest that genetic correlations among cognitive abilities are epiphenomenal in the sense that multiple genetically independent brain mechanisms could affect each ability, creating genetic correlations among abilities. However, the genetic principles of *pleiotropy* (each gene affects many traits) and *polygenicity* (many genes affect each trait) suggest that generalist genes may have their effects further upstream, creating genetic correlations among brain structures and functions, a prediction that supports a network view of brain structure and function (Deary et al., 2010; Plomin & Kovas, 2005).

In summary, multivariate genetic research—from both twin studies and SNP-based analyses—suggests that most of the genetic action is general across diverse cognitive abilities rather than specific to each ability. *g* is a good target for gene-hunting because it indexes these generalist genes.

IDENTIFYING GENES

Finding genes associated with cognitive abilities will have far-reaching ramifications at all levels of understanding from DNA to brain to behavior. Despite its complexity, cognitive ability is a reasonable candidate for molecular genetic research because it is one of the most heritable domains of behavior.

The first attempts to find genes associated with cognitive ability focused on genes involved in brain function (Payton, 2009). One problem with such a candidate gene approach is that we often do not have strong hypotheses as to which genes are true candidate genes. Indeed, the general rule of pleiotropy suggests that most of the thousands of genes expressed in the brain could be considered as candidates. Moreover, many genetic associations are in non-coding regions of DNA rather than in traditional genes, as described in Chapter 10. The major problem for candidate gene association studies is that reports of associations have failed to replicate, suggesting that published reports of associations are false-positive results caused by the use of samples underpowered to detect the small effect sizes that seem to be the source of heritability for complex traits. Strong support for this conclusion comes from a recent study of nearly 10,000 individuals that was not able to replicate associations for ten of the most frequently reported candidate gene associations (Chabris et al., 2012; Franić et al., 2015).

Another candidate gene strategy for identifying associations for cognitive abilities is to focus on intermediate phenotypes—often called *endophenotypes*—that are presumed to be simpler genetically and thus more likely to yield associations of large effect size that can be detected with small samples (Goldberg & Weinberger, 2004; Winterer & Goldman, 2003). As discussed in Chapter 10, although all levels of analysis from genes to g are important to study in their own right and in terms of understanding pathways between genes and behavior, it seems unlikely that brain endophenotypes will prove to be simpler genetically or be more useful in identifying genes associated with cognitive abilities than studying cognitive abilities themselves (Kovas & Plomin, 2006).

As discussed in Chapter 9, attempts to find genes associated with complex traits like cognitive ability have gone beyond looking for candidate genes to conducting systematic scans of the genome using GWA strategies. SNP arrays have made it possible to conduct GWA studies with hundreds of thousands of SNPs. Similar to results from other GWA studies of complex traits in the life sciences, the first GWA studies of g did not identify replicable associations (Butcher, Davis, Craig, & Plomin, 2008; Davies et al., 2011; Davis et al., 2010; Need et al., 2009). These GWA studies were powered to detect associations that account for as little as 0.5 percent of the variance, less than a 1 IQ point difference, which suggests that there may be no associations of large effect on IQ in the population.

A "brute force" strategy to narrow the missing heritability gap is to use the common SNPs currently available on microarrays with much larger samples in order to detect smaller effect sizes. As indicated earlier, SNP heritability estimates indicate that the common SNPs on current SNP arrays tag at least half of the heritability of cognitive ability. A consortium of studies of childhood intelligence with a total sample of nearly 18,000 found no significant associations for individual SNPs even though in this study an association that accounted for only 0.25 percent of the variance would be detected as statistically significant (Benyamin et al., 2014), suggesting that even larger samples will be needed to account for the missing heritability of g. Indeed, a recent meta-analysis of more than 50,000 adults reported 13 genomewide significant SNP associations (Davies et al., 2015). Nonetheless, a polygenic score based on these GWA results accounted for only 1.2 percent of the variance of g in independent samples, indicating again that the effect sizes are extremely small, and that the missing heritability gap remains wide.

The power of a brute force strategy can be seen in a GWA meta-analysis of a "proxy" variable of years of schooling, which correlates moderately with cognitive ability. Because this variable is included as part of the demographic description of most GWA studies, it was possible to conduct GWA meta-analysis based on more than 329,000 adults. This GWA yielded 74 associations that were significant with genomewide correction for multiple testing (Okbay et al., 2016). The largest effect size accounted for only 0.02 percent of the variance in years of schooling, which is about one month of schooling per allele. A polygenic score accounted for 4 percent of the variance in years of schooling. A similar polygenic score from an earlier, smaller GWA analysis also correlated with school achievement (Ward et al., 2014) and cognitive abilities (Krapohl & Plomin, 2015; Rietveld et al., 2014b).

Genomewide association studies have also begun to be reported for other cognitive abilities, including reading ability (Luciano, Montgomery, Martin, Wright, & Bates,

2011b; Meaburn, Harlaar, Craig, Schalkwyk & Plomin, 2008), mathematics ability (Docherty et al., 2010), memory tasks (Papassotiropoulos et al., 2006), and information-processing measures (Cirulli et al., 2010; Luciano et al., 2011a; Need et al., 2009). These first GWA studies suggest a familiar refrain: No associations of sufficiently large effect size have emerged that reach genomewide significance, suggesting that heritability is caused by many genes of small effect. As in other domains, the major strategy for identifying these genes of small effect is to increase the sample sizes by conducting meta-analyses across studies. A remarkable example of this approach is a meta-analysis of nearly 20,000 individuals with structural MRI data from 17 studies, which identified with genomewide significance a SNP associated with hippocampal volume and another SNP associated with intracranial volume (Stein et al., 2012). Although these SNPs accounted for only 0.3 percent of the variance, they also cor-related significantly with g.

As indicated in Chapter 9, another strategy for finding the elusive genes respon-sible for missing heritability is to investigate rarer variants than those currently avail-able on SNP microarray platforms, which use the most common SNPs with minor allele frequencies greater than 5 percent because such SNPs are most useful for tagging the entire genome. As discussed in Chapter 12, the role of rare variants is well-established in single-gene syndromes that involve cognitive disability. However, it remains unclear to what extent low frequency and rare alleles contribute to the genetic architecture of complex traits like cognitive ability in the general popula-tion. There have been reports of finding no association between cognitive ability and low frequency copy number variants (Kirkpatrick et al., 2014; MacLeod et al., 2012; McRae, Wright, Hansell, Montgomery, & Martin, 2013). Microarrays with rarer SNPs in exomes are now available and are being used in GWA studies of the normal sample, but initial reports suggest that rarer SNPs will not close much of the miss-ing heritability gap (Luciano et al., 2015; Marioni et al., 2014; Spain et al., 2015). As discussed in Chapter 9, research is moving toward sequencing the entire genome so that all DNA variation can be detected—common as well as rare DNA variants of all kinds, not just SNPs.

Finding genes that account for the heritability of cognitive abilities has impor-tant implications for society as well as for science (Plomin, 1999). The grandest impli-cation for science is that these genes will serve as an integrating force across diverse disciplines, with DNA as the common denominator, and will open up new scientific horizons for understanding learning and memory. In terms of implications for society, it should be emphasized that no public policies necessarily follow from finding genes associated with cognitive abilities because policy involves values (see Chapter 20). For example, finding genes that predict cognitive ability does not mean that we ought to put all of our resources into educating the brightest children once we identify them genetically. Depending on our values, we might worry more about the children falling off the low end of the bell curve in an increasingly technological society and decide to devote more public resources to those who are in danger of being left behind.

Potential problems related to finding genes associated with cognitive abilities—such as prenatal and postnatal screening, discrimination in education and employment, and group differences—have been considered (Newson & Williamson, 1999; Nuffield Council on Bioethics, 2002). We need to be cautious and to think carefully about societal implications and ethical issues, but there is also much to celebrate here in terms of increased potential for understanding our species' ability to think and learn.

Summary

Animal studies indicate genetic influence on learning, such as the maze-bright and maze-dull selection study of learning in rats. Human studies of general cognitive ability (g) have been conducted for over a century. Family, twin, and adoption studies converge on the conclusion that about half of the total variance of measures of g can be accounted for by genetic factors. For example, twin correlations for g are about 0.85 for identical twins and 0.60 for fraternal twins. Specific cognitive abilities such as verbal and spatial ability and school achievement such as literacy and numeracy are also substantially heritable. Unlike other domains of behavior, these cognitive and learning abilities show evidence for shared environmental influence.

Three genetic findings are special for cognitive abilities. The first special finding is that the heritability of g increases during the life course, reaching levels in adulthood comparable to the heritability of height. The influence of shared environment diminishes sharply after adolescence. Although less well studied than g, specific cognitive abilities appear to show a similar trend. In contrast, school achievement is highly heritable in the early school years and remains high throughout schooling.

The second special finding is that assortative mating is much greater for cognitive abilities than for other traits such as personality and height and weight. This finding has important implications for the genetic architecture of cognitive abilities.

The third special finding is that, to a major extent, the same genes affect diverse cognitive and learning abilities, referred to as the Generalist Genes Hypothesis. g indexes these generalist genes for cognitive abilities.

Attempts to identify some of the genes responsible for the heritability of cognitive abilities have begun, including candidate gene studies and genomewide association studies. This research has demonstrated that many genes of small effect are responsible for the heritability of cognitive abilities. Nonetheless, SNP-based heritability estimates suggest that common SNPs can explain most of the heritability of cognitive abilities; thus, the major strategy for finding genes associated with cognitive abilities and the genetic correlations among them is to increase the sample size of GWA analyses.

CHAPTER **TWELVE**

Cognitive Disabilities

In an increasingly technological world, cognitive disabilities are important liabilities. More is known about genetic causes of cognitive disabilities than about any other area of behavioral genetics. Many single genes and chromosomal abnormalities that contribute to general cognitive disability are known. Although most of these are rare, together they account for a substantial amount of cognitive disability, especially *severe disability*, which is often defined as intelligence quotient (IQ) scores below 50. (The average IQ in the population is 100, with a standard deviation of 15, which means that about 95 percent of the population have IQ scores between 70 and 130.) Less is known about mild cognitive disability (IQs from 50 to 70) and specific cognitive disabilities, such as reading disability, even though they are much more common. In this chapter, we discuss the genetics of these types of cognitive disabilities. Dementia, which is the focus of intense research, is considered in Chapter 19 on aging.

The American Psychiatric Association's *Diagnostic and Statistical Manual of Mental Disorders-5* (DSM-5) refers to general cognitive disability as intellectual disability, previously called mental retardation. For example, DSM-5 defines *intellectual disability* as impairments in cognitive abilities that impact adaptive functioning in skills such as language and reading, in the social domain such as empathy and social judgment, and in the practical domain such as personal care and job responsibilities. We will use the term *general cognitive disability* when referring to low IQ and *specific cognitive disability* when referring to specific learning disabilities such as those in reading or mathematics. Four levels of general cognitive disability are considered: mild (IQ 50 to 70), moderate (IQ 35 to 50), severe (IQ 20 to 35), and profound (IQ below 20). About 85 percent of all individuals with IQs below 70 are classified as mild, most of whom can live independently and hold a job. Individuals with IQs from 35 to 50 usually have good self-care skills and can carry on simple conversations. Although they generally do not live independently and in the past were usually institutionalized, today they often live in the community in special residences or with their families. People with IQs from 20 to 35 can learn some self-care skills and understand language, but they have trouble speaking and require considerable supervision. Individuals with IQs below 20 may understand simple communication but usually cannot speak; they remain institutionalized.

GENERAL COGNITIVE DISABILITY: QUANTITATIVE GENETICS

In the behavioral sciences, it is now widely accepted that genetics substantially influences general cognitive ability; this belief is based on evidence presented in Chapter 11. Although one might expect that low IQ scores are also due to genetic factors, this conclusion does not necessarily follow. For example, cognitive disability can be caused by environmental trauma, such as birth problems, nutritional deficiencies, or head injuries. A sibling study suggests that moderate and severe cognitive disability may be due largely to nonheritable factors. In a study of over 17,000 white children, 0.5 percent were moderately to severely disabled (Nichols, 1984). As shown in Figure 12.1, the siblings of these children showed no cognitive disability. The siblings' average IQ was 103, with a range of 85 to 125. In other words, moderate to severe cognitive disability showed no **familial** resemblance. In contrast, siblings of mildly disabled children tend to have lower than average IQ scores (see Figure 12.1), as would be expected

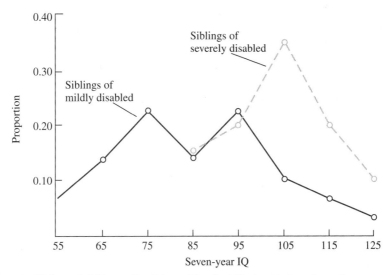

FIGURE 12.1 Siblings of children with mild cognitive disability tend to have lower than average IQs. In contrast, siblings of severely disabled children tend to have normal IQs. These trends suggest that mild disability is familial but severe disability is not. (Data from Nichols, 1984.)

for an inherited trait. The average IQ for these siblings of mildly disabled children (1.2 percent of the sample were mildly disabled) was only 85. A similar result was found in the largest family study of mild cognitive disability, which considered 80,000 relatives of 289 mentally disabled individuals (Reed & Reed, 1965). This family study showed that mild mental disability is very strongly familial. If one parent is mildly disabled, the risk for cognitive disability in the children is about 20 percent. If both parents are mildly disabled, the risk is nearly 50 percent.

These findings have been supported in a study involving more than a million sibling pairs (Reichenberg et al., 2015). This study also analyzed data for 9000 twin pairs using a technique called DF extremes analysis, which is described later in this chapter. These analyses led to the conclusion that moderate to severe cognitive disability is genetically different from the normal distribution of intelligence. In contrast, mild cognitive disability is only quantitatively, but not qualitatively, different for the normal distribution. In other words, the same genetic and environmental factors are responsible for mild cognitive disability and normal variation in cognitive ability. As we shall see, most common disabilities (>1 percent frequency), such as reading disability, are like mild cognitive disability in that they represent the low quantitative end of the same genetic and environmental factors responsible for the normal range of individual differences in ability.

As discussed in the following section, there are hundreds of single-gene causes of cognitive disability that are inherited from generation to generation; however, these are so rare that they may not appear in large samples that have not been selected for severe disability. Although most moderate and severe cognitive disability may not be inherited from generation to generation, it can be caused by noninherited (called *de novo*) DNA events, such as new gene mutations and new chromosomal abnormalities, as well as by environmental events. DNA sequencing research is discovering many new noninherited dominant mutations responsible for such sporadic cases. In fact, DNA sequencing promises to be a powerful approach for identifying *de novo* mutations of any kind—from a single nucleotide base pair to deletions and duplications of parts of chromosomes—responsible for sporadic cases of severe cognitive disability (Gilissen et al., 2014).

GENERAL COGNITIVE DISABILITY: SINGLE-GENE DISORDERS

The classic single-gene cause of severe cognitive disability is PKU. A newer discovery is fragile X syndrome; both of which are mentioned in Chapter 3. We will first discuss these two single-gene disorders, which are known for their effect on cognitive disability, and then we will discuss Rett syndrome, a common cause of cognitive disability in females.

Until recently, much of what was known about these disorders, as well as the chromosomal disorders described in the next section, came from studies of patients in institutions. These earlier studies painted a gloomy picture. But more recent systematic surveys of entire populations show a wide range of individual differences, including individuals whose cognitive functioning is in the normal range. These genetic disorders shift the IQ distribution downward, but a wide range of individual differences remains.

Phenylketonuria

The most well-known inherited form of moderate cognitive disability is phenylketonuria (PKU), which occurs in about 1 in 10,000 births, although its frequency varies widely from a high of 1 in 5000 in Ireland to a low of 1 in 100,000 in Finland. In the untreated condition, IQ scores are often below 50, although the range includes some near-normal IQs. As mentioned in Chapter 3, PKU is a single-gene recessive disorder that previously accounted for about 1 percent of mildly disabled individuals in institutions. PKU is the best example of the usefulness of finding genes related to behavior. Knowledge that PKU is caused by a single gene led to an understanding of how the genetic defect causes cognitive disability. Mutations in the *PAH* gene that produces the enzyme phenylalanine hydroxylase lead to an enzyme that does not work properly, that is, one that is less efficient in breaking down phenylalanine. Phenylalanine comes from food, especially red meats; if it cannot be broken down properly, it builds up and damages the developing brain. The precise brain pathways by which the mutation causes cognitive disability are not known (de Groot, Hoeksma, Blau, Reijngoud, & van Spronsen, 2010).

Although PKU is inherited as a simple single-gene recessive disorder, the molecular genetics of PKU is not so simple (Scriver & Waters, 1999). The *PAH* gene, which is on chromosome 12, shows more than 500 different disease-causing mutations, some of which cause milder forms of cognitive disability (Mitchell et al., 2011). Similar findings have emerged for many classic single-gene disorders. Different mutations can do different things to the gene's product, and this variability makes understanding the disease process more difficult. It also makes DNA diagnosis more difficult, although DNA sequencing can identify any mutation. A mouse model of a mutation in the *PAH* gene shows similar phenotypic effects and has been widely used to investigate effects on brain and behavioral development (Martynyuk, van Spronsen, & Van der Zee, 2010).

To allay fears about how genetic information will be used in the future, it is important to note that knowledge about the single-gene cause of PKU did not lead to sterilization programs or genetic engineering. Instead, an environmental intervention—a diet low in phenylalanine—was found to prevent the development of cognitive disability. Widespread screening at birth for this genetic effect began in 1961, a program demonstrating that genetic screening can be accepted when a relatively simple intervention is available (Guthrie, 1996). However, despite screening and intervention, PKU individuals still tend to have a slightly lower IQ, especially when the low phenylalanine diet has not been strictly followed (Brumm & Grant, 2010).

It is generally recommended that the diet be maintained as long as possible, at least through adolescence, and some suggest throughout life (Gentile, Ten Hoedt, & Bosch, 2010). PKU women must return to a strict low-phenylalanine diet before becoming pregnant to prevent their high levels of phenylalanine from damaging the fetus (Mitchell et al., 2011).

Fragile X Syndrome

As mentioned in Chapter 3, fragile X syndrome is the second most common cause of cognitive disability after Down syndrome and is the most common inherited form. It is twice as common in males as in females. The frequency of fragile X is usually given as 1 in 5000 males and 1 in 10,000 females (Rooms & Kooy, 2011). At least 2 percent of the male residents of schools for cognitively disabled persons have fragile X syndrome. Most fragile X males are moderately disabled, but many are only mildly disabled and some have normal intelligence. Only about one-half of girls with fragile X are affected because one of the two X chromosomes for girls inactivates, as mentioned in Chapter 4. Although fragile X syndrome is a major source of the greater incidence of cognitive disability in boys, more than 90 other genes on the X chromosome have been implicated in cognitive disability (Gecz, Shoubridge, & Corbett, 2009).

For fragile X males, IQ declines after childhood. In addition to lowered IQ, about three-quarters of fragile X males show large, often protruding, ears and a long face with a prominent jaw. They also often show unusual behaviors such as odd speech, poor eye contact (gaze aversion), and flapping movements of the hands. Language difficulties range from an absence of speech to mild communication difficulties. Often observed is a speech pattern called *cluttering*, in which talk is fast, with occasional garbled, repetitive, and disorganized speech. Spatial ability tends to be affected more than verbal ability. Comprehension of language is often better than expression and better than expected on the basis of an average IQ of about 70. Parents frequently report overactivity, impulsivity, and inattention.

Until the gene for fragile X was found in 1991, the disorder's inheritance was puzzling (Verkerk et al., 1991). It did not conform to a simple X-linkage pattern because its risk increased across generations. Fragile X syndrome is caused by an expanded triplet repeat (CGG) on the X chromosome ($Xq27.3$). The disorder is called *fragile X* because the many repeats cause the chromosome to be fragile at that point and to break during laboratory preparation of chromosomes. The disorder is now diagnosed on the basis of DNA sequence. Parents who inherit X chromosomes with a normal number of repeats (6 to 40 repeats) can produce eggs or sperm with an expanded number of repeats (up to 200 repeats), called a *premutation*. This premutation does not cause cognitive disability in their offspring, but it is unstable and often leads to much greater expansions (more than 200 repeats) in later generations, especially when the premutated X chromosome is inherited through the mother. The risk that a premutation will expand to a full mutation increases over four generations from 5 to 50 percent, although it is not yet possible to predict when a premutation will expand to a full mutation. The mechanism by which expansion occurs is not known. The full mutation causes fragile X in almost all males but in only half of the females. Females are mosaics for fragile X in the sense that one X chromosome is inactivated, so some cells will have the full mutation and others will be normal (Willemsen, Levenga, & Oostra, 2011). As a result, females with the full mutation have much more variable symptoms. The triplet repeat is in an untranslated region at the beginning of a gene (*fragile X mental retardation-1, FMR1*) that, when expanded to a full mutation, prevents that gene from being transcribed. The mechanism by which the full mutation prevents transcription is *DNA methylation*, a developmental mechanism for genetic regulation, as discussed in Chapter 10. DNA methylation prevents transcription by binding a methyl group to DNA, usually at CG repeat sites. The full mutation for fragile X, with its hundreds of CGG repeats, causes hypermethylation and thus shuts down transcription of the *FMR1* gene. The gene's protein product (FMRP) binds RNA, which means that the gene product regulates expression of other genes. FMRP facilitates translation of hundreds of neuronal RNAs; thus, the absence of FMRP causes diverse problems. Research on fragile X is moving rapidly from molecular genetics to neurobiology (Cook, Nuro, & Murai, 2014). Researchers hope that, once the functions of FMRP are understood, it can be artificially supplied. In addition, methods for identifying carriers of premutations have improved; these screening tests will help people carrying premutations to avoid producing children who have a larger expansion and therefore suffer from fragile X syndrome (Rooms & Kooy, 2011).

Rett Syndrome

Rett syndrome is a common single-gene cause of general cognitive disability that occurs only in females (1 in 10,000) (Neul et al., 2010). The disorder shows few effects in infancy, although the head, hands, and feet are slow to grow. Cognitive development is normal during infancy but, by school age, girls with Rett syndrome are generally unable to talk and about half are unable to walk, with an average IQ of about 55 (Neul et al., 2010). Women with Rett syndrome seldom live beyond age 60, and are prone to seizures and gastrointestinal disorders. This single-gene disorder was mapped to the long arm of the X chromosome (Xq28) and then to a specific gene (*MECP2*, which encodes methyl-CpG-binding protein-2) (Amir et al., 1999). *MECP2* is a gene involved in the methylation process that silences other genes during development and thus has diffuse effects throughout the brain (Lyst & Bird, 2015). For example, *MECP2* regulates *BDNF*, which affects many aspects of neuronal development and thus has widespread effects when its expression is disrupted in individuals with Rett syndrome (Li & Pozzo-Miller, 2014). The effects are variable in females because of random X-chromosome inactivation in females (see Chapter 4). Males with *MECP2* mutations usually die before or shortly after birth. Intensive efforts are underway to design therapeutic strategies using mouse models and cells from patients with Rett syndrome (Liyanage & Rastegar, 2014).

Other Single-Gene Disorders

The average IQ scores of individuals with the most common single-gene causes of general cognitive disability are summarized in Figure 12.2. It should be remembered, however, that the range of cognitive functioning is very wide for these disorders. The defective allele shifts the IQ distribution downward, but a wide range of individual IQs remains. More than 250 other single-gene disorders, whose primary defect is something other than cognitive disability, also show effects on IQ (Inlow & Restifo, 2004; Raymond, 2010). Three of the most common disorders are Duchenne muscular dystrophy, Lesch-Nyhan syndrome, and neurofibromatosis. Duchenne muscular dystrophy is a disorder of muscle tissue caused by a recessive gene on the X chromosome that occurs in 1 in 3500 males and usually leads to death by age 20. The average IQ of males with the disorder is 85, although it is not known how the gene affects the brain (D'Angelo et al., 2011). Lesch-Nyhan syndrome is another rare X-linked recessive disorder, with an incidence of about 1 in 20,000 male births; many medical problems occur that lead to death before age 30. The most striking feature of this disorder is compulsive self-injurious behavior, reported in over 85 percent of cases (Anderson & Ernst, 1994). In terms of cognitive disability, most individuals have moderate or severe learning difficulties, with an average IQ of about 70, and speech is usually impaired, although memory for both recent and past events appears to be unaffected. Neurofibromatosis type 1 is caused by a single dominant allele that is surprisingly common (about 1 in 3000 births) for a dominant allele, which may be related to the fact that most individuals with neurofibromatosis survive until middle age, after the reproductive years. Although the disorder is known for skin tumors and tumors in nerve tissue,

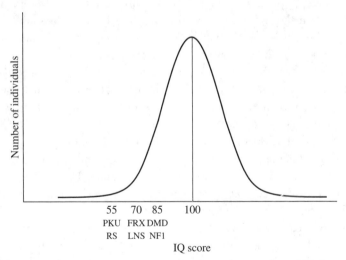

FIGURE 12.2 Single-gene causes of general cognitive disability: phenylketonuria (PKU), Rett syndrome (RS), fragile X syndrome (FRX), Lesch-Nyhan syndrome (LNS), Duchenne muscular dystrophy (DMD), and neurofibromatosis type 1 (NF1). Despite the lower average IQs, a wide range of cognitive functioning is found.

the majority of affected individuals also have learning difficulties, with an average IQ of about 85 (Shilyansky, Lee, & Silva, 2010).

Although there are hundreds of such rare single-gene disorders, together they account for only a small portion of cognitive disability and its heritability. Most cognitive disability is mild; it represents the low end of the normal distribution of general cognitive ability and is caused by many genes of small effect as well as multiple environmental factors, as discussed in Chapter 11.

GENERAL COGNITIVE DISABILITY: CHROMOSOMAL ABNORMALITIES

DNA not only affects general cognitive ability at the level of single genes, as described in the previous section. It also has effects at the level of the addition or deletion of an entire chromosome and everything in between, including insertions and deletions of large and small parts of chromosomes. The visual analysis of chromosomes themselves is being replaced by DNA sequencing, which can detect insertions and deletions down to the level of a single nucleotide (Ostrer, 2011). In general, insertions and deletions of DNA, big or small, are detrimental to cognitive development. The history of the field of *cytogenetics*—a branch of genetics concerned with the study of the structure and function of the cell, especially the chromosomes—is described in an autobiographical account of one of the pioneers of the field (Jacobs, 2014).

This section on chromosomal abnormalities begins with descriptions of the classic whole-chromosome abnormalities that affect cognitive development: Down syndrome and chromosomal abnormalities involving the X chromosome.

Down Syndrome

Down syndrome is caused by a trisomy of chromosome 21 (Roizen & Patterson, 2003). It was one of the first identified genetic disorders, and its 150-year history parallels the history of genetic research (Patterson & Costa, 2005). It is the single most important cause of general cognitive disability and occurs in about 1 in 1000 births. It is so common that its general features are probably familiar to everyone (Figure 12.3). Although more than 300 abnormal features have been reported for Down syndrome children, a handful of specific physical disorders are diagnostic because they occur so frequently. These features include increased neck tissue, muscle weakness, speckled iris of the eye, open mouth, and protruding tongue. Some symptoms, such as increased neck tissue, become less prominent as the child grows, whereas other symptoms, such as cognitive disability and short stature, become more prominent. About two-thirds of affected individuals have hearing deficits, and one-third have heart defects, leading to an average life span of 50 years (Zigman, 2013). As first noted by Langdon Down, who identified the disorder in 1866, children with Down syndrome appear to be obstinate but otherwise generally amiable.

FIGURE 12.3 Three-year-old girl with Down syndrome. (Monkey Business Images/Getty Images.)

The most striking feature of Down syndrome is general cognitive disability (Lott & Dierssen, 2010). As is the case for all single-gene and chromosomal effects on general cognitive ability, affected individuals show a wide range of IQs. The average IQ among children with Down syndrome is 55, with only the top 10 percent falling within the lower end of the normal range of IQs. By adolescence, language skills are generally at about the level of a 3-year-old child. Most individuals with Down syndrome who reach the age of 45 suffer from the cognitive decline of dementia, which was an early clue suggesting that a gene related to dementia might be on chromosome 21 (see Chapter 19).

Down syndrome is an example of an exception to Mendel's laws because it does not run in families. Most cases are created anew each generation by nondisjunction of chromosome 21, as explained in Chapter 4. Another important feature of Down syndrome is that it occurs much more often in women giving birth later in life. Nondisjunction explains why the incidence of Down syndrome is higher among the offspring of older mothers. All the immature eggs of a female mammal are present before birth. These eggs have both members of each pair of chromosomes. Each month, one of the immature eggs goes through the final stage of cell division. Nondisjunction is more likely to occur as the female grows older and activates immature eggs that have been dormant for decades. In contrast, fresh sperm are produced all the time. For this reason, the incidence of Down syndrome is not affected by the age of the father.

Advances in genetics have stimulated a resurgence of research on Down syndrome with the hope of ameliorating at least some of its symptoms (Lana-Elola, Watson-Scales, Fisher, & Tybulewicz, 2011). The fundamental problem is that because there are three copies of chromosome 21, its several hundred genes are overexpressed. Mouse models have played an important role in understanding cognitive deficits in Down syndrome (Das & Reeves, 2011; Guedj, Bianchi, & Delabar, 2014).

Sex Chromosome Abnormalities

Extra X chromosomes also cause cognitive disabilities, although the effect is highly variable, which is the reason why many cases remain undiagnosed (Hong & Reiss, 2014; Lanfranco, Kamischke, Zitzmann, & Nieschlag, 2004). In males, an extra X chromosome causes XXY male syndrome, often called Klinefelter syndrome. As indicated in Chapter 4, even though X is a large chromosome with many genes, extra X chromosomes are largely inactivated, as happens with normal females, who have two X chromosomes; however, some genes on the extra X chromosome escape inactivation in XXY males (Tuttelmann & Gromoll, 2010). XXY male syndrome is the most common chromosomal abnormality in males, occurring in about 1 in 500 male births. The major problems involve low testosterone levels after adolescence, leading to infertility, small testes, and breast development. Early detection and hormonal therapy are important to alleviate the condition, although infertility remains (Herlihy & McLachlan, 2015). Males with XXY male syndrome have an average IQ of about 85; most have speech and language problems as well as poor school performance (Mandoki, Sumner, Hoffman, & Riconda, 1991).

In females, an extra X chromosome (called *triple X syndrome*) occurs in about 1 in 1000 births. Females with triple X show an average IQ of about 85 (Tartaglia, Howell, Sutherland, Wilson, & Wilson, 2010). Unlike XXY males, XXX females have normal sexual development and are able to conceive children; they have so few problems that they are rarely detected clinically. Their scores on verbal tests (such as on vocabulary) are lower than their scores on nonverbal tests (such as puzzles), and many require speech therapy (Bishop et al., 2011). For both XXY and XXX individuals, head circumference at birth is smaller than average, a feature suggesting that the cognitive deficits may be prenatal in origin. As is generally the case for chromosomal abnormalities, structural brain imaging research indicates diffuse effects (Giedd et al., 2007).

In addition to having an extra X chromosome, it is possible for males to have an extra Y chromosome (XYY) and for females to have just one X chromosome (XO, called *Turner syndrome*). There is no equivalent syndrome of males with a Y chromosome but no X because this is fatal. XYY males, about 1 in 1000 male births, are taller than average after adolescence and have normal sexual development. More than 95 percent of XYY males do not even know they have an extra Y chromosome. Although XYY males have fewer cognitive problems than XXY males, about half have speech difficulties as well as language and reading problems (Leggett, Jacobs,

Nation, Scerif, & Bishop, 2010). Their average IQ is about 10 points lower than that of their siblings with normal sex chromosomes. Juvenile delinquency is also associated with XYY. The XYY syndrome was the center of a furor in the 1970s, when it was suggested that such males are more violent, a suggestion possibly triggered by the notion of a "super male" with exaggerated masculine characteristics caused by an extra Y chromosome; however, this idea is not supported by research.

Turner syndrome females (XO) occur in about 1 in 2500 female births, although 98 percent of XO fetuses miscarry, accounting for 10 percent of the total number of spontaneous abortions. The main problems are short stature and abnormal sexual development; infertility is common. Puberty rarely occurs without hormone therapy, which makes early diagnosis important (Lee & Conway, 2014); even with therapy, the individual is infertile because she does not ovulate. Hormonal treatment is now standard, and many XO women have conceived with in vitro fertilization (Stratakis & Rennert, 2005). Although verbal IQ is about normal, nonverbal IQ is lower, about 90, and social cognition is also impaired (Hong, Dunkin, & Reiss, 2011).

Small Chromosomal Deletions

As noted earlier, chromosomal abnormalities do not just involve a whole chromosome. Three classic small chromosomal deletions that affect cognitive development are Angelman syndrome, Prader-Willi syndrome, and Williams syndrome. After describing these disorders, we will turn to research that uses new DNA techniques to identify even smaller deletions.

A small deletion in chromosome 15 (15q11) causes Angelman syndrome (1 in 20,000 births) if the deletion comes from the mother's egg or Prader-Willi syndrome (1 in 20,000 births) if it comes from the father's sperm. In most cases, the deletion occurs spontaneously (*de novo*) in the formation of gametes, although in about 10 percent of the cases mutations inherited by the mother or father are responsible (Williams, Driscoll, & Dagli, 2010). This region of chromosome 15, usually millions of base pairs in length, contains several imprinted genes that are differentially silenced by epigenetic methylation of the DNA, depending on whether the deletion comes from the mother's egg or the father's sperm. This phenomenon in which the expression of a gene depends on whether it is inherited from the mother or from the father is called *genomic imprinting*, even though most methylation marks from the parents' genome are erased so that the infant's epigenome starts with a clean slate (Tang et al., 2015). Angelman syndrome results in moderate cognitive disability, abnormal gait, speech impairment, seizures, and an inappropriately happy demeanor that includes frequent laughing and excitability (Bird, 2014). For one gene in this region (*UBE3A*), the maternal gene is expressed and the paternal gene is silenced so that a deletion that disrupts the maternal gene will cause Angelman syndrome symptoms, whereas a disruption in the paternal gene would not have an effect. In contrast, the paternal copy is expressed for other genes in this same region (e.g., *SNRPN*) and deletions in the paternal copies of these genes can cause Prader-Willi syndrome, which most noticeably involves overeating, temper outbursts, and social problems but also leads to multiple learning difficulties and an average IQ of about 55 (Rice & Einfeld, 2015). New techniques for understanding epigenetic processes are advancing our understanding of how this deletion has its effects on brain development (Mabb, Judson, Zylka, & Philpot, 2011).

Williams syndrome, with an incidence of about 1 in 10,000 births, is caused by a small deletion from chromosome 7 (7q11.2), a region that includes about 25 genes. Most cases are not inherited (*de novo*). Williams syndrome involves disorders of connective tissue that lead to growth retardation and multiple medical problems. General cognitive disability is common (average IQ of 55), and most affected individuals have learning difficulties that require special schooling. Some studies find that language development is less affected than nonverbal abilities (Martens, Wilson, & Reutens, 2008). As adults, most affected individuals are unable to live independently. As is typical of chromosomal abnormalities that include several genes, no consistent brain pathology is found other than a reduction in cerebral volume.

Figure 12.4 summarizes the average effect on IQ of the most common chromosomal causes of general cognitive disability. Again, it should be emphasized that there is a wide range of cognitive functioning around the average IQ scores shown in the figure. In addition to these classic syndromes, DNA sequencing research has revealed that as many as 15 percent of cases of severe cognitive disability may be due to smaller deletions or duplications from a thousand to millions of base pairs that can involve a few genes, dozens of genes, or no genes (coding regions) at all (Topper, Ober, & Das,

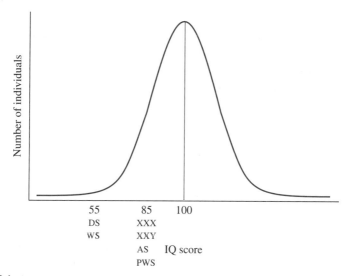

FIGURE 12.4 The most common chromosomal causes of general cognitive disability are Down syndrome (DS) and the sex chromosomal abnormalities XXX and XXY. The average IQs of individuals with XYY and XO are only slightly lower than normal and thus are not listed. Deletions of very small parts of chromosomes contribute importantly to general cognitive disability, but most are rare, such as Angelman syndrome (AS), Prader-Willi syndrome (PWS), and Williams syndrome (WS). For all these chromosomal abnormalities, a wide range of cognitive functioning is found.

2011). As mentioned in Chapter 9, these structural variations in chromosomes are called *copy number variants (CNVs)*. Most CNVs arise *de novo* during meiosis when a DNA segment is deleted on one chromosome and duplicated on the corresponding member of the chromosome pair. As with other chromosomal abnormalities, deletions are generally worse than duplications. There are tens of thousands of CNVs; we all have CNVs peppered throughout our genome without obvious effect, despite all the extra or missing segments of DNA (Zarrei et al., 2015). However, some CNVs, usually rare and *de novo* (i.e., not seen in either parent), affect neurocognitive development (Malhotra & Sebat, 2012). Although therapeutic interventions are not yet available, there is hope for differential diagnosis of cognitive disabilities with genomic sequencing (Willemsen & Kleefstra, 2014) and newborn screening is on the horizon (Beckmann, 2015).

SPECIFIC COGNITIVE DISABILITIES

As its name implies, general cognitive disability has general effects on the ability to learn, which is reflected in difficulties at school. We use the term *specific cognitive disabilities* in relation to school-related difficulties such as those affecting reading, communication, and mathematics. Behavioral genetic research brings genetics to the field of educational psychology, which has been slow to recognize the importance of genetic influence (Haworth & Plomin, 2011; Wooldridge, 1994), even though teachers in the classroom do (Walker & Plomin, 2005). This section focuses on low performance in cognitive processes related to academic achievement, whereas Chapter 11 described genetic research on the normal range of variation in these processes. We begin with reading disability because reading is the primary problem for about 80 percent of children with a diagnosed learning disorder. We then consider communication disorders, mathematics disability, and, finally, the interrelationships of learning disabilities.

Reading Disability

As many as 10 percent of children have difficulty learning to read. Children with reading disability (also known as *dyslexia*, for example, in DSM-5) read slowly and often with poor comprehension. When reading aloud, they perform poorly. For some, specific causes can be identified, such as cognitive disability, brain damage, sensory problems, and deprivation. However, many children without such problems find it difficult to read.

Family studies have shown that reading disability runs in families. The largest family study included 1044 individuals in 125 families with a reading-disabled child and 125 matched control families (DeFries, Vogler, & LaBuda, 1986). Siblings and parents of the reading-disabled children performed significantly worse on reading tests than did siblings and parents of control children. The first major twin study indicated that familial resemblance for reading disability involves genetic factors (DeFries, Knopik, & Wadsworth, 1999). For more than 250 twin pairs in which at least one member of the pair was reading disabled, twin concordances were 66 percent for identical twins and 36 percent for fraternal twins, a result suggesting substantial genetic influence. Large twin studies found similar results in the early school years for both reading disability and reading ability in the United Kingdom (Kovas et al., 2007) and the United States (Hensler et al., 2010). However, in all of these studies, shared environmental influence is modest, typically accounting for less than 20 percent of the variance (Willcutt et al., 2010).

As part of DeFries and colleagues' twin study, a new method was developed to estimate the genetic contribution to the mean difference between the reading-disabled probands and the mean reading ability of the population. This type of analysis, called *DF extremes analysis* after its creators (DeFries & Fulker, 1985), assesses the extent to which the quantitative scores of MZ and DZ partners (co-twins) of selected index cases (probands) regress differentially to the population mean. In other words, to the extent that genetic influences are responsible for the difference between the probands and the rest of the population, co-twins should be more similar to the probands for MZ twins than for DZ twins. This comparison of MZ and DZ co-twin means yields an estimate of *group heritability*, an index of the extent to which the extreme scores of probands is due to genetic influences, in contrast to the usual heritability estimate, which refers to differences between individuals rather than to mean differences between groups. Finding significant group heritability implies that there are genetic links between the disorder, however assessed, and the quantitative trait. That is, if the measure of extremes (or a diagnosis) were not linked genetically to the quantitative trait, group heritability would be zero. DF extremes analysis is conceptually similar to the liability-threshold model described in Box 3.3. The major difference is that the liability-threshold model assumes a continuous dimension even though it assesses a dichotomous disorder, usually a diagnosis. In contrast, DF extremes analysis assesses rather than assumes a continuum. As described earlier in this chapter, moderate to severe general cognitive disability is etiologically distinct from the normal distribution of *g*, as indicated by DF extremes analysis (Nichols, 1984; Reichenberg et al., 2015). Additional support comes from research finding that rare single-gene mutations and chromosomal abnormalities often cause moderate to severe general cognitive disability but do not contribute importantly to variation in the normal range of cognitive ability. In contrast, mild cognitive disability appears to be quantitatively, not qualitatively, different from normal variation in cognitive ability. That is, mild cognitive disability is the low end of the same genetic and environmental influences responsible for variation in the normal distribution of cognitive ability. Results for reading disability and other common disabilities discussed in this section are similar to those for mild cognitive disability rather than more severe cognitive disability. Phrased more provocatively, these findings from DF extremes analysis suggest that common disorders such as reading disability are not really disorders—they are merely the low end of the normal distribution (Plomin et al., 2009). This view fits with the basic quantitative genetic model, which assumes that genetic influence for complex traits is due to many genes of small effect size that contribute to a normal quantitative trait distribution (Chapter 3). What we call disorders and disabilities are the low end of these quantitative trait distributions. This hypothesis predicts that when genes associated with reading disability are identified, the same genes will be associated with normal variation in reading ability.

Early molecular genetic research on reading disability assumed that the target was a single major gene rather than many genes of small effect in the population (Bishop, 2015). Various modes of transmission have been proposed, especially autosomal dominant transmission and X-linked recessive transmission. The autosomal dominant hypothesis takes into account the high rate of familial resemblance but fails to account for the fact that about a fifth of reading-disabled individuals do not have affected relatives. An X-linked recessive hypothesis is suggested when a disorder occurs more often in males than in females, as is the case for reading disability. However, the X-linked recessive hypothesis does not work well as an explanation of reading disability. As described in Chapter 3, one of the hallmarks of X-linked recessive transmission is the absence of father-to-son transmission, since sons inherit their X chromosome only from their mother. Contrary to the X-linked recessive hypothesis, reading disability is transmitted from father to son as often as from mother to son. It is now generally accepted that, like most complex disorders, reading disability is caused by multiple genes as well as by multiple environmental factors (Fisher & DeFries, 2002).

One of the most exciting findings in behavioral genetics in the past two decades is that the first quantitative trait locus for a human behavioral disorder was reported for reading disability, using sib-pair QTL linkage analysis (Cardon et al., 1994). As explained in Chapter 9, siblings can share zero, one, or two alleles for a particular DNA marker. If siblings who share more alleles are also more similar for a quantitative trait such as reading ability, then QTL linkage is likely. QTL linkage analysis is much more powerful when one sibling is selected because of an extreme score on the quantitative trait. When one sibling was selected for reading disability, the reading ability score of the co-sibling was also lower when the two siblings shared alleles for markers on the short arm of chromosome 6 ($6p21$). Significant linkage was also found for markers in this region in an independent sample of fraternal twins and in several replication studies in the broader region of the short arm of chromosome 6 (Fisher & DeFries, 2002). Despite these consistent linkage results, it has been difficult to identify the specific genes responsible for the QTL linkage among the hundreds of genes in this gene-rich region of chromosome 6, but the search has narrowed to two genes very close together at $6p22$: *KIAA0319* and *DCDC2* (Carrion-Castillo, Franke, & Fisher, 2013). Genes in this region and a dozen other candidate genes reported to be associated with reading disability provide plausible pathways among genes, brain, and behavior that involve the growth and migration of neurons (Poelmans, Buitelaar, Pauls, & Franke, 2011). There have been far fewer candidate gene association studies for reading than for other behaviors, perhaps because there are no obvious candidate genes and also because linkage analysis has dominated reading research. A meta-analysis of three small genomewide association studies of reading and language disability found no significant associations

(Gialluisi et al., 2014), suggesting that the combined influence of many genes with relatively small effect are also responsible for reading difficulties.

Reading disability is generally assumed to be preceded by language problems (Pennington & Bishop, 2009), and genetic influences on reading disability and on language and speech disorders overlap substantially (Haworth et al., 2009a; Newbury, Monaco, & Paracchini, 2014). Language and speech disorders are the topic of the following section.

Communication Disorders

DSM-5 includes four types of communication disorders: language, speech, stuttering, and social communication. Several family studies, examining communication disorders broadly, indicate that communication disorders are familial (Stromswold, 2001). Twin studies suggest that this familial resemblance is genetic in origin. A review of twin studies of language disability yields twin concordances of 75 percent for MZ twins and 43 percent for DZ twins (Stromswold, 2001). Using DF extremes analysis, the average weighted group heritability was 43 percent for language disabilities (Plomin & Kovas, 2005). A large twin study of language delay in infancy found high heritability, even at 2 years of age (Dale et al., 1998). The only adoption study of communication disorders confirms the twin results, suggesting substantial genetic influence (Felsenfeld & Plomin, 1997).

The high heritability of communication disorders has attracted attention from molecular genetics (Smith et al., 2010). A high-profile paper reported a mutation in a gene (*FOXP2*) that accounted for an unusual type of speech-language impairment that includes deficits in oro-facial motor control in one family (Lai, Fisher, Hurst, Vargha-Khadem, & Monaco, 2001). In the media, this finding was unfortunately trumpeted as "the" gene for language, whereas in fact the mutation has not been found outside the original family (Meaburn, Dale, Craig, & Plomin, 2002; Newbury et al., 2002). Several linkages and candidate gene associations have been reported with communication disorders (Fisher & Vernes, 2015). The first genomewide association study found no significant associations (Nudel et al., 2014).

Stuttering affects about 5 percent of preschool children, but most make a full recovery. Family studies of stuttering over the past 50 years have shown that about a third of stutterers have other stutterers in their families (Kidd, 1983). Twin studies indicate that stuttering is highly heritable (Fagnani, Fibiger, Skytthe, & Hjelmborg, 2011), especially stuttering that persists past early childhood (Dworzynski, Remington, Rijsdijk, Howell, & Plomin, 2007). However, genomewide linkage studies have not yielded consistent results (Fisher, 2010).

Mathematics Disability

DSM-5 classifies problems with comprehending numbers as *dyscalculia*, which means "counting badly." For poor performance on tests of mathematics, the first twin study suggested moderate genetic influence (Alarcón, DeFries, Light, & Pennington, 1997).

Although different aspects of mathematics performance are highly correlated, timed tests, called *fluency measures*, have been shown to have significant independent genetic influence from untimed tests (Petrill et al., 2012). A study using U.K. National Curriculum scores of 7-year-olds reported concordances for mathematics disability of about 70 percent for MZ twins and 40 percent for DZ twins and a DF extremes group heritability estimate of 65 percent (Oliver et al., 2004). Results obtained from a meta-analysis of twin studies for mathematics disability yielded a highly similar group heritability estimate of 0.61 (Plomin & Kovas, 2005). The first genomewide association study of mathematics disability found no genetic associations of large effect (Docherty et al., 2010). Similar to reading disability and all common disorders, these results suggest that mathematics disability is quantitatively, not qualitatively, different from normal variation in mathematics ability. This implies that the heritability of mathematics disability is caused by many genes of small effect, a conclusion that will be seen repeatedly in subsequent chapters for all common disorders and complex traits.

Comorbidity among Specific Cognitive Disabilities

Learning disabilities are distinguished from each other and from other cognitive disabilities because they are thought to be distinct disabilities. However, it is increasingly recognized that there is a great deal of comorbidity among these disabilities (Butterworth & Kovas, 2013). Two multivariate genetic analyses suggest that there is substantial genetic overlap between reading and mathematics disabilities (Knopik, Alarcón, & DeFries, 1997; Kovas et al., 2007). Extending DF extremes analysis to bivariate analysis, genetic correlations of 0.53 and 0.67 between reading and mathematics disability were reported. In other words, many of the genes that affect reading disability also affect mathematics disability. The reach of these general effects of genes for cognitive disabilities extends beyond reading and mathematics disability to communication disorders and general cognitive disability (Haworth et al., 2009a) and even further to other disorders such as hyperactivity, especially inattentiveness (Greven, Kovas, Willcutt, Petrill, & Plomin, 2014). These multivariate genetic results for cognitive disabilities, which are similar to those seen for cognitive abilities (Chapter 11), suggest that when DNA studies find genes associated with one cognitive or learning disability, most of these genes will also be associated with other disabilities (Mascheretti et al., 2014).

Summary

Results of sibling and twin studies suggest that moderate to severe cognitive disability is genetically different from the normal distribution of individual differences in general cognitive ability. Recent DNA studies confirm this hypothesis by finding many new noninherited (*de novo*) mutations responsible for sporadic cases of moderate to severe cognitive disability. Moreover there are more than 250 inherited single-gene disorders, most extremely rare, that include cognitive disability among their symptoms. A classic disorder is PKU, caused by a recessive mutation on chromosome 12.

The discovery of fragile X syndrome is especially important because it is the most common cause of inherited cognitive disability (1 in several thousand males, half as common in females). It is caused by a triplet repeat (CGG) on the X chromosome that expands over several generations until it reaches more than 200 repeats, when it causes cognitive disability in males. A common single-gene cause of severe cognitive disability in females is Rett syndrome. Other single-gene mutations known primarily for other effects also contribute to cognitive disability, such as those for Duchenne muscular dystrophy, Lesch-Nyhan syndrome, and neurofibromatosis.

For all of the single-gene disorders, the defective allele shifts the IQ distribution downward, but a wide range of individual IQs remains. Also, although there are hundreds of such rare single-gene disorders, together they account for only a tiny portion of cognitive disability. Most cognitive disability is mild and appears to be the low end of the normal distribution of general cognitive ability and caused by many QTLs of small effect as well as multiple environmental factors (see Chapter 11).

Chromosomal abnormalities play an important role in cognitive disability. The most common cause of cognitive disability is Down syndrome, caused by the presence of three copies of chromosome 21. Down syndrome occurs in about 1 in 1000 births and is responsible for about 10 percent of cognitively disabled individuals in institutions. Risk for cognitive disability is also increased by having an extra X chromosome (XXY males, XXX females). An extra Y chromosome (XYY males) or a missing X chromosome (Turner females) cause less disability. XYY males have speech and language problems; Turner females (XO) generally perform less well on nonverbal tasks such as spatial tasks. Small deletions of chromosomes can result in cognitive disability, as in Angelman syndrome, Prader-Willi syndrome, and Williams syndrome. Similar to single-gene disorders, there is a wide range of cognitive functioning around the lowered average IQ scores found for all these chromosomal causes of cognitive disability. An exciting area of research uses exome and whole-genome sequencing to detect subtle chromosomal abnormalities, especially *de novo* (noninherited) deletions and duplications called *copy number variants* (*CNVs*), that might account for as many as 15 percent of sporadic cases of severe cognitive disability.

Twin studies suggest genetic influence for specific cognitive disabilities, including reading disability, communication disorders, and mathematics disability. For these cognitive disabilities, DF extremes analysis suggests that genetic and environmental influences have effects at the low end of the normal distribution of cognitive abilities that are similar to their effects on the rest of the distribution. For reading disability, a replicated linkage on chromosome 6 was the first QTL linkage discovered for human behavioral disorders; two genes in this region are the best candidates, although a dozen other candidate gene regions have been proposed. Several linkages and candidate gene associations have also been proposed for communication disorders and mathematics disability. The substantial comorbidity between specific cognitive disabilities is largely due to genetic factors, meaning that the same genes affect different learning disabilities although there are also disability-specific genes.

CHAPTER THIRTEEN

Schizophrenia

P sychopathology has been, and continues to be, one of the most active areas of behavioral genetic research, largely because of the social importance of mental illness. One out of two persons in the United States has some form of disorder during their lifetime, and one out of five persons suffered from a disorder within the last year (Steel et al., 2014). The costs in terms of suffering to patients and their friends and relatives, as well as the economic costs, make psychopathology one of the most pressing problems today.

The genetics of psychopathology led the way toward the acceptance of genetic influence in psychology and psychiatry. The history of psychiatric genetics is described in Box 13.1. This chapter and the next two provide an overview of what is known about the genetics of several major categories of psychopathology: schizophrenia, mood disorders, and anxiety disorders. Other disorders, such as posttraumatic stress disorder, somatic symptom disorders, and eating disorders, are also briefly reviewed, as are disorders usually first diagnosed in childhood: autism spectrum disorder, attention-deficit/hyperactivity disorder, and tic disorders. Other major categories in the DSM-5 include personality disorders (Chapter 16), substance-related disorders (Chapter 17), and cognitive disorders such as dementia (Chapter 19). The DSM-5 includes several other disorders for which no genetic research is as yet available (e.g., dissociative disorders such as amnesia and fugue states). Much has been written about the genetics of psychopathology, including several texts (Jang, 2005; Kendler & Prescott, 2007) and edited books (e.g., Dodge & Rutter, 2011; Hudziak, 2008; MacKillop & Munafò, 2013; Rhee & Ronald, 2014; Ritsner, 2009). Many questions remain concerning diagnosis, most notably the extent of comorbidity and heterogeneity (Cardno et al., 2012). Diagnoses to date depend on symptoms, and it is possible that the same symptoms have different causes and that different symptoms could have the same causes (Ritsner & Gottesman, 2011). One of the hopes for genetic research is that it can begin to provide diagnoses based on causes rather than symptoms. We will return to this issue in Chapter 14.

This chapter focuses on schizophrenia, the most highly studied area in behavioral genetic research on psychopathology. Schizophrenia involves persistent abnormal beliefs (delusions), hallucinations (especially hearing voices), disorganized speech (odd associations and rapid changes of subject), grossly disorganized behavior, and so-called negative symptoms, such as flat affect (lack of emotional response) and avolition (lack of motivation). A diagnosis of schizophrenia requires that such symptoms occur for at least six months. It usually strikes in late adolescence or early adulthood. Early onset in adolescence tends to be gradual but has a worse prognosis. Although it derives from Greek words meaning "split mind," schizophrenia has nothing to do with the notion of a "split personality."

More genetic research has focused on schizophrenia than on other areas of psychopathology for three reasons. First, it is the most severe form of psychopathology and one of the most debilitating of all disorders (Üstün et al., 1999). Second, it is so common, with a lifetime risk in nearly 1 percent of the population (Saha, Chant, Welham, & McGrath, 2005). Third, it generally lasts a lifetime, although a few people recover, especially if they have had just one episode (Robinson, Woerner, McMeniman, Mendelowitz, & Bilder, 2004); there are signs, however, that recovery rates are improving (AlAqeel & Margolese, 2013). Unlike patients of two decades ago, most people with schizophrenia are no longer institutionalized, because drugs can control some of their worst symptoms. Nonetheless, schizophrenics still occupy half the beds in mental hospitals, and those discharged make up about 10 percent of the homeless population (Folsom & Jeste, 2002). It has been estimated that the cost to our society of schizophrenia alone rivals that of cancer (Kennedy, Altar, Taylor, Degtiar, & Hornberger, 2014).

FAMILY STUDIES

The basic genetic results for schizophrenia were described in Chapter 3 to illustrate genetic influence on complex disorders. Family studies consistently show that schizophrenia is familial (Ritsner & Gottesman, 2011). In contrast to the base rate of about 1 percent lifetime risk in the population, the risk for relatives increases with genetic relatedness to the schizophrenic proband: 4 percent for second-degree relatives and 9 percent for first-degree relatives.

The average risk of 9 percent for first-degree relatives differs for parents, siblings, and offspring of schizophrenics. In 14 family studies of over 8000 schizophrenics, the median risk was 6 percent for parents, 9 percent for siblings, and 13 percent for offspring (Gottesman, 1991; Ritsner & Gottesman, 2011). The low risk for parents of schizophrenics (6 percent) is probably due to the fact that schizophrenics are less likely to marry and those who do marry have relatively few children. For this reason, parents of schizophrenics are less likely than expected to be schizophrenic. When

BOX 13.1 The Beginnings of Psychiatric Genetics: Bethlem Royal and Maudsley Hospitals

Founded in London in 1247, Bethlem Hospital is one of the oldest institutions in the world caring for people with mental disorders. However, there have been times in Bethlem's long history when it was associated with some of the worst images of mental illness, and it gave us the origin of the word *bedlam.* Perhaps the most famous portrayal is in the final scene of Hogarth's series of paintings *A Rake's Progress,* which shows the Rake's decline into madness at Bethlem (see figure). Hogarth's portrayal assumes that madness is the consequence of high living and therefore, it is implied, a wholly environmental affliction.

The observation that mental disorders have a tendency to run in families is ancient, but among the first efforts to record this association systematically were those at Bethlem Hospital. Records from the 1820s show that one of the routine questions that doctors had to attempt to answer about the

illness of a patient they were admitting was "whether hereditary?" This, of course, predated the development of genetics as a science, and it was not until a hundred years later that the first research group on psychiatric genetics was established in Munich, Germany, under the leadership of Emil Kraepelin. The Munich department attracted many visitors and scholars, including a mathematically gifted young psychiatrist from Maudsley Hospital, Eliot Slater, who obtained a fellowship to study psychiatric genetics there. In 1935, Slater returned to London and started his own research group, which led to the creation in 1959 of the Medical Research Council's (MRC) Psychiatric Genetics Unit at what is now the Institute of Psychiatry, Psychology and Neuroscience. The Bethlem and Maudsley Twin Register, set up by Slater in 1948, was among the important resources that underpinned a number of influential studies, and Slater introduced sophisticated statistical approaches to

schizophrenics do become parents, the rate of schizophrenia in their offspring is high (13 percent). The risk is the same regardless of whether the mother or the father is schizophrenic. When both parents are schizophrenic, the risk for their offspring shoots up to 46 percent. Siblings provide the least biased risk estimate, and their risk (9 percent) is in between the estimates for parents and for offspring. Although the risk of 9 percent is high, nine times the population risk of 1 percent, it should be remembered that the majority of schizophrenics do not have a schizophrenic first-degree relative.

The family design provides the basis for genetic high-risk studies of the development of children whose mothers were schizophrenic. In one of the first such studies, begun in the early 1960s in Denmark, 200 such offspring were followed until their forties (Parnas et al., 1993). In the high-risk group whose mothers were schizophrenic, 16 percent were diagnosed as schizophrenic (whereas 2 percent in the low-risk group were schizophrenic), and the children who eventually became schizophrenic had mothers whose schizophrenia was more severe. These children experienced a less data evaluation. The MRC Psychiatric Genetics Unit became one of the key centers for training and played a major role in the career development of many overseas postdoctoral students, including Irving Gottesman, Leonard Heston, Peter McGuffin, and Ming Tsuang.

In 1971, Slater published the first psychiatric genetics textbook in English, *The Genetics of Mental Disorders* (Slater & Cowie, 1971). Later in the 1970s, following Slater's retirement, psychiatric genetics became temporarily unfashionable in the United Kingdom but was continued as a scientific discipline in North America and mainland Europe by researchers trained by Slater or influenced by his work.

William Hogarth, *A Rake's Progress*, 1735. Plate 8. The British Museum. (William Hogarth/Culture Club/Getty Images.)

Eliot Slater. (The Estate of Eliot Slater.)

stable home life and more institutionalization, reminding us that family studies do not disentangle nature and nurture in the way adoption studies do. The children who became schizophrenic were more likely to have had birth complications, particularly prenatal viral infection (Cannon et al., 1993). They also showed attention problems in childhood, especially problems in "tuning out" incidental stimuli like the ticking of a clock (Hollister, Mednick, Brennan, & Cannon, 1994). Another high-risk study found similar results in childhood and also found more personality disorders in the offspring of schizophrenic parents when the offspring were young adults (Erlenmeyer-Kimling et al., 1995).

TWIN STUDIES

Twin studies show that genetics contributes importantly to familial resemblance for schizophrenia. As was shown in Figure 3.8, the probandwise concordance for MZ twins is 48 percent and the concordance for DZ twins is 17 percent. In a meta-analysis of 14 twin studies of schizophrenia using a liability-threshold model (see Chapter 3), these concordances suggest a heritability of liability of about 80 percent (Sullivan et al., 2003a). More recent studies continue to confirm these earlier findings, yielding probandwise concordances of 41 to 65 percent in MZ and 0 to 28 percent in DZ pairs (Cardno et al., 2012).

A dramatic case study involved identical quadruplets, called the Genain quadruplets, all of whom were schizophrenic, although they varied considerably in severity of the disorder (DeLisi et al., 1984) (Figure 13.1). For 14 pairs of reared-apart identical twins in which at least one member of each pair became schizophrenic, 9 pairs (64 percent) were concordant (Gottesman, 1991).

Despite the strong and consistent evidence for genetic influence provided by the twin studies, it should be remembered that the average concordance for identical twins is only about 50 percent. In other words, half of the time these genetically identical pairs of individuals are discordant for schizophrenia, an outcome that provides strong evidence for the importance of nongenetic factors.

Because differences within pairs of identical twins cannot be genetic in origin, the co-twin control method can be used to study nongenetic reasons why one identical twin is schizophrenic and the other is not. One early study of discordant identical

FIGURE 13.1 Identical quadruplets (known under the fictitious surname Genain), each of whom developed symptoms of schizophrenia between the ages of 22 and 24. (©AP Images.)

twins found few life history differences except that the schizophrenic co-twins were more likely to have had birth complications and some neurological abnormalities (Mosher, Polling, & Stabenau, 1971). Follow-up studies also found differences in brain structures and more frequent birth complications for the schizophrenic co-twin in discordant identical twin pairs (Torrey, Bowler, Taylor, & Gottesman, 1994). Recent research has found epigenetic (DNA methylation) differences within pairs of identical twins discordant for schizophrenia (Dempster et al., 2011); however, there are inconsistent findings for copy number variation (CNV) differences between affected and unaffected MZ twins (Bloom et al., 2013).

An interesting finding has emerged from another use of discordant twins: studying their offspring or other first-degree relatives. Discordant identical twins provide direct proof of nongenetic influences because the twins are identical genetically yet discordant for schizophrenia. Even though one twin in discordant pairs is spared from schizophrenia for environmental reasons, that twin still carries the same high genetic risk as the twin who is schizophrenic. That is why nearly all studies find rates of schizophrenia as high in the families of discordant as in concordant identical twin pairs (Gottesman & Bertelsen, 1989; McGuffin, Farmer, & Gottesman, 1987).

ADOPTION STUDIES

Results of adoption studies agree with those of family and twin studies in pointing to genetic influence in schizophrenia. As described in Chapter 6, the first adoption study of schizophrenia by Leonard Heston in 1966 is a classic study. The results (see Box 6.1) showed that the risk of schizophrenia in adopted offspring of schizophrenic birth mothers was 11 percent (5 of 47), much greater than the 0 percent risk for 50 adoptees whose birth parents had no known mental illness. The risk of 11 percent is similar to the risk for offspring reared by their schizophrenic biological parents. This finding not only indicates that family resemblance for schizophrenia is largely genetic in origin, but it also implies that growing up in a family with schizophrenics does not increase the risk for schizophrenia beyond the risk due to heredity.

Box 6.1 also mentioned that Heston's results have been confirmed and extended by other adoption studies. Two Danish studies began in the 1960s with 5500 children adopted between 1924 and 1947 as well as 10,000 of their 11,000 biological parents. One of the studies (Rosenthal, Wender, Kety, & Schulsinger, 1971; Rosenthal et al., 1968) used the adoptees' study method. This method is the same as that used in Heston's study, but important experimental controls were added. At the time of these studies, birth parents were typically teenagers when they placed children for adoption. Consequently, because schizophrenia does not usually occur until later in life, often neither the adoption agencies nor the adoptive parents were aware of the diagnosis. In addition, both schizophrenic fathers and mothers were studied to assess whether Heston's results, which involved only mothers, were influenced by prenatal maternal factors.

This study began by identifying biological parents who had been admitted to a psychiatric hospital. Biological mothers or fathers who were diagnosed as schizophrenic and whose children had been placed in adoptive homes were selected. This procedure yielded 44 birth parents (32 mothers and 12 fathers) who were diagnosed as chronic schizophrenics. Their 44 adopted children were matched to 67 control adoptees whose birth parents had no psychiatric history, as indicated by the records of psychiatric hospitals. The adoptees, with an average age of 33, were interviewed for three to five hours by an interviewer blind to the status of their birth parents.

Three (7 percent) of the 44 proband adoptees were chronic schizophrenics, whereas none of the 67 control adoptees were (Figure 13.2). Moreover, 27 percent of the probands showed schizophrenic-like symptoms, whereas 18 percent of the controls had similar symptoms. Results were similar for 69 proband adoptees whose parents were selected by using broader criteria for schizophrenia. Results were also similar regardless of whether the mother or the father was schizophrenic. The unusually high rates of psychopathology in the Danish control adoptees may have occurred because the study relied on hospital records to assess the psychiatric status of the birth parents. For this reason, the study may have overlooked psychiatric problems of control parents that had not come to the attention of psychiatric hospitals. To follow up this possibility, the researchers interviewed the birth parents of the control adoptees and found that one-third fell in the schizophrenic spectrum. Thus, the researchers concluded that "our controls are a poor control group and our technique of selection has minimized the differences between the control and index groups" (Wender, Rosenthal, Kety, Schulsinger, & Welner, 1974, p. 127). This bias is conservative in terms of demonstrating genetic influence.

An adoptees study in Finland confirmed these results (Tienari et al., 2004). About 10 percent of adoptees who had a schizophrenic biological parent showed some form of psychosis, whereas 1 percent of control adoptees had similar disorders. This study also suggested genotype-environment interaction, because adoptees whose biological parents were schizophrenic were more likely to have schizophrenia-related disorders when the adoptive families functioned poorly.

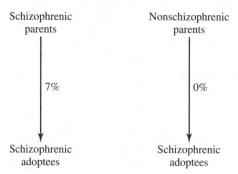

FIGURE 13.2 Danish adoption study of schizophrenia: adoptees' study method.

The second Danish study (Kety et al., 1994) used the adoptees' family method, focusing on 47 of the 5500 adoptees diagnosed as chronically schizophrenic. A matched control group of 47 nonschizophrenic adoptees was also selected. The biological and adoptive parents and siblings of the index and control adoptees were interviewed. The rate of chronic schizophrenia was 5 percent (14 of 279) for the first-degree biological relatives of schizophrenic adoptees and 0 percent (1 of 234) for the biological relatives of the control adoptees. The adoptees' family method also provides a direct test of the influence of the environmental effect of having a schizophrenic relative. If familial resemblance for schizophrenia is caused by the family environment created by schizophrenic parents, schizophrenic adoptees should be more likely to come from adoptive families with schizophrenia, relative to the control adoptees. To the contrary, 0 percent (0 of 111) of the adoptive parents and siblings of the schizophrenic adoptees were schizophrenic—like the 0 percent incidence (0 of 117) for the adoptive parents and siblings of control adoptees (Figure 13.3).

This study also included many biological half siblings of the adoptees (Kety, 1987). Such a situation arises when biological parents place a child for adoption and then later have another child with a different partner. The comparison of biological half siblings who have the same father (paternal half siblings) with those who have the same mother (maternal half siblings) is particularly useful for examining the possibility that the results of adoption studies may be affected by prenatal factors rather than by heredity. The resemblance between paternal half siblings is less likely to be influenced by prenatal factors because they were born to different mothers. Among half siblings of schizophrenic adoptees, 16 percent (16 of 101) were schizophrenic; among half siblings of control adoptees, only 3 percent (3 of 104) were schizophrenic. The results were the same for maternal and paternal half siblings, an outcome suggesting that prenatal factors are not likely to be of major importance in the origin of schizophrenia.

In summary, the adoption studies clearly point to genetic influence. Moreover, adoptive relatives of schizophrenic probands do not show increased risk for schizophrenia. These results, similar to the twin results, imply that familial resemblance for schizophrenia is due to heredity rather than to shared family environment. Recent research estimating heritability directly from DNA provides additional confirmation of genetic influence on schizophrenia (S. H. Lee et al., 2012).

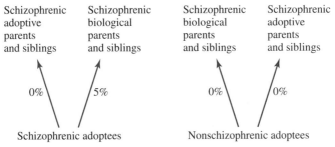

FIGURE 13.3 Danish adoption study of schizophrenia: adoptees' family method.

SCHIZOPHRENIA OR SCHIZOPHRENIAS?

Is schizophrenia one disorder or is it a heterogeneous collection of disorders? When the disorder was named in 1908, it was called "the schizophrenias." Multivariate genetic analysis can address this fundamental issue of heterogeneity. The classic subtypes of schizophrenia—such as catatonic (disturbance in motor behavior), paranoid (persecution delusions), and disorganized (both thought disorder and flat affect are present)—are not supported by genetic research. That is, although schizophrenia runs in families, the particular subtype does not. This result is seen most dramatically in a follow-up of the Genain quadruplets (DeLisi et al., 1984). Although they were all diagnosed as schizophrenic, their symptoms varied considerably.

There is evidence that more severe schizophrenia is more heritable than milder forms (Gottesman, 1991). Furthermore, the evidence from both early studies and more recent work, using multivariate statistical methods such as cluster analysis, suggests that the classic "disorganized" subtype of schizophrenia, even if it does not "breed true," shows an especially high rate of affected family members (Cardno et al., 1999; Farmer, McGuffin, & Gottesman, 1987).

Another approach to the problem of heterogeneity divides schizophrenia on the basis of family history (Murray, Lewis, & Reveley, 1985), although there are problems with this approach (Eaves, Kendler, & Schulz, 1986) and there is clearly no simple dichotomy (Jones & Murray, 1991). These typologies seem more likely to represent a continuum from less to more severe forms of the same disorder rather than genetically distinct disorders (McGuffin et al., 1987).

As discussed in Chapter 10, a related strategy is to search for endophenotypes (Gottesman & Gould, 2003). Many potential endophenotypes have been suggested for schizophrenia, including various structural and functional markers in the brain, olfactory deficits, and attention and memory deficits (Ritsner & Gottesman, 2011). One additional example of a behavioral endophenotype in schizophrenia research is called *smooth-pursuit eye tracking*. This term refers to the ability to follow a moving object smoothly with one's eyes without moving the head (Levy, Holzman, Matthysse, & Mendell, 1993). Some studies have shown that schizophrenics whose eye tracking is jerky tend to have more negative symptoms and that their relatives with poor eye tracking are more likely to show schizophrenic-like behaviors (Clementz, McDowell, & Zisook, 1994). However, other research does not support this hypothesis (Torrey et al., 1994). More recent efforts from the Consortium on the Genetics of Schizophrenia consider a wide range of neurocognitive and neurophysiological assessments as potential endophenotypes (Seidman et al., 2015; Swerdlow, Gur, & Braff, 2015). The hope is that such endophenotypes will clarify the inheritance of schizophrenia and assist attempts to find specific genes responsible for schizophrenia.

Although some researchers assume that schizophrenia is heterogeneous and needs to be split into subtypes, others argue in favor of the opposite approach, lumping schizophrenia-like disorders into a broader spectrum of schizoid disorders

(Farmer et al., 1987; McGue & Gottesman, 1989). Because schizophrenia co-occurs with various other disorders, including depression, anxiety, and substance abuse disorders, future analyses of such comorbidity may shed new light on the genetic factors that underlie schizophrenia and related disorders (Ritsner & Gottesman, 2011; Cardno & Owen, 2014). Recent studies also suggest that schizophrenia and bipolar disorder frequently co-occur (Laursen, Agerbo, & Pedersen, 2009) and that such comorbidity is due primarily to genetic influences (Lichtenstein et al., 2009; Pol et al., 2012; Cardno & Owen, 2014). This finding, based largely on twin studies, has been strongly supported by SNP-based methods (Bulik-Sullivan et al., 2015a; Lee et al., 2013).

IDENTIFYING GENES

Before the new DNA markers were available, attempts were made to associate classic genetic markers, such as blood groups, with schizophrenia. For example, several early studies suggested a weak association of schizophrenia marked by paranoid delusions with the major genes encoding human leukocyte antigens (HLAs) of the immune response, a gene cluster associated with many diseases (McGuffin & Sturt, 1986).

Although schizophrenia was one of the first behavioral domains put under the spotlight of molecular genetic analysis, it has been slow to reveal evidence for specific genes. During the euphoria of the 1980s, when the new DNA markers were first being used to find genes for complex traits, some claims were made for linkage, but they could not be replicated. The first was a claim for linkage with an autosomal dominant gene on chromosome 5 for Icelandic and British families (Sherrington et al., 1988). However, combined data from five other studies in other countries failed to confirm the linkage (McGuffin et al., 1990).

More than 20 genomewide linkage scans (with more than 350 genetic markers) have been published, but none have suggested a gene of major effect for schizophrenia (Riley & Kendler, 2006). Hundreds of reports of linkage for schizophrenia in the 1990s led to a confusing picture because few studies were replicated. However, greater clarity has emerged since around 2000. For example, a meta-analysis of 20 genomewide linkage scans of schizophrenia in diverse populations indicated greater consistency of linkage results than previously recognized (Lewis et al., 2003). Significant linkage was found on the long arm of chromosome 2 (2q); linkage was suggested for ten other regions, including 6p and 8p. It has been difficult to detect linkage signals because linkage analysis requires very large samples to discern small effects.

Association studies of schizophrenia have also provided their own challenges. Over 1000 genes have been tested for association with schizophrenia, making it one of the most studied disorders through a candidate gene approach (Gejman, Sanders, & Kendler, 2011). Despite this fact, there is considerable inconsistency in the results. Multiple genes have been suggested, such as *neuregulin 1* on chromosome 8 (Stefansson et al., 2002) and *dysbindin* at 6p22.3 (Straub et al., 2002), as well as other genes related to neurotransmitters expressed in the brain, such as dopamine. However, many of these findings do not replicate across individual studies, possibly due in part to small effect sizes, small sample sizes, or the selective reporting of positive results.

More recently, efforts have been made to try to resolve some of these issues. Larger samples obtained by combining studies, such as those of the Psychiatric Genomics Consortium (PGC; http://www.med.unc.edu/pgc), are showing greater power to detect genes that increase risk for schizophrenia. By the end of 2013, genomewide association studies (GWAS), which systematically look at the whole genome, had detected around 22 nonoverlapping possible loci (Ripke et al., 2011). Moreover, as mentioned in Chapter 9, success has also been found when looking at the risk across a set of genes. For example, the International Schizophrenia Consortium has found that hundreds of genes, each with small individual effects, contribute to the risk for developing the disorder (Purcell et al., 2009). Not only was this polygenic score higher in people with schizophrenia, it was also higher in people with bipolar disorder than controls (Kavanagh, Tansey, O'Donovan, & Owen, 2015). The overall conclusions from these studies were that (i) common variants are important to the etiology of schizophrenia but act in a polygenic fashion (i.e., no common variant individually contributes substantially to liability) (Bulik-Sullivan et al., 2015b; Gratten, Wray, Keller, & Visscher, 2014), (ii) larger sample sizes are needed, and (iii) there is substantial genetic overlap between adult-onset disorders, especially schizophrenia and bipolar disorder (Bulik-Sullivan et al., 2015a; Kavanagh et al., 2015).

During the past few years, the PGC sample sizes have more than doubled and meta-analyses of these PGC datasets have resulted in 108 distinct genomic loci associations with schizophrenia (Schizophrenia Working Group of the Psychiatric Genomics Consortium, 2014). Follow-up efforts found that some of these associations were enriched in brain-specific *gene enhancers* (a short 50–1500 bp region of DNA that can be bound with proteins to activate transcription of a gene), including those involved in immune function. Despite the results of this landmark study, plausible functional variants could not be identified for some of the findings, suggesting that we are still limited in our understanding of the underlying biology of schizophrenia.

In addition to these efforts within the realm of common genetic variation, there is also growing interest in the importance of rare variants on risk for schizophrenia. Before exome sequencing became popular (see Chapter 9), there was growing evidence that copy number variants (CNVs, see Chapter 9) were seen more frequently in individuals with schizophrenia. Rare and large CNVs associated with schizophrenia have been found on several chromosomes, and these investigations, particularly of *de novo* CNVs, have helped to provide an explanation for some of the biological processes underlying schizophrenia (see Kavanagh et al., 2015, for a review). This is, in part, because CNVs tend to affect many genes and because the effects of CNVs are not specific. Many of the CNVs implicated in schizophrenia are also associated with at least one other disorder, such as autism spectrum disorder or attention-deficit/hyperactivity disorder (ADHD, see Chapter 15). More recent efforts, particularly those of two exome sequencing studies that screened most of the coding exome for rare variants that might affect risk (Fromer et al., 2014; Purcell et al., 2014), suggest that *de novo* single nucleotide variant mutations and small insertions and deletions (*indels*) might play less of a role in schizophrenia than indicated by earlier studies. While the exome sequencing studies lacked power to implicate specific genes and rare mutations, these results collectively suggest a very complex genetic architecture underlying this disorder that includes both rare and common genetic variation.

Summary

Psychopathology is the most active area of research in behavioral genetics. For schizophrenia, lifetime risk is about 1 percent in the general population, 10 percent in first-degree relatives whether reared together or adopted apart, 17 percent for fraternal twins, and 48 percent for identical twins. This pattern of results indicates substantial genetic influence as well as nonshared environmental influence. Genetic high-risk studies and co-twin control studies suggest that birth complications and attention problems in childhood are weak predictors of schizophrenia, which usually strikes in early adulthood. Genetic influence has been found utilizing both the adoptees' study method, like that used in the first adoption study by Heston, and the adoptees' family method. More severe schizophrenia may be more heritable than less severe forms. Recent research suggests that there is substantial genetic overlap between schizophrenia and other psychiatric disorders, especially bipolar disorder.

There has been considerable progress in research on the molecular genetics of schizophrenia in the past few years. Linkage studies with schizophrenia have begun to yield consistent results and, combined with results from recent genomewide association studies and rare variant studies, have led to the identification of several genes or regions that have significant but small associations with schizophrenia. Overall, genetic liability to schizophrenia results from multiple genes of small effect.

CHAPTER **FOURTEEN**

Other Adult Psychopathology

Although schizophrenia has been the most highly studied disorder in behavioral genetics, in recent years the spotlight has turned to mood disorders. In this chapter, we provide an overview of genetic research on mood disorders as well as other adult psychopathology. The chapter ends with a discussion of the extent to which genes that affect one disorder also affect other disorders.

MOOD DISORDERS

Mood disorders involve severe swings in mood, not just the "blues" that all people feel on occasion. For example, over 50 percent of all suicides are by people diagnosed as having mood disorders (Isometsä, 2014). There are two major categories of mood disorders: major depressive disorder, consisting of episodes of depression, and bipolar disorder, in which there are episodes of both depression and mania.

Major depressive disorder usually has a slow onset over weeks or even months. Each episode typically lasts several months and ends gradually. Characteristic features include depressed mood, loss of interest in usual activities, disturbance of appetite and sleep, loss of energy, and thoughts of death or suicide. Major depressive disorder affects an astounding number of people. In a U.S. survey, the lifetime risk is about 17 percent, with about half of these in a severe or very severe category; risk is two times greater for women than for men after adolescence (Kessler et al., 2012; see National Comorbidity Study at http://www.hcp.med.harvard.edu/ncs/ for more information about prevalence of psychopathology). Moreover, the problem is getting worse: Each successive generation born since World War II has higher rates of depression (Burke, Burke, Roe, & Regier, 1991), and prevalence rates more than doubled from the early 1990s to the early 2000s (Compton, Conway, Stinson, & Grant, 2006). These temporal trends could possibly be due to changes in environmental influences, diagnostic criteria, or clinical referral rates. Major depressive disorder is sometimes called *unipolar depression* because it involves only depression. In contrast, *bipolar disorder*, also known as manic-depressive illness, is a disorder in which the mood of the affected individual alternates between the depressive pole and the other pole of mood, called *mania*. Mania involves euphoria, inflated self-esteem, sleeplessness, talkativeness, racing thoughts, distractibility, hyperactivity, and reckless behavior. Mania typically begins and ends suddenly, and it lasts from several days to several months. Mania is sometimes difficult to diagnose; for this reason the DSM (the American Psychiatric Association's *Diagnostic and Statistical Manual of Mental Disorders*) has distinguished *bipolar I disorder*, with a clear manic episode, from *bipolar II disorder*, with a less clearly defined manic episode. Bipolar disorder is much less common than major depression, with an incidence of about 4 percent in the adult population and no gender difference (Kessler et al., 2012).

Family Studies

For more than 70 years, family studies have shown increased risk for first-degree relatives of individuals with mood disorders (Slater & Cowie, 1971). Since the 1960s, researchers have considered major depression and bipolar disorder separately. In seven family studies of major depression, the family risk was 9 percent on average, whereas risk in control samples was about 3 percent (McGuffin & Katz, 1986). Age-corrected morbidity risk estimates that take into account lifetime risk (see Chapter 3) are about twice as high (Sullivan, Neale, & Kendler, 2000). A review of 18 family studies of bipolar I and II disorder yielded an average risk of 9 percent, as compared to less than 1 percent in control individuals (Smoller & Finn, 2003). (See Figure 14.1.) The risks in these studies are low relative to the frequency of the disorder mentioned earlier because these studies focused on severe depression and bipolar disorder, cases that often required hospitalization.

It has been hypothesized that the distinction between unipolar major depression and bipolar disorder is primarily a matter of severity; bipolar disorder may be a more severe form of depression (McGuffin & Katz, 1986). The basic multivariate finding from family studies is that relatives of unipolar probands are not at increased risk for bipolar disorder (less than 1 percent), but relatives of bipolar probands are at increased risk (14 percent) for unipolar depression (Smoller & Finn, 2003). If we postulate that bipolar disorder is a more severe form of depression, this model would explain why familial risk is greater for bipolar disorder, why bipolar probands have an excess of unipolar relatives, and why unipolar probands do not have many relatives with bipolar disorder. However, a twin study discussed in the next section and a recent family study do not provide much support for the hypothesis that bipolar disorder is a more severe form of unipolar depression (Axelson et al., 2015; McGuffin et al., 2003). Identifying genes associated with these disorders will provide crucial evidence for resolving such issues, although to date the findings are mixed. A meta-analysis of gene variants in the methylenetetrahydrofolate reductase (*MTHFR*) gene and schizophrenia, bipolar disorder, and unipolar major depression found an

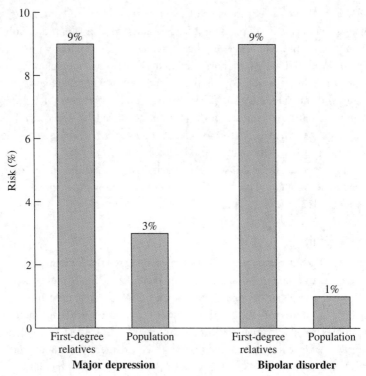

FIGURE 14.1 Family studies of mood disorders.

association with the combined disorders for one *MTHFR* variant, suggesting a shared genetic influence on the three disorders (Peerbooms et al., 2011), although at least one additional meta-analysis suggests that these findings are limited to Asian and African populations (Hu et al., 2014). Other genes have also been associated with both bipolar disorder and unipolar depression, further supporting the likelihood of a common genetic liability to these disorders (e.g., Schulze et al., 2014).

Are some forms of depression more familial? For example, there is a long history of trying to subdivide depression into reactive (triggered by an event) and endogenous (coming from within) subtypes, but family studies provide little support for this distinction (Rush & Weissenburger, 1994). However, severity and especially recurrence show increased familiality for major depressive disorder (Janzing et al., 2009; Milne et al., 2009; Sullivan et al., 2000). Early onset appears to increase familial risk for bipolar disorder (Smoller & Finn, 2003). Drug use and suicide attempts are also familial features of bipolar disorder (Schulze, Hedeker, Zandi, Rietschel, & McMahon, 2006). Another potentially promising direction for subdividing depression is in terms of response to drugs (Binder & Holsboer, 2006). For example, there is some evidence that the therapeutic response to specific antidepressants tends to run in families (Tsuang & Faraone, 1990). A well-known drug treatment for bipolar disorder is lithium; responsiveness to lithium appears to be strongly familial (Grof et al., 2002).

Twin Studies

Twin studies yield evidence for moderate genetic influence for mood disorders. For major depressive disorder, six twin studies yielded average twin probandwise concordances of 0.43 for MZ twins and 0.28 for DZ twins (Sullivan et al., 2000). Liability-threshold model fitting of these data estimated heritability of liability as 0.37, with no shared environmental influence. The largest twin study to date yielded highly similar results: 0.38 heritability and no shared environmental influence (Kendler, Gatz, Gardner, & Pedersen, 2006a). However, family studies suggest that more severe depression might be more heritable. In line with this suggestion, the only clinically ascertained major depressive disorder twin sample large enough to perform model-fitting analyses estimated heritability of liability as 70 percent (McGuffin, Katz, Watkins, & Rutherford, 1996). However, it is also possible that the higher heritability of depression in the clinical sample represents higher reliability of clinical assessment. Some have argued that there are multiple forms of major depression and that it cannot be considered a homogeneous single disorder (Goldberg, 2011). Findings from a large twin study of the DSM symptoms for major depression yielded three genetic factors rather than a single underlying genetic factor, supporting the idea that there are multiple forms of major depression and that each may have different genetic underpinnings (Kendler, Aggen, & Neale, 2013).

For bipolar disorder, average twin concordances were 72 percent for MZ twins and 40 percent for DZ twins in early studies (Allen, 1976); three more recent twin studies yield average twin concordances of 65 percent and 7 percent, respectively (Smoller & Finn, 2003). Two twin studies of bipolar disorder using different samples from different countries yield strikingly similar results: MZ and DZ twin concordances were 40 percent and 5 percent in a U.K. study (McGuffin et al., 2003) and 43 percent and 6 percent in a Finnish study (Kieseppa, Partonen, Haukka, Kaprio, & Lonnqvist, 2004). Model-fitting liability-threshold analyses suggest extremely high heritabilities of liability (0.89 and 0.93, respectively) and no shared environmental influence. The average MZ and DZ twin concordances for the five more recent studies described above are 55 percent and 7 percent, respectively (Figure 14.2).

As mentioned earlier, one of the most important goals of genetic research is to provide diagnostic classifications based on etiology rather than symptoms. For example, are unipolar depression and bipolar disorder genetically distinct? One twin study investigated the model described earlier that bipolar disorder is a more extreme version of major depressive disorder (McGuffin et al., 2003). Part of the problem in addressing this issue is that conventional diagnostic rules assume that an individual has either unipolar or bipolar disorder and that bipolar disorder trumps unipolar disorder. However, in this twin study, this diagnostic assumption was relaxed and a genetic correlation of 0.65 was found between depression and mania, a finding that supports the model that bipolar disorder is a more extreme version of unipolar depression. However, 70 percent of the genetic variance on mania was independent of depression, a finding that does not support the model. A model that explicitly

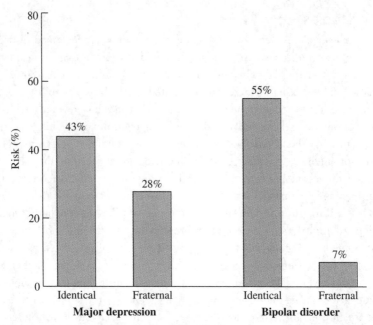

FIGURE 14.2 Approximate twin results for mood disorders.

tested the assumption that bipolar disorder is a more extreme form of unipolar depression was rejected, but so was a model in which the two disorders were assumed to be genetically distinct. This lack of resolution is probably due to a lack of power. Although this was the largest clinically ascertained twin study, there were only 67 pairs in which at least one twin was diagnosed with bipolar disorder and 244 pairs in which at least one twin was diagnosed with unipolar depression. Resolution of this important diagnostic issue can be addressed definitively when genes are identified for the two disorders.

As in the research on schizophrenia (Chapter 13), a study of offspring of identical twins discordant for bipolar disorder has been reported (Bertelsen, 1985). Similar to the results for schizophrenia, the same 10 percent risk for mood disorder was found in the offspring of the unaffected twin and in the offspring of the affected twin. This outcome implies that the identical twin who does not succumb to bipolar disorder nonetheless transmits a liability for the illness to offspring to the same extent as does the ill twin.

Adoption Studies

Results of adoption research on mood disorders are mixed. The largest study began with 71 adoptees with a broad range of mood disorders (Wender et al., 1986). Mood disorders were found in 8 percent of the 387 biological relatives of the probands, a risk only slightly greater than the risk of 5 percent for the 344 biological relatives of control adoptees. The biological relatives of the probands showed somewhat greater rates of alcoholism (5 percent versus 2 percent) and of attempted or actual suicide (7 percent versus 1 percent). Two other adoption studies relying on medical records of depression found little evidence for genetic influence (Cadoret, O'Gorman, Heywood, & Troughton, 1985a; von Knorring, Cloninger, Bohman, & Sigvardsson, 1983). Although the sample size is necessarily small, 12 pairs of identical twins reared apart have been identified in which at least one member of each pair had suffered from major depression (Bertelsen, 1985). Eight of the 12 pairs (67 percent) were concordant for major depression, which is consistent with a hypothesis of at least some genetic influence on depression.

An adoption study that focused on adoptees with bipolar disorder found stronger evidence for genetic influence (Mendlewicz & Rainer, 1977). The rate of bipolar disorder in the birth parents of the bipolar adoptees was 7 percent, but it was 0 percent for the parents of control adoptees. As in the family studies, birth parents of these bipolar adoptees also showed elevated rates of unipolar depression (21 percent) relative to the rate for birth parents of control adoptees (2 percent), a result suggesting that the two disorders are not distinct genetically. Adoptive parents of the bipolar and control adoptees differed little in their rates of mood disorders.

SNP-Based Heritability

As described in Chapter 7, SNP-based heritability can be estimated from DNA in large samples of unrelated individuals. SNP heritability estimates have been reported for major depressive disorder (32 percent; Lubke et al., 2012), as well as variability in nonsomatic depression (21 percent; Laurin et al., 2015), age at onset (17 to 51 percent, depending on the sample; Ferentinos et al., 2015; Power et al., 2012), variability in response to pharmacological treatment (42 to 47 percent; Tansey et al., 2013; Palmer et al., in press), and symptoms of appetite and insomnia (30 percent; Pearson et al., 2016). These data suggest that aspects of major depressive disorder can be accounted for by the additive aggregate contribution of common SNPs, each contributing a small amount of variance to depression-related phenotypes.

Identifying Genes

For decades, the greater risk of major depression for females led to the hypothesis that a dominant gene on the X chromosome might be involved. As explained in Chapter 3, females can inherit the gene on either of their two X chromosomes, whereas males can only inherit the gene on the X chromosome they receive from their mother. Although initially linkage was reported between depression and color blindness, which is caused by genes on the X chromosome (Chapter 3), studies of DNA markers on the X chromosome failed to confirm linkage (Baron, Freimer, Risch, Lerer, & Alexander, 1993). Father-to-son inheritance is common for both major depression and bipolar disorder, which argues against X-linkage inheritance. Moreover, as mentioned earlier, bipolar disorder shows little sex difference. For these reasons, X linkage seems unlikely (Hebebrand, 1992).

In 1987, researchers reported linkage between bipolar disorder and markers on chromosome 11 in a genetically isolated community of Old Order Amish in Pennsylvania (Egeland et al., 1987). Unfortunately, this highly publicized finding was not replicated in other studies. The original report was withdrawn when follow-up research on the original pedigree with additional data showed that the evidence for linkage disappeared (Kelsoe et al., 1989).

These false starts led to greater caution in the search for genes for mood disorders. Linkage studies of major depressive disorder have lagged behind those for schizophrenia and bipolar disorder because, as discussed above, major depressive disorder appears to be less heritable, at least in community-based samples (McGuffin, Cohen, & Knight, 2007). Three early genomewide linkage studies of major depressive disorder converged on linkage at $15q$ (Camp et al., 2005; Holmans et al., 2007; McGuffin et al., 2005). Follow-up fine mapping showed modestly positive evidence for linkage at $15q25$-$q26$ (Levinson et al., 2007). Recent reviews of genomewide association (GWA) studies of major depression have concluded that no significant associations have been found (Cohen-Woods, Craig, & McGuffin, 2013; Flint & Kendler, 2014). Two loci on chromosome 10 have been identified for major depressive disorder using a highly selected sample with a severe subtype (CONVERGE Consortium, 2015). Although these new findings did not robustly replicate using a mega-analysis of European studies, they suggest that focusing on subtypes of major depression may prove to be an important approach in identifying genes associated with depression.

Genomewide linkage scans of bipolar disorder led to a surprising discovery. A meta-analysis of 11 linkage studies with more than 1200 individuals diagnosed as having bipolar disorder found strong evidence for linkage at $13q$ and $22q$ (Badner & Gershon, 2002). The same study also conducted a meta-analysis of 18 linkage studies of schizophrenia and found the strongest evidence for linkage in the same two regions, $13q$ and $22q$, in addition to other regions. Subsequent analyses using multiple combined datasets support the finding of genes common to both bipolar disorder and schizophrenia (e.g., Purcell et al., 2009). More recent GWA studies have supported the finding that bipolar disorder and schizophrenia are associated with the same common SNPs (Cross-Disorder Group of the Psychiatric Genomics Consortium, 2013a), although these associations were in a different region ($3p21$) and were also associated with major depressive disorder. Associations for bipolar disorder at a chromosome $3p21$ locus have been replicated (e.g., Chen et al., 2013) and several studies have identified new SNPs associated with bipolar disorder using genomewide approaches (e.g., Mühleisen et al., 2015; Chen et al., 2013). Two of the genes that have been associated with bipolar disorder in multiple studies are CACNA1C and ANK3 (see Shinozaki & Potash, 2014, and Gatt, Burton, Williams, & Schofield, 2015, for reviews).

Because of the large number of genes that have been associated with bipolar disorder, with only a handful consistently replicated, it has been difficult to interpret these findings. One strategy that has been used is to conduct studies designed to clarify the potential functional role of the gene variation on brain activity or psychological functioning. For example, one such study found that healthy subjects carrying the form of the gene *CACNA1C* that has been associated with bipolar disorder had lower levels of extraversion and higher harm avoidance, trait anxiety, paranoid ideation, and high startle reactivity (Roussos, Giakoumaki, Georgakopoulos, Robakis, & Bitsios, 2011). More recently, the gene *CACNA1C* and other genes commonly associated with both bipolar disorder and schizophrenia (e.g., *ANK3*) were examined in regard to their impact on human brain structure and function (Gurung & Prata, 2015). Most of the genes examined were also related to neuroimaging phenotypes that have been found to be important in schizophrenia and bipolar disorder. For example, *CACNA1C* was associated with white and grey matter volume, regional activation and functional connectivity during executive tasks, and facial affect recognition. These findings and others examining functional relevance of gene variation are critical for understanding not just which genes may be associated with disorder, but also why they are associated.

ANXIETY DISORDERS

A wide range of disorders involve anxiety (panic disorder, generalized anxiety disorder, and phobias). In *panic disorder,* recurrent panic attacks come on suddenly and unexpectedly, usually lasting for several minutes. Panic attacks often lead to a fear of being in a situation that might bring on more panic attacks (e.g., *agoraphobia,* which literally means "fear of the marketplace"). *Generalized anxiety* refers to a more chronic state of diffuse anxiety marked by excessive and uncontrollable worrying. In a *phobia,* the fear is attached to a specific stimulus, such as fear of heights (*acrophobia*), enclosed places (*claustrophobia*), or social situations (*social phobia*).

Anxiety disorders are usually not as crippling as schizophrenia or severe depressive disorders. However, they are the most common form of mental illness, with a lifetime prevalence of 29 percent (Kessler et al., 2005a), and can lead to other disorders, notably depression and alcoholism. Median age of onset is much earlier for anxiety (age 11) than for mood disorders (age 30). The lifetime risks for anxiety disorders are 5 percent for panic disorder, 6 percent for generalized anxiety disorder, 13 percent for specific phobias, and 12 percent for social phobia. Panic disorder, generalized anxiety disorder, and specific phobias are twice as common in women as in men.

There has been much less genetic research on anxiety disorders than on schizophrenia and mood disorders. In general, results for anxiety disorders appear to be similar to those for depression in suggesting moderate genetic influence, as compared to the more substantial genetic influence seen for schizophrenia and bipolar disorder. As discussed later, the similarity in results for anxiety and depression may be caused by genetic overlap between them. Nonetheless, we will briefly review evidence for genetic influence for panic disorder, generalized anxiety disorder, and phobias.

A review of eight family studies of panic disorder yielded an average morbidity risk of 13 percent in first-degree relatives of cases and 2 percent in controls (Shih, Belmonte, & Zandi, 2004). In an early twin study of panic disorder, the concordance rates for identical and fraternal twins were 31 percent and 10 percent, respectively (Torgersen, 1983). In two large twin studies with nonclinical samples, the heritability of liability was about 40 percent, with no evidence of shared environmental influence (Kendler, Gardner, & Prescott, 2001; Mosing et al., 2009a); in two other large twin studies, heritability was approximately 30 percent, with no shared environmental influence (López-Solà et al., 2014; Tambs et al., 2009). A meta-analysis of five twin studies yielded a similar liability heritability (43 percent), with no shared environmental influence (Hettema, Neale, & Kendler, 2001a). No adoption data are available for panic disorder or any other anxiety disorders.

Generalized anxiety disorder appears to be as familial as panic disorder, but the evidence for heritability is weaker. A review of family studies indicates an average risk of about 10 percent among first-degree relatives as compared to a risk of 2 percent in controls (Eley, Collier, & McGuffin, 2002). However, two twin studies found no evidence for genetic influence (Andrews, Stewart, Allen, & Henderson, 1990; Torgersen, 1983); three other twin studies suggested modest genetic influence of about 20 percent and little shared environmental influence (Hettema, Prescott, & Kendler, 2001b; Kendler, Neale, Kessler, Heath, & Eaves, 1992; Scherrer et al., 2000). Two additional twin studies found a somewhat higher heritability for generalized anxiety disorder of around 30 percent (López-Solà et al., 2014; Tambs et al., 2009), although for one of the studies nearly all of this genetic variance was shared with other anxiety disorders. A recent report estimated modest SNP heritability, around 10 percent, for any anxiety disorder (Otowa et al., 2016).

Phobias show familial resemblance: 30 percent familial risk versus 10 percent in controls for specific phobias excluding agoraphobia (Fyer, Mannuzza, Chapman, Martin, & Klein, 1995), 5 percent versus 3 percent for agoraphobia (Eley et al., 2002), and 20 percent versus 5 percent for social phobia (Stein et al., 1998). A meta-analysis of ten published twin studies of phobias found an average heritability around 0.30 for phobias of animals, situations, and blood-injury-injection, with some evidence of modest shared environmental influences only for situational and blood-injury-injection phobias (Van Houtem et al., 2013). Although there is little evidence of shared environmental influence, phobias are learned, even fears of evolutionarily fear-relevant stimuli such as snakes and spiders. An interesting twin study of fear conditioning showed moderate genetic influence on individual differences in learning and extinguishing fears (Hettema, Annas, Neale, Kendler, & Fredrikson, 2003).

OTHER DISORDERS

As mentioned earlier, the DSM includes many other categories of disorders. We know about the genetics of only a handful of these other disorders. These include post-traumatic stress disorder (PTSD), depressive disorder with seasonal pattern, somatic symptom disorders (including chronic fatigue), eating disorders, and obsessive-compulsive disorders. Other disorders are discussed in later chapters: impulse-control disorders such as hyperactivity in Chapter 15, antisocial personality disorder in Chapter 16, and substance abuse disorders in Chapter 17.

Several studies have examined the genetics of posttraumatic stress disorder (PTSD). Diagnosis of PTSD depends on experiencing a prior traumatic event that threatens death or serious injury, such as war, assault, or natural disaster, witnessing such an event, or learning that the traumatic event occurred to a close family member or close friend. PTSD symptoms include re-experiencing the trauma (intrusive memories and nightmares) and denying the trauma (emotional numbing). One survey estimated that the lifetime risk for one PTSD episode is about 1 percent (Davidson, Hughes, Blazer, & George, 1991). The risk is much higher, of course, in those who have experienced trauma. For example, after a plane crash, as many as one-half of the survivors develop PTSD (Smith, North, McColl, & Shea, 1990). About 10 percent of U.S. veterans of the Vietnam War still suffered from PTSD many years later (Weiss et al., 1992). Response to trauma appears to show familial resemblance (Eley et al., 2002). The Vietnam War provided an opportunity to conduct a twin study of PTSD because more than 4000 twin pairs were veterans of the war. A series of studies of these twins began by dividing the sample into those who served in Southeast Asia (who were much more likely to experience trauma) and those who did not (True et al., 1993). The results were similar for both groups regardless of the type of trauma experienced: Heritabilities of 15 PTSD symptoms were all about 40 percent, and there was no evidence of shared environmental influence. A large all-female twin study of PTSD found that genetic influences accounted for 72 percent of the variance in PTSD with the remaining variance due to nonshared environmental effects (Sartor et al., 2011).

Depressive disorder with seasonal pattern (formerly called *seasonal affective disorder* or *SAD*) is a type of major depression that occurs seasonally, typically in the fall or winter (Rosenthal et al., 1984). Family and twin studies suggest results similar to those for depression, with modest heritability (about 30 percent) and little shared environmental influence (Sher, Goldman, Ozaki, & Rosenthal, 1999). However, one twin study reported heritability twice as high (Jang, Lam, Livesley, & Vernon, 1997). It is noteworthy that this study was conducted in British Columbia (Canada) and yielded very high rates of SAD compared to the other studies, which suggests the possibility that the higher heritability and prevalence in the Canadian samples might be due to the northern latitude and more severe winters of Canada (Jang, 2005). A recent GWA study found overlap in genetic risk for seasonality and bipolar disorder, major depression, and schizophrenia, providing some support for the seasonal pattern category introduced in the DSM-5 (Byrne et al., 2015).

In somatic symptom and related disorders, psychological conflicts lead to physical symptoms such as stomach pains. There are several disorders in this category but only somatic symptom disorders have been examined in genetic studies. *Somatization disorder* involves multiple symptoms with no apparent physical cause. Somatic symptom disorders show some genetic influence in family, twin, and adoption studies

(Guze, 1993). Somatic symptom disorder, which is much more common in women than in men, shows strong familial resemblance for women, but for men it is related to increased family risk for antisocial personality (Guze, Cloninger, Martin, & Clayton, 1986; Lilienfeld, 1992). An adoption study suggests that this link between somatic symptom disorder in women and antisocial behavior in men may be genetic in origin (Bohman, Cloninger, von Knorring, & Sigvardsson, 1984). Biological fathers of adopted women with somatic symptom disorder showed increased rates of antisocial behavior and alcoholism. A twin study of somatic distress symptoms in an unselected sample showed genetic as well as shared environmental influence; it also suggested that some of the genetic influence is independent of depression and phobia (Gillespie, Zhu, Heath, Hickie, & Martin, 2000).

Chronic fatigue refers to fatigue of more than six months' duration that cannot be explained by a physical or other psychiatric disorder. Family studies suggest that chronic fatigue is moderately familial (Albright, Light, Light, Bateman, & Cannon-Albright, 2011; Walsh, Zainal, Middleton, & Paykel, 2001). A twin study of diagnosed chronic fatigue found concordance rates of 55 percent in MZ twins and 19 percent in DZ twins (Buchwald et al., 2001). Twin studies of chronic fatigue symptoms in unselected samples yielded mixed results. Most twin studies found modest genetic and shared environmental influences (Sullivan, Evengard, Jacks, & Pedersen, 2005; Sullivan, Kovalenko, York, Prescott, & Kendler, 2003b), even in childhood (Farmer, Scourfield, Martin, Cardno, & McGuffin, 1999). In another study, fatigue-related symptoms were found to be due mostly to shared environmental influences in women and to genetic and nonshared environmental influences in men (Schur, Afari, Goldberg, Buchwald, & Sullivan, 2007). A set of studies that examined chronic fatigue symptoms and other somatic symptoms found that the symptoms could be explained by genetic and nonshared environmental influences (Kato, Sullivan, Evengard, & Pedersen, 2009; Kato, Sullivan, & Pedersen, 2010).

Eating disorders include *anorexia nervosa* (extreme dieting and avoidance of food) and *bulimia nervosa* (binge eating followed by vomiting), both of which occur mostly in adolescent girls and young women, and a new category called *binge eating disorder* (binge eating and feelings of lack of control and distress). Both anorexia nervosa and bulimia nervosa appear to run in families (Eley et al., 2002); in twin studies, both appear to be moderately heritable, with little influence of shared environment (Trace, Baker, Peñas-Lledó, & Bulik, 2013). For example, the largest twin study of anorexia found a heritability of liability of 56 percent and no shared environmental influence (Bulik et al., 2006). A sibling adoption study of disordered eating yielded a similar pattern of findings, with genetic influences accounting for more than half of the variance and no shared environmental influences (Klump, Suisman, Burt, McGue, & Iacono, 2009). Eating disorders is an area that is especially promising for studies of the interplay between genes and environment (Bulik, 2005), including biological factors such as puberty and hormone exposure that may moderate genetic and environmental influences (see Klump, 2013, for a review).

Obsessive-compulsive disorders (OCDs) are indicated by intrusive, repetitive, and persistent thoughts, urges, or images that cause distress and that result in excessive or repetitive ritualistic behaviors, such as repeated hand washing in response to an obsession with hygiene. Family studies have tended to yield inconsistent findings for OCD because of differences in diagnostic criteria and small sample sizes. A review of family studies of OCD reported an average risk of 7 percent for family members and 3 percent for controls for studies using consistent criteria and larger sample sizes (Shih et al., 2004). Genetic influences accounted for around 40 percent of the variance, while shared environmental effects accounted for less than 10 percent of the variance in a meta-analysis of 14 reports of twin studies of obsessive-compulsive symptoms (Taylor, 2011), and two large twin studies of OCD symptoms found heritability of around 40 percent with no significant shared environmental influence (López-Solà et al., 2014; Mataix-Cols et al., 2013). SNP heritability estimates for obsessive-compulsive symptoms suggest that 14 percent of the variance can be accounted for by the additive aggregate contribution of common SNPs (den Braber et al., 2016).

CO-OCCURRENCE OF DISORDERS

The co-occurrence, or *comorbidity,* of psychiatric disorders is striking. People with one disorder have almost a 50 percent chance of having more than one disorder during a 12-month period (Kessler, Chiu, Demler, Merikangas, & Walters, 2005b). In addition, more serious disorders are much more likely to involve comorbidity. Are these really different disorders that co-occur, or does the co-occurrence call into question current diagnostic systems? Diagnostic systems are based on phenotypic descriptions of symptoms rather than on causes. Genetic research offers the hope of systems of diagnosis that take into account evidence on causation. As explained in Chapter 7 and the Appendix, multivariate genetic analysis of twin and adoption data can be used to ask whether genes that affect one trait also affect another trait.

Hundreds of genetic studies have addressed this key question of comorbidity in psychopathology. Earlier in this chapter, we considered the surprising finding of genetic overlap between major depressive disorder and bipolar disorder as well as the even more surprising possibility of genetic overlap between bipolar disorder and schizophrenia. Scores of multivariate family and twin studies have examined comorbidity across the many anxiety disorders as well as between anxiety disorders and other disorders such as depression and alcoholism. Rather than describe studies that compare two or three disorders (see, for example, Jang, 2005; McGuffin, Gottesman, & Owen, 2002), we will provide an overview of multivariate genetic results that point to a surprising degree of genetic comorbidity.

For example, consider the diverse anxiety disorders. A multivariate genetic analysis of lifetime diagnoses of major anxiety disorders indicated substantial genetic overlap among generalized anxiety disorder, panic disorder, agoraphobia, and social phobia (Hettema, Prescott, Myers, Neale, & Kendler, 2005). The only specific genetic effects were found for specific phobias such as fear of animals. Differences between the disorders are largely caused by nonshared environmental factors. Results were similar for men and women despite the much greater frequency of anxiety disorders in women. A subsequent twin study examined panic disorder, generalized anxiety disorder, phobias, OCD, and PTSD (Tambs et al., 2009). Again, all of the anxiety disorders were influenced by a common genetic factor, with only phobias and OCD showing some specific genetic influences; no shared environmental influences were significant for any of the disorders.

Broadening this multivariate genetic approach beyond anxiety disorders to include major depression yields the most surprising finding in this area: Anxiety (especially generalized anxiety disorder) and depression are largely the same thing genetically. This finding was initially reported in a paper in 1992 for lifetime estimates (Kendler et al., 1992), with results summarized in Figure 14.3. Heritability of liability in this study was 42 percent for major depression and 69 percent for generalized anxiety disorder. There was no significant shared environmental influence; nonshared environment accounted for the remainder of the liability of the two disorders. The amazing finding was the genetic correlation of 1.0 between the two disorders, indicating that the same genes affect depression and anxiety. Nonshared environmental influences correlated 0.51, suggesting that nonshared environmental factors differentiate the disorders to some extent. These findings for lifetime estimates of depression and anxiety were replicated using one-year prevalences obtained from follow-up interviews (Kendler, 1996). A review of 23 twin studies and 12 family studies confirms that anxiety and depression are largely the same disorder genetically and that the disorders are differentiated by nonshared environmental factors (Middeldorp, Cath, Van Dyck, & Boomsma, 2005). Chapter 15 describes more work in this area that has focused on children and adolescents, rather than

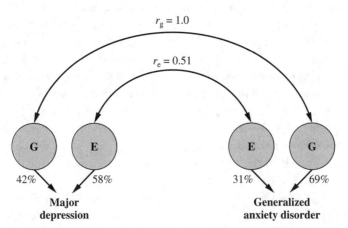

FIGURE 14.3 Multivariate genetic results for major depression and generalized anxiety disorder. (Data from Kendler, Neale, Kessler, Heath, & Eaves, 1992. Copyright 1992 by the American Medical Association.)

adults, with the aim of understanding how these disorders develop and co-occur across development.

Going beyond depression and anxiety disorders to include drug abuse and antisocial behavior suggests a genetic structure of common psychiatric disorders (not including schizophrenia and bipolar disorder) that differs substantially from current diagnostic classifications based on symptoms (Kendler, Prescott, Myers, & Neale, 2003b). Genetic research suggests two broad categories of disorders, called *internalizing* and *externalizing*. Internalizing disorders include depression and anxiety disorders; externalizing disorders include alcohol and other drug abuse as well as antisocial behavior in adulthood (and conduct disorder in childhood). Internalizing disorders can be separated into an anxious/misery factor, which includes depression and anxiety disorders, and a fear factor, which includes phobias. Both internalizing factors are involved in panic disorder. As discussed in Chapter 16, the internalizing disorders might represent the extreme of the broad personality trait called *neuroticism*.

The disparate externalizing disorders (Chapters 15–17) are part of a general genetic factor, although both alcohol dependence and other drug abuse include some disorder-specific genetic effects. The genetic structure of internalizing and externalizing disorders applies equally to men and women despite the much greater risk of internalizing disorders for women and externalizing disorders for men. Because few disorders show shared environmental influence, it does not affect the structure. Nonshared environment largely contributes to heterogeneity rather than comorbidity. Thus, the phenotypic structure of comorbidity is largely driven by the genetic structure (Krueger, 1999).

These multivariate genetic results predict that when genes are found that are associated with any of the internalizing disorders, the same genes are highly likely to be associated with other internalizing disorders. Similarly, genes associated with any of the externalizing disorders will likely be associated with the other externalizing disorders but not with the internalizing disorders. This result suggests that genetic influences are broad in their effect in psychopathology. It mirrors a similar finding concerning "generalist genes" in the area of cognitive abilities (see Chapter 11).

Identifying Genes

Although multivariate genetic research suggests that the genetic action lies at the level of broad categories of internalizing and externalizing disorders, molecular genetic research on anxiety disorders has focused on traditional diagnoses. Moreover, not nearly as much molecular genetic research has been conducted on these disorders as compared to the mood disorders. As a result, linkage studies have not yet converged, and the "usual suspect" candidate gene studies have not yet revealed replicable results (e.g., Eley et al., 2002; Jang, 2005; Smoller, Block, & Young, 2009).

Panic disorder has been studied most, in part because it appears to be more heritable than the other anxiety disorders and in part because it can be so debilitating. Five early linkage studies of panic disorder did not yield consistent results

(Villafuerte & Burmeister, 2003), suggesting that genetic effects may be relatively small. However, subsequent reports have yielded more promising results, suggesting linkage on 15q and possibly 2q (Fyer et al., 2006) as well as for regions that are specific for different forms of panic or phobic disorder (Smoller et al., 2009). As with other complex traits, candidate gene associations have largely failed to replicate (e.g., Maron, Hettema, & Shlik, 2010; Shimada-Sugimoto, Otowa & Hettema, 2015). The strongest case so far can be made for an association between panic disorder in females and a functional polymorphism (Val158Met) in the catechol-O-methyltransferase (*COMT*) gene (McGrath et al., 2004; Rothe et al., 2006), a polymorphism that has been reported to be associated with many other common disorders and complex traits (Craddock, Owen, & O'Donovan, 2006). Similar mixed results are beginning to emerge for candidate gene studies of OCD (Hemmings & Stein, 2006; Stewart et al., 2007), although a meta-analysis of 230 polymorphisms in 113 studies of OCD suggests that 20 of the associations identified were significant in one of the two-stage meta-analyses (Taylor, 2013). Two GWA studies for OCD suggest that genes in glutamatergic, serotonergic, and dopaminergic systems may be important (Mattheisen et al., 2014; Stewart et al., 2013). Linkage and candidate gene association studies of eating disorders have also been mixed (Slof-Op 't Landt et al., 2005); although GWA studies have been conducted, they have been underpowered for detecting genome-wide significance (e.g., Boraska et al., 2014). A GWA study of depression using sets of SNPs selected from GWA studies for their association with a particular phenotype found evidence for significant associations for many genetic loci of small effect that influence both depression and anxiety (Demirkan et al., 2011). Thus, although there is some evidence for genes related to specific disorders, there is also emerging evidence of substantial overlap in the genes across multiple disorders, a finding supported by several studies discussed earlier, including the GWA study reporting associations of four SNPs with five psychiatric disorders (Cross-Disorder Group of the Psychiatric Genomics Consortium, 2013a, 2013b). As more studies consider multiple diagnoses, it is likely that, consistent with findings from twin studies, genes will be identified that are related to broad categories of disorders.

Summary

Moderate genetic influence has been found for major depressive disorder, and substantial genetic influence has been found for bipolar disorder. More severe and recurrent forms of these mood disorders are more heritable. Bipolar disorder may be a more severe form of depression. Surprisingly, molecular genetic studies for bipolar disorder suggest linkages and associations similar to those found for schizophrenia.

Anxiety disorders yield quantitative genetic results that are similar to depression—moderate genetic influence with little evidence of shared environmental influence. Some evidence for genetic influence has also been found for depressive disorder with seasonal pattern, somatic symptom disorders, chronic fatigue, eating disorders, and obsessive-compulsive disorder.

Some of the most far-reaching genetic findings in psychopathology concern genetic comorbidity. Genetic research has begun to call into question the fundamental diagnostic distinction between schizophrenia and bipolar disorder, including the molecular genetic findings of similar linkages and associations for the two disorders. The most striking finding regarding the mood disorders is that major depressive disorder and generalized anxiety disorder are the same disorder from a genetic perspective. Multivariate genetic research suggests a genetic structure of common psychiatric disorders that includes just two broad categories, internalizing and externalizing disorders.

CHAPTER **FIFTEEN**

Developmental Psychopathology

S chizophrenia is typically diagnosed in adulthood. Other disorders emerge in childhood. General cognitive disability, learning disorders, and communication disorders were discussed in Chapter 12. Other DSM diagnostic categories that first appear in childhood include pervasive developmental disorders (e.g., autistic disorder), attention-deficit and disruptive behavior disorders (e.g., attention-deficit/ hyperactivity disorder, conduct disorder), anxiety disorders, tic disorders (e.g., Tourette disorder), elimination disorders (e.g., enuresis), and, most recently, mood disorders. In a nationwide sample of unselected households with children from 8 to 15 years of age, 12 percent of children met 12-month criteria for diagnosis of disruptive disorders (attention-deficit/hyperactivity disorder or conduct disorder), mood or anxiety disorder (depression, dysthymia, anxiety or panic), or eating disorder (Merikangas et al., 2010). Even more surprising is that approximately 14 percent of those children met the criteria for two or more of the disorders.

Only in the past two decades has genetic research begun to focus on disorders of childhood (Rutter, Silberg, O'Connor, & Simonoff, 1999). Developmental psychopathology is not limited to childhood: It considers change and continuity throughout the life course, including disorders such as dementia, which develops later in life (see Chapters 12 and 19). However, genetic research on childhood disorders has blossomed recently, as is reflected in this chapter. One reason to consider childhood disorders is that some disorders that emerge in childhood persist into adulthood, either in the same form or in a different but related form. Median age of onset is much earlier for anxiety disorders (age 11) and impulse-control disorders (age 11) than for mood disorders (age 30). Half of all lifetime cases of diagnosed disorders start by age 14, which suggests that interventions aimed at prevention or early treatment need to focus on childhood and adolescence (Kessler et al., 2005a), especially because only half of the children aged 8 to 15 who met criteria for diagnosis for a mental health disorder had sought treatment with a mental health professional (Merikangas et al., 2010). However, the main reason for the increased interest in the genetics of childhood disorders is that the two major childhood disorders—autism and attention-deficit/hyperactivity disorder—have been shown to be among the most heritable of all mental disorders, as described in the following sections.

AUTISM

Autism was once thought to be a childhood version of schizophrenia, but it is now known to be a distinct disorder marked by abnormalities in social relationships, communication deficits, and restricted interests. As traditionally diagnosed, it is relatively uncommon; however, a 2010 survey by the U.S. Centers for Disease Control and Prevention found higher rates for autism than previously reported, about 1 in 68 children, with rates almost five times higher in boys than girls (http://www.cdc.gov /ncbddd/autism/data.html). Even higher rates, 1 in 38 children, have been reported in a study that screened over 55,000 children in a South Korean community (Kim et al., 2011). During the 1990s, there was a fivefold increase in the diagnosis of autism, in part because of heightened awareness and changing diagnostic criteria (Muhle, Trentacoste, & Rapin, 2004), and the rates have continued to increase in the 2000s. The diagnosis of autism has been broadened to *autism spectrum disorder* (ASD) representing a continuum of symptoms. Traditionally, a diagnosis of autism was limited to children who showed impairments in all three areas (social, communication, interests) before 3 years of age. In contrast, *Asperger syndrome* was diagnosed if children were impaired in the social and interests domains but appeared to have normal language and cognitive development before 3 years of age. The "other" diagnosis was used for children who showed severe impairment in just one or two of the domains. Most researchers now consider these three disorders as part of a single continuum or spectrum of disorder. In the early 2000s, great concern among parents was driven by media reports that the supposed increase in ASD was caused environmentally by the measles-mumps-rubella (MMR) vaccine. However, the evidence on this putative environmental cause of ASD has been consistently negative (Taylor, Swerdfeger, & Eslick, 2014a).

Family and Twin Studies

When Kanner (1943) first characterized autism in 1943, he assumed it was caused "constitutionally." However, in subsequent decades, autism was thought to be environmentally caused, either by cold and rejecting parents or by brain damage (Hanson & Gottesman, 1976). Genetics did not seem to be important because there were no reported cases of an autistic child having an autistic parent and because the risk to siblings was only about 5 percent (Bailey, Phillips, & Rutter, 1996; Smalley, Asarnow, & Spence, 1988). However, this rate of 5 percent was 100 times greater than the population rate of autism as diagnosed in those original studies, a difference implying strong familial resemblance. The reason why autistic children do not have autistic parents is that few severely autistic individuals marry and have children.

In 1977, the first systematic twin study of autism began to change the view that autism was environmental in origin (Folstein & Rutter, 1977). Four of 11 pairs of identical twins were concordant for autism, whereas none of 10 pairs of fraternal twins were. These pairwise concordance rates of 36 and 0 percent rose to 92 and 10 percent when the diagnosis was broadened to include communication and social problems. Co-twins of autistic children are more likely to have communication problems as well as social difficulties. In a follow-up of the twin sample into adult life, problems with social relationships were prominent (Le Couteur et al., 1996). These findings were replicated in other twin studies (Ronald & Hoekstra, 2011). A conservative estimate of the concordance in MZ pairs is 60 percent. A review of four independent twin studies suggests a heritability of liability for autism greater than 90 percent (Freitag, 2007). Twin and family studies of ASD find similar results, suggesting substantial heritability with little evidence of shared environmental influence (e.g., Colvert et al., 2015; Risch et al., 2014; Sandin et al., 2014; but see Hallmayer et al., 2011, for a contrasting view of the role of shared environment).

On the basis of these twin and family findings, views regarding autism have changed radically. Instead of being seen as an environmentally caused disorder, it is now considered to be one of the most heritable mental disorders (Freitag, 2007; Ronald & Hoekstra, 2011). One unusual aspect of genetic research on autism is that, as traditionally diagnosed, autism is so severe that it nearly always results in affected children being seen by clinical services rather than remaining undetected in the community (Thapar & Scourfield, 2002). As a result, nearly all twin studies have been based on clinical cases rather than community samples. However, recent research has considered ASD as a continuum that extends well into common behavioral problems seen in undiagnosed children in the community. This trend was driven in part by the results of early family studies in which relatives of autistic individuals were found to have some communication and social difficulties (Bailey, Palferman, Heavey, & Le Couteur, 1998). Twin studies have also generally supported the hypothesis that the genetic and environmental causes of ASD symptoms are distributed continuously throughout the population and that the etiology of autistic traits does not differ across the full range of severity (e.g., Colvert et al., 2015; Lundstrom et al., 2012; Robinson et al., 2011; but see Frazier et al., 2014 for an exception). This is an emerging rule in behavioral genetics—that disorders are actually the quantitative extreme of a continuum of normal variation (see Chapters 13 and 14).

In contrast to the assumption that autism involves a triad of impairments—poor social interaction, language and communication problems, and restricted range of interests and activities—twin studies of ASD symptoms in community samples have found evidence for genetic heterogeneity, especially between social impairments (interaction and communication) and nonsocial impairments (interests and activities). Several multivariate genetic analyses of the triad of symptoms have found high heritability (about 80 percent) for each of the three types of symptoms but surprisingly low genetic correlations among them (e.g., Ronald, Happé, Price, Baron-Cohen, & Plomin, 2006; Taylor et al., 2014b). These findings suggest that, although some children by chance have all three types of symptoms, the ASD triad of symptoms are different genetically. This surprising conclusion, which contradicts the traditional diagnosis of autism, is supported by cognitive and brain data (Happé, Ronald, & Plomin, 2006).

Identifying Genes

Quantitative genetic evidence suggesting substantial genetic influence on autism led to autism being the early target of affected sib-pair linkage analysis after the success of QTL linkage in the area of reading disability in 1994 (see Chapter 12). In 1998, an international collaborative linkage study reported evidence of a locus on chromosome 7 (7q31-q33) in a study of 87 affected sibling pairs (International Molecular Genetic Study of Autism Consortium, 1998). This 7q linkage was replicated in other studies, although several studies did not replicate the linkage (Trikalinos et al., 2006). No specific gene has been implicated reliably (De Rubeis & Buxbaum, 2015). Many other linkage regions have been reported in several genomewide linkage studies, but none has been replicated in more than two studies (Ma et al., 2007). Despite the sex difference in ASD, no consistent evidence for linkage to the X chromosome has emerged.

As with other common disorders, these linkage results could be viewed as demonstrating that there are no genes of sufficiently large effect size to be detected by sib-pair linkage analyses with samples of fewer than many hundreds of affected sibling pairs. The most straightforward way to address the issue of power to detect smaller QTL effect sizes is to increase the sample size, although it is difficult to obtain such samples because only about 5 percent of the siblings of autistic children are also autistic. One large-scale collaborative project conducted a sib-pair linkage analysis of more than 1000 families across 19 countries, involving 120 scientists from more than 50 institutions (Szatmari et al., 2007). Although previously reported linkages were not replicated, including the linkage on 7q, linkage was suggested for 11p12-q13. Linkage results appeared stronger when families with copy number variants (see Chapter 9) were removed from the analysis.

Similar to other disorders, hundreds of candidate gene associations have been reported but no consistent associations have as yet been found (Geschwind, 2011; Xu et al., 2012). Although many genomewide association (GWA) studies have also been conducted, the results of such studies have been similarly inconclusive for finding a particular gene or set of genes associated with ASD, with two notable exceptions. First, a study of over 50,000 individuals used a genomewide approach to examine associations of SNPs with five psychiatric disorders, including ASD (Cross-Disorders Group of the Psychiatric Genetics Consortium, 2013a; 2013b). Although none of the SNPs were uniquely associated with ASD, three were significantly associated with both ASD and schizophrenia (Kavanagh et al., 2015). Second, a meta-analysis of 8 studies examining a susceptibility locus on chromosome 2 (*SLC25A12*) found evidence for an association between two SNPs in *SLC25A12* and susceptibility for ASD (Liu et al., 2015).

One explanation for the dearth of findings from GWA and genomewide linkage studies is their focus on common variants. There is accumulating evidence that as many as 10 percent of ASD cases can be accounted for by rare mutations due to copy number variants (CNVs) (Levy et al., 2011). Although CNVs are usually *de novo* mutations, there is evidence that these rare variants may also be inherited as recessive mutations that increase risk for ASD when homozygous (e.g., Krumm et al., 2015). Because autism does run in families, rare CNVs cannot be the only explanation for ASD. Instead, common variants as well as CNVs are likely to play a role.

In an effort to organize the vast number of genes identified for autism and to provide a resource for researchers, a recent review and analysis of existing data identified more than 2000 genes, 4500 CNVs, and 158 linkage regions reported to be associated with ASD (Xu et al., 2012). This information is in an online searchable database (http://autismkb.cbi.pku.edu.cn/). As this work moves forward, the multivariate genetic research described above indicating genetic heterogeneity for the three types of symptoms suggests that molecular genetic studies might profit by focusing more on the three types of symptoms separately rather than beginning with diagnoses of autism, which requires the presence of all three impairments.

ATTENTION-DEFICIT/HYPERACTIVITY DISORDER

Attention-deficit/hyperactivity disorder (ADHD), as defined by DSM-5, refers to children who exhibit very high activity, have a poor attention span, and act impulsively. Findings from the National Survey of Children's Health in the United States estimated that 11 percent of children had ever received an ADHD diagnosis by adolescence with boys greatly outnumbering girls (Visser et al., 2014; see also: http://www.cdc.gov/ncbddd/adhd/features/key-findings-adhd72013.html). European psychiatrists have tended to take a more restricted approach to diagnosis, with an emphasis on hyperactivity that not only is severe and pervasive across situations but also is of early onset and unaccompanied by high anxiety (Polanczyk, de Lima, Horta, Biederman, & Rohde, 2007; Taylor, 1995). There is continuing uncertainty about the merits of these narrower and broader approaches to diagnosis (Polanczyk, Willcutt, Salum, Kieling, & Rohde, 2014). However conceptualized, ADHD usually continues into adolescence and, depending on the criteria used, may persist into adulthood (Faraone, Biederman, & Mick, 2006).

Twin Studies

ADHD runs in families, with first-degree relatives five times more likely to be diagnosed as compared to controls (Biederman et al., 1992) and with greater familial risk when ADHD persists into adulthood (Faraone, Biederman, & Monuteaux, 2000).

Twin studies have consistently shown a strong genetic effect on hyperactivity regardless of whether it is measured by questionnaire (Nikolas & Burt, 2010) or by standardized and detailed interviewing (Eaves et al., 1997), regardless of whether it is rated by parents or teachers (Saudino, Ronald, & Plomin, 2005), and regardless of whether it is treated as a continuously distributed dimension of symptoms (Thapar, Langley, O'Donovan, & Owen, 2006) or as a clinical diagnosis (Gillis, Gilger, Pennington, & DeFries, 1992; Larsson, Chang, D'Onofrio & Lichtenstein, 2014). A heritability estimate of 76 percent was computed for pooled findings across 20 twin studies (Faraone et al., 2005), and a more recent meta-analysis of 21 studies confirmed these findings with a heritability estimate of about 70 percent for hyperactivity and around 56 percent for inattention (Nikolas & Burt, 2010). These results suggest that heritability is greater for ADHD than for other childhood disorders with the exception of autism.

As is almost always the case in behavioral genetics, stability of ADHD symptoms is largely driven by genetics (e.g., Kan et al., 2013; Larsson, Dilshad, Lichtenstein, & Barker, 2011; Pingault et al., 2015). As is usually the case for psychopathology, heritability appears to be greater for persistent ADHD that extends into adulthood (Faraone, 2004). An unusual aspect of ADHD results is that DZ correlations are often lower than expected relative to MZ correlations, especially for parental ratings. This could be due to a contrast effect in which parents inflate differences between their DZ twins, but this pattern of twin results is also consistent with **nonadditive genetic variance** (e.g., Eaves et al., 1997; Hudziak, Derks, Althoff, Rettew, & Boomsma, 2005; Nikolas & Burt, 2010), as discussed in Chapter 16. Although adoption studies to date have been few and quite limited methodologically (McMahon, 1980), they lend some support to the hypothesis of genetic influence for ADHD (e.g., Cantwell, 1975). Two children-of-twins studies (Chapter 6) attempted to clarify the joint roles of genetic and environmental influences in the development of ADHD in children of alcoholics and found that maternal alcohol use disorder and ADHD relate to child ADHD largely via genetic effects (Knopik et al., 2006; Knopik et al., 2009b).

The activity and attention components of ADHD are both highly heritable (Greven, Asherson, Rijsdijk, & Plomin, 2011a; Nikolas & Burt, 2010). Multivariate genetic twin analyses of the inattention and hyperactivity components of ADHD indicate substantial genetic overlap between the two components, providing genetic justification for the syndrome of ADHD (e.g., Greven, Rijsdijk, & Plomin, 2011b; Larsson, Lichtenstein, & Larsson, 2006; Merwood et al., 2014). Another multivariate issue concerns the genetic overlap between parental and teacher ratings of ADHD, both of which are highly heritable. Multivariate genetic analyses suggest some genetic overlap but also some genetic effects specific to parents and teachers (McLoughlin, Rijsdijk, Asherson, & Kuntsi, 2011; Thapar et al., 2006) with another large adolescent twin study finding a similar pattern of results for parent, teacher, and self-ratings of ADHD symptoms (Merwood et al., 2013). In other words, these results predict that to some extent different genes will be associated with ADHD viewed by parents in the home and ADHD viewed by teachers in school. In addition, pervasive ADHD that is seen both at home and in school is more heritable than ADHD specific to just one situation (Thapar et al., 2006), and hyperactivity-impulsivity and inattention are seen, in part, as distinct by both parents and teachers (McLoughlin et al., 2011).

Identifying Genes

As was the case for autism, the consistent evidence of a large genetic contribution to ADHD attracted the attention of molecular geneticists. However, this recognition came later for ADHD than for autism and at a time when molecular genetic studies had moved on from linkage to association studies in an attempt to identify QTLs of small effect size. Because GWA was not available at that time, these early studies were limited to candidate genes. Interest has centered on genes involved in the dopamine pathway because many children with ADHD improve when given psychostimulants, such as methylphenidate, which affect dopamine pathways. The dopamine transporter gene *DAT1* was an obvious candidate because methylphenidate inhibits the dopamine transporter mechanism and *DAT1* knock-out mice are hyperactive (Caron, 1996). An exciting initial finding of an association for *DAT1* (Cook et al., 1998) was replicated in three studies but failed to replicate in three other studies (Thapar & Scourfield, 2002). Somewhat stronger results were found for two other dopamine genes that code for dopamine receptors called *DRD4* and *DRD5*. Two meta-analyses found small (**odds ratios** of about 1.2 to 1.3) but significant associations for dopamine-related genes (*DRD4* and *DRD5*), although only one of the meta-analyses found *DAT1* to be significant (Gizer, Ficks, & Waldman, 2009; Li, Sham, Owen, & He, 2006). As expected from the multivariate genetic results indicating substantial genetic overlap between ADHD symptoms, these patterns of associations are similar across symptoms (Thapar et al., 2006).

Associations have been reported for more than 30 other candidate genes, but none have been consistently replicated (see Li, Chang, Zhang, Gao, & Wang, 2014 for a review). Although candidate gene association studies dominated the early genetic research on ADHD, genomewide linkage screens have been reported, including a meta-analysis of seven independent linkage scans (Zhou et al., 2008), a bivariate linkage scan for ADHD and reading disability (Gayán et al., 2005), and a follow-up fine-mapping study of nine candidate linkage regions (Ogdie et al., 2004). No consistent linkage regions have been identified.

Similar to ASD, many GWA studies have been conducted for ADHD with no clear and consistent findings. One study took a systematic approach to search for common variants using both a standard SNP GWA analysis and a more focused, hypothesis-driven approach guided by findings from studies of CNVs (Stergiakouli et al., 2012). This study reported convergence between the SNP- and CNV-guided analyses for *CHRNA7* and some overlap in regions across the two approaches for cholesterol-related and central nervous system pathways. Another study focusing on CNVs also found evidence for involvement of the *CHRNA7* gene, which is also associated with comorbid conduct disorder (Williams et al., 2012). The findings from the many studies focused on CNVs in individuals with ADHD, including at least one genomewide CNV study, have indicated that there is likely to be a role for CNVs in understanding how genes contribute to the development of ADHD, but more work remains to be done. A database of ADHD genes (*ADHDgene:* http://adhd.psych.ac.cn/) has been created that includes SNPs, CNVs and other variants, genes, and chromosomal regions gleaned from published genetic studies of ADHD (Zhang et al., 2012).

DISRUPTIVE BEHAVIOR DISORDERS

Disruptive behavior disorders include oppositional defiant disorder and conduct disorder. In earlier versions of the DSM these disorders were clustered with ADHD, but they are now considered a different category of disorders, although they do often occur together. Because conduct disorder is the most well-studied of these disorders in genetic research, that is our focus here.

Genetic studies of conduct disorder yield results quite different from those for ADHD. DSM-5 criteria for conduct disorder include aggression, destruction of property, deceitfulness or theft, and other serious violations of rules such as running away from home. Some 5 to 10 percent of children and adolescents meet these diagnostic criteria, with boys again greatly outnumbering girls (Cohen et al., 1993; Rutter et al., 1997). In contrast to ADHD, the combined data from several early twin studies of juvenile delinquency yield concordance rates of 87 percent for identical twins and 72 percent for fraternal twins, rates that suggest only modest genetic influence and substantial shared environmental influence (McGuffin & Gottesman, 1985). This pattern is broadly supported by the results of a twin study of self-reported teenage antisocial behavior in U.S. Army Vietnam-era veterans (Lyons et al., 1995). However, many twin studies of delinquent acts and conduct disorder symptoms in normative samples of adolescents have shown greater genetic influence (Thapar et al., 2006) as well as substantial shared environmental influences (e.g., Bornovalova, Hicks, Iacono, & McGue, 2010; Burt, 2009a).

Heterogeneity in antisocial behavior symptoms also contributes to some of the inconsistencies in the published research findings on conduct problems. For example, there is evidence from several twin studies that aggressive antisocial behavior is more heritable than nonaggressive antisocial behavior (e.g., Burt & Neiderhiser, 2009; Eley, Lichtenstein, & Stevenson, 1999) (Figure 15.1). Moreover, different genetic factors affect aggressive and nonaggressive conduct problems (Burt, 2013; Gelhorn et al., 2006). Genetic effects are probably greatest with respect to early-onset aggressive antisocial behavior that is accompanied by hyperactivity and that shows a strong tendency to persist into adulthood as antisocial personality disorder (e.g., Moffitt,

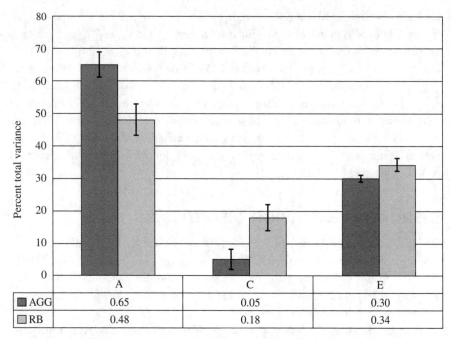

FIGURE 15.1 Genetic, shared environmental, and nonshared environmental influences on aggressive (AGG) and nonaggressive rule-breaking (RB) behaviors. A = additive genetic variance; C = common (shared) environmental variance; E = nonshared environmental variance. (Data from S. A. Burt, "Are there meaningful etiological differences within antisocial behavior? Results of a meta-analysis," *Child Psychology Review, 29,* (2009), 163–178.)

1993; Robins & Price, 1991; Rutter et al., 1999). (See Chapter 16 for a discussion of personality disorders, including antisocial personality disorder.) In addition, antisocial behavior that is persistent across situations (home, school, laboratory) is more heritable (Arseneault et al., 2003; Baker, Jacobson, Raine, Lozano, & Bezdjian, 2007a). In contrast, environmentally mediated risks are probably strongest with respect to nonaggressive juvenile delinquency that has an onset in the adolescent years and does not persist into adult life. The development of conduct disorder and antisocial behavior is a rich vein for studies of gene-environment interplay (Jaffee, Strait, & Odgers, 2012; Moffitt, 2005), as discussed in Chapter 8.

Another aspect of genetic heterogeneity in childhood antisocial behavior is callous-unemotional personality, which involves psychopathic tendencies such as lack of empathy and guilt. In a large twin study of 7-year-old children rated by their teachers, antisocial behavior accompanied by callous-unemotional tendencies was highly heritable (80 percent), with no shared environmental influence, whereas antisocial behavior without callous-unemotional tendencies was only modestly heritable (30 percent) and showed moderate shared environmental influence (35 percent) (Viding, Blair, Moffitt, & Plomin, 2005). These findings persisted longitudinally; moreover, children who showed high or increasing levels of callous-unemotional traits during middle childhood and high levels of conduct problems had the most problematic outcomes at age 12 (Fontaine, McCrory, Boivin, Moffitt, & Viding, 2011).

ANXIETY DISORDERS

The median age of onset for anxiety disorders is 11 years (Kessler et al., 2005a); for this reason, some genetic research has considered anxiety in childhood, with recent work identifying relatively stable anxiety symptoms in preschool-aged children (Edwards, Rapee, & Kennedy, 2010b; Silberg et al., 2015). Several studies have used a sample of over 4500 twin pairs from the United Kingdom to examine anxiety and related symptoms from early childhood to adolescence. In one study, this research team found three components of anxiety in 4-year-old children comparable to adult anxiety disorders (see Chapter 14): generalized anxiety, fears, and obsessive-compulsive behaviors (Eley et al., 2003). Two components are specific to childhood: separation anxiety and shyness/inhibition. Heritability was greatest for obsessive-compulsive behaviors and shyness/inhibition (both over 60 percent), with no evidence of shared environmental influence. Another report examining the same sample of twins during middle childhood found moderate stability in parent reports of anxiety symptoms from age 7 to 9, with genetic influences accounting for approximately half of the variance in symptoms (Trzaskowski, Zavos, Haworth, Plomin, & Eley, 2012). The stability in each type of anxiety symptom was due primarily to genetic influences, whereas change from one type of symptom to another over time was due mostly to shared environmental influences. These findings highlight the need for longitudinal research and for examining multiple symptoms.

A study of obsessive-compulsive symptoms in the United States and the Netherlands also found high heritability (55 percent) in both countries in twins aged 7, 10, and 12 (Hudziak et al., 2004). Heritabilities of generalized anxiety and fears were about 40 percent in the same study, while for fears, there was some evidence of shared environmental influence, which is similar to results for specific fears in adults (Chapter 14). Heritability of obsessive-compulsive behavior symptoms was also found to be high from early childhood (4 years) to adolescence (age 16 years), with the majority of the stability in symptoms over time due to genetic influences (Krebs, Waszczuk, Zavos, Bolton, & Eley, 2015). A similar pattern of findings was found in a longitudinal study of fears and phobias for 2490 Swedish twins followed from middle childhood (age 8–9) to early adulthood (age 19–20) (Kendler et al., 2008b). For three categories of fears—animal, blood/injury, and situational—this study showed relatively stable genetic influence over time, decreasing shared environmental influences, and increasing nonshared environmental influences. An interesting developmental pattern of genetic effects also emerged, with only a modest amount of genetic influence from middle childhood persisting into young adulthood and with new genetic influences (or innovations) emerging at each age, especially during early adolescence (age 13–14).

Separation anxiety is interesting because in addition to showing moderate heritability (about 40 percent), substantial shared environmental influence was also found (35 percent) (Feigon, Waldman, Levy, & Hay, 2001). It is noteworthy that studies of maternal attachment of young children, which is indexed in part by separation anxiety, have also found evidence for shared environmental influence (Fearon et al., 2006; O'Connor & Croft, 2001; Roisman & Fraley, 2006). However, a follow-up of 4-year-old U.K. twins at 6 years of age using DSM-IV diagnoses of separation anxiety disorder found high heritability of liability (73 percent) and no shared environmental influence (Bolton et al., 2006), although there were significant shared environmental influences on the covariation between specific phobia and separation anxiety symptoms in a subset of the same sample (Eley, Rijsdijk, Perrin, O'Connor, & Bolton, 2008). These results are not necessarily contradictory: The studies that found shared environmental influence and modest heritability analyzed individual differences throughout the distribution, whereas the Bolton et al. study focused on the diagnosable extreme of separation anxiety.

Multivariate genetic analysis of the study of 4-year-old twins indicated that the five components of anxiety were moderately correlated genetically, although obsessive-compulsive behaviors were least related genetically to the others (Eley et al., 2003). A subsequent analysis of 7- and 9-year-old twins yielded a similar pattern of findings, with anxiety-related behaviors showing common variance due to genetic and shared environmental influences and specific genetic and nonshared environmental influences on each subtype (Hallett, Ronald, Rijsdijk, & Eley, 2009). These findings were replicated in a study examining 378 pairs of Italian twin children (Ogliari et al., 2010). Specifically, genetic and nonshared environmental influences explained the covariation among generalized anxiety, panic, social phobia, and separation anxiety.

The strong genetic overlap between anxiety and depression in adulthood (Chapter 14) suggests that depressive symptoms might also be profitably studied in childhood (Thapar & Rice, 2006). Two twin studies found differences pre- and post-adolescence in the etiology of the association between anxiety and depression, with common genetic influences for anxiety and depression symptoms present in postadolescence but not preadolescence (Silberg, Rutter, & Eaves, 2001; Waszczuk, Zavos, Gregory, & Eley, 2014). Several studies have examined genetic and environmental influences on depressive symptoms and on the covariation among depressive and anxiety symptoms during childhood and adolescence (e.g., Brendgen et al., 2009; Franić, Dolan, Borsboom, van Beijsterveldt, & Boomsma, 2014b; Lamb et al., 2010). Many studies have found evidence for substantial genetic influences on internalizing behavior—a construct that includes both depression and anxiety symptoms—and that stability in internalizing behavior from childhood through adolescence and adulthood can be explained primarily by genetic influences (e.g., Nivard et al., 2015; O'Connor, Neiderhiser, Reiss, Hetherington, & Plomin, 1998). A review of this work indicates that genes substantially influence stability in both anxiety and depression from age 7 to 12, but not from age 3 to 7, and that the high degree of comorbidity between these disorders is due largely to genetic influences (Franić, Middeldorp, Dolan, Ligthart, & Boomsma, 2010).

OTHER DISORDERS

Although schizophrenia and bipolar disorder do not generally appear until early adulthood, genetic research on possible childhood forms of these disorders has been motivated by the principle that more severe forms of disorders are likely to have an earlier onset (Nicolson & Rapoport, 1999). In relation to childhood-onset schizophrenia, relatives of affected individuals are at increased risk of schizophrenia, suggesting a link between the child and adult forms of the disorder (Nicolson et al., 2003). The only twin study of childhood schizophrenia yielded high heritability, although the sample size was small (Kallmann & Roth, 1956). More recent work has examined child and adolescent deficits in social adjustment and schizotypal personality as precursors of the development of schizophrenia using a twin-family design, finding that schizophrenia was associated with these deficits for primarily genetic reasons (Picchioni et al., 2010). Psychotic experiences (i.e., paranoia, hallucinations, cognitive disorganization) usually precede the onset of psychosis and have been shown to be moderately heritable with some shared environmental influence in a large adolescent twin sample, suggesting that early manifestations of schizophrenia can be detected (Zavos et al., 2014). Interesting results concerning links with adult schizophrenia are emerging from molecular genetic research incorporating brain endophenotypes (Addington et al., 2005; Gornick et al., 2005; Mullin et al., 2015).

Childhood bipolar disorder appears to be more likely in families with adult bipolar disorder (Pavuluri, Birmaher, & Naylor, 2005). Linkage, candidate gene, and GWA studies of childhood bipolar disorder have been reported, but no consistent results have emerged (Althoff, Faraone, Rettew, Morley, & Hudziak, 2005; Doyle et al., 2010; McGough et al., 2008; Nurnberger et al., 2014). When genes are identified that are responsible for the high heritabilities of adult schizophrenia and bipolar disorder, one of the next research questions will be whether these genes are also associated with juvenile forms of these disorders. A recent report used polygenic scores derived from adult GWA studies of schizophrenia and bipolar disorder but found no associations with a broad range of behavioral problems in adolescents (Krapohl et al., 2015).

Other childhood disorders for which some genetic data are available include enuresis (bedwetting) and tics. Enuresis in children after age 4 is common, about 7 percent for boys and 3 percent for girls. An early family study found substantial familial resemblance (Hallgren, 1957). Strong genetic influence was found in three small twin studies (Bakwin, 1971; Hallgren, 1957; McGuffin, Owen, O'Donovan, Thapar, & Gottesman, 1994). A large study of adult twins reporting retrospectively on enuresis in childhood yielded substantial heritability (about 70 percent) for both males and females (Hublin, Kaprio, Partinen, & Koskenvuo, 1998). However, an equally large study of 3-year-old twins found only moderate genetic influence on nocturnal bladder control as reported by parents for boys (about 30 percent) and an even smaller effect in girls (about 10 percent) (Butler, Galsworthy, Rijsdijk, & Plomin, 2001). A large epidemiological family study found that risk for severe childhood nocturnal enuresis was greater when mothers or fathers experienced nocturnal enuresis, and urinary incontinence was nearly 10 times higher in children when fathers were incontinent (with a lower risk from mothers of only about 3 times higher), indicating a strong familial influence (von Gontard, Heron, & Joinson, 2011). Candidate gene studies have not yielded replicable results (von Gontard, Schaumburg, Hollmann, Eiberg, & Rittig, 2001), although a meta-analysis suggests a role for the *ADRB3* gene in women (Cartwright et al., 2015).

Tic disorders involve involuntary twitching of certain muscles, especially of the face, that typically begins in childhood. A twin study indicated that heritability of tics in children and adolescents was modest (about 30 percent) (Ooki, 2005). The same study showed that stuttering was highly heritable (about 80 percent) but that tics and stuttering are genetically different. Genetic research has focused on the most severe form, called *Tourette disorder*. Tourette disorder is rare (about 0.4 percent), whereas simple tics are much more common. Although family studies show little familial resemblance for simple tics, relatives of probands with chronic, severe tics characteristic of Tourette disorder are at increased risk for tics of all kinds (Pauls, 1990), for OCD (Pauls, Towbin, Leckman, Zahner, & Cohen, 1986), and for ADHD (Pauls, Leckman, & Cohen, 1993). A twin study of Tourette disorder found concordances of 53 percent for identical twins and 8 percent for fraternal twins (Price, Kidd, Cohen, Pauls, & Leckman, 1985). A family study of Tourette disorder patients from the United States and the Netherlands estimated moderate heritability for tics and different levels of heritability based on the types of tics (de Haan, Delucchi, Mathews, & Cath, 2015). Molecular genetic studies have so far not yielded replicable results. Linkage studies of large family pedigrees have been reported (e.g., Verkerk et al., 2006), but no clear major-gene linkages have been detected. The largest genomewide QTL linkage study of Tourette disorder suggested linkage on chromosome 2*p* (The Tourette Syndrome Association International Consortium for Genetics, 2007). Although there have been many candidate gene studies of tic disorders, the candidate gene approach has not led to replicable associations.

OVERVIEW OF TWIN STUDIES OF CHILDHOOD DISORDERS

Genetic research on childhood disorders has increased dramatically, in part fueled by the finding of high heritabilities for ASD and ADHD. A general summary of twin results for the major domains of childhood psychopathology is presented in Figure 15.2. In addition to the high heritabilities of ASD and its components and of ADHD and its components, heritability is also exceptionally high for aggressive conduct disorder, obsessive-compulsive symptoms, and shyness. Just as interesting, however, are the moderate heritabilities for nonaggressive conduct disorder, generalized anxiety, fears, and separation anxiety. Especially noteworthy is the evidence for shared environmental influence for nonaggressive conduct disorder and separation anxiety. Nearly all of these results in childhood are based on parent or teacher reports of children's behavior. Twin studies of psychopathology in adolescence using

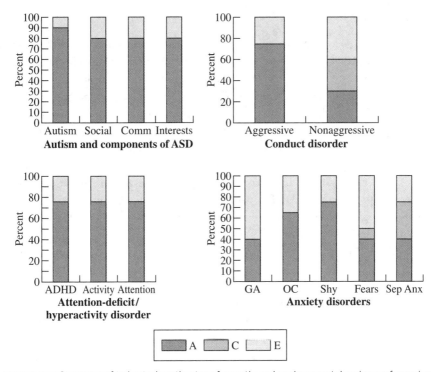

FIGURE 15.2 Summary of twin study estimates of genetic and environmental variances for major domains of childhood psychopathology. The components of autism spectrum disorder (ASD) are social relationships, communication deficits, and restricted interests. The five aspects of anxiety disorders are generalized anxiety (GA), obsessive-compulsive behaviors (OC), shyness/inhibition (Shy), fears, and separation anxiety (Sep Anx). A = additive genetic variance; C = common (shared) environmental variance; E = nonshared environmental variance.

interviews and self-reports with the twins themselves yielded quite different results (Ehringer, Rhee, Young, Corley, & Hewitt, 2006; Lewis, Haworth & Plomin, 2014).

SNP-BASED HERITABILITY FINDINGS FOR CHILDHOOD DISORDERS

To date, relatively few studies of child and adolescent psychopathology have met the requirements for estimating SNP heritability (see Box 7.1). Nonetheless, a few studies have reported SNP heritability estimates for ASD, ADHD, and oppositional defiant disorder symptoms (Cross-Disorder Group of the Psychiatric Genomics Consortium, 2013a; Pappa et al., 2015; Yang et al., 2013). SNP heritability was estimated as 0.17 for ASD, 0.28 to 0.45 for ADHD, and 0.20 for oppositional defiant disorder symptoms. These estimates are lower than those reported by twin studies, especially for ASD and ADHD, although when both common and rare variants were included (Yang et al., 2013) the estimates were higher.

Summary

Two decades ago, autism was thought to be an environmental disorder. Now, twin studies suggest that it is one of the most heritable disorders. Although the results of linkage studies and candidate gene studies have not as yet been successful, there is accumulating evidence that rare variants (e.g., CNVs) play an important role. This lack of success in finding common variants might be due in part to the possibility that the components of the autistic triad—abnormalities in social relationships, communication deficits, and restricted interests—are different genetically, even though each is highly heritable.

Attention-deficit and disruptive behavior disorders include attention-deficit/hyperactivity disorder (ADHD), which is highly heritable and shows no shared environmental influence. Multivariate genetic research suggests that its components of activity and attention overlap genetically, providing support for the construct of ADHD. Candidate gene studies of ADHD have yielded two dopamine receptor genes that show small but significant associations.

Genetic research suggests that conduct disorder is heterogeneous, with aggressive conduct disorder showing substantial genetic influence and no shared environmental influence, in contrast to nonaggressive conduct disorder, which shows only modest genetic influence and moderate shared environmental influence.

Twin studies of parental ratings of anxiety in childhood suggest an interestingly diverse pattern of results. The highest heritability emerges for shyness, which is one of the most highly heritable personality traits (Chapter 16). Heritability is also very high for obsessive-compulsive symptoms, although results in adulthood are more mixed (Chapter 16). Heritability is more modest for generalized anxiety, which is comparable to results in adulthood (Chapter 14). These three aspects of anxiety show no evidence for shared environmental influence, which is similar to results for adult psychopathology but is even more surprising in childhood because children are living with their families. In contrast, fears and especially separation anxiety are notable for evidence of shared environmental influence.

Some genetic influence has also been reported for childhood schizophrenia, childhood bipolar disorder, enuresis, and chronic tics, although much less genetic research has targeted these disorders.

CHAPTER **SIXTEEN**

Personality and Personality Disorders

I f you were asked what someone is like, you would probably describe various personality traits, especially those depicting extremes of behavior. "Jennifer is full of energy, very sociable, and unflappable." "Steve is conscientious, quiet, but quick tempered." Genetic researchers have been drawn to the study of personality because, within psychology, personality has always been the major domain for studying the normal range of individual differences, with the abnormal range being the provenance of psychopathology. A general rule emerging from behavioral genetic research is that common disorders are the quantitative extreme of the same genetic and environmental factors that contribute to the normal range of variation. In other words, some psychopathology may be the extreme of normal variation in personality. We will return to the links between personality and psychopathology later in this chapter, after we have described basic research on personality.

Personality traits are relatively enduring individual differences in behavior that are stable across time and across situations (John, Robins, & Pervin, 2008). In the 1970s, there was an academic debate about whether personality exists, a debate reminiscent of the nature-nurture debate. Some psychologists argued that behavior is more a matter of the situation than of the person, but it is now generally accepted that both are important and can interact (Kenrick & Funder, 1988; Rowe, 1987). Cognitive abilities (Chapters 11 and 12) also fit the definition of enduring individual differences, but they are usually considered separately from personality. Another definitional issue concerns *temperament*, personality traits that emerge early in life and, according to some researchers (e.g., Buss & Plomin, 1984), may be more heritable. However, there are many different definitions of temperament (Goldsmith et al., 1987), and the supposed distinction between temperament and personality will not be emphasized here.

Genetic research on personality is extensive and is described in several books (Benjamin, Ebstein, & Belmaker, 2002; Cattell, 1982; Eaves, Eysenck, & Martin, 1989;

Loehlin, 1992; Loehlin & Nichols, 1976; Wright, 1998) and dozens of reviews (e.g., Turkheimer, Pettersson & Horn, 2014). We will provide only an overview of this huge literature because its basic message is quite simple: Genes make a major contribution to individual differences in personality whereas shared environment does not; environmental influence on personality is almost entirely of the nonshared variety.

SELF-REPORT QUESTIONNAIRES

The vast majority of genetic research on personality involves self-report questionnaires administered to adolescents and adults. Such questionnaires include a range of dozens to hundreds of items, such as "I am usually shy when meeting people I don't know well" or "I am easily angered." People's responses to these questionnaires are remarkably stable, even over several decades (Costa & McCrae, 1994).

Forty years ago, a landmark study involving 750 pairs of adolescent twins and dozens of personality traits reached two major conclusions that have stood the test of time (Loehlin & Nichols, 1976). First, nearly all personality traits show moderate heritability. This conclusion might seem surprising because you would expect some traits to be highly heritable and other traits not to be heritable at all. Second, although environmental variance is also important, virtually all the environmental variance makes children growing up in the same family no more similar than children in different families. This category of environmental effects is called *nonshared environment*. The second conclusion is also surprising because theories of personality from Freud onward assumed that parenting played a critical shared environmental role in personality development. This important finding is discussed in Chapter 7.

Genetic research on personality has focused on five broad dimensions of personality, called the *Five-Factor Model (FFM)*, that encompass many aspects of personality (Goldberg, 1990). The best-studied of these are extraversion and neuroticism. *Extraversion* includes sociability, impulsiveness, and liveliness. *Neuroticism* (emotional instability) involves moodiness, anxiousness, and irritability. These two traits plus the three others included in the FFM create the acronym OCEAN: *openness* to experience (culture), *conscientiousness* (conformity, will to achieve), extraversion, *agreeableness* (likability, friendliness), and neuroticism.

Genetic results for extraversion and neuroticism are summarized in Table 16.1 (Loehlin, 1992). In five large twin studies in five different countries, with a total sample size of 24,000 pairs of twins, results indicate moderate genetic influence. Correlations are about 0.50 for identical twins and about 0.20 for fraternal twins. Studies of twins reared apart also indicate genetic influence, as do adoption studies of extraversion. Adoption results point to less genetic influence than do the twin studies. Heritability was estimated as 40 percent across all personality traits in two large-scale meta-analyses (Polderman et al., 2015; Vukasovic & Bratko, 2015). The latter meta-analysis also confirmed the finding suggested in Table 16.1 that twin studies yield higher heritability estimates (47 percent) as compared to family and adoption studies (22 percent).

TABLE 16.1

Twin, Family, and Adoption Results for Extraversion and Neuroticism

Type of Relative	Correlation	
	Extraversion	Neuroticism
Identical twins reared together	0.51	0.46
Fraternal twins reared together	0.18	0.20
Identical twins reared apart	0.38	0.38
Fraternal twins reared apart	0.05	0.23
Nonadoptive parents and offspring	0.16	0.13
Adoptive parents and offspring	0.01	0.05
Nonadoptive siblings	0.20	0.09
Adoptive siblings	-0.07	0.11

SOURCE: *Loehlin (1992)*.

Lower heritability in adoption than in twin studies could be due to nonadditive genetic variance, which makes identical twins more than twice as similar as fraternal twins and other first-degree relatives (Eaves et al., 1999b; Eaves, Heath, Neale, Hewitt, & Martin, 1998; Keller, Coventry, Heath, & Martin, 2005; Loehlin, Neiderhiser, & Reiss, 2003; Plomin, Corley, Caspi, Fulker, & DeFries, 1998). It could also be due to a special environmental effect that boosts identical twin similarity, which implies that twin study estimates of heritability might be inflated (Plomin & Caspi, 1999).

The fact that the heritability estimates are much less than 100 percent implies that environmental factors are important, but, as mentioned earlier, this environmental influence is almost entirely due to nonshared environmental effects. As discussed in Chapter 7, the message is not that family experiences are unimportant but rather that the relevant experiences are specific to each child in the family. This finding was ignored when it was first noted (Loehlin & Nichols, 1976) and controversial when it was first highlighted (Plomin & Daniels, 1987), but it is now widely accepted because it has consistently replicated (Plomin, 2011; Turkheimer et al., 2014). The acceptance is so complete that the focus now is on finding *any* shared environmental influence for personality. For example, it has been suggested that shared environmental influence may be more important at the extremes of personality (Pergadia et al., 2006b). It has also been suggested that adoption data find more evidence of shared environmental influence (Matteson, McGue, & Iacono, 2013), although the results in Table 16.1 provide little support for this hypothesis because the average correlations are 0.03 between adoptive parents and their adopted children and 0.02 between adoptive siblings.

Heritabilities in the 30 to 50 percent range are typical of personality results (Figure 16.1), although much less genetic research has been done on the other three traits of the FFM. Also, openness to experience, conscientiousness, and agreeableness

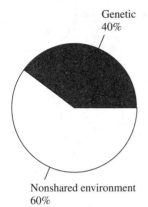

Genetic
40%

Nonshared environment
60%

FIGURE 16.1 Genetic results for personality traits assessed by self-report questionnaires are remarkably similar, suggesting that 30 to 50 percent of the variance is due to genetic factors. Environmental variance is also important, but hardly any environmental variance is due to shared environmental influence.

have been measured differently in different studies because, until recently, no standard measures were available. A model-fitting summary of family, twin, and adoption data for scales of personality thought to be related to these three traits yielded heritability estimates of 45 percent for openness to experience, 38 percent for conscientiousness, and 35 percent for agreeableness, with no evidence of shared environmental influence (Loehlin, 1992). The first genetic study to use a measure specifically designed to assess the FFM factors found similar estimates in an analysis of twins reared together and twins reared apart, except that agreeableness showed lower heritability (12 percent) (Bergeman et al., 1993). Other twin studies yielded heritabilities of about 40 percent for all of the FFM factors including agreeableness (Franić, Borsboom, Dolan, & Boomsma, 2014; Jang, Livesley, & Vernon, 1996). There has been recent interest in the FFM dimension of conscientiousness, which has been popularized in education as "grit." Grit, which predicts academic achievement, is thought to be more malleable than other predictors such as intelligence; training grit has been set as a priority by the U.S. and U.K. education departments (Duckworth & Gross, 2014). However, a recent twin study shows that grit is the same trait genetically as conscientiousness and yields the same results as other personality traits: moderate genetic influence and no shared environmental influence (Rimfeld, Kovas, Dale, & Plomin, 2016).

Do these broad FFM factors represent the best level of analysis for genetic research? Multivariate genetic research supports the FFM structure in that the genetic structure is similar to the phenotypic structure (Turkheimer et al., 2014). Nonetheless, subtraits within each FFM factor show significant unique genetic variance not shared with other traits in the factor, suggesting that there is more to personality than the FFM factors (Franić et al., 2014a; Jang et al., 2006; Jang, McCrae, Angleitner, Riemann, & Livesley, 1998; Loehlin, 1992). For example, extraversion includes diverse traits such as sociability, impulsiveness, and liveliness, as well as activity, dominance, and sensation seeking. Each of these traits has received some attention in genetic research but not nearly as much as the more global traits of extraversion and neuroticism.

Several theories of personality development have been proposed about other ways in which personality should be sliced, and similar results have been found for the different traits highlighted in these theories (Kohnstamm, Bates, & Rothbart, 1989). For example, a neurobiologically oriented theory organizes personality into four different domains: novelty seeking, harm avoidance, reward dependence, and persistence (Cloninger, 1987). Similar twin study results have been found for these dimensions (Heiman, Stallings, Young, & Hewitt, 2004; Stallings, Hewitt, Cloninger, Heath, & Eaves, 1996). A study that combined multiple personality scales from different measures using latent factors found three dimensions that showed heritabilities of about 50 to 65 percent and no evidence of shared environmental influences (Ganiban et al., 2009a). The heritabilities are somewhat higher than usual for personality because they are estimated from reliable variance from latent personality constructs rather than from estimates of total variance.

One of the most surprising findings from genetic research on personality questionnaires is that all traits show moderate genetic influence (usually about 40 percent heritability) and little influence of shared environment. It is also surprising that studies have not found any personality traits assessed by self-report questionnaire that consistently show low or no heritability in twin studies. Moreover, there is no evidence that any traits are consistently more heritable than any others (Turkheimer et al., 2014). This is in contrast to childhood psychopathology (Chapter 15), where some disorders are more heritable than others and some disorders yield more shared environmental influence than others.

The conclusion that heritability is modest for all personality traits is supported by SNP-based heritability estimates of self-report questionnaires of personality, which are about 10 percent (Genetics of Personality Consortium et al., 2015; Rietveld et al., 2013a; Verweij et al., 2012; Vinkhuyzen et al., 2012a), including an analysis of the FFM factors (Power & Pluess, 2015). As mentioned in previous chapters, SNP heritability estimates are usually about half the twin heritability, but for personality, the SNP heritability estimates are only about one-quarter the twin estimates. This extra-wide gap between SNP heritability and twin heritability for personality could be due to nonadditive genetic variance or inflated twin estimates, as discussed earlier.

OTHER MEASURES OF PERSONALITY

All of the research described in the previous section relied on self-report questionnaires. Are the ubiquitous results showing moderate heritability and little shared environment somehow due to the use of self-report questionnaires? A new direction for research on personality is to incorporate multiple methods of assessment (Saudino & Micalizzi, 2015). A study of more than 1000 adult twin pairs in Germany and Poland compared results from self-report questionnaires and from ratings by peers for measures of the FFM personality factors (Riemann, Angleitner, & Strelau, 1997). Each twin's personality was rated by two different peers. The average correlation between the two peer ratings was 0.61, a result indicating substantial agreement concerning each twin's personality. The averaged peer ratings correlated 0.55 with the twins' self-report ratings, a result indicating moderate validity of self-report ratings. Figure 16.2 shows the results of twin analyses for self-report data and peer ratings averaged across two peers. The results for self-report ratings are similar to those in other studies. The exciting result is that peer ratings also show significant genetic influence, although somewhat less than self-report ratings. For two of the five traits (extraversion and agreeableness), peer ratings suggest greater influence of shared environment than do self-report ratings, although these differences are not statistically significant. Importantly, multivariate genetic analysis indicates that the same genetic factors are largely involved in self-report and peer ratings, a result providing strong evidence for the genetic validity of self-report ratings. An earlier study used twin reports about each other, and it also found similar evidence for genetic influence on personality traits, whether assessed by self-report or by the co-twin (Heath, Neale, Kessler, Eaves, & Kendler, 1992).

Genetic researchers interested in personality in childhood were forced to use measures other than self-report questionnaires. For the past 30 years, this research has relied primarily on ratings by parents, but twin studies using parent ratings have yielded odd results. Correlations for identical twins are high and correlations for fraternal twins are very low, sometimes even negative. It is likely that these results are due to contrast effects, which result when parents of fraternal twins contrast the twins (Plomin, Chipuer, & Loehlin, 1990). For example, parents might report that one twin is the active twin and the other is the inactive twin, even though, relative to other children that age, the twins are not really very different from each other (Carey, 1986; Eaves, 1976; Neale & Stevenson, 1989).

In contrast to parent ratings in twin studies, which yield inflated estimates of heritability, adoption studies using parent ratings in childhood find little evidence

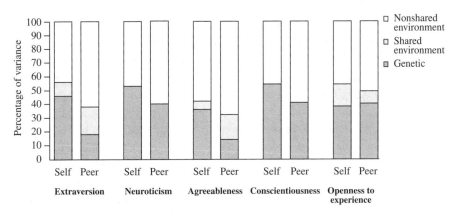

FIGURE 16.2 Genetic (dark blue), shared environment (light blue), and nonshared environment (white) components of variance for self-report ratings and peer ratings for the FFM personality traits. Components of variance were calculated from identical twin (660 pairs) and same-sex fraternal twin (200 pairs) correlations presented by Riemann and colleagues (1997). (Data from Plomin & Caspi, 1999.)

for genetic influence (Loehlin, Willerman, & Horn, 1982; Plomin, Coon, Carey, DeFries, & Fulker, 1991; Scarr & Weinberg, 1981; Schmitz, 1994). A combined twin study and stepfamily study of parent ratings of adolescents found significantly greater heritability estimates for twins than for nontwins and confirmed that parent ratings are subject to contrast effects (Saudino, McGuire, Reiss, Hetherington, & Plomin, 1995). As mentioned in relation to self-report questionnaires, such findings might also be due to nonadditive genetic variance. However, the weight of evidence indicates that genetic results for parent ratings of personality are due in part to contrast effects (Mullineaux, Deater-Deckard, Petrill, Thompson, & DeThorne, 2009; Saudino, Wertz, Gagne, & Chawla, 2004).

Other measures of children's personality, such as behavioral ratings by observers, show more reasonable patterns of results in both twin and adoption studies (Braungart, Plomin, DeFries, & Fulker, 1992; Cherny et al., 1994; Goldsmith & Campos, 1986; Lemery-Chalfant, Doelger, & Goldsmith, 2008; Matheny, 1980; Plomin et al., 1993; Plomin & Foch, 1980; Plomin, Foch, & Rowe, 1981; Saudino, 2012; Saudino, Plomin, & DeFries, 1996; Wilson & Matheny, 1986). For example, genetic influence has been found in observational studies of young twins for a dimension of fearfulness called *behavioral inhibition* (Matheny, 1989; Robinson, Kagan, Reznick, & Corley, 1992), for shyness (Cherny et al., 1994; Eggum-Wilkens, Lemery-Chalfant, Aksan, & Goldsmith, 2015), for effortful control during middle childhood (Lemery-Chalfant et al., 2008), and for activity level measured by actometers that record movement (Saudino, 2012; Saudino & Eaton, 1991). Because evidence for genetic influence is so widespread, even for observational measures, it is interesting that observer ratings of personality in the first few days of life have found no evidence for genetic influence (Riese, 1990) and that individual differences in smiling in infancy also show no genetic influence (Plomin, 1987).

OTHER FINDINGS

Genetic research on personality will be accelerated by research showing the association between personality and psychopathology and by molecular genetic studies of personality. Both of these trends will be discussed later in this chapter. As just described, another example of new directions for personality research is increasing interest in measures other than self-report questionnaires.

In this section, we highlight three examples of new directions for personality research that go beyond the typical personality result, that is, heritabilities of about 40 percent and little shared environmental influence. These examples are research on personality in different situations, studies of developmental change and continuity, and the role of personality in the interplay between nature and nurture. Two other relatively new areas of genetic research—well-being and self-esteem—deserve a mention even though they yield the typical result. Although well-being has only recently become a focus for genetic research (Pluess, 2015), a meta-analysis of well-being as well as happiness and life satisfaction based on 10 studies including 56,000 individuals yielded a heritability estimate of 36 percent and no evidence of shared environmental influence (Bartels, 2015). (Well-being is also discussed in Chapter 18 in relation to health psychology.) Self-esteem, also referred to as a sense of self-worth, is interesting because it was thought to be an aspect of personality due solely to family environment and immune from genetic influence (Harter, 1983). However, twin and adoption studies yield the typical personality result, with heritabilities of about 40 percent but no influence of shared environment in childhood (Neiderhiser & McGuire, 1994; Van Ryzin et al., 2015), adolescence (Kamakura, Ando, & Ono, 2007; McGuire, Neiderhiser, Reiss, Hetherington, & Plomin, 1994; Neiss, Stevenson, Legrand, Iacono, & Sedikides, 2009), and adulthood (Roy, Neale, & Kendler, 1995; Svedberg et al., 2014).

Situations

It is interesting, in relation to the person-situation debate mentioned earlier, that some evidence suggests that genetic factors are involved in situational change as well as in stability of personality across situations (Phillips & Matheny, 1997). For example, in one study, observers rated the adaptability of infant twins in two laboratory settings: unstructured free play and test taking (Matheny & Dolan, 1975). Adaptability differed to some extent across these situations, but identical twins changed in more similar ways than fraternal twins did, an observation implying that genetics contributes to change as well as to continuity across situations for this personality trait. Similar results were found in a more recent study of person-situation interaction (Borkenau, Riemann, Spinath, & Angleitner, 2006). A twin study using a questionnaire to assess personality in different situations also found that genetic factors contribute to personality changes across situations (Dworkin, 1979). Even patterns of responding across items of personality questionnaires show genetic influence (Eaves & Eysenck, 1976; Hershberger, Plomin, & Pedersen, 1995).

Development

Does heritability change during development? Unlike general cognitive ability, which shows increases in heritability throughout the life span (Chapter 11), it is more difficult to draw general conclusions concerning personality development, in part because there are so many personality traits. In general, heritability appears to increase during infancy (Goldsmith, 1983; Loehlin, 1992), starting with zero heritability for personality during the first days of life (Riese, 1990). Of course, what is assessed as personality during the first few days of life is quite different from what is assessed later in development, and the sources of individual differences might also be quite different in neonates. In childhood, parent ratings are often used which, as indicated earlier, overestimate genetic influence. Throughout the rest of the life span using self-ratings, meta-analyses indicate that heritability does not change (Briley & Tucker-Drob, 2014; Polderman et al., 2015; Turkheimer et al., 2014).

A second important question about development concerns the genetic contribution to either continuity or change from age to age. For cognitive ability, genetic factors largely contribute to stability from age to age rather than to change, although some evidence can be found, especially in childhood, for genetically influenced change (Chapter 11). Although less well-studied than cognitive ability, developmental findings for personality appear to be similar. The first report of a longitudinal genetic analysis over an age span of a decade in adulthood concluded that 80 percent of the phenotypic stability of personality was mediated genetically (McGue et al., 1993a), which has been confirmed in recent meta-analyses throughout the life span (Briley & Tucker-Drob, 2014; Turkheimer et al., 2014).

Nature-Nurture Interplay

Another new direction for genetic research on personality involves the role of personality in explaining a fascinating finding discussed in Chapter 8: Environmental measures widely used in psychological research show genetic influence. Genetic research consistently shows that family environment, peer groups, social support, and life events often show as much genetic influence as measures of personality. Personality is a good candidate to explain some of this genetic influence because personality can affect how people select, modify, construct, or perceive their environments. For example, genetic influence on personality in adulthood has been reported to contribute to genetic influence on parenting in three studies (Chipuer & Plomin, 1992; Losoya, Callor, Rowe, & Goldsmith, 1997; McAdams, Gregory & Eley, 2013), although not in another (Vernon, Jang, Harris, & McCarthy, 1997).

Genetic influence on perceptions of life events can be entirely accounted for by the FFM personality factors (Saudino et al., 1997). These findings are not limited to self-report questionnaires. For example, genetic influence found on an observational measure of home environments can be explained entirely by genetic influence on a tester-rated measure of attention called *task orientation* (Saudino & Plomin, 1997).

PERSONALITY AND SOCIAL PSYCHOLOGY

Social psychology focuses on the behavior of groups, whereas individual differences are in the spotlight for personality research. For this reason, there is not nearly as much genetic research relevant to social psychology as there is for personality. However, some areas of social psychology border on personality, and genetic research has begun at these borders. Three examples are relationships, attitudes, and behavioral economics.

Relationships

Genetic research has addressed parent-offspring relationships, romantic relationships, and sexual orientation. As discussed in Chapter 8, relationships between parents and offspring, especially their warmth (such as affection and support), consistently show genetic influence. Dozens of twin and adoption studies have found similar results that point to substantial genetic influences in most aspects of relationships, not just between parents and offspring but also between siblings, peers, friends, and spouses (Horwitz & Neiderhiser, 2015; Plomin, 1994). A major area of developmental research on parent-offspring relationships involves attachment between infant and caregiver, as assessed in the so-called *Strange Situation,* a laboratory-based assessment in which mothers briefly leave their child with an experimenter and then return (Ainsworth, Blehar, Waters, & Wall, 1978). Sibling concordance of about 60 percent has been reported for attachment classification (van IJzendoorn et al., 2000; Ward, Vaughn, & Robb, 1988). The first systematic twin study of attachment using the Strange Situation found only modest genetic influence and substantial influence of shared environment (O'Connor & Croft, 2001). Three subsequent studies using the Strange Situation also found modest heritability and substantial shared environmental influence (Bokhorst et al., 2003; Fearon et al., 2006; Roisman & Fraley, 2006), although another twin study based on observations rather than the Strange Situation found evidence for greater genetic influence (Finkel, Wille, & Matheny, 1998). As described in Chapter 15, twin studies of separation anxiety disorder, which is related to attachment, also generally show modest heritability and substantial shared environmental influence. In summary, attachment seems to be an exception to the typical personality findings.

Like parent-offspring relationships, romantic relationships differ widely in various aspects, such as closeness and passion. The first genetic study of styles of romantic love is interesting because it showed no genetic influence (Waller & Shaver, 1994). The average twin correlations for six scales (for example, companionship and passion) were 0.26 for identical twins and 0.25 for fraternal twins, results implying some shared environmental influence but no genetic influence, which contrasts sharply with the typical results for personality. Similar results have been found for initial attraction in mate selection (Lykken & Tellegen, 1993). In other words, genetics may play no role in the type of romantic relationships we choose. Although more research is needed to pin down the role of genetics in initial attraction, research suggests that genetic factors are important when the *quality* of romantic relationships is considered. There are now a handful of studies that have examined self-report, partner report, and observational ratings of relationship quality in married and long-term cohabitating twins; these studies have yielded heritability estimates ranging from about 15 to 35 percent and no shared environmental influence (Spotts et al., 2004, 2006). There is also some evidence that personality accounts for nearly half of the genetic variance in relationship quality (Spotts et al., 2005). Therefore, although genetic factors may not influence the type of romantic relationships we choose, they may affect our satisfaction with those relationships.

For sexual orientation, results are not yet clear. An early twin study of male homosexuality reported remarkable concordance rates of 100 percent for identical twins and 15 percent for fraternal twins (Kallmann, 1952). However, a later twin study found less extreme concordances of 52 and 22 percent, respectively, and a concordance of 22 percent for genetically unrelated adoptive brothers (Bailey & Pillard, 1991); other twin studies found even less genetic influence and more influence of shared environment (Bailey, Dunne, & Martin, 2000; Kendler, Thornton, Gilman, & Kessler, 2000). A small twin study of lesbians also yielded evidence for moderate genetic influence (Bailey, Pillard, Neale, & Agyei, 1993). A population-based study of nearly 4000 Swedish twins found heritabilities ranging from 34 to 39 percent and no shared environmental influences for the total number of same-sex partners for men and much lower heritability, of around 20 percent, and modest shared environmental influence (~15 percent) for women (Langstrom, Rahman, Carlstrom, & Lichtenstein, 2010). This area of research received considerable attention because of reports of linkage between homosexuality and a region at the tip of the long arm of the X chromosome (*Xq28;* Hamer, Hu, Magnuson, Hu, & Pattatucci, 1993; Hu et al., 1995). The X chromosome was targeted because it was thought that male homosexuality is more likely to be transmitted from the mother's side of the family, but later studies did not find an excess of maternal transmission (Bailey et al., 1999). The X linkage was not replicated in a subsequent study (Rice, Anderson, Risch, & Ebers, 1999), although a recent follow-up provides some support for X linkage (Sanders et al., 2015). No genomewide association studies have as yet been reported. When genetic research touches on especially sensitive issues such as sexual orientation, it is important to keep in mind earlier discussions (see Chapter 7) about what it does and does not mean to show genetic influence (Bailey et al., 2016; Pillard & Bailey, 1998).

Attitudes and Political Behavior

Social scientists have long been interested in the impact of group processes on change and continuity in attitudes and beliefs. Although it is recognized that social factors are not solely responsible for attitudes, it has been a surprise to find that genetics makes a major contribution to individual differences in attitudes. A core dimension of attitudes is *traditionalism,* which involves conservative versus liberal views on a wide range of issues. A measure of this attitudinal dimension was included in an adoption study of personality as a control variable because it was not expected to be heritable (Scarr & Weinberg, 1981). However, the results indicated that this measure was as heritable as the personality measures but also showed shared environmental influence. A recent meta-analysis of 12,000 twin pairs from nine studies in five countries confirmed these results for various aspects of political ideology, with heritability estimates of about 40 percent and shared environment estimates of about 20 percent (Hatemi et al., 2014). Genetic influence on political attitudes correlates with genetic influence on traditional personality traits but longitudinal analyses suggest that personality traits are not causal (Hatemi & Verhulst, 2015).

Genetic research extends beyond political attitudes to political behaviors (Fowler & Schreiber, 2008; Hatemi & McDermot, 2011). For example, one study in a large American twin sample found that political party identification was due mostly to shared environmental influences, while the intensity of party identification was equally split between genetic and nonshared environmental influences (Hatemi, Alford, Hibbing, Martin, & Eaves, 2009). Other studies have reported that political participation is heritable (Baker, Barton, Lozano, Raine, & Fowler, 2006; Fowler, Baker, & Dawes, 2008).

Religious attitudes have also been the focus of genetic research, as seen in a special issue of the journal *Twin Research* (Eaves, D'Onofrio, & Russell, 1999). Research suggests that the heritability of religiousness increases and shared environmental influence decreases from adolescence to adulthood (Kandler & Riemann, 2013; Koenig, McGue, Krueger, & Bouchard, 2005).

Sometimes these results are held up for ridicule: How can attitudes about politics or religion be heritable? We hope that by now you can answer this question (see Chapter 8), but it has been put particularly well in the context of social attitudes:

> We may view this as a kind of cafeteria model of the acquisition of social attitudes. The individual does not inherit his ideas about fluoridation, royalty, women judges, and nudist camps; he learns them from his culture. But his genes may influence which ones he elects to put on his tray. Different cultural institutions—family, church, school, books, television—like different cafeterias, serve up somewhat different menus, and the choices a person makes will reflect those offered him as well as his own biases. (Loehlin, 1997, p. 48)

This theme of nature operating via nurture was discussed in Chapter 8.

Social psychology traditionally uses the experimental approach rather than investigating naturally occurring variation. There is a need to bring together these two research traditions. For example, Tesser (1993), a social psychologist, separated attitudes into those that were more heritable (such as attitudes about the death penalty) and those that were less heritable (such as attitudes about coeducation and the truth of the Bible). In standard social psychology experimental situations, the more heritable items were found to be less susceptible to social influence and more important in interpersonal attraction (Tesser, Whitaker, Martin, & Ward, 1998), a result replicated in a recent study (Schwab, 2014).

Behavioral Economics

Another area of genetic research related to personality is behavioral economics. For example, results obtained from twin and adoption studies of vocational interests are similar to those that have been reported for personality questionnaires (Betsworth et al., 1994; Roberts & Johansson, 1974; Scarr & Weinberg, 1978a). Evidence for genetic influence was also found in twin studies of work values (Keller, Bouchard, Segal, & Dawes, 1992) and job satisfaction (Arvey, Bouchard, Segal, & Abraham, 1989; Judge, Ilies & Zhang, 2012).

Recent genetic research in behavioral economics has also begun to focus on other behaviors central to economics, such as investor behavior (Barnea, Cronqvist, & Siegel, 2010), financial decision making (Cesarini, Johannesson, Lichtenstein, Sandewall, & Wallace, 2010; MacKillop, 2013), philanthropy (Cesarini, Dawes, Johannesson, Lichtenstein, & Wallace, 2009), self-employment and entrepreneurship (van der Loos et al., 2013), and economic risk-taking (Le, Miller, Slutske, &

Martin, 2010; Zhong et al., 2009; Zyphur, Narayanan, Arvey, & Alexander, 2009). The field is moving quickly toward molecular genetic research (Beauchamp et al., 2011; Koellinger et al., 2010). For example, SNP-based heritability estimates support twin research in finding significant genetic influence in behavioral economics (Benjamin et al., 2012).

PERSONALITY DISORDERS

To what extent is psychopathology the extreme manifestation of normal dimensions of personality? It has long been suggested that this is the case for some psychiatric disorders (e.g., Cloninger, 2002; Eysenck, 1952; Livesley, Jang, & Vernon, 1998). As noted earlier, an important general lesson from behavioral genetic research on psychopathology (Chapters 13–15) as well as cognitive disabilities (Chapter 12) is that common disorders are the quantitative extreme of the same genetic and environmental factors that contribute to the normal range of variation. With cognitive disabilities such as reading disability, it is easy to see what normal variation is— variation in reading ability is normally distributed, and reading disability is the low end of that distribution. However, what are the dimensions of normal variation in personality that are associated with depression or other types of psychopathology?

Chapter 14 ended with a multivariate genetic model that proposes two broad categories of psychopathology. The internalizing category includes depression and anxiety disorders, and the externalizing category includes antisocial behavior and drug abuse. One of the most important findings from genetic research on personality is the extent of genetic overlap between the internalizing category of psychopathology and the personality factor of neuroticism. As mentioned earlier, neuroticism does not mean *neurotic* in the sense of being nervous; neuroticism refers to a general dimension of emotional instability, which includes moodiness, anxiousness, and irritability. Twin studies found that genetic factors shared between neuroticism and internalizing disorders accounted for between one-third and one-half of the genetic risk (Hettema et al., 2006; Kendler & Gardner, 2011; Mackintosh, Gatz, Wetherell, & Pedersen, 2006). Another study reported genetic correlations of about 0.50 between neuroticism and major depression (Kendler et al., 2006a). Similar findings had emerged from earlier multivariate genetic studies (Eaves et al., 1989).

In summary, the internalizing category of psychopathology is similar genetically to the personality factor of neuroticism. What about the externalizing category of psychopathology? Although it would be wonderfully symmetrical if extraversion predicted externalizing psychopathology, this is not the case (Khan, Jacobson, Gardner, Prescott, & Kendler, 2005). However, several studies have shown that aspects of extraversion—especially novelty seeking, impulsivity, and disinhibition—predict externalizing psychopathology (Krueger, Caspi, Moffitt, Silva, & McGee, 1996). Two different twin studies have addressed the causes of overlap between disinhibitory dimensions of personality and externalizing psychopathology; both found that some of the overlap is genetic in origin, although most of the genetic influence on disinhibitory personality is independent of externalizing psychopathology (Krueger et al., 2002; Young et al., 2009). In contrast, a recent twin study found that FFM personality factors can explain all of the genetic influences on behavior problems in adolescence (Lewis et al., 2014).

All of this research suggests some genetic overlap between personality and psychopathology. Much genetic research on this topic has focused on an area of psychopathology called *personality disorders*. Unlike psychopathology, described in Chapters 13–15, personality disorders are personality traits that cause significant impairment or distress. People with personality disorders regard their disorder as part of who they are, their personality, rather than as a condition that can be treated. That is, they do not feel that they were once well and are now ill. Although the reliability, validity, and utility of diagnosing personality disorders have long been questioned, research has addressed the genetics of personality disorders and their links to normal personality and to other psychopathology (Jang, 2005; Nigg & Goldsmith, 1994; Torgersen, 2009). Increasingly, personality disorders are being considered as dimensions rather than categories, which will increase genetic research on their links with personality (Zachar & First, 2015).

DSM-5 recognizes ten personality disorders, but only three have been investigated systematically in genetic research: schizotypal, obsessive-compulsive, and antisocial personality disorders. A meta-analysis of twin studies with measures related to personality disorders of any kind yielded results similar to those for personality: heritability of about 40 percent and no shared environmental influence (Polderman et al., 2015).

Schizotypal Personality Disorder

Schizotypal personality disorder involves less intense schizophrenic-like symptoms and, like schizophrenia, clearly runs in families (Baron, Gruen, Asnis, & Lord, 1985; Siever et al., 1990). The results of a small twin study suggested genetic influence, yielding 33 percent concordance for identical twins and 4 percent for fraternal twins (Torgersen et al., 2000). Twin studies using dimensional measures of schizotypal symptoms in unselected samples of twins also found evidence for genetic influence, with heritability estimates ranging widely from about 20 to 80 percent (Claridge & Hewitt, 1987; Coolidge, Thede, & Jang, 2001; Kendler et al., 2008a; Kendler et al., 2006c; Torgersen, 2009).

Genetic research on schizotypal personality disorder focuses on its relationship to schizophrenia and has consistently found an excess of the disorder among first-degree relatives of schizophrenic probands. A summary of such studies found that the risks of schizotypal personality disorder are 11 percent for the first-degree relatives of schizophrenic probands and 2 percent for control families (Nigg & Goldsmith, 1994).

Adoption studies have played an important role in showing that the disorder is part of the genetic spectrum of schizophrenia. For example, in a Danish adoption study (see Chapter 13), the rate of schizophrenia was 5 percent in the biological first-degree relatives of schizophrenic adoptees but 0 percent in their adoptive relatives and relatives of control adoptees (Kety et al., 1994). When schizotypal personality disorder was included in the diagnosis, the rates rose to 24 and 3 percent, respectively, implying greater genetic influence for the spectrum of schizophrenia that includes schizotypal personality disorder (Kendler, Gruenberg, & Kinney, 1994). Twin studies also suggest that schizotypal personality disorder is genetically related to schizophrenia (Farmer et al., 1987), especially for the negative (anhedonia) rather than the positive (delusions) aspects of schizotypy (Torgersen et al., 2002). Studies using community samples of twins suggest that the negative and positive aspects of schizotypy differ genetically (Linney et al., 2003) and that schizotypy is genetically related to the schizophrenia spectrum (Jang, Woodward, Lang, Honer, & Livesley, 2005). Recent genetic research considers subclinical psychotic experiences more generally as a heritable personality trait that is normally distributed in the population (Zavos et al., 2014) and that predicts genetic liability for psychosis (Binbay et al., 2012), although some research disagrees (Zammit et al., 2014).

Obsessive-Compulsive Personality Disorder

Obsessive-compulsive personality disorder sounds as if it is a milder version of the obsessive-compulsive type of anxiety disorder (OCD, described in Chapter 14); family studies provide some empirical support for this. However, the diagnostic criteria for these two disorders are quite different. The compulsion of OCD is a single sequence of specific behaviors, whereas the personality disorder is more pervasive, involving a general preoccupation with trivial details that leads to difficulties in making decisions and getting anything accomplished. Only one small twin study of diagnosed obsessive-compulsive personality disorder has been reported, and it found substantial genetic influence (Torgersen et al., 2000). However, twin studies of obsessional symptoms in unselected samples of twins suggest modest heritability (Kendler et al., 2008a; Torgersen, 1980; Young, Fenton, & Lader, 1971). Family studies indicate that obsessional traits are more common (about 15 percent) in relatives of probands with obsessive-compulsive disorder than in controls (5 percent) (Rasmussen & Tsuang, 1984). Furthermore, results obtained from a recent twin study examining symptoms of obsessive-compulsive disorder and obsessive-compulsive personality traits suggest common genetic influences (Taylor, Asmundson, & Jang, 2011). This finding implies that obsessive-compulsive personality disorder might be part of the spectrum of the obsessive-compulsive type of anxiety disorder.

Antisocial Personality Disorder and Criminal Behavior

Much more genetic research has focused on antisocial personality disorder (ASPD) than on other personality disorders. ASPD includes such chronic behaviors as breaking the law, lying, and conning others for personal profit or pleasure but also includes more cognitive and personality-based criteria such as impulsivity, aggressiveness, disregard for safety of self and others, and lack of remorse for having hurt, mistreated, or stolen from others. Although ASPD shows early roots, the vast majority of juvenile delinquents and children with conduct disorders do not develop antisocial personality disorder (Robins, 1978). For this reason, there is a need to distinguish conduct disorder that is limited to adolescence from antisocial behavior that persists throughout the life span (Caspi & Moffitt, 1995; Kendler, Aggen, & Patrick, 2012; Moffitt, 1993). ASPD affects about 1 percent of females and 4 percent of males from 13 to 30 years of age (American Psychiatric Association, 2013; Kessler et al., 1994). The prevalence of the disorder is much higher in selected populations, such as prisons, where there is a preponderance of violent offenders, with 47 percent of male prisoners and 21 percent of female prisoners having ASPD (Fazel & Danesh, 2002). Similarly, the prevalence of ASPD is higher among patients in alcohol or other drug abuse treatment programs than in the general population, suggesting a link between ASPD and substance abuse and dependence (Moeller & Dougherty, 2001).

Family studies show that ASPD runs in families (Nigg & Goldsmith, 1994), and an adoption study found that familial resemblance is largely due to genetic rather than to shared environmental factors (Schulsinger, 1972). Although no twin studies of diagnosed ASPD are available, there are over 100 twin and adoption studies on antisocial behavior. A meta-analysis of 52 independent twin and adoption studies of antisocial behavior found evidence for significant shared environmental influences (16 percent) as well as significant genetic effects, including additive and nonadditive influences (41 percent), and nonshared environmental influences (43 percent) (Rhee & Waldman, 2002). More recent meta-analyses, though, suggest slightly higher heritabilities of 50 to 60 percent and similar magnitudes of shared environmental influences of about 15 percent (Burt, 2009a; Ferguson, 2010). However, both shared environmental influences and heritability were lower in parent-offspring studies than in twin and sibling studies, which could signal developmental changes between childhood (offspring) and adulthood (parents), in contrast to twins, who are exactly the same age. These meta-analyses agree that, while genetic influences are important to antisocial behavior in childhood through adulthood, the magnitude of familial effects (genetic and shared environmental influences) decreases somewhat with age and nonfamilial influences increase with age (Ferguson, 2010; Rhee & Waldman, 2002). Moreover, as is typically found in longitudinal genetic analyses, genetics and shared environment largely contribute to stability and nonshared environment contributes to change during development (Burt, McGue, & Iacono, 2010).

There have been questions about whether the criteria for ASPD reflect one disorder (or a single dimension) or whether ASPD is better represented by multiple dimensions that capture variation in this personality domain (Burt, 2009a). A recent multivariate twin study of ASPD symptoms suggests that two factors comprise ASPD: aggressive-disregard and disinhibition (Kendler et al., 2012a). Scores on the genetic aggressive-disregard factor are more strongly associated with risk for conduct disorder and early and heavy alcohol use; in contrast, scores on the genetic disinhibition factor are more strongly associated with novelty seeking and major depression

(Kendler et al., 2012a). Interestingly, both genetic factors predicted cannabis, cocaine, and alcohol dependence, which suggests two potential pathways that might explain the association between ASPD and substance use disorders, a topic we turn to shortly.

A type of antisocial personality disorder called *psychopathy* has recently become the target of genetic research because of its prediction of violent crime and recidivism (Viding & McCrory, 2012). Although there is no precise equivalent in DSM-5, psychopathic personality disorder involves a lack of empathy, callousness, irresponsibility, and manipulativeness (Hare, 1993; Viding, 2004). As discussed in Chapter 15, psychopathic tendencies appear to be highly heritable in childhood and adolescence, with no influence of shared environment. The overlap between psychopathic personality and antisocial behavior is largely genetic in origin (Larsson et al., 2007). Furthermore, psychopathic personality during adolescence predicts antisocial behavior in adults, and genetic factors contribute to this association (Forsman, Lichtenstein, Andershed, & Larsson, 2010).

ASPD is genetically correlated with both criminal behavior and substance use. Two adoption studies of birth parents with criminal records found increased rates of ASPD in their adopted offspring (Cadoret & Stewart, 1991; Crowe, 1974), suggesting that genetics contributes to the relationship between criminal behavior and ASPD. Most genetic research in this area has focused on criminal behavior itself, rather than on ASPD, because crime can be assessed objectively by using criminal records. However, criminal behavior, although important in its own right, is only moderately associated with ASPD. About 40 percent of male criminals and 8 percent of female criminals qualify for a diagnosis of ASPD (Robins & Regier, 1991). Clearly, breaking the law cannot be equated with psychopathology (Rutter, 1996).

A classic twin study of criminal behavior included male twins born in Denmark from 1881 to 1910 (Christiansen, 1977). For more than one thousand twin pairs, genetic influence was found for criminal convictions, with an overall concordance of 51 percent for male identical twins and 30 percent for male-male fraternal twins. In multiple twin studies of adult criminality, identical twins are consistently more similar than fraternal twins (Raine, 1993). The average concordances for identical and fraternal twins are 52 and 21 percent, respectively. A recent study based on more than 20,000 twin pairs in Sweden estimated 45 percent heritability for all criminal convictions, with similar heritabilities for violent, white-collar, and property convictions (Kendler et al., 2015b).

Adoption studies are also consistent with the hypothesis of significant genetic influence on adult criminality, although adoption studies point to less genetic influence than do twin studies. It has been hypothesized that twin studies overestimate genetic effects because identical twins are more likely to be partners in crime (Carey, 1992). Adoption studies include both the adoptees' study method (Cloninger, Sigvardsson, Bohman, & von Knorring, 1982; Crowe, 1972) and the adoptees' family method (Cadoret et al., 1985a). One of the best studies used the adoptees' study method, beginning with more than 14,000 adoptions in Denmark between 1924 and

1947 (Mednick, Gabrielli, & Hutchings, 1984). Using court convictions as an index of criminal behavior, the researchers found evidence for genetic influence and for genotype-environment interaction, as shown in Figure 16.3. Adoptees were at greater risk for criminal behavior when their birth parents had criminal convictions, a finding implying genetic influence. Unlike the twin study just described, this adoption study (and others) found genetic influence for crimes against property but not for violent crimes (Bohman, Cloninger, Sigvardsson, & von Knorring, 1982; Brennan et al., 1996). Evidence for genotype-environment interaction was also suggested. Adoptive parents with criminal convictions had no effect on the criminal behavior of adoptees unless the adoptees' birth parents also had criminal convictions. A more recent study of adoptees included in the National Longitudinal Study of Adolescent Health found that those adoptees who had a birth father or birth mother who had ever been arrested were significantly more likely to be arrested, sentenced to probation, incarcerated, and arrested multiple times than adoptees whose birth parents had never been arrested (Beaver, 2011).

A Swedish adoption study of criminality using the adoptees' family method found evidence for genotype-environment interaction as well as interesting interactions with alcohol abuse, which greatly increases the likelihood of violent crimes (Bohman, 1996; Bohman et al., 1982). When adoptees' crimes did not involve alcohol abuse, their biological fathers were found to be at increased risk for nonviolent crimes. In contrast, when adoptees' crimes involved alcohol abuse, their biological fathers were not at increased risk for crime. These findings suggest that genetics contributes to criminal behavior but not to alcohol-related crimes, which are likely to be more violent.

Evidence from family, twin, and adoption studies consistently suggests a common underlying vulnerability to ASPD and substance use disorders. For example, relatives of alcohol-dependent individuals show significant familial aggregation of ASPD

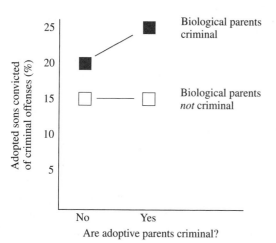

FIGURE 16.3 Evidence for genetic influence and genotype-environment interaction for criminal behavior in a Danish adoption study. (Data from Mednick et al., 1984.)

(Nurnberger et al., 2004), and family history of alcohol use disorder is associated with ASPD. Large twin studies indicate that this familiality is due, in part, to genetic influences that contribute to the co-occurrence of ASPD and substance use disorders (Agrawal, Jacobson, Prescott, & Kendler, 2004; Fu et al., 2002; Hicks, Krueger, Iacono, McGue, & Patrick, 2004). Adoption studies provide additional support for a genetic link between ASPD and substance use. Male adoptees who were at increased biological risk for ASPD showed increased aggressiveness, conduct problems, ASPD, and eventual substance dependence (Cadoret, Yates, Troughton, Woodworth, & Stewart, 1995a), a finding that was replicated in female adoptees (Cadoret, Yates, Troughton, Woodworth, & Stewart, 1996).

IDENTIFYING GENES

In contrast to molecular genetic research on psychopathology, molecular genetic research on personality has received much less attention. The field began in 1996 with reports from two studies of an association between a DNA marker for a certain neuroreceptor gene (*DRD4*, dopamine D_4 receptor) and the personality trait of novelty seeking in unselected samples (Benjamin et al., 1996; Ebstein et al., 1996). *DRD4* is the gene mentioned in Chapter 15 that has been reported to show an association with attention-deficit/hyperactivity disorder (ADHD). Individuals high in novelty seeking are characterized as impulsive, exploratory, fickle, excitable, quick-tempered, and extravagant. However, many studies have failed to replicate the association with novelty seeking (Jang, 2005). A meta-analysis of 17 studies of extraversion rather than the narrow trait of novelty seeking also found no significant association (Munafo et al., 2003).

As noted in Chapter 12, early reports of an association between XYY males and violence were overblown. However, as described in Chapter 8, the *MAOA* gene on the X chromosome has been associated with antisocial behavior in individuals who suffered severe childhood maltreatment, a genotype-environment interaction (Caspi et al., 2002). This finding has held up in a recent meta-analysis (Byrd & Manuck, 2014).

Previous chapters (see especially Chapter 9) indicated that candidate gene findings have a poor record of replicating, and this is also the case in the personality domain (Munafo & Flint, 2011). A recent review of 369 studies of candidate gene associations reported for all personality traits found no clear consensus on any associations (Balestri et al., 2014). Several genomewide association (GWA) studies have been reported for the FFM factors, which have been summarized and reanalyzed in a meta-analysis that included over 20,000 individuals (de Moor et al., 2012). Three SNPs emerged as genomewide significant but these did not replicate in independent samples. The largest GWA meta-analysis for personality, which included more than 60,000 participants from 29 studies, focused on neuroticism (Genetics of Personality Consortium et al., 2015). One SNP showed genomewide significance but it did not replicate in independent samples. GWA studies for other traits mentioned in this chapter have also come up empty-handed, for example, for political attitudes (Hatemi et al., 2014), behavioral economics (Benjamin et al., 2012), and antisocial behavior (Tielbeek et al., 2012).

This first wave of GWA studies for personality supports the conclusion reached in previous chapters: The heritability of complex traits and common disorders is due to many genes of small effect (Plomin, DeFries, Knopik & Neiderhiser, 2016). The largest effect sizes are extremely small, generally less than .05 percent (Turkheimer et al., 2014), which means that most published studies, especially candidate gene studies, have been dramatically underpowered to detect such small effects.

Summary

More twin data are available from self-report personality questionnaires than from any other domain of psychology, and they consistently yield evidence for moderate genetic influence for dozens of personality dimensions. Most well-studied are extraversion and neuroticism, with heritability estimates of about 50 percent for extraversion and about 40 percent for neuroticism across twin and adoption studies, although twin studies yield higher heritability estimates than do adoption studies. Other personality traits assessed by personality questionnaire also show heritabilities ranging from 30 to 50 percent. There is no replicated example of zero heritability for any specific personality trait, nor is there evidence that any personality trait is more heritable than others. Environmental influence is almost entirely due to non-shared environmental factors. These surprising findings are not limited to self-report questionnaires. For example, a twin study using peer ratings yielded similar results. Although the degree of genetic influence suggested by twin studies using parent ratings of their children's personalities appears to be inflated by contrast effects, more objective measures, such as behavioral ratings by observers, indicate genetic influence in twin and adoption studies.

New directions for genetic research include looking at personality continuity and change across situations and across time. Results indicate that genetic factors are largely responsible for continuity and that change is largely due to environmental factors. Other new findings include the central role that personality plays in producing genetic influence on measures of the environment. Another new direction for research lies at the border with social psychology. For example, genetic influence has been found for relationships, such as parent-offspring relationships, quality of romantic relationships and sexual orientation. Other examples include evidence for genetic influence on political attitudes and behavioral economics.

A major new direction for genetic research on personality is to consider its role in psychopathology. For example, depression and other internalizing forms of psychopathology are, to a large extent, the genetic extreme of normal variation in the major personality dimension of neuroticism. Personality disorders, which are at the border between personality and psychopathology, are another growth area for genetic research in personality. It is likely that some personality disorders are part of the genetic continuum of psychopathology: schizotypal personality disorder and schizophrenia, and obsessive-compulsive personality disorder and obsessive-compulsive anxiety disorder. Most genetic research on personality disorders has focused on antisocial personality disorder and its relationship to criminal behavior and substance abuse. From adolescence to adulthood, genetic influence increases and shared environmental influence decreases for symptoms of antisocial personality disorder, including juvenile delinquency and adult criminal behavior.

SNP-based heritability estimates for personality (about 10 percent) are only one-quarter of twin study estimates of heritability (about 40 percent). Early reports of candidate gene associations have generally not replicated. The first wave of GWA studies for personality suggests that its heritability is due to many genes of small effect.

CHAPTER **SEVENTEEN**

Substance Use Disorders

Alcohol use disorders, nicotine use, and abuse of other drugs are major health-related behaviors. Externalizing behaviors, such as attention-deficit/hyperactivity disorder (ADHD) and conduct disorder (see Chapter 15), have long been proposed as etiologic predictors of later alcohol and drug problems (Groenman et al., 2013; Palmer et al., 2013; Zucker, Heitzeg, & Nigg, 2011). More specifically, as discussed in Chapter 15, substance use is part of a general genetic factor of externalizing disorders, but alcohol and other drugs include significant disorder-specific genetic effects (Kendler et al., 2003b; Vrieze, McGue, Miller, Hicks, & Iacono, 2013). Most behavioral genetic research in this area has focused on alcohol dependence or alcohol-related behavior and, to a lesser extent, nicotine dependence. There is also an increasing focus on cannabis use research.

ALCOHOL DEPENDENCE

Twin and Adoption Research on Alcohol-Related Phenotypes

There are many steps in the pathway to alcohol dependence, for example: whether or not to drink alcohol, the amount one drinks, the way one drinks, and the subsequent development of tolerance and dependence. Each of these steps might involve different genetic mechanisms. For this reason, alcohol dependence is likely to be highly heterogeneous. Nonetheless, numerous family studies have shown that alcohol use disorders run in families, although the studies vary widely in the size of the effect and in diagnostic criteria. For males, alcohol dependence in a first-degree relative is by far the single best predictor of alcohol dependence. For example, a family study of 1212 alcohol-dependent probands and their 2755 siblings found an average risk for lifetime diagnosis of alcohol dependence of about 50 percent in male siblings and

25 percent in female siblings (Bierut et al., 1998). According to the U.S. Centers for Disease Control and Prevention (CDC), the risk rates in the general population are about 17 percent for men and 8 percent for women. Assortative mating for alcohol use is substantial (correlation of about 0.40), which is thought to be caused by initial selection of the spouse rather than the effect of living with the spouse (Grant et al., 2007; Hicks, Foster, Iacono, & McGue, 2013). Assortative mating of this magnitude could inflate estimates of shared environment and could also create a genotype-environment correlation in which children are more likely to experience both genetic and environmental risks. (See Chapter 11 for more discussion of assortative mating.)

Twin and adoption studies indicate that genetic factors play a major role in the familial aggregation of alcohol dependence. In a Danish adoption study, alcohol dependence in men was associated with alcohol dependence in birth parents but not adoptive parents (Goodwin, Schulsinger, Hermansen, Guze, & Winokur, 1973; Goodwin, Schulsinger, Knop, Mednick, & Guze, 1977). A similar association between alcohol dependence in adopted sons and their birth fathers was reported in Sweden (Cloninger, Bohman, & Sigvardsson, 1981; Sigvardsson, Bohman, & Cloninger, 1996). Likewise, the Iowa adoption studies (Cadoret, 1994; Cadoret, O'Gorman, Troughton, & Heywood, 1985a; Cadoret, Troughton, & O'Gorman, 1987) showed a significantly elevated risk for alcohol dependence in adopted sons and daughters from an alcoholic birth family background, compared to control adoptees, consistent with a genetic influence on alcohol dependence. Two recent adoption studies from the United States (Hicks et al., 2013; McGue et al., 2007) and Sweden (Kendler et al., 2015a) also support the role of genetics in parent-child transmission of alcohol dependence, and further suggest that parents pass on to their (biological) offspring a nonspecific, genetic liability to multiple externalizing disorders (Hicks et al., 2013; Kendler et al., 2015a).

Numerous large twin studies on alcohol abuse, alcohol dependence, and other alcohol-related outcomes yield comparable results. The results of adult twin studies on various drinking-related behaviors are highly consistent, with genetic effects accounting for 40 to 60 percent of the variance across measures of quantity and frequency of use as well as problem use and dependence (Dick, Prescott, & McGue, 2009a; Hicks et al., 2013). Early twin studies suggested higher heritability for alcohol dependence in males (Legrand, McGue, & Iacono, 1999); however, this sex difference is not seen in more recent twin studies (Knopik et al., 2004; Prescott, 2002). Twin studies of adolescent alcohol-related variables, however, yield much more variable results. Studies of adolescent alcohol use disorders are uncommon because diagnostic criteria are typically not met until early adulthood (Lynskey, Agrawal, & Heath, 2010). As such, the few genetic studies of adolescent alcohol dependence symptoms suggest small and nonsignificant genetic effects (Knopik, Heath, Bucholz, Madden, & Waldron, 2009a; Rose, Dick, Viken, Pulkkinen, & Kaprio, 2004), with shared environment playing a larger role. Regarding alcohol initiation in adolescence, results again suggest a large role for shared environment and a small yet significant role for genetic effects (Fowler et al., 2007). An interesting developmental finding is that shared environment appears to be related to the initial use of alcohol in adolescence and young adulthood but not to later alcohol abuse (Dick et al., 2014; Pagan et al., 2006).

Consistent with shared environment being important for adolescent alcohol-related outcomes, adoption studies yield some evidence for the influence of shared environment that is specific to siblings and not shared between parents and offspring (Hicks et al., 2013). For example, in an adoption study of alcohol use and misuse among adolescents, the correlation between problem drinking in parents and adolescent alcohol use was 0.30 for biological offspring but only 0.04 for adoptive offspring (McGue, Sharma, & Benson, 1996). Despite the lack of resemblance between adoptive parents and their adopted offspring, adoptive sibling pairs who were not genetically related correlated 0.24. Moreover, the adoptive sibling correlation was significantly greater for same-sex siblings ($r = 0.45$) than for opposite-sex siblings ($r = 0.01$). These results suggest the reasonable hypothesis that sibling effects (or perhaps peer effects) may be more important than parent effects in the use of alcohol in adolescence. However, as mentioned earlier, assortative mating might be responsible, at least in part, for apparent shared environmental influences (Grant et al., 2007).

The majority of research discussed to this point has focused on alcohol dependence or alcohol use disorder. As mentioned above, alcohol dependence is a multifactorial disorder characterized by symptoms that include, but are not limited to, tolerance, withdrawal, and using alcohol in larger amounts or for longer periods than intended. These symptoms are hypothesized to index vulnerability in biological systems that influence alcohol dependence. Recent work using adult twins suggests that each of the symptoms that comprise alcohol dependence are heritable (estimates ranging from 36 to 59 percent) (Kendler, Aggen, Prescott, Crabbe, & Neale, 2012b). Further, these symptoms may not reflect a single dimension of genetic liability but rather reflect three underlying dimensions that index risk for: (i) tolerance and heavy use; (ii) loss of control with alcohol associated social dysfunction; and (iii) withdrawal and continued use despite problems. These results are consistent with those for traits that have clear laboratory animal parallels, such as tolerance and withdrawal (described below). More recent efforts using SNP-based heritability also find significant genetic influences on a subset of alcohol dependence symptoms (tolerance, using longer than intended, continued use despite problems, and activities given up) as well as overall alcohol dependence diagnosis (Palmer et al., 2015b; Vrieze et al., 2013; Yang et al., 2014). SNP-based genetic correlations across alcohol dependence symptoms suggest that the same genes affect multiple symptoms (Palmer et al., 2015b).

It is clear that both genes and environment play an important role in alcohol-related phenotypes; perhaps unsurprisingly, these genetic and environmental factors are likely to coact in a complex fashion (Enoch, 2012; Guerrini, Quadri, & Thomson, 2014). Quantitative genetic research on alcohol use behaviors has provided several examples of genotype-environment interaction (see Chapter 8; see also Young-Wolff, Enoch, & Prescott, 2011, for a review). Heritability has been reported to be lower for those with later age of onset (Agrawal et al., 2009), for married individuals (Heath, Jardine, & Martin, 1989), for individuals with a religious upbringing (Koopmans, Slutske, van Baal, & Boomsma, 1999) and from stricter and closer families (Miles, Silberg, Pickens, & Eaves, 2005), in regions with lower alcohol sales (Dick, Rose, Viken, Kaprio, & Koskenvuo, 2001), and for individuals with peers who are less deviant (Dick et al., 2007; Kendler, Gardner, & Dick, 2011). These findings suggest that genetic risk for alcohol use is greater in more permissive environments (unmarried, nonreligious upbringing, greater alcohol availability, more peers reporting alcohol use). While adoption studies are fewer in number, they also suggest genotype-environment inter-action. In studies of Swedish adoptees, adopted children who had both genetic risk (an alcohol-dependent birth parent) and environmental risk (an alcohol-dependent adoptive parent) were most likely to abuse alcohol (Sigvardsson et al., 1996). Addition-ally, having a birth father with a history of criminality (Chapter 16) interacted with unstable home environment to increase antisocial alcoholism in males (Cloninger et al., 1982). The Iowa adoption studies also suggest that birth family interacted with psychopathology in the adoptive parent and parental conflict in the adoptive home environment to increase risk for the development of alcoholism in females (Cutrona et al., 1994).

Animal Research on Alcohol-Related Phenotypes

Psychopharmacogenetics, which concerns the genetic effects on behavioral responses to drugs, is one of the most prolific areas of behavioral genetic research using ani-mal models. The larger field of *pharmacogenetics* (Roses, 2000), often called ***pharmaco-genomics*** in recognition of the ability to examine genetic effects on a genomewide basis, focuses on genetic differences in positive and negative effects of drugs in order to individualize and optimize drug therapy (Evans & Relling, 2004; Goldstein, Tate, & Sisodiya, 2003). Most research in psychopharmacogenetics involves alco-hol (Bloom & Kupfer, 1995; Broadhurst, 1978; Crabbe & Harris, 1991). For example, studies in *Drosophila* have examined susceptibility to the effects of alcohol by measur-ing the degree of sensitivity and tolerance to the sedative or motor-impairing effects of alcohol (e.g., Scholz, Ramond, Singh, & Heberlein, 2000). Recent work has also demonstrated that *Drosophila* can model many features of addiction, such as increased consumption over time, the overcoming of aversive stimuli in order to consume alco-hol, and relapse after periods of alcohol deprivation (Devineni & Heberlein, 2013).

Using a mouse model, researchers discovered in 1959 that inbred strains of mice differ markedly in their preference for drinking alcohol, an observation that implies genetic influence (McClearn & Rodgers, 1959). Studies spanning more than 150 gen-erations of mice find similar results, suggesting that this is a highly heritable trait that is very stable over time (Wahlsten et al., 2006). Moreover, research also suggests that preference drinking is a reasonable model for alcohol's reinforcing effects (Green & Grahame, 2008). Inbred strain differences have also been found for other behavioral responses to alcohol (see Crabbe, 2012, for a review).

Selection studies provide especially powerful demonstrations of genetic influence. For example, one classic study successfully selected for sensitivity to the effects of alcohol (McClearn, 1976). When mice are injected with the mouse equivalent of several drinks, they will "sleep it off" for various lengths of time. "Sleep time" in response to alcohol injections was measured by the time it took mice to right themselves after being placed on their backs in a cradle (Figure 17.1). Selection for this measure of alcohol sensitivity was successful, an outcome providing a powerful demonstration of the importance of genetic factors (Figure 17.2). After 18 generations of selective breeding, the long-sleep (LS) animals "slept" for an average of two hours. Many of the short-sleep (SS) mice were not even knocked out, and their average "sleep time" was only about ten minutes. By generation 15, there was no overlap between the LS and SS lines (Figure 17.3). That is, every mouse in the LS line slept longer than any mouse in the SS line.

Alcohol has a combination of effects during consumption. Specifically, there are stimulatory effects during the first part of a drinking session that are rewarding, but after a peak alcohol level is reached, alcohol has sedating properties that are aversive. The extent to which genetic variation may disproportionately alter the balance between these effects may have profound implications on drinking behavior. If, due to genetic differences, individuals experience the rewarding effects of alcohol but not the aversive sedating effects, then they may be more likely to drink excessively in a

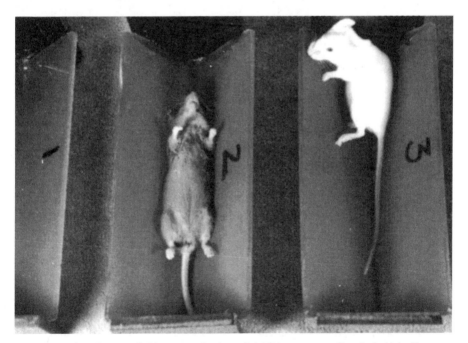

FIGURE 17.1 The "sleep cradle" for measuring loss of righting response after alcohol injections in mice. In cradle 2, a long-sleep mouse is still on its back, sleeping off the alcohol injection. In cradle 3, a short-sleep mouse has just begun to right itself. (Courtesy of E. A. Thomas.)

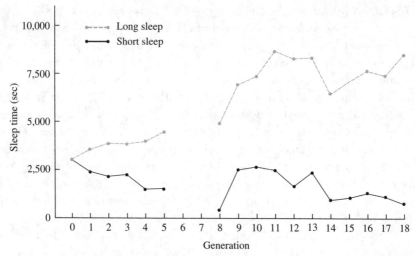

FIGURE 17.2 Results of alcohol sleep-time selection study. Selection was suspended during generations 6 through 8. (Data from G. E. McClearn, unpublished.)

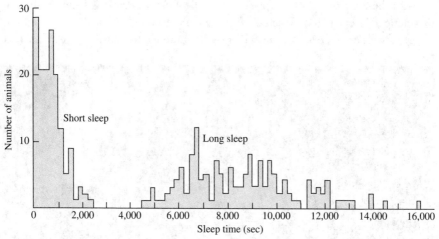

FIGURE 17.3 Distributions of alcohol sleep time after 15 generations of selection. (Data from G. E. McClearn, unpublished.)

fashion that may lead to dependence. By contrast, if an individual finds the sedating properties of alcohol particularly severe (consistent with the LS mice), this may lead to less drinking and a subsequent decrease in the risk for developing alcohol dependence. Since SS and LS mice are selectively bred and provide strong evidence for the genetic basis of these alcohol-related effects, they can serve as a critical translational bridge between animal research methods and understanding how genetic differences may influence the risk for alcohol dependence.

The steady divergence of the lines over 18 generations indicates that many genes affect this measure. If just one or two genes were involved, the lines would completely diverge in a few generations. Other selection studies include successful selection in mice for susceptibility to seizures during withdrawal from alcohol dependence and for voluntary alcohol consumption in rats (Crabbe, Kosobud, Young, Tam, & McSwigan, 1985; Green & Grahame, 2008). These are powerful genetic effects. For example, mice in the line selected for susceptibility to seizures are so sensitive to withdrawal that they show symptoms after a single injection of alcohol. Interestingly, however, seizure-prone and seizure-resistant selected lines do not differ in their functional tolerance to ethanol (Crabbe, Kendler, & Hitzemann, 2013). In functional tolerance, the amount of drug that remains in contact with the tissue of interest has not changed, but the target tissue no longer responds in the same way. This finding has also been found in inbred strains and, to a lesser extent, recombinant inbred strains (see Crabbe et al., 2013 for a review) and supports human work suggesting that genetic risk factors for tolerance to alcohol and alcohol withdrawal are only weakly related (Kendler et al., 2012b; Palmer et al., 2015b). Animal genetic models, including mice, rats, and *Drosophila,* continue to be widely used for behavioral genetic research on alcohol-related traits as well as for molecular genetic research (Awofala, 2011; Crabbe et al., 2013; Devineni & Heberlein, 2013).

Molecular Genetic Research on Alcohol-Related Phenotypes

Alcohol dependence in humans has long been a target for molecular genetic studies in order to identify genes that contribute to the risk for developing the disorder (see Rietschel & Treutlein, 2013, for a review). Whole-genome linkage studies using various populations, including Irish (Prescott et al., 2006), African American (Gelernter et al., 2009), and Native American families (Ehlers et al., 2004; Long et al., 1998), as well as the Collaborative Genetics of Alcoholism (COGA) study (Foroud et al., 2000; Reich et al., 1998), have consistently reported linkage to a region on the long arm of chromosome 4 that contains the alcohol dehydrogenase (*ADH*) gene cluster family. A linkage region on the short arm of chromosome 4, close to the cluster of gamma-aminobutyric acid (GABA) receptors, has also been consistently reported (Long et al., 1998; Reich et al., 1998).

As the genes that code for alcohol-metabolizing enzymes are well-known (Lovinger & Crabbe, 2005), the aldehyde dehydrogenase gene (*ALDH2*) and the alcohol dehydrogenase (*ADH*) genes are the best-established genes in which polymorphisms may be associated with risk for alcohol dependence (see Kimura & Higuchi, 2011, for a review). Figure 17.4 presents a simplified model of these genetic influences on the role of alcohol dependence as well as several illustrative candidate genes, which are discussed below. One particularly interesting and consistent finding based on the results of candidate gene studies involves the *ALDH2* polymorphism. There is evidence that the *ALDH2* polymorphism is associated with both the drinking behavior of healthy people and the risk for alcohol dependence. An *ALDH2* allele (*ALDH2*2*) that leads to inactivity of a key enzyme in the metabolism of alcohol occurs in 25 percent of Chinese and

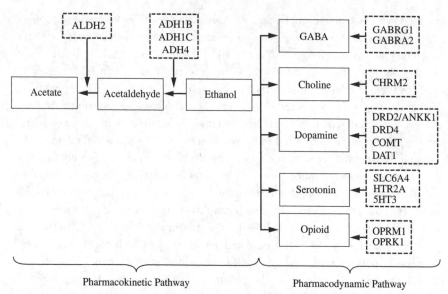

FIGURE 17.4 A network model of genes involved in alcohol dependence via alterations to ethanol's pharmacokinetics and pharmacodynamics. The left-hand side of the figure indicates the pharmacokinetic pathway that metabolizes ethanol into acetate. The right-hand side indicates the pharmacodynamic pathways that reflect ethanol's molecular pharmacological effects on multiple neurotransmitter systems. Dashed boxes contain a list of candidate genes that most likely affect the respective systems. See Palmer and colleagues (2012) for a review of these biological pathways.

40 percent of Japanese but is hardly ever found in Caucasians. The resulting buildup of acetaldehyde leads to unpleasant symptoms, such as flushing and nausea, when alcohol is consumed. This is an example of a mutant allele that protects against the development of alcoholism. This genetic variant results in reduced alcohol consumption and has been implicated as the reason why rates of alcoholism are much lower in Asian than in Caucasian populations. In fact, being homozygous for the *ALDH2*2* allele almost completely prevents individuals from becoming alcoholics (Higuchi et al., 2004). The same unpleasant symptoms described here are produced by the drug disulfiram (Antabuse), which is the basis for an alcoholism therapy used to deter drinking.

Associations for other candidate genes have been reported (see Rietschel & Treutlein, 2013, for a review), especially genes that code for receptors for GABA (Enoch et al., 2009), cholinergic muscarinic receptor-2 (*CHRM2;* Luo et al., 2005), dopamine (McGeary, 2009; van der Zwaluw et al., 2009), serotonin (Enoch, Gorodetsky, Hodgkinson, Roy, & Goldman, 2011), and opioids (Anton et al., 2008). Efforts are now underway to test for moderation of specific gene effects by environmental risk factors. For example, three studies looking at three different genes have suggested that parental monitoring moderates the association between externalizing behavior, including alcohol use and *GABRA2* (Dick et al., 2009b), *CHRM2* (Dick et al., 2011), and a dopaminergic pathway gene, catechol-O-methyl transferase (*COMT;*

Laucht et al., 2012). More specifically, and supportive of quantitative genetic findings of G × E in alcohol use, these three studies suggest that the association between the genotype and externalizing behavior is stronger in environments with lower parental monitoring. Despite these interesting and encouraging results, the only consistent findings from classical genomewide association (GWA) studies of alcohol dependence are those implicating the alcohol-metabolizing enzyme genes, which have shown associations for alcohol dependence and alcohol consumption phenotypes (see Hart & Kranzler, 2015, for a review). Specifically, *ALDH2* is consistently associated with alcohol phenotypes in East Asian populations (Park et al., 2013; Quillen et al., 2014) and *ADH1B* in European American and African American populations (Frank et al., 2012; Gelernter et al., 2014a). In other words, the SNPs in the genes encoding metabolizing enzymes are among the common variants with the largest effects on alcohol dependence risk (Hart & Kranzler, 2015). In contrast, associations with other candidate genes for alcohol dependence such as *DRD2, OPRM1,* and *COMT* have not yet been replicated in GWA studies (Olfson and Bierut, 2012).

Pharmacogenomic studies of rodents have been successfully used to identify QTLs associated with alcohol-related behavior (Ehlers et al., 2010). For example, QTLs for alcohol preference drinking have been linked to mouse chromosome 9 (Phillips, Belknap, Buck, & Cunningham, 1998; Tabakoff et al., 2008) and to rat chromosome 4 (Spence et al., 2009). QTLs for acute alcohol withdrawal and acute functional tolerance in mice have been mapped to mouse chromosome 1 (Kozell, Belknap, Hofstetter, Mayeda, & Buck, 2008) and chromosome 4 (Bennett et al., 2015), respectively. Alcohol-preference related behaviors have also been mapped to chromosome 4 (Belknap & Atkins, 2001; Saba et al., 2011). Other QTLs have been mapped for other alcohol-related responses in mice, such as alcohol-induced loss of righting reflex (Crabbe et al., 1999a; Lovinger & Crabbe, 2005).

QTL research in animal models is especially exciting because it can nominate candidate QTLs that can then be tested in human QTL research (Lovinger & Crabbe, 2005). For example, over 90 percent of the mouse and human genomes include regions of conserved synteny. In other words, there are regions in the mouse and human genomes in which the gene order in the most common ancestor has been conserved in both species (Ehlers et al., 2010). Knock-out studies in mice also demonstrate the effects of specific genes on behavioral responses to alcohol. For example, knocking out a serotonin receptor gene in mice leads to increased alcohol consumption (Crabbe et al., 1996). Knocking out certain dopaminergic receptors results in supersensitivity to alcohol (Rubinstein et al., 1997) and reduced alcohol preference drinking (Savelieva, Caudle, Findlay, Caron, & Miller, 2002). Such differences in brain sensitivity to ethanol in human populations could be responsible for addiction in general (Martinez & Narendran, 2010) as well as the lethal consequences of binge drinking in some individuals (Heath et al., 2003).

Recent studies have used genomic approaches (Chapter 10) to shed light on the molecular pathways underlying alcohol response and addiction (Awofala, 2011;

Tabakoff et al., 2009). Such approaches, using mice, rats, and *Drosophila*, combine genetic marker information, gene expression, and complex phenotypes to ascertain the candidate genes and gene product interaction pathways that significantly influence the variation in expression of a particular phenotype in animal models. Findings from animal models are then compared to what is known in humans. A more recent effort took the opposite approach. Juraeva and colleagues (2015) combined pathway analysis with functional follow-up in *Drosophila* and a small-scale human laboratory study to identify risk genes for alcohol dependence. Using **gene set analysis** in a human sample (1333 alcohol dependent cases and 2168 controls), they identified 19 gene sets. Six of these gene sets included the gene *XRCC5*, which was then knocked down in *Drosophila*. The mutant flies exhibited lower sensitivity to ethanol than controls. The authors subsequently conducted an alcohol intravenous self-administration study in humans and found a significant association between maximum blood-alcohol concentration and *XRCC5* genotype, suggesting that *XRCC5* may be a possible candidate for alcohol dependence. In summary, these approaches collectively suggest that human and animal models can be mutually informative in determining candidate pathways and networks of genes that play an important role in determining the behavioral response to alcohol (Awofala, 2011).

NICOTINE DEPENDENCE

One of the most common and potentially hazardous environmental exposures that negatively influences health and development is exposure to cigarette smoke. The CDC (2014) has reported that almost 20 percent of adults in the United States—approximately 42 million people—smoked cigarettes in 2003, and most of them were dependent on nicotine. Previous work has found over 4000 chemicals in cigarette smoke, including nicotine, benzo[a]pyrene, and carbon monoxide, and more than 40 of these chemicals have been established as known carcinogens (Thielen, Klus, & Mueller, 2008). Cigarette smoking has been linked to several diseases and disabling conditions, including heart disease and lung diseases (U.S. Department of Health and Human Services, 2014). Further, for every individual who dies from a disease associated with smoking, 30 more people battle at least one major illness attributable to smoking (CDC, 2014). Several studies have singled out tobacco use as the world's leading preventable cause of death (CDC, 2014). By some estimates, up to 6 million deaths worldwide can be attributed to smoking, and current trend data predict that tobacco use will cause more than 8 million deaths a year by 2030 (World Health Organization, 2011). In the United States, tobacco use has been implicated in 20 percent of deaths per year, or 480,000 deaths annually, and approximately 41,000 of these have been attributed to secondhand smoke exposure (U.S. Department of Health and Human Services, 2014). On average, smokers die more than a decade earlier than nonsmokers (Jha et al., 2013). Although nicotine is an environmental agent, smoking behaviors aggregate in families due to genetic predispositions as well as environmental influences (Rose, Broms, Korhonen, Dick, & Kaprio, 2009). Individual differences in susceptibility to nicotine's addictive properties and harmful effects are also influenced by genetic factors.

Twin Research on Smoking-Related Phenotypes

Multiple phenotypes are associated with smoking and nicotine dependence, including smoking initiation, smoking persistence, tolerance to nicotine, smoking cessation, regular smoking, number of cigarettes smoked per day, and nicotine withdrawal (see Rose et al., 2009, for a detailed review). Considerable genetic research has investigated smoking initiation, which appears to be different from the reasons people persist or continue to smoke. While the heritability of nicotine dependence, smoking persistence, and regular smoking, for example, can be assessed only in those who have already started to smoke, the genetic effects on smoking initiation can be examined among all persons in the population (Rose et al., 2009). A meta-analysis of 17 twin cohorts from six studies of smoking initiation across three countries concluded that genetic factors play a significant role (Li, Cheng, Ma, & Swan, 2003). This meta-analysis included studies from 1993 to 1999. Since that time, at least ten additional twin studies of over 60,000 twin pairs from five countries (Finland, Australia, the United States, the Netherlands, and Turkey) have examined genetic effects on smoking initiation (e.g., Broms, Silventoinen, Madden, Heath, & Kaprio, 2006; Do et al., 2015; Hamilton et al., 2006; Morley et al., 2007; Öncel, Dick, Maes, & Aliev, 2014; Vink, Willemsen, & Boomsma, 2005). Among adult twins, genetic influences are substantial and explain, on average, about 50 percent or more of the variance. However, the estimates vary widely across studies. Studies on smoking initiation suggest heritabilities of about 0.20 to 0.75 for women and about 0.30 to 0.65 for men (reviewed in Rose et al., 2009). This range could be explained by various definitions of smoking initiation (e.g., age of first cigarette, age of initiation of regular smoking) as well as the likelihood that the magnitude of genetic effects varies with time and place (Chapter 7 on heritability; Kendler et al., 1999). More recent studies are also investigating genetic effects on reactions to first cigarette use, such as dizziness or headache. Evidence suggests that how people experience their initial few cigarettes is due to both heritable contributions and environmental experiences unique to the person (Agrawal, Madden, Bucholz, Heath, & Lynskey, 2014b; Haberstick, Ehringer, Lessem, Hopfer, & Hewitt, 2011).

Smoking persistence also shows substantial genetic variance and very little influence of shared environment (Rose et al., 2009). Most studies that focus on smoking persistence test for a genetic correlation between smoking initiation and persistence using a special case of the liability-threshold model (Chapter 3) called a two-stage model. This model estimates the amount of genetic and environmental overlap between the first stage of initiation and the second stage of persistence (or dependence) and has been applied to other domains of substance use as well (Heath, Martin, Lynskey, Todorov, & Madden, 2002). In a sample of U.S. twins, genetic influences that contribute to smoking initiation and persistence differ substantially (Do et al., 2015; Maes et al., 2004). Similar results were reported in a Finnish twin sample, with genetic effects influencing smoking initiation accounting for only about 3 percent of the variance in smoking persistence (Broms et al., 2006). Another interesting multivariate result is that the genetics of persistent smoking appears to be mediated by genetic vulnerability to nicotine withdrawal (Pergadia, Heath, Martin, & Madden, 2006a).

When considering nicotine dependence, as defined by various diagnostic criteria, multiple large twin studies all point to genetic influence on adult nicotine dependence. A classic early study including 12,000 twin pairs from Sweden, of whom half smoked, suggested that if one twin currently smoked, the probability that the co-twin smoked was 75 percent for identical twins and 63 percent for fraternal twins (Medlund, Cederlof, Floderus-Myrhed, Friberg, & Sorensen, 1977). Subsequent heritability estimates are even higher across several cultures, suggesting that about 60 percent of the risk for nicotine dependence is due to genetic influence. Studies also suggest that the time to first cigarette after waking, with a heritability of 55 percent, appears to tap a pattern of heavy, uninterrupted, and automatic smoking and may be a good single-item measure of nicotine dependence (Baker et al., 2007b) and genetic risk for nicotine dependence (Haberstick et al., 2007). It should be noted that these results refer to smoking cigarettes. An interesting study found that smoking tobacco in pipes and cigars showed no genetic influence and substantial shared environmental influence (Schmitt, Prescott, Gardner, Neale, & Kendler, 2005). More recent studies using SNP-heritability approaches report SNP heritability estimates of 36 percent for DSM-III nicotine dependence (Vrieze et al., 2013) and 26 to 33 percent for DSM-IV nicotine dependence measures (Bidwell et al., 2016), suggesting that common SNPs account for a relatively large portion of genetic effects detected using traditional biometrical twin modeling approaches.

While there are many adult twin studies of smoking behavior, the literature on adolescent twin studies is less extensive. Unlike adolescent alcohol-related behaviors, in which shared environment appears significant, there is less evidence for the role of shared environmental influences on adolescent smoking-related behaviors (Lynskey et al., 2010). Rather, adolescent twin studies demonstrate the importance of genetic factors in smoking behaviors at this earlier developmental stage; however, the range of heritability estimates is large (25 to 80 percent) and, similar to adult studies, dependent on the smoking variable of interest (Do et al., 2015). Nicotine withdrawal, however, shows remarkable similarity across adolescent and adult smokers, with genetic effects accounting for 50 percent of the variance in nicotine withdrawal (Pergadia et al., 2010).

Quantitative genetic research on genotype-environment interaction for smoking-related behaviors has not been as extensive as that for alcohol use. What little has been done has primarily focused on adolescents. Genetic influences on adolescent smoking decreased at higher levels of parental monitoring (Dick et al.,

2007), but increased with self-reported religiosity (Timberlake et al., 2006). A recent study examined whether changes in smoking policies (i.e., more explicit warnings on cigarette packages, smoke-free working and leisure environments, and media campaigns designed to prevent adolescent smoking) led to a change in the contribution of genetic influences to smoking behaviors (Vink & Boomsma, 2011). While the prevalence of smoking has decreased in recent years, there has been no change in the relative contribution of genetic and environmental factors, providing little or no evidence of genotype-environment interactions.

Molecular Genetic Research on Smoking-Related Phenotypes

Despite the wide range of heritability estimates, there is consistent support for an important role of genetics for most smoking behaviors. However, estimates of heritability provide no information about what specific genes are involved. Early molecular genetic studies of smoking-related outcomes yielded inconsistent results (reviewed in Ho & Tyndale, 2007), perhaps because none were specifically designed to study nicotine dependence.

The strongest and most consistent genetic contributions to nicotine dependence come from genes that are associated with differences in nicotine's pharmacokinetics (i.e., the absorption, distribution, and metabolism of nicotine in the body) and with differences in pharmacodynamics (i.e., genetic variation that impacts nicotine's effects on an individual) (Bierut, 2011; MacKillop, Obasi, Amlung, McGeary & Knopik, 2010). A simplified model of these influences can be seen in Figure 17.5, which includes the primary metabolic pathways, neurotransmitter systems, and illustrative candidate genes.

Variation in nicotine metabolism plays an important role in cigarette consumption. Twin studies of nicotine metabolism suggest a heritability of 60 percent, and the major contributor to genetic variation in this metabolic pathway is the *CYP2A6 gene* (Swan et al., 2005), whose enzyme is primarily responsible for the metabolism of nicotine to cotinine. Recent GWA meta-analyses confirm the importance of the *CYP2A6* region on chromosome 19 as variants in this region were associated with number of cigarettes smoked per day (Agrawal et al., 2012; Thorgeirsson et al., 2010; Tobacco and Genetics Consortium, 2010). Many of the other genes involved in the nicotine metabolism pathway are also promising candidate genes (see MacKillop et al., 2010, for a review).

In addition to metabolic pathways, neurotransmitters are another target for nicotine, especially nicotinic receptor stimulation, which is involved in nicotine's psychoactive effects on cognitive variables, such as attention, learning, and memory (Benowitz, 2008). A robust finding suggests that genetic variation in the nicotinic receptor subunit cluster (for example, *CHRNA3*), located on chromosome 15, alters risk for becoming a heavy smoker (Bierut, 2011). There appear to be at least two distinct variants that contribute to heavy smoking in this region on chromosome 15

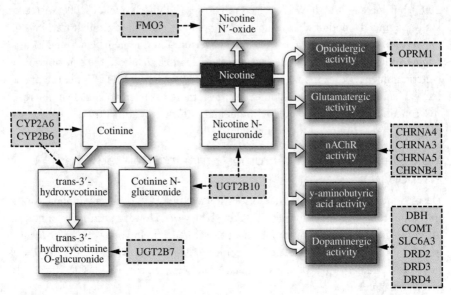

FIGURE 17.5 A model of genes involved in nicotine dependence via alterations to nicotine's pharmacokinetics and pharmacodynamics. Solid arrows indicate pharmacokinetic pathways that metabolize nicotine and pharmacodynamic pathways that reflect nicotine's molecular pharmacological effects on multiple neurotransmitter systems. Dashed arrows indicate candidate genes and their points of putative influence. (From Springer, Current Cardiovascular Risk Reports, The Role of Genetics in Nicotine Dependence: Mapping the Pathways from Genome to Syndrome, Volume 4, 2010, pp. 446-453, by James MacKillop, Ezemenari M. Obasi, Michael T. Amlung, John E. McGeary, Valerie S. Knopik, © Springer Science+Business Media, LLC 2010. With permission of Springer Science+Business Media.)

(Saccone et al., 2010; Tobacco and Genetics Consortium, 2010) and age of first regular tobacco use (Stephens et al., 2013). Other neurotransmitter systems, such as the endogenous opioid system, are also being investigated, although the effects are small and inconclusive (see Agrawal et al., 2012, for a review).

Recent transgenic studies in mice involving the deletion and replacement of nicotinic acetylcholine receptor subunits have begun to identify the molecular mechanisms underlying nicotine addiction (see Hall, Markou, Levin, & Uhi, 2012, and Marks, 2013, for reviews). Just as nicotine stimulates nicotine receptors and enhances cognitive functioning (e.g., attention), loss of receptor function impairs cognitive performance (Poorthuis, Goriounova, Couey, & Mansvelder, 2009). For example, mice lacking one of the subunits of the receptor show abnormalities in certain types of memory (Granon, Faure, & Changeux, 2003), social interaction (Granon et al., 2003), and decision making (Maubourguet, Lesne, Changeux, Maskos, & Faure, 2008). Molecular methods designed to turn specific genes "on" and "off" have revealed distinct contributions of certain subunits of the nicotinic acetylcholine receptor to the short-term effects of nicotine, including the acute behavioral effects (Changeux, 2010; Hall et al., 2012).

OTHER DRUGS

Inbred strain, selection studies, and knock-out models in mice have documented genetic influence on sensitivity to almost all drugs subject to abuse (Crabbe & Harris, 1991; Uhl, Drgonova, & Hall, 2014). Human studies are difficult to conduct because drugs such as amphetamines, heroin, and cocaine are illegal and exposure to these drugs changes over time (Seale, 1991). Although addictions such as cocaine or opiate dependence are less common, they have been considered more devastating socially, cause more physical illness, and are thought of as extremes of addiction (Bierut, 2011). Family studies have shown about an eightfold increased risk of drug abuse in relatives of probands with drug abuse for a wide range of drugs such as cannabis, sedatives, opioids, and cocaine (Merikangas et al., 1998; Merikangas & McClair, 2012). Two major twin studies of a broad range of drug abuse have been conducted in the United States, one involving veterans of the U.S. war in Vietnam (Tsuang, Bar, Harley, & Lyons, 2001) and the other involving twins in Virginia (Kendler, Myers, & Prescott, 2007b). Both studies yielded evidence of substantial heritabilities of liability (about 30 percent to 70 percent) and little evidence of shared environmental influence across various drugs of abuse. Similar results have been found in a twin study in Norway (Kendler, Aggen, Tambs, & Reichborn-Kjennerud, 2006b). A SNP-based heritability analysis found that common and rare SNPs accounted for 46 percent of the variance in illicit drugs (Vrieze et al., 2014).

A focus of recent research has been on developmental issues (Zucker, 2006). For example, as found for alcohol, shared family environmental factors are more important for initiation, but genetic factors are largely responsible for subsequent use and abuse (Kendler & Prescott, 1998; Rhee et al., 2003). A slightly different picture is seen for cannabis initiation and problematic use in a meta-analysis of 28 studies of cannabis initiation and 24 studies of cannabis use, which found that genetic factors contribute to about 50 percent of the vulnerability for both initiation and problem use (Verweij et al., 2010). SNPs collectively explain about 25 percent of the variance in cannabis initiation (Minică et al., 2015) and 20 percent of the variance in DSM-5 cannabis use disorder (Agrawal et al., 2014a).

Multivariate genetic analyses indicate that the same genes largely mediate vulnerability across different drugs, with additive genetic factors explaining more than 60 percent of the common liability to drug dependence (Palmer et al., 2012) but shared environmental influence in adolescence being more drug specific (Young, Rhee, Stallings, Corley, & Hewitt, 2006). SNP heritability studies also support an additive effect of common SNPs that is shared across multiple indicators of drug problems (Palmer et al., 2015a). A systematic review of the literature also supports a common liability to multiple facets of substance dependence, particularly etiological factors, such as genetics (Vanyukov et al., 2012). This common liability model of addiction has gained more consistent support than the *gateway hypothesis*— the theory that the use of less deleterious drugs may lead to a future risk of using more dangerous hard drugs (Gelernter & Kranzler, 2010; Vanyukov et al., 2012).

The gateway hypothesis has been tested using various approaches. A novel method, called *Mendelian randomization* (Davey Smith & Ebrahim, 2003), uses Mendel's second law of independent assortment to examine the causal effect of environmental exposure, such as exposure to drugs of abuse. For example, the *ALDH2* gene was used in a Mendelian randomization test of the gateway hypothesis (Davey Smith & Hemani, 2014; Irons, McGue, Iacono, & Oetting, 2007). The gateway hypothesis would predict that the *ALDH2*-deficient genotypic group, which was much less exposed to alcohol, would be less likely to use other drugs if alcohol exposure is a gateway to the use of other drugs. The results of the study strongly disconfirmed this gateway hypothesis because the *ALDH2*-deficient genotypic group was just as likely to use other drugs despite using alcohol much less than the *ALDH2*-normal group.

The molecular genetics of other drug-related behaviors has been examined in mice, especially for transgenic models of responses to opiates, cocaine, and amphetamine. More than three dozen transgenic mouse models have been established for responses to these drugs (Sora, Li, Igari, Hall, & Ikeda, 2010). Much QTL research in mice has also been conducted (Crabbe et al., 2010), including genes involved in reward mechanisms as well as drug preference and response (Goldman, Oroszi, & Ducci, 2005).

GWA studies of use of drugs other than alcohol and nicotine are beginning to be reported. As is the case for alcoholism, GWA studies, including genomewide copy number variant (CNV) studies (Li et al., 2014), of addiction to other drugs, such as heroin and methamphetamine, report many associations with small effect sizes but no large effects (Gelernter & Kranzler, 2010; Yuferov, Levran, Proudnikov, Nielsen, & Kreek, 2010). GWA (Agrawal et al., 2011; Agrawal et al., 2014a; Sherva et al., 2016) and gene-based tests (Minică et al., 2015; Verweij et al., 2013) for cannabis use yield similar results. However, more recent studies with larger samples and (in some cases) built-in replication datasets have begun to identify putative risk variants for opioid dependence (Gelernter et al., 2014b), opioid sensitivity (Nishizawa et al., 2014), and cocaine dependence (Gelernter et al., 2014c).

COMPLEXITIES OF STUDYING THE GENETICS OF SUBSTANCE USE

It is often implicitly assumed that there is substantial specificity between genetic factors and specific types of substance dependence, but there is a growing and strong empirical basis for believing that most of the genetic variance is shared (MacKillop et al., 2010). For example, nicotine dependence and alcoholism are both comorbid with depression, smoking co-occurs with schizophrenia, alcohol use co-occurs with antisocial behavior, and, as outlined above, various types of substance use tend to occur together, such as alcohol use and smoking or cigarette smoking and cannabis use (Agrawal et al., 2012). It is both plausible and probable that the pathways from genes to substance use and abuse are not a result of independent and additive effects, but rather involve a highly complex system that includes interactions among many genes with pleiotropic effects (MacKillop et al., 2010).

Summary

Results of twin and adoption studies of alcohol-related behaviors suggest moderate heritability and little evidence for shared environmental influences. Several examples of genotype-environment interaction have been reported in which genetic risk for alcohol-related outcomes is greater in more permissive environments. As is the case for alcohol-related behaviors, moderate genetic influence and little shared environmental influence have been found for smoking and other drug use, although shared environmental influence plays a larger role for initiation of smoking. Multivariate studies suggest that common genes mediate vulnerability across various drugs. Pharmacogenetics has been a very active area of research, using animal models of drug use and abuse, especially for alcohol. For example, selection studies have documented genetic influence on many behavioral responses to drugs. Many QTLs for alcohol-related behavior in mice have been identified. In human populations, GWA studies are beginning to yield some consistent findings for alcohol, smoking, and, to a lesser extent, other drugs, such as cannabis, methamphetamine, and heroin.

CHAPTER **EIGHTEEN**

Health Psychology

Genetic research in psychology has focused on cognitive disabilities and abilities (Chapters 11–12), psychopathology (Chapters 13–15), personality (Chapter 16), and substance use (Chapter 17). The reason for this focus is that these are the areas of psychology that have had the longest history of research on individual differences. Much less is known about the genetics of other major domains of psychology that have not traditionally emphasized individual differences, such as perception, learning, and language. The purpose of this chapter is to provide an overview of genetic research in a relatively newer area, *health psychology*, sometimes called psychological or behavioral medicine because it lies at the intersection between psychology and medicine. Specifically, health psychology is concerned with understanding how biological, psychological, environmental, and cultural factors are involved in physical health and illness. Research in this area focuses on the role of behavior in promoting health and in preventing and treating disease. Although genetic research in this area is relatively new, some conclusions can be drawn about relevant topics such as body weight and subjective well-being. Momentum in these areas adds to the relevance of **genetic counseling** for health psychology outcomes.

GENETICS AND HEALTH PSYCHOLOGY

Most of the central issues about the role of behavior in promoting health and in preventing and treating disease have only just begun to be addressed in genetic research. For example, the first book on genetics and health psychology was not published until 1995 (Turner, Cardon, & Hewitt, 1995). However, in the past 20 years, thousands of papers have been published related to health psychology, suggesting that this is an area of exponential growth. We will focus on two areas relevant to genetics and health psychology: body weight and subjective well-being.

Body Weight and Obesity

Obesity and overweight are becoming more widespread and are worldwide clinical and public health burdens (Kelly, Yang, Chen, Reynolds, & He, 2008). In the United States, more than one-third of adults and 17 percent of youth are obese (Ogden, Carroll, Kit, & Flegal, 2014). Obesity is a major health risk for several medical disorders, including diabetes, heart disease, and cancer, as well as for mortality (Flegal, Kit, Orpana, & Graubard, 2013; Gallagher & LeRoith, 2015; Nimptsch & Pischon, 2015). Although it is often assumed that individual differences in weight are largely due to environmental factors, twin and adoption studies consistently lead to the conclusion that genetics accounts for the majority of the variance for weight (Grilo & Pogue-Geile, 1991), body mass index, and other measures of obesity and regional fat distribution (such as skinfold thickness and waist circumference) (Herrera, Keildson, & Lindgren, 2011; Llewellyn & Wardle, 2015). For example, as illustrated in Figure 18.1, twin correlations for weight based on thousands of pairs of twins are 0.80 for identical twins and 0.43 for fraternal twins. Identical twins reared apart correlate 0.72. Biological parents and their adopted-away offspring are almost as similar in weight (0.23) as are nonadoptive parents and their offspring (0.26), who share both nature and nurture. Adoptive parents and their offspring, and adoptive siblings, who share nurture but not nature, do not resemble each other at all for weight.

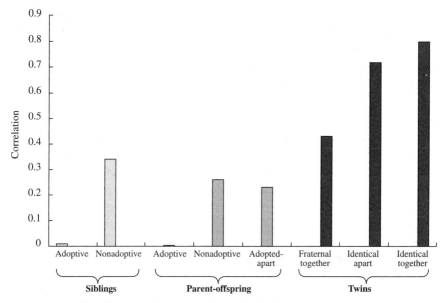

FIGURE 18.1 Family, adoption, and twin correlations for body weight. (Data from Grilo & Pogue-Geile, 1991.)

Together, the results in Figure 18.1 imply a heritability of about 70 percent for body weight. A heritability of about 70 percent has also been found across eight European countries despite average differences in weight, with some suggestion of greater shared environmental influence for women (Schousboe et al., 2003). Similar results are also found for *body mass index (BMI)*, which corrects weight on the basis of height (i.e., weight [kg]/height [m2]), and for *skinfold thickness*, which is an index of fatness (Grilo & Pogue-Geile, 1991; Maes, Neale, & Eaves, 1997; Nan et al., 2012). There are relatively few genetic studies of overweight or obesity, in part because weight shows a continuous distribution, a situation rendering diagnostic criteria somewhat arbitrary (Bray, 1986). For both children and adults, overweight and obesity classifications are typically based on BMI. In general, BMI between the 5th and 85th percentiles is considered normal, and BMI greater than the 95th percentile is considered overweight or, more recently, obese (Krebs et al., 2007).

Using an obesity cutoff based on BMI, twin studies have indicated similarly high heritabilities for obesity in childhood (Dubois et al., 2012; Silventoinen, Rokholm, Kaprio, & Sorensen, 2010), preadolescence (Nan et al., 2012) and adulthood (Silventoinen & Kaprio, 2009). A parent-offspring family study indicates that the risk of obesity in adult offspring is 20 percent if both parents are obese, 8 percent if only one parent is obese, and only 1 percent if neither parent is obese (Jacobson, Torgerson, Sjostrom, & Bouchard, 2007).

The dramatic increase in obesity throughout the world is sometimes thought to deny a role for genetics, but, as discussed in Chapter 7, the causes of population means and variances are not necessarily related. That is, the mean population increase in weight is probably due to the increased availability and reduced costs of energy-dense food, increased portion sizes, increased consumption of added sugars, and a reduction in physical activity (Llewellyn & Wardle, 2015; Skelton, Irby, Grzywacz, & Miller, 2011; Skinner & Skelton, 2014). However, despite our increasingly "obesogenic" environments, a wide range of variation in weight remains—many people are still thin. Obesogenic environments could shift the entire distribution upward while the causes of individual differences, including genetic causes, could remain unchanged (Wardle, Carnell, Haworth, & Plomin, 2008b).

As also emphasized in Chapter 7, finding genetic influence does not mean that the environment is unimportant. Anyone can lose weight if they stop eating. The issue is not what *can* happen but rather what *does* happen. That is, to what extent are the obvious differences in weight among people due to genetic and environmental differences that exist in a particular population at a particular time? The answer provided by the research summarized in Figure 18.1 (which is consistent with more recent studies) is that genetic differences largely account for individual differences in weight. If everyone ate the same amount and exercised the same amount, people would still differ in weight for genetic reasons.

This conclusion was illustrated dramatically in an interesting study of dietary intervention in 12 pairs of identical twins (Bouchard et al., 1990). For three months, the twins were given excess calories and kept in a controlled sedentary environment. Individuals differed greatly in how much weight they gained, but members of identical twin pairs correlated 0.50 in weight gain. Similar twin studies show that the effects on weight of physical activity and exercise are also influenced by genetic factors (den Hoed et al., 2013; Fagard, Bielen, & Amery, 1991; Heitmann et al., 1997).

Such studies do not indicate the mechanisms by which genetic effects occur. For example, even though genetic differences appear when calories and exercise are controlled, in the world outside the laboratory, genetic contributions to individual differences might be mediated by individual differences in proximal processes such as food intake and metabolism (Naukkarinen, Rissanen, Kaprio, & Pietilainen, 2012; Silventoinen et al., 2010). In other words, individual differences in eating habits and in the tendency to exercise, although typically assumed to be environmental factors responsible for body weight, are influenced by genetic factors. Twin studies suggest that genetic factors do affect many aspects of eating, such as appetite (Carnell, Haworth, Plomin, & Wardle, 2008; van Jaarsveld, Boniface, Llewellyn, & Wardle, 2014); the number, timing, and composition of meals; degree of hunger and sense of fullness after eating (de Castro, 1999; Llewellyn, van Jaarsveld, Johnson, Carnell, & Wardle, 2010; Llewellyn & Wardle, 2015); eating styles, such as emotional eating and uncontrolled eating (Tholin, Rasmussen, Tynelius, & Karlsson, 2005); speed of eating and enjoyment of food (Llewellyn et al., 2010); and food preferences in general (Breen, Plomin, & Wardle, 2006).

Previous chapters have indicated that environmental variance is of the nonshared variety for most areas of behavioral research. This is also the case for body weight. As noted in relation to Figure 18.1, adoptive parents and their adopted children and adoptive siblings do not resemble each other at all for weight. This finding is surprising because theories of weight and obesity have largely focused on weight control by means of dieting, yet individuals growing up in the same families do not resemble each other for environmental reasons (Grilo & Pogue-Geile, 1991). Attitudes toward eating, weight, and appetite also show substantial heritability and no influence of shared family environment (Llewellyn & Wardle, 2015; Rutherford, McGuffin, Katz, & Murray, 1993). The next step in this research is to identify environmental factors that differ for children growing up in the same family. For example, although it is reasonable to assume that children in the same family share similar diets, this may not be the case. The difficulty lies in the fact that the biological and environmental determinants of weight and obesity are intertwined, and include diverse child, family, and community characteristics.

The prevalence of overweight and obesity has increased over time and also increases with age (Ogden et al., 2014). Thus, it is important to examine the relative contributions of genetics and environment to BMI over time, as this could potentially provide valuable insight into the causes of the obesity epidemic (Duncan et al., 2009). Genetic factors that affect body weight begin to have their effects in early childhood (Meyer, 1995). In fact, in a recent study of 23 twin birth cohorts from four countries,

BMI was found to be strongly influenced by genetic factors in both males and females as early as five months of age (Dubois et al., 2012). Longitudinal genetic studies are especially informative. The first longitudinal twin study from birth through adolescence found no heritability for birth weight, increasing heritability during the first year of life, and stable heritabilities of 60 to 70 percent thereafter (see Figure 18.2 for identical and fraternal twin correlations; Matheny, 1990). These results have consistently been replicated in other twin studies in childhood (e.g., Dellava, Lichtenstein, & Kendler, 2012; Estourgie-van Burk, Bartels, van Beijsterveldt, Delemarre-van de Waal, & Boomsma, 2006; Pietilainen et al., 1999). A recent longitudinal study found that heritability of BMI increased from 43 percent at age 4 to 82 percent at age 10, and confirmed these results using genomewide SNP-heritability and polygenic risk score approaches (Llewellyn, Trzaskowski, Plomin, & Wardle, 2014a). In a systematic review and analysis of about 8,000 MZ and 9,900 DZ twin pairs from twelve published studies, heritability of BMI was found to be high across preadolescence, young adulthood, and late adulthood, ranging from 60 to 80 percent (Figure 18.3; see Nan et al., 2012). Longitudinal twin studies that examined the change in BMI from adolescence to young adulthood also indicate that, while the magnitude of genetic influences is largely stable, different sets of genes may underlie the rate of change during this developmental period (Ortega-Alonso, Pietilainen, Silventoinen, Saarni, & Kaprio, 2012).

Similar to most other behaviors and phenotypes discussed earlier in this book, there is keen interest in the role of gene-environment interplay in the risk for obesity (Llewellyn & Wardle, 2015). For example, heritability estimates may vary depending on certain environmental factors. Heritability of BMI has been reported to be

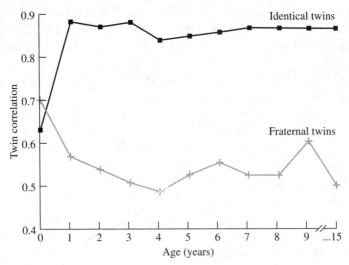

FIGURE 18.2 Identical and fraternal twin correlations for weight from birth to 15 years of age. (Data from Matheny, 1990.)

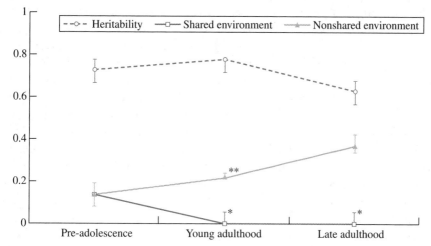

FIGURE 18.3 Genetic and environmental contributions to BMI from preadolescence to adulthood. *Lower limit of confidence interval is 0. **Lower limit of confidence interval is 0.20. (Data from Nan et al., 2012.)

lower among adults with higher income levels (Johnson & Krueger, 2005) and among young adults who exercise frequently (Mustelin, Silventoinen, Pietilainen, Rissanen, & Kaprio, 2009; Silventoinen et al., 2009). It has also been suggested that genetic and common environmental effects on BMI may be moderated by parental education level, with lower heritability if parental education was limited (i.e., not having completed high school) or mixed (one parent with limited education and one parent with a higher educational level). Common environment did not affect variation of adolescent BMI in highly educated families but did influence BMI in families with limited parental education (Lajunen, Kaprio, Rose, Pulkkinen, & Silventoinen, 2012). Recent work has focused on the *behavioral susceptibility theory (BST)*, which proposes that individuals who inherit a more avid appetite or lower sensitivity to satiety are more likely to overeat in response to the food environment (see Llewellyn & Wardle, 2015, for a review).

As mentioned previously, many of these ostensible environmental measures are heritable. For example, individual differences in physical activity and appetite during adulthood are due in part to genetic influences (Mustelin et al., 2012; van Jaarsveld et al., 2014). Thus, despite the increased information that is now available about the predictors of BMI, the picture is becoming increasingly complex.

Molecular genetic studies Obesity is the target of intense molecular genetic research, initially because of the so-called obese gene in mice. Mouse models have historically been very important in uncovering the genetic architecture of obesity and related traits, and advances in these models continue to provide insight into the etiology of weight-related diseases (see Mathes, Kelly, & Pomp, 2011, for a review). In the 1950s, a recessive mutation that caused obesity was discovered in mice. When these obese mice were given blood from a normal mouse, they lost weight, a result suggesting that the obese mice were missing some factor important in control of weight. The gene was cloned and was found to be similar to a human gene (Zhang et al., 1994). The gene's product, a hormone called *leptin*, was shown to reduce weight in mice by decreasing appetite and increasing energy use (Halaas et al., 1995). However, with rare exceptions (Montague et al., 1997), obese humans do not appear to have defects in the leptin gene. The gene that codes for the leptin receptor in the brain has also been cloned from another mouse mutant (Chua et al., 1996). Mutations in this gene might contribute to genetic risk for obesity. Up to 3 percent of patients with severe obesity have been found to have a loss-of-function mutation in the leptin receptor (Farooqi et al., 2007; van der Klaauw & Farooqi, 2015). Interestingly, the obesity phenotype in individuals with defects in the leptin gene or its receptor is very similar, illustrating that leptin is a key piece of the body weight and obesity puzzle (Ramachandrappa & Farooqi, 2011).

Another biological system that has received interest is the melanocortin system (van der Klaauw & Farooqi, 2015). Many of the effects of leptin on the body are mediated by the central nervous system, particularly the hypothalamus. When leptin binds to leptin receptors in this area of the brain, it stimulates the melanocortin system. It is this stimulation that actually suppresses food intake (Ramachandrappa & Farooqi, 2011). A particular gene in this system, *MC4R*, has been associated with obesity in humans (Vaisse, Clement, Guy-Grand, & Froguel, 1998; Yeo et al., 1998), and targeted disruption of *MC4R* in mice leads to increased food intake and increased lean mass and growth (Huszar et al., 1997). It is believed that these hypothalamic pathways interact with other brain centers to coordinate appetite, regulate metabolism, and influence energy expenditure (van der Klaauw & Farooqi, 2015). In other words, obesity-related traits are highly complex and are likely to be regulated by multiple genes that impact many systems, and these genes are likely to interact not only with one another but also with environmental stimuli (Mathes et al., 2011).

As with most complex traits, major single-gene effects on human obesity are rare and often involve severe disorders. In addition, hundreds of genes in mice have been shown to affect body weight when mutated or otherwise altered (Mathes et al., 2011; Rankinen et al., 2006). However, multiple genes of various effect sizes are likely to be responsible for the substantial genetic contribution to common overweight and obesity. Genomewide association (GWA) approaches have identified genes that increase risk for common forms (i.e., not due to a single gene) of obesity, as defined by BMI, waist circumference, waist:hip ratio, and body fat percentage. To date, more than 80 genetic loci have been identified by GWA approaches, and many of these have been replicated in different populations and ethnicities (Locke et al., 2015). The gene that has been consistently associated with common obesity, *FTO*, explains about 1 percent of the variance of BMI (Frayling et al., 2007) and has been linked to various appetitive characteristics, such as higher food intake (Cecil, Tavendale, Watt, Hetherington, & Palmer, 2008; Wardle, Llewellyn, Sanderson, & Plomin, 2009) and lower satiety responsiveness (Wardle et al., 2008a). As predicted by quantitative genetic research, the SNP in the *FTO* gene is associated with body weight throughout the distribution, not just with the obese end of the distribution. Also as predicted by quantitative genetic research, the SNP is not associated with birth weight but shows correlations with body weight beginning at 7 years of age.

MC4R, which was suggested initially through candidate gene studies, has also been identified via multiple GWA studies to be associated with BMI (Zeggini et al., 2007), waist circumference (Chambers et al., 2008), higher energy and fat intake (Qi, Kraft, Hunter, & Hu, 2008), and early-onset obesity (Farooqi et al., 2003). A meta-analysis of BMI in 250,000 adult individuals confirmed 14 of the previously identified obesity genes, including *FTO* and *MC4R,* and also identified 18 new loci related to obesity (Speliotes et al., 2010). When looking at childhood obesity, a meta-analysis of 5530 obese cases and 8318 controls yielded two novel loci (Bradfield et al., 2012). These loci were also found in a more recent meta-analysis of BMI in 339,224 individuals (Locke et al., 2015). Researchers have been using findings from meta-analysis to guide creation of polygenic risk scores. For example, risk scores comprised of the 34 loci identified in meta-analyses in adults (Speliotes et al., 2010) and children (Bradfield et al., 2012) were used to examine how satiety plays a role in genetic influence on obesity (Llewellyn, Trzaskowski, van Jaarsveld, Plomin, & Wardle, 2014b). Researchers found that low satiety responsiveness (or appetite regulation) is one of the mechanisms through which genetic predisposition leads to weight gain in an environment rich with food.

The message is clear that common variants appear to contribute small, yet potentially meaningful, effects to obesity-related phenotypes. However, as discussed in Chapter 10, there are other types of genetic variation, including copy number variants and rare variants found at lower frequencies in the population (Figure 18.4, see van der Klaauw & Farooqi, 2015). Recent evidence integrating CNV and gene expression levels in adipose tissue, suggests that a CNV encompassing the salivary amylase gene (*AMY1*), which is involved in carbohydrate metabolism, is associated with BMI and obesity (Falchi et al., 2014).

Epigenetics and obesity-related outcomes Epigenetic modifications, such as DNA methylation and imprinting (see Chapter 10), have also been suggested to affect obesity through their impact on gene expression (Desai, Jellyman, & Ross, 2015). Recall that genomic imprinting influences the genetic expression of alleles as a function of whether the allele came from the father or the mother. One example is Prader-Willi syndrome (Chapter 12), which results from a paternal deletion at 15*q*11-13 and is characterized by severe early-onset obesity due to satiety dysfunction (Shapira et al., 2005; Williams et al., 2010). Epigenetic variation can also be induced by early environmental influences, and DNA methylation has been suggested to affect fetal

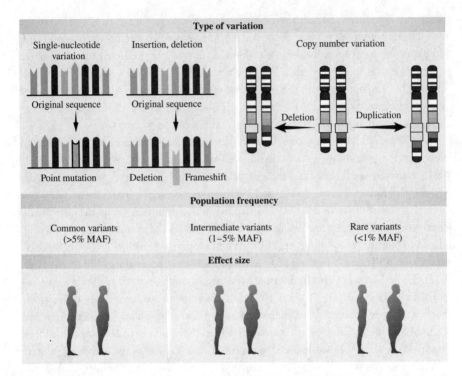

FIGURE 18.4 Types of genetic variation contributing to body weight. MAF = minor allele frequency. (Information from van der Klaauw AA, Farooqi IS. The hunger genes: pathways to obesity. *Cell.* 2015 Mar 26;161(1):119-32. doi: 10.1016/j.cell.2015.03.008. Review. PubMed PMID: 25815990.)

growth, later metabolism, and risk for other chronic diseases (Herrera et al., 2011; Maccani & Marsit, 2009; Zheng, Xiao, Zhang, & Yu, 2014).

Although obese mothers tend to have obese children (Dabelea et al., 2008), maternal weight loss prior to pregnancy via clinical intervention can reduce the risk of obesity in children by providing a less obesogenic prenatal environment (Smith et al., 2009). However, in obese women, it is difficult to distinguish genetic and environmental contributions to offspring obesity. Animal models of maternal obesity have begun to shed some light on the possible interaction between the environment and the epigenetic mechanisms that might affect expression of genes associated with increased BMI and other obesity-related traits (see Lavebratt, Almgren, & Ekström, 2012, for a review). For example, the *MC4R* gene shows reduced methylation following long-term exposure to a high-fat diet in mice (Widiker, Kaerst, Wagener, & Brockmann, 2010). A high-fat diet also modifies methylation of the leptin promoter in rats (Milagro et al., 2009). Importantly, genetic and epigenetic factors are intimately intertwined. As more becomes known about the role of genetics and epigenetics in obesity, that information can be combined with known environmental risks in order to gain a more comprehensive picture of the etiology of obesity-related outcomes (Smith & Ryckman, 2015, Desai et al., 2015).

New directions in genetics of obesity and weight gain The vast majority of studies, only a small fraction of which are discussed above, have focused on the observable outcome, or phenotype, of weight. Research is now emerging that attempts to uncover the effect of our genetic makeup on our gut microbiome (Goodrich et al., 2014; Mathes et al., 2011). The *gut microbiome* is a population of microbial species that interact with gastrointestinal tissues and may ultimately affect body weight, obesity, and other nutritionally relevant traits. The hypothesis is that lean and obese individuals have different gut microbial populations that affect energy extraction and later deposit of fat stores from consumed food, which could influence the host's weight gain environmentally (Turnbaugh & Gordon, 2009). However, the host's genome could also affect the function of the gut microbiome (Goodrich et al., 2014). Studies using animal models have begun to investigate these questions and suggest that genetic variations found in the host affect the function of the gut microbiome, which then influences the development of obesity (see Mathes et al., 2011, for a review). Studies of obese and lean twins have begun to dissect the relative contributions of host genotype and environmental exposures, such as diet, to shaping the microbial and viral landscape of our gut microbiota (Reyes et al., 2010; Turnbaugh et al., 2009). Results suggest that, although the human gut microbiome is shared to some extent among family members, gut microbiomes also contain a variety of specific (i.e., non-shared) bacteria that affect individuals' ability to extract energy from their diet and deposit it into fat, in part as a function of the individuals' genotypes (Hansen et al., 2011; Turnbaugh et al., 2009).

Subsequent research has moved beyond the comparison of gut microbiota from twin pairs discordant for obesity in order to begin to determine the causal mechanisms underlying the association between the microbiome and obesity. In a transformative study, fecal samples from obese and lean co-twins were transplanted into germ-free mice fed with a low-fat diet. Mice who harbored the obese twin's microbiota exhibited increased total-body and fat mass as well as obesity-related metabolic phenotypes, which were not related to daily food consumption (Ridaura et al., 2013). Further tests suggested that housing the mice harboring the obese twin's microbiota with mice harboring the lean twin's microbiota could "rescue" or prevent the development of increased body mass and obesity-related phenotypes in the obese mice (Ridaura et al., 2013). Further work in germ-free mice has identified a particular gut bacterium, *Christensenella minuta*, that can influence obesity-related phenotypes. When *C. minuta* was added to an obese person's fecal sample that was subsequently transplanted into a recipient mouse, the effect was a leaner mouse (Goodrich et al., 2014). This is consistent with data suggesting that leaner people have a greater abundance of *C. minuta* in their gut than obese individuals (Ley, 2015).

Weight loss Epigenetic modifications and the gut microbiome may affect body weight, but the results of twin and family studies summarized in this chapter clearly indicate that individual differences in body weight are highly heritable. Although this high heritability may have some relevance for the success or failure of individual weight-loss efforts, it does not imply that environmental factors are unimportant. Obviously, exercise and caloric restriction can result in weight reduction. Unfortunately, however, such intended weight loss is often only temporary (Elfhag & Rössner, 2005). In fact, in young and middle-age adults, intentional weight loss and strict dieting are often correlated with overeating (Keski-Rakhonen et al., 2005; Smith, Williamson, Bray, & Ryan, 1999). While intentional weight loss and overeating, on the surface, appear to be on opposite ends of the eating behavior spectrum, there is evidence to suggest that there is a positive correlation due in part to shared genetic effects. Specifically, about a third of the genetic factors between intentional weight loss and overeating are shared, while less than 10 percent of environmental risk factors are shared (Wade, Treloar, Heath, & Martin, 2009). This genetic correlation between intentional weight loss and overeating, coupled with the high heritability for body weight, implies that permanent changes in lifestyle may be required to maintain reduced body weight (Elfhag & Rossner, 2005).

Subjective Well-Being and Health

Subjective well-being, life satisfaction, and their relation to health constitute a growing area of research in behavioral genetics (Pluess, 2015). Research suggests, perhaps unsurprisingly, that a lower subjective well-being is associated with chronic health problems (Strine, Chapman, Balluz, Moriarty, & Mokdad, 2008), depression (Greenspoon & Saklofske, 2001), poorer quality of life, increased health care costs, early retirement, and mortality (Gill et al., 2006; Katon et al., 2004). Positive well-being, on the other hand, is related to longevity and may add several years to the life span (Steptoe, Deaton, & Stone, 2015).

Twin studies suggest that about 35 percent of the variance in subjective well-being is due to genetic influences (Bartels, 2015). Moreover, continuity of subjective well-being over time also appears to be influenced by genetic factors (Roysamb, Tambs, Reichborn-Kjennerud, Neale, & Harris, 2003). The phenotypic relationships between subjective well-being and self-reported health, sleep, physical activity, and psychopathology are due, at least in part, to genetic overlap (Bartels, Cacioppo, van Beijsterveldt, & Boomsma, 2013; Mosing, Zietsch, Shekar, Wright, & Martin, 2009b; Paunio et al., 2009; Waller, Kujala, Kaprio, Koskenvuo, & Rantanen, 2010). The positive effects of exercise on subjective well-being are also thought to be attributable to common genetic factors (Bartels, de Moor, van der Aa, Boomsma, & de Geus, 2012).

Less is known about the molecular genetic underpinnings of subjective well-being or self-rated health. A genomewide linkage scan for subjective happiness suggested QTLs of interest on chromosomes 1 and 19 (Bartels et al., 2010); however, replication and additional studies are needed. Recent GWA efforts have yielded no significant findings for self-rated health (Mosing et al., 2010b). SNP heritability estimates suggest that only 4% of the variance in subjective well-being, as measured by feelings of happiness and enjoyment of life, can be accounted for by the additive effects of common SNPs (Okbay et al., in press; Rietveld et al., 2013a). A recent GWA study of well-being in nearly 300,000 individuals identified three genome-wide significant associations; a polygenic score accounted for about one percent of the variance (Okbay et al., 2016). Consequently, it appears that self-rated health and subjective well-being are likely to be due to the contribution of multiple genes of small effect rather than a few genes of major effect.

Increasing interest is being paid to the relationships between subjective well-being, happiness, and healthy aging (Steptoe et al., 2015). Mental health is increasingly defined not only by the absence of illness but also by the presence of subjective well-being (Sadler, Miller, Christensen, & McGue, 2011). It is clear that subjective well-being predicts favorable life outcomes, including better mental and somatic health, as well as longevity. Further, this body of research has prompted interventions and public health initiatives that are focused on increasing happiness and well-being, particularly among older adults. This will be discussed more in Chapter 19.

HEALTH PSYCHOLOGY AND GENETIC COUNSELING

It is clear that we are at the dawn of a new era in which behavioral genetic research is moving beyond the demonstration of the importance of heredity to the identification of specific genes. For example, saliva and blood samples collected in clinics are now often sent to laboratories for DNA extraction (even though each of us does not yet have a memory key with our complete DNA sequence). As described in Chapter 9, hundreds of thousands of DNA polymorphisms can be genotyped on SNP chips at a modest cost. In the past, this type of information was available for single-gene disorders, such as fragile X syndrome, as well as for the QTL association between apolipoprotein E and late-onset dementia. However, there are now companies that offer the ease of obtaining genetic risk prediction at a low cost for anyone willing to send a saliva sample.

As is the case with most important advances, identifying genes for behavior will raise new ethical issues (e.g., Pergament & Ilijic, 2014). These issues are already beginning to affect genetic counseling (Box 18.1). Genetic counseling is expanding from the diagnosis and prediction of rare, untreatable single-gene conditions to the prediction of common, often treatable or preventable conditions (Karanjawala & Collins, 1998). Although there are many unknowns in this uncharted terrain, the benefits of identifying genes for understanding the etiology of behavioral disorders and dimensions seem likely to outweigh the potential abuses. The judicious use of genetic and genomic information has significant, but as yet untested, potential to enhance the clinical care and prevention of chronic diseases. That is, it can help us to understand the etiology of disease and also aid in providing treatment recommendations for patients' health behaviors

BOX 18.1 Genetic Counseling

Genetic counseling is an important interface between the behavioral sciences and genetics and goes well beyond simply conveying information about genetic risks and burdens. It helps individuals come to terms with the information by dispelling mistaken beliefs and allaying anxiety in a nondirective manner that aims to inform rather than to advise. In the United States, over 3000 health professionals have been certified as genetic counselors, and about half of these were trained in 2-year master's programs (Mahowald, Verp, & Anderson, 1998). For more information about genetic counseling as a profession, including practice guidelines and perspectives, see the National Society of Genetic Counselors (http://www.nsgc.org/), which sponsors the *Journal of Genetic Counseling* and has a useful link called "How to Become a Genetic Counselor." For more general information about professional education in genetic counseling, see the National Coalition for Health Professional Education in Genetics (http://www.nchpeg.org/).

Until recently, most genetic counseling was requested by parents who had an affected child and were concerned about risk for other children. Now genetic risk is often assessed directly by means of DNA testing. As more genes are identified for disorders, genetic counseling is increasingly involved in issues related to prenatal diagnoses, prediction, and intervention. This new information will create new ethical dilemmas. Huntington disease provides a good example. It used to be that if you had a parent with the disease, you knew you would have a 50 percent chance of developing the disease. However, with the discovery of the gene responsible for Huntington disease, in almost all cases it is now possible to diagnose whether a fetus or an adult will have the disease. Would you want to take the test? It turns out that the majority of people at risk choose not to take the test, largely because there is as yet no

(Cho et al., 2012; Green & Guyer, 2011). Health psychologists are at the forefront of research investigating the effects of genetic testing on patient attitudes, beliefs, and health-related behaviors (Godino, Turchetti, Jackson, Hennessy, & Skirton, 2015; McBride, Koehly, Sanderson, & Kaphingst, 2010). For example, there is some evidence that when patients are provided with genetic testing results, their preventative behavior increases (Taylor & Wu, 2009). Recent systematic reviews of the impact of genetic risk information on chronic adult diseases found some psychological benefits of including genetic information in treatment of chronic diseases, but it concluded that many gaps in knowledge must be addressed before genetic science can be effectively translated into clinical practice (Godino et al., 2015; McBride et al., 2010). New studies are being designed that try to address these gaps in order to increase the clinical and personal utility of genetic testing (e.g., Cho et al., 2012).

cure (Maat-Kievit et al., 2000). If you did take the test, the results would likely affect knowledge of risk for your relatives. Do your relatives have the right to know, or is their right *not* to know more important? One generally accepted rule is that informed consent is required for testing; moreover, children should not be tested before they become adults unless a treatment becomes available.

A growing area is prenatal genetic screening, which provides parents with information about the health of the fetus. Genomewide tests, including diagnostic whole-exome and whole-genome sequencing, have improved the ability to detect clinically significant findings, but have also increased the chance of detecting incidental findings and variants of uncertain significance. This brings about considerable challenges surrounding how these results are communicated to parents (Westerfield, Darilek, van den Veyver, 2014).

Another increasingly important problem concerns the availability of genetic information to employers and insurance companies. These issues are most pressing for single-gene disorders like Huntington disease, in which a single gene is necessary and sufficient to develop the disorder. For most behavioral disorders, however, genetic risks will involve QTLs that are probabilistic risk factors rather than certain causes of the disorder. A major new dilemma concerns the burgeoning industry of marketing genetic tests directly to consumers (Biesecker & Marteau, 1999; Wade & Wilfond, 2006). Although genetic counseling has traditionally focused on single-gene and chromosomal disorders, increasingly the field is encompassing complex disorders including behavioral disorders (Finn & Smoller, 2006). Despite the ethical dilemmas that arise with the new genetic information, it should also be emphasized that these findings have the potential for profound improvements in the prediction, prevention, and treatment of diseases.

Summary

Interesting genetic results are emerging in the domain of health psychology. One example of genetic research on health psychology concerns body weight and obesity. Although most theories of weight gain are environmental, genetic research consistently shows substantial genetic influence on individual differences in body weight, with heritabilities of about 70 percent. Also interesting in light of environmental theories is the consistent finding that shared family environment does not affect weight. Longitudinal studies indicate that genetic influences on weight are surprisingly stable after infancy, although there is some evidence for genetic change even during adulthood. Body weight and obesity are the target of much molecular genetic research in mice and humans, with increasing success. Subjective well-being is another example of an area where genetic research, both quantitative and molecular, is beginning to expand.

CHAPTER NINETEEN

Aging

U nderstanding the factors that promote healthy aging is an area of great social significance. The average age in most societies is increasing, primarily as a result of improvements in health care. For example, in the United States, 45 million people were age 65 and older in 2013, and this number is expected to rise to nearly 100 million by 2060, an increase from 14 percent to 22 percent (Administration on Aging, 2014). Those 85 and older are projected to triple in the United States (Ortman, Velkoff, & Hogan, 2014) and worldwide (United Nations, 2013). Although obvious changes occur later in life, it is not possible to lump older individuals into a category of "the elderly" because older adults differ greatly biologically and psychologically. For the purposes of this chapter we define the latter part of the life span as age 50 and older, and the "older old" as age 70 and above. The question for genetics is the extent to which genetic factors contribute to individual differences in functioning later in life.

This chapter will focus on behavioral genetic research on cognitive aging, physical health, and longevity. Research in these areas has provided critical insights about these aspects of aging that would not have been possible without using the strategies available in behavioral genetics (Figure 19.1). The explosion of molecular genetic research on cognitive decline, dementia, and longevity in the elderly has added momentum to genetic research on behavioral aging, and has provided some of the most well-replicated evidence of a specific gene involved in development.

COGNITIVE AGING

Many twin studies have assessed how cognitive function changes with age across the life span, leading to the surprising finding that heritability of general cognitive ability *increases* with age (Chapter 11) with some drop-off in the older old as shown in Figure 19.2 (Finkel & Pedersen, 2004). There is also some indication that the

FIGURE 19.1 Ninety-three-year-old MZ twins participating in a twin study of cognitive functioning late in life and photos of them going back to childhood (McClearn et al., 1997). Not only do MZ twins continue to look physically similar late in life, they also continue to perform similarly on measures of cognitive ability. (Photo collage of 93-year-old MZ twins from the cover of *Science* Vol. 276, no. 5318, 6 June 1997. Republished with permission of AAAS.)

patterns of genetic and environmental influences on cognitive aging may differ for some specific cognitive abilities (Reynolds & Finkel, 2015; Tucker-Drob & Briley, 2014). Therefore, examining overall cognitive ability may not capture the nuances of cognitive aging, especially in the older old.

General Cognitive Ability

Twin and adoption studies have found that heritability of general cognitive ability reaches a peak in later adulthood of about 80 percent (Finkel & Reynolds, 2009; Pedersen, 1996). The stability in general cognitive ability throughout adulthood

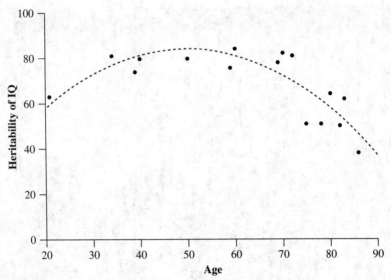

FIGURE 19.2 Summary of heritability estimates for general cognitive ability across the adult life span. (Data from Finkel & Reynolds, 2009.)

is also very high and is due nearly entirely to genetic influences (Tucker-Drob & Briley, 2014). Some studies have found that the heritability in general cognitive ability decreases slightly in the older old, which seems to be the result of *increased* nonshared environmental influences (Reynolds et al., 2005; Finkel & Reynolds, 2014; Johnson, McGue, & Dreary, 2014). In other words, environmental influences unique to each member of the twin pair have a greater impact on individual differences in general cognitive ability during later adulthood. There are other reports, however, that do not find a decrease in heritability in the older old (McGue & Christensen, 2013; Lee, Henry, Trollor, & Sachdev, 2010b). Until more data become available for twin samples over age 80, it may not be possible to resolve this issue definitively (Reynolds & Finkel, 2014); however, the findings for increasing heritability on general cognitive ability up to age 70 are clear and have been replicated in multiple studies and meta-analyses.

Specific Cognitive Abilities

As described in Chapter 11, specific cognitive abilities, such as verbal ability, spatial ability, and memory, are the components that make up general cognitive ability. Not mentioned in the discussion of specific cognitive abilities in Chapter 11 is a distinction often made in the field of cognitive aging between "fluid" abilities, such as spatial ability, which decline with age, and "crystallized" abilities, such as vocabulary, which increase with age (Baltes, 1993; Reynolds, Finkel, & Zavala, 2014). This finding has led some to hypothesize that fluid abilities are more biologically based and crystallized abilities more culturally based (Lindenberger, 2001). However, genetic research so far has found that fluid and crystallized abilities are equally heritable (Finkel & Reynolds, 2009; Pedersen, 1996). Interestingly, genetic and environmental influences on the stability of fluid and crystalized abilities may differ. One meta-analysis found greater genetic stability for fluid than for crystalized abilities (Tucker-Drob & Briley, 2014).

Although less is known about specific cognitive abilities throughout the life span, evidence suggests that, for many domains, the pattern of genetic and environmental influences over time is similar to that seen for general cognitive ability. Two meta-analyses of findings for specific cognitive abilities from twin and family studies suggest that heritability tends to increase with age (Reynolds & Finkel, 2015; Tucker-Drob & Briley, 2014), consistent with the findings for general cognitive ability. There is, however, one report that does not find an increase in heritability for adults over age 65 for cognitive abilities assessed across multiple domains (Polderman et al., 2015).

There are some differences in how genetic and environmental factors influence change in specific cognitive abilities depending on the domain examined (Finkel, Reynolds, McArdle, & Pedersen, 2005). For example, although verbal ability is highly heritable, change in verbal ability with age was due entirely to nonshared environmental influences. In contrast, for processing speed, heritability was high both at baseline and for change. A different analysis of the same sample across a longer time span (up to age 96) found that there was substantial overlap in genetic influences on cognitive change across domains, as well as genetic influences unique to specific cognitive abilities, especially for memory change for those age 65 and older (Tucker-Drob, Reynolds, Finkel & Pedersen, 2014). This highlights the need to consider both general and specific cognitive abilities in order to get a more complete understanding of the behavioral genetics of cognitive aging.

Dementia

Although aging is a highly variable process, as many as one quarter of individuals over age 85 worldwide suffer severe cognitive decline known as *dementia* (Gatz, Jang, Karlsson, & Pedersen, 2014; Prince et al., 2013). Prior to age 65, the incidence is 1 percent or less (Figure 19.3). Among the elderly, dementia accounts for more days of hospitalization than any other psychiatric disorder (Cumings & Benson, 1992) and has a substantial impact on the quality of life both for the individual with dementia and their family and caregivers (Alzheimer's Disease International, 2015). The number of diagnosed dementia patients is projected to nearly double every 20 years (Alzheimer's Disease International, 2015).

More than half of all cases of dementia involve Alzheimer disease (AD), which has been studied for more than a century (Gatz et al., 2014). AD occurs very gradually over many years, beginning with loss of memory for recent events. This mild memory loss affects many older individuals but is much more severe in individuals with AD. Irritability and difficulty in concentrating are also often noted. Memory gradually worsens to include simple behaviors, such as forgetting to turn off the stove or bath water and wandering off and getting lost. Eventually—sometimes after 3 years,

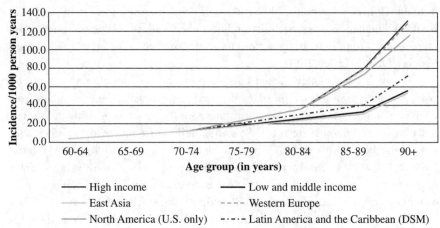

FIGURE 19.3 Annual incidence of dementia for world regions estimated from meta-analyses. (Data from Alzheimer's Disease International, 2015.)

sometimes after 15 years—individuals with AD become bedridden. Biologically, AD involves extensive changes in brain nerve cells, including plaques and tangles (described later) that build up and result in death of the nerve cells. Although these plaques and tangles occur to some extent in most older people, in individuals with AD they are much more numerous and widespread.

Another type of dementia is the result of the cumulative effect of multiple small strokes in which blood flow to the brain becomes blocked, thus damaging the brain. This type of dementia is called *multiple-infarct dementia (MID)*. (An *infarct* is an area damaged as a result of a stroke.) Unlike AD, MID is usually more abrupt and involves focal symptoms such as loss of language rather than general cognitive decline. Co-occurrence of AD and MID is seen in about one third of all cases. The DSM-5 recognizes several other kinds of dementias, called *neurocognitive disorders*, including major or mild neurocognitive disorders due to Parkinson disease, AIDS, head trauma, and Huntington disease (Chapter 3).

Surprisingly little is known about the quantitative genetics of either AD or MID. Family studies of AD probands estimate risk to first-degree relatives of nearly 50 percent by age 85, when the data are adjusted for age of the relatives (McGuffin, Owen, O'Donovan, Thapar, & Gottesman, 1994; Green et al., 2002). Until recently, the only twin study of dementia was one reported over 60 years ago. That twin study, which did not distinguish AD and MID, found concordances of 43 percent for identical twins and 8 percent for fraternal twins, results suggesting moderate genetic influence (Kallmann & Kaplan, 1955). Although subsequent heritability estimates for dementias like MID have not been significantly different from zero (Ferencz & Gerritsen, 2015; Gatz, Reynolds, Finkel, Pedersen, & Walters, 2010), more recent twin studies find evidence of substantial genetic influence on AD, with concordances two times greater for identical than for fraternal twins in Finland (Räihä, Kapiro, Koskenvuo,

Rajala, & Sourander, 1996), Norway (Bergem, Engedal, & Kringlen, 1997), Sweden (Gatz et al., 1997), and the United States (Plassman & Breitner, 1997). In the largest twin study to date, liability to AD yielded a heritability estimate of 0.58 (Gatz et al., 2006). SNP-based heritability estimates support the findings of genetic influences on AD with common SNPs accounting for about 30 percent of the total variance (Ridge et al., 2013; Lee et al., 2013).

Some of the most important molecular genetic findings for behavioral disorders have come from research on dementia (Bettens, Sleegers, & Van Broeckhoven, 2013). Early research focused on a rare (1 in 10,000) type of Alzheimer disease that appears before 65 years of age and shows evidence for autosomal dominant inheritance. Three genes have been identified that contribute to this rare form of the disorder (Bekris, Yu, Bird, & Tsuang, 2010). However, the great majority of Alzheimer cases occur after 65 years of age, typically in persons in their seventies and eighties. A major advance toward understanding late-onset Alzheimer disease is the discovery of a strong allelic association with a gene (for apolipoprotein E) on chromosome 19 (Corder et al., 1993). This *APOE* gene has three alleles (confusingly called alleles 2, 3, and 4). The frequency of allele 4 is about 40 percent in individuals with Alzheimer disease and 15 percent in control samples. This result translates to about a sixfold increased risk for late-onset Alzheimer disease for individuals who have one or two of these alleles.

Allele 4 of the *APOE* gene, although a risk factor, is neither necessary nor sufficient for developing dementia. For instance, nearly half of patients with late-onset Alzheimer disease do not have that allele. Assuming a liability-threshold model, allele 4 accounts for about 15 percent of the variance in liability (Owen, Liddle, & McGuffin, 1994). Because apolipoprotein E is known for its role in transporting lipids throughout the body, its association with late-onset AD was puzzling at first. However, the product of allele 4 has multiple effects in the brain that lead to the plaques common in AD and, eventually, to the death of nerve cells (Tanzi & Bertram, 2005).

Because the *APOE* gene does not account for all the genetic influence on AD, the search is on for other genes responsible for the heritability of AD. A meta-analysis of over one thousand reports of associations with over 500 candidate genes found evidence for significant associations for more than a dozen susceptibility QTLs, although results are often inconsistent (Bertram, McQueen, Mullin, Blacker, & Tanzi, 2007). Genomewide association (GWA) studies consistently confirm the association with the *APOE* gene, but more than a dozen studies yielded inconsistent results for other associations until three large-scale studies including data from 43,000 individuals provided compelling evidence for small effects of variants in four novel susceptibility genes that might lead to synaptic disintegration (Hollingworth, Harold, Jones, Owen, & Williams, 2011). Subsequent meta-analyses and GWA studies suggested additional risk loci (e.g., Lambert et al., 2013), but including risk loci identified in GWA studies in genetic risk prediction models found only minimal improvement for predicting AD beyond other variables such as age, sex, and the *APOE* gene (reviewed in Gatz et al., 2014). More than a dozen knock-out mouse models of AD-related genes have been generated, and several of the mutants show β-amyloid deposits and plaques, although no animal model has as yet been shown to have all of the expected AD effects, including the critical effects on memory (Bekris et al., 2010).

Genes and Normal Cognitive Aging

Much less work has been done on the molecular genetics of normal cognitive aging. There is, however, an indication that the *APOE* gene plays an important role, along with another gene in the lipid metabolism pathway, *SORL1* (Davies et al., 2012; Reynolds et al., 2013). GWA studies have found that many of the same genes associated with AD are also associated with general cognitive function (Davies et al., 2015; Zhang & Pierce, 2014).

HEALTH AND AGING

As discussed in Chapter 18, there is increasing interest in the relationship between subjective well-being and healthy aging. That is, what is important is not just how long we live but how well we live—not just adding years to our life but adding life to our years. Subjective well-being is also important because it indexes how healthy an individual feels and it is related to mental health. In addition, two aspects of physical functioning are most often examined in research on aging: physiological functioning, which includes things like obesity, cardiovascular health, and lung function; and behavioral physical functioning, which includes things like muscle strength that allow for independent functioning in daily life.

Physiological Functioning

Twin studies have found heritabilities of about 40 percent for blood pressure, the most common indicator of cardiovascular health included in twin studies (Vinck, Fagard, Loos, & Vlietinck, 2001), and similar heritabilities for hypertension (elevated blood pressure) (McCaffery, Papandonatos, Lyons, & Niaura, 2008; Kupper et al., 2005). Interestingly, the handful of longitudinal studies of blood pressure suggest that genetic influences decrease with age (Finkel et al., 2003). More sophisticated measures of cardiovascular health, such as heart rate variability, show heritabilities similar to those found for blood pressure, ranging from 30 to 55 percent, depending on how the tests are conducted (Li et al., 2009a; Uusitalo et al., 2007). Studies have also looked at *serum lipids*, indicators of cholesterol levels in the blood, as an indicator of cardiovascular health and find heritabilities for serum lipids of around 50 to 60 percent (e.g., Goode, Cherny, Christian, Jarvik, & De Andrade, 2007; Nilsson, Read, Berg, & Johansson, 2009). The heritability of serum lipids changes after age 50 (Goode et al., 2007; Heller, de Faire, Pedersen, Dahlen, & McClearn, 1993), and results obtained from longitudinal studies suggest that new genetic influences on serum lipids may emerge at midlife (Middelburg, Martin & Whitfield, 2006).

Behavioral and Physical Functioning

During adulthood, heritability for upper and lower body strength ranges from 30 to 60 percent (Finkel et al., 2003; Frederiksen et al., 2002; Tiainen et al., 2004; Tiainen et al., 2005) and is stable across adulthood (McGue & Christensen, 2013). Activities of daily living are especially important during later adulthood and include behaviors like walking, balance, and chair stands (rising from a chair). Heritability estimates are generally low to moderate, with no indication that genetic influences contribute to change with age (Christensen, Gaist, Vaupel, & McGue, 2002; Christensen, Frederiksen, Vaupel, & McGue, 2003a; Finkel, Ernsth-Bravell, & Pedersen, 2014a).

Self-Rated Health

Self-rated health is a commonly used measure in studies of aging populations as the measure captures not only general physical health but also personality and cognitive status (Finkel, Pedersen, Berg, & Johansson, 2000). It has also been found to predict longevity independent of objective health measures (Idler & Benyamini, 1997). Heritability for self-rated health is moderate, ranging from 25 to 40 percent (Christensen, Holm, McGue, Corder, & Vaupel, 1999; Svedberg, Lichtenstein, & Pedersen, 2001). A recent report from a consortium of over 12,000 twin pairs found that heritability on self-rated health generally was less in late adulthood (Franz et al., 2016). As might be expected given the nature of the construct of self-rated health, much of the genetic variance is shared with other constructs such as depression (Mosing, Pedersen, Martin, & Wright, 2010a) and cognitive function (Svedberg, Gatz, & Pedersen, 2009).

For psychopathology and personality, the few genetic studies in later life yield results similar to those described in Chapters 14–16 for research earlier in life (Bergeman, 1997). For example, for depression in later life, twin studies indicate modest heritabilities (e.g., Gatz, Pedersen, Plomin, Nesselroade, & McClearn, 1992; Johnson, McGue, Gaist, Vaupel, & Christensen, 2002b; McGue & Christensen, 2013). There are also genetically influenced links between cognitive abilities and mental health. For example, in a sample of male twins assessed longitudinally, low cognitive ability during early adulthood (age 20) predicted depressive symptoms during later life (age 51–60), with most of the correlation due to genetic influences (Franz et al., 2011). For personality, *Type A behavior*—hard-driving and competitive behavior that is of special interest because of its reputed link with heart attacks—shows moderate heritability typical of other personality measures in older twins (Pedersen et al., 1989b). Another interesting personality domain is *locus of control,* which refers to the extent that outcomes are believed to be due to one's own behavior or chance. For some older individuals, this sense of control declines, and this change is related to deterioration in psychological functioning and poor health. A twin study later in life found moderate genetic influence for two aspects of locus of control: sense of responsibility and life direction (Pedersen, Gatz, Plomin, Nesselroade, & McClearn, 1989a). However, the key variable of the perceived role of luck—in other words, a lack of control—in determining life's outcomes showed no genetic influence and substantial shared environmental influence. Another study of twins in late life (average age 59) was more consistent with findings for personality earlier in the life span, finding modest genetic influences on locus of control and no shared environmental influences (Mosing et al., 2012). This more recent finding of genetic but not shared environmental influences on locus of control is not surprising given the high stability of personality throughout adulthood. When the stability of personality is examined for genetic and environmental influences, genetic influences are found to account for the majority of the stability in later life (Johnson, McGue, & Krueger, 2005; Read, Vogler, Pedersen, & Johansson, 2006). GWA studies of self-rated health have been inconclusive (e.g., Mosing et al., 2010b), suggesting that this is a construct that is likely to be influenced by many genes of small effect.

Molecular Genetics and Physical Health

As described in Chapter 18, the molecular genetics of physical health has been an area of intense focus, with many publications of GWA studies and meta-analyses of genes related to various aspects of physical health. Interestingly, the genes that have been identified as important for BMI and obesity during young adulthood do not seem to be important during later adulthood (e.g., Graff et al., 2013), a finding that suggests that genetic and environmental factors related to BMI and obesity during later adulthood may be different than those for younger adulthood. It is also possible that nonshared environmental influences may have increased importance for physical health during the latter portion of the life span, as has been found for cognitive aging.

Similar to the quantitative genetic studies discussed above, molecular genetic investigations have also examined heart health in adults through the study of serum lipids. The *APOE* gene is associated with serum lipid profiles, with carriers of allele 4 showing poorer lipid profiles than carriers of the other alleles (Bennet et al., 2007). About a quarter of the genetic variance for serum lipid traits was explained by 95 genes that achieved significance in a GWA study of cholesterol (Teslovich et al., 2010).

Resting heart rate and lung functioning both are indicators of pulmonary health and have been associated with longevity and healthy aging (McClearn, Svartengren, Pedersen, Heller, & Plomin, 1994; Stessman, Jacobs, Stessman-Lande, Gilon, & Leibowitz, 2013). Two genes have been associated with resting heart rate in GWA studies (Deo et al., 2013), both important in processes related to heart function. Nearly 50,000 individuals from 23 studies (ages spanning from 17–97 years across all studies) were examined in a meta-analysis of GWA studies on lung functioning, with 26 significant gene loci identified or confirmed (Soler Artigas et al., 2011). Although 14 of the loci identified or confirmed (e.g., *MFAP2* on chromosome 1 and *ZKSCAN3* on chromosome 6) have been associated with other complex traits and disease, many of the other loci had not previously been associated with pulmonary function. This meta-analysis also found that more than half of the novel loci showed consistent effects on lung function in a different sample of children, suggesting that lung function decline in adults and the elderly may be due to the same genes important for lung development.

LONGEVITY

The famous U.S. Supreme Court Justice Oliver Wendell Holmes quipped that "those wishing long lives should advertise for a couple of parents, both belonging to long-lived families" (cited by Cohen, 1964, p. 133). Research, however, indicates only modest genetic influence on longevity, with heritabilities of about 25 percent from twin studies (Finkel, Gerritsen, Reynolds, Dahl, & Pedersen, 2014b) and about 10 percent using common SNPs (Pilling et al., 2016), although genetic influence on longevity may increase at the most advanced ages (Hjelmborg et al., 2006). The most consistent evidence from molecular genetic studies suggests that polymorphisms in the *APOE* gene (e.g., Novelli et al., 2008) and *FOXOA3* gene (Flachsbart et al., 2009; Li et al., 2009b; Wilicox et al., 2008) are associated with longer life (see Wheeler & Kim, 2011, for a review). *APOE* is hypothesized to be associated with individual differences in human longevity, probably because of its links with cardiovascular disease (Christensen, Johnson, & Vaupel, 2006b). The *FOXOA3* gene is part of the insulin signaling pathway. GWA studies have identified a few additional gene associations, although additional replication is needed (Brooks-Wilson, 2013; Hindorff et al., 2011; Nebel et al., 2011).

Much genetic research in nonhuman species—especially mice, fruit flies, and nematode worms—has shown that mutations in the insulin signaling pathway affect the life span (reviewed in Martin, 2011; Tissenbaum, 2012; Wheeler & Kim, 2011). The insulin signaling pathway is related to processes like oxidative stress resistance and metabolism regulation in animals and humans (Barbieri, Bonafè, Franceschi, & Paolisso, 2003). Animal models are continuing to aid in efforts to identify genes associated with longevity (Kenyon, 2010). For example, according to the Human Aging Genomic Resources (http://genomics.senescence.info/), 126 genes in the mouse have been identified as being related to aging (Tacutu et al., 2013). In the fruit fly *Drosophila melanogaster*, selective breeding, QTL analysis, and mutational analysis have identified 170 genes related to the aging process. In the nematode worm (*C. elegans*), more than 800 genes have been found to influence life span.

Longevity research also presents an excellent example of gene-by-environment interaction. A diet restricted in calories has been shown, across multiple organisms, to extend the life span. This finding was first reported in the 1930s, when it was observed that rats that were underfed, or had restricted caloric intake, lived significantly longer than their normally fed counterparts (McCay, Crowell, & Maynard, 1935). Research in this area has expanded so much that dietary restriction is currently considered a robust life-extending intervention. However, research suggesting life extension due to reduced caloric intake has not been without contradictory findings. Some researchers have reported that restricted diets actually decrease the life span in certain strains of rodents (Harper, Leathers, & Austad, 2006). Researchers attempted to address this inconsistency by examining the efficacy of caloric restriction on life span across a range of genotypes (Liao, Rikke, Johnson, Diaz, & Nelson, 2010). Among 41 recombinant inbred strains of mice (Chapter 5), it was reported that dietary restriction shortened the life span in more strains than it increased the life span. Moreover, strain-specific "lengths of life span" under restricted or normal diets were not correlated, meaning that genetic determinants of longevity differ under the two dietary conditions (Liao et al., 2010). There is also recent evidence that meal timing and the microbiome are both crucial to the effectiveness of caloric restriction with some genetic variation in response also being indicated (Fontana & Partridge, 2015). Thus, it appears that dietary restriction might not be a universal intervention for increasing the life span because it depends on the genetic background of the individual or organism.

Summary

With recent dramatic increases in the number of people over age 65, there is a need for continued research on healthy aging. Dementia and cognitive decline in later life are intense areas of molecular genetic research. For both general and specific cognitive abilities, twin and adoption studies indicate that heritability increases during adulthood. To better understand healthy aging, there has been an increased focus on physiological functioning and indicators of physical health and activities of daily living. Molecular genetic studies of more objective health measures, such as blood pressure and serum lipids, have been fruitful in identifying risk genes that account for substantial amounts of variance. Genetic influences on longevity are only moderate, with much research focusing on molecular genetics and using animal studies.

CHAPTER **TWENTY**

The Future of Behavioral Genetics

P redicting the future of behavioral genetics is not a matter of crystal ball gazing. The momentum of recent developments makes the field certain to thrive, especially as behavioral genetics continues to flow beyond psychology and psychiatry into the mainstream of research in diverse fields from neuroscience to economics. This momentum is propelled by new findings, methods, and projects, both in quantitative genetics and in molecular genetics.

Another reason for optimism about the continued growth of genetics in the behavioral sciences is that so many more researchers have incorporated genetic strategies into their studies. This trend has grown much stronger now that the price of admission to genetic research is just some saliva from which DNA is extracted, not difficult-to-obtain samples of twins or adoptees. Although caution is also warranted (Chapter 9), this easy access to genetics is important because the best behavioral genetic research is likely to be done by behavioral scientists who are not primarily geneticists. Experts from behavioral domains will focus on traits and theories that are pivotal to those domains and interpret their research findings in ways that will achieve the most impact. As described in the Preface, the goal of this book is to share with you our excitement about behavioral genetics and to whet your appetite for learning about genetics in the behavioral sciences. We hope that this introduction will inspire some readers to contribute to the field. Although we believe that the field of behavioral genetics has made some of the most important discoveries in the behavioral sciences, there is much left to do.

QUANTITATIVE GENETICS

Some of the most important findings in the behavioral sciences have come from quantitative genetic studies. Recently, a top-ten list of behavioral genetic findings has been proposed (Plomin, DeFries, Knopik & Neiderhiser, 2016). All ten findings have been discussed in previous chapters, such as the heritability of intelligence increases throughout development (Chapter 11), age-to-age stability is mainly due to genetics (Chapters 11 and 16), and most measures of the "environment" show significant genetic influence (Chapter 8). These are "big" findings, both in terms of effect size and potential impact on the behavioral sciences. In the context of current concerns about replication in science (Pashler & Wagenmakers, 2012), an important feature of behavioral genetic research is that it replicates (Plomin et al., 2016).

Quantitative genetic research will continue to make important advances for at least three reasons. First, quantitative genetic methods estimate the cumulative effect of genetic influence regardless of the number of genes involved or the magnitude or complexity of their effects. If we could find all the genes responsible for heritability, there would no longer be any need for quantitative genetic research because genetic influence could be assessed directly from each individual's DNA rather than being assessed indirectly by genetic relatedness, as in twin and adoption studies. However, it seems highly unlikely that most—let alone all—of the genes responsible for the heritability for any complex trait will be identified in the foreseeable future (Chapter 9).

The second reason is that quantitative genetics is as much about the environment as it is about genetics, whereas molecular genetics is fundamentally about genetics. Just as quantitative genetic methods can be used to estimate the cumulative effect of genetic influences without identifying the individual genes involved, these methods can also estimate the cumulative effect of environmental influences without identifying the specific factors that are responsible for the environmental influence. Quantitative genetics can investigate environmental influences while controlling for genetics as well as study genetic influences while controlling for environmental influences (Chapter 8). For this reason, quantitative genetics provides the best available evidence for the importance of the environment in the behavioral sciences (Chapters 11–19). It has also made some of the most important discoveries about how the environment affects behavior. One example is the finding that environmental influences typically operate on an individual-by-individual basis, not generally on a family-by-family basis (Chapter 7). Another example is the finding that many putative environmental measures show substantial genetic influence (Chapter 8). In the proposed list of top-ten findings from behavioral genetics mentioned above, four of the findings involve the environment, discoveries that could only have been made using genetically sensitive research designs.

The third reason is that a quantitative genetic technique has been developed that estimates genetic influence from chance genetic similarity among unrelated individuals as estimated from SNPs. SNP heritability, described in Chapter 7, will be increasingly used because it does not require special relatives such as twins or adoptees. Although SNP heritability requires thousands of individuals genotyped on hundreds of thousands of SNPs, these are also the requirements of genomewide association analysis (Chapter 9), which means that many studies are available that meet these requirements for SNP heritability. Multivariate SNP-based quantitative genetics is especially useful to estimate genetic correlations between traits (as discussed in Chapters 11 and 17).

The future will no doubt witness the application of quantitative genetic research to other behavioral traits. Behavioral genetics has only scratched the surface of possible applications, even within the domains of cognitive abilities (Chapter 11), cognitive disabilities (Chapter 12), psychopathology (Chapters 13–15), personality (Chapter 16), and substance abuse (Chapter 17). For example, for cognitive abilities, most research has focused on general cognitive ability and major group factors of specific cognitive abilities. The future of quantitative genetic research in this area lies in more fine-grained analyses of cognitive abilities and in the use of information-processing, cognitive psychology, and neuroimaging approaches to cognition. For psychopathology, genetic research has just begun to consider disorders other than schizophrenia, the major mood disorders, and substance use disorders. Much remains to be learned about disorders in childhood, for example. Approaching psychopathology as quantitative traits rather than qualitative disorders is a major new direction for quantitative genetic research. Personality and substance abuse are such complex domains that they can keep researchers busy for decades, especially as they go beyond self-report questionnaires and interviews to other measures such as neuroimaging. A rich territory for future exploration is the link between psychopathology and personality.

Cognitive disabilities and abilities, psychopathology, personality, and substance abuse have been the targets for the vast majority of genetic research in the behavioral sciences because these areas have traditionally considered individual differences. Two other areas that are beginning to be explored genetically were described in Chapters 18 and 19: health psychology and aging. Some of the oldest areas of psychology — perception, learning, and language, for example — as well as some of the newest areas of research, such as neuroscience, have not emphasized individual differences and, as a result, are only beginning to be explored systematically from a genetic perspective. Other disciplines in the social and behavioral sciences are beginning to catch on to genetics, most notably economics and political science, with other fields — such as demography, education, and sociology — sure to follow.

Genetic research in the behavioral sciences will continue to move beyond simply demonstrating that genetic factors are important. The questions *whether* and *how much* genetic factors affect behavioral dimensions and disorders represent important first steps in understanding the origins of individual differences. But these are only first steps. The next steps involve the question *how* — that is, determining the mechanisms by which genes have their effect. How do genetic effects unfold developmentally? What are the biological pathways between genes and behavior? How do nature and nurture interact and correlate? Examples of these three directions for genetic research in psychology — developmental genetics, multivariate genetics, and "environmental" genetics — have been presented throughout the preceding chapters. The future will see more research of this type as behavioral genetics continues to move beyond merely documenting genetic influence.

Developmental genetic analysis considers change as well as continuity during development throughout the human life span. Two types of developmental questions can be asked. First, do genetic and environmental components of variance change during development? The most striking example to date involves intelligence for which genetic effects become increasingly important throughout the life span. Shared family environment is important in childhood, but its influence becomes negligible after adolescence. The second question concerns the role of genetic and environmental factors in age-to-age change and continuity during development. Using general cognitive ability again as an example, we find a surprising degree of genetic continuity from childhood to adulthood. However, some evidence has been found for genetic change as well, for example, during the transition from early to middle childhood, when formal schooling begins. Interesting developmental discoveries are not likely to be limited to cognitive development or childhood — it just so happens that most developmental genetic research so far has focused on children's cognitive development, although aging will increasingly be the target for developmental research (Chapter 19).

Multivariate genetic research addresses the covariance between traits rather than the variance of each trait considered by itself. A surprising finding in relation to specific cognitive abilities is that the same genetic factors affect most cognitive abilities and disabilities (Chapter 11 and 12). For psychopathology, a key question is why so many disorders co-occur. Multivariate genetic research suggests that genetic overlap between disorders may be responsible for this comorbidity (Chapter 14). Another basic question in psychopathology involves heterogeneity. Are there subtypes of disorders that are genetically distinct? Multivariate genetic research is critical for investigating the causes of comorbidity and heterogeneity as well as for identifying the most heritable constellations (comorbidity) and components (heterogeneity) of psychopathology (Chapters 13–15), an area of inquiry that could impact treatment efforts such as drug design and discovery as well as diagnosis. Another fundamental question is the extent to which genetic and environmental effects on disorders are merely the quantitative extremes of the same genetic and environmental factors that affect the rest of the distribution. Or are disorders qualitatively different from the normal range of behavior? A major goal of future research will be to test the validity of current symptom-based diagnostic schemes and ultimately to create an etiology-based scheme that recognizes quantitative dimensions as well as qualitative diagnoses.

Another general direction for multivariate genetic research is to investigate the mechanisms by which genetic factors influence behavior by identifying genetic correlations between behavior and biological processes such as those assessed by neuroimaging. It cannot be assumed that the nexus of associations between biology and behavior is necessarily genetic in origin. Multivariate genetic analysis is needed to investigate the extent to which genetic factors mediate these associations.

"Environmental" genetics will continue to explore the interface between nature and nurture. As mentioned earlier, genetic research has made some of the most important discoveries about the environment in recent decades, especially non-shared environment and the role of genetics in experience (Chapter 6). One of the major challenges for behavioral genetics is to identify the specific environmental factors responsible for the widespread influence of nonshared environment. MZ twins provide an especially sharp scalpel to dissect nonshared environment because MZ co-twins differ only for reasons of nonshared environment. An even broader topic is understanding how genes influence experience, which is part of the biggest question of all: How do genetic and environmental influences covary and interact to influence behavior? More discoveries about environmental mechanisms can be predicted as the environment continues to be investigated in the context of genetically sensitive designs. New multivariate quantitative genetic methods have recently been developed that aim to distinguish environmental causation from correlation (Chapter 8). Much remains to be learned about interactions and correlations between nature and nurture.

In summary, no crystal ball is needed to predict that quantitative genetic research will continue to flourish as it turns to other areas of behavior and, especially, as it goes beyond the rudimentary questions of *whether* and *how much* to ask the question *how*. Such research will become increasingly important as it guides molecular genetic research to the most heritable components and constellations throughout the human life span as they interact and correlate with the environment. In return, developmental, multivariate, and "environmental" behavioral genetics will be transformed by molecular genetics.

MOLECULAR GENETICS

To answer questions about how genes influence behavior, nothing can be more important than identifying specific genes responsible for the widespread genetic influence on behavior. However, the quest is to find not *the* gene for a trait, but rather the multiple genes that are associated with the trait in a probabilistic rather than a predetermined manner. The breathtaking pace of molecular genetics (Chapter 9) leads us to predict that behavioral scientists will increasingly use DNA markers as a tool in their research to identify the relevant genetic differences among individuals.

Even though DNA markers individually predict only a small amount of variance of a trait (Plomin et al., 2016), they can be used together as polygenic scores in any research that considers individual differences, without the need for special family-based samples such as twins or adoptees (Wray et al., 2014). Moreover, polygenic predictors using DNA markers would have the distinct advantage of making predictions for specific individuals rather than a general prediction for all members of a family. Aiding this prediction that behavioral scientists will routinely use DNA in their research is the fact that DNA is inexpensive to obtain and DNA arrays make genotyping increasingly inexpensive, even for complex traits for which hundreds or thousands of DNA markers are genotyped.

Polygenic predictions will eventually transform quantitative genetic research, taking the developmental, multivariate, and gene-environment interplay issues discussed throughout this book to the next level. As indicated in previous chapters, this is already happening in several areas of research (Krapohl et al., 2015). Polygenic predictors will also facilitate research on the links among the genome, epigenome, transcriptome, proteome, neurome, and eventually behavior (Chapter 10).

In contrast to bottom-up functional genomics research, top-down behavioral genomics research using polygenic scores is likely to pay off more quickly in terms of prediction, diagnosis, intervention, and prevention of behavioral disorders. Behavioral genomics represents the long-term future of behavioral genetics, when we are likely to have polygenic predictors that account for some of the ubiquitous genetic influence for many behavioral dimensions and disorders. Bottom-up functional genomics will eventually meet top-down behavioral genomics in the brain. The grandest implication for science is that DNA will serve as a common denominator integrating diverse disciplines. Clinically, polygenic predictors will be key to personalized genomics, which hopes to predict risk, identify treatment interactions, and propose interventions to prevent problems before they appear. A particularly promising area is the prediction of responses to drug treatments.

As indicated in Chapter 9, it has been predicted that in the next few years, rather than screening newborns for just a few known genetic mutations like phenylketonuria, we will sequence all of the 3 billion nucleotide base pairs of their genomes. Sequencing whole genomes will yield all DNA variants. We predict that most of these variants will be altogether different from traditional ones, deletions and duplications of long stretches of DNA being a recent example (Chapter 9); such rare DNA variants may have relatively large effects that will account for at least some of the "missing heritability." When whole-genome sequences become available, it will cost little to use this information. The promise and problems of these developments were discussed in the section on genetic counseling in Chapter 18. The impact on behavioral genetics is that this same whole-genome sequence information could also be available for use in behavioral research.

One of the great strengths of DNA analysis is that it can be used to predict risk long before a disorder appears. This predictive ability will allow research on interventions that can prevent the disorder rather than trying to reverse a disorder once it appears and has already caused collateral damage. Molecular genetics may also eventually lead to personalized genomics — individualized gene-based diagnoses and treatment programs.

For these reasons, it is crucial that behavioral scientists be prepared to take advantage of the exciting developments in molecular genetics. In the same way that we now assume that computer literacy is an essential goal to be achieved during elementary and secondary education, students in the behavioral sciences must be taught about genetics in order to prepare them for this future. Otherwise, this opportunity for behavioral scientists will slip away by default to geneticists, and genetics is much too important a topic to be left to geneticists! Clinicians use the acronym "DNA" to note that a client "did not attend"—it is critical to the future of the behavioral sciences that DNA mean deoxyribonucleic acid rather than "did not attend."

IMPLICATIONS OF NATURE AND NURTURE

The controversy that swirled around behavioral genetics research during the 1970s has largely faded, as indicated, for example, by the dramatic increase in the number of journal publications (Chapter 1). These new findings from behavioral genetics research lead to two general messages. The first message is that genes play a surprisingly important role across all behavioral traits. This has resulted in an increasing acceptance of genetic influence in the behavioral sciences that is now growing into a tidal wave that that threatens to engulf the equally important second message: Individual differences in complex behavioral traits are due at least as much to environmental influences as they are to genetic influences (Plomin et al., 2016).

The first message will become more prominent during the next decade as more genes are identified that contribute to the widespread influence of genetics in the behavioral sciences. As explained in Chapter 7, it should be emphasized that genetic effects on complex traits describe *what is*. Such findings do not predict *what could be* or prescribe *what should be*. Genes are not destiny. Genetic effects on complex traits represent probabilistic propensities, not predetermined programming. A related point is that, for complex traits such as behavioral traits, quantitative genetic effects refer to average effects in a population, not to a particular individual. For example, one of the strongest DNA associations with a complex behavioral disorder is the association between allele 4 of the gene encoding apolipoprotein E and late-onset dementia (Chapter 19). Unlike simple single-gene disorders, this QTL association does not mean that allele 4 is necessary or sufficient for the development of dementia. Many people with dementia do not have the allele, and many people with the allele do not have dementia. A particular gene may be associated with a large average increase in risk for a disorder, but it is likely to be a weak predictor at an individual level. The importance of this point concerns the dangers of labeling individuals on the basis of population averages.

The relationship between genetics and equality is an issue that lurks in the shadows, causing a sense of unease about genetics. The main point is that finding genetic differences among individuals does not compromise the value of social equality. The essence of a democracy is that all people should have legal equality *despite* their genetic differences. Knowledge alone by no means accounts for societal and political decisions. Values are just as important as knowledge in the decision-making process. Decisions, both good and bad, can be made with or without knowledge. Nonetheless, scientific findings are often misused, and scientists, like the rest of the population, need to be concerned with reducing such misuse. We firmly believe, however, that better decisions can be made with knowledge than without. There is nothing to be gained by sticking our heads in the sand and pretending that genetic differences do not exist.

Finding widespread genetic influence creates new problems to consider. For example, could evidence for genetic influence be used to justify the status quo? Will people at genetic risk be labeled and discriminated against? As genetic variants are found that predict behavioral traits, will parents use them prenatally to select "designer" children? (See Chapter 18.) New knowledge also provides new opportunities. For example, identifying genes associated with a particular disorder could make it more likely that environmental preventions and interventions that are especially effective for the disorder can be found. Knowing that certain children have increased genetic risk for a disorder could make it possible to prevent or ameliorate the disorder before it appears, rather than trying to treat the disorder after it appears and causes other problems.

Two other points should be made in this regard. First, most powerful scientific advances create new problems. For example, consider prenatal screening for genetic defects. This advance has obvious benefits in terms of detecting chromosomal and genetic disorders before birth. Combined with abortion, prenatal screening can relieve parents and society of the tremendous burden of severe birth defects. However, it also raises ethical problems concerning abortion and creates the possibility of abuses, such as compulsory screening. Despite the problems created by advances in science, we would not want to cut off the flow of knowledge and its benefits in order to avoid having to confront such problems.

The second point is that it is wrong to assume that environmental explanations are good and that genetic explanations are dangerous. Tremendous harm was done by the environmentalism that prevailed until the 1960s, when the pendulum swung back to a more balanced view that recognized genetic as well as environmental influences. For example, environmentalism led to blaming children's problems on what their parents did to them in the first few years of life. Imagine that, in the 1950s, you were among the 1 percent of parents who had a child who became schizophrenic in late adolescence. You faced a lifetime of concern. And then you were told that the schizophrenia was caused by what you did to the child in the first few years. The sense of guilt would have been overwhelming. Worst of all, such parent blaming was not correct. There is no evidence that early parental treatment causes schizophrenia. Although the environment is important, whatever the salient environmental factors might be, they are not shared family environmental factors. Most important, we now know that schizophrenia is substantially influenced by genetic factors and individual-specific environmental factors.

Our hope for the future is that the next generation of behavioral scientists will wonder what the nature-nurture fuss was all about. We hope they will say, "Of course, we need to consider nature and nurture to understand behavior." The conjunction between nature and nurture is truly *and*, not *versus*.

The basic message of behavioral genetics is that each of us is an individual. Recognition of, and respect for, individual differences is essential to the ethic of individual worth. Proper attention to individual needs, including provision of the environmental circumstances that will optimize the development of each person, is a utopian ideal and no more attainable than other utopias. Nevertheless, we can approach this ideal more closely if we recognize, rather than ignore, individuality. Acquiring the requisite knowledge regarding the genetic and environmental etiologies of individual differences in behavior warrants a high priority because human individuality is the fundamental natural resource of our species.

APPENDIX

Statistical Methods in Behavioral Genetics

Shaun Purcell

1 INTRODUCTION

Quantitative genetics offers a powerful theory and various methods for investigating the genetic and environmental etiology of any characteristic that can be measured, including both continuous and discrete traits. As discussed in Chapter 9, quantitative genetics and molecular genetics are coming together in the study of complex quantitative traits. In both fields, powerful statistical and epidemiological methods have been developed to address a series of related questions:

- Do genes influence this outcome?
- What types of genetic effects are at work?
- Can genetic effects explain the relationships between this and other outcomes?
- Where are the genes located?
- What specific form(s) of the genes cause certain outcomes?
- Do genetic effects operate similarly across different populations and environments?

This Appendix introduces some of the methods behind these research questions, in a manner designed to provide the rationale behind the methods as well as an appreciation of the directions in which the field is developing, including molecular genetics. Both quantitative genetics (with an emphasis on the components of variance model-fitting approaches to complex traits) and molecular genetics (with an emphasis on linkage and association approaches to gene mapping) are covered.

We begin with a brief overview of some of the statistical tools that are commonly used in behavioral genetic research: variance, covariance, correlation, regression, and matrices. Although one need not be a fully trained statistician to use most behavioral genetic methods, understanding the main statistical concepts that underlie

BOX A.1 Behavioral Genetic Interactive Models

The *Behavioral Genetic Interactive Modules* are a series of freely available interactive computer programs with accompanying textual guides designed to convey a sense of the methods of modern behavioral genetic analysis to students and researchers new to the field. Currently, 11 modules covering the material in this Appendix can be accessed from the website at http://pngu.mgh.harvard.edu/purcell/bgim/. Taken together, the modules listed below lead from the basic statistical foundations of quantitative genetic analysis to an introduction to some of the more advanced analytical techniques.

Variance is designed to introduce the concept of variance: what it represents, how it is calculated, and how it can be used to assess individual differences in any quantitative trait. Standardized scores are also introduced.

Covariance demonstrates how the covariance statistic can be used to represent association between two measures.

Correlation & Regression is an exploration of the relationship among variance, covariance, correlation, and regression coefficients.

Matrices provides a simple matrix calculator.

Single Gene Model introduces the basic biometrical model used to describe the effects of individual genes, in terms of additive genetic values and dominance deviations.

Variance Components: ACE illustrates the partitioning of variance into additive genetic, shared environmental, and nonshared environmental components in the context of MZ and DZ twins.

Families demonstrates the relationship between additive and dominance genetic variance, shared and non-shared environmental variance, and expected familial correlations for different types of relatives.

Model Fitting 1 defines a simple path diagram to model the covariance between observed variables and allows the user to manually adjust path coefficients to find the best-fitting model; it includes a twin ACE model and nested models that can be compared with the full ACE model.

Model Fitting 2 performs a maximum-likelihood analysis of univariate twin data and presents the parameter estimates for nested submodels.

Multivariate Analysis models the genetic and environmental etiology of two traits.

Extremes Analysis illustrates DF extremes analysis as well as individual differences analysis, in order to explore how these two methods can inform us about links between normal variation and extreme scores.

For individuals wishing to take their study of statistical analysis further, a guide is provided to help you get started on analyzing your own data as well as simulated data sets that can be used to explore these methods further. Behavioral genetic analyses using widely available statistics packages such as *Stata* are described, as well as an introduction to *Mx*, a powerful, freely available model-fitting package by Mike Neale.

About the Author

Shaun Purcell develops statistical and computational tools for the design of genetic studies, the detection of gene variants influencing complex human traits, and the dissection of these effects within the larger context of other genetic and environmental factors. He is currently an associate professor at Mount Sinai School of Medicine, in New York, and is on the faculty at Harvard Medical School, based at the Analytic and Translational Genetics Unit, Massachusetts General Hospital. He is also an associate member of the Broad Institute of Harvard and MIT, and the Stanley Center for Psychiatric Research. As an undergraduate from 1992 to 1995, he studied experimental psychology at Oxford University; in 1996, he had the opportunity to develop an interest in statistical methods while working toward a master's of science degree at University College London. In 1997, he joined the Social, Genetic and Developmental Psychiatry (SGDP) Research Centre at the Institute of Psychiatry in London,

(Courtesy of Shaun Purcell.)

to embark on a Ph.D. with Pak Sham and Robert Plomin, working on a project designed to map quantitative trait loci for anxiety and depression. His current work involves whole genome association and whole exome sequencing studies of bipolar disorder and schizophrenia, and the development of statistical and computational tools for such studies.

quantitative genetic research enables one to appreciate the ideas, assumptions, and limitations behind the methods.

Next, the classical quantitative genetic model is introduced, which relates the properties of a single gene to variation in a quantitative phenotype. This relatively simple model forms the basis for the majority of quantitative genetic methods. We then examine how the analysis of familial correlations can be used to infer the underlying etiological nature of a trait, given our knowledge of the way genes work. The basic model partitions the variance of a single trait into portions attributable to additive genetic effects, shared environmental effects, and nonshared environmental effects. The tools of model fitting and path analysis are introduced in this context. Extensions to the basic model are also considered: multivariate analysis, analysis of extremes, and interactions between genes and environments, for example.

Finally, we see how molecular genetic information on specific loci can be incorporated. In this way, the chromosomal positions of genes can be mapped. This work leads the way to the study of gene function at a molecular level—the vital next step if we really want to know *how* our genes make us what we are.

1.1 Variation and Covariation: Statistical Descriptions of Individual Differences

Behavioral genetics is concerned with the study of individual differences: detecting the factors that make individuals in a population different from one another. As a first step, it is concerned with gauging the relative importance of genetic and environmental factors that cause individual differences. To assess the importance of these factors, we need to be able to *measure* individual differences. This task requires some elementary statistical theory.

A population is defined as the complete set of all individuals in a group under study. Examples of populations would include sets such as all humans, all female Americans aged 20 to 25 in the year 2000, or all the stars in a galaxy. We might measure a characteristic, such as talkativeness, intelligence, weight, or temperature, for each of the individuals in a population. We are concerned with assessing how these characteristics vary both *within* populations (e.g., among 2-year-old males) and *between* them (e.g., male versus female infants).

If all the individuals in a set are studied, population statistics such as the average or the variance can be calculated exactly. However, it is usually not practical to measure every individual in the population, so we resort to *sampling* individuals from the population. A key concept in sampling is that, ideally, it should be conducted at *random*. A nonrandom sample, such as only the tallest 20 percent of 11-year-old girls, would give an inflated (biased) estimate of the average height of 11-year-old girls. An estimate of the average height in the population gathered from a random sample would not, *on average*, be biased. However, it is important to recognize that an estimate of the population mean made on the basis of a random sample will vary somewhat from the population mean. The amount of this variation will depend on the sample size and on chance. We need to know how much we expect this variation to be so that we know how accurate estimates of the population parameters are. This assessment of accuracy is critical when we want to compare populations.

Once we have defined a population, various *parameters* such as the mean, range, and variance can be described for the trait that we wish to study. Similarly, when we have a sample of the population, we can calculate *statistics* from the sample that correspond to the parameters of the population. It is not always the case that the measure of the sample statistic is the best estimate of the corresponding population parameter. This discrepancy distinguishes descriptive from inferential statistics. Descriptive statistics simply describe the sample; inferential statistics are used to get estimates of the parameters of the entire population.

1.1.1 The mean The arithmetic mean is one of the simplest and most useful statistics. It is a measure of the center of a distribution and is the familiar average statistic used in everyday speech. It is very simple to compute, being the sum of all observations' values divided by the number of observations in the sample:

$$\mu = \Sigma x/N$$

where Σx is the sum of all observations in the set of size N. Strictly speaking, the mean is only labeled μ (pronounced "mu") if it is computed from the entire population. Usually, the mean will be calculated from a sample, and the mean of a variable, say x, is written as $\bar{x}$ (read as "x bar").

The mean is especially useful when comparing groups. Given an estimate of how accurate the means are, it becomes possible to compare means for two or more groups. Examples might include whether women are more verbally skilled than men, whether albino mice are less active than other mice, or whether light moves faster than sound.

Some physical measures, such as the number of inches of rainfall per year, are obviously well ordered, such that the difference between 15 and 16 inches is the same as the difference between 21 and 22 inches—namely, 1 inch. Many physical measurements have the same scale throughout the distribution, which is called an *interval* scale. In behavioral research, however, it is often difficult to get measures that are on an interval scale. Some measures are *binary*, consisting simply of the presence or absence of a disease or symptom. The mean of a binary variable scored 0 for absent and 1 for present indicates the proportion of the sample that has the symptom or disease present, so again the mean is a useful summary. However, not all measures can be effectively summarized as means. The trouble starts when there are several ordered categories, such as "Not at all/Sometimes/Quite often/Always." Even if these items are scored 0, 1, 2, and 3, the mean tells us little about the frequencies in each category. This problem is even greater when the categories cannot be ordered, such as religious affiliation. Here the mean would be of no use at all.

1.1.2 Variance Variance is a statistic that tells us how spread out scores are. This is a measure of individual differences in the population, the focus of most behavioral genetic analyses. Variances are also important when assessing differences between group means. Behavioral genetic analyses are typically less focused on group differences, although such analyses are central to most quantitative sciences. For example, a researcher may wish to ask whether a control group significantly differs from an experimental one on a measure, or whether boys and girls differ in the amount that they eat. Testing differences between means is often carried out with a statistical method called the analysis of variance (ANOVA). In fact, individual differences are treated as the "error" term in ANOVA.

The usual approach to calculating the variance, established by R. A. Fisher (1922), one of the founders of quantitative genetics, is to take the average of the squared deviations from the mean. Fisher showed that the squared deviations from the mean had more desirable statistical properties than other measures of variance that might be considered, such as the average absolute difference. In particular, the average squared deviation is the most accurate statistic.

Calculating the variance (often written as s^2) is straightforward:

1. Calculate the mean.
2. Express the scores as deviations from the mean.
3. Square the deviations and sum them.
4. Divide the sum by the number of observations minus 1.

Or, written as a formula:

$$s^2 = \frac{\sum (x - \bar{x})^2}{N - 1}$$

A second commonly used approach involves computing the contribution of each observation to the variance and correcting for the mean at the end. This alternative method produces the same answer, but it can be more efficient for computers to use. Note that $N - 1$ instead of N is used to calculate the average squared deviation in order to produce unbiased estimates of variance—for technical, statistical reasons.

Variances range from zero upward: There is no such thing as a negative variance. A variance of zero would indicate no variation in the sample (i.e., all individuals would have to have exactly the same score). The greater the spread in scores, the greater the variance.

With binary "yes/no" or "affected/unaffected" traits, measuring the variance is difficult. We may imagine that a binary trait is observed because there is an underlying normal distribution of *liability* to the trait, caused by the additive effects of a large number of factors, each of small effect. The binary trait that we observe arises because there is a threshold, and only those with liability above threshold express the trait. We cannot directly observe the underlying liability, so typically we assume that it has variance of unity (1). If the variance of the underlying distribution were increased, it would simply change the proportion of subjects that are above threshold. That is, changing the variance is equivalent to changing the threshold. Distinguishing between mean changes and variance changes is not generally possible with binary data, but it is possible if the data are ordinal, with at least three ordered categories.

Having measured the variance, quantitative genetic analysis aims to partition it—that is, to divide the total variance into parts attributable to genetic and environmental components. This task requires the introduction of another statistical concept, covariance. Before turning to covariance, we will take a brief digression to consider another way of expressing scores that facilitates comparisons of means and variances.

1.1.3 Standardized scores Different types of measures have different scales, which can cause problems when making comparisons between them. For example, differences in height could be expressed in either metric or common (imperial) terms. In a population, the absolute value of variance in height will depend on the scale used to measure it—the unit of variance will be either centimeters squared or inches squared. If we take the square root of variance, we obtain a measure of spread that has the same unit of the observed trait, called the *standard deviation (s)*. The standard deviation also has several convenient statistical properties. If a trait is normally distributed (bell-shaped curve), then 95 percent of all observations will lie within two standard deviations on either side of the mean.

The example of measuring height demonstrates the difficulties that may be encountered when we wish to compare differently scaled measures. In the case of metric and common measurements of height, which both measure the same thing, the problem of scale can be easily overcome by using standard conversion formulas. In psychology, however, measurements often will have no fixed scale. A questionnaire that measures extraversion might have a scale from 0 to 12, from 1 to 100, or from -4 to $+4$. If scale is arbitrary, it makes sense to make all measures have the same, standardized scale.

Suppose we have data on two reliable questionnaire measures of extraversion, A and B, each from a different population. Say measure A has a range of 0 to 12 and a mean score of 6.4, whereas measure B has a range of 0 to 50 with a mean of 24. If we were to assess two individuals, one scoring 8 on measure A and the other scoring 30 on measure B, how could we tell which person is the more extraverted? The most commonly used technique is to *standardize* our measures. The formula for calculating a standardized score z from a raw score x is

$$z = \frac{x - \bar{x}}{\sqrt{s_x^2}}$$

where s_x^2 is the variance of x. That is, we reexpress the scores in standard deviation units. For example, if we calculate that measure A has a variance of 4, then the standard deviation is $\sqrt{4} = 2$. If we express scores as the number of standard deviations away from the mean, then a score of 2 raw-score units above the mean on measure A is $+1$ standard deviation units. Raw scores equaling the raw-score mean will become 0 in standard deviation units. A raw score of 2 will become $(2 - 6.4)/2 = -2.2$. Therefore, a score of 8 on measure A corresponds to a standardized score of $(8 - 6.4)/2 = 0.8$ standard deviation units above the mean.

We can also do the same for measure B, to be able to make scale-independent comparisons between our two measures of extraversion. If measure B is found to have a variance of 8 (and therefore a standard deviation of $\sqrt{8}$), then a raw score of 30 corresponds to a standardized score of $(30 - 24)/\sqrt{8} = 2.1$. We can therefore conclude that individual B is more extraverted than individual A (i.e., $2.1 > 0.8$) (Figure A.1). Converting the measures into standardized scores also allows statistical tests of the significance of such differences (the z-test).

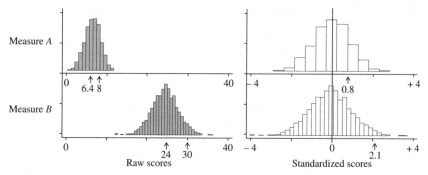

FIGURE A.1 Standardized scores. Raw scores on the two measures cannot be directly equated. Standardizing both measures to have a mean of 0 and a standard deviation of 1 facilitates the comparison of measures *A* and *B*.

Standardized scores are said to have *zero sum* property (they will always have a mean of 0) and unit standard deviation (i.e., a standard deviation of 1). As we have seen, standardizing is useful when comparing different measures of the same thing. Indeed, standardizing can be used to compare different measures of different things (e.g., whether a particular individual is more extreme in height or in extraversion).

However, there are some situations in which standardized scores can be misleading. Standardizing within groups (i.e., using the estimates of the mean and standard deviation from that group) will destroy between-group differences. All groups will end up with means of zero, which will hide any true between-group variation. Note that it was implicit in the example above that measures *A* and *B* are both reliable, and that the two populations are equivalent with respect to the distribution of "true" extraversion.

1.1.4 Covariance Another fundamental statistic that underlies behavioral genetic theory is *covariance*. Covariance is a statistic that informs us about the relationship between two characteristics (e.g., height and weight). Such a statistic is called a *bivariate* statistic, in contrast to the mean and variance, which are both *univariate* statistics. If two variables are associated (i.e., they *covary* together), we may have reason to believe that this covariation occurs because one characteristic influences the other. Alternatively, we might suspect that both characteristics have a common cause. Covariance, by itself, however, cannot tell us *why* two variables are associated: It is only a measure of the magnitude of association. Figure A.2 shows four possible relationships between two variables, *X* and *Y*, each of which could result in a similar covariance between the two variables. For example, it is clearly wrong to think of an individual's weight as *causing* his or her height, whereas it is fair to say that an individual's height does, in part, determine that person's weight—it should be noted that care is needed in the interpretation of *all* statistics. The methods of path analysis (as reviewed later) do offer an opportunity to begin to "tease apart" causation from

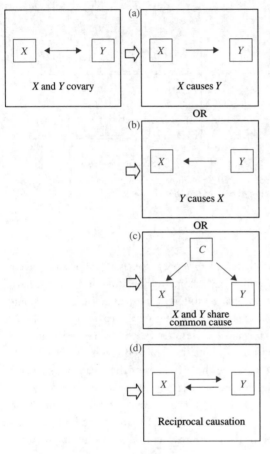

FIGURE A.2 Causes of covariation. Two variables can covary for a number of reasons: (a, b) One variable might cause the other, or (c) both variables might be influenced by a third variable (*C*), or (d) both variables might influence the other. The covariance statistic cannot by itself discriminate among these alternatives.

"mere" correlation, especially when applied to data sets that differ in genetic or environmental factors.

A sensible first step when investigating the relationship between two continuous variables is to begin with a *scatterplot*. The scatterplot shown in Figure A.3 represents 200 observations. In this example, it is apparent that the two measures are not independent. As X increases (the scale for X increases toward the right), we see that the scores on Y also tend to increase. Covariance is a measure that attempts to quantify this kind of relationship (as do *correlation* and *regression coefficients*, introduced later).

Calculating the covariance proceeds in much the same way as calculating the variance. However, instead of squaring the deviations from the mean, we calculate the cross-product of the deviations of the first variable with those of the second. To compute the covariance, we would

1. Calculate the mean of X.
2. Calculate the mean of Y.

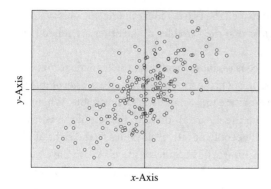

FIGURE A.3 Scatterplot representing 200 observations measured on two variables, X and Y. As can be seen, X and Y are not independent, because observations with higher values for X also tend to have higher values for Y.

3. Express the scores as deviations from the means.
4. Calculate the product of the deviations for each data pair and sum them.
5. Divide by $N - 1$ to obtain an estimate of the covariance.

Written as a formula, the covariance is

$$\text{Cov}_{XY} = \frac{\sum(X - \bar{X})(Y - \bar{Y})}{N - 1}$$

Covariance values can range between plus and minus infinity. Negative values imply that high scores on one measure tend to be associated with low scores on the other measure. A covariance of 0 implies that there is no *linear* relationship between the two measures.

That covariance measures only linear association is an important issue: Consider the two scatterplots in Figure A.4. Neither of these two bivariate data sets displays any *linear* association between the two variables, so both have a covariance of zero.

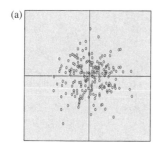
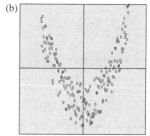

FIGURE A.4 Covariance and independence. The covariance statistic represents linear association. Both scatterplots represent data sets with a covariance of zero. (a) The two variables in this data set are truly independent; that is, the average value of one variable is independent of the value of the other. (b) The variables in this data set are not linearly related, but they are clearly not independent.

However, there is a clear difference between the two data sets: in one, the observations are truly *independent*, whereas it is clear that the variables in the other are related but not in a linear way.

A key to understanding covariance is to understand what the formula for its calculation is really doing. Figure A.5 represents the four quadrants of a scatterplot. The lines intersecting in the middle represent the mean value for each variable. When the scores are expressed as deviations from the mean, all those to the left of the vertical line (or below the horizontal line) will become negative; all values to the right of the vertical line (or above the horizontal line) will become positive. As we have seen, covariance is calculated by summing the products of these deviations. Therefore, because both the product of two positive numbers and the product of two negative numbers are positive whereas the product of one positive and one negative number is always negative, the contribution each observation makes to the covariance will depend on which quadrant it falls in. Observations in the top-right and bottom-left quadrants (both numbers above the mean and both numbers below the mean, respectively) will make a positive contribution to the covariance. The farther away from the origin (the bivariate point where the two means intersect), the larger this contribution will be. Observations in the other two quadrants will tend to decrease the covariance. If all bivariate data points were evenly distributed across this space, the positive contributions to the covariance would tend to be canceled out by an equal number of negative contributions, resulting in a near zero covariance statistic. A large positive covariance would imply that the bulk of data points fall in the bottom-left and top-right quadrants; a large negative covariance would imply that the bulk of data points fall in the top-left and bottom-right quadrants.

1.1.5 Variance of a sum Covariance is also important for calculating the variance of a sum of two variables. This statistic is relevant to our later discussion of the basic quantitative genetic model. Say you have variables X and Y and you know their variances and the covariance between them. What would the variance of $(X + Y)$ be? If all the data are available, you may decide to calculate a new variable that is the sum of

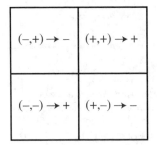

FIGURE A.5 Calculating covariance. The contribution each observation makes to the covariance will depend on the quadrant in which it falls.

the two variables and then calculate its variance in the ordinary manner. Alternatively, if you know only the summary statistics, you can use the formula:

$$\text{Var}(X + Y) = \text{Var}(X) + \text{Var}(Y) + 2\text{Cov}(X,Y)$$

In other words, the variance of a sum is the sum of the two variances plus twice the covariance between the two measures. If two variables are uncorrelated, then the covariance term will be zero and the variance of the sum is simply the sum of the variances. As will be seen later, the mathematics of variance is critical in the formulation of the genetic model for describing complex traits.

1.1.6 Correlation and regression We have seen how using standardized scores can help when working with measures that have different scales. When creating a standardized score, we use information about the variance of a measure to rescale the raw data. As mentioned earlier, the covariance between two measures is dependent on the scales of the raw data and can range from plus to minus infinity. We can use information about the variance of two measures to standardize their covariance statistic, in a manner analogous to creating standardized scores. A covariance statistic standardized in this way is called a *correlation*.

The correlation is calculated by dividing the covariance by the square root of the product of the two variances for each measure. Therefore, the correlation between X and Y (r_{XY}) is

$$r_{XY} = \frac{\text{Cov}_{XY}}{\sqrt{s_X^2 s_Y^2}}$$

where Cov_{XY} is the covariance and s_X^2 and s_Y^2 are the variances. If both X and Y are standardized variables (i.e., s_X and s_Y, and therefore also s_X^2 and s_Y^2, both equal 1), then the correlation will be the same as the covariance (as can be seen in the formula above).

Correlations (typically labeled r) always range from $+1$ to -1. A correlation of $+1$ indicates a perfect positive *linear* relationship between two variables. A correlation of -1 represents a perfect negative linear relationship. A correlation of 0 implies no linear relationship between the two variables (in the same way that a covariance of 0 implies no linear relationship). The kind of correlations we might expect to observe in the real world are likely to fall somewhere between 0 and $+1$. How exactly do we interpret correlations of intermediate values? Does, for example, a correlation of 0.4 mean that the two measures are the same 40 percent of the time? In short, no. What it reflects, as seen in the equation above, is the proportion of variance that is shared by the two measures. (The square of a correlation, r^2, is a commonly used statistic that indicates the proportion of variance in one variable that can be predicted by the other. For correlations between relatives, the unsquared correlation, representing the proportion of variance common to both family members, is more useful.)

Regression is related to correlation in that it also examines the relationship between two variables. Regression is concerned with *prediction* in that it asks whether knowing the value of one variable for an individual helps us to guess what the value of another variable will be.

Regression coefficients (often called *b*) can be calculated by using a method similar to that used to calculate correlation coefficients. The regression coefficient of "y on x" (i.e., given *X*, what is our best guess for the value of *Y*) divides the covariance between *X* and *Y* by the variance of the variable (*X*) from which we are making the prediction (rather than standardizing the covariance by dividing by the product of the standard deviations of *X* and *Y*):

$$b = \frac{\text{Cov}_{XY}}{s_X^2}$$

Given this regression coefficient, an equation relating *X* and *Y* can be written:

$$\hat{Y} = bX + c$$

where *c* is called the regression constant. As plotted in Figure A.6, this equation describes a straight line (the *least squares regression line*) that can be drawn through the observed points and represents the best prediction of *Y* given information on

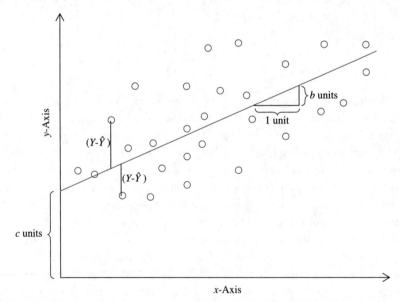

FIGURE A.6 Linear regression. The regression of a line of best fit between *X* and *Y* is represented by the equation $\hat{Y} = bX + c$. For each unit increase in *X*, we expect *Y* to increase *b* units. The two vertical lines represent the deviations between the expected and actual values of *Y*. The sum of the deviations squared is used to calculate the residual variance of *Y*, that is, the variance in *Y* not accounted for by *X*. The regression constant *c* represents the value of *Y* when *X* is zero (at the origin).

X ($\hat{Y}$, pronounced "y hat"). The equation implies that for an increase of one unit in X, Y will increase an average of b units.

Regression equations can also be used to analyze more complicated, nonlinear relationships between two variables. For example, the variable Y might be a function of the square of X as well as of X itself. We would therefore include this higher-order term in the equation to describe the relationship between X and Y:

$$\hat{Y} = b_1 X^2 + b_2 X + c$$

This equation describes a nonlinear least squares regression line (i.e., a parabolic curve if b_1 doesn't equal zero).

It is possible to calculate the discrepancy, or error, between the predicted values of Y given X and the actual values of Y observed in the sample ($Y - \hat{Y}$). These discrepancies are called the *residuals*, and it is often useful to calculate the variance of the residuals. From the first regression equation given above, if X and Y were totally unrelated, then b would be estimated near zero and c would be the mean of Y (because this value represents the *best guess* of Y if you don't have any other information). In this case, residual error variance would be the same as the variance of Y. To the extent that knowing X actually does help you guess Y, the regression coefficient will become significantly nonzero and the error term will decrease.

We can partition the variance in a variable, Y, into the part that is associated with another variable X and the part that is independent of X. In terms of a regression of Y on X, this partitioning is reflected in the variance of the predicted Y values (the variance of $\hat{Y}$) as opposed to the variance of the residuals (the variance of ($Y - \hat{Y}$)). The correlation between the two variables can actually be used to estimate these values in a straightforward way:

$$s_{\hat{Y}}^2 = r^2 s_Y \quad \text{and} \quad s_{Y - \hat{Y}}^2 = (1 - r^2) \; s_{\hat{Y}}^2.$$

A common regression-based technique can be used to "regress out" or "adjust for" the effects of one variable on another. For example, we may wish to study the relationship between verbal ability and gender in children. However, we also know that verbal ability is age related, and we do not want the effects of age to confound this analysis. We can calculate an age-adjusted measure of verbal ability by performing a regression of verbal ability on age. For every individual, we subtract their predicted value (given their age) from their observed value to create a new variable that reflects verbal ability without the effects of age-related variation: The new variable will not correlate with age. If there were any mean differences in age between boys and girls in the sample, then the effects of these on verbal ability have been effectively removed.

1.1.7 Matrices Reading behavioral genetic journal articles and books, one is likely to come across *matrices* sooner or later: "In QTL linkage the variance-covariance *matrix* for the sibship is modeled in terms of alleles shared identical-by-descent" or "The *matrix* of genotypic means can be observed. . . ." What are matrices and why do we use them? This section presents a brief introduction to matrices that will place such sentences in context.

Matrices are commonly used in behavioral genetics to represent information in a concise and easy-to-manipulate manner. A matrix is simply a block of *elements* organized in rows and columns. For example,

$$\begin{bmatrix} 34 & 23 \\ 56 & 17 \\ 65 & 38 \end{bmatrix}$$

is a matrix with three rows and two columns. Typically, a matrix will be organized such that each row and column has an associated meaning. In this example, the matrix might reflect scores for three students (each row representing one student) on English and French exams (the first column representing the score for English, the second for French). Elements are often indexed by their row and column: s_{ij} refers to the ith student's score on the jth test.

The matrix above represents raw data. In a similar way, the spreadsheet of values in statistical programs such as SPSS can be thought of as one large matrix. Perhaps the most commonly encountered form of matrix is the *correlation matrix*, which is used to represent descriptive statistics of raw data (correlations) in an orderly fashion. In a correlation matrix, the element in the ith row and jth column represents the pair-wise correlation between the ith and jth variables.

Here is a correlation matrix between three different variables:

$$\begin{bmatrix} 1.00 & 0.73 & 0.14 \\ 0.73 & 1.00 & 0.37 \\ 0.14 & 0.37 & 1.00 \end{bmatrix}$$

Correlation matrices have several easily recognizable properties. First, a correlation matrix will always be *square*—having the same number of rows as columns. For n variables, the correlation matrix will be an $n \times n$ matrix. The *diagonal* of a square matrix is the set of elements for which the row number equals the column number, so in terms of correlations, these elements represent the correlation of a variable with itself, which will always be 1. Additionally, correlation matrices will always be *symmetric* about the diagonal—that is, element r_{ij} equals r_{ji}. This symmetry represents the simple fact that the correlation between A and B is the same as the correlation between B and A. It is common practice not to write the redundant upper off-diagonal elements if a matrix is known to be symmetric. Our correlation matrix would be written

$$\begin{bmatrix} 1.00 & & \\ 0.73 & 1.00 & \\ 0.14 & 0.37 & 1.00 \end{bmatrix}$$

Correlation matrices are often presented in journal articles in tabular form to summarize correlational analyses.

A closely related type of matrix that occurs more often in behavioral genetic analysis is the *variance-covariance* matrix. In place of correlations, the elements of an $n \times n$ variance-covariance matrix are n variances along the diagonal and $(n-1)n/2$ covariances in the lower off-diagonal. A correlation matrix is a *standardized* variance-covariance matrix, just as a correlation is a standardized covariance. The variance-covariance matrix for the three variables in the correlation matrix above might be

$$\begin{bmatrix} 2.32 & & \\ 1.43 & 1.64 & \\ 0.43 & 0.98 & 4.21 \end{bmatrix}$$

A variance-covariance matrix can be transformed into a correlation matrix: $r_{ij} = v_{ij}/\sqrt{v_{ii}v_{jj}}$, where r_{ij} are the new elements of the correlation matrix and v_{ij} are the elements of the variance-covariance matrix. (This is essentially a reformulation of the equation for calculating correlations given above in matrix notation.) Note that information is lost about the relative magnitude of variances among the different variables in a correlation matrix (because they are all standardized to 1). As mentioned earlier, because correlations are not scale dependent, however, they are easier to interpret than covariances and therefore better for descriptive purposes.

Matrices can be added to or subtracted from each other as long as both matrices have the same number of rows and the same number of columns:

$$\begin{bmatrix} 4 & -5 \\ 1 & 2 \end{bmatrix} + \begin{bmatrix} -2 & x \\ 0 & y \end{bmatrix} = \begin{bmatrix} 2 & x-5 \\ 1 & y+2 \end{bmatrix}$$

Note that here the elements of the sum matrix are not simple numerical terms—elements of matrices can be as complicated as you want. The beauty of matrix notation is that we can label matrices so that we can refer to many elements with a simple letter, say, **A**. (Matrices are generally written in bold type.)

$$\mathbf{A} = \begin{bmatrix} 4 & 5 \\ 1 & 2 \end{bmatrix}$$

$$\mathbf{B} = \begin{bmatrix} -2 & x \\ 0 & y \end{bmatrix}$$

$$\mathbf{A} - \mathbf{B} = \begin{bmatrix} 6 & -5-x \\ 1 & 2-y \end{bmatrix}$$

The other common matrix algebra operations are multiplication, inversion, and transposition. Matrix multiplication does not work in the same way as matrix addition (that kind of element-by-element multiplication is actually called a *Kronecker product*). Unlike normal multiplication, where $ab = ba$, in matrix multiplication $\mathbf{AB} \neq \mathbf{BA}$. For $\mathbf{A}$ to be multiplied by $\mathbf{B}$, matrix $\mathbf{A}$ must have the same number of columns as $\mathbf{B}$ has rows. The resulting matrix has as many rows as $\mathbf{A}$ and as many columns as $\mathbf{B}$. Each element is the sum of products across each row of $\mathbf{A}$ and each column of $\mathbf{B}$. Following are two examples:

$$\begin{bmatrix} a & c & e \\ b & d & f \end{bmatrix} \begin{bmatrix} g & h & i \\ j & k & l \\ m & n & o \end{bmatrix} = \begin{bmatrix} ag+cj+em & ah+ck+en & ai+cl+eo \\ bg+dj+fm & bh+dk+fn & bi+dl+fo \end{bmatrix}$$

$$\begin{bmatrix} 3 & 3 & 0 \\ 1 & -2 & 5 \end{bmatrix} \begin{bmatrix} 7 & 2 \\ 3 & 2 \\ 8 & 4 \end{bmatrix} = \begin{bmatrix} 30 & 12 \\ 41 & 18 \end{bmatrix}$$

The equivalent to division is called matrix inversion and is complex to calculate, especially for large matrices. Only square matrices have an inverse, written $\mathbf{A}^{-1}$. Matrix inversion plays a central role in solving model-fitting problems.

Finally, the transpose of a matrix, $\mathbf{A}'$, is matrix $\mathbf{A}$ but with rows and columns swapped. Therefore, if $\mathbf{A}$ were a 3×2 matrix, then $\mathbf{A}'$ will be a 2×3 matrix (note that rows are given first):

$$\begin{bmatrix} 2 & 3 \\ 0 & -1 \\ -2 & 1 \end{bmatrix}' = \begin{bmatrix} 2 & 0 & -2 \\ 3 & -1 & 1 \end{bmatrix}$$

There is a great deal more to matrix algebra than the simple examples presented here. Basic familiarization with the types of matrices and matrix operations is useful, however, if only to realize that when behavioral genetic articles and books refer to matrices they are not necessarily talking about anything particularly complicated. The main utility of matrices is their convenience of presentation—it is the actual meaning of the elements that is important.

2 QUANTITATIVE GENETICS

2.1 The Biometric Model

When we say that a trait is *heritable* or *genetic*, we are implying that at least one gene has a measurable effect on that trait. Although most behavioral traits appear to depend on many genes, it is still important to review the properties of a single gene because the more complex models are built upon these foundations. We will begin by examining the basic quantitative genetic model that mathematically describes the genetic and environmental underpinnings of a trait.

2.1.1 Allele and genotype The pair of alleles that an individual carries at a particular locus constitutes what we call the *genotype* at that locus. Imagine that, at a particular locus, two forms of a gene, labeled A_1 and A_2 (this would be called a *biallelic* locus), exist in the population. Because individuals have two copies of every gene (one from their father, one from their mother), individuals will possess one of three genotypes: They may have either two A_1 alleles or two A_2, in which case they are said to be *homozygous* for that particular allele. Alternatively, they may carry one copy of each allele, in which case they are said to be *heterozygous* at that locus. We would write the three genotypes as A_1A_1, A_1A_2, and A_2A_2 (or, using different notation, *AA, Aa,* and *aa*).

For biallelic loci, the two alleles will occur in the population at particular frequencies. If we counted all the alleles in a population and three-fourths were A_1, then we say that A_1 has an allelic frequency of 0.75. Because these frequencies must sum to 1, we know that the A_2 allele has a frequency of 0.25. It is common practice to denote the allelic frequencies of a biallelic locus as p and q (so here, p is the allelic frequency of the A_1 allele, 0.75, and q is the frequency of A_2, 0.25). Given these, we can predict the genotypic frequencies. Formally, if the two alleles A_1 and A_2 have allelic frequencies p and q, then, with random mating, we would expect to observe the three genotypes A_1A_1, A_1A_2, and A_2A_2 at frequencies p^2, $2pq$, and q^2, respectively. (See Box 3.2.)

2.1.2 Genotypic values Next, we need a way to describe any effects of the alleles at a locus on whatever trait we are interested in. A locus is said to be *associated with* a trait if some of its alleles are associated with different mean levels of that trait in the population. For qualitative diseases (i.e., diseases that are either present or not present), a single allele may be necessary and sufficient to develop the disease. In this case, the disease-predisposing allele acts in either a dominant or a recessive manner. Carrying a dominant allele will result in the disease irrespective of the other allele at that locus; conversely, if the disease-predisposing allele is recessive, then the disease will only develop in individuals homozygous for that allele.

For a quantitative trait, however, we need some way of specifying *how much* an allele affects the trait. Considering only a locus with two alleles, A_1 and A_2, we define the average value of one of the homozygotes (say, A_1A_1) as a and the average value of the other homozygote (A_2A_2) as $-a$. The value of the heterozygote (A_1A_2) is labeled d and is dependent on the mode of gene action. If there is no dominance, d will be zero (i.e., the midpoint of the two homozygotes' scores). If the A_1 allele is dominant to A_2, then d will be greater than zero. If dominance is complete (i.e., if the observed value for A_1A_2 equals that of A_1A_1), then $d = +a$.

2.1.3 Additive effects Observed genotypic values for a single locus can be defined in terms of an *additive genetic value* and a *dominance deviation*. The additive genetic value of a locus relates to the average effect of an allele. As illustrated in Figure A.7, the

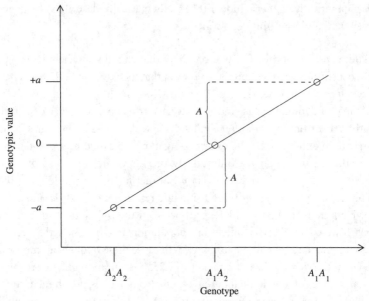

FIGURE A.7 Additive genetic values. The number of A_1 alleles predicts additive genetic values. Because there is no dominance (and assuming equal allelic frequency), the additive genetic values equal the genotypic values. (A, value added by each A_1 allele.)

additive genetic value is the genotypic value expected from the number of a particular allele (say, A_1) at that locus, either 0, 1, or 2 (each A_1 allele increases an individual's score by A units).

Additive genetic values are important in behavioral genetics because they represent the extent to which genotypes "breed true" from parents to offspring. If a parent has one copy of a certain allele, say, A_1, then each offspring has a 50 percent chance of receiving an A_1 allele. If an offspring receives an A_1 allele, then its additive effect will contribute to the phenotype to exactly the same extent as it did to the parent's phenotype. That is, it will lead to increased parent-offspring resemblance on the phenotype, irrespective of other alleles at that locus or at other loci.

2.1.4 Dominance deviation   Dominance is the extent to which the effects of alleles at a locus do not simply "add up" to produce genotypic values. The *dominance deviation* is the difference between actual genotypic values and what would be expected under a strictly additive model. Figure A.8 represents the deviations (labeled D) of the expected (or additive) genotypic values from the actual genotypic values that occur if there is an effect of dominance at the locus.

Dominance genetic variance represents genetic influence that does not "breed true." Saying that the effect of a locus involves dominance is equivalent to saying that an individual's genotypic value results from the *combination* of alleles at that particular

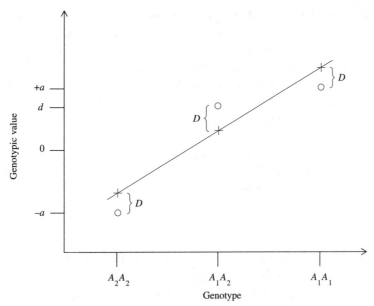

FIGURE A.8 Dominance deviations. The genotypic values (circles) deviate from the expected values under an additive model (crosses) when there is dominance (i.e., d ≠ 0). (D, deviation from expected attributed to dominance.)

locus. However, offspring receive only one allele from each parent, not a combination of two alleles. Genetic influence due to dominance will not be transmitted from parent to offspring, therefore. In this way, additive and dominance genetic values are defined so as to be independent of each other.

2.1.5 Polygenic model Not only can we consider the additive and nonadditive effects at a single locus, we can also sum these effects across loci. This concept is the essence of the polygenic extension of the single-gene model. Just as additive genetic values are the summation of the average effects of two alleles at a single locus, they can also be summed across the many loci that may influence a particular phenotypic character. Similarly, dominance deviations from additive genetic values can also be summed for all the loci influencing a character. Thus, it is relatively easy to generalize the single-gene model to a polygenic one with many loci, each with its own additive and nonadditive effects. Under an *additive* polygenic model, the genetic effect G on the phenotype represents the sum of effects from different loci.

$$G = G_1 + G_2 + \ldots + G_N$$

This expression implies that the effects of different alleles simply add up—that is, there is no interaction between alleles where the effect of one allele, say, G_1 is modified by the presence of the allele with effect G_2. The polygenic model needs to consider the possibility that the effects of different loci do not add up independently but interact with each other—an interaction called *epistasis*. For example, imagine two loci, each with an allele that increases an individual's score by one point on a particular trait. If there were no epistasis, having a risk allele at both loci would increase the score by two points. If there were epistasis, however, having risk alleles at both loci might possibly lead to a ten-point increase. Epistasis therefore complicates analysis, but there is evidence that such phenomena might be quite prevalent for certain complex traits. In other words, dominance is *intralocus* interaction between alleles, whereas epistasis is *interlocus* interaction, that is, between loci.

The total genetic contribution to a phenotype is G, which is the sum of all additive genetic effects A, all dominance deviations D, and all epistatic interaction effects I:

$$G = A + D + I$$

2.1.6 Phenotypic values and variance components model Quantitative genetic theory states that every individual's phenotype is made up of genetic and environmental contributions. No behavioral phenotype will be entirely determined by genetic effects, so we should always expect an environmental effect, E, which also includes measurement error, on the phenotype P. In algebraic terms,

$$P = G + E$$

where, for convenience, we assume that P represents an individual's deviation from the population mean rather than an absolute score. In any case, behavioral genetics is not primarily interested in the score of any one individual. Rather, the focus is on explaining the causes of phenotypic differences in a population—why some individuals are more extraverted than others, or why some individuals are alcoholic, for example.

In fact, there is often no direct way of determining the relative magnitude of genetic and environmental deviations for any one individual, certainly if one has not obtained DNA from individuals. However, in a sample of individuals, especially of genetically related individuals, it is possible to estimate the variances of the terms P, G, and E. This approach is called the *variance components approach*, and it relies on the equation that showed us how to calculate the variance of a sum.

Recall that

$$\text{Var}(X + Y) = \text{Var}(X) + \text{Var}(Y) + 2\text{Cov}(X, Y)$$

Turning this expression around, it gives us a method for partitioning the variance of a variable that is a composite of constituent parts. That is, our goal is to "decompose the variance" of a trait into the constituent parts of genetic and environmental sources of variation.

For simplicity, we will assume no epistasis, so $P = G + E = A + D + E$. The variance of P is equal to the sum of the variance of the separate components, A, D, and E, plus twice the covariance between them:

$$\text{Var}(P) = \text{Var}(A + D + E)$$
$$= \text{Var}(A) + \text{Var}(D) + \text{Var}(E) + 2\text{Cov}(A, D) + 2\text{Cov}(A, E) + 2\text{Cov}(D, E)$$

which begins to look unmanageable until we realize that we can use some theoretical assumptions of our model to constrain this equation. By definition, additive genetic influences are independent of dominance deviations. That is, $\text{Cov}(A, D)$ will necessarily equal zero, so this term can be dropped from the model. Another assumption that we may wish to make (but one that is not necessarily true) is that genetic and environmental influences are uncorrelated. This is equivalent to saying that $\text{Cov}(A, E)$ and $\text{Cov}(D, E)$ equal zero and can be dropped from the model. We will see later that there are detailed reasons why this assumption might not hold (what is called a *gene-environment correlation*) (see also Chapter 8). For the time being, however, our simplified model reads:

$$\text{Var}(P) = \text{Var}(A) + \text{Var}(D) + \text{Var}(E)$$

A note on notation: Variances are often written in other ways. For example, above we have denoted additive genetic variance as $\text{Var}(A)$. As we will see, this term is often written differently, depending on the context (mainly for historical reasons). In formal model fitting, the lowercase Greek letter sigma squared with a subscript (σ_A^2) might be used. A similar value calculated in the context of comparing familial correlations (narrow-sense heritability, introduced later) is typically labeled h^2, whereas it is written as a^2 in the context of path analysis (also introduced later). Under most circumstances, however, these all refer to roughly the same thing.

In conclusion, it might not seem that we have achieved very much in simply considering variances instead of values. However, as will be discussed, quantitative genetic methods can use these models to estimate the relative contribution of genetic and environmental influences to phenotypic variance.

2.1.7 Environmental variation Because the nature of environmental effects is more varied and changeable than the underlying nature of genetic influence, it is not possible to decompose this term into constituent parts in a straightforward way. That is, if we detect genetic influence, then we know that this effect must result from at least one gene—and we know something about the properties of genes.

However, if we detect environmental influence on a trait, we cannot assume any one mechanism. But behavioral genetics is able to investigate environmental influences in two main ways. As we will see later, family-based studies using twins or adoptive relatives allow environmental influences to be partitioned into those shared between relatives (i.e., those that make relatives resemble each other) and those that are nonshared (i.e., those that do not make relatives resemble each other). This type of analysis is not at the level of specific, measured environmental variables.

A second approach is to actually measure a specific aspect of the environment (e.g., parental socioeconomic status, or nutritional content of diet) and incorporate it into genetic analysis. For example, we may wish to partition out the variation in the trait due to a measured environmental source if we consider it to represent a cause of *nuisance* or *noise* variance in the trait (i.e., to treat it as a covariate). Alternatively, we may believe that an environment is important in the expression of genetic influence. For example, we might suspect that stress might bring out genetic vulnerabilities toward depression. Therefore, depression might be expected to show greater genetic influence for individuals experiencing stress. In this case, we would not want to adjust for the effects of the environmental variable. Such a circumstance is named a gene-environment interaction ($G \times E$ interaction). In terms of the quantitative genetic model,

$$P = G + E + (G \times E)$$

where ($G \times E$) does not necessarily represent a multiplication effect but rather any interactive effect of genes and environment that is independent of their main effects.

2.2 Estimating Variance Components

In the previous section we outlined a simple biometric model, describing the variation in observed phenotypes in terms of various genetic and environmental sources of variation. In this section, we consider how we can use family data to estimate some of the key parameters of such models, with a focus on heritability as estimated from the classical twin study, introducing maximum likelihood estimation and model fitting.

2.2.1 Genes and families Until now, we have built a general genetic model of the etiology of variation in a trait among individuals. A major step in quantitative genetics is to incorporate knowledge of basic laws of heredity to allow us to extend our model to include the covariance between relatives. Conceptually, most behavioral genetic analysis contrasts phenotypic similarity between related individuals (which is measured) with their genetic similarity (which is known from genetics). If individuals who are more closely related genetically also tend to be more similar on a measured trait, then this tendency is evidence for that trait being heritable—that is, the trait is at least partially influenced by genes.

When we study families, we are not only interested in the variance of a trait—the main focus is on the covariance between relatives. Earlier we saw how we can study two variables, such as height and weight, and ask whether they are associated with each other. In a similar way, covariances and correlations can also be used to ask whether a single variable is associated between family members. For example, do brothers and sisters tend to be similar in height or not? If we measured height in sibling pairs, we could calculate the covariance between an individual's height and the sibling's height. If the covariance equaled zero, this would imply that brothers and sisters are no more likely to have similar heights than any two unrelated individuals picked at random from the population. If the covariance is greater than zero, this would imply that taller individuals tend to have taller brothers and sisters. Quantitative genetic analysis attempts to determine the factors that can make relatives similar—their shared nature or their shared nurture.

2.2.2 Genetic relatedness in families An individual has two copies of every gene, one paternally inherited and one maternally inherited. When an individual passes one copy of each gene to its offspring, there is an equal chance that either the paternally inherited gene or the maternally inherited gene will be transmitted. From these two simple facts, we can calculate the expected proportion of gene sharing between individuals of different genetic relatedness. Siblings who share both biological parents will share either zero, one, or two alleles at each locus. For autosomal loci, there is a 50 percent chance that siblings will share the same paternal allele (two ways of sharing, two ways of not sharing, all with equal probability) and, correspondingly, a 50 percent chance of sharing the same maternal allele. Therefore, siblings stand a $0.50 \times 0.50 = 0.25$ (25 percent) chance of sharing both paternal and maternal alleles; a $(1.00 - 0.50) \times (1.00 - 0.50) = 0.25$ (25 percent) chance of sharing no alleles; a $1.00 - 0.25 - 0.25 = 0.50$ (50 percent) chance of sharing one allele. The average, or expected, alleles shared is therefore $(0 \times 0.25) + (1 \times 0.5) + (2 \times 0.25) = 1$. Therefore, in the average case, siblings will share half of the additive genetic variation that could potentially contribute to phenotypic variation because they share one out of two alleles. Because siblings stand only a 25 percent chance of sharing *both* alleles, in the average case, siblings will share a quarter of the dominance genetic variation that could potentially contribute to phenotypic variation.

For other types of relatives, we can work out their expected genetic relatedness in terms of genetic components of variance. Parent-offspring pairs always share precisely one allele: They will share half of the additive genetic effects that contribute to variation in the population but none of the dominance genetic effects. Half siblings, who have only one parent in common, share only a quarter of additive genetic variance but no dominance variance (because they can never inherit two alleles at the same locus from the same parent).

The majority of behavioral genetic studies focus on twins. Genetically, full sibling pairs and DZ twin pairs are equivalent. So, whereas DZ twins will only share half the additive genetic variance and one-fourth of the dominance variance, MZ twins share all their genetic makeup, so additive and dominance genetic variance components will be completely shared.

These coefficients of genetic relatedness are summarized in Table A.1. Sharing additive and dominance genetic variance contributes to the phenotypic correlation between relatives. As mentioned earlier, correlations between relatives directly estimate the proportion of variance shared between them. So we can think of the

TABLE A.1
Coefficients of Genetic Relatedness

Related Pair	Proportion of Additive Genetic Variation Shared	Proportion of Dominance Genetic Variation Shared
Parent and offspring (PO)	1/2	0
Half siblings (HS)	1/4	0
Full siblings (FS)	1/2	1/4
Nonidentical twins (DZ)	1/2	1/4
Identical twins (MZ)	1	1

familial correlation as the sum of all the shared components of variance between two relatives.

Not only genes are shared between most relatives, however. Individuals that are genetically related are more likely to experience similar environments than unrelated individuals are. If an environmental factor influences a variable, then sharing this environment will also contribute to the phenotypic correlation between relatives. As explained in Chapter 7, behavioral genetics conceptually divides environmental influences into two distinct types with regard to their impact on families. Environments that are shared by family members *and* that tend to make members more similar on a particular trait are called *shared environmental* influences. In contrast, *nonshared environmental* influences do not result in family members becoming more alike for a given trait.

Most behavioral genetic analysis focuses on three components of variance: additive genetic, shared environmental, and nonshared environmental. As we will see, this tripartite approach underlies the estimation of heritability by comparing twin correlations and is the basic model used in more sophisticated model-fitting analysis. This model is often referred to as the ACE model. (A stands for additive genetic effects, C for common (shared) environment, and E for nonshared environment.)

2.2.3 Heritability As explained in Chapter 7, heritability is the proportion of phenotypic variance that is attributable to genotypic variance. There are two types of heritability: *broad-sense heritability* refers to all sources of genetic variance, whether the genes operate in an additive manner or not. *Narrow-sense heritability* refers only to the proportion of phenotypic variance explained by additive genetic effects. Narrow-sense heritability therefore gives an indication of the extent to which a trait will "breed true" — that is, the degree of parent-offspring similarity that is expected. Broad-sense heritability, on the other hand, gives an indication of the extent to which genetic factors of any kind are responsible for trait variation in the population.

We are able to estimate the heritability of a trait by comparing correlations between certain types of family members. For simplicity, we will assume that the only influences on a trait are additive genetic effects and environmental effects that are either shared or nonshared between family members. We can describe the correlation we observe between different types of relatives in terms of the components of variance they share. For example, we expect the correlation between full siblings to represent half the additive genetic variance and, by definition, all the shared environmental variance but none of the nonshared environmental variance. As mentioned earlier, additive genetic variance is typically labeled h^2 in this context (representing narrow-sense heritability). The shared environmental variance is labeled c^2 (nonshared environment is e^2). Therefore,

$$r_{FS} = \frac{h^2}{2} + c^2$$

Suppose we observed for full siblings a correlation of 0.45 for a trait. We would not be able to work out what h^2 and c^2 are from this information alone because, as reflected in the equation above, nature and nurture are shared by siblings. However, by comparing sets of correlations between certain different types of relatives, we are able to estimate the relative balance of genetic and environmental effects. The most common study design uses MZ and DZ twin pairs. The correlations expressed in terms of shared variance components are therefore

$$r_{MZ} = h^2 + c^2$$

$$r_{DZ} = \frac{h^2}{2} + c^2$$

Subtracting the second equation from the first gives

$$r_{MZ} - r_{DZ} = h^2 - \frac{h^2}{2} + c^2 - c^2$$

$$= \frac{h^2}{2}$$

$$h^2 = 2(r_{MZ} - r_{DZ})$$

That is, narrow-sense heritability is calculated as twice the difference between the correlations observed for MZ and DZ twin pairs. The proportion of variance attributable to shared environmental effects can easily be estimated as the difference between the MZ correlation and the heritability ($c^2 = r_{MZ} - h^2$). Because we have estimated these two variance components from correlations, which are standardized, h^2 and c^2 represent *proportions* of variance. The final component of variance we are interested in is nonshared environmental variance, e^2. This statistic does not appear in the equations describing the correlations between relatives, of course. However, we know that h^2, c^2, and e^2 must sum to 1 if they represent proportions, so

$$h^2 + c^2 + e^2 = 1$$
$$[2(r_{MZ} - r_{DZ})] + [r_{MZ} - 2(r_{MZ} - r_{DZ})] + e^2 = 1$$
$$\therefore r_{MZ} + e^2 = 1$$
$$\therefore e^2 = 1 - r_{MZ}$$

This conclusion is intuitive: Because MZ twins are genetically identical, any variance that is not shared between them (i.e., the extent to which the MZ twin correlation is not 1) must be due to nonshared environmental sources of variance.

Let's consider an example: Suppose we observe a correlation of 0.64 in MZ twins and 0.44 in DZ twins. Taking twice the difference between the correlations, we can conclude that the trait has a heritability of 0.4 $[= 2 \times (0.64 - 0.44)]$. That is, 40 percent of variation in the population from which we sampled is attributable to the additive effects of genes. The shared family environment therefore accounts for 24 percent ($c^2 = 0.64 - 0.4 = 0.24$) of the variance; the nonshared environment accounts for 36 percent ($e^2 = 1 - 0.64 = 0.36$).

A pattern of results such as those just described would suggest that genes play a significant role in individual differences for this trait, differences between people being roughly half due to nature, half due to nurture. We have made several assumptions, however, in order to arrive at this conclusion. These assumptions will be considered more fully in the context of model fitting, but we will mention two immediate assumptions. First, we have assumed that dominance is not important for this trait (not to mention other more complex interactions such as epistasis). We have assumed that all genetic effects are additive (which is why h^2 represents narrow-sense heritability). If this assumption were not true, the heritability estimate would be biased. Second, we have assumed that MZ and DZ twins only differ in terms of the genetic relatedness. That is, the same shared environment term, c^2, appears in both MZ and DZ equations. If parents treat identical twins more similarly than they treat nonidentical twins, this assumption could result in higher MZ correlations relative to DZ correlations. This assumption, which is in theory testable, is called the *equal environments assumption* (see Chapter 6). Violations of this assumption would overestimate the importance of genetic effects.

Other types of relatives can be studied to calculate heritability; for example, we could compare correlations for full siblings and half siblings. Not all comparisons will be informative, however. Comparing the correlation for full siblings and the correlation for parent and offspring will not help to estimate heritability (because these relatives do not differ in terms of shared additive genetic variance). It is preferable to study twins for several reasons. It can be shown that for statistical reasons, twins afford greater accuracy in determining heritability because larger proportions of variance are shared by MZ twins. Additionally, twins are more closely matched for age, familial, and social influences than are half siblings or parents and offspring. The interpretation of the shared environment is much less clear for parents and offspring.

Quantitative genetic studies can also contrast family members who are genetically similar but have not shared any environmental influences. This comparison is the basis of the adoption study. The simplest form of adoption study is that of MZ twins reared apart. Because MZ twins reared apart are genetically identical but do not share any environmental influences, the correlation directly estimates heritability. That is, if there has been no selective placement, any tendency for MZ twins reared apart to be similar must be attributable to the influences of shared genes.

2.2.4 Model fitting and the classical twin design Simple comparisons between twin correlations can indicate whether genetic influences are important for a trait. This is the important first question that any quantitative genetic analysis must ask. Here we will examine some of the more formal statistical techniques that can be used to analyze genetically informative data and to ask other, more involved questions.

Model-fitting approaches involve constructing a model that describes some observed data. In the quantitative genetic studies, the observed data that we model are typically the variance-covariance matrices for family members. The model will then consist of a variance-covariance matrix formulated in terms of various *parameters*. These will typically be the variance components (additive genetic and so on) we encountered earlier. Various combinations of different values for the model parameters will generate different expected variance-covariance matrices. The goal of model fitting is twofold: (1) to select the model with the smallest number of parameters that (2) generates expectations that match the observed data as closely as possible. As we will see, there is a payoff between the number of parameters in a model and the accuracy with which it can model the observed data.

If we were to fit the ACE model to observed MZ and DZ twin data, the three parameter estimates selected to match the expected variance-covariance matrices with the observed ones would correspond directly to the estimates of heritability, and of shared and nonshared environmental influences that we calculated earlier in a relatively straightforward manner. Why would we ever want to perform more complicated model fitting? There are several good reasons: First, these calculations are only valid *if* the ACE model is a true reflection of reality. Model fitting allows different types of models to be explicitly tested and compared. Model fitting also facilitates the calculation of confidence intervals around the parameter estimates. It is common to read something such as "$h^2 = 0.35 \ (0.28 - 0.42)$," which means that the heritability was estimated at 35 percent, but there is a 95 percent chance that, even if it is not exactly 35 percent, it at least lies within the range of 28 to 42 percent. Model fitting can also incorporate many different types of family structures, model multivariate data, and include any *measured* genetic or environmental information we may have, in order to improve our estimates and explore potential interactions of genetic and environmental effects, or to test whether specific loci are associated with the trait or not.

Let's start from basics. Imagine that we have measured a trait in a population of twins. We have not measured any DNA, nor have we measured any other environmental factors that might influence the trait. We summarize our data as two variance-covariance matrices, one for MZ twin pairs and one for DZ twin pairs; so our "observed data" are six unique statistics:

$$\begin{bmatrix} \text{Var}_1^{MZ} & \\ \text{Cov}_{12}^{MZ} & \text{Var}_2^{MZ} \end{bmatrix}$$

$$\begin{bmatrix} \text{Var}_1^{DZ} & \\ \text{Cov}_{12}^{DZ} & \text{Var}_2^{DZ} \end{bmatrix}$$

Using our knowledge of the quantitative genetic model as outlined earlier, we can begin to construct a model that describes the two variance-covariance matrices for the twins. That is, we assume that observed trait variation is due to a certain mixture of additive genetic, dominance genetic, shared environmental, and nonshared environmental effects (we will ignore epistasis and other interactions).

Model fitting begins by creating an explicit model for the variance-covariance matrix for families, in terms of genetic and environmental variance components. Returning to the basic genetic model, phenotype, P, is a function of additive, A, and dominance, D, genetic effects. Additionally, we include environmental effects, which are either shared, C, or nonshared, E. (*Note:* The basic model did not make this distinction because it is primarily formulated to describe variation in a population of *unrelated* individuals, i.e., E referred to *all* environmental effects.)

$$P = A + D + C + E$$

In terms of variances, therefore, remembering all the assumptions outlined under the single-gene model that apply at this step (no gene-environment correlation, for example), we obtain

$$\sigma_P^2 = \sigma_A^2 + \sigma_D^2 + \sigma_C^2 + \sigma_E^2$$

where, using the model-fitting notation, $\sigma^2_{A/D/C/E}$ (pronounced "sigma") stands for the components of variance associated with the four types of effect and σ^2_P is the phenotypic variance.

To construct our twin model, we need to explicitly write out every element of the variance-covariance matrices in terms of the parameters of the model. We have already defined the trait variance in terms of the variance components:

$$\sigma_A^2 + \sigma_D^2 + \sigma_C^2 + \sigma_E^2$$

We will write this term for all four variance elements in the model. Note that we are modeling variances and covariances instead of correlations; this is often done in model fitting because it captures more information (the variance and covariance) than a correlation does. The σ^2_A parameter will not directly estimate narrow-sense heritability — we need to divide the additive genetic variance component by the total variance:

$$\sigma^2_A/(\sigma^2_A + \sigma^2_D + \sigma^2_C + \sigma^2_E)$$

We make the assumption that components of variance are identical for all individuals. That is, we write the same expression for all four variance elements. This assumption implies that the effects of genes and environments on an individual are not altered by that individual being a member of an MZ or DZ twin pair. Additionally, it assumes that individuals were not assigned a Twin 1 or Twin 2 label in a way that might make Twin 1's variance differ from Twin 2's variance. For example, if the first-born twin was always coded as Twin 1, then, depending on the nature of the trait, this assumption might not be warranted. (This problem is sometimes avoided by "double-entering" twin pairs so that each individual is entered twice, once as Twin 1 and once as Twin 2, when calculating the observed variance-covariance matrices. This method will, of course, ensure that Twin 1 and Twin 2 have equal variances.)

The covariance term between twins is also a function of the components of variance, in terms of the extent to which they are shared between twins, as stated earlier. All additive and dominance genetic variance, as well as shared environmental variance, is shared by MZ twins. These components contribute to the covariance between MZ twins fully. DZ twins share one-half the additive genetic variance, one-fourth the dominance genetic variance, all the shared environmental variance, and none of the nonshared environmental variance. The contributions of these components to the DZ covariance are in proportion to these coefficients of sharing.

Therefore, for MZ twin pairs, the variance-covariance matrix is modeled as

$$\begin{bmatrix} \sigma^2_A + \sigma^2_D + \sigma^2_C + \sigma^2_E & \\ \sigma^2_A + \sigma^2_D + \sigma^2_C & \sigma^2_A + \sigma^2_D + \sigma^2_C + \sigma^2_E \end{bmatrix}$$

whereas, for DZ twins, it is

$$\begin{bmatrix} \sigma^2_A + \sigma^2_D + \sigma^2_C + \sigma^2_E & \\ \dfrac{\sigma^2_A}{2} + \dfrac{\sigma^2_D}{4} + \sigma^2_C & \sigma^2_A + \sigma^2_D + \sigma^2_C + \sigma^2_E \end{bmatrix}$$

These two matrices represent our model. Different values of σ^2_A, σ^2_D, σ^2_C, and σ^2_E will result in different *expected* variance-covariance matrices. These matrices are "expected," in the sense that, *if* the values of the model parameters were true, then these are the averaged matrices we would expect to observe if we repeated the experiment a very large number of times.

As an example, consider a trait with a variance of 5. Imagine that variation in this trait was entirely due to an equal balance of additive genetic effects and non-shared environmental effects. In terms of the model, this assumption is equivalent to saying that σ^2_A and σ^2_E both equal 2.5, whereas σ^2_D and σ^2_C both equal 0. If this were true, then what variance-covariance matrices would we *expect* to observe for MZ and DZ twins? Simply substituting these values, we would expect to observe for MZ twins,

$$\begin{bmatrix} 2.5+0+0+2.5 & \\ 2.5+0+0 & 2.5+0+0+2.5 \end{bmatrix} = \begin{bmatrix} 5 & \\ 2.5 & 5 \end{bmatrix}$$

and for DZ twins,

$$\begin{bmatrix} 2.5+0+0+2.5 & \\ \dfrac{2.5}{2}+\dfrac{0.0}{4}+0 & 2.5+0+0+2.5 \end{bmatrix} = \begin{bmatrix} 5 & \\ 1.25 & 5 \end{bmatrix}$$

To recap, we have seen how a specific set of parameter values will result in a certain expected set of variance-covariance matrices for twins. This result is, in itself, not very useful. We do not know the true values of these parameters — these are the very values we are trying to discover! Model fitting helps us to estimate the parameter values most likely to be true by evaluating the expected values produced by very many sets of parameter values. The set of parameter values that produces expected matrices that most closely match the observed matrices are selected as the *best-fit parameter estimates*. These represent the best estimates of the true parameter values. Because of the iterative nature of model fitting (evaluating very many different sets of parameter values), it is a computationally intensive technique that can only be performed by using computers.

2.2.5 An example of the model-fitting principle Suppose that, for a certain trait, we observe the following variance-covariance matrices for MZ and DZ pairs, respectively (note that the observed variances are similar although not identical):

$$\begin{bmatrix} 2.81 & \\ 2.13 & 3.02 \end{bmatrix}$$

$$\begin{bmatrix} 3.17 & \\ 1.54 & 3.06 \end{bmatrix}$$

The model fitting would start by substituting *any* set of parameters to generate the expected matrices. Suppose we substituted $\sigma^2_A = 0.7$, $\sigma^2_D = 0.2$, $\sigma^2_C = 1.2$, and $\sigma^2_E = 0.8$. These values only represent a "first guess" that will be evaluated and improved on by the model-fitting process. These values imply that 24 percent $[0.7/(0.7 + 0.2 + 1.2 + 0.8)]$ of phenotypic variation is attributable to additive genetic effects. If these were the true values, the variance-covariance matrix we would expect to observe for MZ twins is

$$\begin{bmatrix} 0.7+0.2+1.2+0.8 & \\ 0.7+0.2+1.2 & 0.7+0.2+1.2+0.8 \end{bmatrix} = \begin{bmatrix} 2.9 & \\ 2.1 & 2.9 \end{bmatrix}$$

whereas, for DZ twins, it is

$$\begin{bmatrix} 0.7+0.2+1.2+0.8 & \\ \dfrac{0.7}{2}+\dfrac{0.2}{4}+1.2 & 0.7+0.2+1.2+0.8 \end{bmatrix} = \begin{bmatrix} 2.9 & \\ 1.6 & 2.9 \end{bmatrix}$$

Comparing these expectations with the observed statistics, we can see that they are numerically similar but not exactly the same. We need an exact method for determining *how good* the fit between the expected and observed matrices is. Model fitting can therefore proceed, changing the parameter values to increase the *goodness of fit* between the model-dependent expected values and the sample-based observed values. When a set of values has been found that cannot be beaten for goodness of fit, these will be presented as the "output" from the model-fitting programs, the best-fit estimates. This process is called *optimization.* It would be very inefficient to evaluate *every* possible set of parameter values. For most models, evaluating every set would in fact be virtually impossible, given current computing technology. Rather, optimization will try to change the parameters in an intelligent way. One way of thinking about this process is as a form of a "hotter-colder" game: The aim is to increasingly refine your guess as to where the hidden object is, rather than exhaustively searching every inch of the room.

There are many indices of fit—one simple one is the chi-squared (χ^2, pronounced "ki," as in *kite*) goodness-of-fit statistic. This statistic essentially evaluates the magnitude of the discrepancies between expected and observed values by comparing how likely the observed data are under the model. The χ^2 goodness-of-fit statistic can be formally tested for significance in order to indicate whether or not the model provides a good approximation of the data. If the χ^2 goodness-of-fit statistic is low (i.e., nonsignificant), it indicates that the observed values *do not significantly deviate* from the expected values. However, a low χ^2 value does not necessarily mean that the parameter values being tested are the best-fit estimates. As we have mentioned, different values for the four parameters might provide a better fit (i.e., an even lower χ^2 goodness-of-fit-statistic).

Just because we can write down a model that we believe to be an accurate description of the real-world processes affecting a trait, it does not necessarily mean that we can derive values for its parameters. In the preceding example, we would not be able to estimate the four parameters (additive and dominance genetic variances, shared and nonshared environmental variances) from our twin data. In simple terms, we are asking too many questions of too little information.

Consider what happens when we change the parameter values to see whether we can improve the fit of the model. Try substituting $\sigma^2_A = 0.1$, $\sigma^2_D = 0.6$, $\sigma^2_C = 1.4$, and $\sigma^2_E = 0.8$ instead, and you will notice that we obtain the same two expected variance-covariance matrices for both MZ and DZ twins as we did under the previous set of parameters. Both sets of parameters would therefore have an identical fit, so we would not be able to distinguish these two alternative explanations of the observations. This phenomenon can make model fitting very difficult or even impossible. This is an instance of a model not being *identified*.

2.2.6 The ACE model Although we will not follow the proof here, researchers have demonstrated that we cannot ask about additive genetic effects, dominance genetic effects, *and* shared environmental effects simultaneously if the only information we have is from MZ and DZ twins reared together.

In virtually every circumstance, we will wish to retain the nonshared environmental variance component in the model. We wish to retain it partly because random measurement error is modeled as a nonshared environmental effect and we do not wish to have a model that assumes no measurement error (it is unlikely to fit very well). Most commonly, we would then model additive genetic variance and shared environmental variance. As mentioned earlier, such a model is called the ACE model.

If we had reason to suspect that dominance genetic variance might be affecting a trait, then we might fit an ADE model instead. If the MZ twin correlation is more than twice the DZ twin correlation, one explanation is that dominance genetic effects play a large role for that trait (an explanation that might suggest fitting an ADE model).

The ACE model (and the ADE model) is an identified model. That is, the best fit between the expected and observed matrices is produced by one and only one set of parameter values. As long as the twin covariances are both positive and the MZ covariance is not smaller than the DZ covariance (both of which are easily justified biologically as reasonable demands), the ACE model will always be able to select a unique set of parameters that best account for the observed statistics.

If we were to model standardized scores (so that differences in the observed variance elements could not reduce fit), then under the ACE model the best-fitting parameters will always have a χ^2 goodness of fit of precisely zero. Such a model is called a *saturated* model. Imagine that, for a standardized trait (i.e., one with a variance of 1), we found an MZ covariance of 0.6 (this can be considered as the MZ twin correlation, of course) and a DZ covariance of 0.4. There is, in fact, one and only one set of values for the three parameters of the ACE model that will produce expected values that exactly match these observed values. In this case, these are $\sigma^2_A = 0.4$, $\sigma^2_C = 0.2$, and $\sigma^2_E = 0.4$. Substituting these into the model, we obtain for MZ twins,

$$\begin{bmatrix} 0.4 + 0.2 + 0.4 & \\ 0.4 + 0.2 & 0.4 + 0.2 + 0.4 \end{bmatrix} = \begin{bmatrix} 1.0 & \\ 0.6 & 1.0 \end{bmatrix}$$

and for DZ twins,

$$\begin{bmatrix} 0.4 + 0.2 + 0.4 & \\ \dfrac{0.4}{2} + 0.2 & 0.4 + 0.2 + 0.4 \end{bmatrix} = \begin{bmatrix} 1.0 & \\ 0.4 & 1.0 \end{bmatrix}$$

There are no other values that σ^2_A, σ^2_C, and σ^2_E can take to produce the same expected variance-covariance matrices. This property does not mean that these values will necessarily reflect the true balance of genetic and environmental effects—they will only reflect the true values if the model (ACE or ADE or whatever) is a good one. All parameter estimates are model dependent: We can only conclude that, *if* the ACE model is a good model, then this result is the balance of genetic and environmental effects. We are able to test different models relative to one another, however, in order to get a sense of whether or not the model is a fair approximation of the underlying reality. We can only compare models if they are *nested,* however. A model is nested in another model if and only if that model results from constraining to zero one or more of the variance components in the larger model. For example, we may suspect that the shared environment plays no significant role for a given trait. We can test this supposition by fixing the shared environment variance component to zero and comparing the fit of the full model with the fit of this reduced model. Nesting is important because it forms the basis for testing and selecting between different models of our data.

A general principle of science is parsimony: to always prefer a simpler theory if it accounts equally well for the observations. This concept, often referred to as *Occam's razor,* is explicit in model fitting. Having derived estimates for genetic and environmental variance components under an ACE model, we might ask whether we could drop the shared environment term from the model. Might our simpler AE model provide a comparable fit to the data? Instead of estimating the shared environment variance component, we assume that it is zero (which is equivalent to ignoring it or removing it from the model). The AE model is therefore nested in the ACE model. We are able to calculate the goodness of fit of the ACE model, which estimates three parameters to explain the data, and the goodness of fit for the AE model, which only estimates two parameters to explain the same data. Any model with fewer parameters will not fit as well as a sensible model with more parameters. The question is whether or not the reduction in fit is *significantly* worse relative to the "advantage" of having fewer parameters in a more parsimonious model.

In our example, the ACE model will estimate $\sigma^2_A = 0.4$, $\sigma^2_C = 0.2$, and $\sigma^2_E = 0.4$. As we saw earlier, substituting these values and *only* these values will produce expected variance-covariance matrices that match the observed perfectly (because we are modeling standardized scores, or correlations). In contrast, consider what happens under the AE model with the same data. Table A.2 shows that the AE model is unable to account for this particular set of observed values. Such a model is said to be *underidentified*. This condition is not necessarily problematic: In general, under-identified models are to be favored. Because a saturated model will *always* be able to fit the observed data perfectly, the goodness of fit does not really mean anything. However, if an underidentified model *does* fit the data, then we should take notice—it is not fitting out of mere statistical necessity. Perhaps it is a better, more parsimonious model of the data. Table A.2 represents three different sets of the values for the two parameters that attempt to explain the observed data. As the table shows, the AE model does not seem able to model our observed statistics quite as well as the ACE model.

If we run a model-fitting program such as *Mx*, we can formally determine which values for σ^2_A and σ^2_E give the best fit for the AE model and whether or not this fit is significantly worse than that of the saturated ACE model. Additionally, we can fit a CE model (which implies that any covariation between twins is not due to genetic factors) and an E model (which implies that there is no significant covariation between twins in any case). The results are presented in Table A.3, showing the optimized parameter values for the different models.

Because these models are not saturated, they cannot necessarily guarantee a perfect fit to the data. Adjusting one parameter to perfectly fit the MZ twin covariance pulls the DZ twin covariance or the variance estimate out of line, and vice versa. We see here that the AE model has estimated the variance and MZ covariance quite

TABLE A.2
Fit of AE Model to Three Parameter Value Sets

Parameters			MZ	DZ
σ^2_A	σ^2_E	Variance	Covariance	Covariance
OBSERVED				
—	—	1.0	0.6	0.4
EXPECTED				
0.6	0.4	1.0	0.6	0.3
0.7	0.3	1.0	0.7	0.35
0.8	0.2	1.0	0.8	0.4

TABLE A.3
Best-Fit Univariate Parameter Estimates

Parameters		Variance	MZ Covariance	DZ Covariance	χ^2	df^a
AE Model						
σ^2_A	σ^2_E					
0.609	0.382	0.991	0.609	0.304	1.91	4
CE Model						
σ^2_C	σ^2_E					
0.5	0.5	1.000	0.500	0.500	6.75	4
E Model	σ^2_E					
	1.000	1.000	0.000	0.000	92.47	5

$^a df$, degrees of freedom.

accurately in selecting the optimized parameters $\sigma^2_A = 0.609$ and $\sigma^2_E = 0.382$ but the expected DZ covariance departs substantially from the observed value of 0.4. But is this departure significant? The last two columns give the χ^2 and associated *degrees of freedom (df)* of the test. Because we have six observed statistics, from which we are estimating two parameters under the AE model, we say that we have $6 - 2 = 4$ degrees of freedom. The degrees of freedom therefore represent a measure of how simple or complex a model is—we need to know this when deciding which is the most parsimonious model. The E model, for example, estimates only one parameter and so has $6 - 1 = 5$ degrees of freedom.

The test of whether a nested, simpler model is more parsimonious is quite simple: We look at the difference in χ^2 goodness of fit between the two models. The difference in degrees of freedom between the two models is used to determine whether or not the difference in fit is significant. If the difference is significant, then we say that the nested submodel does *not* provide a good account of the data when compared with the goodness of fit of the fuller model. The χ^2 statistics calculated in our example in Table A.3 are dependent on sample size—these figures are based on 150 MZ twins and 150 DZ twins.

The ACE model estimates three parameters from the six observed statistics, so it has three degrees of freedom; the χ^2 is always 0.0 because the model is saturated. Therefore, the difference in fit between the ACE and AE models is $1.91 - 0 = 1.91$ with $4 - 3 = 1$ degree of freedom. Looking up this χ^2 value in significance tables tells us that it is not significant at the $p = 0.05$ level (in fact, $p = 0.17$). A p value lower than 0.05 indicates that the observed results would be expected to arise less than 5 percent of the time by chance alone, if there were in reality no effect. This is commonly accepted to be sufficient evidence to reject a null hypothesis, which states that no effect is present. Therefore, because the AE model does not show a signifi-cant reduction in fit relative to the ACE model, this result provides evidence that the shared environment is not important (i.e., that σ^2_C is not substantially greater than 0.0) for this trait.

What about the CE and E models, though? The CE model fit is reduced by a χ^2 value of 6.75, also for a gain of one degree of freedom. This reduction in fit is signif-icant at the $p = 0.05$ level ($p = 0.0093$). This significant reduction in goodness of fit suggests that additive genetic effects are important for this trait (i.e., that $\sigma^2_A > 0.0$). Unsurprisingly, the E model shows an even greater reduction in fit ($\Delta\chi^2 = 92.47$ for two degrees of freedom: $p < 0.00001$), thus confirming the obvious fact that the members of both types of twins do in fact show a reasonable degree of resemblance to each other.

2.2.7 Path analysis The kind of model fitting we have described so far is intimately related to a field of statistics called *path analysis*. Path analysis provides a visual and intuitive way to describe and explore any kind of model that describes some observed data. The *paths*, drawn as arrows, reflect the statistical effect of one variable on another, independent of all the other variables—what are called *partial regression coefficients*. The *variables* can be either measured traits (squares) or the *latent* (unmeasured; circles) variance components of our model. The twin ACE model can be represented as the path diagram in Figure A.9.

The curved, double-headed arrows between latent variables represent the covar-iance between them. The 1.0/0.5 on the covariance link between the two *A* latent variables indicates that for MZ twins, this covariance link is 1.0; for DZ twins, 0.5. The covariance links between the *C* and *E* terms therefore represent the previously

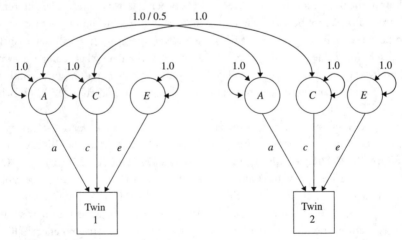

FIGURE A.9 ACE path diagram. This path diagram is equivalent to the matrix formulation of the ACE model. Path coefficients (*a*, *c*, and *e*) rather than variance components (which are assumed to be 1) are estimated.

defined sharing of these variance components between twins (i.e., no link implies a 0 covariance). The double-headed arrow loops on each latent variable represent the variance of that variable. In our previous model fitting, we estimated the variances of these latent variables, calling them σ^2_A, σ^2_C, and σ^2_E. In our path diagram, we have fixed all the variances to 1.0. Instead, we estimate the path coefficients, which we have labeled as a, c, and e. The differences here are largely superficial: The diagram and the previous models are mathematically identical.

To understand a path diagram and how it relates to the kind of models we have discussed, we need to acquaint ourselves with a few basic rules of path analysis. The covariance between two variables is represented by tracing along all the paths that connect the two variables. There are certain rules about the directions in which paths can or cannot be traced, how loops in paths are dealt with, and so on, but the principle is simple. For each path, we multiply all the path coefficients together with the variances of any latent variables traced through. We sum these paths to calculate the expected covariance. The variance for the first twin is therefore a (up the first path) times 1.0 (the variance of latent variable A) times a (back down the path) plus the same for the paths to latent variables C and E. This equals $(a \times 1.0 \times a) + (c \times 1.0 \times c) + (e \times 1.0 \times e) = a^2 + c^2 + e^2$. So instead of estimating the variance components, we have written the model to estimate the path coefficients. This approach is used for practical reasons (e.g., it means that estimates of variance always remain positive, being the square of the path coefficient). The covariance between twins is derived in a similar way. When we trace the two paths between the twins, we get $(a \times 1.0 \times a) + (c \times 1.0 \times c)$ for MZ twins and $(a \times 0.5 \times a) + (c \times 1.0 \times c)$ for DZ twins. That is, $a^2 + c^2$ for MZ twins and $0.5a^2 + c^2$ for DZ twins, as before.

So we have seen how a properly constructed path diagram implies an expected variance-covariance (or correlation) matrix for the observed variables in the model. As noted, it is standard for the parameters in path diagrams to be path coefficients instead of variance components, although, for most basic purposes, this substitution makes very little difference. Any path diagram can be converted into a model that can be written down as algebraic terms in the elements of variance-covariance matrices, and vice versa.

2.2.8 Multivariate analysis So far we have focused on the analysis of only one phenotype at a time. This method is often called a *univariate* approach—studying the genetic-environmental nature of the *variance of one trait*. If multiple measures have been assessed for each individual, however, a model-fitting approach easily extends to analyze the genetic-environmental basis of the *covariance between multiple traits*. Is, for example, the correlation between depression and anxiety due to genes that influence both traits, or is it largely due to environments that act as risk factors for both depression and anxiety? If we think of a correlation as essentially reflecting shared causes somewhere in the etiological pathways of the two traits, multivariate genetic analysis can tell us something about the nature of these shared causes. The development of multivariate quantitative genetics is one of the most important advances in behavioral genetics during the past two decades.

The essence of multivariate genetic analysis is the analysis of *cross-covariance* in relatives. That is, we can ask whether trait X is associated with another family member's trait Y. Path analysis provides an easy way to visualize multivariate analysis. The path diagram for a multivariate genetic analysis of two measures is shown in Figure A.10. The new parameters in this model are r_A, r_C, and r_E. These symbols represent the *genetic correlation,* the *shared environmental correlation,* and the *nonshared environmental correlation,* respectively. A genetic correlation of 1.0 would imply that all additive genetic influences on trait X also impact on trait Y. A shared environmental correlation of 0 would imply that the environmental influences that make twins more similar on measure X are independent of the environmental influences that make twins more similar on measure Y. The phenotypic correlation between X and Y can therefore be dissected into genetic and environmental constituents. A high genetic correlation implies that if a gene were found for one trait, there is a reasonable chance that this gene would also influence the second trait.

Multivariate analysis can model more than two variables—as many measures as we wish can be included. In matrix terms, instead of modeling a 2×2 matrix, we model a $2n \times 2n$ matrix, where n is the number of variables in the model. In a bivariate case, if we call the measures X and Y in Twins 1 and 2 (such that X_1 represents measure X for Twin 1), then the variance-covariance matrix would be

$$\begin{bmatrix} \mathrm{Var}(X_1) \\ \mathrm{Cov}(X_1X_2) & \mathrm{Var}(X_2) \\ \mathrm{Cov}(X_1Y_1) & \mathrm{Cov}(X_2Y_1) & \mathrm{Var}(Y_1) \\ \mathrm{Cov}(X_1Y_2) & \mathrm{Cov}(X_2Y_2) & \mathrm{Cov}(Y_1Y_2) & \mathrm{Var}(Y_2) \end{bmatrix}$$

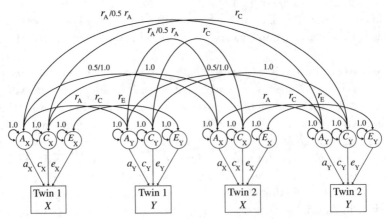

FIGURE A.10 Multivariate ACE path diagram. This path diagram represents a multivariate ACE model. The expected variance-covariance matrix (given in Table A.4) can be derived from this diagram by tracing the paths.

giving us ten unique pieces of information. Along the diagonal, we have four variances—each measure in each twin. The terms $\text{Cov}(X_1Y_1)$ and $\text{Cov}(X_2Y_2)$ are the phenotypic covariances between X and Y for the first and second twin, respectively. The terms $\text{Cov}(X_1X_2)$ and $\text{Cov}(Y_1Y_2)$ are the univariate cross-twin covariances; the final two terms $\text{Cov}(X_1Y_2)$ and $\text{Cov}(X_2Y_1)$ are the cross-twin cross-trait covariances.

The corresponding multivariate ACE model for the expected variance-covariance matrix would be written in terms of univariate parameters as before (three parameters for measure X and three for measure Y) as well as three parameters for the genetic, shared environmental, and nonshared environmental correlations between the two measures (where G is the coefficient of relatedness; i.e., either 1.0 or 0.5 for MZ or DZ twins). Table A.4 presents the elements of this matrix in tabular form.

The shaded area in Table A.4 represents the cross-trait part of the model, which looks more complex than it really is. In path diagram terms, the phenotypic (within-individual) cross-trait covariance results from three paths. The first path includes the additive genetic path for measure $X(a_X)$ multiplied by the genetic correlation between the two traits (r_A) and the additive genetic path for measure $Y(a_Y)$. The shared environmental and nonshared environmental paths are constructed in a similar way. The cross-twin cross-trait correlations are identical, except that there are no nonshared environmental components (by definition) and there is a coefficient of relatedness, G, to determine the magnitude of shared additive genetic variance for MZ and DZ twins. Be careful in the interpretation of a *nonshared environmental correlation;* remember that this term means *nonshared* between family members, not *trait-specific.* Any environmental effect that family members do not have in common and that influences more than one trait will induce a nonshared environmental correlation between these traits.

TABLE A.4
Variance-Covariance Matrix for a Multivariate Genetic Model

	Twin 1 Measure X	Twin 2 Measure X	Twin 1 Measure Y	Twin 2 Measure Y
Twin 1 Measure X	$a_X^2 + c_X^2 + e_X^2$			
Twin 2 Measure X	$Ga_X^2 + c_X^2$	$a_X^2 + c_X^2 + e_X^2$		
Twin 1 Measure Y	$r_A a_X a_Y +$ $r_C c_X c_Y +$ $r_E e_X e_Y$	$Gr_A a_X a_Y +$ $r_C c_X c_Y$	$a_Y^2 + c_Y^2 + e_Y^2$	
Twin 2 Measure Y	$Gr_A a_X a_Y +$ $r_C c_X c_Y$	$r_A a_X a_Y +$ $r_C c_X c_Y +$ $r_E e_X e_Y$	$Ga_Y^2 + c_Y^2$	$a_Y^2 + c_Y^2 + e_Y^2$

Genetic, shared environmental, and nonshared environmental correlations are independent of univariate heritabilities. That is, two traits might both have low heritabilities but a high genetic correlation. This would mean that, although there are probably only a few genes of modest effect that influence both these traits, whichever gene influences one trait is very likely to influence the other trait also. In this way, the analysis of these three etiological correlations can begin to tell us not just *whether* two traits are correlated but also *why* they are correlated.

Imagine that we have measured three traits, X, Y, and Z, in a sample of MZ and DZ twins (400 MZ pairs, 400 DZ pairs). What might a multivariate genetic analysis be able to tell us about the relationships between these traits? Looking at the phenotypic correlations, we observe that each trait is moderately correlated with the other two:

$$\begin{bmatrix} 1.00 & & \\ 0.42 & 1.00 & \\ 0.30 & 0.45 & 1.00 \end{bmatrix}$$

Naturally, we would be interested in the twin correlations for these measures—both the univariate and cross-trait twin correlations. For MZ twins, we might observe

$$\begin{bmatrix} 0.78 & & \\ 0.44 & 0.91 & \\ 0.08 & 0.39 & 0.70 \end{bmatrix}$$

whereas for DZ twins, we might see

$$\begin{bmatrix} 0.40 & & \\ 0.23 & 0.61 & \\ 0.04 & 0.23 & 0.58 \end{bmatrix}$$

The twin correlations along the diagonal therefore represent univariate twin correlations. For example, we can see that the correlation between MZ twins for trait Y is 0.91. The off-diagonal elements represent the cross-twin cross-trait correlations. For example, the correlation between an individual's trait X with their co-twin's trait Y is 0.23 for DZ twins. Submitting our data to formal model-fitting analysis gives optimized estimates for the univariate parameters (heritability, proportion of variance attributable to shared environment, proportion of variance attributable to nonshared environment) shown in Table A.5.

That is, traits X and Y both appear to be strongly heritable. Trait Z appears less heritable, although one-fourth of the variation in the population of twins is still due to genetic factors. The more interesting results emerge when the multivariate structure of the data is examined. The best-fitting parameter estimates for the genetic

TABLE A.5
Best-Fit Univariate Parameter Estimates

Trait	Optimized Estimate (%)[a]		
	h^2	c^2	e^2
X	74	4	22
Y	60	31	9
Z	23	47	30

[a]h^2, heritability or additive genetic variance; c^2, shared environmental variance; e^2, nonshared environmental variance.

correlation matrix, the shared environment correlation matrix, and the nonshared environment correlation matrix, respectively, are presented in the following matrices:

$$
\begin{bmatrix} 1.00 & & \\ 0.44 & 1.00 & \\ 0.11 & 0.75 & 1.00 \end{bmatrix}
\quad
\begin{bmatrix} 1.00 & & \\ 0.98 & 1.00 & \\ 0.17 & 0.26 & 1.00 \end{bmatrix}
\quad
\begin{bmatrix} 1.00 & & \\ 0.10 & 1.00 & \\ 0.89 & 0.46 & 1.00 \end{bmatrix}
$$

Genetic correlation   Shared environmental   Nonshared environmental
matrix   correlation matrix   correlation matrix

These correlations tell an interesting story about the underlying nature of the association between the three traits. Although on the surface, traits X, Y, and Z appear to be all moderately intercorrelated, behavioral genetic analysis has revealed a nonuniform pattern of underlying genetic and environmental sources of association.

The genetic correlation between traits Y and Z is high ($r_A = 0.75$), so any genes impacting on Y are likely to also affect Z, and vice versa. The contribution of shared genetic factors to the phenotypic correlation between two traits is called the *bivariate heritability*. This statistic is calculated by tracing the genetic paths that contribute to the phenotypic correlation: in this case, a_Y and r_A (Y-Z correlation) and a_Z. In other words, the bivariate heritability is the product of the square root of both univariate heritabilities multiplied by the genetic correlation. In the case of traits Y and Z, this statistic equals $\sqrt{0.60} \times 0.75 \times \sqrt{0.23} = 0.28$. As shown in an earlier matrix, the phenotypic correlation between traits Y and Z is 0.45. Therefore, over half (62 percent = $0.28/0.45$) of the correlation between traits Y and Z can be explained by shared genes. Note that we take the square root of the univariate heritabilities because, in path analysis terms, we only trace up the path once—in calculating the univariate heritability, we would come back down that path, therefore squaring the estimate.

The same logic can be applied to the environmental influences. Focusing on traits Y and Z, tracing the paths for shared and nonshared environmental influences yields values of 0.10 ($\sqrt{0.31}$ × 0.26 × $\sqrt{0.47}$) and 0.07 ($\sqrt{0.09}$ × 0.46 × $\sqrt{0.30}$) for the bivariate estimates. Note that these add up to the phenotypic correlation, as expected (0.28 + 0.10 + 0.07 = 0.45).

In contrast, the correlation between traits X and Z ($r = 0.30$) is not predominantly mediated by shared genetic influence: $\sqrt{0.74}$ × 0.11 × $\sqrt{0.23}$ = 0.04; only 13 percent of this phenotypic correlation is due to genes.

An interesting aspect of this kind of analysis is that it could potentially reveal a strong genetic overlap between two heritable traits even when the phenotypic correlation is near 0. This scenario could arise if there were, for example, a negative nonshared environmental correlation (i.e., certain environments [nonshared between family members] tend to make individuals dissimilar for two traits). Consider the following example: Two traits both have univariate heritabilities of 0.50 and no shared environmental influences, so the nonshared environment will account for the remaining 50 percent of the variance. If the traits had a genetic correlation of 0.75 but a nonshared environmental correlation of −0.75, then the phenotypic correlation would be 0. The phenotypic correlation is the sum of the chains of paths ($\sqrt{0.5}$ × 0.75 × $\sqrt{0.5}$) + ($\sqrt{0.5}$ × −0.75 × $\sqrt{0.5}$) = 0.0. This example shows that the phenotypic correlation by itself does not necessarily tell you very much about the shared etiologies of traits.

The preceding model is just one form of multivariate model. Different models that make different assumptions about the underlying nature of the traits can be fitted to test whether a more parsimonious explanation fits the data. For example, the *common-factor independent-pathway* model assumes that each measure has specific (subscript "S") genetic and environmental effects as well as general (subscript "C") genetic and environmental effects that create the correlations between all the measures. Figure A.11 shows a schematic path diagram for a three-trait version of this model. (*Note:* The diagram represents only one twin for convenience—the full model would have the three traits for both twins and the A and C latent variables would have the appropriate covariance links between twins.) In this path diagram, the general factors are at the bottom.

A similar but more restricted model, the *common-factor common-pathway* model, assumes that the common genetic *and* environmental effects load onto a latent variable, L, that in turn loads onto all the measures in the model. This model is said to be more restricted in that, because fewer parameters are estimated, the expected variance-covariance is not as free to model any pattern of phenotypic, cross-twin same-trait and cross-twin cross-trait, correlations. Figure A.12 represents this model (again, for only one twin).

The common-factor independent-pathway model is nested in the more general multivariate model presented earlier; the common-factor common-pathway model is nested in both. These models can therefore be tested against each other to see which provides the most parsimonious explanation of the observations. Note that these multivariate models can also vary in terms of whether they are ACE, ADE, CE, AE, or E models.

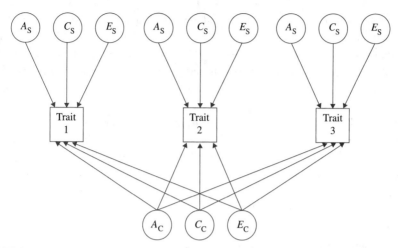

FIGURE A.11 Common-factor independent-pathway multivariate path diagram. This is a partial diagram, for one twin. *A*, additive genetic effects; *C*, shared environmental effects; *E*, nonshared environmental effects; S (subscript), specific effects; C (subscript), general effects.

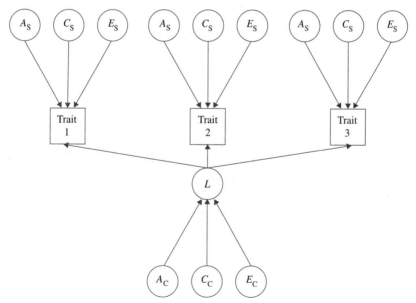

FIGURE A.12 Common-factor common-pathway multivariate path diagram. This is a partial diagram, for one twin. *A*, additive genetic effects; *C*, shared environmental effects; *E*, nonshared environmental effects; S (subscript), specific effects; C (subscript), general effects; *L*, latent variable.

A more specific form of multivariate model that has received a lot of interest is the *longitudinal* model. This model is appropriate for designs that take repeated measures of a trait over a period of time (say, IQ at 5, 10, 15, and 20 years of age). Such models can be used to unravel the etiology of continuity and change in a trait over time and are especially powerful for studying the interaction of genetic makeup and environment.

2.2.9 Complex effects including gene-environment interaction

For the sake of simplicity (and parsimony), all the ACE-type models we have looked at so far have made various assumptions about the nature of the genetic and environmental influences that operate on the trait. Nature does not always conform to our expectations, however. In this section, we will briefly review some of the "complexities" that can be incorporated into models of genetic and environmental influence.

As mentioned earlier, an important feature of the model-fitting approach is that, as well as being flexible, it tends to make the assumptions of the model quite apparent. One such assumption is the *equal environments assumption* that MZ and DZ twins receive equally similar environments (see Chapter 6). The assumption is implicit in the model—we estimate the same parameter for shared environmental effects for MZ and DZ twins. This assumption might not always be true in practice. Can we account for potential inequalities of environment in our model? Unfortunately, not without collecting more information. The model-fitting approach is flexible, but it cannot do everything—this problem is an example of how experimental design and analysis should work hand-in-hand to tackle such questions. For example, research has compared MZ twins who have been mistakenly brought up as DZ twins, and vice versa, to study whether MZ twins are in fact treated more similarly, as indicated in Chapter 6.

Another assumption of the models used so far is random mating in the population. When nonrandom (or assortative) mating occurs (Chapter 11), then loci for a trait will be correlated between spouses. This unexpected correlation will lead to siblings and DZ twins sharing more than half their genetic variation, a situation that will bias the estimates derived from our models. In model fitting, the effects of assortative mating can be modeled (and therefore accounted for) if appropriate parental information is gathered.

Covariance between relatives on any trait can arise from a number of different sources that are not considered in our basic models. As mentioned earlier, shared causation is not the only process by which covariation can arise. The phenotype of one twin might *directly* influence the phenotype of the other, for example, because the co-twin is very much part of a twin's environment. Having an aggressive co-twin may influence levels of aggression as a result of the direct exposure to the co-twin's aggressive behavior. Such an effect is called *sibling interaction*. In the context of multivariate analysis, it is possible that trait X actually causes trait Y in the same individual, rather than a gene or environment impacting on both. These situations can be modeled by using fairly standard approaches. If such factors are important but are ignored in model fitting, they will bias estimates of genetic and environmental influence.

Another way in which the basic model might be extended is to account for possible *heterogeneity* in the sample. Genetic and environmental influences may be different for boys and girls on the same trait, or for young versus old people. Heritability is only a sample-based statistic: A heritability of 70 percent means that 70 percent of the variation *in the sample* can be accounted for by genetic effects. This outcome could be because the trait is completely heritable in 70 percent of the sample and not at all heritable in 30 percent. Such a sample would be called *heterogeneous*—there is something different and potentially interesting about the 30 percent that we may wish to study. The standard model-fitting approaches we have studied so far would leave the researcher oblivious to such effects.

To uncover heterogeneity, various approaches can be taken. Potential indices of heterogeneity (e.g., sex or age) can be incorporated into a model, for example. We could ask, Does heritability increase with age? Or we could test a model having separate parameter estimates for boys and girls for genetic effects against the nested model with only one parameter for both sexes. Same-sex and opposite-sex DZ twins can be modeled separately to test for quantitative and qualitative etiological differences between males and females. This design is called a *sex-limitation model,* and it can ask whether the magnitude of genetic and environmental effects are similar in males and females. Additionally, such designs are potentially able to test whether the *same* genes are important for both sexes, irrespective of magnitude of effect.

Other complications include *nonadditivity,* such as epistasis, gene-environment interaction, and gene-environment correlation. These three types of effects were defined under the preceding biometric model section. Epistasis is any gene-gene interaction; $G \times E$ interaction is the interaction between genetic effects and environments; G-E correlation occurs when certain genes are associated with certain environments. As an example of epistasis, imagine that an allele at locus A only predisposes toward depression if that individual also has a certain allele at locus B. As an example of gene-environment interaction, the allele at locus A may have an effect only for individuals living in deprived environments. These types of effects complicate model fitting because there are many forms in which they could occur. Normal twin study designs do not offer much hope for identifying them. An MZ correlation that is much higher than twice the DZ correlation would be suggestive of epistasis, but the models cannot really go any further in quantifying such effects.

Although model fitting can often be extended to incorporate more complex effects, it is not generally possible to include *all* these "modifications" at the same time. Successful approaches will typically select specific types of models that should be fitted a priori, on the basis of existing etiological knowledge of the traits under study.

One exciting development in model fitting involves incorporating measured variables for individuals into the analysis. Measuring alleles at specific loci, or specific environmental variables, makes the detection of specific, complex, interactive effects feasible, as well as forming the basis for modern techniques for mapping genes, as we will review in the final section.

2.2.10 Environmental mediation Behavioral genetic studies have convincingly demonstrated that genes play a significant role in many complex human traits and diseases. As a result, rather than just estimating heritability and other genetic quantities of interest, an increasingly important application of genetically informative designs, such as the twin study, is to shed light on the nature of *environmental effects*.

Although we might know that an environment and an outcome show a statistical correlation, we often do not understand the true nature of that association. For example, an association might be causal if the environment directly affects the outcome. Alternatively, the association might only arise as a reflection of some other underlying shared, possibly genetic, factor that influences both environment and the outcome. As illustrated in detail in Chapter 8, many "environmental" measures do indeed show genetic influence. By using a genetically informative design to control for genetic factors, researchers are able to make stronger inferences about environmental factors. A simple but powerful design is to focus on environmental measures that predict phenotypic differences between MZ twins.

2.2.11 Extremes analysis When we partition the variance of a trait into portions attributable to genetic or environmental effects, we are analyzing the sources of *individual differences* across the entire range of the trait. When looking at a quantitative trait, we may be more interested in one end, or extreme, of that trait. Instead of asking what makes individuals different for a trait, we might want to ask what makes individuals score high on that trait.

Consider a trait such as reading ability. Low levels of reading ability have clinical significance; individuals scoring very low will tend to be diagnosed as having reading disability. We may want to ask what makes people reading disabled, rather than what influences individuals' reading ability. We could perform a qualitative analysis where the dependent variable is simply a *Yes* or a *No* to indicate whether or not individuals are reading disabled (i.e., low scoring). If we have used a quantitative trait measure (such as a score on a reading ability task) that we believe to be related to reading disability, we may wish to retain this extra information. Indeed, we can ask whether reading disability is etiologically related to the continuum of reading ability or whether it represents a distinct syndrome. In the latter case, the factors that tend to make individuals score lower on a reading ability task in the entire population will not be the same as the factors that make people reading disabled. A regression-based method for analyzing twin data, DF (DeFries-Fulker) extremes analysis, addresses such questions, by analyzing means as opposed to variances. The methodology for DF extremes analysis is described in Chapter 12.

3 MOLECULAR GENETICS

Mapping genes for quantitative traits (quantitative trait loci, or QTLs) and diseases is a fast-developing area in behavioral genetics. The goal is to identify either the chromosomal region in which a QTL resides (via *linkage analysis*) or to pinpoint the specific variants or genes involved (via *association analysis*). The starting point for both of these molecular genetic approaches is to collect DNA, either from families or samples of unrelated individuals, and directly measure the genotype (one or more variants) to study their relationship with the phenotype. The process of measuring genotypes is called *genotyping,* where we obtain the genotype for one or more *markers* (DNA variants) in each individual. Genotyping technology has evolved rapidly over the past few decades: Whereas early studies might have considered only a handful of markers, modern molecular genetic studies can now genotype a million variants or more in *genomewide association studies,* the current state-of-the-art.

Here we will briefly review the two complementary techniques of linkage and association analysis. Linkage tests whether or not the pattern of inheritance within families at a specific locus correlates with the pattern of trait similarity. Association, on the other hand, directly tests whether specific alleles at specific markers are correlated with increased or decreased scores on a trait or with prevalence of disease.

Although there are other molecular techniques that can be applied to complex behavioral traits, we restrict our focus in this section to approaches that correlate genotype marker data to phenotype. Other approaches not covered here include *expression analysis* using microarrays (to see whether patterns of gene expression, the amount of RNA produced in particular cell types, is related to phenotype), *DNA sequencing* (to study a region's entire DNA code for each individual, for example, to see whether rare mutations, that are not represented by common, polymorphic markers, are related to phenotype), and *epigenetics* (looking at features of the genome other than the standard inherited variation of DNA bases, such as methylation patterns).

3.1 Linkage Analysis

As described in Chapter 3, Mendel coined two famous "laws," based on his studies with garden peas. His first law, the "law of segregation," basically states that each person gets a paternal and a maternal copy of each gene, and which copy they pass on to each of their offspring is random. His second law, the "law of independent assortment," further states that which copy (i.e., the paternal or maternal) of a particular gene an individual passes on to his or her child does not depend on which copy of any other gene is passed on. In other words, Mendel believed that the transmission of any two genes is statistically independent, in the same way two coin tosses are, implying four equally likely possible combinations.

Mendel did not get it 100 percent right, however. There is an important exception, which is when the two genes, let's call them *A* and *B*, are close to each other on the same chromosome. In this case, we would say that *A* and *B* are *linked* or *in linkage*. Importantly, we can exploit the property of linkage (that nearby genes tend to be cotransmitted from a parent to its offspring) to localize genes that affect phenotypes, in *linkage analysis*, as described below.

3.1.1 Patterns of gene flow in families If genes *A* and *B* were on different chromosomes, then Mendel's second law would hold. But consider what happens when they are not, as shown in Figure A.13. This figure shows a possible set of transmissions from a father and mother to their child for a stretch of this chromosome, which contains both genes *A* and *B*, very close to each other. For this whole region, the father

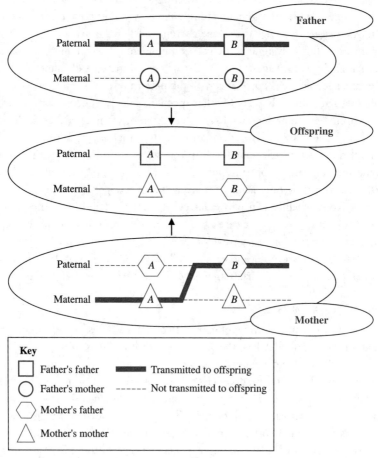

FIGURE A.13 Recombination of chromosomes during meiosis.

transmits to his child the copy he received from his own father. In contrast, we see that during meiosis (the process of forming the sex cells) the mother's paternal and maternal chromosomes have experienced a *recombination event*, such that the mother transmits a mosaic of her own mother's and father's chromosomes.

Whether or not a recombination occurs at any one position is more or less a random process. Importantly, the farther away two points on a chromosome are, the more likely they are to be separated by a recombination event (technically, separated by *an odd number of recombination events*, as more than one can occur per chromosome). Two genes that are very close to each other on the same chromosome will tend not to be separated by recombination, however, and so they will tend to be cotransmitted from parent to offspring (i.e., either both are transmitted, or neither is). As mentioned above, this tendency is called linkage.

3.1.2 Genome scans using linkage But what is the relevance of linkage to gene mapping? How does it help us find genes that influence particular phenotypes? First, linkage analysis has been centrally important in creating maps of the genome: By studying whether or not particular DNA variants are cotransmitted in families, researchers were able to infer the relative order and positions of these markers along each chromosome. Second, linkage analysis can help to detect genotype-phenotype correlations. Instead of considering markers at two genes, *A* and *B*, it is possible to consider linkage between a marker and a phenotype. If the marker and the phenotype are similarly cotransmitted in families, we can infer the presence of a phenotype-influencing gene that is linked to the marker.

A typical linkage analysis might involve genotyping a couple of hundred highly informative microsatellite markers (ones with many alleles) spaced across the genome, in a collection of families with multiple generations or multiple offspring. Often, the markers that are tested are not themselves assumed to be functional for the trait — they are merely selected because they are polymorphic in the population. The markers are used to statistically reconstruct the pattern of gene flow within these families for all positions along a chromosome. Such a study, often called a *genome scan*, provides an elegant way to search the entire genome for regions that might harbor phenotype-related genes. For disease traits, the simplest form of linkage analysis is to consider families with at least two affected siblings. If a region is linked with disease, we would expect the two siblings to have inherited the exact same stretch of chromosome from their parents more often than expected by chance, as a consequence of their sharing the same disease.

In practice, there are many complexities and many flavors of linkage analysis (e.g., for larger families, for continuous as well as disease traits, using different statistical models and assumptions, including variance components frameworks as described above that also incorporate marker data). Classical (parametric) linkage analysis relies on small numbers of large families (pedigrees) and explicitly models the distance between a test marker locus and a putative disease locus. The term *disease locus* (as opposed to QTL) reflects the fact that classical linkage is primarily concerned with mapping genes for dichotomous disease-like traits. Classical linkage requires that a model for the disease locus be specified a priori, in terms of allelic frequencies and mode of action (recessive or dominant). Figure A.14 shows an example of a pedigree in which a dominant gene is causing disease.

The approach of classical linkage is not so well suited to complex traits, however, for it is hard to specify any one model if we expect a large number of loci of small effect to impact on a trait. The alternative, nonparametric, or allele sharing, approach to linkage simply tests whether allele sharing at a locus correlates with trait similarity, as described above for affected sibling pairs. For quantitative traits, linkage analysis is often performed in nuclear families using a variance components framework similar to that described above for twin analysis. Using marker data, we can partition a sample of sibling pairs into those that share 0, 1, or 2 copies of the exact same parental DNA at any particular position along each chromosome. If the test locus is linked to the trait, then the sibling correlation should increase with the amount of sharing. Considering any one position, it is as if we are effectively splitting the siblings into unrelated pairs (those sharing 0 at that particular position), parent-offspring pairs (those sharing 1) and MZ twins (those sharing 2) and fitting the kind of quantitative genetic model described above, comparing these groups in the same way we compare MZ and DZ twins.

In general, linkage analysis has proven spectacularly successful in mapping many rare disease genes of large effect (for example, see Chapters 9 and 12). For many complex traits (which are often highly heritable but not influenced by only one or two major genes), linkage analysis has been less directly useful. Although linkage analysis can effectively search the entire genome with a relatively small number of markers, it lacks power to detect genes of small effect and has limited resolution. In many cases, collecting enough informative families might also be difficult.

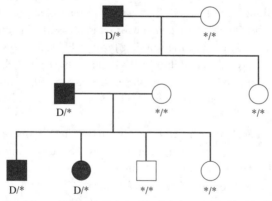

FIGURE A.14 A pedigree for a dominant disease (D) allele transmitted by the father. The asterisks refer to alleles other than D.

3.2 Association Analysis

Over the past decade, association analysis has become the approach of choice for many researchers attempting to map genes of small effect for complex traits. In many ways, association analysis asks a simpler question compared to linkage analysis. Whereas linkage analysis dissects patterns of genotypic and phenotypic sharing between related individuals, association analysis directly tests whether there is a genotype-phenotype correlation. Association is typically more powerful than linkage analysis to detect small effects, but it is necessary to genotype a much greater number of markers to cover the same genomic area. Traditionally, researchers would tend to restrict association analysis to a few "candidate" genes, or regions of the genome implicated by previous linkage studies. Modern advances in genotyping technology, which allow a million or more markers to be genotyped per individual, have made very large scale studies feasible.

3.2.1 Population-based association analysis Imagine that a particular gene with two alleles, A_1 and A_2, is thought to be a QTL for a quantitative measure of cognitive ability. To test this hypothesis, a researcher might collect a sample of unrelated individuals, measured for this phenotype and genotyped for this particular locus (so we know whether an individual has A_1A_1, A_1A_2, or A_2A_2 genotype), and then ask whether the phenotype depends on genotype. The actual analysis might be a regression of phenotype (the dependent variable) on genotype (the independent variable, coded as the number of A_1 alleles an individual has, i.e., 0, 1, or 2). Similarly, if the phenotype was, instead, a disease, one might perform a *case-control study* in which a sample of cases (people with a particular disease, for example) are ascertained along with a control sample (people without the disease, but ideally who are otherwise well-matched to the case sample). If the frequency of a particular allele or genotype is significantly higher (or lower) in cases relative to controls, one would conclude that the gene shows an association with disease. For example, as discussed in Chapter 19, the frequency of the *ApoE4* allele of the gene that encodes apolipoprotein E is about 40 percent in individuals with Alzheimer disease and about 15 percent in controls.

Consider the following example of a disease-based association analysis. The basic data for a single biallelic marker can be presented in a 3×2 contingency table of disease status by genotype. In this case, the cell counts refer to the number of individuals in each of the six categories.

	Case	Control
A_1A_1	64	41
A_1A_2	86	88
A_2A_2	26	42

One could perform a test of association based on a chi-squared test of independence for a contingency table. Often, however, such data are instead collapsed into allele counts, as opposed to genotype counts. In this case, each individual contributes twice (if the marker is autosomal): A_1A_1 individuals contribute two A_1 alleles, A_2A_2 individuals contribute two A_2 alleles, and A_1A_2 individuals contribute one of each. The 2 × 2 contingency table now represents the number of "case alleles" and "control alleles." A test based on this table implicitly assumes a simple dosage model for the effect of each allele, which will be more powerful, if true, than a genotypic analysis.

	Case	Control
A_1	64 × 2 + 86 = 214	41 × 2 + 88 = 170
A_2	26 × 2 + 86 = 138	42 × 2 + 88 = 172

Pearson's chi-squared statistic for this table is 8.63 (which has an associated p-value of 0.003, as this is a 1 degree of freedom test). Standard statistical software packages can be used to calculate this kind of association statistic. Often the effect will be described as an *odds ratio,* where a value of 1 indicates no effect, a value significantly greater than 1 represents a risk effect (of A_1 in this case), and a value significantly less than 1 represents a protective effect. If the four cells of a 2 × 2 table are labeled a, b, c and d:

	Case	Control
A_1	a	c
A_2	b	d

then the odds ratio is calculated ad/bc. In this example, the odds ratio is therefore $(214 \times 172)/(138 \times 170) = 1.57$, indicating that A_1 increases risk for disease. For many complex traits, researchers expect very small odds ratios, such as 1.2 or 1.1, for individual markers; such small effects are statistically hard to detect. If the disease is rare, an odds ratio can be interpreted as a *relative risk,* meaning, in this example, that each extra copy of the A_1 allele an individual possesses increases his or her risk of disease by a factor of 1.57. So if A_2A_2 individuals have a baseline risk of disease of 1%, then A_1A_2 individuals would have an expected risk of 1.57% and A_1A_1 individuals would have a risk of 1.57% × 1.57% = 2.46%.

3.2.2 Population stratification and family-based association

In the previous section, we noted that samples should be well-matched. In any association study, it is particularly critical that samples be well-matched in terms of ethnicity. Failure to adequately match can result in *population stratification* (a type of confounding) which causes spurious results in which between-group differences confound the search for biologically relevant within-group effects. For example, imagine a case/control study where the sample actually comes from two distinct ethnic groups. Further, imagine that one group is overrepresented in cases versus controls (this might be because the disease is more prevalent in one group, or it might just reflect differences in how cases and controls were ascertained). Any gene that is more common in one of the ethnic groups than in the other will now show an obligatory statistical association with disease because of this third, confounding variable, ethnicity. Almost always, these associations will be completely spurious (i.e., the gene has no causal association with disease).

That correlation does not imply causation is, of course, a maxim relevant to any epidemiological study. But often in genetics we are less concerned with proving causality, per se, than we are with having *useful* correlational evidence (i.e., that could be used in locating a nearby causal disease gene, as described below in the section on indirect association). The problem with population stratification is that it will tend to throw up a very large number of red herrings that have absolutely no useful interpretation.

Luckily there are a number of ways to avoid the possible confounding due to population stratification in association studies. The most obvious is to apply sound experimental and epidemiological principles of randomization and appropriate sampling protocols. Another alternative is to use families to test for association, as most family members are necessarily well-matched for ethnicity. For example, for siblings discordant for Alzheimer disease, we would expect that the affected siblings would have a higher frequency of the *ApoE4* allele of the gene encoding apolipoprotein E than would the unaffected members of the sibling pairs. Note that this is distinct from linkage analysis, which is based on sharing of chromosomal regions within families rather than testing the effects of specific alleles across families.

A common family-based association design is the *transmission/disequilibrium test* (TDT), which involves sampling affected individuals and their parents; in effect, the control individuals are created as "ghost-siblings" of cases, using the alleles that the *parents did not transmit* to their affected offspring. The test focuses only on parents who are heterozygous (e.g., have both an A_1 and an A_2 allele) and asks whether one allele was more often transmitted to affected offspring. If neither allele is associated with disease, we would expect 50:50 transmission of both alleles, as stated by Mendel's first law.

Although family-based association designs control against population stratification (and allow for some other specific hypotheses to be tested, for example, imprinting effects, in which the parental origin of an allele matters), they are in general less efficient, as more individuals must be sampled to achieve the same power as a population-based design. Recently, due to the increasing ability to genotype large numbers of markers, another approach to population stratification has emerged. By using markers randomly selected from across the genome, it is possible to empirically derive and control for ancestry in population-based studies using statistical methods.

3.2.3 Indirect association and haplotype analysis In linkage analysis, the actual markers tested are not themselves assumed to be functional; they are merely proxies that provide information on the inheritance patterns of chromosomal regions. Similarly, in association analysis we do not necessarily assume the marker being tested is the functional, causal variant. This is because when we test any one marker, more often than not we are also implicitly testing the effects of surrounding markers, as alleles at nearby positions will be correlated at the population level. This phenomenon is closely related to linkage, described above, and is in fact called *linkage disequilibrium.*

A correlation between markers at the population level means that knowing a person's genotype at one marker tells you something about their genotype at a second marker. This correlation between markers, or linkage disequilibrium, actually reflects our shared ancestry. Over many generations, recombination has rearranged the genome, but like an imperfectly shuffled deck of cards, some traces of the previous order still exist. Because we inherit stretches of chromosomes that contain many alleles, certain strings of alleles will tend to be preserved by chance. Unless these strings are broken by recombination, the strings of alleles that sit on the same chromosomal stretch of DNA (called *haplotypes*) may become common at the population level. Considering three markers, A, B, and C (each with alleles coded 1 and 2), there may be only three common haplotypes in the population

$$
\begin{array}{ll}
A_1 \, B_1 \, C_1 & 80\% \\
A_2 \, B_2 \, C_2 & 12\% \\
A_1 \, B_2 \, C_2 & 8\%
\end{array}
$$

In this example, possessing an A_2 allele makes you much more likely also to possess B_2 and C_2 alleles (100% of the time, in fact) than if you possess an A_1 allele (now only $8/(8 + 80) = 9\%$ of the time). We would, therefore, say that marker A is in linkage disequilibrium with B and C (and vice versa).

Linkage disequilibrium leads to indirect association; for example, if B were the true QTL, then performing an association analysis at A would still recover some of the true signal, due to the correlation in alleles, although it would be somewhat attenuated. In contrast, genotyping C instead of B would recover all the information, as it is a perfect proxy for B.

It is possible to use haplotype information in association analysis, by testing haplotypes instead of genotypes. In the above example, we might ask whether the number of copies of the $A_2B_2C_2$ haplotype that an individual possesses predicts the phenotype. By combining multiple markers in this way (called *haplotype-based association analysis*), one can extract extra information without extra genotyping. For example, imagine a fourth, ungenotyped locus, D. In this case, the $A_1B_2C_2$ haplotype is a perfect proxy for D (as it is completely correlated with the D_2 allele) whereas none of the three original individual markers are.

$$A_1 B_1 C_1 D_1 \qquad 80\%$$
$$A_2 B_2 C_2 D_1 \qquad 12\%$$
$$A_1 B_2 C_2 D_2 \qquad 8\%$$

Any one individual will possess two of these haplotypes (one paternally, one maternally inherited), for example, $A_1 B_1 C_1$ and $A_2 B_2 C_2$ if we consider just the three genotyped markers. We do not usually observe haplotypes directly, however. Instead, we observe genotypes, which in this case would be $A_1 A_2$ for the first marker, $B_1 B_2$ for the second, and $C_1 C_2$ for the last. As illustrated in Figure A.15, in themselves, genotypes do not contain information about haplotypes, so it might not always be possible to determine unambiguously which haplotypes an individual has. (A particular combination of genotypes might be compatible with more than one pair of haplotypes.) However, statistical techniques can be used to estimate the frequencies of the different possible haplotypes, which in turn can be used to guess which pair of haplotypes is most likely given the genotypes for an individual (this process is called *haplotype phasing*).

3.2.4 The HapMap and genomewide association studies

In the example above, wouldn't it have been great if we knew in advance that markers B and C were perfect proxies for each other, or that marker D could be predicted by a haplotype of A, B and C? Knowing that, we would probably not want to waste money genotyping all the markers, when genotyping a subset would give exactly the same information. In fact, now we usually do know in advance, thanks to the HapMap Project (http://www .hapmap.org/). This was a large, international survey of patterns of linkage disequilibrium across the genome, performed in a number of different populations, focusing on single nucleotide polymorphisms (SNPs), the most common form of variation in the human genome. SNPs are biallelic markers, with the alleles being two of A, C, G and T (i.e., the four nucleotide bases of DNA).

For many common variants, the HapMap shows that there are lots of perfect proxies in the genome; that is, there is a lot of redundancy. This means that it is possible to measure almost all common variation in the human genome using a much

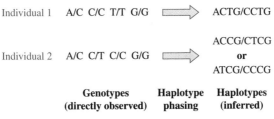

FIGURE A.15 Observed genotypes and inferred haplotypes.

smaller set of SNPs. This concept is called *tagging* and effectively determines how to optimally choose which markers to genotype.

Based on large-scale genomic efforts such as the HapMap and new genotyping technologies, association analysis has recently been taken to its logical conclusion: the *genomewide association study* (GWAS, Chapter 9). As the name suggests, this involves genotyping hundreds of thousands of markers, usually in large case/control samples. The hope is that such studies combine the power of association analysis with the genomewide, unbiased coverage of the previous generation of linkage genome scans.

Websites

Associations

The Behavior Genetics Association, with links to its journal, *Behavior Genetics:*
> http://www.bga.org/

The International Society for Twin Studies is an international, multidisciplinary scientific organization whose purpose is to further research and public education in all fields related to twins and twin studies. Its website is linked to the society's journal, *Twin Research and Human Genetics:*
> http://www.twinstudies.org/

The International Society of Psychiatric Genetics is a worldwide organization that aims to promote and facilitate research in the genetics of psychiatric disorders, substance use disorders, and allied traits. With links to associated journals, *Psychiatric Genetics and Neuropsychiatric Genetics:*
> http://www.ispg.net/

The American Society of Human Genetics, with links to its journal, *American Journal of Human Genetics:*
> http://www.ashg.org/

The European Society of Human Genetics, with links to its journal, *European Journal of Human Genetics:*
> http://www.eshg.org/

The Human Genome Organization (HUGO), the international organization of scientists involved in human genetics:
> http://www.hugo-international.org/

The International Behavioral and Neural Genetics Society (IBANGS) works to promote the field of neurobehavioral genetics. With links to its journal *Genes, Brain and Behavior.*
> http://www.ibngs.org/

The Psychiatric Genomics Consortium (PGC) conducts mega-analyses of genomewide genetic data for psychiatric disorders. This website provides information about the organization, implementation, and results of the PGC.
> http://www.med.unc.edu/pgc

Databases and Genome Browsers

EMBL-EBI, the European Molecular Biology Laboratory's (EMBL) European Bioinformatics Institute (EBI), is the European node for globally coordinated efforts to collect and disseminate biological data:
> http://www.ebi.ac.uk/

NCBI, the National Center for Biotechnology Information, is the U.S. node of the European Bioinformatics Institute:
> http://www.ncbi.nlm.nih.gov/

Ensembl, the EBI and Wellcome Trust Sanger Institute's genome browser:
> http://www.ensembl.org/

Gene Weaver, powered by the Ontological Discovery Environment, is a curated repository of genomic experimental results with an accompanying tool set for dynamic integration of these data sets, enabling

users to interactively address questions about sets of biological functions and their relations to sets of genes.
http://www.GeneWeaver.org

The genome browser maintained by the University of California Santa Cruz (UCSC) is an interactive open source website offering graphical access to genome sequence data from a variety of vertebrate and invertebrate species and major model organisms:
http://genome.ucsc.edu/

NCBI's Online Mendelian Inheritance in Man (OMIM) database is a catalog of human genes and genetic disorders. The database contains textual information, pictures, and reference material:
http://www.ncbi.nlm.nih.gov/omim/

Phenotype Based Gene Analyzer (Phenolyzer) is a tool focusing on discovering genes based on user-specific disease/phenotype terms.
http://phenolyzer.usc.edu/

Resources

Behavioral Genetic Interactive Modules are based on the Appendix to this text by Shaun Purcell:
http://pngu.mgh.harvard.edu/purcell/bgim/

The OpenMx forum contains useful information on twin model fitting in *Mx:*
http://openmx.psyc.virginia.edu/forums/

R is a free software environment for statistical computing and graphics. *Bioconductor* is an open source and open development software project for the analysis and comprehension of genomic data using the *R* environment:
http://www.r-project.org/

http://www.bioconductor.org/

The Jackson Laboratory, Mouse Genome Informatics, is an excellent resource for mouse genetics:
http://www.informatics.jax.org/

National Institutes of Health (NIH) Model Organisms for Biomedical Research provides the latest information on animal models used in genetic research:
http://www.nih.gov/science/models/

The DNA Learning Center of Cold Spring Harbor Laboratory is a science center devoted entirely to genetics and provides much information online, including an animated primer on the basics of DNA, genes, and heredity:
http://www.dnalc.org/

The Allen Brain Atlas is a collection of online public resources integrating extensive gene expression and neuroanatomical data, with a novel suite of search and viewing tools:
http://www.brain-map.org/

The GWAS Catalog is a catalog of published genomewide association studies:
http://www.ebi.ac.uk/gwas/

Microarray Technology

Affymetrix and Illumina are two of the leading suppliers of microarray technology:
http://www.affymetrix.com/estore/

http://www.illumina.com/

Public Understanding of Genetics

Your Genome is a website, curated by the Wellcome Trust's Sanger Institute, that is intended to help people understand genetics and genomic science and its implications:
http://www.yourgenome.org/

The Genetic Science Learning Center is an outreach education program at the University of Utah. Its aim is to help people understand how genetics affects their lives and society. This is an introductory guide to molecular genetics:
http://learn.genetics.utah.edu/

The Genetics Home Reference provides consumer-friendly information about the effects of genetic variations on human health:
http://ghr.nlm.nih.gov/

Information about genetic counseling is available from the website of the National Society of Genetic Counselors:
http://www.nsgc.org/

Glossary

active genotype-environment correlation A correlation between genetic and environmental influences that occurs when individuals select or construct environments with effects that covary with their genetic propensities.

additive genetic variance Individual differences caused by the independent effects of alleles or loci that "add up." In contrast to *nonadditive genetic variance,* in which the effects of alleles or loci interact.

adoption studies A range of studies that use the separation of biological and social parentage brought about by adoption to assess the relative importance of genetic and environmental influences. Most commonly, the strategy involves a comparison of adoptees' resemblance to their biological parents, who did not rear them, and to their adoptive parents. May also involve the comparison of genetically related siblings and genetically unrelated (adoptive) siblings reared in the same family.

adoptive siblings Genetically unrelated children adopted by the same family and reared together.

affected sib-pair linkage design A QTL linkage design that involves pairs of siblings who meet criteria for a disorder. Linkage with DNA markers is assessed by allele sharing within the pairs of siblings—whether they share 0, 1, or 2 alleles for a DNA marker. (See Box 9.2.)

allele An alternative form of a gene at a locus, for example, A_1 versus A_2.

allele sharing Presence of zero, one, or two of the parents' alleles in two siblings (a sibling pair, or sib pair).

allelic association An association between allelic frequencies and a phenotype. For example, the frequency of allele *4* of the gene that encodes apolipoprotein E is about 40 percent for individuals with Alzheimer disease and 15 percent for control individuals who do not have the disorder.

allelic frequency Population frequency of an alternate form of a gene. For example, the frequency of the PKU allele is about 1 percent. (In contrast, see *genotypic frequency.*)

alternative splicing The process by which mRNA is reassembled to create different transcripts that are then translated into different proteins. More than half of human genes are alternatively spliced.

amino acid One of the 20 building blocks of proteins, specified by a triplet code of DNA.

amniocentesis A medical procedure used for prenatal diagnosis in which a small amount of amniotic fluid is extracted from the amnion surrounding a developing fetus. Because some of the fluid contains cells from the fetus, fetal chromosomes can be examined and fetal genes can be tested.

anticipation See *genetic anticipation.*

assortative mating Nonrandom mating that results in similarity between spouses. Assortative mating can be negative ("opposites attract") but is usually positive.

autosome Any chromosome other than the X or Y sex chromosomes. Humans have 22 pairs of autosomal chromosomes and 1 pair of sex chromosomes.

band (chromosomal) A chromosomal segment defined by staining characteristics.

base pair (bp) One step in the spiral staircase of the double helix of DNA, consisting of adenine bonded to thymine, or cytosine bonded to guanine.

behavioral genomics The study of how genes in the genome function at the behavioral level of analysis. In contrast to *functional genomics,* behavioral genomics is a top-down approach to understanding how genes work in terms of the behavior of the whole organism.

bioinformatics Techniques and resources to study the genome, transcriptome, and proteome, such as DNA sequences and functions, gene expression maps, and protein structures.

candidate gene A gene whose function suggests that it might be associated with a trait. For example, dopamine genes are considered as candidate genes for hyperactivity because the drug most commonly used to treat hyperactivity, methylphenidate, acts on the dopamine system.

candidate gene-by-environment interaction Genotype-environment interaction in which an association between a particular (candidate) gene and a phenotype differs in different environments.

carrier An individual who is heterozygous at a given locus, carrying both a normal allele and a mutant recessive allele, and who appears normal phenotypically.

centimorgan (cM) Measure of genetic distance on a chromosome. Two loci are 1 cM apart if there is a 1 percent chance of recombination due to crossover in a single generation. In humans, 1 cM corresponds to approximately 1 million base pairs.

centromere A chromosomal region without genes where the chromatids are held together during cell division.

children-of-twins (COT) design A study that includes parents who are twins and the children of each twin.

chorion Sac within the placenta that surrounds the embryo. Two-thirds of the time, identical twins share the same chorion.

chromatid One of the two copies of DNA making up a duplicated chromosome, which are joined at their centromeres for the process of cell division (mitosis or meiosis). They are normally identical but may have slight differences in the case of mutations. They are called sister chromatids as long as they are joined by the centromeres, during which time they can recombine. When they separate, the strands are called daughter chromosomes.

chromosome A structure that is composed mainly of chromatin, which contains DNA, and resides in the nucleus of cells. Latin for "colored body" because chromosomes stain differently from the rest of the cell. (See also *autosome.*)

chromosome substitution strains (CSSs) CSSs are created by introducing individual chromosomes from a donor inbred strain into a host inbred strain resulting in a panel of 22 mouse strains that vary on a single chromosome from two well-characterized inbred strains.

coding region The portion of a gene's DNA composed of exons that code for proteins.

codon A sequence of three base pairs that codes for a particular amino acid or the end of a chain.

comorbidity Presence of more than one disorder or disease in an individual.

concordance Presence of a particular condition in two family members, such as twins.

copy number variant (CNV) A structural variation that involves duplication or deletion of long stretches of DNA (one thousand to many thousands of base pairs in length), often encompassing protein-coding genes as well as noncoding genes. CNVs account for more than 10 percent of the human genome.

correlation An index of resemblance that ranges from -1.00 to 1.00, where 0.00 indicates no resemblance.

crossover See *recombination.*

developmental genetic analysis Analysis of change and continuity of genetic and environmental parameters during development. Applied to longitudinal data, assesses genetic and environmental influences on age-to-age change and continuity.

DF extremes analysis An analysis of familial resemblance that takes advantage of quantitative scores of the relatives of probands rather than just assigning a dichotomous diagnosis to the relatives and assessing concordance. (In contrast, see *liability-threshold model.*)

diallel design Complete intercrossing of three or more inbred strains and comparing all possible F_1 crosses between them.

diathesis-stress A type of genotype-environment interaction in which individuals at genetic risk for a disorder (diathesis) are especially sensitive to the effects of risky (stress) environments.

direct association An association between a trait and a DNA marker that is the functional polymorphism that causes the association. In contrast to *indirect association,* in which the DNA marker is not the functional polymorphism.

dizygotic (DZ) Fraternal, or nonidentical, twins; literally, "two zygotes."

DNA (deoxyribonucleic acid) The double-stranded molecule that encodes genetic information. The two strands are held together by hydrogen bonds between two of the four bases, with adenine bonded to thymine, and cytosine bonded to guanine.

DNA marker A polymorphism in DNA itself, such as a single-nucleotide polymorphism (SNP) or copy number variant (CNV).

DNA methylation An epigenetic process by which gene expression is inactivated by the addition of a methyl group.

DNA sequence The order of base pairs on a single chain of the DNA double helix.

dominance The effect of one allele depends on that of another. A dominant allele produces the same phenotype in an individual regardless of whether one or two copies are present. (Compare with *epistasis,* which refers to nonadditive effects between genes at different loci.)

effect size The proportion of individual differences for the trait in the population accounted for by a particular factor. For example, heritability estimates the effect size of genetic differences among individuals.

electrophoresis A method used to separate DNA fragments by size. When an electrical charge is applied to DNA fragments in a gel, smaller fragments travel farther.

endophenotype An "inside" or intermediate phenotype that does not involve overt behavior.

environmentality Proportion of phenotypic differences among individuals that can be attributed to environmental differences in a particular population.

epigenetics DNA modifications that affect gene expression without changing the DNA sequence that can be "inherited" when cells divide; can be involved in long-term developmental changes in gene expression.

epigenome Epigenetic events throughout the genome that influence gene expression.

epistasis Nonadditive interaction between genes at different loci. The effect of one gene depends on that of another. (Compare with *dominance,* which refers to nonadditive effects between alleles at the same locus.)

equal environments assumption In twin studies, the assumption that environments are similar for identical and fraternal twins.

evocative genotype-environment correlation A correlation between genetic and environmental influences that occurs when individuals evoke environmental effects that covary with their genetic propensities

extended children-of-twins (ECOT) design A study that combines a children-of-twins design and a comparable sample of twins who are children and their parents.

exon DNA sequence transcribed into messenger RNA and translated into protein. (Compare with *intron*.)

expanded triplet repeat A repeating sequence of three base pairs, such as the CGG repeat responsible for fragile X, that increases in number of repeats over several generations.

expression QTL (eQTL) Treating gene expression as a phenotype, QTLs can be identified that account for genetic influence on gene expression.

F_1, F_2 The offspring in the first and second generations following mating between two inbred strains.

familial Resemblance among family members.

family study Assessing the resemblance between genetically related parents and offspring, and between siblings living together. Resemblance can be due to heredity or to shared family environment.

first-degree relative See *genetic relatedness*.

fragile X syndrome Fragile sites are breaks in chromosomes that occur when chromosomes are stained or cultured. Fragile X is a fragile site on the X chromosome that is the second most important cause after Down syndrome of intellectual disability in males, and is due to an expanded triplet repeat.

full siblings Individuals who have both biological (birth) parents in common.

functional genomics The study of gene function that traces pathways between genes, brain, and behavior. Usually implies a bottom-up approach that begins with molecules in a cell, in contrast to *behavioral genomics*.

gamete Mature reproductive cell (sperm or ovum) that contains a haploid (half) set of chromosomes.

gene The basic unit of heredity. A sequence of DNA bases that codes for a particular product. Includes DNA sequences that regulate transcription. (See also *allele; locus*.)

gene expression Transcription of DNA into mRNA.

gene expression profiling Using microarrays to assess the expression of all genes in the genome simultaneously.

gene frequency Refers to frequency of alleles (e.g., A_1 or A_2) in a sample or population.

gene map Visual representation of the relative distances between genes or genetic markers on chromosomes.

gene set analysis A test for association between biologically meaningful sets of genes and a phenotype.

gene silencing Suppressing expression of a gene but not altering it and, thus, not heritable.

gene targeting Mutations that are created in a specific gene and can then be transferred to an embryo.

Generalist Genes Hypothesis A term referring to the substantial genetic correlations among cognitive abilities.

genetic anticipation The severity of a disorder becomes greater or occurs at an earlier age in subsequent generations. In some disorders, this phenomenon is known to be due to the intergenerational expansion of DNA repeat sequences.

genetic correlation A statistic indexing the extent to which genetic influences on one trait are correlated with genetic influences on another trait independent of the heritabilities of the traits.

genetic counseling Conveys information about genetic risks and burdens, and helps individuals come to terms with the information and make their own decisions concerning actions.

genetic relatedness The extent to which relatives have genes in common. *First-degree relatives* of the proband (parents and siblings) are 50 percent similar genetically. *Second-degree relatives* of the proband (grandparents, aunts, and uncles) are 25 percent similar genetically. *Third-degree relatives* of the proband (first cousins) are 12.5 percent similar genetically.

genome All the DNA sequences of an organism. The human genome contains about 3 billion DNA base pairs.

genomewide association study (GWAS) An association study that assesses DNA variation throughout the genome.

genomewide gene-by-environment interaction A method for searching for genotype-environment interaction that assesses DNA variation throughout the genome.

genomic imprinting The process by which an allele at a given locus is expressed differently depending on whether it is inherited from the mother or the father.

genotype An individual's combination of alleles at a particular locus.

genotype-environment correlation Experiences that are correlated with genetic propensities. In molecular genetic research, genotype-environment correlation refers to the actual correlation between genotype and an environmental measure.

genotype-environment interaction Genetic sensitivity or susceptibility to environments. Genotype-environment interaction is usually limited to statistical interactions, such as genetic effects that differ in different environments. For example, the association between a genotype for a particular gene and a phenotype might differ in different environments.

genotypic frequency The frequency of alleles considered two at a time as they are inherited in individuals. The genotypic frequency of PKU individuals (homozygous for the recessive PKU allele) is 0.0001. The genotypic frequency of PKU carriers (who are heterozygous for the PKU allele) is 0.02.

In contrast, the *allelic frequency* of the recessive PKU allele is 0.01. (See Box 3.2.)

half siblings Individuals who have just one biological (birth) parent in common.

haploid genotype (haplotype) The DNA sequence on one chromosome. In contrast to *genotype*, which refers to a pair of chromosomes, the DNA sequence on one chromosome is called a *haploid genotype*, which has been shortened to *haplotype*.

haplotype block A series of single-nucleotide polymorphisms (SNPs) on a chromosome that are very highly correlated (i.e., seldom separated by recombination). The HapMap Project has systematized haplotype blocks for several ethnic groups (http://hapmap.ncbi.nlm.nih.gov/).

Hardy-Weinberg equilibrium Allelic and genotypic frequencies remain the same, generation after generation, in the absence of forces such as natural selection that change these frequencies. If a two-allele locus is in Hardy-Weinberg equilibrium, the frequency of genotypes is $p^2 + 2pq + q^2$, where p and q are the frequencies of the two alleles.

heritability The proportion of phenotypic differences among individuals that can be attributed to genetic differences in a particular population. *Broad-sense heritability* involves all additive and nonadditive sources of genetic variance, whereas *narrow-sense heritability* is limited to additive genetic variance.

heterozygosity The presence of different alleles at a given locus on both members of a chromosome pair.

homozygosity The presence of the same allele at a given locus on both members of a chromosome pair.

imprinting See *genomic imprinting.*

inbred strain A strain of animal that has been created by mating brothers and sisters for at least 20 generations, resulting in nearly genetically identical individuals.

inbred strain study Comparing inbred strains, for example on behavioral traits.

Differences between strains can be attributed to their genetic differences when the strains are reared in the same laboratory environment. Differences within strains estimate environmental influences, because all individuals within an inbred strain are virtually identical genetically.

inbreeding Mating between genetically related individuals.

independent assortment Mendel's second law of heredity. It states that the inheritance of genes at one locus is not affected by the inheritance of genes at another locus. Exceptions to the law occur when genes are inherited which are close together on the same chromosome. Such linkages make it possible to map genes to chromosomes.

index case See *proband*.

indirect association An association between a trait and a DNA marker that is not itself the functional polymorphism that causes the association. In contrast to *direct association*, in which the DNA marker itself is the functional polymorphism.

instinct An innate behavioral tendency.

intron DNA sequence within a gene that is transcribed into messenger RNA but spliced out before the translation into protein. (Compare with *exon*.)

knock-out Inactivation of a gene by gene targeting.

liability-threshold model A model that assumes that dichotomous disorders are due to underlying genetic liabilities that are distributed normally. The disorder appears only when a threshold of liability is exceeded.

lifetime expectancy See *morbidity risk estimate*.

linkage Loci that are close together on a chromosome. Linkage is an exception to Mendel's second law of independent assortment, because closely linked loci are not inherited independently within families.

linkage analysis A technique that detects linkage between DNA markers and traits,

used to map genes to chromosomes. (See also *DNA marker; linkage; mapping*.)

linkage disequilibrium A violation of Mendel's law of independent assortment in which genes are uncorrelated. It is most frequently used to describe how close DNA markers are together on a chromosome; linkage disequilibrium of 1.0 means that the alleles of the DNA markers are perfectly correlated; 0.0 means that there is complete random association (linkage equilibrium).

locus (plural, loci) The site of a specific gene on a chromosome. Latin for "place."

mapping Linkage of DNA markers to a chromosome and to specific regions of chromosomes.

meiosis Cell division that occurs during gamete formation and results in halving the number of chromosomes, so that each gamete contains only one member of each chromosome pair.

messenger RNA (mRNA) Processed RNA that leaves the nucleus of the cell and serves as a template for protein synthesis in the cell body cytoplasm.

methylation An epigenetic process by which gene expression is inactivated by adding a methyl group to a chromosome region.

microarray Commonly known as gene chips, microarrays are slides the size of a postage stamp with hundreds of thousands of DNA sequences that serve as probes to detect gene expression (RNA microarrays), methylation (DNA methylation microarrays), or single-nucleotide polymorphisms (DNA microarrays).

microRNA A class of non-coding RNA with just 21–25 nucleotides that can degrade or silence gene expression by binding with messenger RNA.

microsatellite marker Two, three, or four DNA base pairs that are repeated up to a hundred times. Unlike SNPs which generally have just two alleles, microsatellite markers often have many alleles that are inherited in a Mendelian manner.

missing heritability The difference between the genomewide identified associations and reported heritability estimates from quantitative genetic studies, such as twin and family designs.

mitosis Cell division that occurs in somatic cells in which a cell duplicates itself and its DNA.

model fitting A technique for testing the fit between a model of genetic and environmental relatedness against the observed data. Different models can be compared, and the best-fitting model is used to estimate genetic and environmental parameters.

molecular genetics The investigation of the effects of specific genes at the DNA level. In contrast to *quantitative genetics*, which partitions phenotypic variances and covariances into genetic and environmental components.

monozygotic (MZ) Identical twins; literally, "one zygote."

morbidity risk estimate The chance of being affected during one's lifetime.

multivariate genetic analysis Quantitative genetic analysis of the covariance between traits.

mutation A heritable change in DNA base pair sequences.

natural selection The driving force in evolution in which the frequency of alleles change as a function of the differential reproduction of individuals and survival of their offspring.

neurome Effects of the genome throughout the brain.

nonadditive genetic variance Individual differences due to nonlinear interactions between alleles at the same (dominance) or different (epistasis) loci. (In contrast, see *additive genetic variance*.)

non-coding RNA (ncRNA) DNA that is transcribed into RNA but not translated into amino acid sequences. Examples include *introns* and *microRNA*.

nondisjunction Uneven division of members of a chromosome pair during meiosis.

nonshared environmental influences Environmental influences that do not contribute to resemblance between family members.

nucleus The part of the cell that contains chromosomes.

odds ratio An effect size statistic for association calculated as the odds of an allele in cases divided by the odds of the allele in controls. An odds ratio of 1.0 means that there is no difference in allele frequency between cases and controls.

passive genotype-environment correlation A correlation between genetic and environmental influences that occurs when children inherit genes with effects that covary with their parent's environment.

pedigree A family tree. Diagram depicting the genealogical history of a family, especially showing the inheritance of a particular condition in the family members.

pharmacogenetics and -genomics The genetics and genomics of responses to drugs.

phenotype An observed characteristic of an individual that results from the combined effects of genotype and environment.

pleiotropy Multiple effects of a gene.

polygenic trait A trait influenced by many genes.

polymerase chain reaction (PCR) A method to amplify a particular DNA sequence.

polymorphism A locus with two or more alleles. Greek for "multiple forms."

population genetics The study of allelic and genotypic frequencies in populations and the forces that change these frequencies, such as natural selection.

posttranslational modification Chemical change to polypeptides (amino acid sequences) after they have been translated from mRNA.

premutation Production of eggs or sperm with an unstable expanded number of repeats (up to 200 repeats for fragile X).

primer A short (usually 20-base) DNA sequence that marks the starting point for DNA replication. Primers on either side of a polymorphism mark the boundaries of a DNA sequence that is to be amplified by polymerase chain reaction (PCR).

proband The index case from whom other family members are identified.

proteome All the proteins translated from RNA (*transcriptome*).

psychopharmacogenetics The genetics of behavioral responses to drugs.

QTL linkage analysis Linkage analysis that searches for linkages of small effect size, quantitative trait loci (QTLs). Most widely used is the affected sib-pair QTL linkage design.

qualitative disorder An either-or trait, usually a diagnosis.

quantitative dimension Traits that are continuously distributed within a population, for example, general cognitive ability, height, and blood pressure.

quantitative genetics A theory of multiple-gene influences that, together with environmental variation, result in quantitative (continuous) distributions of phenotypes. Quantitative genetic methods (such as the twin and adoption methods for human analysis, and inbred strain and selection methods for nonhuman analysis) estimate genetic and environmental contributions to phenotypic variance and covariance in a population.

quantitative trait locus (QTL; plural: quantitative trait loci, QTLs) A gene in multiple-gene systems that contributes to quantitative (continuous) variation in a phenotype.

recessive An allele that produces its effect on a phenotype only when two copies are present.

recombinant inbred strains Inbred strains derived from brother-sister matings from an initial cross of two inbred progenitor strains. Called *recombinant* because, in the F_2 and subsequent generations, chromosomes from the progenitor strains recombine and exchange parts. Used to map genes and identify quantitative trait loci.

recombination During meiosis, chromosomes exchange parts by a crossing over of chromatids.

recombinatorial hotspot Chromosomal location subject to much recombination. Often marks the boundaries of haplotype blocks.

repeat sequence Short sequences of DNA—two, three, or four nucleotide bases of DNA—that repeat a few times to a few dozen times. Used as DNA markers.

restriction enzyme Recognizes specific short DNA sequences and cuts DNA at that site.

ribosome A small dense structure in the cell body (cytoplasm) that assembles amino acid sequences in the order dictated by mRNA.

RNA interference (RNAi) The use of double-stranded RNA to change the expression of the gene that shares its sequence. Also called *small interfering RNA* (siRNA) because it degrades complementary RNA transcripts.

second-degree relative See *genetic relatedness.*

segregation The process by which two alleles at a locus, one from each parent, separate during heredity. Mendel's law of segregation is his first law of heredity.

selective breeding Breeding for a phenotype over several generations by selecting parents with high scores on the phenotype, mating them, and assessing their offspring to determine the response to selection. Bidirectional selection studies also select in the other direction, that is, for low scores.

selective placement Adoption of children into families in which the adoptive parents are similar to the children's biological parents.

sex chromosome See *autosome.*

shared environmental influences Environmental factors that make family members similar.

single nucleotide polymorphism (SNP) The most common type of DNA polymorphism which involves a difference in a single nucleotide. SNPs (pronounced "snips") can produce a change in an amino acid sequence (called *nonsynonymous*, i.e., not synonymous).

small interfering RNA (siRNA) See *RNA interference (RNAi)*.

SNP-based heritability analysis A technique to estimate the extent to which phenotypic variance for a trait can potentially be explained by all the single-nucleotide polymorphisms (SNPs) on a microarray. For a sample of thousands of individuals, overall genotypic similarity pair by pair is used to predict phenotypic similarity. Does not identify specific allelic associations.

SNP heritability Heritability estimated directly from DNA differences between individuals.

somatic cells All cells in the body except for the sex cells that produce gametes.

stabilizing selection Selection that maintains genetic variation within a population, for example, selection for intermediate phenotypic values.

structural equation modeling (SEM) A statistical method for testing a conceptual or theoretical model. In behavioral genetics this method is used to estimate heritability and environmentality based on the similarity and differences among family members.

synapse A junction between two nerve cells, through which impulses pass by diffusion of a neurotransmitter, such as dopamine or serotonin.

synteny Loci on the same chromosome; related to *linkage*.

synteny homology Similar ordering of loci in chromosomal regions in different species.

targeted mutation A process by which a gene is changed in a specific way to alter its function, such as knock-outs. Called *transgenics* when the mutated gene is transferred from another species.

third-degree relative See *genetic relatedness*.

transcription The synthesis of an RNA molecule from DNA in the cell nucleus.

transcriptome RNA transcribed from all the DNA in the genome.

transfer RNA (tRNA) A type of RNA molecule that helps decode a messenger RNA sequence into a protein.

transgenic Containing foreign DNA. For example, gene targeting can be used to replace a gene with a nonfunctional substitute in order to knock out the gene's functioning.

translation Assembly of amino acids into peptide chains on the basis of information encoded in messenger RNA. Occurs on ribosomes in the cell cytoplasm.

triplet codon See *codon*.

triplet repeat See *expanded triplet repeat*.

trisomy Having three copies of a particular chromosome due to nondisjunction.

twin correlation Correlation of twin 1 with twin 2. Typically computed separately for MZ and DZ twins. Used to estimate genetic and environmental influences.

twin study Comparing the resemblance of identical and fraternal twins to estimate genetic and environmental components of variance.

whole-genome amplification Using a few restriction enzymes in polymerase chain reactions (PCRs) to chop up and amplify the entire genome. This makes microarrays possible.

whole-genome sequencing (also known as full-genome sequencing) Determining the complete sequence of nucleotide base pairs for a genome.

X-linked trait A phenotype influenced by a gene on the X chromosome. X-linked recessive diseases occur more frequently in males because they only have one X chromosome.

zygote The cell, or fertilized egg, resulting from the union of a sperm and an egg (ovum).

References

1000 Genomes Project Consortium. (2012). An integrated map of genetic variation from 1,092 human genomes. *Nature, 491*(7422), 56–65.

Ackerman, P. L., Beier, M. E., & Boyle, M. O. (2005). Working memory and intelligence: the same or different constructs? *Psychological Bulletin, 131*(1), 30–60. doi:10.1037/0033-2909.131.1.30

Addington, A. M., Gornick, M., Duckworth, J., Sporn, A., Gogtay, N., Bobb, A., . . . Straub, R. E. (2005). GAD1 (2q31.1), which encodes glutamic acid decarboxylase (GAD67), is associated with childhood-onset schizophrenia and cortical gray matter volume loss. *Molecular Psychiatry, 10*(6), 581–588.

ADHDgene. (2014). ADHDgene: A Genetic Database for Attention Deficit Hyperactivity Disorder. *An Overview of ADHDgene, 40,* D1003–D1009.

Administration on Aging. (2014). A profile of older Americans: 2014. U.S. Department of Health and Human Services.

Aebersold, R., & Mann, M. (2003). Mass spectrometry-based proteomics. *Nature, 422*(6928), 198–207. doi:10.1038/nature01511

Agrawal, A., Jacobson, K. C., Prescott, C. A., & Kendler, K. S. (2002). A twin study of sex differences in social support. *Psychological Medicine, 32*(7), 1155-1164.

Agrawal, A., Jacobson, K. C., Prescott, C. A., & Kendler, K. S. (2004). A twin study of personality and illicit drug use and abuse/dependence. *Twin Research, 7*(1), 72–81. doi:10.1375/13690520460741462

Agrawal, A., Lynskey, M. T., Bucholz, K. K., Kapoor, M., Almasy, L., Dick, D. M., . . . Hancock, D. B. (2014a). DSM-5 cannabis use disorder: A phenotypic and genomic perspective. *Drug and Alcohol Dependence, 134,* 362–369.

Agrawal, A., Lynskey, M. T., Hinrichs, A., Grucza, R., Saccone, S. F., Krueger, R., . . . Consortium, G. (2011). A genome-wide association study of DSM-IV cannabis dependence. *Addiction Biology, 16*(3), 514–518. doi:10.1111/j.1369-1600.2010.00255.x

Agrawal, A., Madden, P. A. F., Bucholz, K. K., Heath, A. C., & Lynskey, M. T. (2014b). Initial reactions to tobacco and cannabis smoking: A twin study. *Addiction, 109*(4), 663–671.

Agrawal, A., Sartor, C. E., Lynskey, M. T., Grant, J. D., Pergadia, M. L., Grucza, R., . . . Heath, A. C. (2009). Evidence for an interaction between age at first drink and genetic influences on DSM-IV alcohol dependence symptoms. *Alcoholism — Clinical and Experimental Research, 33*(12), 2047–2056. doi:10.1111/j.1530-0277.2009.01044.x

Agrawal, A., Verweij, K. J. H., Gillespie, N. A., Heath, A. C., Lessov-Schlaggar, C. N., Martin, N. G., . . . Lynskey, M. T. (2012). The genetics of addiction — a translational perspective. *Translational Psychiatry, 2*(7), e140.

Ainsworth, M. D. S., Blehar, M. C., Waters, E., & Wall, S. (1978). *Patterns of attachment: A psychological study of the Strange Situation.* Hillsdale, NJ: Erlbaum.

AlAqeel, B., & Margolese, H. C. (2013). Remission in schizophrenia: Critical and systematic review. *Harvard Review of Psychiatry, 20*(6), 281–297.

Alarcón, M., DeFries, J. C., Light, J. G., & Pennington, B. F. (1997). A twin study of mathematics disability. *Journal of Learning Disabilities, 30*(6), 617–623.

Alarcón, M., Plomin, R., Fulker, D. W., Corley, R., & DeFries, J. C. (1999). Molarity not modularity: Multivariate genetic analysis of specific cognitive abilities in parents and their 16-year-old children in the Colorado Adoption Project. *Cognitive Development, 14,* 175–193. doi:10.1016/S0885-2014(99)80023-9

Albright, F., Light, K., Light, A., Bateman, L., & Cannon-Albright, L. A. (2011). Evidence for a heritable predisposition to Chronic Fatigue Syndrome. *BMC Neurology, 11,* 62. doi:10.1186/1471-2377-11-62

Allen, G. (1975). *Life science in the twentieth century.* New York: John Wiley.

Allen Institute for Brain Science. (2014). Allen Human Brain Atlas. Retrieved from http://human.brain-map.org

Allen, M. G. (1976). Twin studies of affective illness. *Archives of General Psychiatry, 33,* 1476–1478.

Allis, C. D., Caparros, M.-L., Jenuwein, T., Reinberg, D., & Lachlan, M. (2015). *Epigenetics* (2nd ed.): Cold Spring Harbor Laboratory Press.

Althoff, R. R., Faraone, S. V., Rettew, D. C., Morley, C. P., & Hudziak, J. J. (2005). Family, twin, adoption, and molecular genetic studies of juvenile bipolar disorder. *Bipolar Disorders, 7*(6), 598–609.

Altmuller, J., Palmer, L. J., Fischer, G., Scherb, H., & Wjst, M. (2001). Genomewide scans of complex human diseases: True linkage is hard to find. *American Journal of Human Genetics, 69*(5), 936–950.

Altshuler, D. L., Durbin, R. M., Abecasis, G. R., Bentley, D. R., Chakravarti, A., Clark, A. G., . . . 1000 Genomes Project Consortium (2010a). A map of human genome variation from population-scale sequencing. *Nature, 467*(7319), 1061–1073. doi:10.1038/nature09534

Altshuler, D. M., Gibbs, R. A., Peltonen, L., Dermitzakis, E., Schaffner, S. F., Yu, F., . . . McEwen, J. E. (2010b). Integrating common and rare genetic variation in diverse human populations. *Nature, 467*(7311), 52–58. doi:10.1038/nature09298

Alzheimer's Disease International. (2015). *World Alzheimer Report 2015: The Global Impact of Dementia. An analysis of prevalence, incidence, cost and trends.*

American Psychiatric Association. (2013). *Diagnostic and Statistical Manual of Mental Disorders. Fifth Edition (DSM-5).* Washington, DC: American Psychiatric Association.

Amir, R. E., Van den Veyer, I. B., Wan, M., Tran, C. Q., Francke, U., & Zoghbi, H. Y. (1999). Rett syndrome is caused by mutations in X-linked MECP2, encoding methyl-CpG-binding protein 2. *Nature Genetics, 23*(2), 185–188.

Anderson, L. T., & Ernst, M. (1994). Self-injury in Lesch-Nyhan disease. *Journal of Autism and Developmental Disorders, 24*(1), 67–81.

Andrews, G., Stewart, G., Allen, R., & Henderson, A. S. (1990). The genetics of six neurotic disorders: A twin study. *Journal of Affective Disorders, 19*(1), 23–29.

Anholt, R. R., & Mackay, T. F. (2004). Quantitative genetic analyses of complex behaviours in *Drosophila. Nature Reviews Genetics, 5*(11), 838–849.

Anton, R. F., Oroszi, G., O'Malley, S., Couper, D., Swift, R., Pettinati, H., & Goldman, D. (2008). An evaluation of mu-opioid receptor (OPRM1) as a predictor of naltrexone response in the treatment of alcohol dependence. *Archives of General Psychiatry, 65*(2), 135–144. doi:10.1001/archpsyc.65.2.135

Ardiel, E. L., & Rankin, C. H. (2010). An elegant mind: Learning and memory in *Caenorhabditis elegans. Learning and Memory, 17*(4), 191–201. doi:10.1101/lm.960510

Arseneault, L., Moffitt, T. E., Caspi, A., Taylor, A., Rijsdijk, F. V., Jaffee, S. R., . . . Measelle, J. R. (2003). Strong genetic effects on cross-situational antisocial behaviour among 5-year-old children according to mothers, teachers, examiner-observers, and twins' self-reports. *Journal of Child Psychology & Psychiatry & Allied Disciplines, 44*(6), 832–848.

Arvey, R. D., Bouchard, T. J., Jr., Segal, N. L., & Abraham, L. M. (1989). Job satisfaction: Environmental and genetic components. *Journal of Applied Psychology, 74*(2), 187–192.

Asbury, K., Dunn, J. F., & Plomin, R. (2006). Birthweight-discordance and differences in early parenting relate to monozygotic twin differences in behaviour problems and academic achievement at age 7. *Developmental Science, 9*(2), F22–F31. doi:10.1111/j.1467-7687.2006.00469.x

Asbury, K., & Plomin, R. (2013). *G is for genes: The impact of genetics on education and achievement* (Vol. 24). New York: Wiley & Sons.

Aschard, H., Lutz, S., Maus, B., Duell, E. J., Fingerlin, T. E., Chatterjee, N., . . . Van Steen, K. (2012). Challenges and opportunities in genome-wide environmental interaction (GWEI) studies. *Human Genetics, 131*(10), 1591–1613.

Ashbrook, D. G., Williams, R. W., Lu, L., & Hager, R. (2015). A cross-species genetic analysis identifies candidate genes for mouse anxiety and human bipolar disorder. *Frontiers in Behavioral Neuroscience, 9*(171).

Avinun, R., & Knafo, A. (2013). Parenting as a reaction evoked by children's genotype: A meta-analysis of children-as-twins studies. *Personality and Social Psychology Review, 18*(1), 87–102.

Awofala, A. A. (2011). Genetic approaches to alcohol addiction: Gene expression studies and recent candidates from *Drosophila. Invertebrate Neuroscience, 11*(1), 1–7. doi:10.1007/s10158-010-0113-y

Axelson, D., Goldstein, B., Goldstein, T., Monk, K., Yu, H., Hickey, M. B., ... Merranko, J. (2015). Diagnostic precursors to bipolar disorder in offspring of parents with bipolar disorder: A longitudinal study. *American Journal of Psychiatry, 172*(7), 638–646.

Aylor, D. L., Valdar, W., Foulds-Mathes, W., Buus, R. J., Verdugo, R. A., Baric, R. S., ... Churchill, G. A. (2011). Genetic analysis of complex traits in the emerging Collaborative Cross. *Genome Research, 21*(8), 1213–1222. doi:10.1101/gr.111310.110

Ayorech, Z., Selzam, S., Smith-Woolley, E., Knopik, V. S., Neiderhiser, J. M., DeFries, J. C., & Plomin, R. (2016). Publication trends over fifty-five years of behavioral genetics research. *Behavior Genetics* [Epub ahead of print]. doi: 10.1007/s10519-016-9786-2

Baddeley, A. D. (2007). *Working memory, thought, and action.* Oxford: Oxford University Press.

Badner, J. A., & Gershon, E. S. (2002). Meta-analysis of whole-genome linkage scans of bipolar disorder and schizophrenia. *Molecular Psychiatry, 7*(4), 405–411. doi:10.1038/sj.mp.4001012

Bae, H. T., Sebastiani, P., Sun, J. X., Andersen, S. L., Daw, E. W., Terracciano, A., Ferrucci, L., & Perls, T. T. (2013). Genome-wide association study of personality traits in the Long Life Family Study. *Frontiers in Genetics, 4*, 65.

Bailey, A., Palferman, S., Heavey, L., & Le Couteur, A. (1998). Autism: The phenotype in relatives. *Journal of Autism and Developmental Disorders, 28*(5), 369–392.

Bailey, A., Phillips, W., & Rutter, M. (1996). Autism: Towards an integration of clinical, genetic, neuropsychological, and neurobiological perspectives. *Journal of Child Psychology and Psychiatry, 37*, 89–126.

Bailey, J. M., Dunne, M. P., & Martin, N. G. (2000). Genetic and environmental influences on sexual orientation and its correlates in an Australian twin sample. *Journal of Personality and Social Psychology, 78*(3), 524–536.

Bailey, J. M., & Pillard, R. C. (1991). A genetic study of male sexual orientation. *Archives of General Psychiatry, 48*, 1089–1096.

Bailey, J. M., Pillard, R. C., Dawood, K., Miller, M. B., Farrer, L. A., Trivedi, S., & Murphy, R. L. (1999). A family history study of male sexual orientation using three independent samples. *Behavior Genetics, 29*, 79–86.

Bailey, J. M., Pillard, R. C., Neale, M. C., & Agyei, Y. (1993). Heritable factors influence sexual orientation in women. *Archives of General Psychiatry, 50*, 217–223.

Bailey, J. M., Vasey, P. L., Diamond, L. M., Breedlove, S. M., Vilain, E., & Epprecht, M. (2016). Sexual orientation, controversy, and science. *Psychological Science in the Public Interest, 17*(2), 45–101. doi:10.1177/1529100616637616

Baker, L. A., Barton, M., Lozano, D. I., Raine, A., & Fowler, J. H. (2006). The Southern California Twin Register at the University of Southern California: II. *Twin Research and Human Genetics, 9*(6), 933–940. doi:10.1375/183242706779462912

Baker, L. A., Jacobson, K. C., Raine, A., Lozano, D. I., & Bezdjian, S. (2007a). Genetic and environmental bases of childhood antisocial behavior: A multi-informant twin study. *Journal of Abnormal Psychology, 116*(2), 219–235. doi:10.1037/0021-843x.116.2.219

Baker, T. B., Piper, M. E., McCarthy, D. E., Bolt, D. M., Smith, S. S., Kim, S.-Y., ... Transdisciplinary Tobacco Use Research Center Tobacco Dependence Phenotype Workgroup. (2007b). Time to first cigarette in the morning as an index of ability to quit smoking: implications for nicotine dependence. *Nicotine & Tobacco Research: Official Journal of the Society for Research on Nicotine and Tobacco, 9*(Suppl 4), S555–S570.

Bakwin, H. (1971). Enuresis in twins. *American Journal of Diseases in Children, 21*, 222–225.

Balestri, M. (2014). Genetic modulation of personality traits a systematic review of the literature. *International Clinical Psychopharmacology, 29*(1), 1–15. doi:10.1097/YIC.0b013e328364590b

Balestri, M., Calati, R., Serretti, A., & De Ronchi, D. (2014). Genetic modulation of personality traits: A systematic review of the literature. *International Clinical Psychopharmacology, 29*(1), 1–15. doi:10.1097/YIC.0b013e328364590b

Ball, H. A., Arseneault, L., Taylor, A., Maughan, B., Caspi, A., & Moffitt, T. E. (2008). Genetic and environmental influences on victims, bullies and bully-victims in childhood. *Journal of Child Psychology and Psychiatry, 49*(1), 104–112. doi:10.1111/j.1469-7610.2007.01821.x

Baltes, P. B. (1993). The aging mind: Potential and limits. *Gerontologist, 33*, 580–594.

Bamshad, M. J., Ng, S. B., Bigham, A. W., Tabor, H. K., Emond, M. J., Nickerson, D. A., & Shendure, J. (2011). Exome sequencing as a tool for Mendelian disease gene discovery. *Nature Reviews Genetics, 12*(11), 745–755. doi:10.1038/nrg3031

Banaschewski, T., Becker, K., Scherag, S., Franke, B., & Coghill, D. (2010). Molecular genetics of attention-deficit/hyperactivity disorder: An overview. *European Child and Adolescent Psychiatry, 19*(3), 237–257. doi:10.1007/s00787-010-0090-z

Barash, Y., Calarco, J. A., Gao, W., Pan, Q., Wang, X., Shai, O., ... Frey, B. J. (2010). Deciphering the splicing code. *Nature, 465*(7294), 53–59.

Barbieri, M., Bonafè, M., Franceschi, C., & Paolisso, G. (2003). Insulin/IGF-I-signaling pathway: An evolutionarily conserved mechanism of longevity from yeast to humans. *American Journal of Physiology-Endocrinology and Metabolism, 285*(5), E1064–E1071.

Barclay, N. L., Eley, T. C., Buysse, D. J., Maughan, B., & Gregory, A. M. (2011). Nonshared environmental influences on sleep quality: A study of monozygotic twin differences. *Behavior Genetics, 42*(2), 234–244. doi:10.1007/s10519-011-9510-1

Barnea, A., Cronqvist, H., & Siegel, S. (2010). Nature or nurture: What determines investor behavior? *Journal of Financial Economics, 98*(3), 583–604. doi:10.1016/j.jfineco.2010.08.001

Baron, M., Freimer, N. F., Risch, N., Lerer, B., & Alexander, J. R. (1993). Diminished support for linkage between manic depressive illness and X-chromosome markers in three Israeli pedigrees. *Nature Genetics, 3,* 49–55.

Baron, M., Gruen, R., Asnis, L., & Lord, S. (1985). Familial transmission of schizotypal and borderline personality disorder. *American Journal of Psychiatry, 142,* 927–934.

Bartels, M. (2015). Genetics of wellbeing and its components satisfaction with life, happiness, and quality of life: A review and meta-analysis of heritability studies. *Behavior Genetics, 45*(2), 137–156. doi:10.1007/s10519-015-9713-y

Bartels, M., Cacioppo, J., van Beijsterveldt, T. C. E. M., & Boomsma, D. (2013). Exploring the association between well-being and psychopathology in adolescents. *Behavior Genetics, 43*(3), 177–190. doi:10.1007/s10519-013-9589-7

Bartels, M., de Moor, M. H. M., van der Aa, N., Boomsma, D. I., & de Geus, E. J. C. (2012). Regular exercise, subjective wellbeing, and internalizing problems in adolescence: Causality or genetic pleiotropy? *Frontiers in Genetics, 3,* 4.

Bartels, M., Rietveld, M. J., van Baal, G. C., & Boomsma, D. I. (2002). Heritability of educational achievement in 12-year-olds and the overlap with cognitive ability. *Twin Research, 5*(6), 544–553.

Bartels, M., Saviouk, V., de Moor, M. H. M., Willemsen, G., van Beijsterveldt, T. C. E. M., Hottenga, J.-J., ... Boomsma, D. I. (2010). Heritability and genome-wide linkage scan of subjective happiness. *Twin Research and Human Genetics, 13*(2), 135–142.

Bassell, G. J., & Warren, S. T. (2008). Fragile X syndrome: Loss of local mRNA regulation alters synaptic development and function. *Neuron, 60*(2), 201–214. doi:10.1016/j.neuron.2008.10.004

Bates, G. P. (2005). History of genetic disease: The molecular genetics of Huntington disease—a history. *Nature Reviews Genetics, 6*(10), 766–773.

Bearden, C. E., & Freimer, N. B. (2006). Endophenotypes for psychiatric disorders: Ready for primetime? *Trends in Genetics, 22*(6), 306–313.

Beauchamp, J. P., Cesarini, D., Johannesson, M., van der Loos, M. J. H. M., Koellinger, P. D., Groenen, P. J. F., ... Christakis, N. A. (2011). Molecular Genetics and Economics. *Journal of Economic Perspectives, 25*(4), 57–82. doi:10.1257/jep.25.4.57

Beaver, K. M. (2011). Genetic influences on being processed through the criminal justice system: Results from a sample of adoptees. *Biological Psychiatry, 69*(3), 282–287. doi:10.1016/j.biopsych.2010.09.007

Beaver, K. M., Boutwell, B. B., Barnes, J. C., & Cooper, J. A. (2009). The biosocial underpinnings to adolescent victimization results from a longitudinal sample of twins. *Youth Violence and Juvenile Justice, 7*(3), 223–238. doi:10.1177/1541204009333830

Beck, J. A., Lloyd, S., Hafezparast, M., Lennon-Pierce, M., Eppig, J. T., Festing, M. F. W., & Fisher, E. M. C. (2000). Genealogies of mouse inbred strains. *Nature Genetics, 24*(1), 23–25.

Beckmann, J. S. (2015). Can we afford to sequence every newborn baby's genome? *Human Mutation, 36*(3), 283–286.

Bekris, L. M., Yu, C.-E., Bird, T. D., & Tsuang, D. W. (2010). Genetics of Alzheimer disease. *Journal of Geriatric Psychiatry and Neurology, 23*(4), 213–227. doi:10.1177/0891988710383571

Belknap, J. K., & Atkins, A. L. (2001). The replicability of QTLs for murine alcohol preference drinking behavior across eight independent studies. *Mammalian Genome, 12*(12), 893–899.

Bellott, D. W., Hughes, J. F., Skaletsky, H., Brown, L. G., Pyntikova, T., Cho, T.-J., ... Page, D. C. (2014). Mammalian Y chromosomes retain widely expressed dosage-sensitive regulators. *Nature, 508*(7497), 494–499. doi:10.1038/nature13206

Benjamin, D. J., Cesarini, D., van der Loos, M. J. H. M., Dawes, C. T., Koellinger, P. D., Magnusson, P. K. E., ... Visscher, P. M. (2012). The genetic architecture of economic and political preferences. *Proceedings of the National Academy of Sciences of the United States of America, 109*(21), 8026–8031. doi:10.1073/pnas.1120666109

Benjamin, J., Ebstein, R., & Belmaker, R. H. (2002). *Molecular genetics and the human personality.* Washington, DC: American Psychiatric Press.

Benjamin, J., Li, L., Patterson, C., Greenburg, B. D., Murphy, D. L., & Hamer, D. H. (1996). Population and familial association between the D4 dopamine receptor gene and measures of novelty seeking. *Nature Genetics, 12,* 81–84.

Bennet, A. M., Di Angelantonio, E., Ye, Z., Wensley, F., Dahlin, A., Ahlbom, A., ... de Faire, U. (2007). Association of apolipoprotein E genotypes with lipid levels and coronary risk. *JAMA, 298*(11), 1300–1311.

Bennett, B., Carosone-Link, P., Zahniser, N. R., & Johnson, T. E. (2006). Confirmation and fine mapping of ethanol sensitivity quantitative trait loci, and candidate gene testing in the LXS recombinant inbred mice. *Journal of Pharmacology and Experimental Therapeutics, 319*(1), 299–307.

Bennett, B., Larson, C., Richmond, P. A., Odell, A. T., Saba, L. M., Tabakoff, B., . . . Radcliffe, R. A. (2015). Quantitative trait locus mapping of acute functional tolerance in the LXS recombinant inbred strains. *Alcoholism: Clinical and Experimental Research, 39*(4), 611–620.

Benoit, C.-E., Rowe, W. B., Menard, C., Sarret, P., & Quirion, R. (2011). Genomic and proteomic strategies to identify novel targets potentially involved in learning and memory. *Trends in Pharmacological Sciences, 32*(1), 43–52. doi:10.1016/j.tips.2010.10.002

Benowitz, N. L. (2008). Neurobiology of nicotine addiction: implications for smoking cessation treatment. *American Journal of Medicine, 121*(4 Suppl 1), S3–10. doi:10.1016/j.amjmed.2008.01.015

Benyamin, B., Pourcain, B., Davis, O. S., Davies, G., Hansell, N. K., Brion, M. J., . . . Visscher, P. M. (2014). Childhood intelligence is heritable, highly polygenic and associated with FNBP1L. *Molecular Psychiatry, 19*(2), 253–258. doi:10.1038/mp.2012.184

Benzer, S. (1973). Genetic dissection of behavior. *Scientific American, 229*(6), 24–37.

Bergem, A. L. M., Engedal, K., & Kringlen, E. (1997). The role of heredity in late-onset Alzheimer disease and vascular dementia: A twin study. *Archives of General Psychiatry, 54*(3), 264–270.

Bergeman, C. S. (1997). *Aging: Genetic and environmental influences.* Newbury Park, CA: Sage.

Bergeman, C. S., Chipuer, H. M., Plomin, R., Pedersen, N. L., McClearn, G. E., Nesselroade, J. R., . . . McCrae, R. R. (1993). Genetic and environmental effects on openness to experience, agreeableness, and conscientiousness: An adoption/ twin study. *Journal of Personality, 61*, 159–179. doi:10.1111/j.1467-6494.1993.tb01030.x

Bergeman, C. S., Plomin, R., McClearn, G. E., Pedersen, N. L., & Friberg, L. (1988). Genotype-environment interaction in personality development: Identical twins reared apart. *Psychology and Aging, 3*, 399–406. doi:10.1037/0882-7974.3.4.399

Bergeman, C. S., Plomin, R., Pedersen, N. L., & McClearn, G. E. (1991). Genetic mediation of the relationship between social support and psychological well-being. *Psychology and Aging, 6*(4), 640–646. doi:10.1037/0882-7974.6.4.640

Bergeman, C. S., Plomin, R., Pedersen, N. L., McClearn, G. E., & Nesselroade, J. R. (1990). Genetic and environmental influences on social support: The Swedish Adoption/Twin Study of Aging. *Journal of Gerontology, 45*(3), 101–106.

Berkman, M. B., & Plutzer, E. (2010). *Evolution, creationism, and the battle to control America's classrooms.* Cambridge: Cambridge University Press.

Berkman, M. B., & Plutzer, E. (2011). Defeating creationism in the courtroom, but not in the classroom. *Science, 331*(6016), 404–405. doi:10.1126/science.1198902

Bernards, R. (2006). Exploring the uses of RNAi—gene knockdown and the Nobel Prize. *The New England Journal of Medicine, 355*(23), 2391–2393.

Bertelsen, A. (1985). Controversies and consistencies in psychiatric genetics. *Acta Paediatrica Scandinavica, 71*, 61–75.

Bertram, L., McQueen, M. B., Mullin, K., Blacker, D., & Tanzi, R. E. (2007). Systematic meta-analyses of Alzheimer disease genetic association studies: The AlzGene database. *Nature Genetics, 39*(1), 17–23.

Betjemann, R. S., Johnson, E. P., Barnard, H., Boada, R., Filley, C. M., Filipek, P. A., . . . Pennington, B. F. (2010). Genetic covariation between brain volumes and IQ, reading performance, and processing speed. *Behavior Genetics, 40*(2), 135–145. doi:10.1007/s10519-009-9328-2

Betsworth, D. G., Bouchard, T. J., Jr., Cooper, C. R., Grotevant, H. D., Hansen, J. I. C., Scarr, S., & Weinberg, R. A. (1994). Genetic and environmental influences on vocational interests assessed using adoptive and biological families and twins reared apart and together. *Journal of Vocational Behavior, 44*, 263–278.

Bettens, K., Sleegers, K., & Van Broeckhoven, C. (2013). Genetic insights in Alzheimer's disease. *The Lancet Neurology, 12*(1), 92–104.

Bickle, J. (2003). *Philosophy and neuroscience: A ruthlessly reductive account.* Boston: Kluwer Academic.

Bidwell, L. C., Palmer, R. H. C., Brick, L., McGeary, J. E., & Knopik, V. S. (2016). Genomewide single nucleotide polymorphism heritability of nicotine dependence as a multidimensional phenotype. *Psychological Medicine*, 1–11.

Biederman, J., Faraone, S. V., Keenan, K., Benjamin, J., Krifcher, B., Moore, C., . . . Steingard, R. (1992). Further evidence for family-genetic risk factors in attention deficit hyperactivity disorder. Patterns of comorbidity in probands and relatives psychiatrically and pediatrically referred samples. *Archives of General Psychiatry, 49*(9), 728–738.

Bierut, L. J. (2011). Genetic vulnerability and susceptibility to substance dependence. *Neuron, 69*(4), 618–627. doi:10.1016/j.neuron.2011.02.015

Bierut, L. J., Dinwiddie, S. H., Begleiter, H., Crowe, R. R., Hesselbrock, V., Nurnberger, J. I., . . . Reich, T. (1998). Familial transmission of substance dependence: Alcohol, marijuana, cocaine, and habitual smoking—A report from the Collaborative Study on the Genetics of Alcoholism. *Archives of General Psychiatry, 55*(11), 982–988. doi:10.1001/archpsyc.55.11.982

Biesecker, B. B., & Marteau, T. (1999). The future of genetic counseling: An international perspective. *Nature Genetics, 22*, 133–137.

Binbay, T., Drukker, M., Elbi, H., Tanık, F. A., Özkınay, F., Onay, H., . . . Alptekin, K. (2012). Testing the psychosis continuum: Differential impact of genetic and nongenetic risk factors and comorbid psychopathology across the entire spectrum of psychosis. *Schizophrenia Bulletin, 38*(5), 992–1002.

Binder, E. B., & Holsboer, F. (2006). Pharmacogenomics and antidepressant drugs. *Annals of Medicine, 38*(2), 82–94.

Bird, A. (2007). Perceptions of epigenetics. *Nature, 447*(7143), 396–398. doi:10.1038/nature05913

Bird, L. M. (2014). Angelman syndrome: Review of clinical and molecular aspects. *The Application of Clinical Genetics, 7*, 93.

Bishop, D. V. M. (2015). The interface between genetics and psychology: Lessons from developmental dyslexia. *Proceedings of the Royal Society of London B: Biological Sciences, 282*(1806), 20143139.

Bishop, D. V. M., Jacobs, P. A., Lachlan, K., Wellesley, D., Barnicoat, A., Boyd, P. A., . . . Scerif, G. (2011). Autism, language and communication in children with sex chromosome trisomies. *Archives of Disease in Childhood, 96*(10), 954–959. doi:10.1136/adc.2009.179747

Björklund, A., Lindahl, M., & Plug, E. (2006). The origins of intergenerational associations: Lessons from Swedish adoption data. *The Quarterly Journal of Economics, 121*(3), 999–1028. doi:10.2307/25098815

Blokland, G. A. M., de Zubicaray, G. I., McMahon, K. L., & Wright, M. J. (2012). Genetic and environmental influences on neuroimaging phenotypes: A meta-analytical perspective on twin imaging studies. *Twin Research and Human Genetics, 15*(03), 351–371.

Blokland, G. A. M., McMahon, K. L., Thompson, P. M., Martin, N. G., de Zubicaray, G. I., & Wright, M. J. (2011). Heritability of working memory brain activation. *Journal of Neuroscience, 31*(30), 10882–10890. doi:10.1523/jneurosci.5334-10.2011

Bloom, F. E., & Kupfer, D. J. (1995). *Psychopharmacology: A fourth generation of progress.* New York: Raven Press.

Bloom, R. J., Kähler, A. K., Collins, A. L., Chen, G., Cannon, T. D., Hultman, C., & Sullivan, P. F. (2013). Comprehensive analysis of copy number variation

in monozygotic twins discordant for bipolar disorder or schizophrenia. *Schizophrenia Research, 146*(1), 289–290.

Boardman, J. D., Alexander, K. B., & Stallings, M. C. (2011). Stressful life events and depression among adolescent twin pairs. *Biodemography and Social Biology, 57*(1), 53–66. doi:10.1080/19485565.2011.574565

Bobori, C. (2015). Molecular genetics of Huntington's disease. In P. Vlamos & A. Alexiou (Eds.), *GeNeDis 2014* (pp. 59–65). Springer.

Bohman, M. (1996). Predisposition to criminality: Swedish adoption studies in retrospect. In G. R. Bock & J. A. Goode (Eds.), *Genetics of Criminal and Antisocial Behaviour* (Vol. 194, pp. 99–114).

Bohman, M., Cloninger, C. R., Sigvardsson, S., & von Knorring, A. L. (1982). Predisposition to petty criminals in Swedish adoptees. I. Genetic and environmental heterogeneity. *Archives of General Psychiatry, 39*, 1233–1241.

Bohman, M., Cloninger, C. R., von Knorring, A. L., & Sigvardsson, S. (1984). An adoption study of somatoform disorders. III. Cross-fostering analysis and genetic relationship to alcoholism and criminality. *Archives of General Psychiatry, 41*(9), 872–878.

Boker, S., Neale, M., Maes, H., Wilde, M., Spiegel, M., Brick, T., . . . Brandmaier, A. (2012). OpenMx 1.2 User Guide.

Boker, S., Neale, M., Maes, H., Wilde, M., Spiegel, M., Brick, T., . . . Fox, J. (2011). OpenMx: An open source extended structural equation modeling framework. *Psychometrika, 76*(2), 306–317. doi:10.1007/s11336-010-9200-6

Bokhorst, C. L., Bakermans-Kranenburg, M. J., Fearon, R. M., van IJzendoorn, M. H., Fonagy, P., & Schuengel, C. (2003). The importance of shared environment in mother-infant attachment security: A behavioral genetic study. *Child Development, 74*(6), 1769–1782.

Bolton, D., Eley, T. C., O'Connor, T. G., Perrin, S., Rabe-Hesketh, S., Rijsdijk, F. V., & Smith, P. (2006). Prevalence and genetic and environmental influences on anxiety disorders in 6-year-old twins. *Psychological Medicine, 36*(3), 335–344. doi:10.1017/S0033291705006537

Bolton, D., & Hill, J. (2004). *Mind, meaning and mental disorder: The nature of causal explanation in psychology and psychiatry.* Oxford: Oxford University Press.

Boomsma, D., Busjahn, A., & Peltonen, L. (2002). Classical twin studies and beyond. *Nature Reviews Genetics, 3*(11), 872–882.

Boraska, V., Franklin, C. S., Floyd, J. A. B., Thornton, L. M., Huckins, L. M., Southam, L., . . . Treasure, J.

(2014). A genome-wide association study of anorexia nervosa. *Molecular Psychiatry, 19*(10), 1085–1094.

Borkenau, P., Riemann, R., Spinath, F. M., & Angleitner, A. (2006). Genetic and environmental influences on Person x Situation profiles. *Journal of Personality, 74*(5), 1451–1480.

Bornovalova, M. A., Hicks, B. M., Iacono, W. G., & McGue, M. (2010). Familial transmission and heritability of childhood disruptive disorders. *American Journal of Psychiatry, 167*(9), 1066–1074. doi:10.1176/appi.ajp.2010.09091272

Bouchard, T. J., Jr., Lykken, D. T., McGue, M., Segal, N. L., & Tellegen, A. (1990). Sources of human psychological differences: The Minnesota Study of Twins Reared Apart. *Science, 250,* 223–228.

Bouchard, T. J., Jr., & McGue, M. (1981). Familial studies of intelligence: A review. *Science, 212,* 1055–1059.

Bouchard, T. J., Jr., & Propping, P. (1993). *Twins as a tool of behavioral genetics.* Chichester, UK: John Wiley & Sons.

Bovet, D. (1977). Strain differences in learning in the mouse. In A. Oliverio (Ed.), *Genetics, environment and intelligence* (pp. 79–92). Amsterdam: North-Holland.

Bowes, L., Maughan, B., Caspi, A., Moffitt, T. E., & Arseneault, L. (2010). Families promote emotional and behavioural resilience to bullying: Evidence of an environmental effect. *Journal of Child Psychology and Psychiatry, 51*(7), 809–817. doi:10.1111/j.1469-7610.2010.02216.x

Bradfield, J. P., Taal, H. R., Timpson, N. J., Scherag, A., Lecoeur, C., Warrington, N. M., ... Thiering, E. (2012). A genome-wide association meta-analysis identifies new childhood obesity loci. *Nature Genetics, 44*(5), 526–531.

BrainCloud. (2011). BrainCloud. Retrieved from http://braincloud.jhmi.edu/

BrainSpan. (2011). BrainSpan: Atlas of the developing human brain. Retrieved from http://www.brainspan.org/

Braungart, J. M., Fulker, D. W., & Plomin, R. (1992a). Genetic mediation of the home environment during infancy: A sibling adoption study of the HOME. *Developmental Psychology, 28,* 1048–1055. doi:10.1037/0012-1649.28.6.1048

Braungart, J. M., Plomin, R., DeFries, J. C., & Fulker, D. W. (1992b). Genetic influence on tester-rated infant temperament as assessed by Bayley's Infant Behavior Record: Nonadoptive and adoptive siblings and twins. *Developmental Psychology, 28,* 40–47. doi:10.1037/0012-1649.28.1.40

Bray, G. A. (1986). Effects of obesity on health and happiness. In K. E. Brownell & J. P. Foreyt (Eds.), *Handbook of eating disorders: Physiology,*

psychology and treatment of obesity anorexia and bulimia (pp. 1–44). New York: Basic Books.

Breen, F. M., Plomin, R., & Wardle, J. (2006). Heritability of food preferences in young children. *Physiology & Behavior, 88*(4–5), 443–447. doi:10.1016/j.physbeh.2006.04.016

Brendgen, M., Boivin, M., Dionne, G., Barker, E. D., Vitaro, F., Girard, A., ... Perusse, D. (2011). Gene-environment processes linking aggression, peer victimization, and the teacher-child relationship. *Child Development, 82*(6), 2021–2036. doi:10.1111/j.1467-8624.2011.01644.x

Brendgen, M., Boivin, M., Vitaro, F., Girard, A., Dionne, G., & Perusse, D. (2008). Gene-environment interaction between peer victimization and child aggression. *Development and Psychopathology, 20*(2), 455–471. doi:10.1017/s0954579408000229

Brendgen, M., Vitaro, F., Boivin, M., Girard, A., Bukowski, W. M., Dionne, G., ... Perusse, D. (2009). Gene-environment interplay between peer rejection and depressive behavior in children. *Journal of Child Psychology and Psychiatry, 50*(8), 1009–1017. doi:10.1111/j.1469-7610.2009.02052.x

Brennan, P. A., Mednick, S. A., & Jacobsen, B. (1996). Assessing the role of genetics in crime using adoption cohorts. In G. R. Bock & J. A. Goode (Eds.), *Genetics of criminal and anti-social behaviour* (pp. 115–128). Chichester, UK: Wiley.

Brett, D., Pospisil, H., Valcárcel, J., Reich, J., & Bork, P. (2002). Alternative splicing and genome complexity. *Nature Genetics, 30,* 29–30.

Briley, D. A., & Tucker-Drob, E. M. (2013). Explaining the increasing heritability of cognitive ability across development: A meta-analysis of longitudinal twin and adoption studies. *Psychological Science, 24*(9), 1704–1713.

Briley, D. A., & Tucker-Drob, E. M. (2014). Genetic and environmental continuity in personality development: A meta-analysis. *Psychological Bulletin, 140*(5), 1303–1331.

Broadhurst, P. L. (1978). *Drugs and the inheritance of behaviour.* New York: Plenum.

Broms, U., Silventoinen, K., Madden, P. A., Heath, A. C., & Kaprio, J. (2006). Genetic architecture of smoking behavior: A study of Finnish adult twins. *Twin Research and Human Genetics, 9*(1), 64–72.

Brooker, R. J., Neiderhiser, J. M., Ganiban, J. M., Leve, L. D., Shaw, D. S., & Reiss, D. (2014). Birth and adoptive parent anxiety symptoms moderate the link between infant attention control and internalizing problems in toddlerhood. *Development and Psychopathology, 26*(02), 347–359.

Brooks-Wilson, A. R. (2013). Genetics of healthy aging and longevity. *Human Genetics, 132*(12), 1323–1338.

Brouwer, S. I., van Beijsterveldt, T. C., Bartels, M., Hudziak, J. J., & Boomsma, D. I. (2006). Influences on achieving motor milestones: A twin-singleton study. *Twin Research and Human Genetics, 9*(3), 424–430.

Brumm, V. L., & Grant, M. L. (2010). The role of intelligence in phenylketonuria: A review of research and management. *Molecular Genetics and Metabolism, 99*, S18–S21. doi:10.1016/j.ymgme.2009.10.015

Buchner, D. A., & Nadeau, J. H. (2015). Contrasting genetic architectures in different mouse reference populations used for studying complex traits. *Genome Research.*

Buchwald, D., Herrell, R., Ashton, S., Belcourt, M., Schmaling, K., Sullivan, P., . . . Goldberg, J. (2001). A twin study of chronic fatigue. *Psychosomatic Medicine, 63*(6), 936–943.

Buck, K. J., Rademacher, B. S., Metten, P., & Crabbe, J. C. (2002). Mapping murine loci for physical dependence on ethanol. *Psychopharmacology (Berl). 160*(4), 398–407.

Bulik, C. M. (2005). Exploring the gene-environment nexus in eating disorders. *Journal of Psychiatry & Neuroscience, 30*(5), 335–339.

Bulik, C. M., Sullivan, P. F., Tozzi, F., Furberg, H., Lichtenstein, P., & Pedersen, N. L. (2006). Prevalence, heritability, and prospective risk factors for anorexia nervosa. *Archives of General Psychiatry, 63*(3), 305–312.

Bulik, C. M., Sullivan, P. F., Wade, T. D., & Kendler, K. S. (2000). Twin studies of eating disorders: A review. *International Journal of Eating Disorders, 27*(1), 1–20.

Bulik-Sullivan, B., Finucane, H. K., Anttila, V., Gusev, A., Day, F. R., Perry, J. R. B., . . . Price, A. L. (2015a). An atlas of genetic correlations across human diseases and traits. *Nature Genetics 47*(11):1236–1241. doi:10.1038/ng.3406.

Bulik-Sullivan, B. K., Loh, P.-R., Finucane, H. K., Ripke, S., Yang, J., Patterson, N., . . . Neale, B. M. (2015b). LD Score regression distinguishes confounding from polygenicity in genome-wide association studies. *Nature Genetics, 47*(3), 291–295.

Burke, K. C., Burke, J. D., Roe, D. S., & Regier, D. A. (1991). Comparing age at onset of major depression and other psychiatric disorders by birth cohorts in five U.S. community populations. *Archives of General Psychiatry, 48*, 789–795.

Burks, B. (1928). The relative influence of nature and nurture upon mental development: A comparative study on foster parent–foster child resemblance. *Yearbook of the National Society for the Study of Education, Part 1, 27*, 219–316.

Burt, C. (1966). The genetic determination of differences in intelligence. *British Journal of Psychology, 57*, 137–153.

Burt, S. A. (2009a). Are there meaningful etiological differences within antisocial behavior? Results of a meta-analysis. *Clinical Psychology Review, 29*(2), 163–178. doi:10.1016/j.cpr.2008.12.004

Burt, S. A. (2009b). Rethinking environmental contributions to child and adolescent psychopathology: A meta-analysis of shared environmental influences. *Psychological Bulletin, 135*(4), 608–637. doi:10.1037/a0015702

Burt, S. A. (2013). Do etiological influences on aggression overlap with those on rule breaking? A meta-analysis. *Psychological Medicine, 43*(09), 1801–1812.

Burt, S. A., Klahr, A., & Klump, K. (2015). Do non-shared environmental influences persist over time? An examination of days and minutes. *Behavior Genetics, 45*(1), 24–34. doi:10.1007/s10519-014-9682-6

Burt, S. A., Klahr, A. M., Neale, M. C., & Klump, K. L. (2013). Maternal warmth and directiveness jointly moderate the etiology of childhood conduct problems. *Journal of Child Psychology and Psychiatry, 54*(10), 1030–1037.

Burt, S. A., & Klump, K. L. (2014). Parent–child conflict as an etiological moderator of childhood conduct problems: An example of a "bioecological" gene–environment interaction. *Psychological Medicine, 44*(05), 1065–1076.

Burt, S. A., Krueger, R. F., McGue, M., & Iacono, W. (2003). Parent-child conflict and the comorbidity among childhood externalizing disorders. *Archives of General Psychiatry, 60*(5), 505–513.

Burt, S. A., McGue, M., & Iacono, W. G. (2010). Environmental contributions to the stability of antisocial behavior over time: Are they shared or non-shared? *Journal of Abnormal Child Psychology, 38*(3), 327–337. doi:10.1007/s10802-009-9367-4

Burt, S. A., McGue, M., Krueger, R. F., & Iacono, W. G. (2005). How are parent-child conflict and childhood externalizing symptoms related over time? Results from a genetically informative cross-lagged study. *Development and Psychopathology, 17*(1), 145–165.

Burt, S. A., & Neiderhiser, J. M. (2009). Aggressive versus nonaggressive antisocial behavior: Distinctive etiological moderation by age. *Developmental Psychology, 45*(4), 1164–1176. doi:10.1037/a0016130

Buss, A. H., & Plomin, R. (1984). *Temperament: Early developing personality traits.* Hillsdale, NJ: Lawrence Erlbaum.

Busto, G. U., Cervantes-Sandoval, I., & Davis, R. L. (2010). Olfactory learning in *Drosophila. Physiology, 25*(6), 338–346. doi:10.1152/physiol.00026.2010

Butcher, L. M., Davis, O. S. P., Craig, I. W., & Plomin, R. (2008). Genome-wide quantitative trait locus association scan of general cognitive ability using pooled DNA and 500K single nucleotide polymorphism microarrays. *Genes, Brain and Behavior, 7*(4), 435–446. doi:10.1111 /j.1601-183X.2007.00368.x

Butler, R. J., Galsworthy, M. J., Rijsdijk, F., & Plomin, R. (2001). Genetic and gender influences on nocturnal bladder control: A study of 2900 3-year-old twin pairs. *Scandinavian Journal of Urology & Nephrology* (35), 177–183. doi:10.1080 /003655901750291917

Butterworth, B., & Kovas, Y. (2013). Understanding neurocognitive developmental disorders can improve education for all. *Science, 340*(6130), 300–305.

Byrd, A. L., & Manuck, S. B. (2014). MAOA, childhood maltreatment, and antisocial behavior: Meta-analysis of a gene-environment interaction. *Biological Psychiatry, 75*(1), 9–17. doi:http://dx.doi .org/10.1016/j.biopsych.2013.05.004

Byrne, E. M., Raheja, U. K., Stephens, S. H., Heath, A. C., Madden, P. A., Vaswani, D., . . . Gehrman, P. R. (2015). Seasonality shows evidence for polygenic architecture and genetic correlation with schizophrenia and bipolar disorder. *Journal of Clinical Psychiatry, 76*(2), 128–134.

Cadoret, R. J. (1994). Genetic and environmental contributions to heterogeneity in alcoholism: findings from the Iowa adoption studies. *Annals of the New York Academy of Sciences, 708*, 59–71.

Cadoret, R. J., Cain, C. A., & Crowe, R. R. (1983). Evidence from gene-environment interaction in the development of adolescent antisocial behaviour. *Behavior Genetics, 13*, 301–310.

Cadoret, R. J., O'Gorman, T. W., Heywood, E., & Troughton, E. (1985a). Genetic and environmental factors in major depression. *Journal of Affective Disorders, 9*, 155–164.

Cadoret, R. J., O'Gorman, T. W., Troughton, E., & Heywood, E. (1985b). Alcoholism and antisocial personality: Interrelationships, genetic and environmental factors. *Archives of General Psychiatry, 42*(2), 161–167.

Cadoret, R. J., & Stewart, M. A. (1991). An adoption study of attention deficit/hyperactivity/ aggression and their relationship to adult antisocial personality. *Comprehensive Psychiatry, 32*(1), 73–82.

Cadoret, R. J., Troughton, E., & O'Gorman, T. W. (1987). Genetic and environmental factors in alcohol abuse and antisocial personality. *Journal of Studies on Alcohol, 48*(1), 1–8.

Cadoret, R. J., Yates, W. R., Troughton, E., Woodworth, G., & Stewart, M. A. (1995a). Genetic-environmental interaction in the genesis of aggressivity and conduct disorders. *Archives of General Psychiatry, 52*, 916–924.

Cadoret, R. J., Yates, W. R., Troughton, E., Woodworth, G., & Stewart, M. A. (1995b). Adoption study demonstrating two genetic pathways to drug abuse. *Archives of General Psychiatry, 52*, 42–52.

Cadoret, R. J., Yates, W. R., Troughton, E., Woodworth, G., & Stewart, M. A. (1996). An adoption study of drug abuse/dependency in females. *Comprehensive Psychiatry, 37*(2), 88–94. doi:10.1016 /s0010-440x(96)90567-2

Caldwell, B. M., & Bradley, R. H. (1984). *Home observation for measurement of the environment (HOME)—Revised edition.* University of Arkansas at Little Rock.

Caldwell, B. M., & Bradley, R. H. (2003). *Home observation for measurement of the environment: Administration manual.* Tempe, AZ: Family & Human Dynamics Research Institute, Arizona State University.

Calvin, C. M., Deary, I. J., Webbink, D., Smith, P., Fernandes, C., Lee, S. H., . . . Visscher, P. M. (2012). Multivariate genetic analyses of cognition and academic achievement from two population samples of 174,000 and 166,000 school children. *Behavior Genetics, 42*(5), 699–710.

Camp, N. J., Lowry, M. R., Richards, R. L., Plenk, A. M., Carter, C., Hensel, C. H., . . . Cannon-Albright, L. A. (2005). Genome-wide linkage analyses of extended Utah pedigrees identifies loci that influence recurrent, early-onset major depression and anxiety disorders. *American Journal of Medical Genetics. Part B, Neuropsychiatric Genetics, 135*(1), 85–93.

Cannon, T. D., Mednick, S. A., Parnas, J., Schulsinger, F., Praestholm, J., & Vestergaard, A. (1993). Developmental brain abnormalities in the offspring of schizophrenic mothers: I. Contributions of genetic and perinatal factors. *Archives of General Psychiatry, 50*, 551–564.

Cantwell, D. P. (1975). Genetic studies of hyperactive children: Psychiatric illness in biological and adopting parents. In R. R. Fieve, D. Rosenthal, & H. Brill (Eds.), *Genetic research in psychiatry* (pp. 273–280). Baltimore: Johns Hopkins University Press.

Capecchi, M. R. (1994). Targeted gene replacement. *Scientific American* (March), 52–59.

Capron, C., & Duyme, M. (1989). Assessment of the effects of socioeconomic status on IQ in a full cross-fostering study. *Nature, 340*, 552–554.

Capron, C., & Duyme, M. (1996). Effect of socioeconomic status of biological and adoptive parents on WISC-R subtest scores of their French adopted children. *Intelligence, 22*(3), 259–275.

Cardno, A. G., Jones, L. A., Murphy, K. C., Sanders, R. D., Asherson, P., Owen, M. J., &

McGuffin, P. (1999). Dimensions of psychosis in affected sibling pairs. *Schizophrenia Bulletin, 25*(4), 841–850.

Cardno, A. G., & Owen, M. J. (2014). Genetic relationships between schizophrenia, bipolar disorder, and schizoaffective disorder. *Schizophrenia Bulletin.* doi:10.1093/schbul/sbu016

Cardno, A. G., Rijsdijk, F. V., West, R. M., Gottesman, I. I., Craddock, N., Murray, R. M., & McGuffin, P. (2012). A twin study of schizoaffective-mania, schizoaffective-depression, and other psychotic syndromes. *American Journal of Medical Genetics. Part B Neuropsychiatric Genetics, 159b*(2), 172–182. doi:10.1002/ajmg.b.32011

Cardon, L. R., Fulker, D. W., DeFries, J. C., & Plomin, R. (1992). Multivariate genetic analysis of specific cognitive abilities in the Colorado Adoption Project at age 7. *Intelligence, 16*, 383–400. doi:10.1016/0160-2896(92)90016-K

Cardon, L. R., Smith, S. D., Fulker, D. W., Kimberling, W. J., Pennington, B. F., & DeFries, J. C. (1994). Quantitative trait locus for reading disability on chromosome 6. *Science, 266*, 276–279.

Carey, G. (1986). Sibling imitation and contrast effects. *Behavior Genetics, 16*, 319–341.

Carey, G. (1992). Twin imitation for anti-social behavior: Implications for genetic and family environmental research. *Journal of Abnormal Psychology, 101*, 18–25.

Carmelli, D., Swan, G. E., & Cardon, L. R. (1995). Genetic mediation in the relationship of education to cognitive function in older people. *Psychology and Aging, 10*, 48–53.

Carnell, S., Haworth, C. M. A., Plomin, R., & Wardle, J. (2008). Genetic influence on appetite in children. *International Journal of Obesity, 32*(10), 1468–1473. doi:10.1038/ijo.2008.127

Caron, M. G. (1996). Images in neuroscience. Molecular biology, II. A dopamine transporter mouse knockout. *American Journal of Psychiatry, 153*(12), 1515.

Carrion-Castillo, A., Franke, B., & Fisher, S. E. (2013). Molecular genetics of dyslexia: An overview. *Dyslexia, 19*(4), 214–240.

Carroll, J. B. (1993). *Human cognitive abilities.* New York: Cambridge University Press.

Carroll, J. B. (1997). Psychometrics, intelligence, and public policy. *Intelligence, 24*, 25–52.

Cartwright, R., Kirby, A. C., Tikkinen, K. A. O., Mangera, A., Thiagamoorthy, G., Rajan, P., . . . Bennett, P. (2015). Systematic review and meta-analysis of genetic association studies of urinary symptoms and prolapse in women. *American Journal of Obstetrics and Gynecology, 212*(2), 199. e1–199e.24.

Caspi, A., Hariri, A. R., Holmes, A., Uher, R., & Moffitt, T. E. (2010). Genetic sensitivity to the environment: the case of the serotonin transporter gene and its implications for studying complex diseases and traits. *Focus, 8*(3), 398–416.

Caspi, A., McClay, J., Moffitt, T. E., Mill, J., Martin, J., Craig, I. W., . . . Poulton, R. (2002). Role of genotype in the cycle of violence in maltreated children. *Science, 297*(5582), 851–854.

Caspi, A., & Moffitt, T. E. (1995). The continuity of maladaptive behaviour: From description to understanding of antisocial behaviour. In D. Cicchetti & D. J. Cohen (Eds.), *Developmental psychopathology* (pp. 472–511). New York: Wiley.

Caspi, A., Sugden, K., Moffitt, T. E., Taylor, A., Craig, I. W., Harrington, H., . . . Poulton, R. (2003). Influence of life stress on depression: Moderation by a polymorphism in the 5-HTT gene. *Science, 301*(5631), 386–389.

Cattell, R. B. (1982). *The inheritance of personality and ability.* New York: Academic Press.

Cech, T. R., & Steitz, J. A. (2014). The noncoding RNA revolution—trashing old rules to forge new ones. *Cell, 157*(1), 77–94. doi:http://dx.doi.org/10.1016/j.cell.2014.03.008

Cecil, J. E., Tavendale, R., Watt, P., Hetherington, M. M., & Palmer, C. N. A. (2008). An obesity-associated FTO gene variant and increased energy intake in children. *New England Journal of Medicine, 359*(24), 2558–2566. doi:10.1056/NEJMoa0803839

Centers for Disease Control and Prevention. (2014). Attention-deficit/hyperactivity disorder (ADHD). Key findings: Trends in the parent-report of health care provider-diagnosis and medication treatment for ADHD: United States, 2003–2011.

Cesarini, D., Dawes, C. T., Johannesson, M., Lichtenstein, P., & Wallace, B. (2009). Genetic variation in preferences for giving and risk taking. *The Quarterly Journal of Economics, 124*(2), 809–842. doi:10.1162/qjec.2009.124.2.809

Cesarini, D., Johannesson, M., Lichtenstein, P., Sandewall, Ö., & Wallace, B. (2010). Genetic variation in financial decision-making. *The Journal of Finance, 65*(5), 1725–1754. doi:10.1111/j.1540-6261.2010.01592.x

Chabris, C. F., Hebert, B. M., Benjamin, D. J., Beauchamp, J., Cesarini, D., van der Loos, M., . . . Laibson, D. (2012). Most reported genetic associations with general intelligence are probably false positives. *Psychological Science, 23*(11), 1314–1323. doi:10.1177/0956797611435528

Chambers, J. C., Elliott, P., Zabaneh, D., Zhang, W., Li, Y., Froguel, P., . . . Kooner, J. S. (2008). Common genetic variation near MC4R is associated with waist circumference and insulin resistance. *Nature Genetics, 40*(6), 716–718. doi:10.1038/ng.156

Champagne, F. A., & Curley, J. P. (2009). Epigenetic mechanisms mediating the long-term effects of maternal care on development. *Neuroscience and Biobehavioral Reviews, 33*(4), 593–600.

Changeux, J.-P. (2010). Nicotine addiction and nicotinic receptors: Lessons from genetically modified mice. *Nature Reviews Neuroscience, 11*(6), 389–401. doi:10.1038/nrn2849

Chen, C. H., Gutierrez, E. D., Thompson, W., Panizzon, M. S., Jernigan, T. L., Eyler, L. T., . . . Dale, A. M. (2012). Hierarchical genetic organization of human cortical surface area. *Science, 335*(6076), 1634–1636. doi:10.1126/science.1215330

Chen, C. H., Panizzon, M. S., Eyler, L. T., Jernigan, T. L., Thompson, W., Fennema-Notestine, C., . . . Dale, A. M. (2012). Genetic influences on cortical regionalization in the human brain. *Neuron, 72*(4), 537–544. doi:10.1016/j.neuron.2011.08.021

Chen, D. T., Jiang, X., Akula, N., Shugart, Y. Y., Wendland, J. R., Steele, C. J. M., . . . McMahon, F. J. (2013). Genome-wide association study meta-analysis of European and Asian-ancestry samples identifies three novel loci associated with bipolar disorder. *Molecular Psychiatry, 18*(2), 195–205.

Cherny, S. S., Fulker, D. W., Emde, R. N., Robinson, J., Corley, R. P., Reznick, J. S., . . . DeFries, J. C. (1994). Continuity and change in infant shyness from 14 to 20 months. *Behavior Genetics, 24,* 365–379. doi:10.1007/BF01067538

Cherny, S. S., Fulker, D. W., & Hewitt, J. K. (1997). Cognitive development from infancy to middle childhood. In R. J. Sternberg & E. L. Grigorenko (Eds.), *Intelligence, heredity and environment* (pp. 463–482). Cambridge: Cambridge University Press.

Chesler, E. J. (2014). Out of the bottleneck: The Diversity Outcross and Collaborative Cross mouse populations in behavioral genetics research. *Mammalian Genome, 25*(1–2), 3–11.

Chesler, E. J., Lu, L., Shou, S., Qu, Y., Gu, J., Wang, J., . . . Williams, R. W. (2005). Complex trait analysis of gene expression uncovers polygenic and pleiotropic networks that modulate nervous system function. *Nature Genetics, 37*(3), 233–242.

Chesler, E. J., Miller, D. R., Branstetter, L. R., Galloway, L. D., Jackson, B. L., Philip, V. M., . . . Manly, K. F. (2008). The Collaborative Cross at Oak Ridge National Laboratory: Developing a powerful resource for systems genetics. *Mammalian Genome, 19*(6), 382–389. doi:10.1007/s00335-008-9135-8

Cheung, V. G., Conlin, L. K., Weber, T. M., Arcaro, M., Jen, K. Y., Morley, M., & Spielman, R. S.

(2003). Natural variation in human gene expression assessed in lymphoblastoid cells. *Nature Genetics, 33*(3), 422–425.

Chiang, M.-C., Barysheva, M., Shattuck, D. W., Lee, A. D., Madsen, S. K., Avedissian, C., . . . Thompson, P. M. (2009). Genetics of brain fiber architecture and intellectual performance. *Journal of Neuroscience, 29*(7), 2212–2224. doi:10.1523/jneurosci.4184-08.2009

Chipuer, H. M., & Plomin, R. (1992). Using siblings to identify shared and non-shared HOME items. *British Journal of Developmental Psychology, 10,* 165–178.

Chipuer, H. M., Rovine, M. J., & Plomin, R. (1990). LISREL modeling: Genetic and environmental influences on IQ revisited. *Intelligence, 14,* 11–29. doi:10.1016/0160-2896(90)90011-H

Cho, A. H., Killeya-Jones, L. A., O'Daniel, J. M., Kawamoto, K., Gallagher, P., Haga, S., . . . Ginsburg, G. S. (2012). Effect of genetic testing for risk of type 2 diabetes mellitus on health behaviors and outcomes: Study rationale, development and design. *BMC Health Services Research, 12,* 16. doi:10.1186/1472-6963-12-16

Chow, B. W.-Y., Ho, C. S.-H., Wong, S. W.-L., Waye, M. M. Y., & Bishop, D. V. M. (2011). Genetic and environmental influences on Chinese language and reading abilities. *PLoS One, 6*(2), e166040. doi:10.1371/journal.pone.0016640

Christensen, K., Frederiksen, H., Vaupel, J. W., & McGue, M. (2003a). Age trajectories of genetic variance in physical functioning: A longitudinal study of Danish twins aged 70 years and older. *Behavior Genetics, 33*(2), 125–136.

Christensen, K., Gaist, D., Vaupel, J. W., & McGue, M. (2002). Genetic contribution to rate of change in functional abilities among Danish twins aged 75 years or more. *American Journal of Epidemiology, 155*(2), 132–139.

Christensen, K., Holm, N. V., McGue, M., Corder, L., & Vaupel, J. W. (1999). A Danish population-based twin study on general health in the elderly. *Journal of Aging and Health, 11*(1), 49–64.

Christensen, K., Johnson, T. E., & Vaupel, J. W. (2006b). The quest for genetic determinants of human longevity: Challenges and insights. *Nature Review Genetics, 7*(6), 436–448.

Christensen, K., Petersen, I., Skytthe, A., Herskind, A. M., McGue, M., & Bingley, P. (2006a). Comparison of academic performance of twins and singletons in adolescence: Follow-up study. *British Medical Journal, 333*(7578), 1095–1097.

Christiansen, K. O. (1977). A preliminary study of criminality among twins. In S. Mednick & K. O. Christiansen (Eds.), *Biosocial bases of criminal behavior* (pp. 89–108). New York: Gardner Press, Inc.

Christiansen, L., Frederiksen, H., Schousboe, K., Skytthe, A., Wurmb-Schwark, N., Christensen, K., & Kyvik, K. (2003b). Age- and sex-differences in the validity of questionnaire-based zygosity in twins. *Twin Research, 6*(4), 275–278.

Chua, S. C., Jr., Chung, W. K., Wu-Peng, X. S., Zhang, Y., Liu, S. M., Tartaglia, L., & Leibel, R. L. (1996). Phenotypes of mouse *diabetes* and rat *fatty* due to mutations in the OB (leptin) receptor. *Science, 271*, 994–996.

Cirulli, E. T., Kasperaviciute, D., Attix, D. K., Need, A. C., Ge, D., Gibson, G., & Goldstein, D. B. (2010). Common genetic variation and performance on standardized cognitive tests. *European Journal of Human Genetics, 18*(7), 815–819. doi:10.1038/ejhg.2010.2

Civelek, M., & Lusis, A. J. (2014). Systems genetics approaches to understand complex traits. *Nature Reviews Genetics, 15*(1), 34–48.

Claridge, G., & Hewitt, J. K. (1987). A biometrical study of schizotypy in a normal population. *Personality and Individual Differences, 8*, 303–312.

Clementz, B. A., McDowell, J. E., & Zisook, S. (1994). Saccadic system functioning among schizophrenic patients and their first-degree biological relatives. *Journal of Abnormal Psychology, 103*, 277–287.

Cloninger, C. R. (1987). A systematic method for clinical description and classification of personality variants. A proposal. *Archives of General Psychiatry, 44*(6), 573–588.

Cloninger, C. R. (2002). The relevance of normal personality for psychiatrists. In J. Benjamin, R. Ebstein, & R. H. Belmaker (Eds.), *Molecular Genetics and Human Personality* (pp. 33–42). New York: American Psychiatric Press.

Cloninger, C. R., Bohman, M., & Sigvardsson, S. (1981). Inheritance of alcohol abuse: Cross-fostering analysis of adopted men. *Archives of General Psychiatry, 38*, 861–868.

Cloninger, C. R., Sigvardsson, S., Bohman, M., & von Knorring, A. L. (1982). Predisposition to petty criminality in Swedish adoptees: II. Cross fostering analysis of gene-environment interaction. *Archives of General Psychiatry, 39*, 1242–1247.

Cobb, J. P., Mindrinos, M. N., Miller-Graziano, C., Calvano, S. E., Baker, H. V., Xiao, W., . . . Young, V. (2005). Application of genome-wide expression analysis to human health and disease. *Proceedings of the National Academy of Sciences USA, 102*(13), 4801–4806.

Cohen, B. H. (1964). Family patterns of mortality and life span. *Quarterly Review of Biology, 39*, 130–181.

Cohen, P., Cohen, J., Kasen, S., Velez, C. N., Hartmark, C., Johnson, J., . . . Streuning, E. L. (1993). An epidemiological study of disorders in late childhood and adolescence: I. Age- and gender-specific prevalence. *Journal of Child Psychology and Psychiatry, 34*(6), 851–867.

Cohen-Woods, S., Craig, I. W., & McGuffin, P. (2013). The current state of play on the molecular genetics of depression. *Psychological Medicine, 43*(04), 673–687.

Colantuoni, C., Lipska, B. K., Ye, T. Z., Hyde, T. M., Tao, R., Leek, J. T., . . . Kleinman, J. E. (2011). Temporal dynamics and genetic control of transcription in the human prefrontal cortex. *Nature, 478*(7370), 519–523. doi:10.1038/nature10524

Collins, F. (2006). *The language of God: A scientist presents evidence for belief.* New York: Simon & Schuster.

Collins, F. S. (2010). *The language of life: DNA and the revolution in personalised medicine.* New York: Harper Collins.

Collins, F. S. (2015). Exceptional opportunities in medical science: A view from the National Institutes of Health. *JAMA, 313*(2), 131–132. doi:10.1001/jama.2014.16736

Colom, R., Rebollo, I., Abad, F. J., & Shih, P. C. (2006). Complex span tasks, simple span tasks, and cognitive abilities: A reanalysis of key studies. *Memory and Cognition, 34*(1), 158–171. doi:10.3758/bf03193395

Colvert, E., Tick, B., McEwen, F., Stewart, C., Curran, S. R., Woodhouse, E., . . . Garnett, T. (2015). Heritability of autism spectrum disorder in a UK population-based twin sample. *JAMA Psychiatry, 72*(5), 415–423.

Compton, W. M., Conway, K. P., Stinson, F. S., & Grant, B. F. (2006). Changes in the prevalence of major depression and comorbid substance use disorders in the United States between 1991–1992 and 2001–2002. *American Journal of Psychiatry, 163*(12), 2141–2147. doi:10.1176/appi.ajp.163.12.2141

Conrad, D. F., Pinto, D., Redon, R., Feuk, L., Gokcumen, O., Zhang, Y. J., . . . Hurles, M. E. (2010). Origins and functional impact of copy number variation in the human genome. *Nature, 464*(7289), 704–712.

CONVERGE Consortium, Cai, N., Bigdeli, T. B., Kretzschmar, W., Li, Y., Liang, J., . . . Hu, Z. (2015). Sparse whole-genome sequencing identifies two loci for major depressive disorder. *Nature, 523*, 588–591.

Cook, D., Nuro, E., & Murai, K. K. (2014). Increasing our understanding of human cognition through the study of Fragile X Syndrome. *Developmental Neurobiology, 74*(2), 147–177.

Cook, E. H., Jr., Courchesne, R. Y., Cox, N. J., Lord, C., Gonen, D., Guter, S. J., . . . Courchesne, E.

(1998). Linkage-disequilibrium mapping of autistic disorder, with 15q11-13 markers. *American Journal of Human Genetics, 62*(5), 1077–1083.

Coolidge, F. L., Thede, L. L., & Jang, K. L. (2001). Heritability of personality disorders in childhood: A preliminary investigation. *Journal of Personality Disorders, 15*(1), 33–40. doi:10.1521 /pedi.15.1.33.18645

Cooper, R. M., & Zubek, J. P. (1958). Effects of enriched and restricted early environments on the learning ability of bright and dull rats. *Canadian Journal of Psychology, 12*, 159–164.

Corder, E. H., Saunders, A. M., Strittmatter, W. J., Schmechel, D. E., Gaskell, P. C., Small, G. W., . . . Pericak Vance, M. A. (1993). Gene dose of apolipoprotein E type 4 allele and the risk of Alzheimer's disease in late onset families. *Science, 261*(5123), 921–923.

Coren, S. (2005). *The intelligence of dogs: A guide to the thoughts, emotions, and inner lives of our canine companions.* New York: Simon & Schuster.

Correa, C. R., & Cheung, V. G. (2004). Genetic variation in radiation-induced expression phenotypes. *American Journal of Human Genetics, 75*(5), 885–890.

Cortez, D., Marin, R., Toledo-Flores, D., Froidevaux, L., Liechti, A., Waters, P. D., . . . Kaessmann, H. (2014). Origins and functional evolution of Y chromosomes across mammals. *Nature, 508*(7497), 488–493. doi:10.1038 /nature13151

Costa, P. T., & McCrae, R. R. (1994). Stability and change in personality from adolescent through adulthood. In C. F. Haverson, Jr., G. A. Kohnstamm, & R. P. Martin (Eds.), *The developing structure of temperament and personality from infancy to adulthood* (pp. 139–150). Hillsdale, NJ: Erlbaum.

Crabbe, J. C. (2012). Translational behaviorgenetic studies of alcohol: Are we there yet? *Genes, Brain and Behavior, 11*(4), 375–386.

Crabbe, J. C., & Harris, R. A. (1991). *The genetic basis of alcohol and drug actions.* New York: Plenum.

Crabbe, J. C., Kendler, K. S., & Hitzemann, R. J. (2013). Modeling the diagnostic criteria for alcohol dependence with genetic animal models *Behavioral Neurobiology of Alcohol Addiction* (pp. 187–221): Springer.

Crabbe, J. C., Kosobud, A., Young, E. R., Tam, B. R., & McSwigan, J. D. (1985). Bidirectional selection for susceptibility to ethanol withdrawal seizures in *Mus musculus. Behavior Genetics, 15*, 521–536.

Crabbe, J. C., Phillips, T. J., & Belknap, J. K. (2010). The complexity of alcohol drinking: Studies in rodent genetic models. *Behavior Genetics, 40*(6), 737–750. doi:10.1007/s10519-010-9371-z

Crabbe, J. C., Phillips, T. J., Buck, K. J., Cunningham, C. L., & Belknap, J. K. (1999a). Identifying genes for alcohol and drug sensitivity: Recent progress and future directions. *Trends in Neurosciences, 22*, 173–179.

Crabbe, J. C., Phillips, T. J., Feller, D. J., Hen, R., Wenger, C. D., Lessov, C. N., & Schafer, G. L. (1996). Elevated alcohol consumption in null mutant mice lacking 5-HT 1B serotonin receptors. *Nature Genetics, 14*(1), 98–101.

Crabbe, J. C., Wahlsten, D., & Dudek, B. C. (1999b). Genetics of mouse behavior: Interactions with laboratory environment. *Science, 284*, 1670–1672.

Craddock, N., Owen, M. J., & O'Donovan, M. C. (2006). The catechol-O-methyl transferase (COMT) gene as a candidate for psychiatric phenotypes: evidence and lessons. *Molecular Psychiatry, 11*(5), 446–458.

Crawley, J. N. (2003). Behavioral phenotyping of rodents. *Comparative Medicine, 53*(2), 140–146.

Crawley, J. N. (2007). *What's wrong with my mouse: Behavioral phenotyping of transgenic and knockout mice* (Vol. 2). Wilmington, DE: Wiley-Liss.

Cretu, D., Diamandis, E. P., & Chandran, V. (2013). Delineating the synovial fluid proteome: Recent advancements and ongoing challenges in biomarker research. *Critical Reviews in Clinical Laboratory Sciences, 50*(2), 51–63. doi:10.3109 /10408363.2013.802408

Cross-Disorder Group of the Psychiatric Genomics Consortium. (2013a). Genetic relationship between five psychiatric disorders estimated from genome-wide SNPs. *Nature Genetics, 45*(9), 984–994.

Cross-Disorder Group of the Psychiatric Genomics Consortium. (2013b). Identification of risk loci with shared effects on five major psychiatric disorders: A genome-wide analysis. *The Lancet, 381*(9875), 1371–1379.

Crowe, R. R. (1972). The adopted offspring of women criminal offenders: A study of their arrest records. *Archives of General Psychiatry, 27*, 600–603.

Crowe, R. R. (1974). An adoption study of antisocial personality. *Archives of General Psychiatry, 31*, 785–791.

Crusio, W. E. (2004). Flanking gene and genetic background problems in genetically manipulated mice. *Biological Psychiatry, 56*(6), 381–385. doi:10.1016/j.biopsych.2003.12.026

Cumings, J. L., & Benson, D. F. (1992). *Dementia: A clinical approach.* Boston, MA: Butterworth.

Cutrona, C. E., Cadoret, R. J., Suhr, J. A., Richards, C. C., Troughton, E., Schutte, K., & Woodworth, G. (1994). Interpersonal variables in the prediction of alcoholism among adoptees—evidence for gene-environment interactions. *Comprehensive Psychiatry, 35*(3), 171–179. doi:10.1016/0010-440x(94)90188-0

D'Angelo, M. G., Lorusso, M. L., Civati, F., Comi, G. P., Magri, F., Del Bo, R., . . . Bresolin, N. (2011). Neurocognitive profiles in Duchenne muscular dystrophy and gene mutation site. *Pediatric Neurology, 45*(5), 292–299. doi:10.1016/j.pediatrneurol.2011.08.003

Dabelea, D., Mayer-Davis, E. J., Lamichhane, A. P., D'Agostino, R. B., Liese, A. D., Vehik, K. S., . . . Hamman, R. F. (2008). Association of intrauterine exposure to maternal diabetes and obesity with type 2 diabetes in youth—The SEARCH Case-Control Study. *Diabetes Care, 31*(7), 1422–1426. doi:10.2337/dc07-2417

Dale, P. S., Simonoff, E., Bishop, D. V. M., Eley, T. C., Oliver, B., Price, T. S., . . . Plomin, R. (1998). Genetic influence on language delay in two-year-old children. *Nature Neuroscience, 1*(4), 324–328. doi:10.1038/1142

Darvasi, A. (1998). Experimental strategies for the genetic dissection of complex traits in animal models. *Nature Genetics, 18,* 19–24.

Darwin, C. (1859). *On the origin of species by means of natural selection, or the preservation of favoured races in the struggle for life.* London: John Murray.

Darwin, C. (1868). *The variation of animals and plants under domestication* (Vol. 2): O. Judd.

Darwin, C. (1871). *The descent of man and selection in relation to sex.* London: John Murray.

Darwin, C. (1896). *Journal of researchers into the natural history and geology of the countries visited during the voyage of H. M. S. Beagle round the world under the command of Capt. Fitz Roy, T. N.* New York: Appleton.

Das, I., & Reeves, R. H. (2011). The use of mouse models to understand and improve cognitive deficits in Down syndrome. *Disease Models & Mechanisms, 4*(5), 596–606. doi:10.1242/dmm.007716

Davey Smith, G., & Ebrahim, S. (2003). "Mendelian randomization": Can genetic epidemiology contribute to understanding environmental determinants of disease? *International Journal of Epidemiology, 32*(1), 1–22.

Davey Smith, G., & Hemani, G. (2014). Mendelian randomization: genetic anchors for causal inference in epidemiological studies. *Human Molecular Genetics, 23*(R1), R89–R98.

Davidson, J. R. T., Hughes, D., Blazer, D. G., & George, L. (1991). Posttraumatic stress disorder in the community: An epidemiological study. *Psychological Medicine, 21,* 713–721.

Davies, G., Armstrong, N., Bis, J. C., Bressler, J., Chouraki, V., Giddaluru, S., . . . Lahti, J. (2015). Genetic contributions to variation in general cognitive function: A meta-analysis of genome-wide association studies in the CHARGE consortium (N=53949). *Molecular Psychiatry, 20*(2), 183–192.

Davies, G., Harris, S. E., Reynolds, C. A., Payton, A., Knight, H. M., Liewald, D. C., . . . Corley, J. (2012). A genome-wide association study implicates the APOE locus in nonpathological cognitive ageing. *Molecular Psychiatry, 19*(1), 76–87.

Davies, G., Tenesa, A., Payton, A., Yang, J., Harris, S. E., Liewald, D., . . . Deary, I. J. (2011). Genome-wide association studies establish that human intelligence is highly heritable and polygenic. *Molecular Psychiatry, 16*(10), 996–1005. doi:10.1038/mp.2011.85

Davis, O. S. P., Butcher, L. M., Docherty, S. J., Meaburn, E. M., Curtis, C. J. C., Simpson, A., . . . Plomin, R. (2010). A three-stage genome-wide association study of general cognitive ability: Hunting the small effects. *Behavior Genetics, 40,* 759–767. doi:10.1007/s10519-010-9350-4

Davis, O. S. P., Haworth, C. M. A., & Plomin, R. (2009). Learning abilities and disabilities: Generalist genes in early adolescence. *Cognitive Neuropsychiatry, 14,* 312–331. doi:10.1080/13546800902797106

Davis, R. L. (2011). Traces of *Drosophila* memory. *Neuron, 70*(1), 8–19. doi:10.1016/j.neuron.2011.03.012

Dawkins, R. (2006). *The god delusion.* London: Bantam Press.

Daxinger, L., & Whitelaw, E. (2012). Understanding transgenerational epigenetic inheritance via the gametes in mammals. *Nature Reviews Genetics, 13*(3), 153–162.

de Castro, J. M. (1999). Behavioral genetics of food intake regulation in free-living humans. *Nutrition, 15,* 550–554.

De Groot, M. J., Hoeksma, M., Blau, N., Reijngoud, D. J., & van Spronsen, F. J. (2010). Pathogenesis of cognitive dysfunction in phenylketonuria: review of hypotheses. *Molecular Genetics and Metabolism, 99,* S86–S89.

de Haan, M. J., Delucchi, K. L., Mathews, C. M., & Cath, D. C. (2015). Tic symptom dimensions and their heritabilities in Tourette's syndrome. *Psychiatric Genetics, 25*(3), 112–118.

de Moor, M. H. M., Costa, P. T., Terracciano, A., Krueger, R. F., de Geus, E. J. C., Toshiko, T., . . . Boomsma, D. I. (2012). Meta-analysis of genome-wide association studies for personality. *Molecular Psychiatry, 17*(3), 337–349. doi:10.1038/mp.2010.128

De Rubeis, S., & Buxbaum, J. D. (2015). Recent advances in the genetics of autism spectrum disorder. *Current Neurology and Neuroscience Reports, 15*(6), 1–9.

Deary, I. J. (2000). *Looking down on human intelligence: From psychometrics to the brain.* Oxford: Oxford University Press.

Deary, I. J. (2012). Intelligence. In S. T. Fiske, D. L. Schacter, & S. E. Taylor (Eds.), *Annual Review of Psychology* (Vol. 63, pp. 453–482).

Deary, I. J. (2013). Intelligence. *Current Biology, 23*(16), R673–R676. doi:http://dx.doi.org/10.1016/j.cub.2013.07.021

Deary, I. J., Penke, L., & Johnson, W. (2010). The neuroscience of human intelligence differences. *Nature Reviews Neuroscience, 11*(3), 201–211.

Debener, S., Ullsperger, M., Siegel, M., & Engel, A. K. (2006). Single-trial EEG-fMRI reveals the dynamics of cognitive function. *Trends in Cognitive Sciences, 10*(12), 558–563.

Deeb, S. S. (2006). Genetics of variation in human color vision and the retinal cone mosaic. *Current Opinion in Genetics & Development, 16*(3), 301–307. doi:http://dx.doi.org/10.1016/j.gde.2006.04.002

DeFries, J. C., & Fulker, D. W. (1985). Multiple regression analysis of twin data. *Behavior Genetics, 15*, 467–473. doi:10.1007/BF01066239

DeFries, J. C., Gervais, M. C., & Thomas, E. A. (1978). Response to 30 generations of selection for open-field activity in laboratory mice. *Behavior Genetics, 8*, 3–13.

DeFries, J. C., Johnson, R. C., Kuse, A. R., McClearn, G. E., Polovina, J., Vandenberg, S. G., & Wilson, J. R. (1979). Familial resemblance for specific cognitive abilities. *Behavior Genetics, 9*, 23–43.

DeFries, J. C., Knopik, V. S., & Wadsworth, S. J. (1999). Colorado Twin Study of reading disability. In D. D. Duane (Ed.), *Reading and attention disorders: Neurobiological correlates* (pp. 17–41). Baltimore, MD: York Press.

DeFries, J. C., Vandenberg, S. G., & McClearn, G. E. (1976). Genetics of specific cognitive abilities. *Annual Review of Genetics, 10*, 179–207.

DeFries, J. C., Vogler, G. P., & LaBuda, M. C. (1986). Colorado Family Reading Study: An overview. In J. L. Fuller & E. C. Simmel (Eds.), *Perspectives in Behavior Genetics* (pp. 29–56). Hillsdale, NJ: Erlbaum.

DeLisi, L. E., Mirsky, A. F., Buchsbaum, M. S., van Kammen, D. P., Berman, K. F., Caton, C., ... Karoum, F. (1984). The Genain quadruplets 25 years later: A diagnostic and biochemical followup. *Psychiatric Research, 13*, 59–76.

Dellava, J. E., Lichtenstein, P., & Kendler, K. S. (2012). Genetic variance of body mass index from childhood to early adulthood. *Behavior Genetics, 42*(1), 86–95. doi:10.1007/s10519-011-9486-x

Demirkan, A., Penninx, B. W., Hek, K., Wray, N. R., Amin, N., Aulchenko, Y. S., ... Middeldorp, C. M. (2011). Genetic risk profiles for depression and anxiety in adult and elderly cohorts. *Molecular Psychiatry, 16*(7), 773–783. doi:10.1038/mp.2010.65

Dempster, E. L., Pidsley, R., Schalkwyk, L. C., Owens, S., Georgiades, A., Kane, F., ... Mill, J. (2011). Disease-associated epigenetic changes in monozygotic twins discordant for schizophrenia and bipolar disorder. *Human Molecular Genetics, 20*(24), 4786–4796. doi:10.1093/hmg/ddr416

den Braber, A., Zilhão, N. R., Fedko, I. O., Hottenga, J. J., Pool, R., Smit, D. J., ... Boomsma, D. I. (2016). Obsessive-compulsive symptoms in a large population-based twin-family sample are predicted by clinically based polygenic scores and by genome-wide SNPs. *Translational Psychiatry, 6*, e731. doi:10.1038/tp.2015.223

den Hoed, M., Brage, S., Zhao, J. H., Westgate, K., Nessa, A., Ekelund, U., ... Loos, R. J. F. (2013). Heritability of objectively assessed daily physical activity and sedentary behavior. *The American Journal of Clinical Nutrition, 98*(5), 1317–1325.

Deo, R., Nalls, M. A., Avery, C. L., Smith, J. G., Evans, D. S., Keller, M. F., ... Quibrera, P. M. (2013). Common genetic variation near the connexin-43 gene is associated with resting heart rate in African Americans: A genome-wide association study of 13,372 participants. *Heart Rhythm, 10*(3), 401–408.

Derks, E. M., Dolan, C. V., & Boomsma, D. I. (2006). A test of the equal environment assumption (EEA) in multivariate twin studies. *Twin Research and Human Genetics, 9*(3), 403–411.

Desai, M., Jellyman, J. K., & Ross, M. G. (2015). Epigenomics, gestational programming and risk of metabolic syndrome. *International Journal of Obesity, 39*(4), 633–641.

Devineni, A. V., & Heberlein, U. (2013). The evolution of *Drosophila melanogaster* as a model for alcohol research. *Annual Review of Neuroscience, 36*, 121–138.

Dewey, F. E., Grove, M. E., Pan, C., Goldstein, B. A., Bernstein, J. A., Chaib, H., ... David, S. P. (2014). Clinical interpretation and implications of whole-genome sequencing. *JAMA, 311*(10), 1035–1045.

Dick, D., Prescott, C. A., & McGue, M. (2009a). The genetics of substance use and substance use disorders. In Y.-K. Kim (Ed.), *Handbook of Behavior Genetics* (pp. 433–453).

Dick, D. M., Agrawal, A., Keller, M. C., Adkins, A., Aliev, F., Monroe, S., ... Sher, K. J. (2015). Candidate gene–environment interaction research reflections and recommendations. *Perspectives on Psychological Science, 10*(1), 37–59.

Dick, D. M., Cho, S. B., Latendresse, S. J., Aliev, F., Nurnberger, J. I., Edenberg, H. J., ... Bucholz, K.

(2014). Genetic influences on alcohol use across stages of development: GABRA2 and longitudinal trajectories of drunkenness from adolescence to young adulthood. *Addiction Biology, 19*(6), 1055–1064.

Dick, D. M., Latendresse, S. J., Lansford, J. E., Budde, J. P., Goate, A., Dodge, K. A., ... Bates, J. E. (2009b). Role of GABRA2 in trajectories of externalizing behavior across development and evidence of moderation by parental monitoring. *Archives of General Psychiatry, 66*(6), 649–657.

Dick, D. M., Meyers, J. L., Latendresse, S. J., Creemers, H. E., Lansford, J. E., Pettit, G. S., ... Huizink, A. C. (2011). CHRM2, parental monitoring, and adolescent externalizing behavior: Evidence for gene-environment interaction. *Psychological Science, 22*(4), 481–489. doi:10.1177/0956797611403318

Dick, D. M., Pagan, J. L., Viken, R., Purcell, S., Kaprio, J., Pulkkinen, L., & Rose, R. J. (2007). Changing environmental influences on substance use across development. *Twin Research and Human Genetics, 10*(2), 315–326. doi:10.1375/twin.10.2.315

Dick, D. M., Rose, R. J., Viken, R. J., Kaprio, J., & Koskenvuo, M. (2001). Exploring gene-environment interactions: Socioregional moderation of alcohol use. *Journal of Abnormal Psychology, 110*(4), 625–632.

Do, E. K., Prom-Wormley, E. C., Eaves, L. J., Silberg, J. L., Miles, D. R., & Maes, H. H. (2015). Genetic and environmental influences on smoking behavior across adolescence and young adulthood in the Virginia Twin Study of Adolescent Behavioral Development and the Transitions to Substance Abuse Follow-Up. *Twin Research and Human Genetics, 18*(01), 43–51.

Dobzhansky, T. (1964). *Heredity and the nature of man.* New York: Harcourt, Brace & World.

Docherty, S. J., Davis, O. S. P., Kovas, Y., Meaburn, E. L., Dale, P. S., Petrill, S. A., ... Plomin, R. (2010). A genome-wide association study identifies multiple loci associated with mathematics ability and disability. *Genes, Brain and Behavior, 9*(2), 234–247. doi:10.1111/j.1601-183X.2009.00553.x

Dodge, K. A., & Rutter, M. (2011). *Gene-environment interactions in developmental psychopathology.* New York: Guilford Press.

Doudna, J. A., & Charpentier, E. (2014). The new frontier of genome engineering with CRISPR-Cas9. *Science, 346*(6213). doi:10.1126/science.1258096.

Doyle, A. E., Biederman, J., Ferreira, M. A. R., Wong, P., Smoller, J. W., & Faraone, S. V. (2010). Suggestive linkage of the Child Behavior Checklist Juvenile Bipolar Disorder phenotype to 1p21, 6p21, and 8q21. *Journal of the American Academy of Child and Adolescent Psychiatry, 49*(4), 378–387. doi:10.1016/j.jaac.2010.01.008

Doyle, G. A., Schwebel, C. L., Ruiz, S. E., Chou, A. D., Lai, A. T., Wang, M. J., ... Ferraro, T. N. (2014). Analysis of candidate genes for morphine preference quantitative trait locus Mop2. *Neuroscience, 277*, 403–416.

Dubois, L., Ohm Kyvik, K., Girard, M., Tatone-Tokuda, F., Perusse, D., Hjelmborg, J., ... Martin, N. G. (2012). Genetic and environmental contributions to weight, height, and BMI from birth to 19 years of age: An international study of over 12,000 twin pairs. *PLoS One, 7*(2), e30153.

Duckworth, A., & Gross, J. J. (2014). Self-control and grit related but separable determinants of success. *Current Directions in Psychological Science, 23*(5), 319–325.

Duncan, A. E., Agrawal, A., Grant, J. D., Bucholz, K. K., Madden, P. A. F., & Heath, A. C. (2009). Genetic and environmental contributions to BMI in adolescent and young adult women. *Obesity, 17*(5), 1040–1043. doi:10.1038/oby.2008.643

Duncan, L. E., & Keller, M. C. (2011). A critical review of the first 10 years of candidate gene-by-environment interaction research in psychiatry. *American Journal of Psychiatry, 168*(10), 1041–1049. doi:10.1176/appi.ajp.2011.11020191

Dunn, J. F., & Plomin, R. (1990). *Separate lives: Why siblings are so different.* New York: Basic Books.

Duyme, M., Dumaret, A. C., & Tomkiewicz, S. (1999). How can we boost IQs of "dull children"?: A late adoption study. *Proceedings of the National Academy of Sciences of the United States of America, 96*, 8790–8794.

Dworkin, R. H. (1979). Genetic and environmental influences on person-situation interactions. *Journal of Research in Personality, 13*, 279–293.

Dworzynski, K., Remington, A., Rijsdijk, F., Howell, P., & Plomin, R. (2007). Genetic etiology in cases of recovered and persistent stuttering in an unselected, longitudinal sample of young twins. *American Journal of Speech-Language Pathology, 16*(2), 169–178. doi:10.1044/1058-0360(2007/021)

Eaves, L., Foley, D., & Silberg, J. (2003). Has the "Equal Environments" assumption been tested in twin studies? *Twin Research, 6*(6), 486–489.

Eaves, L. J. (1976). A model for sibling effects in man. *Heredity, 36*, 205–214.

Eaves, L. J., D'Onofrio, B., & Russell, R. (1999a). Transmission of religion and attitudes. *Twin Research, 2*, 59–61.

Eaves, L. J., Eysenck, H., & Martin, N. G. (1989). *Genes, culture, and personality: An empirical approach.* London: Academic Press.

Eaves, L. J., & Eysenck, H. J. (1976). Genetical and environmental components of inconsistency and unrepeatability in twins' responses to a neuroticism questionnaire. *Behavior Genetics, 6*, 145–160.

Eaves, L. J., Heath, A. C., Martin, N. G., Maes, H., Neale, M., Kendler, K., . . . Corey, L. (1999b). Comparing the biological and cultural inheritance of personality and social attitudes in the Virginia 30,000 study of twins and their relatives. *Twin Research, 2,* 62–80.

Eaves, L. J., Heath, A. C., Neale, M. C., Hewitt, J. K., & Martin, N. G. (1998). Sex differences and non-additivity in the effects of genes in personality. *Twin Research, 1,* 131–137.

Eaves, L. J., Kendler, K. S., & Schulz, S. C. (1986). The familial sporadic classification: Its power for the resolution of genetic and environmental etiological factors. *Journal of Psychiatric Research, 20,* 115–130.

Eaves, L. J., Prom, E. C., & Silberg, J. L. (2010). The mediating effect of parental neglect on adolescent and young adult anti-sociality: A longitudinal study of twins and their parents. *Behavior Genetics, 40*(4), 425–437. doi:10.1007/s10519-010-9336-2

Eaves, L. J., Silberg, J. L., Meyer, J. M., Maes, H. H., Simonoff, E., Pickles, A., . . . Hewitt, J. K. (1997). Genetics and developmental psychopathology: 2. The main effects of genes and environment on behavioral problems in the Virginia Twin Study of Adolescent Behavioral Development. *Journal of Child Psychology and Psychiatry, 38*(8), 965–980.

Ebstein, R. P., Novick, O., Umansky, R., Priel, B., Osher, Y., Blaine, D., . . . Belmaker, R. H. (1996). Dopamine D 4 receptor (D 4 DR) exon III polymorphism associated with the human personality trait novelty-seeking. *Nature Genetics, 12,* 78–80.

Edwards, S. L., Rapee, R. M., & Kennedy, S. (2010b). Prediction of anxiety symptoms in preschool-aged children: Examination of maternal and paternal perspectives. *Journal of Child Psychology and Psychiatry, 51*(3), 313–321. doi:10.1111/j.1469-7610.2009.02160.x

Egeland, J. A., Gerhard, D. S., Pauls, D. L., Sussex, J. N., Kidd, K. K., Allen, C. R., . . . Housman, D. E. (1987). Bipolar affective disorders linked to DNA markers on chromosome 11. *Nature, 325*(26), 783–787.

Eggum-Wilkens, N. D., Lemery-Chalfant, K., Aksan, N., & Goldsmith, H. H. (2015). Self-conscious shyness: Growth during toddlerhood, strong role of genetics, and no prediction from fearful shyness. *Infancy, 20*(2), 160–188.

Ehlers, C. L., Gilder, D. A., Wall, T. L., Phillips, E., Feiler, H., & Wilhelmsen, K. C. (2004). Genomic screen for loci associated with alcohol dependence in mission Indians. *American Journal of Medical Genetics Part B: Neuropsychiatric Genetics, 129B*(1), 110–115. doi:10.1002/ajmg.b.30057

Ehlers, C. L., Walter, N. A. R., Dick, D. M., Buck, K. J., & Crabbe, J. C. (2010). A comparison of selected quantitative trait loci associated with alcohol use phenotypes in humans and mouse models. *Addiction Biology, 15*(2), 185–199. doi:10.1111/j.1369-1600.2009.00195.x

Ehringer, M. A., Rhee, S. H., Young, S., Corley, R., & Hewitt, J. K. (2006). Genetic and environmental contributions to common psychopathologies of childhood and adolescence: A study of twins and their siblings. *Journal of Abnormal Child Psychology, 34*(1), 1–17. doi:10.1007/s10802-005-9000-0

Elam, K. K., Harold, G. T., Neiderhiser, J. M., Reiss, D., Shaw, D. S., Natsuaki, M. N., . . . Leve, L. D. (2014). Adoptive parent hostility and children's peer behavior problems: Examining the role of genetically informed child attributes on adoptive parent behavior. *Developmental Psychology, 50*(5), 1543–1552. doi:10.1037/a0035470

Eley, T. C., Bolton, D., O'Connor, T. G., Perrin, S., Smith, P., & Plomin, R. (2003). A twin study of anxiety-related behaviours in pre-school children. *Journal of Child Psychology and Psychiatry, 44*(7), 945–960. doi:10.1111/1469-7610.00179

Eley, T. C., Collier, D., & McGuffin, P. (2002). Anxiety and eating disorders. In P. McGuffin, M. J. Owen, & I. I. Gottesman (Eds.), *Psychiatric Genetics & Genomics* (pp. 303–340). Oxford: Oxford University Press.

Eley, T. C., Lichtenstein, P., & Stevenson, J. (1999). Sex differences in the aetiology of aggressive and non-aggressive antisocial behavior: Results from two twin studies. *Child Development, 70*(1), 155–168.

Eley, T. C., Rijsdijk, F. V., Perrin, S., O'Connor, T. G., & Bolton, D. (2008). A multivariate genetic analysis of specific phobia, separation anxiety and social phobia in early childhood. *Journal of Abnormal Child Psychology, 36*(6), 839–848. doi:10.1007/s10802-008-9216-x

Elfhag, K., & Rössner, S. (2005). Who succeeds in maintaining weight loss? A conceptual review of factors associated with weight loss maintenance and weight regain. *Obesity Reviews, 6*(1), 67–85. doi:10.1111/j.1467-789X.2005.00170.x

Enoch, M.-A. (2012). The influence of gene–environment interactions on the development of alcoholism and drug dependence. *Current Psychiatry Reports, 14*(2), 150–158.

Enoch, M.-A., Hodgkinson, C. A., Yuan, Q., Albaugh, B., Virkkunen, M., & Goldman, D. (2009). GABRG1 and GABRA2 as independent predictors for alcoholism in two populations. *Neuropsychopharmacology, 34*(5), 1245–1254. doi:10.1038/npp.2008.171

Enoch, M. A., Gorodetsky, E., Hodgkinson, C., Roy, A., & Goldman, D. (2011). Functional genetic variants that increase synaptic serotonin and 5-HT3 receptor sensitivity predict alcohol and drug dependence. *Molecular Psychiatry, 16*(11), 1139–1146. doi:10.1038/mp.2010.94

Erlenmeyer-Kimling, L. (1972). Gene-environment interactions and the variability of behavior. In L. Ehrman, G. S. Omenn, & E. Caspari (Eds.), *Genetics, Environment, and Behavior* (pp. 181–208). San Diego: Academic Press.

Erlenmeyer-Kimling, L., & Jarvik, L. F. (1963). Genetics and intelligence: A review. *Science, 142,* 1477–1479.

Erlenmeyer-Kimling, L., Squires-Wheeler, E., Adamo, U. H., Bassett, A. S., Cornblatt, B. A., Kestenbaum, C. J., . . . Gottesman, I. I. (1995). The New York high-risk project: Psychoses and cluster A personality disorders in offspring of schizophrenic parents at 23 years of follow-up. *Archives of General Psychiatry, 52,* 857–865.

Estourgie-van Burk, G. F., Bartels, M., van Beijsterveldt, T. C., Delemarre-van de Waal, H. A., & Boomsma, D. I. (2006). Body size in five-year-old twins: Heritability and comparison to singleton standards. *Twin Research and Human Genetics, 9*(5), 646–655.

Evans, W. E., & Relling, M. V. (2004). Moving towards individualized medicine with pharmacogenomics. *Nature., 429*(6990), 464–468.

Eyler, L. T., Prom-Wormley, E., Panizzon, M. S., Kaup, A. R., Fennema-Notestine, C., Neale, M. C., . . . Kremen, W. S. (2011). Genetic and environmental contributions to regional cortical surface area in humans: A magnetic resonance imaging twin study. *Cerebral Cortex, 21*(10), 2313–2321. doi:10.1093/cercor/bhr013

Eysenck, H. J. (1952). *The scientific study of personality.* London: Routledge & Kegan Paul.

Fagard, R., Bielen, E., & Amery, A. (1991). Heritability of aerobic power and anaerobic energy generation during exercise. *Journal of Applied Physiology, 70,* 357–362.

Fagnani, C., Fibiger, S., Skytthe, A., & Hjelmborg, J. V. B. (2011). Heritability and environmental effects for self-reported periods with stuttering: A twin study from Denmark. *Logopedics Phoniatrics Vocology, 36*(3), 114–120. doi:10.3109/14015439.2010.534503

Falchi, M., El-Sayed Moustafa, J. S., Takousis, P., Pesce, F., Bonnefond, A., Andersson-Assarsson, J. C., . . . Froguel, P. (2014). Low copy number of the salivary amylase gene predisposes to obesity. *Nature Genetics, 46*(5), 492–497. doi:10.1038/ng.2939

Falconer, D. S. (1965). The inheritance of liability to certain diseases estimated from the incidence among relatives. *Annals of Human Genetics, 29,* 51–76.

Falconer, D. S., & MacKay, T. F. C. (1996). *Introduction to quantitative genetics* (4th ed). Harlow, UK: Longman.

Faraone, S. V. (2004). Genetics of adult attention-deficit/hyperactivity disorder. *Psychiatric Clinics of North America, 27*(2), 303–321.

Faraone, S. V., Biederman, J., & Mick, E. (2006). The age-dependent decline of attention deficit hyperactivity disorder: A meta-analysis of follow-up studies. *Psychological Medicine, 36*(2), 159–165. doi:10.1017/s003329170500471x

Faraone, S. V., Biederman, J., & Monuteaux, M. C. (2000). Attention-deficit disorder and conduct disorder in girls: Evidence for a familial subtype. *Biological Psychiatry, 48*(1), 21–29.

Faraone, S. V., Perlis, R. H., Doyle, A. E., Smoller, J. W., Goralnick, J. J., Holmgren, M. A., & Sklar, P. (2005). Molecular genetics of attention-deficit/hyperactivity disorder. *Biological Psychiatry, 57*(11), 1313–1323.

Farmer, A., Scourfield, J., Martin, N., Cardno, A., & McGuffin, P. (1999). Is disabling fatigue in childhood influenced by genes? *Psychological Medicine, 29*(2), 279–282.

Farmer, A. E., McGuffin, P., & Gottesman, I. I. (1987). Twin concordance for DSM-III schizophrenia: Scrutinizing the validity of the definition. *Archives of General Psychiatry, 44,* 634–641.

Farooqi, I. S., Keogh, J. M., Yeo, G. S. H., Lank, E. J., Cheetham, T., & O'Rahilly, S. (2003). Clinical spectrum of obesity and mutations in the melanocortin 4 receptor gene. *New England Journal of Medicine, 348*(12), 1085–1095. doi:10.1056/NEJMoa022050

Farooqi, I. S., Wangensteen, T., Collins, S., Kimber, W., Matarese, G., Keogh, J. M., . . . O'Rahilly, S. (2007). Clinical and molecular genetic spectrum of congenital deficiency of the leptin receptor. *New England Journal of Medicine, 356*(3), 237–247. doi:10.1056/NEJMoa063988

Fazel, S., & Danesh, J. (2002). Serious mental disorder in 23,000 prisoners: a systematic review of 62 surveys. *The Lancet, 359*(9306), 545–550. doi:10.1016/s0140-6736(02)07740-1

Fearon, R. M., Reiss, D., Leve, L. D., Shaw, D. S., Scaramella, L. V., Ganiban, J. M., & Neiderhiser, J. M. (2015). Child-evoked maternal negativity from 9 to 27 months: Evidence of gene–environment correlation and its moderation by marital distress. *Development and Psychopathology, 27*(4 Pt 1), 1251-1265.

Fearon, R. M., van IJzendoorn, M. H., Fonagy, P., Bakermans-Kranenburg, M. J., Schuengel, C., & Bokhorst, C. L. (2006). In search of shared and nonshared environmental factors in security of attachment: A behavior-genetic study of the association between sensitivity and attachment security. *Developmental Psychology, 42*(6), 1026–1040.

Federenko, I. S., Schlotz, W., Kirschbaum, C., Bartels, M., Hellhammer, D. H., & Wust, S. (2006).

The heritability of perceived stress. *Psychological Medicine, 36*(3), 375–385.

Feigon, S. A., Waldman, I. D., Levy, F., & Hay, D. A. (2001). Genetic and environmental influences on separation anxiety disorder symptoms and their moderation by age and sex. *Behavior Genetics, 31*, 403–411.

Feinberg, M. E., Button, T. M. M., Neiderhiser, J. M., Reiss, D., & Hetherington, E. M. (2007). Parenting and adolescent antisocial behavior and depression: Evidence of genotype x parenting environment interaction. *Archives of General Psychiatry, 64*(4), 457–465. doi:10.1001/archpsyc.64.4.457

Felsenfeld, S., & Plomin, R. (1997). Epidemiological and offspring analyses of developmental speech disorders using data from the Colorado Adoption Project. *Journal of Speech, Language, and Hearing Research, 40*, 778–791.

Ferencz, B., & Gerritsen, L. (2015). Genetics and underlying pathology of dementia. *Neuropsychological Review, 25*(1), 113–124.

Ferentinos, P., Koukounari, A., Power, R., Rivera, M., Uher, R., Craddock, N., . . . Lewis, C. M. (2015). Familiality and SNP heritability of age at onset and episodicity in major depressive disorder. *Psychological Medicine, 45*(10), 2215–2225. doi:10.1017/S0033291715000215

Ferguson, C. J. (2010). Genetic contributions to antisocial personality and behavior: A meta-analytic review from an evolutionary perspective. *Journal of Social Psychology, 150*(2), 160–180.

Filiou, M. D., Turck, C. W., & Martins-de-Souza, D. (2011). Quantitative proteomics for investigating psychiatric disorders. *Proteomics Clinical Applications, 5*(1–2), 38–49. doi:10.1002/prca.201000060

Finkel, D., Ernsth-Bravell, M., & Pedersen, N. L. (2014a). Sex differences in genetic and environmental influences on longitudinal change in functional ability in late adulthood. *The Journals of Gerontology Series B: Psychological Sciences and Social Sciences, 70*(5), 709–717.

Finkel, D., Gerritsen, L., Reynolds, C. A., Dahl, A. K., & Pedersen, N. L. (2014b). Etiology of individual differences in human health and longevity. *Annual Review of Gerontology and Geriatrics, 34*(1), 189–227.

Finkel, D., & Pedersen, N. L. (2000). Contribution of age, genes, and environment to the relationship between perceptual speed and cognitive ability. *Psychology and Aging, 15*(1), 56–64. doi:10.1037/0882-7974.15.1.56

Finkel, D., & Pedersen, N. L. (2004). Processing speed and longitudinal trajectories of change for cognitive abilities: The Swedish Adoption/Twin Study of Aging. *Aging Neuropsychology and Cognition, 11*(2–3), 325–345.

Finkel, D., Pedersen, N. L., Berg, S., & Johansson, B. (2000). Quantitative genetic analysis of biobehavioral markers of aging in Swedish studies of adult twins. *Journal of Aging and Health, 12*(1), 47–68.

Finkel, D., Pedersen, N. L., Reynolds, C. A., Berg, S., De Faire, U., & Svartengren, M. (2003). Genetic and environmental influences on decline in biobehavioral markers of aging. *Behavior Genetics, 33*(2), 107–123.

Finkel, D., & Reynolds, C. A. (2009). Behavioral genetic investigations of cognitive aging. In Y.-K. Kim (Ed.), *Handbook of behavior genetics* (pp. 101–111). New York: Springer.

Finkel, D., & Reynolds, C. A. (2014). *Behavior genetics of cognition across the lifespan.* New York: Springer.

Finkel, D., Reynolds, C. A., McArdle, J. J., & Pedersen, N. L. (2005). The longitudinal relationship between processing speed and cognitive ability: Genetic and environmental influences. *Behavior Genetics, 35*(5), 535–549.

Finkel, D., Wille, D. E., & Matheny, A. P., Jr. (1998). Preliminary results from a twin study of infant–caregiver attachment. *Behavior Genetics, 28*, 1–8.

Finn, C. T., & Smoller, J. W. (2006). Genetic counseling in psychiatry. *Harvard Review of Psychiatry, 14*(2), 109–121.

Fisher, R. A. (1918). The correlation between relatives on the supposition of Mendelian inheritance. *Transactions of the Royal Society of Edinburgh, 52*, 399–433.

Fisher, S. E. (2010). Genetic susceptibility to stuttering. *New England Journal of Medicine, 362*(8), 750–752. doi:10.1056/NEJMe0912594

Fisher, S. E., & DeFries, J. C. (2002). Developmental dyslexia: Genetic dissection of a complex cognitive trait. *Nature Reviews Neuroscience, 3*, 767–780.

Fisher, S. E., & Vernes, S. C. (2015). Genetics and the language sciences. *Annual Review of Linguistics, 1*(1), 289–310.

Flachsbart, F., Caliebeb, A., Kleindorp, R., Blanche, H., von Eller-Eberstein, H., Nikolaus, S., . . . Nebel, A. (2009). Association of FOXO3A variation with human longevity confirmed in German centenarians. *Proceedings of the National Academy of Sciences of the United States of America, 106*(8), 2700–2705. doi:10.1073/pnas.0809594106

Flegal, K. M., Kit, B. K., Orpana, H., & Graubard, B. I. (2013). Association of all-cause mortality with overweight and obesity using standard body mass index categories: A systematic review and meta-analysis. *JAMA, 309*(1), 71-82. doi:10.1001/jama.2012.113905

Fletcher, R. (1990). *The Cyril Burt scandal: Case for the defense.* New York: Macmillan.

Flint, J., Corley, R., DeFries, J. C., Fulker, D. W., Gray, J. A., Miller, S., & Collins, A. C. (1995). A simple genetic basis for a complex psychological trait in laboratory mice. *Science, 269*(5229), 1432–1435.

Flint, J., & Kendler, K. S. (2014). The genetics of major depression. *Neuron, 81*(3), 484–503.

Flint, J., & Munafo, M. R. (2007). The endophenotype concept in psychiatric genetics. *Psychological Medicine, 37*(2), 163–180.

FlyAtlas 2. FlyAtlas 2. Retrieved from http://flyatlas.gla.ac.uk

FlyAtlas. FlyAtlas: The *Drosophila* gene expression atlas. Retrieved from http://flyatlas.org

Folsom, D., & Jeste, D. V. (2002). Schizophrenia in homeless persons: A systematic review of the literature. *Acta Psychiatrica Scandinavica, 105*(6), 404–413.

Folstein, S., & Rutter, M. (1977). Infantile autism: A genetic study of 21 twin pairs. *Journal of Child Psychology and Psychiatry, 18*, 297–321.

Fontaine, N. M. G., McCrory, E. J. P., Boivin, M., Moffitt, T. E., & Viding, E. (2011). Predictors and outcomes of joint trajectories of callous-unemotional traits and conduct problems in childhood. *Journal of Abnormal Psychology, 120*(3), 730–742. doi:10.1037/a0022620

Fontana, L., & Partridge, L. (2015). Promoting health and longevity through diet: From model organisms to humans. *Cell, 161*(1), 106–118.

Foroud, T., Edenberg, H. J., Goate, A., Rice, J., Flury, L., Koller, D. L., . . . Reich, T. (2000). Alcoholism susceptibility loci: Confirmation studies in a replicate sample and further mapping. *Alcoholism: Clinical and Experimental Research, 24*(7), 933–945. doi:10.1097/00000374-200007000-00001

Forsman, M., Lichtenstein, P., Andershed, H., & Larsson, H. (2010). A longitudinal twin study of the direction of effects between psychopathic personality and antisocial behaviour. *Journal of Child Psychology and Psychiatry, 51*(1), 39–47. doi:10.1111/j.1469-7610.2009.02141.x

Fountoulakis, M., & Kossida, S. (2006). Proteomics-driven progress in neurodegeneration research. *Electrophoresis, 27*(8), 1556–1573.

Fountoulakis, M., Tsangaris, G. T., Maris, A., & Lubec, G. (2005). The rat brain hippocampus proteome. *Journal of Chromatography B, 819*(1), 115–129.

Fowler, J. H., Baker, L. A., & Dawes, C. T. (2008). Genetic variation in political participation. *American Political Science Review, 102*(2), 233–248. doi:10.1017/s0003055408080209

Fowler, J. H., & Schreiber, D. (2008). Biology, politics, and the emerging science of human nature. *Science, 322*(5903), 912–914. doi:10.1126/science.1158188

Fowler, T., Lifford, K., Shelton, K., Rice, F., Thapar, A., Neale, M. C., . . . van den Bree, M. B. (2007). Exploring the relationship between genetic and environmental influences on initiation and progression of substance use. *Addiction, 102*(3), 413–422. doi:10.1111/j.1360-0443.2006.01694.x

Fraga, M. F., Ballestar, E., Paz, M. F., Ropero, S., Setien, F., Ballestar, M. L., . . . Esteller, M. (2005). Epigenetic differences arise during the lifetime of monozygotic twins. *Proceedings of the National Academy of Sciences (USA), 102*(30), 10604–10609.

Franić, S., Borsboom, D., Dolan, C. V., & Boomsma, D. I. (2014a). The Big Five personality traits: Psychological entities or statistical constructs? *Behavior Genetics, 44*(6), 591–604.

Franić, S., Dolan, C. V., Borsboom, D., van Beijsterveldt, C. E. M., & Boomsma, D. I. (2014b). Three-and-a-half-factor model? The genetic and environmental structure of the CBCL/6–18 internalizing grouping. *Behavior Genetics, 44*(3), 254–268.

Franić, S., Dolan, C. V., Broxholme, J., Hu, H., Zemojtel, T., Davies, G. E., . . . Hottenga, J.-J. (2015). Mendelian and polygenic inheritance of intelligence: A common set of causal genes? Using next-generation sequencing to examine the effects of 168 intellectual disability genes on normal-range intelligence. *Intelligence, 49*, 10–22.

Franić, S., Middeldorp, C. M., Dolan, C. V., Ligthart, L., & Boomsma, D. I. (2010). Childhood and adolescent anxiety and depression: Beyond heritability. *Journal of the American Academy of Child and Adolescent Psychiatry, 49*(8), 820–829. doi:10.1016/j.jaac.2010.05.013

Frank, J., Cichon, S., Treutlein, J., Ridinger, M., Mattheisen, M., Hoffmann, P., . . . Zill, P. (2012). Genome-wide significant association between alcohol dependence and a variant in the ADH gene cluster. *Addiction Biology, 17*(1), 171–180.

Franz, C. E., Finkel, D., Panizzon, M. S., Spoon, K., Christensen, K., Gatz, M., . . . IGEMS Consortium. (2016). Facets of subjective health from early adulthood to old age. *Journal of Aging and Health.* doi:10.1177/0898264315625488

Franz, C. E., Lyons, M. J., O'Brien, R., Panizzon, M. S., Kim, K., Bhat, R., . . . Xian, H. (2011). A 35-year longitudinal assessment of cognition and midlife depression symptoms: The Vietnam Era Twin Study of Aging. *The American Journal of Geriatric Psychiatry, 19*(6), 559–570.

Frayling, T. M., Timpson, N. J., Weedon, M. N., Zeggini, E., Freathy, R. M., Lindgren, C. M., . . . McCarthy, M. I. (2007). A common variant in the FTO gene is associated with Body Mass Index and predisposes to childhood and adult obesity. *Science, 316,* 889–894.

Frazer, K. A., Ballinger, D. G., Cox, D. R., Hinds, D. A., Stuve, L. L., Gibbs, R. A., . . . Skol, A. (2007). A second generation human haplotype map of over 3.1 million SNPs. *Nature, 449*(7164), 851–853. doi:10.1038/nature06258

Frazier, T. W., Thompson, L., Youngstrom, E. A., Law, P., Hardan, A. Y., Eng, C., & Morris, N. (2014). A twin study of heritable and shared environmental contributions to autism. *Journal of Autism and Developmental Disorders, 44*(8), 2013–2025.

Frederiksen, H., Gaist, D., Christian Petersen, H., Hjelmborg, J., McGue, M., Vaupel, J. W., & Christensen, K. (2002). Hand grip strength: A phenotype suitable for identifying genetic variants affecting mid- and late-life physical functioning. *Genetic Epidemiology, 23*(2), 110–122.

Freitag, C. M. (2007). The genetics of autistic disorders and its clinical relevance: A review of the literature. *Molecular Psychiatry, 12*(1), 2–22.

Friedman, N. P., Miyake, A., Corley, R. P., Young, S. E., DeFries, J. C., & Hewitt, J. K. (2006). Not all executive functions are related to intelligence. *Psychological Science, 17*(2), 172–179. doi:10.1111/j.1467-9280.2006.01681.x

Friedman, N. P., Miyake, A., Young, S. E., DeFries, J. C., Corley, R. P., & Hewitt, J. K. (2008). Individual differences in executive functions are almost entirely genetic in origin. *Journal of Experimental Psychology-General, 137*(2), 201–225. doi:10.1037/0096-3445.137.2.201

Fromer, M., Pocklington, A. J., Kavanagh, D. H., Williams, H. J., Dwyer, S., Gormley, P., . . . Ruderfer, D. M. (2014). De novo mutations in schizophrenia implicate synaptic networks. *Nature, 506*(7487), 179–184.

Fu, Q. A., Heath, A. C., Bucholz, K. K., Nelson, E., Goldberg, J., Lyons, M. J., . . . Eisen, S. A. (2002). Shared genetic risk of major depression, alcohol dependence, and marijuana dependence: Contribution of antisocial personality disorder in men. *Archives of General Psychiatry, 59*(12), 1125–1132. doi:10.1001/archpsyc.59.12.1125

Fuller, J. L., & Thompson, W. R. (1960). *Behavior genetics.* New York: Wiley.

Fuller, J. L., & Thompson, W. R. (1978). *Foundations of behavior genetics.* St Louis, MO: Mosby.

Fullerton, J. (2006). New approaches to the genetic analysis of neuroticism and anxiety. *Behavior Genetics, 36*(1), 147–161.

Fullerton, J., Cubin, M., Tiwari, H., Wang, C., Bomhra, A., Davidson, S., . . . Flint, J. (2003). Linkage analysis of extremely discordant and concordant sibling pairs identifies quantitative-trait loci that influence variation in the human personality trait neuroticism. *American Journal of Human Genetics, 72*(4), 879–890.

Fyer, A. J., Hamilton, S. P., Durner, M., Haghighi, F., Heiman, G. A., Costa, R., . . . Knowles, J. A. (2006). A third-pass genome scan in panic disorder: Evidence for multiple susceptibility loci. *Biological Psychiatry, 60*(4), 388–401.

Fyer, A. J., Mannuzza, S., Chapman, T. F., Martin, L. Y., & Klein, D. F. (1995). Specificity in familial aggregation of phobic disorders. *Archives of General Psychiatry, 52*(7), 564–573.

Gallagher, E. J., & LeRoith, D. (2015). Obesity and diabetes: The increased risk of cancer and cancer-related mortality. *Physiological Reviews, 95*(3), 727–748.

Galton, F. (1865). Hereditary talent and character. *Macmillan's Magazine, 12,* 157–166 & 318–327.

Galton, F. (1869). *Hereditary genius: An enquiry into its laws and consequences.* Cleveland, OH: World.

Galton, F. (1876). The history of twins as a criterion of the relative powers of nature and nurture. *Royal Anthropological Institute of Great Britain and Ireland Journal, 6,* 391–406.

Galton, F. (1883). *Inquiries into human faculty and its development.* London: Macmillan.

Ganiban, J. M., Chou, C., Haddad, S., Lichtenstein, P., Reiss, D., Spotts, E. L., & Neiderhiser, J. M. (2009a). Using behavior genetics methods to understand the structure of personality. *European Journal of Developmental Science, 3*(2), 195–214.

Ganiban, J. M., Ulbricht, J. A., Spotts, E. L., Lichtenstein, P., Reiss, D., Hansson, K., & Neiderhiser, J. M. (2009b). Understanding the role of personality in explaining associations between marital quality and parenting. *Journal of Family Psychology, 23*(5), 646–660. doi:10.1037/a0016091

Gao, W., Li, L., Cao, W., Zhan, S., Lv, J., Qin, Y., . . . Hu, Y. (2006). Determination of zygosity by questionnaire and physical features comparison in Chinese adult twins. *Twin Research and Human Genetics, 9*(2), 266–271.

Gatt, J. M., Burton, K. L., Williams, L. M., & Schofield, P. R. (2015). Specific and common genes implicated across major mental disorders: A review of meta-analysis studies. *Journal of Psychiatric Research, 60,* 1–13.

Gatz, M., Jang, J. Y., Karlsson, I. K., & Pedersen, N. L. (2014). Dementia: Genes, environments, interactions. In D. Finkel & C. A. Reynolds (Eds.), *Behavior genetics of cognition across the lifespan* (pp. 201–231). New York: Springer.

Gatz, M., Pedersen, N. L., Berg, S., Johansson, B., Johansson, K., Mortimer, J. A., . . . Ahlbom, A.

(1997). Heritability for Alzheimer's disease: The study of dementia in Swedish twins. *Journals of Gerontology Series A: Biological Science and Medical Science, 52,* M117–M125.

Gatz, M., Pedersen, N. L., Plomin, R., Nesselroade, J. R., & McClearn, G. E. (1992). Importance of shared genes and shared environments for symptoms of depression in older adults. *Journal of Abnormal Psychology, 101,* 701–708. doi:10.1037/0021-843X.101.4.701

Gatz, M., Reynolds, C. A., Finkel, D., Pedersen, N. L., & Walters, E. (2010). Dementia in Swedish twins: Predicting incident cases. *Behavior Genetics, 40*(6), 768–775.

Gatz, M., Reynolds, C. A., Fratiglioni, L., Johansson, B., Mortimer, J. A., Berg, S., . . . Pedersen, N. L. (2006). Role of genes and environments for explaining Alzheimer disease. *Archives of General Psychiatry, 63*(2), 168–174.

Gavrilov, K., & Saltzman, W. M. (2012). Therapeutic siRNA: Principles, challenges, and strategies. *The Yale Journal of Biology and Medicine, 85*(2), 187.

Gayán, J., Willcutt, E. G., Fisher, S. E., Francks, C., Cardon, L. R., Olson, R. K., . . . DeFries, J. C. (2005). Bivariate linkage scan for reading disability and attention-deficit/hyperactivity disorder localizes pleiotropic loci. *Journal of Child Psychology & Psychiatry, 46*(10), 1045–1056.

Ge, X., Natsuaki, M. N., Martin, D. M., Leve, L. D., Neiderhiser, J. M., Shaw, D. S., . . . Reiss, D. (2008). Bridging the divide: Openness in adoption and postadoption psychosocial adjustment among birth and adoptive parents. *Journal of Family Psychology, 22*(4), 529–540. doi:10.1037/a0012817

Gecz, J., Shoubridge, C., & Corbett, M. (2009). The genetic landscape of intellectual disability arising from chromosome X. *Trends in Genetics, 25*(7), 308–316. doi:10.1016/j.tig.2009.05.002

Gejman, P. V., Sanders, A. R., & Kendler, K. S. (2011). Genetics of schizophrenia: New findings and challenges. In A. Chakravarti & E. Green (Eds.), *Annual Review of Genomics and Human Genetics* (Vol. 12, pp. 121–144).

Gelernter, J., & Kranzler, H. R. (2010). Genetics of drug dependence. *Dialogues in Clinical Neuroscience, 12*(1), 77–84.

Gelernter, J., Kranzler, H. R., Panhuysen, C., Weiss, R. D., Brady, K., Poling, J., & Farrer, L. (2009). Dense genomewide linkage scan for alcohol dependence in African Americans: Significant linkage on chromosome 10. *Biological Psychiatry, 65*(2), 111–115. doi:10.1016/j.biopsych.2008.08.036

Gelernter, J., Kranzler, H. R., Sherva, R., Almasy, L., Koesterer, R., Smith, A. H., . . . Rujescu, D. (2014a). Genome-wide association study of alcohol dependence: Significant findings in African- and European-Americans including novel risk loci. *Molecular Psychiatry, 19*(1), 41–49.

Gelernter, J., Kranzler, H. R., Sherva, R., Koesterer, R., Almasy, L., Zhao, H., & Farrer, L. A. (2014b). Genome-wide association study of opioid dependence: Multiple associations mapped to calcium and potassium pathways. *Biological Psychiatry, 76*(1), 66–74.

Gelernter, J., Sherva, R., Koesterer, R., Almasy, L., Zhao, H., Kranzler, H. R., & Farrer, L. (2014c). Genome-wide association study of cocaine dependence and related traits: FAM53B identified as a risk gene. *Molecular Psychiatry, 19*(6), 717–723.

Gelhorn, H., Stallings, M., Young, S., Corley, R., Rhee, S. H., Christian, H., & Hewitt, J. (2006). Common and specific genetic influences on aggressive and nonaggressive conduct disorder domains. *Journal of the American Academic of Child and Adolescent Psychiatry, 45*(5), 570–577.

Genetics of Personality Consortium, de Moor, M. H. M., Van Den Berg, S. M., Verweij, K. J. H., Krueger, R. F., Luciano, M., . . . Amin, N. (2015). Meta-analysis of genome-wide association studies for neuroticism, and the polygenic association with major depressive disorder. *JAMA Psychiatry, 72*(7), 642–650.

Gentile, J. K., Ten Hoedt, A. E., & Bosch, A. M. (2010). Psychosocial aspects of PKU: Hidden disabilities—a review. *Molecular Genetics and Metabolism, 99,* S64–S67.

Geschwind, D. H. (2011). Genetics of autism spectrum disorders. *Trends in Cognitive Sciences, 15*(9), 409–416. doi:10.1016/j.tics.2011.07.003

Ghazalpour, A., Doss, S., Zhang, B., Wang, S., Plaisier, C., Castellanos, R., . . . Horvath, S. (2006). Integrating genetic and network analysis to characterize genes related to mouse weight. *PLoS Genetics, 2*(8), e130.

Ghosh, R., Bloom, J. S., Mohammadi, A., Schumer, M. E., Andolfatto, P., Ryu, W., & Kruglyak, L. (2015). Genetics of intra-species variation in avoidance behavior induced by a thermal stimulus in *C. elegans.* bioRxiv. doi:http://dx.doi.org/10.1101/014290

Gialluisi, A., Newbury, D. F., Wilcutt, E. G., Olson, R. K., DeFries, J. C., Brandler, W. M., . . . Simpson, N. H. (2014). Genome-wide screening for DNA variants associated with reading and language traits. *Genes, Brain and Behavior, 13*(7), 686–701.

Gibbs, R. A., Weinstock, G. M., Metzker, M. L., Muzny, D. M., Sodergren, E. J., Scherer, S., . . . Collins, F. (2004). Genome sequence of the Brown Norway rat yields insights into mammalian evolution. *Nature, 428*(6982), 493–521.

Giedd, J. N., Clasen, L. S., Wallace, G. L., Lenroot, R. K., Lerch, J. P., Wells, E. M., . . . Samango-Sprouse, C. A. (2007). XXY (Klinefelter syndrome): A pediatric quantitative brain magnetic resonance imaging case-control study. *Pediatrics, 119*(1), e232–e240.

Gilissen, C., Hehir-Kwa, J. Y., Thung, D. T., van de Vorst, M., van Bon, B. W. M., Willemsen, M. H., . . . Schenck, A. (2014). Genome sequencing identifies major causes of severe intellectual disability. *Nature, 511*(7509).

Gill, S. C., Butterworth, P., Rodgers, B., Anstey, K. J., Villamil, E., & Melzer, D. (2006). Mental health and the timing of men's retirement. *Social Psychiatry and Psychiatric Epidemiology, 41*(7), 515–522. doi:10.1007/s00127-006-0064-0

Gillespie, N. A., Zhu, G., Heath, A. C., Hickie, I. B., & Martin, N. G. (2000). The genetic aetiology of somatic distress. *Psychological Medicine, 30*(5), 1051–1061.

Gillham, N. W. (2001). *A life of Sir Francis Galton: From African exploration to the birth of Eugenics.* Oxford: Oxford University Press.

Gillis, J. J., Gilger, J. W., Pennington, B. F., & DeFries, J. C. (1992). Attention deficit disorder in reading-disabled twins: Evidence for a genetic etiology. *Journal of Abnormal Child Psychology, 20,* 303–315.

Giot, L., Bader, J. S., Brouwer, C., Chaudhuri, A., Kuang, B., Li, Y., . . . Rothberg, J. M. (2003). A protein interaction map of *Drosophila melanogaster. Science, 302*(5651), 1727–1736.

Giros, B., Jaber, M., Jones, S. R., Wightman, R. M., & Caron, M. G. (1996). Hyperlocomotion and indifference to cocaine and amphetamine in mice lacking the dopamine transporter. *Nature, 379,* 606–612.

Gizer, I. R., Ficks, C., & Waldman, I. D. (2009). Candidate gene studies of ADHD: A meta-analytic review. *Human Genetics, 126*(1), 51–90.

Glahn, D. C., Knowles, E. E. M., McKay, D. R., Sprooten, E., Raventós, H., Blangero, J., . . . Almasy, L. (2014). Arguments for the sake of endophenotypes: Examining common misconceptions about the use of endophenotypes in psychiatric genetics. *American Journal of Medical Genetics Part B: Neuropsychiatric Genetics, 165*(2), 122–130. doi:10.1002/ajmg.b.32221

Godinho, S. I., & Nolan, P. M. (2006). The role of mutagenesis in defining genes in behaviour. *European Journal of Human Genetics, 14*(6), 651–659.

Godino, L., Turchetti, D., Jackson, L., Hennessy, C., & Skirton, H. (2015). Impact of presymptomatic genetic testing on young adults: A systematic review. *European Journal of Human Genetics.* doi:10.1038/ejhg.2015.153

Goldberg, D. (2011). The heterogeneity of "major depression." *World Psychiatry, 10*(3), 226–228.

Goldberg, L. R. (1990). An alternative description of personality: The Big Five factor structure. *Journal of Personality and Social Psychology, 59,* 1216–1229.

Goldberg, T. E., & Weinberger, D. R. (2004). Genes and the parsing of cognitive processes. *Trends in Cognitive Science, 8*(7), 325–335.

Goldman, D., Oroszi, G., & Ducci, F. (2005). The genetics of addictions: Uncovering the genes. *Nature Review Genetics, 6*(7), 521–532.

Goldsmith, H. H. (1983). Genetic influences on personality from infancy to adulthood. *Child Development, 54,* 331–355.

Goldsmith, H. H., Buss, A. H., Plomin, R., Rothbart, M. K., Chess, S., Hinde, R. A., & McCall, R. B. (1987). Roundtable: What is temperament? Four approaches. *Child Development, 58,* 505–529. doi:10.2307/1130527

Goldsmith, H. H., & Campos, J. J. (1986). Fundamental issues in the study of early development: The Denver twin temperament study. In M. E. Lamb, A. L. Brown, & B. Rogoff (Eds.), *Advances in developmental psychology* (pp. 231–283). Hillsdale, NJ: Erlbaum.

Goldstein, D. B., Tate, S. K., & Sisodiya, S. M. (2003). Pharmacogenetics goes genomic. *Nature Review Genetics, 4*(12), 937–947.

Goode, E. L., Cherny, S. S., Christian, J. C., Jarvik, G. P., & De Andrade, M. (2007). Heritability of longitudinal measures of body mass index and lipid and lipoprotein levels in aging twins. *Twin Research and Human Genetics, 10*(05), 703–711.

Goodrich, Julia K., Waters, Jillian L., Poole, Angela C., Sutter, Jessica L., Koren, O., Blekhman, R., . . . Ley, Ruth E. (2014). Human genetics shape the gut microbiome. *Cell, 159*(4), 789–799. doi:http://dx.doi.org/10.1016/j.cell.2014.09.053

Goodwin, D. W., Schulsinger, F., Hermansen, L., Guze, S. B., & Winokur, G. (1973). Alcohol problems in adoptees raised apart from alcoholic biological parents. *Archives of General Psychiatry, 28*(2), 238–243.

Goodwin, D. W., Schulsinger, F., Knop, J., Mednick, S., & Guze, S. B. (1977). Alcoholism and depression in adopted-out daughters of alcoholics. *Archives of General Psychiatry, 34*(7), 751–755.

Gornick, M. C., Addington, A. M., Sporn, A., Gogtay, N., Greenstein, D., Lenane, M., . . . Straub, R. E. (2005). Dysbindin (DTNBP1, 6p22.3) is associated with childhood-onset psychosis and endophenotypes measured by the Premorbid Adjustment Scale (PAS). *Journal of Autism and Developmental Disorders, 35*(6), 831–838.

Gottesman, I. I. (1991). *Schizophrenia genesis: The origins of madness.* New York: Freeman.

Gottesman, I. I., & Bertelsen, A. (1989). Confirming unexpressed genotypes for schizophrenia. *Archives of General Psychiatry, 46,* 867–872.

Gottesman, I. I., & Gould, T. D. (2003). The endophenotype concept in psychiatry: Etymology and strategic intentions. *American Journal of Psychiatry, 160*(4), 636–645.

Gottfredson, L. S. (1997). Why g matters: The complexity of everyday life. *Intelligence, 24*(1), 79–132.

Gould, S. J. (2011). *Rocks of ages: Science and religion in the fullness of life.* New York: Ballantine.

Gould, T. D., & Gottesman, I. I. (2006). Psychiatric endophenotypes and the development of valid animal models. *Genes, Brain, and Behavior, 5*(2), 113–119.

Graff, M., Gordon-Larsen, P., Lim, U., Fowke, J. H., Love, S.-A., Fesinmeyer, M., ... Prentice, R. L. (2013). The influence of obesity-related single nucleotide polymorphisms on BMI across the life course: The PAGE study. *Diabetes, 62*(5), 1763–1767.

Granon, S., Faure, P., & Changeux, J. P. (2003). Executive and social behaviors under nicotinic receptor regulation. *Proceedings of the National Academy of Sciences of the United States of America, 100*(16), 9596–9601. doi:10.1073/pnas.1533498100

Grant, J. D., Heath, A. C., Bucholz, K. K., Madden, P. A. F., Agrawal, A., Statham, D. J., & Martin, N. G. (2007). Spousal concordance for alcohol dependence: Evidence for assortative mating or spousal interaction effects? *Alcoholism: Clinical and Experimental Research, 31*(5), 717–728. doi:10.1111/j.1530-0277.2007.00356.x

Grant, S. G., Marshall, M. C., Page, K. L., Cumiskey, M. A., & Armstrong, J. D. (2005). Synapse proteomics of multiprotein complexes: En route from genes to nervous system diseases. *Human Molecular Genetics, 14*(Spec No. 2, Sep 8), R225–R234.

Gratten, J., Wray, N. R., Keller, M. C., & Visscher, P. M. (2014). Large-scale genomics unveils the genetic architecture of psychiatric disorders. *Nature Neuroscience, 17*(6), 782–790.

Green, A. S., & Grahame, N. J. (2008). Ethanol drinking in rodents: Is free-choice drinking related to the reinforcing effects of ethanol? *Alcohol, 42*(1), 1–11. doi:10.1016/j.alcohol.2007.10.005

Green, E. D., & Guyer, M. S. (2011). Charting a course for genomic medicine from base pairs to bedside. *Nature, 470*(7333), 204–213. http://dx.doi.org/10.1038/

Green, R. C., Cupples, L. A., Go, R., Benke, K. S., Edeki, T., Griffith, P. A., ... Bachman, D.

(2002). Risk of dementia among white and African American relatives of patients with Alzheimer disease. *JAMA, 287*(3), 329–336.

Greenspan, R. J. (1995). Understanding the genetic construction of behavior. *Scientific American, 272,* 72–78.

Greenspoon, P. J., & Saklofske, D. H. (2001). Toward an integration of subjective well-being and psychopathology. *Social Indicators Research, 54*(1), 81–108. doi:10.2307/27526929

Gregory, S. G., Barlow, K. F., McLay, K. E., Kaul, R., Swarbreck, D., Dunham, A., ... Prigmore, E. (2006). The DNA sequence and biological annotation of human chromosome 1. *Nature, 441*(7091), 315–321.

Greven, C. U., Asherson, P., Rijsdijk, F. V., & Plomin, R. (2011a). A longitudinal twin study on the association between inattentive and hyperactive-impulsive ADHD symptoms. *Journal of Abnormal Child Psychology, 39*(5), 623–632. doi:10.1007/s10802-011-9513-7

Greven, C. U., Kovas, Y., Willcutt, E. G., Petrill, S. A., & Plomin, R. (2014). Evidence for shared genetic risk between ADHD symptoms and reduced mathematics ability: A twin study. *Journal of Child Psychology and Psychiatry, 55*(1), 39–48.

Greven, C. U., Rijsdijk, F. V., & Plomin, R. (2011b). A twin study of ADHD symptoms in early adolescence: Hyperactivity-impulsivity and inattentiveness show substantial genetic overlap but also genetic specificity. *Journal of Abnormal Child Psychology, 39*(2), 265–275. doi:10.1007/s10802-010-9451-9

Grilo, C. M., & Pogue-Geile, M. F. (1991). The nature of environmental influences on weight and obesity: A behavior genetic analysis. *Psychological Bulletin, 10,* 520–537.

Groenman, A. P., Oosterlaan, J., Rommelse, N., Franke, B., Roeyers, H., Oades, R. D., ... Faraone, S. V. (2013). Substance use disorders in adolescents with attention deficit hyperactivity disorder: A 4-year follow-up study. *Addiction, 108*(8), 1503–1511.

Grof, P., Duffy, A., Cavazzoni, P., Grof, E., Garnham, J., MacDougall, M., ... Alda, M. (2002). Is response to prophylactic lithium a familial trait? *Journal of Clinical Psychiatry, 63*(10), 942–947.

Grotewiel, M., & Bettinger, J. C. (2015). *Drosophila* and *Caenorhabditis elegans* as discovery platforms for genes involved in human alcohol use disorder. *Alcoholism: Clinical and Experimental Research, 39*(8), 1292–1311.

Grubb, S. C., Bult, C. J., & Bogue, M. A. (2014). Mouse phenome database. *Nucleic Acids Research, 42*(D1), D825–D834.

Guedj, F., Bianchi, D. W., & Delabar, J.-M. (2014). Prenatal treatment of Down syndrome: A reality? *Current Opinion in Obstetrics and Gynecology,* *26*(2), 92–103.

Guerrini, I., Quadri, G., & Thomson, A. D. (2014). Genetic and environmental interplay in risky drinking in adolescents: A literature review. *Alcohol and Alcoholism, 49*(2), 138–142.

Gunderson, E. P., Tsai, A. L., Selby, J. V., Caan, B., Mayer-Davis, E. J., & Risch, N. (2006). Twins of mistaken zygosity (TOMZ): Evidence for genetic contributions to dietary patterns and physiologic traits. *Twin Research and Human Genetics, 9*(4), 540–549.

Guo, S. (2004). Linking genes to brain, behavior and neurological diseases: What can we learn from zebrafish? *Genes, Brain, and Behavior, 3*(2), 63–74.

Gurung, R., & Prata, D. P. (2015). What is the impact of genome-wide supported risk variants for schizophrenia and bipolar disorder on brain structure and function? A systematic review. *Psychological Medicine, 45*(12), 2461–2480.

Gusella, J. F., Tazi, R. E., Anderson, M. A., Hobbs, W., Gibbons, K., Raschtchian, R., ... Wallace, M. R. (1984). DNA markers for nervous system diseases. *Science, 225,* 1320–1326.

Gusella, J. F., Wexler, N. S., Conneally, P. M., Naylor, S. L., Anderson, M. A., & Tanzi, R. E. (1983). A polymorphic DNA marker genetically linked to Huntington's disease. *Nature, 306,* 234–238.

Guthrie, R. (1996). The introduction of newborn screening for phenylketonuria. A personal history. *European Journal of Pediatrics, 155*(Suppl.1), S4–5.

Guze, S. B. (1993). Genetics of Briquet's syndrome and somatization disorder: A review of family, adoption and twin studies. *Annals of Clinical Psychiatry, 5,* 225–230.

Guze, S. B., Cloninger, C. R., Martin, R. L., & Clayton, P. J. (1986). A follow-up and family study of Briquet's syndrome. *British Journal of Psychiatry, 149,* 17–23.

GWAS Catalog. (2015). The NHGRI-EBI Catalog of published genome-wide association studies. Retrieved from http://www.ebi.ac.uk/gwas

Haberstick, B. C., Ehringer, M. A., Lessem, J. M., Hopfer, C. J., & Hewitt, J. K. (2011). Dizziness and the genetic influences on subjective experiences to initial cigarette use. *Addiction, 106*(2), 391–399. doi:10.1111/j.1360-0443.2010.03133.x

Haberstick, B. C., Timberlake, D., Ehringer, M. A., Lessem, J. M., Hopfer, C. J., Smolen, A., & Hewitt, J. K. (2007). Genes, time to first cigarette and nicotine dependence in a general population sample of young adults. *Addiction, 102*(4), 655–665.

Haimovich, A. D., Muir, P., & Isaacs, F. J. (2015). Genomes by design. *Nature Reviews Genetics, 16*(9), 501–516.

Halaas, J. L., Gajiwala, K. S., Maffei, M., Cohen, S. L., Chait, B. T., Rabinowitz, D., ... Friedman, J. M. (1995). Weight-reducing effects of the plasma protein encoded by the obese gene. *Science, 269,* 543–546.

Hall, F. S., Markou, A., Levin, E. D., & Uhl, G. R. (2012). Mouse models for studying genetic influences on factors determining smoking cessation success in humans. *Annals of the New York Academy of Sciences, 1248*(1), 39–70.

Hallett, V., Ronald, A., Rijsdijk, F., & Eley, T. C. (2009). Phenotypic and genetic differentiation of anxiety-related behaviors in middle childhood. *Depression and Anxiety, 26*(4), 316–324. doi:10.1002/da.20539

Hallgren, B. (1957). Enuresis, a clinical and genetic study. *Acta Psychiatrica Scandinavica Supplementum 114,* 1–159.

Hallmayer, J., Cleveland, S., Torres, A., Phillips, J., Cohen, B., Torigoe, T., ... Risch, N. (2011). Genetic heritability and shared environmental factors among twin pairs with autism. *Archives of General Psychiatry, 68*(11), 1095–1102. doi:10.1001/archgenpsychiatry.2011.76

Hamer, D. H., Hu, S., Magnuson, V. L., Hu, N., & Pattatucci, A. M. L. (1993). A linkage between DNA markers on the X chromosome and male sexual orientation. *Science, 2*(261), 321–327.

Hamilton, A. S., Lessov-Schlaggar, C. N., Cockburn, M. G., Unger, J. B., Cozen, W., & Mack, T. M. (2006). Gender differences in determinants of smoking initiation and persistence in California twins. *Cancer Epidemiology Biomarkers & Prevention, 15*(6), 1189–1197. doi:10.1158/1055-9965.epi-05-0675

Hannon, G. J. (2002). RNA interference. *Nature, 418*(6894), 244–251.

Hansen, E. E., Lozupone, C. A., Rey, F. E., Wu, M., Guruge, J. L., Narra, A., ... Gordon, J. I. (2011). Pan-genome of the dominant human gut-associated archaeon, *Methanobrevibacter smithii,* studied in twins. *Proceedings of the National Academy of Sciences of the United States of America, 108,* 4599–4606. doi:10.1073/pnas.1000071108

Hanson, D. R., & Gottesman, I. I. (1976). The genetics, if any, of infantile autism and childhood schizophrenia. *Journal of Autism and Developmental Disorders, 6*(3), 209–234.

Happé, F., Ronald, A., & Plomin, R. (2006). Time to give up on a single explanation for autism. *Nature Neuroscience, 9*(10), 1218–1220. doi:10.1038/nn1770

Harakeh, Z., Neiderhiser, J. M., Spotts, E. L., Engels, R. C., Scholte, R. H. J., & Reiss, D. (2008). Genetic factors contribute to the association between peers and young adults smoking:

Univariate and multivariate behavioral genetic analyses. *Addictive Behaviors, 33*(9), 1113–1122. doi:10.1016/j.addbeh.2008.02.017

Hare, R. D. (1993). *Without conscience: The disturbing world of psychopaths among us.* New York: Pocket Books.

Harlaar, N. (2006). *Individual differences in early reading achievement: Developmental insights from a twin study.* University of London.

Harlaar, N., Butcher, L. M., Meaburn, E., Sham, P., Craig, I. W., & Plomin, R. (2005a). A behavioural genomic analysis of DNA markers associated with general cognitive ability in 7-year-olds. *Journal of Child Psychology and Psychiatry, 46*(10), 1097–1107. doi:10.1111/j.1469-7610.2005.01515.x

Harlaar, N., Hayiou-Thomas, M. E., & Plomin, R. (2005b). Reading and general cognitive ability: A multivariate analysis of 7-year-old twins. *Scientific Studies of Reading, 9*(3), 197–218. doi:10.1207/s1532799xssr0903_2

Harold, G. T., Leve, L. D., Barrett, D., Elam, K., Neiderhiser, J. M., Natsuaki, M. N., ... Thapar, A. (2013). Biological and rearing mother influences on child ADHD symptoms: Revisiting the developmental interface between nature and nurture. *Journal of Child Psychology and Psychiatry, 54*(10), 1038–1046. doi:10.1111/jcpp.12100

Harper, J. M., Leathers, C. W., & Austad, S. N. (2006). Does caloric restriction extend life in wild mice? *Aging Cell, 5*(6), 441–449. doi:10.1111/j.1474-9726.2006.00236.x

Harris, J. R. (1998). *The nurture assumption: Why children turn out the way they do.* New York: The Free Press.

Harris, K. M., Halpern, C. T., Whitsel, E., Hussy, J., Tabor, J., Entzel, P., & Udry, J. R. (2009). The National Longitudinal Study of Adolescent Health: Research design.

Harris, T. W., Antoshechkin, I., Bieri, T., Blasiar, D., Chan, J., Chen, W. J., ... Sternberg, P. W. (2010). WormBase: A comprehensive resource for nematode research. *Nucleic Acids Research, 38,* D463–D467. doi:10.1093/nar/gkp952

Hart, A. B., & Kranzler, H. R. (2015). Alcohol dependence genetics: Lessons learned from genome-wide association studies (GWAS) and post-GWAS analyses. *Alcoholism: Clinical and Experimental Research, 39*(8), 1312–1327.

Harter, S. (1983). Developmental perspectives on the self-system. In E. M. Hetherington (Ed.), *Handbook of child psychology: Socialization, personality, and social development* (Vol. 4, pp. 275–385). New York: Wiley.

Hartwell, L., Goldberg, M., Fischer, J., Hood, L., & Aquadro, C. (2014). *Genetics: From genes to genomes* (5th ed.). New York: McGraw-Hill Higher Education.

Hatemi, P., Medland, S., Klemmensen, R., Oskarsson, S., Littvay, L., Dawes, C., ... Martin, N. (2014). Genetic influences on political ideologies: Twin analyses of 19 measures of political ideologies from five democracies and genome-wide findings from three populations. *Behavior Genetics, 44*(3), 282–294. doi:10.1007/s10519-014-9648-8

Hatemi, P. K., Alford, J. R., Hibbing, J. R., Martin, N. G., & Eaves, L. J. (2009). Is there a "party" in your genes? *Political Research Quarterly, 62*(3), 584–600. doi:10.1177/1065912908327606

Hatemi, P. K., & McDermot, R. (Eds.). (2011). *Man is by nature a political animal: Evolution, biology, and politics.* Chicago: University of Chicago Press.

Hatemi, P. K., & Verhulst, B. (2015). Political attitudes develop independently of personality traits. *PLoS One, 10*(3), e0118106.

Havekes, R., Meerlo, P., & Abel, T. (2015). Animal studies on the role of sleep in memory: From behavioral performance to molecular mechanisms. In P. Meerlo, R. M. Benca, & T. Abel (Eds.), *Sleep, neuronal plasticity and brain function* (Vol. 25, pp. 183–206). Berlin, Heidelberg: Springer.

Haworth, C. M. A., Davis, O. S. P., Hanscombe, K. B., Kovas, Y., Dale, P. S., & Plomin, R. (2013). Understanding the science-learning environment: A genetically sensitive approach. *Learning and Individual Differences, 23,* 145–150.

Haworth, C. M. A., Kovas, Y., Harlaar, N., Hayiou-Thomas, E. M., Petrill, S. A., Dale, P. S., & Plomin, R. (2009a). Generalist genes and learning disabilities: A multivariate genetic analysis of low performance in reading, mathematics, language and general cognitive ability in a sample of 8000 12-year-old twins. *Journal of Child Psychology and Psychiatry, 50,* 1318–1325. doi:10.1111/j.1469-7610.2009.02114.x

Haworth, C. M. A., & Plomin, R. (2011). Genetics and education: Towards a genetically sensitive classroom. In K. R. Harris, S. Graham, & T. Urdan (Eds.), *The American Psychological Association handbook of educational psychology* (pp. 529–559). Washington, DC: American Psychological Association.

Haworth, C. M. A., Wright, M. J., Luciano, M., Martin, N. G., de Geus, E. J. C., van Beijsterveldt, C. E. M., ... Plomin, R. (2010). The heritability of general cognitive ability increases linearly from childhood to young adulthood. *Molecular Psychiatry, 15*(11), 1112–1120. doi:10.1038/mp.2009.55

Hawrylycz, M. J., Lein, E. S., Guillozet-Bongaarts, A. L., Shen, E. H., Ng, L., Miller, J. A., ... Riley, Z. L. (2012). An anatomically comprehensive atlas of the adult human brain transcriptome. *Nature, 489*(7416), 391–399.

Hayden, E. C. (2014). The $1,000 genome. *Nature, 507*(7492), 294–295.

Heard, E., & Martienssen, R. A. (2014). Transgenerational epigenetic inheritance: Myths and mechanisms. *Cell, 157*(1), 95–109. doi:http://dx.doi.org/10.1016/j.cell.2014.02.045

Hearnshaw, L. S. (1979). *Cyril Burt, psychologist.* Ithaca, NY: Cornell University Press.

Heath, A. C., Jardine, R., Martin, N. G. (1989). Interactive effects of genotype and social environment on alcohol consumption in female twins. *Journal of Studies on Alcohol, 50*(1), 38–48.

Heath, A. C., Madden, P. A. F., Bucholz, K. K., Nelson, E. C., Todorov, A., Price, R. K., . . . Martin, N. G. (2003). Genetic and environmental risks of dependence on alcohol, tobacco, and other drugs. In R. Plomin, J. C. DeFries, I. W. Craig, & P. McGuffin (Eds.), *Behavioral genetics in the postgenomic era* (pp. 309–334). Washington, DC: American Psychological Association.

Heath, A. C., Martin, N. G., Lynskey, M. T., Todorov, A. A., & Madden, P. A. (2002). Estimating two-stage models for genetic influences on alcohol, tobacco or drug use initiation and dependence vulnerability in twin and family data. *Twin Research, 5*(2), 113–124.

Heath, A. C., Neale, M. C., Kessler, R. C., Eaves, L. J., & Kendler, K. S. (1992). Evidence for genetic influences on personality from self-reports and informant ratings. *Journal of Social and Personality Psychology, 63*, 85–96.

Hebb, D. O. (1949). *The organization of behavior.* New York: Wiley.

Hebebrand, J. (1992). A critical appraisal of X-linked bipolar illness: Evidence for the assumed mode of inheritance is lacking. *British Journal of Psychiatry, 160*, 7–11.

Heiman, N., Stallings, M. C., Young, S. E., & Hewitt, J. K. (2004). Investigating the genetic and environmental structure of Cloninger's personality dimensions in adolescence. *Twin Research, 7*(5), 462–470.

Heisenberg, M. (2003). Mushroom body memoir: From maps to models. *Nature Reviews Neuroscience, 4*(4), 266–275.

Heitmann, B. L., Kaprio, J., Harris, J. R., Rissanen, A., Korkeila, M., & Koskenvuo, M. (1997). Are genetic determinants of weight gain modified by leisure-time physical activity? A prospective study of Finnish twins. *American Journal of Clinical Nutrition, 66*, 672–678.

Heller, D. A., de Faire, U., Pedersen, N. L., Dahlen, G., & McClearn, G. E. (1993). Genetic and environmental influences on serum lipid levels in twins. *New England Journal of Medicine, 328*(16), 1150–1156.

Hemmings, S. M., & Stein, D. J. (2006). The current status of association studies in obsessive-compulsive disorder. *The Psychiatric Clinics of North America, 29*(2), 411–444.

Henderson, N. D. (1967). Prior treatment effects on open field behaviour of mice — A genetic analysis. *Animal Behaviour, 15*, 365–376.

Henderson, N. D. (1972). Relative effects of early rearing environment on discrimination learning in housemice. *Journal of Comparative and Physiological Psychology, 72*, 505–511.

Hensler, B. S., Schatschneider, C., Taylor, J., & Wagner, R. K. (2010). Behavioral genetic approach to the study of dyslexia. *Journal of Developmental and Behavioral Pediatrics, 31*(7), 525–532. doi:10.1097/DBP.0b013e3181ee4b70

Herlihy, A. S., & McLachlan, R. I. (2015). Screening for Klinefelter syndrome. *Current Opinion in Endocrinology, Diabetes and Obesity, 22*(3), 224–229.

Herrera, B. M., Keildson, S., & Lindgren, C. M. (2011). Genetics and epigenetics of obesity. *Maturitas, 69*(1), 41–49.

Herrnstein, R. J., & Murray, C. (1994). *The bell curve: Intelligence and class structure in American life.* New York: Free Press.

Hershberger, S. L., Lichtenstein, P., & Knox, S. S. (1994). Genetic and environmental influences on perceptions of organizational climate. *Journal of Applied Psychology, 79*, 24–33.

Hershberger, S. L., Plomin, R., & Pedersen, N. L. (1995). Traits and metatraits: Their reliability, stability, and shared genetic influence. *Journal of Personality and Social Psychology, 69*(4), 673–684. doi:10.1037/0022-3514.69.4.673

Heston, L. L. (1966). Psychiatric disorders in foster home reared children of schizophrenic mothers. *British Journal of Psychiatry, 112*, 819–825.

Hetherington, E. M., & Clingempeel, W. G. (1992). Coping with marital transitions: A family systems perspective. *Monographs of the Society for Research in Child Development, 57*(2–3), 1–238.

Hettema, J. M., Annas, P., Neale, M. C., Kendler, K. S., & Fredrikson, M. (2003). A twin study of the genetics of fear conditioning. *Archives of General Psychiatry, 60*(7), 702–708.

Hettema, J. M., Neale, M. C., & Kendler, K. S. (2001a). A review and meta-analysis of the genetic epidemiology of anxiety disorders. *American Journal of Psychiatry, 158*(10), 1568–1578.

Hettema, J. M., Neale, M. C., Myers, J. M., Prescott, C. A., Kendler, K. S., Hettema, J. M., . . . Kendler, K. S. (2006). A population-based twin study of the relationship between neuroticism and internalizing disorders. *American Journal of Psychiatry, 163*(5), 857–864.

Hettema, J. M., Prescott, C. A., & Kendler, K. S. (2001b). A population-based twin study of generalized anxiety disorder in men and women. *Journal of Nervous & Mental Disease, 189*(7), 413–420.

Hettema, J. M., Prescott, C. A., Myers, J. M., Neale, M. C., & Kendler, K. S. (2005). The structure of genetic and environmental risk factors for anxiety disorders in men and women. *Archives of General Psychiatry, 62*(2), 182–189.

Hicks, B. M., Foster, K. T., Iacono, W. G., & McGue, M. (2013). Genetic and environmental influences on the familial transmission of externalizing disorders in adoptive and twin offspring. *JAMA Psychiatry, 70*(10), 1076–1083.

Hicks, B. M., Krueger, R. F., Iacono, W. G., McGue, M., & Patrick, C. J. (2004). Family transmission and heritability of externalizing disorders: A twin-family study. *Archives of General Psychiatry, 61*(9), 922–928. doi:10.1001/archpsyc.61.9.922

Higuchi, S., Matsushita, S., Masaki, T., Yokoyama, A., Kimura, M., Suzuki, G., & Mochizuki, H. (2004). Influence of genetic variations of ethanol-metabolizing enzymes on phenotypes of alcohol-related disorders. In S. F. Ali, T. Nabeshima, & T. Yanagita (Eds.), *Current status of drug dependence/abuse studies: Cellular and molecular mechanisms of drugs of abuse and neurotoxicity* (Vol. 1025, pp. 472–480). New York Academy of Science.

Hill, S. Y. (2010). Neural plasticity, human genetics, and risk for alcohol dependence. *International Review of Neurobiology, 91*, 53–94. doi:10.1016/s0074-7742(10)91003-9

Hindorff, L. A., MacArthur, J., Morales, J., Junkins, H. A., Hall, P. N., Klemm, A. K., & Manolio, T. A. (2016). A catalog of published genome-wide association studies. Available at: http://www.genome.gove/gwastudies.

Hirschhorn, J. N., & Daly, M. J. (2005). Genome-wide association studies for common diseases and complex traits. *Nature Reviews Genetics, 6*(2), 95–108.

Hirschhorn, J. N., Lohmueller, K., Byrne, E., & Hirschhorn, K. (2002). A comprehensive review of genetic association studies. *Genetics in Medicine, 4*(2), 45–61.

Hjelmborg, J. V., Iachine, I., Skytthe, A., Vaupel, J. W., McGue, M., Koskenvuo, M., . . . Christensen, K. (2006). Genetic influence on human lifespan and longevity. *Human Genetics, 119*(3), 312–321.

Ho, M. K., & Tyndale, R. F. (2007). Overview of the pharmacogenomics of cigarette smoking. *Pharmacogenomics Journal, 7*(2), 81–98. doi:10.1038/sj.tpj.6500436

Hobcraft, J. (2006). The ABC of demographic behaviour: How the interplays of alleles, brains, and contexts over the life course should shape research aimed at understanding population processes. *Population Studies, 60*(2), 153–187.

Hobert, O. (2003). Behavioral plasticity in *C. elegans:* Paradigms, circuits, genes. *Journal of Neurobiology, 54*(1), 203–223.

Hochberg, Z., Feil, R., Constancia, M., Fraga, M., Junien, C., Carel, J. C., . . . Albertsson-Wikland, K. (2010). Child health, developmental plasticity, and epigenetic programming. *Endocrine Reviews, 32*(2), 159–224. doi:10.1210/er.2009-0039

Hogarth, W. (1735). A rake's progress (pp. Plate 8).

Hollingworth, P., Harold, D., Jones, L., Owen, M. J., & Williams, J. (2011). Alzheimer's disease genetics: Current knowledge and future challenges. *International Journal of Geriatric Psychiatry, 26*(8), 793–802. doi:10.1002/gps.2628

Hollister, J. M., Mednick, S. A., Brennan, P., & Cannon, T. D. (1994). Impaired autonomic nervous system habituation in those at genetic risk for schizophrenia. *Archives of General Psychiatry, 51*, 552–558.

Holmans, P., Weissman, M. M., Zubenko, G. S., Scheftner, W. A., Crowe, R. R., Depaulo, J. R., Jr., . . . Levinson, D. F. (2007). Genetics of recurrent early-onset major depression (GenRED): Final genome scan report. *American Journal of Psychiatry, 164*(2), 248–258.

Hong, D. S., Dunkin, B., & Reiss, A. L. (2011). Psychosocial functioning and social cognitive processing in girls with Turner syndrome. *Journal of Developmental and Behavioral Pediatrics, 32*(7), 512–520. doi:10.1097/DBP.0b013e3182255301

Hong, D. S., & Reiss, A. L. (2014). Cognitive and neurological aspects of sex chromosome aneuploidies. *The Lancet Neurology, 13*(3), 306–318.

Horwitz, B. N., Ganiban, J. M., Spotts, E. L., Lichtenstein, P., Reiss, D., & Neiderhiser, J. M. (2011). The role of aggressive personality and family relationships in explaining family conflict. *Journal of Family Psychology, 25*(2), 174–183. doi:10.1037/a0023049

Horwitz, B. N., Marceau, K., Narusyte, J., Ganiban, J., Spotts, E. L., Reiss, D., . . . Neiderhiser, J. M. (2015). Parental criticism is an environmental influence on adolescent somatic symptoms. *Journal of Family Psychology, 29*(2), 283.

Horwitz, B. N., & Neiderhiser, J. M. (2015). *Behavioral genetics of interpersonal relationships across the lifespan.* New York: Springer.

Hotta, Y., & Benzer, S. (1970). Genetic dissection of the *Drosophila* nervous system by means of mosaics. *Proceedings of the National Academy of Sciences, 67*, 1156–1163.

Hou, J., Chen, Z., Natsuaki, M. N., Li, X., Yang, X., Zhang, J., & Zhang, J. (2013). A longitudinal investigation of the associations among parenting, deviant peer affiliation, and externalizing behaviors: A monozygotic twin differences design. *Twin Research and Human Genetics, 16*(03), 698–706.

Houts, R. M., Caspi, A., Pianta, R. C., Arseneault, L., & Moffitt, T. E. (2010). The challenging pupil in the classroom: The effect of the child on the teacher. *Psychological Science, 21*(12), 1802–1810. doi:10.1177/0956797610388047

Howe, K., Clark, M. D., Torroja, C. F., Torrance, J., Berthelot, C., Muffato, M., . . . Matthews, L. (2013). The zebrafish reference genome sequence and its relationship to the human genome. *Nature, 496*(7446), 498–503.

Hu, C.-Y., Qian, Z.-Z., Gong, F.-F., Lu, S.-S., Feng, F., Wu, Y.-L., . . . Sun, Y.-H. (2014). Methylenetetrahydrofolate reductase (MTHFR) polymorphism susceptibility to schizophrenia and bipolar disorder: an updated meta-analysis. *Journal of Neural Transmission, 122*(2), 307–320.

Hu, S., Pattatucci, A. M. L., Patterson, C., Li, L., Fulker, D. W., Cherny, S. S., . . . Hamer, D. H. (1995). Linkage between sexual orientation and chromosome Xq28 in males but not in females. *Nature Genetics, 11*, 248–256.

Hublin, C., Kaprio, J., Partinen, M., & Koskenvuo, M. (1998). Nocturnal enuresis in a nationwide twin cohort. *Sleep, 21*(6), 579–585.

Hudziak, J. J. (2008). *Developmental psychopathology and wellness: Genetic and environmental influences.* Arlington, VA: American Psychiatric Publishing, Inc.

Hudziak, J. J., Derks, E. M., Althoff, R. R., Rettew, D. C., & Boomsma, D. I. (2005). The genetic and environmental contributions to attention deficit hyperactivity disorder as measured by the Conners' Rating Scales—revised. *American Journal of Psychiatry, 162*(9), 1614–1620.

Hudziak, J. J., Van Beijsterveldt, C. E., Althoff, R. R., Stanger, C., Rettew, D. C., Nelson, E. C., . . . Boomsma, D. I. (2004). Genetic and environmental contributions to the Child Behavior Checklist Obsessive-Compulsive Scale: A cross-cultural twin study. *Archives of General Psychiatry, 61*(6), 608–616.

Hulshoff Pol, H. E., Schnack, H. G., Posthuma, D., Mandl, R. C., Baare, W. F., van Oel, C., . . . Kahn, R. S. (2006). Genetic contributions to human brain morphology and intelligence. *Journal of Neuroscience, 26*(40), 10235–10242. doi:10.1523/jneurosci.1312-06.2006

Human Ageing Genomic Resources. (2016). Human ageing genomic resources. Retrieved from http://genomics.senescence.info/

Human Proteome Map. (2014). Human proteome map. Retrieved from http://humanproteomemap.org/

Human Proteome Organization. (2014). Human proteome project. Retrieved from http://www.thehpp.org

Hunt, E. B. (2011). *Human intelligence.* Cambridge, UK: Cambridge University Press.

Hur, Y.-M., & Craig, J. M. (2013). Twin registries worldwide: An important resource for scientific research. *Twin Research and Human Genetics, 16*(Special Issue 01), 1–12.

Hur, Y.-M., & Shin, J.-S. (2008). Effects of chorion type on genetic and environmental influences on height, weight, and body mass index in South Korean young twins. *Twin Research and Human Genetics, 11*(1), 63–69. doi:10.1375/twin.11.1.63

Husén, T. (1959). *Psychological twin research.* Stockholm: Almqvist & Wiksell.

Huszar, D., Lynch, C. A., Fairchild-Huntress, V., Dunmore, J. H., Fang, Q., Berkemeier, L. R., . . . Lee, F. (1997). Targeted disruption of the melanocortin-4 receptor results in obesity in mice. *Cell, 88*(1), 131–141. doi:10.1016/s0092-8674(00)81865-6

Idler, E. L., & Benyamini, Y. (1997). Self-rated health and mortality: A review of twenty-seven community studies. *Journal of Health and Social Behavior,* 21–37.

Iervolino, A. C., Pike, A., Manke, B., Reiss, D., Hetherington, E. M., & Plomin, R. (2002). Genetic and environmental influences on adolescent peer socialization: Evidence from two genetically sensitive designs. *Child Development, 73*(1), 162–175. doi:10.1111/1467-8624.00398

Illumina. (2015). HiSeq X series of sequencing systems. Retrieved from http://www.illumina.com/content/dam/illumina-marketing/documents/products/datasheets/datasheet-hiseq-x-ten.pdf

Inlow, J. K., & Restifo, L. L. (2004). Molecular and comparative genetics of mental retardation. *Genetics, 166*, 835–881.

International HapMap Project. International HapMap project. Retrieved from http://hapmap.ncbi.nlm.nih.gov

International Human Genome Sequencing Consortium. (2001). Initial sequencing and analysis of the human genome. *Nature, 409*, 860–921.

International Molecular Genetic Study of Autism Consortium. (1998). A full genome screen for autism with evidence for linkage to a region on chromosome 7q. *Human Molecular Genetics, 7*(3), 71–78.

Ioannides, A. A. (2006). Magnetoencephalography as a research tool in neuroscience: State of the art. *Neuroscientist, 12*(6), 524–544.

Ioannidis, J. P., Ntzani, E. E., Trikalinos, T. A., & Contopoulos-Ioannidis, D. G. (2001).

Replication validity of genetic association studies. *Nature Genetics, 29*(3), 306–309.

Ionita-Laza, I., Lee, S., Makarov, V., Buxbaum, Joseph D., & Lin, X. (2013). Sequence kernel association tests for the combined effect of rare and common variants. *American Journal of Human Genetics, 92*(6), 841–853. doi:10.1016/j.ajhg.2013.04.015

Irons, D. E., McGue, M., Iacono, W. G., & Oetting, W. S. (2007). Mendelian randomization: A novel test of the gateway hypothesis and models of gene-environment interplay. *Developmental Psychopathology, 19*(4), 1181–1195. doi:10.1017/s0954579407000612

Isometsä, E. (2014). Suicidal behaviour in mood disorders—who, when, and why? *Canadian Journal of Psychiatry, 59*(3), 120–130.

Jacob, H. J., & Kwitek, A. E. (2002). Rat genetics: Attaching physiology and pharmacology to the genome. *Nature Reviews Genetics, 3*(1), 33–42.

Jacobs, P. A. (2014). An opportune life: 50 years in human cytogenetics. *Annual Review of Genomics and Human Genetics, 15*, 29–46.

Jacobson, K. C., & Rowe, D. C. (1999). Genetic and environmental influences on the relationships between family connectedness, school connectedness, and adolescent depressed mood: Sex differences. *Developmental Psychology, 35*(4), 926–939.

Jacobson, P., Torgerson, J. S., Sjostrom, L., & Bouchard, C. (2007). Spouse resemblance in body mass index: Effects on adult obesity prevalence in the offspring generation. *American Journal of Epidemiology, 165*(1), 101–108.

Jaffee, S. R., Caspi, A., Moffitt, T. E., Dodge, K. A., Rutter, M., Taylor, A., & Tully, L. A. (2005). Nature × nurture: Genetic vulnerabilities interact with physical maltreatment to promote conduct problems. *Development and Psychopathology, 17*(1), 67–84.

Jaffee, S. R., & Price, T. S. (2007). Gene-environment correlations: A review of the evidence and implications for prevention of mental illness. *Molecular Psychiatry, 12*(5), 432–442.

Jaffee, S. R., Strait, L. B., & Odgers, C. L. (2012). From correlates to causes: Can quasi-experimental studies and statistical innovations bring us closer to identifying the causes of antisocial behavior? *Psychological Bulletin, 138*(2), 272–295. doi:10.1037/a0026020

Jang, K. L. (2005). *The behavioral genetics of psychopathology: A clinical guide.* Mahwah, NJ: Lawrence Erlbaum Associates.

Jang, K. L., Lam, R. W., Livesley, W. J., & Vernon, P. A. (1997). The relationship between seasonal mood change and personality: More apparent than real? *Acta Psychiatrica Scandinavica, 95*(6), 539–543.

Jang, K. L., Livesley, W. J., Ando, J., Yamagata, S., Suzuki, A., Angleitner, A., . . . Spinath, F. (2006). Behavioral genetics of the higher-order factors of the Big Five. *Personality and Individual Differences, 41*(2), 261–272.

Jang, K. L., Livesley, W. J., & Vernon, P. A. (1996). Heritability of the Big Five dimensions and their facets: A twin study. *Journal of Personality, 64*, 577–591.

Jang, K. L., McCrae, R. R., Angleitner, A., Riemann, R., & Livesley, W. J. (1998). Heritability of facet-level traits in a cross-cultural twin sample: Support for a hierarchical model of personality. *Journal of Personality and Social Psychology, 74*, 1556–1565.

Jang, K. L., Woodward, T. S., Lang, D., Honer, W. G., & Livesley, W. J. (2005). The genetic and environmental basis of the relationship between schizotypy and personality: A twin study. *Journal of Nervous & Mental Disease, 193*(3), 153–159.

Janzing, J. G., de Graaf, R., ten Have, M., Vollebergh, W. A., Verhagen, M., & Buitelaar, J. K. (2009). Familiality of depression in the community: Associations with gender and phenotype of major depressive disorder. *Social Psychiatry and Psychiatric Epidemiology, 44*(12), 1067–1074. doi:10.1007/s00127-009-0026-4

Jensen, A. R. (1978). Genetic and behavioural effects of nonrandom mating. In R. T. Osbourne, C. E. Noble, & N. Weyl (Eds.), *Human variation: The biopsychology of age, race, and sex* (pp. 51–105). New York: Academic Press.

Jensen, A. R. (1998). *The g factor: The science of mental ability.* Westport, CT: Praeger.

Jha, P., Ramasundarahettige, C., Landsman, V., Rostron, B., Thun, M., Anderson, R. N., . . . Peto, R. (2013). 21st-century hazards of smoking and benefits of cessation in the United States. *New England Journal of Medicine, 368*(4), 341–350.

Jinks, J. L., & Fulker, D. W. (1970). Comparison of the biometrical genetical, MAVA, and classical approaches to the analysis of human behavior. *Psychological Bulletin, 73*, 311–349.

John, O. P., Robins, R. W., & Pervin, L. A. (Eds.) (2008). *Handbook of personality: Theory and research* (3rd ed.). New York: Guilford Press.

Johnson, W., & Krueger, R. F. (2005). Genetic effects on physical health: Lower at higher income levels. *Behavior Genetics, 35*(5), 579–590. doi:10.1007/s10519-005-3598-0

Johnson, W., Krueger, R. F., Bouchard, T. J., Jr., & McGue, M. (2002a). The personalities of twins: Just ordinary folks. *Twin Research, 5*(2), 125–131.

Johnson, W., McGue, M., & Deary, I. J. (2014). Normative cognitive aging. In D. Finkel & C. A. Reynolds (Eds.), *Behavior genetics of cognition across the lifespan.* New York: Springer.

Johnson, W., McGue, M., Gaist, D., Vaupel, J. W., & Christensen, K. (2002b). Frequency and heritability of depression symptomatology in the second half of life: Evidence from Danish twins over 45. *Psychological Medicine, 32*(7), 1175–1185.

Johnson, W., McGue, M., & Krueger, R. F. (2005). Personality stability in late adulthood: A behavioral genetic analysis. *Journal of Personality, 73*(2), 523–552.

Johnson, W., McGue, M., Krueger, R. F., & Bouchard, T. J., Jr. (2004). Marriage and personality: A genetic analysis. *Journal of Personality and Social Psychology, 86*(2), 285–294.

Jones, L. J., & Norton, W. H. J. (2015). Using zebrafish to uncover the genetic and neural basis of aggression, a frequent comorbid symptom of psychiatric disorders. *Behavioural Brain Research, 276*, 171–180.

Jones, P. B., & Murray, R. M. (1991). Aberrant neurodevelopment as the expression of schizophrenia genotype. In P. McGuffin & R. Murray (Eds.), *The new genetics of mental illness* (pp. 112–129). Oxford: Butterworth-Heinemann.

Jones, S. (1999). *Almost like a whale: The origin of species, updated.* New York: Doubleday.

Jones, S. R., Gainetdinov, R. R., Jaber, M., Giros, B., Wightman, R. M., & Caron, M. G. (1998). Profound neuronal plasticity in response to inactivation of the dopamine transporter. *Proceedings of the National Academy of Sciences of the United States of America, 95*, 4029–4034.

Jordan, K. W., Morgan, T. J., & Mackay, T. F. (2006). Quantitative trait loci for locomotor behavior in *Drosophila* melanogaster. *Genetics, 174*(1), 271–284.

Joshi, A. A., Lepore, N., Joshi, S. H., Lee, A. D., Barysheva, M., Stein, J. L., . . . Thompson, P. M. (2011). The contribution of genes to cortical thickness and volume. *Neuroreport, 22*(3), 101–105. doi:10.1097/WNR.0b013e3283424c84

Joynson, R. B. (1989). *The Burt affair.* London: Routledge.

Judge, T. A., Ilies, R., & Zhang, Z. (2012). Genetic influences on core self-evaluations, job satisfaction, and work stress: A behavioral genetics mediated model. *Organizational Behavior and Human Decision Processes, 117*(1), 208–220.

Juraeva, D., Treutlein, J., Scholz, H., Frank, J., Degenhardt, F., Cichon, S., . . . Lang, M. (2015). XRCC5 as a risk gene for alcohol dependence: Evidence from a genome-wide gene-set-based analysis and follow-up studies in *Drosophila* and humans. *Neuropsychopharmacology, 40*(2), 361–371.

Kafkafi, N., Benjamini, Y., Sakov, A., Elmer, G. I., & Golani, I. (2005). Genotype-environment interactions in mouse behavior: A way out of the problem. *Proceedings of the National Academy of Sciences of the United States of America, 102*(12), 4619–4624.

Kallmann, F. J. (1952). Twin and sibship study of overt male homosexuality. *Journal of Human Genetics, 4*, 136–146.

Kallmann, F. J., & Kaplan, O. J. (1955). Genetic aspects of mental disorders in later life. In O. J. Kaplan (Ed.), *Mental disorders in later life* (pp. 26–46). Stanford CA: Stanford University Press.

Kallmann, F. J., & Roth, B. (1956). Genetic aspects of preadolescent schizophrenia. *American Journal of Psychiatry, 112*(8), 599–606.

Kalueff, A. V., Echevarria, D. J., & Stewart, A. M. (2014). Gaining translational momentum: More zebrafish models for neuroscience research. *Progress in Neuro-Psychopharmacology and Biological Psychiatry, 55*, 1–6.

Kamakura, T., Ando, J., & Ono, Y. (2007). Genetic and environmental effects of stability and change in self-esteem during adolescence. *Personality and Individual Differences, 42*(1), 181–190.

Kamin, L. J. (1974). *The science and politics of IQ.* Potomac, MD: Erlbaum.

Kan, K.-J., Dolan, C. V., Nivard, M. G., Middeldorp, C. M., van Beijsterveldt, C. E. M., Willemsen, G., & Boomsma, D. I. (2013). Genetic and environmental stability in attention problems across the lifespan: Evidence from the Netherlands twin register. *Journal of the American Academy of Child & Adolescent Psychiatry, 52*(1), 12–25.

Kandler, C., & Riemann, R. (2013). Genetic and environmental sources of individual religiousness: The roles of individual personality traits and perceived environmental religiousness. *Behavior Genetics, 43*(4), 297–313.

Kanner, L. (1943). Autistic disturbances of affective contact. *Nervous Child, 2*, 217–250.

Karanjawala, Z. E., & Collins, F. S. (1998). Genetics in the context of medical practice. *Journal of the American Medical Association, 280*, 1533–1544.

Karg, K., Burmeister, M., Shedden, K., & Sen, S. (2011). The serotonin transporter promoter variant (5-HTTLPR), stress, and depression meta-analysis revisited: Evidence of genetic moderation. *Archives of General Psychiatry, 68*(5), 444–454. doi:10.1001/archgenpsychiatry.2010.189

Karlsgodt, K. H., Bachman, P., Winkler, A. M., Bearden, C. E., & Glahn, D. C. (2011). Genetic influence on the working memory circuitry: Behavior, structure, function and extensions to illness. *Behavioural Brain Research, 225*(2), 610–622. doi:10.1016/j.bbr.2011.08.016

Kato, K., & Pedersen, N. L. (2005). Personality and coping: A study of twins reared apart and twins reared together. *Behavior Genetics, 35*(2), 147–158.

Kato, K., Sullivan, P. F., Evengard, B., & Pedersen, N. L. (2009). A population-based twin study of functional somatic syndromes. *Psychological Medicine, 39*(3), 497–505. doi:10.1017/s0033291708003784

Kato, K., Sullivan, P. F., & Pedersen, N. L. (2010). Latent class analysis of functional somatic symptoms in a population-based sample of twins. *Journal of Psychosomatic Research, 68*(5), 447–453. doi:10.1016/j.jpsychores.2010.01.010

Katon, W. J., Lin, E. H. B., Russo, J., Von Korff, M., Ciechonowski, P., Simon, G., . . . Young, B. (2004). Cardiac risk factors in patients with diabetes mellitus and major depression. *Journal of General Internal Medicine, 19*(12), 1192–1199. doi:10.1111/j.1525-1497.2004.30405.x

Kavanagh, D. H., Tansey, K. E., O'Donovan, M. C., & Owen, M. J. (2015). Schizophrenia genetics: Emerging themes for a complex disorder. *Molecular Psychiatry, 20*(1), 72–76.

Keller, L. M., Bouchard, T. J., Jr., Segal, N. L., & Dawes, R. V. (1992). Work values: Genetic and environmental influences. *Journal of Applied Psychology, 77*, 79–88.

Keller, M. C., Coventry, W. L., Heath, A. C., & Martin, N. G. (2005). Widespread evidence for non-additive genetic variation in Cloninger's and Eysenck's personality dimensions using a twin plus sibling design. *Behavioral Genetics, 35*(6), 707–721.

Keller, M. C., Garver-Apgar, C. E., Wright, M. J., Martin, N. G., Corley, R. P., Stallings, M. C., . . . Zietsch, B. P. (2013). The genetic correlation between height and IQ: Shared genes or assortative mating. *PLoS Genetics, 9*(4), e1003451.

Kelly, T., Yang, W., Chen, C. S., Reynolds, K., & He, J. (2008). Global burden of obesity in 2005 and projections to 2030. *International Journal of Obesity, 32*(9), 1431–1437. doi:10.1038/ijo.2008.102

Kelsoe, J. R., Ginns, E. I., Egeland, J. A., Gerhard, D. S., Goldstein, A. M., Bale, S. J., . . . Paul, S. M. (1989). Re-evaluation of the linkage relationship between chromosome 11p loci and the gene for bipolar affective disorder in the Old Order Amish. *Nature, 342*, 238–242.

Kendler, K. S. (1996). Major depression and generalised anxiety disorder. Same genes, (partly) different environments—revisited. *British Journal of Psychiatry Supplement*(30), 68–75.

Kendler, K. S. (2001). Twin studies of psychiatric illness: An update. *Archives of General Psychiatry, 58*(11), 1005–1014.

Kendler, K. S. (2005). Toward a philosophical structure for psychiatry. *The American Journal of Psychiatry, 162*(3), 433–440.

Kendler, K. S., Aggen, S. H., Czajkowski, N., Roysamb, E., Tambs, K., Torgersen, S., . . .

Reichborn-Kjennerud, T. (2008a). The structure of genetic and environmental risk factors for DSM-IV personality disorders: A multivariate twin study. *Archives of General Psychiatry, 65*(12), 1438–1446. doi:10.1001/archpsyc.65.12.1438

Kendler, K. S., Aggen, S. H., & Neale, M. C. (2013). Evidence for multiple genetic factors underlying DSM-IV criteria for major depression. *JAMA Psychiatry, 70*(6), 599–607.

Kendler, K. S., Aggen, S. H., & Patrick, C. J. (2012a). A multivariate twin study of the DSM-IV criteria for antisocial personality disorder. *Biological Psychiatry, 71*(3), 247–253. doi:10.1016/j.biopsych.2011.05.019

Kendler, K. S., Aggen, S. H., Prescott, C. A., Crabbe, J., & Neale, M. C. (2012b). Evidence for multiple genetic factors underlying the DSM-IV criteria for alcohol dependence. *Molecular Psychiatry, 17*(12), 1306–1315.

Kendler, K. S., Aggen, S. H., Tambs, K., & Reichborn-Kjennerud, T. (2006b). Illicit psychoactive substance use, abuse and dependence in a population-based sample of Norwegian twins. *Psychological Medicine, 36*(7), 955–962.

Kendler, K. S., & Baker, J. H. (2007). Genetic influences on measures of the environment: A systematic review. *Psychological Medicine, 37*(5), 615–626.

Kendler, K. S., Czajkowski, N., Tambs, K., Torgersen, S., Aggen, S. H., Neale, M. C., & Reichborn-Kjennerud, T. (2006c). Dimensional representations of DSM-IV cluster A personality disorders in a population-based sample of Norwegian twins: A multivariate study. *Psychological Medicine, 36*(11), 1583–1591.

Kendler, K. S., & Eaves, L. J. (1986). Models for the joint effects of genotype and environment on liability to psychiatric illness. *American Journal of Psychiatry, 143*, 279–289.

Kendler, K. S., Gardner, C., & Dick, D. M. (2011). Predicting alcohol consumption in adolescence from alcohol-specific and general externalizing genetic risk factors, key environmental exposures and their interaction. *Psychological Medicine, 41*(7), 1507–1516. doi:10.1017/s003329171000190x

Kendler, K. S., & Gardner, C. O. (2011). A longitudinal etiologic model for symptoms of anxiety and depression in women. *Psychological Medicine, 41*(10), 2035–2045. doi:10.1017/s0033291711000225

Kendler, K. S., Gardner, C. O., Annas, P., Neale, M. C., Eaves, L. J., & Lichtenstein, P. (2008b). A longitudinal twin study of fears from middle childhood to early adulthood: Evidence for a developmentally dynamic genome. *Archives of General Psychiatry, 65*(4), 421–429. doi:10.1001/archpsyc.65.4.421

Kendler, K. S., Gardner, C. O., & Prescott, C. A. (2001). Panic syndromes in a population-based sample of male and female twins. *Psychological Medicine, 31*(6), 989–1000.

Kendler, K. S., Gardner, C. O., & Prescott, C. A. (2003a). Personality and the experience of environmental adversity. *Psychological Medicine, 33*(7), 1193–1202.

Kendler, K. S., Gatz, M., Gardner, C. O., & Pedersen, N. L. (2006a). Personality and major depression: A Swedish longitudinal, population-based twin study. *Archives of General Psychiatry, 63*(10), 1113–1120.

Kendler, K. S., & Greenspan, R. J. (2006). The nature of genetic influences on behavior: Lessons from "simpler" organisms. *The American Journal of Psychiatry, 163*(10), 1683–1694.

Kendler, K. S., Gruenberg, A. M., & Kinney, D. K. (1994a). Independent diagnoses of adoptees and relatives, as defined by DSM-II, in the provincial and national samples of the Danish adoption study of schizophrenia. *Archives of General Psychiatry, 51*, 456–468.

Kendler, K. S., Jacobson, K. C., Gardner, C. O., Gillespie, N., Aggen, S. A., & Prescott, C. A. (2007a). Creating a social world: A developmental twin study of peer-group deviance. *Archives of General Psychiatry, 64*(8), 958–965.

Kendler, K. S., Ji, J., Edwards, A. C., Ohlsson, H., Sundquist, J., & Sundquist, K. (2015a). An extended Swedish national adoption study of alcohol use disorder. *JAMA Psychiatry, 72*(3), 211–218.

Kendler, K. S., Kessler, R. C., Walters, E. E., MacLean, C. J., Neale, M. C., Heath, A. C., & Eaves, L. J. (1995). Stressful life events, genetic liability, and onset of an episode of major depression in women. *American Journal of Psychiatry, 152*, 833–842.

Kendler, K. S., Maes, H. H., Lönn, S. L., Morris, N. A., Lichtenstein, P., Sundquist, J., & Sundquist, K. (2015b). A Swedish national twin study of criminal behavior and its violent, white-collar and property subtypes. *Psychological Medicine, 45*(11), 2253–2262.

Kendler, K. S., Myers, J., & Prescott, C. A. (2007b). Specificity of genetic and environmental risk factors for symptoms of cannabis, cocaine, alcohol, caffeine, and nicotine dependence. *Archives of General Psychiatry, 64*(11), 1313–1320. doi:10.1001/archpsyc.64.11.1313

Kendler, K. S., & Neale, M. C. (2010). Endophenotype: A conceptual analysis. *Molecular Psychiatry, 15*(8), 789–797. doi:10.1038/mp.2010.8

Kendler, K. S., Neale, M. C., Kessler, R. C., Heath, A. C., & Eaves, L. J. (1992). Major depression and generalized anxiety disorder. Same genes, (partly) different environments? *Archives of General Psychiatry, 49*(9), 716–722.

Kendler, K. S., Neale, M. C., Kessler, R. C., Heath, A. C., & Eaves, L. J. (1993). A test of the equal-environment assumption in twin studies of psychiatric illness. *Behavior Genetics, 23*(1), 21–27.

Kendler, K. S., Neale, M. C., Kessler, R. C., Heath, A. C., & Eaves, L. J. (1994). Parental treatment and the equal environment assumption in twin studies of psychiatric illness. *Psychological Medicine, 24*(3), 579–590.

Kendler, K. S., Neale, M. C., Sullivan, P., Corey, L. A., Gardner, C. O., & Prescott, C. A. (1999). A population-based twin study in women of smoking initiation and nicotine dependence. *Psychological Medicine, 29*(2), 299–308.

Kendler, K. S., Ohlsson, H., Sundquist, J., & Sundquist, K. (2015c). Triparental families: A new genetic-epidemiological design applied to drug abuse, alcohol use disorders, and criminal behavior in a Swedish national sample. *American Journal of Psychiatry, 172*(6), 553–560. doi:10.1176/appi.ajp.2014.14091127

Kendler, K. S., & Prescott, C. A. (1998). Cannabis use, abuse, and dependence in a population-based sample of female twins. *American Journal of Psychiatry, 155*, 1016–1022.

Kendler, K. S., & Prescott, C. A. (2007). *Genes, environment and psychopathology: Understanding the causes of psychiatric and substance use disorders.* New York: Guilford Press.

Kendler, K. S., Prescott, C. A., Myers, J., & Neale, M. C. (2003b). The structure of genetic and environmental risk factors for common psychiatric and substance use disorders in men and women. *Archives of General Psychiatry, 60*(9), 929–937.

Kendler, K. S., Thornton, L. M., Gilman, S. E., & Kessler, R. C. (2000). Sexual orientation in a U.S. national sample of twin and nontwin sibling pairs. *American Journal of Psychiatry, 157*, 1843–1846.

Kennedy, J. L., Altar, C. A., Taylor, D. L., Degtiar, I., & Hornberger, J. C. (2014). The social and economic burden of treatment-resistant schizophrenia: A systematic literature review. *International Clinical Psychopharmacology, 29*(2), 63–76.

Kenrick, D. T., & Funder, D. C. (1988). Profiting from controversy: Lessons from the person-situation debate. *American Psychologist, 43*(1), 23.

Kenyon, C. J. (2010). The genetics of ageing. *Nature, 464*(7288), 504–512. doi:10.1038/nature08980

Keski-Rahkonen, A., Neale, B. M., Bulik, C. M., Pietiläinen, K. H., Rose, R. J., Kaprio, J., & Rissanen, A. (2005). Intentional weight loss in young adults: Sex-specific genetic and environmental effects.

Obesity Research, 13(4), 745–753. doi:10.1038 /oby.2005.84

Kessler, R., McGonagle, K. A., Zhao, C. B., Nelson, C. B., Hughes, M., Eshleman, S., . . . Kendler, K. S. (1994). Lifetime and 12-month prevalence of DSM-III-R psychiatric disorders in the United States: Results from the National Comorbidity Study. *Archives of General Psychiatry, 51*, 8–19.

Kessler, R. C., Berglund, P., Demler, O., Jin, R., Merikangas, K. R., & Walters, E. E. (2005a). Lifetime prevalence and age-of-onset distributions of DSM-IV disorders in the National Comorbidity Survey Replication. *Archives of General Psychiatry, 62*(6), 593–602.

Kessler, R. C., Chiu, W. T., Demler, O., Merikangas, K. R., & Walters, E. E. (2005b). Prevalence, severity, and comorbidity of 12-month DSM-IV disorders in the National Comorbidity Survey Replication. *Archives of General Psychiatry, 62*(6), 617–627.

Kessler, R. C., Petukhova, M., Sampson, N. A., Zaslavsky, A. M., & Wittchen, H-U. (2012). Twelve-month and lifetime prevalence and lifetime morbid risk of anxiety and mood disorders in the United States. *International Journal of Methods in Psychiatric Research, 21*(3): 169–184. doi:10.1002/mpr.1359

Kety, S. S. (1987). The significance of genetic factors in the etiology of schizophrenia: Results from the national study of adoptees in Denmark. *Journal of Psychiatric Research, 21*, 423–430.

Kety, S. S., Wender, P. H., Jacobsen, B., Ingraham, L. J., Jansson, L., Faber, B., & Kinney, D. K. (1994). Mental illness in the biological and adoptive relatives of schizophrenic adoptees: Replication of the Copenhagen study in the rest of Denmark. *Archives of General Psychiatry, 51*, 442–455.

Khan, A. A., Jacobson, K. C., Gardner, C. O., Prescott, C. A., & Kendler, K. S. (2005). Personality and comorbidity of common psychiatric disorders. *British Journal of Psychiatry, 186*, 190–196.

Khoury, M. J., Yang, Q. H., Gwinn, M., Little, J. L., & Flanders, W. D. (2004). An epidemiologic assessment of genomic profiling for measuring susceptibility to common diseases and targeting interventions. *Genetics in Medicine, 6*(1), 38–47.

Kidd, K. (1983). Recent progress on the genetics of stuttering. In C. Ludlow & J. Cooper (Eds.), *Genetic Aspects of Speech and Language Disorders* (pp. 197–213). New York: Academic Press.

Kieseppa, T., Partonen, T., Haukka, J., Kaprio, J., & Lonnqvist, J. (2004). High concordance of bipolar I disorder in a nationwide sample of twins. *American Journal of Psychiatry, 161*(10), 1814–1821.

Kile, B. T., & Hilton, D. J. (2005). The art and design of genetic screens: Mouse. *Nature Reviews Genetics, 6*(7), 557–567.

Kim, D. H., & Rossi, J. J. (2007). Strategies for silencing human disease using RNA interference. *Nature Reviews Genetics, 8*(3), 173–184. doi:10.1038 /nrg2006

Kim, M.-S., Pinto, S. M., Getnet, D., Nirujogi, R. S., Manda, S. S., Chaerkady, R., . . . Pandey, A. (2014). A draft map of the human proteome. *Nature, 509*(7502), 575–581. doi:10.1038/nature13302

Kim, Y. S., Leventhal, B. L., Koh, Y. J., Fombonne, E., Laska, E., Lim, E. C., . . . Grinker, R. R. (2011). Prevalence of autism spectrum disorders in a total population sample. *American Journal of Psychiatry, 168*(9), 904–912. doi:10.1176/appi. ajp.2011.10101532

Kimura, M., & Higuchi, S. (2011). Genetics of alcohol dependence. *Psychiatry and Clinical Neurosciences, 65*(3), 213–225. doi:10.1111/j.1440-1819.2011.02190.x

Kirkpatrick, R. M., McGue, M., Iacono, W. G., Miller, M. B., Basu, S., & Pankratz, N. (2014). Low-frequency copy-number variants and general cognitive ability: No evidence of association. *Intelligence, 42,* 98–106.

Klahr, A. M., & Burt, S. A. (2014). Elucidating the etiology of individual differences in parenting: A meta-analysis of behavioral genetic research. *Psychological Bulletin, 140*(2), 544. doi:10.1037/a0034205

Kleinman, J. E., Law, A. J., Lipska, B. K., Hyde, T. M., Ellis, J. K., Harrison, P. J., & Weinberger, D. R. (2011). Genetic neuropathology of schizophrenia: New approaches to an old question and new uses for postmortem human brains. *Biological Psychiatry, 69*(2), 140–145. doi:10.1016/j.biopsych.2010.10.032

Klose, J., Nock, C., Herrmann, M., Stuhler, K., Marcus, K., Bluggel, M., . . . Lehrach, H. (2002). Genetic analysis of the mouse brain proteome. *Nature Genetics, 30*(4), 385–393.

Klump, K. L. (2013). Puberty as a critical risk period for eating disorders: A review of human and animal studies. *Hormones and Behavior, 64*(2), 399–410.

Klump, K. L., Suisman, J. L., Burt, S. A., McGue, M., & Iacono, W. G. (2009). Genetic and environmental influences on disordered eating: An adoption study. *Journal of Abnormal Psychology, 118*(4), 797–805. doi:10.1037/a0017204

Knafo, A., & Plomin, R. (2006). Parental discipline and affection, and children's prosocial behavior: Genetic and environmental link. *Journal of Personality and Social Psychology, 90,* 147–164. doi:10.1037/0022-3514.90.1.147

Knickmeyer, R. C., Kang, C., Woolson, S., Smith, J. K., Hamer, R. M., Lin, W., . . . Gilmore, J. H. (2011). Twin-singleton differences in neonatal brain structure. *Twin Research and Human Genetics, 14*(3), 268–276. doi:10.1375/twin.14.3.268

Knopik, V. S., Alarcón, M., & DeFries, J. C. (1997). Comorbidity of mathematics and reading deficits: Evidence for a genetic etiology. *Behavior Genetics, 27*(5), 447–453. doi:10.1023/A:1025622400239

Knopik, V. S., Heath, A. C., Bucholz, K. K., Madden, P. A. F., & Waldron, M. (2009a). Genetic and environmental influences on externalizing behavior and alcohol problems in adolescence: A female twin study. *Pharmacology Biochemistry and Behavior, 93*(3), 313–321. doi:10.1016/j.pbb.2009.03.011

Knopik, V. S., Heath, A. C., Jacob, T., Slutske, W. S., Bucholz, K. K., Madden, P. A. F., ... Martin, N. G. (2006). Maternal alcohol use disorder and offspring ADHD: Disentangling genetic and environmental effects using a children-of-twins design. *Psychological Medicine, 36*(10), 1461–1471. doi:10.1017/s0033291706007884

Knopik, V. S., Heath, A. C., Madden, P. A. F., Bucholz, K. K., Slutske, W. S., Nelson, E. C., ... Martin, N. G. (2004). Genetic effects on alcohol dependence risk: Re-evaluating the importance of psychiatric and other heritable risk factors. *Psychological Medicine, 34*(8), 1519–1530. doi:10.1017/s0033291704002922

Knopik, V. S., Jacob, T., Haber, J. R., Swenson, L. P., & Howell, D. N. (2009b). Paternal alcoholism and offspring ADHD problems: A children of twins design. *Twin Research and Human Genetics, 12*(1), 53–62.

Koellinger, P., van der Loos, M., Groenen, P., Thurik, A., Rivadeneira, F., van Rooij, F., ... Hofman, A. (2010). Genome-wide association studies in economics and entrepreneurship research: Promises and limitations. *Small Business Economics, 35*(1), 1–18. doi:10.1007/s11187-010-9286-3

Koenig, L. B., McGue, M., Krueger, R. F., & Bouchard, T. J., Jr. (2005). Genetic and environmental influences on religiousness: Findings for retrospective and current religiousness ratings. *Journal of Personality, 73*(2), 471–488.

Koeppen-Schomerus, G., Spinath, F. M., & Plomin, R. (2003). Twins and non-twin siblings: Different estimates of shared environmental influence in early childhood. *Twin Research, 6*(2), 97–105. doi:10.1375/136905203321536227

Kohnstamm, G. A., Bates, J. E., & Rothbart, M. K. (1989). *Temperament in childhood*. New York: Wiley.

Konradi, C. (2005). Gene expression microarray studies in polygenic psychiatric disorders: Applications and data analysis. *Brain Research Reviews, 50*(1), 142–155.

Koopmans, J. R., Slutske, W. S., van Baal, G. C., & Boomsma, D. I. (1999). The influence of religion on alcohol use initiation: Evidence for genotype × environment interaction. *Behavior Genetics, 29*(6), 445–453.

Koscielny, G., Yaikhom, G., Iyer, V., Meehan, T. F., Morgan, H., Atienza-Herrero, J., ... Di Fenza, A. (2014). The International Mouse Phenotyping Consortium Web Portal, a unified point of access for knockout mice and related phenotyping data. *Nucleic Acids Research, 42*(D1), D802–D809.

Koten, J. W., Jr., Wood, G., Hagoort, P., Goebel, R., Propping, P., Willmes, K., & Boomsma, D. I. (2009). Genetic contribution to variation in cognitive function: An fMRI study in twins. *Science, 323*(5922), 1737–1740. doi:10.1126/science.1167371

Kovas, Y., Haworth, C. M. A., Dale, P. S., & Plomin, R. (2007). The genetic and environmental origins of learning abilities and disabilities in the early school years. *Monographs of the Society for Research in Child Development, 72*, 1–144. doi:10.1111/j.1540-5834.2007.00453.x

Kovas, Y., & Plomin, R. (2006). Generalist genes: Implications for the cognitive sciences. *Trends in Cognitive Sciences, 10*(5), 198–203. doi:10.1016/j.tics.2006.03.001

Kovas, Y., Voronin, I., Kaydalov, A., Malykh, S. B., Dale, P. S., & Plomin, R. (2013). Literacy and numeracy are more heritable than intelligence in primary school. *Psychological Science, 24*(10), 2048–2056.

Kozell, L., Belknap, J. K., Hofstetter, J. R., Mayeda, A., & Buck, K. J. (2008). Mapping a locus for alcohol physical dependence and associated withdrawal to a 1.1 Mb interval of mouse chromosome 1 syntenic with human chromosome 1q23.2-23.3. *Genes, Brain and Behavior, 7*(5), 560–567. doi:10.1111/j.1601-183X.2008.00391.x

Krapohl, E., Euesden, J., Zabaneh, D., Pingault, J. B., Rimfeld, K., von Stumm, S., ... Plomin, R. (2015). Phenome-wide analysis of genome-wide polygenic scores. *Molecular Psychiatry.* doi:10.1038/mp.2015.126

Krapohl, E., & Plomin, R. (2015). Genetic link between family socioeconomic status and children's educational achievement estimated from genome-wide SNPs. *Molecular Psychiatry, 21*(3), 437–443.

Krebs, G., Waszczuk, M. A., Zavos, H. M. S., Bolton, D., & Eley, T. C. (2015). Genetic and environmental influences on obsessive–compulsive behaviour across development: A longitudinal twin study. *Psychological Medicine, 45*(07), 1539–1549.

Krebs, N. F., Himes, J. H., Jacobson, D., Nicklas, T. A., Guilday, P., & Styne, D. (2007). Assessment of child and adolescent overweight and obesity. *Pediatrics, 120*, S193–S228. doi:10.1542/peds.2007-2329D

Kroksveen, A. C., Opsahl, J. A., Aye, T. T., Ulvik, R. J., & Berven, F. S. (2011). Proteomics of human cerebrospinal fluid: Discovery and verification of biomarker candidates in neurodegenerative diseases using quantitative proteomics. *Journal of Proteomics, 74*(4), 371–388. doi:http://dx.doi.org/10.1016/j.jprot.2010.11.010

Krueger, R. F. (1999). The structure of common mental disorders. *Archives of General Psychiatry, 56*(10), 921–926.

Krueger, R. F., Caspi, A., Moffitt, T. E., Silva, A., & McGee, R. (1996). Personality traits are differentially linked to mental disorders: A multitrait-multidiagnosis study of an adolescent birth cohort. *Journal of Abnormal Psychology, 105*, 299–312.

Krueger, R. F., Hicks, B. M., Patrick, C. J., Carlson, S. R., Iacono, W. G., & McGue, M. (2002). Etiologic connections among substance dependence, antisocial behavior, and personality: Modeling the externalizing spectrum. *Journal of Abnormal Psychology, 111*(3), 411–424.

Krueger, R. F., Markon, K. E., & Bouchard, T. J., Jr. (2003). The extended genotype: The heritability of personality accounts for the heritability of recalled family environments in twins reared apart. *Journal of Personality, 71*(5), 809–833.

Krumm, N., Turner, T. N., Baker, C., Vives, L., Mohajeri, K., Witherspoon, K., ... He, Z.-X. (2015). Excess of rare, inherited truncating mutations in autism. *Nature Genetics, 47*(6), 582–588.

Kukekova, A. V., Trut, L. N., Chase, K., Kharlamova, A. V., Johnson, J. L., Temnykh, S. V., ... Lark, K. G. (2011). Mapping loci for fox domestication: Deconstruction/reconstruction of a behavioral phenotype. *Behavior Genetics, 41*(4), 593–606. doi:10.1007/s10519-010-9418-1

Kumar, V., Kim, K., Joseph, C., Thomas, L. C., Hong, H., & Takahashi, J. S. (2011). Second-generation high-throughput forward genetic screen in mice to isolate subtle behavioral mutants. *Proceedings of the National Academy of Sciences of the United States of America, 108*, 15557–15564. doi:10.1073/pnas.1107726108

Kupper, N., Willemsen, G., Riese, H., Posthuma, D., Boomsma, D. I., & de Geus, E. J. C. (2005). Heritability of daytime ambulatory blood pressure in an extended twin design. *Hypertension, 45*(1), 80–85.

Labuda, M. C., DeFries, J. C., & Fulker, D. W. (1987). Genetic and environmental covariance-structures among WISC-R subtests: A twin study. *Intelligence, 11*(3), 233–244. doi:10.1016/0160-2896(87)90008-0

Lack, D. (1953). Darwin's finches. *Scientific American, 188*, 67.

Lai, C. S., Fisher, S. E., Hurst, J. A., Vargha-Khadem, F., & Monaco, A. P. (2001). A forkhead-domain gene is mutated in a severe speech and language disorder. *Nature, 413*(6855), 519–523.

Lajunen, H.-R., Kaprio, J., Rose, R. J., Pulkkinen, L., & Silventoinen, K. (2012). Genetic and environmental influences on BMI from late childhood to adolescence are modified by parental education. *Obesity, 20*(3), 583–589. doi:10.1038/oby.2011.304

Lamb, D. J., Middeldorp, C. M., van Beijsterveldt, C. E. M., Bartels, M., van der Aa, N., Polderman, T. J. C., & Boomsma, D. I. (2010). Heritability of anxious-depressive and withdrawn behavior: Age-related changes during adolescence. *Journal of the American Academy of Child and Adolescent Psychiatry, 49*(3), 248–255. doi:10.1016/j.jaac.2009.11.014

Lambert, J.-C., Ibrahim-Verbaas, C. A., Harold, D., Naj, A. C., Sims, R., Bellenguez, C., ... Beecham, G. W. (2013). Meta-analysis of 74,046 individuals identifies 11 new susceptibility loci for Alzheimer's disease. *Nature Genetics, 45*(12), 1452–1458.

Lana-Elola, E., Watson-Scales, S. D., Fisher, E. M. C., & Tybulewicz, V. L. J. (2011). Down syndrome: Searching for the genetic culprits. *Disease Models & Mechanisms, 4*(5), 586–595. doi:10.1242/dmm.008078

Lander, E. S. (2011). Initial impact of the sequencing of the human genome. *Nature, 470*(7333), 187–197. doi:10.1038/nature09792

Lanfranco, F., Kamischke, A., Zitzmann, M., & Nieschlag, E. (2004). Klinefelter's syndrome. *The Lancet, 364*(9430), 273–283.

Langstrom, N., Rahman, Q., Carlstrom, E., & Lichtenstein, P. (2010). Genetic and environmental effects on same-sex sexual behavior: A population study of twins in Sweden. *Archives of Sexual Behavior, 39*(1), 75–80. doi:10.1007/s10508-008-9386-1

Lanphier, E., Urnov, F., Haecker, S. E., Werner, M., & Smolenski, J. (2015). Don't edit the human germ line. *Nature, 519*(7544), 410.

Larsson, H., Chang, Z., D'Onofrio, B. M., & Lichtenstein, P. (2014). The heritability of clinically diagnosed attention deficit hyperactivity disorder across the lifespan. *Psychological Medicine, 44*(10), 2223–2229.

Larsson, H., Dilshad, R., Lichtenstein, P., & Barker, E. D. (2011). Developmental trajectories of DSM-IV symptoms of attention-deficit/hyperactivity disorder: Genetic effects, family risk and associated psychopathology. *Journal of Child Psychology and Psychiatry, 52*(9), 954–963. doi:10.1111/j.1469-7610.2011.02379.x

Larsson, H., Lichtenstein, P., & Larsson, J. O. (2006). Genetic contributions to the development of ADHD subtypes from childhood to adolescence.

Journal of the American Academy of Child and Adolescent Psychiatry, 45(8), 973–981.

Larsson, H., Tuvblad, C., Rijsdijk, F. V., Andershed, H., Grann, M., & Lichtenstein, P. (2007). A common genetic factor explains the association between psychopathic personality and antisocial behavior. *Psychological Medicine, 37*(1), 15–26.

Lau, B., Bretaud, S., Huang, Y., Lin, E., & Guo, S. (2006). Dissociation of food and opiate preference by a genetic mutation in zebrafish. *Genes, Brain and Behavior, 5*(7), 497–505.

Laucht, M., Blomeyer, D., Buchmann, A. F., Treutlein, J., Schmidt, M. H., Esser, G., . . . Banaschewski, T. (2012). Catechol-O-methyltransferase Val158Met genotype, parenting practices and adolescent alcohol use: Testing the differential susceptibility hypothesis. *Journal of Child Psychology and Psychiatry, 53*(4), 351–359. doi:10.1111/j.1469-7610.2011.02408.x

Laurin, C. A., Hottenga, J. J., Willemsen, G., Boomsma, D. I., & Lubke, G. H. (2015). Genetic analyses benefit from using less heterogeneous phenotypes: An illustration with the hospital anxiety and depression scale (HADS). *Genetic Epidemiology, 39*(4): 317–24. doi:10.1002/gepi.21897

Laursen, T. M., Agerbo, E., & Pedersen, C. B. (2009). Bipolar disorder, schizoaffective disorder, and schizophrenia overlap: A new comorbidity index. *Journal of Clinical Psychiatry, 70*(10), 1432–1438. doi:10.4088/JCP.08m04807

Lavebratt, C., Almgren, M., & Ekström, T. J. (2012). Epigenetic regulation in obesity. *International Journal of Obesity, 36*(6), 757–765.

Le, A. T., Miller, P. W., Slutske, W. S., & Martin, N. G. (2010). Are attitudes towards economic risk heritable? Analyses using the Australian twin study of gambling. *Twin Research and Human Genetics, 13*(04), 330–339. doi:doi:10.1375/twin.13.4.330

Le Couteur, A., Bailey, A., Goode, S., Pickles, A., Robertson, S., Gottesman, I. I., & Rutter, M. (1996). A broader phenotype of autism: The clinical spectrum in twins. *Journal of Child Psychology and Psychiatry, 37,* 785–801.

Leahy, A. M. (1935). Nature-nurture and intelligence. *Genetic Psychology Monographs, 17,* 236–308.

Lee, H., Ripke, S., Neale, B., Faraone, S., Purcell, S., Perlis, R., . . . Witte, J. (2013). Genetic relationship between five psychiatric disorders estimated from genome-wide SNPs. *Nature Genetics, 45*(9), 984–994.

Lee, M. C., & Conway, G. S. (2014). Turner's syndrome: Challenges of late diagnosis. *The Lancet Diabetes & Endocrinology, 2*(4), 333–338.

Lee, S. H., DeCandia, T. R., Ripke, S., Schizophrenia Psychiatric Genome-Wide Association Study Consortium, International Schizophrenia Consortium, Molecular Genetics of Schizophrenia Collaboration, . . . Wray, N. R. (2012a). Estimating the proportion of variation in susceptibility to schizophrenia captured by common SNPs. *Nature Genetics, 44*(3), 247–250.

Lee, S. H., Harold, D., Nyholt, D. R., Goddard, M. E., Zondervan, K. T., Williams, J., . . . Visscher, P. M. (2013). Estimation and partitioning of polygenic variation captured by common SNPs for Alzheimer's disease, multiple sclerosis and endometriosis. *Human Molecular Genetics, 22*(4), 832–841.

Lee, T., Henry, J. D., Trollor, J. N., & Sachdev, P. S. (2010b). Genetic influences on cognitive functions in the elderly: A selective review of twin studies. *Brain Research Reviews, 64*(1), 1–13. doi:10.1016/j.brainresrev.2010.02.001

Lee, T., Mosing, M. A., Henry, J. D., Trollor, J. N., Lammel, A., Ames, D., . . . Sachdev, P. S. (2012). Genetic influences on five measures of processing speed and their covariation with general cognitive ability in the elderly: The Older Australian Twins Study. *Behavior Genetics, 42*(1), 96–106. doi:10.1007/s10519-011-9474-1

Leggett, V., Jacobs, P., Nation, K., Scerif, G., & Bishop, D. V. M. (2010). Neurocognitive outcomes of individuals with a sex chromosome trisomy: XXX, XYY, or XXY: A systematic review. *Developmental Medicine and Child Neurology, 52*(2), 119–129. doi:10.1111/j.1469-8749.2009.03545.x

Legrain, P., Aebersold, R., Archakov, A., Bairoch, A., Bala, K., Beretta, L., . . . Omenn, G. S. (2011). The Human Proteome Project: Current state and future direction. *Molecular Cell Proteomics, 10*(7), M111.009993. doi:10.1074/mcp.M111.009993

Legrand, L. N., McGue, M., & Iacono, W. G. (1999). A twin study of state and trait anxiety in childhood and adolescence. *Journal of Child Psychology and Psychiatry, 40*(6), 953–958.

Lein, E. S., Hawrylycz, M. J., Ao, N., Ayres, M., Bensinger, A., Bernard, A., . . . Jones, A. R. (2007). Genome-wide atlas of gene expression in the adult mouse brain. *Nature, 445*(7124), 168–176.

Lemery-Chalfant, K., Doelger, L., & Goldsmith, H. H. (2008). Genetic relations between effortful and attentional control and symptoms of psychopathology in middle childhood. *Infant and Child Development, 17*(4), 365–385. doi:10.1002/icd.581

Lemery-Chalfant, K., Kao, K., Swann, G., & Goldsmith, H. H. (2013). Childhood temperament: Passive gene-environment correlation, gene-environment interaction, and the hidden importance of the family environment. *Development and Psychopathology, 25*(1), 51–63. doi:10.1017/S0954579412000892

Lepage, P., Leclerc, M. C., Joossens, M., Mondot, S., Blottiere, H. M., Raes, J., . . . Dore, J. (2013). A metagenomic insight into our gut's microbiome. *Gut, 62*(1), 146–158.

Lerner, I. M. (1968). *Heredity, evolution and society*. San Francisco: Freeman.

Letwin, N. E., Kafkafi, N., Benjamini, Y., Mayo, C., Frank, B. C., Luu, T., . . . Elmer, G. I. (2006). Combined application of behavior genetics and microarray analysis to identify regional expression themes and gene-behavior associations. *The Journal of Neuroscience, 26*(20), 5277–5287.

Leve, L. D., DeGarmo, D. S., Bridgett, D. J., Neiderhiser, J. M., Shaw, D. S., Harold, G. T., . . . Reiss, D. (2013a). Using an adoption design to separate genetic, prenatal, and temperament influences on toddler executive function. *Developmental Psychology, 49*(6), 1045–1057. doi:10.1037/a0029390

Leve, L. D., Harold, G. T., Ge, X., Neiderhiser, J. M., Shaw, D., Scaramella, L. V., & Reiss, D. (2009). Structured parenting of toddlers at high versus low genetic risk: Two pathways to child problems. *Journal of the American Academy of Child and Adolescent Psychiatry, 48*(11), 1102–1109. doi:10.1097/CHI.0b013e3181b8bfc0

Leve, L. D., Neiderhiser, J. M., Shaw, D. S., Ganiban, J., Natsuaki, M. N., & Reiss, D. (2013b). The Early Growth and Development Study: A prospective adoption study from birth through middle childhood. *Twin Research and Human Genetics, 16*(1), 412–423.

Levinson, D. F., Evgrafov, O. V., Knowles, J. A., Potash, J. B., Weissman, M. M., Scheftner, W. A., . . . Holmans, P. (2007). Genetics of recurrent early-onset major depression (GenRED): Significant linkage on chromosome 15q25-q26 after fine mapping with single nucleotide polymorphism markers. *American Journal of Psychiatry, 164*(2), 259–264.

Levy, D., Ronemus, M., Yamrom, B., Lee, Y. H., Leotta, A., Kendall, J., . . . Wigler, M. (2011). Rare de novo and transmitted copy-number variation in autistic spectrum disorders. *Neuron, 70*(5), 886–897. doi:10.1016/j.neuron.2011.05.015

Levy, D. L., Holzman, P. S., Matthysse, S., & Mendell, N. R. (1993). Eye tracking dysfunction and schizophrenia: A critical perspective. *Schizophrenia Bulletin, 19,* 461–536.

Lewis, C. M., Levinson, D. F., Wise, L. H., DeLisi, L. E., Straub, R. E., Hovatta, I., . . . Helgason, T. (2003). Genome scan meta-analysis of schizophrenia and bipolar disorder, part II: Schizophrenia. *American Journal of Human Genetics, 73*(1), 34–48.

Lewis, G. J., Haworth, C., & Plomin, R. (2014). Identical genetic influences underpin behavior problems in adolescence and basic traits of personality. *Journal of Child Psychology and Psychiatry, 55*(8), 865–875.

Ley, R. E. (2015). The gene-microbe link. *Nature (London), 518*(7540), S7.

Li, D., Sham, P. C., Owen, M. J., & He, L. (2006). Meta-analysis shows significant association between dopamine system genes and attention deficit hyperactivity disorder (ADHD). *Human Molecular Genetics, 15*(14), 2276–2284.

Li, D., Zhao, H., Kranzler, H. R., Li, M. D., Jensen, K. P., Zayats, T., . . . Gelernter, J. (2014). Genome-wide association study of copy number variations (cnvs) with opioid dependence. *Neuropsychopharmacology, 40*(4), 1016–1026.

Li, J., Huo, Y., Zhang, Y., Fang, Z., Yang, J., Zang, T., . . . Xu, X. (2009a). Familial aggregation and heritability of electrocardiographic intervals and heart rate in a rural Chinese population. *Annals of Noninvasive Electrocardiology, 14*(2), 147–152.

Li, M. D., Cheng, R., Ma, J. Z., & Swan, G. E. (2003). A meta-analysis of estimated genetic and environmental effects on smoking behavior in male and female adult twins. *Addiction, 98*(1), 23–31. doi:10.1046/j.1360-0443.2003.00295.x

Li, W., & Pozzo-Miller, L. (2014). BDNF deregulation in Rett syndrome. *Neuropharmacology, 76,* 737–746.

Li, Y., Breitling, R., & Jansen, R. C. (2008). Generalizing genetical genomics: Getting added value from environmental perturbation. *Trends in Genetics, 24*(10), 518–524. doi:10.1016/j.tig.2008.08.001

Li, Y., Wang, W.-J., Cao, H., Lu, J., Wu, C., Hu, F.-Y., . . . Tian, X.-L. (2009b). Genetic association of FOXO1A and FOXO3A with longevity trait in Han Chinese populations. *Human Molecular Genetics, 18*(24), 4897–4904. doi:10.1093/hmg/ddp459

Li, Z., Chang, S.-h., Zhang, L.-y., Gao, L., & Wang, J. (2014). Molecular genetic studies of ADHD and its candidate genes: A review. *Psychiatry Research, 219*(1), 10–24.

Liao, C. Y., Rikke, B. A., Johnson, T. E., Diaz, V., & Nelson, J. F. (2010). Genetic variation in the murine lifespan response to dietary restriction: From life extension to life shortening. *Aging Cell, 9*(1), 92–95. doi:10.1111/j.1474-9726.2009.00533.x

Lichtenstein, P., Harris, J. R., Pedersen, N. L., & McClearn, G. E. (1992). Socioeconomic status and physical health, how are they related? An empirical study based on twins reared apart and twins reared together. *Social Science and Medicine, 36,* 441–450.

Lichtenstein, P., Holm, N. V., Verkasalo, P. K., Iliadou, A., Kaprio, J., Koskenvuo, M., . . . Hemminki, K. (2000). Environmental and heritable factors in the causation of cancer—analysis of cohorts of twins from Sweden, Denmark, and Finland. *The New England Journal of Medicine, 343*(2), 78–85.

Lichtenstein, P., Yip, B. H., Bjork, C., Pawitan, Y., Cannon, T. D., Sullivan, P. F., & Hultman, C. M. (2009). Common genetic determinants of schizophrenia and bipolar disorder in Swedish families: A population-based study. *The Lancet, 373*(9659), 234–239. doi:10.1016/s0140-6736(09)60072-6

Lidsky, A. S., Robson, K., Chandra, T., Barker, P., Ruddle, F., & Woo, S. L. C. (1984). The PKU locus in man is on chromosome 12. *American Journal of Human Genetics, 36*, 527–533.

Lilienfeld, S. O. (1992). The association between antisocial personality and somatization disorders: A review and integration of theoretical models. *Clinical Psychology Review, 12*, 641–662.

Lindblad-Toh, K., Wade, C. M., Mikkelsen, T. S., Karlsson, E. K., Jaffe, D. B., Kamal, M., ... Lander, E. S. (2005). Genome sequence, comparative analysis and haplotype structure of the domestic dog. *Nature, 438*(7069), 803–819.

Lindenberger, U. (2001). Lifespan theories of cognitive development. In N. J. Smelser & P. B. Bates (Eds.), *International encyclopaedia of the social and behavior sciences* (pp. 8848–8854). Oxford: Elsevier.

Linney, Y. M., Murray, R. M., Peters, E. R., MacDonald, A. M., Rijsdijk, F., & Sham, P. C. (2003). A quantitative genetic analysis of schizotypal personality traits. *Psychological Medicine, 33*(5), 803–816.

Lipscomb, S. T., Laurent, H., Neiderhiser, J. M., Shaw, D. S., Natsuaki, M. N., Reiss, D., & Leve, L. D. (2014). Genetic vulnerability interacts with parenting and early care and education to predict increasing externalizing behavior. *International Journal of Behavioral Development, 38*(1), 70–80.

Liu, J., Yang, A., Zhang, Q., Yang, G., Yang, W., Lei, H., ... Zhang, Z. (2015). Association between genetic variants in SLC25A12 and risk of autism spectrum disorders: An integrated meta analysis. *American Journal of Medical Genetics Part B: Neuropsychiatric Genetics, 168*(4), 236–246.

Liu, X., & Davis, R. L. (2006). Insect olfactory memory in time and space. *Current Opinion in Neurobiology, 16*(6), 679–685.

Livesley, W. J., Jang, K. L., & Vernon, P. A. (1998). Phenotypic and genetic structure of traits delineating personality disorder. *Archives of General Psychiatry, 55*, 941–948.

Liyanage, V. R. B., & Rastegar, M. (2014). Rett syndrome and MeCP2. *Neuromolecular Medicine, 16*(2), 231–264.

Llewellyn, C., & Wardle, J. (2015). Behavioral susceptibility to obesity: Gene-environment interplay in the development of weight. *Physiological Behavior.* doi:10.1016/j.physbeh.2015.07.006

Llewellyn, C. H., Trzaskowski, M., Plomin, R., & Wardle, J. (2014a). From modeling to measurement: Developmental trends in genetic influence on adiposity in childhood. *Obesity, 22*(7), 1756–1761. doi:10.1002/oby.20756

Llewellyn, C. H., Trzaskowski, M., van Jaarsveld, C. M., Plomin, R., & Wardle, J. (2014b). Satiety mechanisms in genetic risk of obesity. *JAMA Pediatrics, 168*(4), 338–344. doi:10.1001/jamapediatrics.2013.4944

Llewellyn, C. H., van Jaarsveld, C. H., Johnson, L., Carnell, S., & Wardle, J. (2010). Nature and nurture in infant appetite: Analysis of the Gemini twin birth cohort. *The American Journal of Clinical Nutrition, 91*(5), 1172–1179. doi:10.3945/ajcn.2009.28868

Locke, A. E., Kahali, B., Berndt, S. I., Justice, A. E., Pers, T. H., Day, F. R., ... Speliotes, E. K. (2015). Genetic studies of body mass index yield new insights for obesity biology. *Nature, 518*(7538), 197–206. doi:10.1038/nature14177

Loehlin, J. C. (1989). Partitioning environmental and genetic contributions to behavioral development. *American Psychologist, 44*, 1285–1292.

Loehlin, J. C. (1992). *Genes and environment in personality development.* Newbury Park, CA: Sage Publications Inc.

Loehlin, J. C. (1997). Genes and environment. In D. Magnusson (Ed.), *The lifespan development of individuals: Behavioral, neurobiological, and psychosocial perspectives: a synthesis* (pp. 38–51). New York: Cambridge University Press.

Loehlin, J. C. (2009). History of behavior genetics. In Y.-K. Kim (Ed.), *Handbook of behavior genetics* (pp. 3–11): Springer New York.

Loehlin, J. C. (2010). Is there an active gene-environment correlation in adolescent drinking behavior? *Behavior Genetics, 40*(4), 447–451. doi:10.1007/s10519-010-9347-z

Loehlin, J. C., Horn, J. M., & Willerman, L. (1989). Modeling IQ change: Evidence from the Texas Adoption Project. *Child Development, 60*, 993–1004.

Loehlin, J. C., Horn, J. M., & Willerman, L. (1990). Heredity, environment, and personality change: Evidence from the Texas Adoption Study. *Journal of Personality, 58*, 221–243.

Loehlin, J. C., Neiderhiser, J. M., & Reiss, D. (2003). The behavior genetics of personality and the NEAD study. *Journal of Research in Personality, 37*(5), 373–387.

Loehlin, J. C., & Nichols, J. (1976). *Heredity, environment and personality.* Austin: University of Texas.

Loehlin, J. C., Willerman, L., & Horn, J. M. (1982). Personality resemblances between unwed mothers and their adopted-away offspring. *Journal of Personality and Social Psychology, 42,* 1089–1099.

Lohmueller, K. E., Pearce, C. L., Pike, M., Lander, E. S., & Hirschhorn, J. N. (2003). Meta-analysis of genetic association studies supports a contribution of common variants to susceptibility to common disease. *Nature Genetics, 33*(2), 177–182.

Long, A. D., Macdonald, S. J., & King, E. G. (2014). Dissecting complex traits using the *Drosophila* synthetic population resource. *Trends in Genetics, 30*(11), 488–495.

Long, J., Knowler, W., Hanson, R., Robin, R., Urbanek, M., Moore, E., . . . Goldman, D. (1998). Evidence for genetic linkage to alcohol dependence on chromosomes 4 and 11 from an autosome-wide scan in an American Indian population. *American Journal of Medical Genetics (Neuropsychiatric Genetics), 81,* 216–221.

López-Solà, C., Fontenelle, L. F., Alonso, P., Cuadras, D., Foley, D. L., Pantelis, C., . . . Soriano-Mas, C. (2014). Prevalence and heritability of obsessive-compulsive spectrum and anxiety disorder symptoms: A survey of the Australian Twin Registry. *American Journal of Medical Genetics Part B: Neuropsychiatric Genetics, 165*(4), 314–325.

Losoya, S. H., Callor, S., Rowe, D. C., & Goldsmith, H. H. (1997). Origins of familial similarity in parenting: A study of twins and adoptive siblings. *Developmental Psychology, 33*(6), 1012–1023.

Lott, I. T., & Dierssen, M. (2010). Cognitive deficits and associated neurological complications in individuals with Down's syndrome. *The Lancet Neurology, 9*(6), 623–633.

Lovinger, D. M., & Crabbe, J. C. (2005). Laboratory models of alcoholism: Treatment target identification and insight into mechanisms. *Nature Neuroscience, 8*(11), 1471–1480.

Lubke, G. H., Hottenga, J. J., Walters, R., Laurin, C., de Geus, E. J. C., Willemsen, G., . . . Boomsma, D. I. (2012). Estimating the genetic variance of major depressive disorder due to all single nucleotide polymorphisms. *Biological Psychiatry, 72*(8), 707–709. doi:10.1016/j.biopsych.2012.03.011

Luciano, M., Hansell, N. K., Lahti, J., Davies, G., Medland, S. E., Raikkonen, K., . . . Deary, I. J. (2011a). Whole genome association scan for genetic polymorphisms influencing information processing speed. *Biological Psychology, 86*(3), 193–202. doi:10.1016/j.biopsycho.2010.11.008

Luciano, M., Montgomery, G. W., Martin, N. G., Wright, M. J., & Bates, T. C. (2011b). SNP sets and reading ability: Testing confirmation of a 10-SNP set in a population sample. *Twin Research and Human Genetics, 14*(3), 228–232. doi:10.1375/twin.14.3.228

Luciano, M., Svinti, V., Campbell, A., Marioni, R. E., Hayward, C., Wright, A. F., . . . Prendergast, J. G. D. (2015). Exome sequencing to detect rare variants associated with general cognitive ability: A pilot study. *Twin Research and Human Genetics, 18*(02), 117–125.

Luciano, M., Wright, M. J., Geffen, G. M., Geffen, L. B., Smith, G. A., Evans, D. M., & Martin, N. G. (2003). A genetic two-factor model of the covariation among a subset of Multidimensional Aptitude Battery and Wechsler Adult Intelligence Scale - Revised subtests. *Intelligence, 31*(6), 589–605. doi:10.1016/s0160-2896(03)00057-6

Lundstrom, S., Chang, Z., Rastam, M., Gillberg, C., Larsson, H., Anckarsater, H., & Lichtenstein, P. (2012). Autism spectrum disorders and autistic-like traits: Similar etiology in the extreme end and the normal variation. *Archives of General Psychiatry, 69*(1), 46–52.

Luo, D., Petrill, S. A., & Thompson, L. A. (1994). An exploration of genetic g: Hierarchical factor analysis of cognitive data from the Western Reserve Twin Project. *Intelligence, 18,* 335–348.

Luo, X., Kranzler, H. R., Zuo, L., Wang, S., Blumberg, H. P., & Gelernter, J. (2005). CHRM2 gene predisposes to alcohol dependence, drug dependence and affective disorders: Results from an extended case-control structured association study. *Human Molecular Genetics, 14*(16), 2421–2434. doi:10.1093/hmg/ddi244

Lush, J. L. (1951). Genetics and animal breeding. In L. C. Dunn (Ed.), *Genetics in the twentieth century* (pp. 493–525). New York: Macmillan.

Lykken, D. T. (2006). The mechanism of emergenesis. *Genes, Brain and Behavior, 5*(4), 306–310.

Lykken, D. T., & Tellegen, A. (1993). Is human mating adventitious or the result of lawful choice? A twin study of mate selection. *Journal of Personality and Social Psychology, 65*(1), 56–68.

Lynch, M. A. (2004). Long-term potentiation and memory. *Physiologica, 84*(1), 87–136.

Lynskey, M. T., Agrawal, A., & Heath, A. C. (2010). Genetically informative research on adolescent substance use: Methods, findings, and challenges. *Journal of the American Academy of Child and Adolescent Psychiatry, 49*(12), 1202–1214. doi:10.1016/j.jaac.2010.09.004

Lyons, M. J., Goldberg, J., Eisen, S. A., True, W., Tsuang, M. T., Meyer, J. M., & Henderson, W. G. (1993). Do genes influence exposure to trauma: A twin study of combat. *American Journal of Medical Genetics (Neuropsychiatric Genetics), 48,* 22–27.

Lyons, M. J., True, W. R., Eisen, S. A., Goldberg, J., Meyer, J. M., Faraone, S. V., . . . Tsuang, M. T. (1995). Differential heritability of adult and juvenile antisocial traits. *Archives of General Psychiatry, 52*(11), 906–915.

Lyst, M. J., & Bird, A. (2015). Rett syndrome: A complex disorder with simple roots. *Nature Reviews Genetics, 16*(5), 261–275.

Ma, D. Q., Cuccaro, M. L., Jaworski, J. M., Haynes, C. S., Stephan, D. A., Parod, J., . . . Pericak-Vance, M. A. (2007). Dissecting the locus heterogeneity of autism: Significant linkage to chromosome 12q14. *Molecular Psychiatry, 12*(4), 376–384.

Mabb, A. M., Judson, M. C., Zylka, M. J., & Philpot, B. D. (2011). Angelman syndrome: Insights into genomic imprinting and neurodevelopmental phenotypes. *Trends in Neurosciences, 34*(6), 293–303. doi:10.1016/j.tins.2011.04.001

Maccani, M. A., & Knopik, V. S. (2012). Cigarette smoke exposure-associated alterations to non-coding RNA. *Frontiers in Genetics, 3*, 53. doi:10.3389/fgene.2012.00053

Maccani, M. A., & Marsit, C. J. (2009). Epigenetics in the placenta. *American Journal of Reproductive Immunology, 62*(2), 78–89. doi:10.1111/j.1600-0897.2009.00716.x

MacGillivray, I., Campbell, D. M., & Thompson, B. (1988). *Twinning and twins.* Chichester: Wiley.

Mackay, T. F., & Anholt, R. R. (2006). Of flies and man: *Drosophila* as a model for human complex traits. *Annual Review of Genomics and Human Genetics, 7*, 339–367.

MacKillop, J. (2013). Integrating behavioral economics and behavioral genetics: Delayed reward discounting as an endophenotype for addictive disorders. *Journal of the Experimental Analysis of Behavior, 99*(1), 14–31.

MacKillop, J., & Munafò, M. R. (2013). *Genetic influences on addiction: An intermediate phenotype approach.* MIT Press.

MacKillop, J., Obasi, E., Amlung, M. T., McGeary, J. E., & Knopik, V. S. (2010). The role of genetics in nicotine dependence: Mapping the pathways from genome to syndrome. *Current Cardiovascular Risk Report, 4*(6), 446–453. doi:10.1007/s12170-010-0132-6

Mackintosh, M.-A., Gatz, M., Wetherell, J. L., & Pedersen, N. L. (2006). A twin study of lifetime generalized anxiety disorder (GAD) in older adults: Genetic and environmental influences shared by neuroticism and GAD. *Twin Research and Human Genetics, 9*(01), 30–37.

Mackintosh, N. J. (1995). *Cyril Burt: Fraud or framed?* Oxford: Oxford University Press.

Mackintosh, N. J. (2011). *IQ and human intelligence* (2 ed.). Oxford: Oxford University Press.

MacLeod, A. K., Davies, G., Payton, A., Tenesa, A., Harris, S. E., Liewald, D., . . . Gow, A. J. (2012).

Genetic copy number variation and general cognitive ability. *PLoS One, 7*(12), e37385.

Maes, H. H., Neale, M. C., & Eaves, L. J. (1997). Genetic and environmental factors in relative body weight and human adiposity. *Behavior Genetics, 27*(4), 325–351.

Maes, H. H., Sullivan, P. F., Bulik, C. M., Neale, M. C., Prescott, C. A., Eaves, L. J., & Kendler, K. S. (2004). A twin study of genetic and environmental influences on tobacco initiation, regular tobacco use and nicotine dependence. *Psychological Medicine, 34*(7), 1251–1261.

Maguire, E. A., Gadian, D. G., Johnsrude, I. S., Good, C. D., Ashburner, J., Frackowiak, R. S., & Frith, C. D. (2000). Navigation-related structural change in the hippocampi of taxi drivers. *Proceedings of the National Academy of Sciences of the United States of America, 97*(8), 4398–4403.

Maguire, E. A., Woollett, K., & Spiers, H. J. (2006). London taxi drivers and bus drivers: A structural MRI and neuropsychological analysis. *Hippocampus., 16*(12), 1091–1101.

Maher, B. (2008). Personal genomes: The case of the missing heritability. *Nature, 456*(7218), 18–21.

Mahowald, M. B., Verp, M. S., & Anderson, R. R. (1998). Genetic counseling: Clinical and ethical challenges. *Annual Review of Genetics, 32*, 547–559.

Malhotra, D., & Sebat, J. (2012). CNVs: Harbingers of a rare variant revolution in psychiatric genetics. *Cell, 148*(6), 1223–1241. doi:http://dx.doi.org/10.1016/j.cell.2012.02.039

Malykh, S. B., Iskoldsky, N. V., & Gindina, E. V. (2005). Genetic analysis of IQ in young adulthood: A Russian twin study. *Personality and Individual Differences, 38*(6), 1475–1485.

Mandoki, M. W., Sumner, G. S., Hoffman, R. P., & Riconda, D. L. (1991). A review of Klinefelter's syndrome in children and adolescents. *Journal of the American Academy of Child and Adolescent Psychiatry, 30*, 167–172.

Manolio, T. A., Collins, F. S., Cox, N. J., Goldstein, D. B., Hindorff, L. A., Hunter, D. J., . . . Visscher, P. M. (2009). Finding the missing heritability of complex diseases. *Nature, 461*(7265), 747–753.

Marceau, K., Horwitz, B. N., Narusyte, J., Ganiban, J. M., Spotts, E. L., Reiss, D., & Neiderhiser, J. M. (2013). Gene–environment correlation underlying the association between parental negativity and adolescent externalizing problems. *Child Development, 84*(6), 2031–2046. doi:10.1111/cdev.12094

Marceau, K., Knopik, V. S., Neiderhiser, J. M., Lichtenstein, P., Spotts, E. L., Ganiban, J. M.,

& Reiss, D. (2015a). Adolescent age moderates genetic and environmental influences on parent–adolescent positivity and negativity: Implications for genotype–environment correlation. *Development and Psychopathology, FirstView*, 1–18.

Marceau, K., McMaster, M. T. B., Smith, T. F., Daams, J. G., Beijsterveldt, C. E. M., Boomsma, D. I., & Knopik, V. S. (2016). The prenatal environment in twin studies: A review of chorionicity. *Behavior Genetics, 46*(3), 286–303.

Marceau, K., Narusyte, J., Lichtenstein, P., Ganiban, J. M., Spotts, E. L., Reiss, D., & Neiderhiser, J. M. (2015b). Parental knowledge is an environmental influence on adolescent externalizing. *Journal of Child Psychology and Psychiatry, 56*(2), 130–137. doi:10.1111/jcpp.12288

Margulies, C., Tully, T., & Dubnau, J. (2005). Deconstructing memory in *Drosophila*. *Current Biology, 15*(17), R700–R713.

Marioni, R. E., Penke, L., Davies, G., Huffman, J. E., Hayward, C., & Deary, I. J. (2014). The total burden of rare, non-synonymous exome genetic variants is not associated with childhood or late-life cognitive ability. *Proceedings of the Royal Society of London B: Biological Sciences, 281*(1781), 20140117.

Marks, M. J. (2013). Genetics matters: Thirty years of progress using mouse models in nicotinic research. *Biochemical Pharmacology, 86*(8), 1105–1113.

Maron, E., Hettema, J. M., & Shlik, J. (2010). Advances in molecular genetics of panic disorder. *Molecular Psychiatry, 15*(7), 681–701.

Martens, M. A., Wilson, S. J., & Reutens, D. C. (2008). Research Review: Williams syndrome: A critical review of the cognitive, behavioral, and neuroanatomical phenotype. *Journal of Child Psychology and Psychiatry, 49*(6), 576–608. doi:10.1111/j.1469-7610.2008.01887.x

Martin, G. M. (2011). The biology of aging: 1985-2010 and beyond. *FASEB Journal, 25*(11), 3756–3762. doi:10.1096/fj.11-1102.ufm

Martin, N., Boomsma, D. I., & Machin, G. (1997). A twin-pronged attack on complex traits. *Nature Genetics, 17*, 387–392.

Martin, N. G., & Eaves, L. J. (1977). The genetical analysis of covariance structure. *Heredity, 38*, 79–95. doi:10.1038/hdy.1977.9

Martinez, D., & Narendran, R. (2010). Imaging neurotransmitter release by drugs of abuse. In D. W. Self & J. K. Staley Gottschalk (Eds.), *Behavioral neuroscience of drug addiction* (Vol. 3, pp. 219–245).

Martynyuk, A. E., van Spronsen, F. J., & Van der Zee, E. A. (2010). Animal models of brain dysfunction in phenylketonuria. *Molecular Genetics and Metabolism, 99*, S100–S105. doi:10.1016/j.ymgme.2009.10.181

Mascheretti, S., Riva, V., Giorda, R., Beri, S., Lanzoni, L. F. E., Cellino, M. R., & Marino, C. (2014). KIAA0319 and ROBO1: Evidence on association with reading and pleiotropic effects on language and mathematics abilities in developmental dyslexia. *Journal of Human Genetics, 59*(4), 189–197.

Mataix-Cols, D., Boman, M., Monzani, B., Rück, C., Serlachius, E., Långström, N., & Lichtenstein, P. (2013). Population-based, multigenerational family clustering study of obsessive-compulsive disorder. *JAMA Psychiatry, 70*(7), 709–717.

Matera, A. G., & Wang, Z. (2014). A day in the life of the spliceosome. *Nature Reviews Molecular Cell Biology, 15*(2), 108–121. doi:10.1038/nrm3742

Matheny, A. P., Jr. (1980). Bayley's Infant Behavioral Record: Behavioral components and twin analysis. *Child Development, 51*, 1157–1167.

Matheny, A. P., Jr. (1989). Children's behavioral inhibition over age and across situations: Genetic similarity for a trait during change. *Journal of Personality, 57*(2), 215–235.

Matheny, A. P., Jr. (1990). Developmental behavior genetics: Contributions from the Louisville Twin Study. In M. E. Hahn, J. K. Hewitt, N. D. Henderson, & R. H. Benno (Eds.), *Developmental behavior genetics: Neural, biometrical, and evolutionary approaches* (pp. 25–39). New York: Chapman & Hall.

Matheny, A. P., Jr., & Dolan, A. B. (1975). Persons, situations, and time: A genetic view of behavioral change in children. *Journal of Personality and Social Psychology, 14*, 224–234.

Mather, K., & Jinks, J. L. (1982). *Biometrical genetics: The study of continuous variation* (Vol. 3). New York: Chapman & Hall.

Mathes, W. F., Kelly, S. A., & Pomp, D. (2011). Advances in comparative genetics: Influence of genetics on obesity. *British Journal of Nutrition, 106*, S1–S10. doi:10.1017/s0007114511001905

Matsumoto, J., Sugiura, Y., Yuki, D., Hayasaka, T., Goto-Inoue, N., Zaima, N., . . . Niwa, S. (2011). Abnormal phospholipids distribution in the prefrontal cortex from a patient with schizophrenia revealed by matrix-assisted laser desorption/ionization imaging mass spectrometry. *Analytical and Bioanalytical Chemistry, 400*(7), 1933–1943. doi:10.1007/s00216-011-4909-3

Matteson, L. K., McGue, M., & Iacono, W. G. (2013). Shared environmental influences on personality: A combined twin and adoption approach. *Behavior Genetics, 43*(6), 491–504.

Mattheisen, M., Samuels, J. F., Wang, Y., Greenberg, B. D., Fyer, A. J., McCracken, J. T., . . . Grados, M. A. (2014). Genome-wide association study in obsessive-compulsive disorder:

Results from the OCGAS. *Molecular Psychiatry, 20*(3), 337–344.

Matthews, K. A., Kaufman, T. C., & Gelbart, W. M. (2005). Research resources for *Drosophila:* The expanding universe. *Nature Reviews Genetics, 6*(3), 179–193.

Maubourguet, N., Lesne, A., Changeux, J.-P., Maskos, U., & Faure, P. (2008). Behavioral sequence analysis reveals a novel role for ß2* nicotinic receptors in exploration. *PLoS Computer Biology, 4*(11), e1000229. doi:10.1371/journal.pcbi.1000229

Maxson, S. C. (2009). The genetics of offensive aggression in mice. In Y.-K. Kim (Ed.), *Handbook of behavior genetics* (pp. 301–316). New York: Springer.

Mayford, M., & Kandel, E. R. (1999). Genetic approaches to memory storage. *Trends in Genetics, 15*(11), 463–470.

Mazzeo, S. E., Mitchell, K. S., Bulik, C. M., Aggen, S. H., Kendler, K. S., & Neale, M. C. (2010). A twin study of specific bulimia nervosa symptoms. *Psychological Medicine, 40*(7), 1203–1213. doi:10.1017/s003329170999122x

McAdams, T. A., Gregory, A. M., & Eley, T. C. (2013). Genes of experience: Explaining the heritability of putative environmental variables through their association with behavioural and emotional traits. *Behavior Genetics, 43*(4), 314–328.

McAdams, T. A., Neiderhiser, J. M., Rijsdijk, F. V., Narusyte, J., Lichtenstein, P., & Eley, T. C. (2014). Accounting for genetic and environmental confounds in associations between parent and child characteristics: A systematic review of children-of-twins studies. *Psychological Bulletin, 140*(4), 1138–1173. doi:10.1037/a0036416

McAdams, T. A., Rijsdijk, F. V., Neiderhiser, J. M., Narusyte, J., Shaw, D. S., Natsuaki, M. N., . . . Eley, T. C. (2015). The relationship between parental depressive symptoms and offspring psychopathology: Evidence from a children-of-twins study and an adoption study. *Psychological Medicine, 45*(12):2583–1294.

McBride, C. M., Koehly, L. M., Sanderson, S. C., & Kaphingst, K. A. (2010). The behavioral response to personalized genetic information: Will genetic risk profiles motivate individuals and families to choose more healthful behaviors? *Annual Review of Public Health, 31*, 89–103. doi:10.1146/annurev.publhealth.012809.103532

McCaffery, J. M., Papandonatos, G. D., Lyons, M. J., & Niaura, R. (2008). Educational attainment and the heritability of self-reported hypertension among male Vietnam-era twins. *Psychosomatic Medicine, 70*(7), 781–786.

McCartney, K., Harris, M. J., & Bernieri, F. (1990). Growing up and growing apart: A developmental meta-analysis of twin studies. *Psychological Bulletin, 107*, 226–237.

McCay, C. M., Crowell, M. F., & Maynard, L. A. (1935). The effect of retarded growth upon the length of life span and upon the ultimate body size. *The Journal of Nutrition, 10*(1), 63–79.

McClearn, G. E. (1963). The inheritance of behavior. In L. J. Postman (Ed.), *Psychology in the making* (pp. 144–252). New York: Knopf.

McClearn, G. E. (1976). Experimental behavioural genetics. In D. Barltrop (Ed.), *Aspects of Genetics in Paediatrics* (pp. 31–39). London: Fellowship of Postdoctorate Medicine.

McClearn, G. E., Johansson, B., Berg, S., Pedersen, N. L., Ahern, F., Petrill, S. A., & Plomin, R. (1997). Substantial genetic influence on cognitive abilities in twins 80+ years old. *Science, 276*, 1560–1563. doi:10.1126/science.276.5318.1560

McClearn, G. E., & Rodgers, D. A. (1959). Differences in alcohol preference among inbred strains of mice. *Quarterly Journal of Studies on Alcohol, 52*, 62–67.

McClearn, G. E., Svartengren, M., Pedersen, N. L., Heller, D. A., & Plomin, R. (1994). Genetic and environmental influences on pulmonary function in aging Swedish twins. *Journal of Gerontology, 49*(6), M264–M268.

McGeary, J. (2009). The DRD4 exon 3 VNTR polymorphism and addiction-related phenotypes: A review. *Pharmacology Biochemistry and Behavior, 93*(3), 222–229. doi:10.1016/j.pbb.2009.03.010

McGettigan, P. A. (2013). Transcriptomics in the RNA-seq era. *Current Opinion in Chemical Biology, 17*(1), 4–11. doi:http://dx.doi.org/10.1016/j.cbpa.2012.12.008

McGough, J. J., Loo, S. K., McCracken, J. T., Dang, J., Clark, S., Nelson, S. F., & Smalley, S. L. (2008). CBCL pediatric bipolar disorder profile and ADHD: Comorbidity and quantitative trait loci analysis. *Journal of the American Academy of Child and Adolescent Psychiatry, 47*(10), 1151–1157. doi:10.1097/CHI.0b013e3181825a68

McGrath, M., Kawachi, I., Ascherio, A., Colditz, G. A., Hunter, D. J., & De, V. I. (2004). Association between catechol-O-methyltransferase and phobic anxiety. *American Journal of Psychiatry, 161*(9), 1703–1705.

McGue, M., Bacon, S., & Lykken, D. T. (1993a). Personality stability and change in early adulthood: A behavioral genetic analysis. *Developmental Psychology, 29*, 96–109.

McGue, M., Bouchard, T. J., Jr., Iacono, W. G., & Lykken, D. T. (1993b). Behavioral genetics of cognitive ability: A life-span perspective. In R. Plomin & G. E. McClearn (Eds.), *Nature, nurture, and psychology* (pp. 59–76). Washington, DC: American Psychological Association.

McGue, M., & Christensen, K. (2013). Growing old but not growing apart: Twin similarity in the latter half of the lifespan. *Behavior Genetics, 43*(1), 1–12.

McGue, M., & Gottesman, I. I. (1989). Genetic linkage in schizophrenia: Perspectives from genetic epidemiology. *Schizophrenia Bulletin, 15,* 453–464.

McGue, M., Keyes, M., Sharma, A., Elkins, I., Legrand, L., Johnson, W., & Iacono, W. G. (2007). The environments of adopted and non-adopted youth: Evidence on range restriction from the Sibling Interaction and Behavior Study (SIBS). *Behavior Genetics, 37*(3), 449–462. doi:10.1007 /s10519-007-9142-7

McGue, M., & Lykken, D. T. (1992). Genetic influence on risk of divorce. *Psychological Science, 3,* 368–373.

McGue, M., Sharma, S., & Benson, P. (1996). Parent and sibling influences on adolescent alcohol use and misuse: Evidence from a U.S. adoption court. *Journal of Studies on Alcohol, 57,* 8–18.

McGuffin, P., Cohen, S., & Knight, J. (2007). Homing in on depression genes. *American Journal of Psychiatry, 164*(2), 195–197.

McGuffin, P., Farmer, A. E., & Gottesman, I. I. (1987). Is there really a split in schizophrenia? The genetic evidence. *British Journal of Psychiatry, 50,* 581–592.

McGuffin, P., & Gottesman, I. I. (1985). Genetic influences on normal and abnormal development. In M. Rutter & L. Hersov (Eds.), *Child and adolescent psychiatry: Modern approaches* (Vol. 2, pp. 17–33). Oxford: Blackwell Scientific.

McGuffin, P., Gottesman, I. I., & Owen, M. J. (2002). *Psychiatric genetics and genomics.* Oxford: Oxford University Press.

McGuffin, P., & Katz, R. (1986). Nature, nurture, and affective disorder. In J. W. F. Deakin (Ed.), *The biology of depression* (pp. 26–51). London: Gaskell Press.

McGuffin, P., Katz, R., Watkins, S., & Rutherford, J. (1996). A hospital-based twin register of the heritability of DSM-IV unipolar depression. *Archives of General Psychiatry, 53,* 129–136.

McGuffin, P., Knight, J., Breen, G., Brewster, S., Boyd, P. R., Craddock, N., . . . Farmer, A. E. (2005). Whole genome linkage scan of recurrent depressive disorder from the depression network study. *Human Molecular Genetics, 14*(22), 3337–3345.

McGuffin, P., Owen, M. J., O'Donovan, M. C., Thapar, A., & Gottesman, I. I. (1994). *Seminars in psychiatric genetics.* London, UK: Gaskell.

McGuffin, P., Rijsdijk, F., Andrew, M., Sham, P., Katz, R., & Cardno, A. (2003). The heritability of bipolar affective disorder and the genetic relationship to unipolar depression. *Archives of General Psychiatry, 60*(5), 497–502.

McGuffin, P., & Rivera, M. (2015). The interaction between stress and genetic factors in the etiopathogenesis of depression. *World Psychiatry, 14*(2), 161–163.

McGuffin, P., Sargeant, M., Hetti, G., Tidmarsh, S., Whatley, S., & Marchbanks, R. M. (1990). Exclusion of a schizophrenia susceptibility gene from the chromosome 5q11-q13 region. New data and a reanalysis of previous reports. *American Journal of Human Genetics, 47,* 534–535.

McGuffin, P., & Sturt, E. (1986). Genetic markers in schizophrenia. *Human Heredity, 36*(2), 65–88.

McGuire, S., Neiderhiser, J. M., Reiss, D., Hetherington, E. M., & Plomin, R. (1994). Genetic and environmental influences on perceptions of self-worth and competence in adolescence: A study of twins, full siblings, and step-siblings. *Child Development*(65), 785–799. doi:10.2307/1131418

McGuire, S. E., Deshazer, M., & Davis, R. L. (2005). Thirty years of olfactory learning and memory research in *Drosophila melanogaster. Progress in Neurobiology, 76*(5), 328–347.

McLoughlin, G., Rijsdijk, F., Asherson, P., & Kuntsi, J. (2011). Parents and teachers make different contributions to a shared perspective on hyperactive-impulsive and inattentive symptoms: A multivariate analysis of parent and teacher ratings on the symptom domains of ADHD. *Behavior Genetics, 41*(5), 668–679. doi:10.1007 /s10519-011-9473-2

McMahon, R. C. (1980). Genetic etiology in the hyperactive child syndrome: A critical review. *American Journal of Orthopsychiatry, 50,* 145–150.

McRae, A. F., Matigian, N. A., Vadlamudi, L., Mulley, J. C., Mowry, B., Martin, N. G., . . . Visscher, P. M. (2007). Replicated effects of sex and genotype on gene expression in human lymphoblastoid cell lines. *Human Molecular Genetics, 16*(4), 364–373.

McRae, A. F., Wright, M. J., Hansell, N. K., Montgomery, G. W., & Martin, N. G. (2013). No association between general cognitive ability and rare copy number variation. *Behavior Genetics, 43*(3), 202–207.

Meaburn, E., Dale, P. S., Craig, I. W., & Plomin, R. (2002). Language-impaired children: No sign of the FOXP2 mutation. *Neuroreport, 13*(8), 1075–1077. doi:10.1097/00001756-200206120-00020

Meaburn, E. L., Harlaar, N., Craig, I. W., Schalkwyk, L. C., & Plomin, R. (2008). Quantitative trait locus association scan of early reading disability and ability using pooled DNA and 100K SNP microarrays in a sample of 5760 children. *Molecular Psychiatry, 13,* 729–740. doi:10.1038 /sj.mp.4002063

Meaney, M. J. (2010). Epigenetics and the biological definition of gene × environment interactions. *Child Development, 81*(1), 41–79.

Medlund, P., Cederlof, R., Floderus-Myrhed, B., Friberg, L., & Sorensen, S. (1977). A new Swedish twin registry. *Acta Medica Scandinavica Supplementum, 60*, 1–11.

Mednick, S. A., Gabrielli, W. F., & Hutchings, B. (1984). Genetic factors in criminal behavior: Evidence from an adoption cohort. *Science, 224*, 891–893.

Mendel, G. J. (1866). Versuche ueber Pflanzenhybriden. *Verhandlungen des Naturforschunden Vereines in Bruenn, 4*, 3–47.

Mendlewicz, J., & Rainer, J. D. (1977). Adoption study supporting genetic transmission in manic-depressive illness. *Nature, 268*, 327–329.

Merikangas, K. R., He, J.-P., Brody, D., Fisher, P. W., Bourdon, K., & Koretz, D. S. (2010). Prevalence and treatment of mental disorders among U.S. children in the 2001-2004 NHANES. *Pediatrics, 125*(1), 75–81. doi:10.1542/peds.2008-2598

Merikangas, K. R., & McClair, V. L. (2012). Epidemiology of substance use disorders. *Human Genetics, 131*(6), 779–789.

Merikangas, K. R., Stolar, M., Stevens, D. E., Goulet, J., Preisig, M. A., Fenton, B., . . . Rounsaville, B. J. (1998). Familial transmission of substance use disorders. *Archives of General Psychiatry, 55*(11), 973–979.

Merriman, C. (1924). The intellectual resemblance of twins. *Psychological Monographs, 33*, 1–58.

Merwood, A., Chen, W., Rijsdijk, F., Skirrow, C., Larsson, H., Thapar, A., . . . Asherson, P. (2014). Genetic associations between the symptoms of attention-deficit/hyperactivity disorder and emotional lability in child and adolescent twins. *Journal of the American Academy of Child & Adolescent Psychiatry, 53*(2), 209–220.

Merwood, A., Greven, C. U., Price, T. S., Rijsdijk, F., Kuntsi, J., McLoughlin, G., . . . Asherson, P. J. (2013). Different heritabilities but shared etiological influences for parent, teacher and self-ratings of ADHD symptoms: An adolescent twin study. *Psychological Medicine, 43*(09), 1973–1984.

Meyer, J. M. (1995). Genetic studies of obesity across the life span. In L. R. Cardon & J. K. Hewitt (Eds.), *Behavior genetic approaches to behavioral medicine* (pp. 145–166). New York: Plenum.

Middelberg, R. P., Martin, N. G., & Whitfield, J. B. (2006). Longitudinal genetic analysis of plasma lipids. *Twin Research and Human Genetics, 9*(04), 550–557.

Middeldorp, C. M., Cath, D. C., Van Dyck, R., & Boomsma, D. I. (2005). The co-morbidity of anxiety and depression in the perspective of genetic epidemiology. A review of twin and family studies. *Psychological Medicine, 35*(5), 611–624.

Milagro, F. I., Campion, J., Garcia-Diaz, D. F., Goyenechea, E., Paternain, L., & Martinez, J. A. (2009). High fat diet-induced obesity modifies the methylation pattern of leptin promoter in rats. *Journal of Physiology and Biochemistry, 65*(1), 1–9.

Miles, D. R., Silberg, J. L., Pickens, R. W., & Eaves, L. J. (2005). Familial influences on alcohol use in adolescent female twins: Testing for genetic and environmental interactions. *Journal of Studies of Alcohol, 66*(4), 445–451.

Miller, J. A., Ding, S. L., Sunkin, S. M., Smith, K. A., Ng, L., Szafer, A., . . . & Lein, E. S. (2014). Transcriptional landscape of the prenatal human brain. *Nature 508*, 199–206. doi:10.1038/nature13185

Miller, N., & Gerlai, R. (2007). Quantification of shoaling behaviour in zebrafish (*Danio rerio*). *Behavioural Brain Research, 184*(2), 157–166. doi:10.1016/j.bbr.2007.07.007

Milne, B. J., Caspi, A., Harrington, H., Poulton, R., Rutter, M., & Moffitt, T. E. (2009). Predictive value of family history on severity of illness: The case for depression, anxiety, alcohol dependence, and drug dependence. *Archives of General Psychiatry, 66*(7), 738–747. doi:10.1001/archgenpsychiatry.2009.55

Minică, C. C., Dolan, C. V., Hottenga, J.-J., Pool, R., Fedko, I. O., Mbarek, H., . . . Vink, J. M. (2015). Heritability, SNP-and gene-based analyses of cannabis use initiation and age at onset. *Behavior Genetics, 45*(5), 503–513.

Mistry, M., Gillis, J., & Pavlidis, P. (2013). Meta-analysis of gene coexpression networks in the post-mortem prefrontal cortex of patients with schizophrenia and unaffected controls. *BMC Neuroscience, 14*, 105. doi:10.1186/1471-2202-14-105

Mitchell, J. J., Trakadis, Y. J., & Scriver, C. R. (2011). Phenylalanine hydroxylase deficiency. *Genetics in Medicine, 13*(8), 697–707. doi:10.1097/GIM.0b013e3182141b48

Miyake, A., & Friedman, N. P. (2012). The nature and organization of individual differences in executive functions: Four general conclusions. *Current Directions in Psychological Science, 21*(1), 8–14.

Moberg, T., Lichtenstein, P., Forsman, M., & Larsson, H. (2011). Internalizing behavior in adolescent girls affects parental emotional over-involvement: A cross-lagged twin study. *Behavior Genetics, 41*(2), 223–233. doi:10.1007/s10519-010-9383-8

Moehring, A. J., & Mackay, T. F. (2004). The quantitative genetic basis of male mating behavior in *Drosophila melanogaster*. *Genetics, 167*(3), 1249–1263.

Moeller, F. G., & Dougherty, D. M. (2001). Antisocial personality disorder, alcohol, and aggression. *Alcohol Research & Health, 25*(1), 5–11.

Moffitt, T. E. (1993). Adolescence-limited and life-course-persistent antisocial behavior: A developmental taxonomy. *Psychological Review, 100*(4), 674–701.

Moffitt, T. E. (2005). The new look of behavioral genetics in developmental psychopathology: Gene-environment interplay in antisocial behaviors. *Psychological Bulletin, 131*(4), 533–554.

Monks, S. A., Leonardson, A., Zhu, H., Cundiff, P., Pietrusiak, P., Edwards, S., . . . Schadt, E. E. (2004). Genetic inheritance of gene expression in human cell lines. *American Journal of Human Genetics, 75*(6), 1094–1105.

Montague, C. T., Farooqi, I. S., Whitehead, J. P., Soos, M. A., Rau, H., Wareham, N. J., . . . P'Rahilly, S. (1997). Congenital leptin deficiency is associated with severe early-onset obesity in humans. *Nature, 387*(June), 904–908.

Moressis, A., Friedrich, A. R., Pavlopoulos, E., Davis, R. L., & Skoulakis, E. M. C. (2009). A dual role for the adaptor protein DRK in *Drosophila* olfactory learning and memory. *Journal of Neuroscience, 29*(8), 2611–2625. doi:10.1523/jneurosci.3670-08.2009

Morgan, T. H., Sturtevant, A. H., Muller, H. J., & Bridges, C. B. (1915). *The mechanism of Mendelian heredity.* New York: Holt.

Morley, K. I., Lynskey, M. T., Madden, P. A. F., Treloar, S. A., Heath, A. C., & Martin, N. G. (2007). Exploring the inter-relationship of smoking age-at-onset, cigarette consumption and smoking persistence: Genes or environment? *Psychological Medicine, 37*(9), 1357–1367. doi:10.1017/s0033291707000748

Morley, M., Molony, C. M., Weber, T. M., Devlin, J. L., Ewens, K. G., Spielman, R. S., & Cheung, V. G. (2004). Genetic analysis of genome-wide variation in human gene expression. *Nature, 430*(7001), 743–747.

Mosher, L. R., Polling, W., & Stabenau, J. R. (1971). Identical twins discordant for schizophrenia: Neurological findings. *Archives of General Psychiatry, 24,* 422–430.

Mosing, M. A., Gordon, S. D., Medland, S. E., Statham, D. J., Nelson, E. C., Heath, A. C., . . . Wray, N. R. (2009a). Genetic and environmental influences on the co-morbidity between depression, panic disorder, agoraphobia, and social phobia: A twin study. *Depression and Anxiety, 26*(11), 1004–1011. doi:10.1002/da.20611

Mosing, M. A., Pedersen, N. L., Cesarini, D., Johannesson, M., Magnusson, P. K. E., Nakamura, J., . . . Ullén, F. (2012). Genetic and environmental influences on the relationship between flow proneness, locus of control and behavioral inhibition. *PLoS ONE, 7*(11), e47958. doi:10.1371/journal.pone.0047958

Mosing, M. A., Pedersen, N. L., Martin, N. G., & Wright, M. J. (2010a). Sex differences in the genetic architecture of optimism and health and their interrelation: A study of Australian and Swedish twins. *Twin Research and Human Genetics, 13*(04), 322–329.

Mosing, M. A., Verweij, K. J. H., Medland, S. E., Painter, J., Gordon, S. D., Heath, A. C., . . . Martin, N. G. (2010b). A genome-wide association study of self-rated health. *Twin Research and Human Genetics, 13*(04), 398–403.

Mosing, M. A., Zietsch, B. P., Shekar, S. N., Wright, M. J., & Martin, N. G. (2009b). Genetic and environmental influences on optimism and its relationship to mental and self-rated health: A study of aging twins. *Behavior Genetics, 39*(6), 597–604. doi:10.1007/s10519-009-9287-7

Muhle, R., Trentacoste, S. V., & Rapin, I. (2004). The genetics of autism. *Pediatrics, 113*(5), e472–e486.

Muhleisen, T. W., Leber, M., Schulze, T. G., Strohmaier, J., Degenhardt, F., Treutlein, J., . . . Cichon, S. (2014). Genome-wide association study reveals two new risk loci for bipolar disorder. *Nature Communications, 5.* doi:10.1038/ncomms4339

Mullin, A. P., Sadanandappa, M. K., Ma, W., Dickman, D. K., VijayRaghavan, K., Ramaswami, M., . . . Faundez, V. (2015). Gene dosage in the dysbindin schizophrenia susceptibility network differentially affect synaptic function and plasticity. *The Journal of Neuroscience, 35*(1), 325–338.

Mullineaux, P. Y., Deater-Deckard, K., Petrill, S. A., Thompson, L. A., & DeThorne, L. S. (2009). Temperament in middle childhood: A behavioral genetic analysis of fathers' and mothers' reports. *Journal of Research in Personality, 43*(5), 737–746. doi:10.1016/j.jrp.2009.04.008

Munafo, M. R., Clark, T. G., Moore, L. R., Payne, E., Walton, R., & Flint, J. (2003). Genetic polymorphisms and personality in healthy adults: A systematic review and meta-analysis. *Molecular Psychiatry, 8*(5), 471–484.

Munafo, M. R., Durrant, C., Lewis, G., & Flint, J. (2009). Gene × environment interactions at the serotonin transporter locus. *Biological Psychiatry, 65*(3), 211–219. doi:10.1016/j.biopsych.2008.06.009

Munafo, M. R., & Flint, J. (2011). Dissecting the genetic architecture of human personality. *Trends in Cognitive Sciences, 15*(9), 395–400. doi:10.1016/j.tics.2011.07.007

Murray, R. M., Lewis, S. W., & Reveley, A. M. (1985). Towards an aetiological classification of schizophrenia. *The Lancet, 1,* 1023–1026.

Mustelin, L., Joutsi, J., Latvala, A., Pietilainen, K. H., Rissanen, A., & Kaprio, J. (2012). Genetic influences on physical activity in young adults: A twin study. *Medicine and Science in Sports and Exercise, 44*(7), 1293–1301. doi:10.1249/MSS.0b013e3182479747

Mustelin, L., Silventoinen, K., Pietilainen, K., Rissanen, A., & Kaprio, J. (2009). Physical activity reduces the influence of genetic effects on BMI and waist circumference: A study in young adult twins. *International Journal of Obesity, 33*(1), 29–36.

Nadler, J. J., Zou, F., Huang, H., Moy, S. S., Lauder, J., Crawley, J. N., . . . Magnuson, T. R. (2006). Large-scale gene expression differences across brain regions and inbred strains correlate with a behavioral phenotype. *Genetics, 174*(3), 1229–1236.

Nair, V. S., Pritchard, C. C., Tewari, M., & Ioannidis, J. P. A. (2014). Design and analysis for studying microRNAs in human disease: A primer on -omic technologies. *American Journal of Epidemiology, 180*(2), 140–152. doi:10.1093/aje/kwu135

Nan, C., Guo, B., Warner, C., Fowler, T., Barrett, T., Boomsma, D., . . . Zeegers, M. (2012). Heritability of body mass index in pre-adolescence, young adulthood and late adulthood. *European Journal of Epidemiology, 27*(4), 247–253. doi:10.1007/s10654-012-9678-6

Narusyte, J., Neiderhiser, J. M., Andershed, A.-K., D'Onofrio, B. M., Reiss, D., Spotts, E., . . . Lichtenstein, P. (2011). Parental criticism and externalizing behavior problems in adolescents: The role of environment and genotype-environment correlation. *Journal of Abnormal Psychology, 120*(2), 365–376. doi:10.1037/a0021815

Narusyte, J., Neiderhiser, J. M., D'Onofrio, B. M., Reiss, D., Spotts, E. L., Ganiban, J., & Lichtenstein, P. (2008). Testing different types of genotype-environment correlation: An extended children-of-twins model. *Developmental Psychology, 44*(6), 1591–1603. doi:10.1037/a0013911

Nash, M. W., Huezo-Diaz, P., Williamson, R. J., Sterne, A., Purcell, S., Hoda, F., . . . Sham, P. C. (2004). Genome-wide linkage analysis of a composite index of neuroticism and mood-related scales in extreme selected sibships. *Human Molecular Genetics, 13*(19), 2173–2182. doi:10.1093/hmg/ddh239

National Human Genome Institute. (2010). Retrieved from https://www.genome.gov/

National Society of Genetic Counselors. National Society of Genetic Counselors. Retrieved from www.nsgc.org

Natsuaki, M. N., Ge, X., Leve, L. D., Neiderhiser, J. M., Shaw, D. S., Conger, R. D., . . . Reiss, D. (2010). Genetic liability, environment, and the development of fussiness in toddlers: The roles of maternal depression and parental responsiveness. *Developmental Psychology, 46*(5), 1147–1158. doi:10.1037/a0019659

Natsuaki, M. N., Leve, L. D., Neiderhiser, J. M., Shaw, D. S., Scaramella, L. V., Ge, X., & Reiss, D. (2013). Intergenerational transmission of risk for social inhibition: The interplay between parental responsiveness and genetic influences. *Development and Psychopathology, 25*(1), 261–274. doi:10.1017/S0954579412001010

Naukkarinen, J., Rissanen, A., Kaprio, J., & Pietilainen, K. H. (2012). Causes and consequences of obesity: The contribution of recent twin studies. *International Journal of Obesity, 36*(8), 1017–1024.

NCBI. dbSNP Short Genetic Variations. Retrieved from http://www.ncbi.nlm.nih.gov/SNP/

NCHPEG. (2015). National Coalition for Health Professional Education in Genetics. Retrieved from http://www.nchpeg.org

Neale, B. M., Rivas, M. A., Voight, B. F., Altshuler, D., Devlin, B., Orho-Melander, M., . . . Daly, M. J. (2011). Testing for an unusual distribution of rare variants. *PLoS Genetics, 7*(3), e1001322.

Neale, M. C., & Stevenson, J. (1989). Rater bias in the EASI temperament scales: A twin study. *Journal of Personality and Social Psychology, 56*, 446–455.

Nebel, A., Kleindorp, R., Caliebe, A., Nothnagel, M., Blanché, H., Junge, O., . . . Wichmann, H.-E. (2011). A genome-wide association study confirms APOE as the major gene influencing survival in long-lived individuals. *Mechanisms of Ageing and Development, 132*(6), 324–330.

Need, A. C., Attix, D. K., McEvoy, J. M., Cirulli, E. T., Linney, K. L., Hunt, P., . . . Goldstein, D. B. (2009). A genome-wide study of common SNPs and CNVs in cognitive performance in the CANTAB. *Human Molecular Genetics, 18*(23), 4650–4661. doi:10.1093/hmg/ddp413

Neiderhiser, J. M., & McGuire, S. (1994). Competence during middle childhood. In J. C. DeFries, R. Plomin, & D. W. Fulker (Eds.), *Nature and nurture during middle childhood* (pp. 141–151). Cambridge, MA: Blackwell.

Neiderhiser, J. M., Reiss, D., Hetherington, E. M., & Plomin, R. (1999). Relationships between parenting and adolescent adjustment over time: Genetic and environmental contributions. *Developmental Psychology, 35*(3), 680–692. doi:10.1037/0012-1649.35.3.680

Neiderhiser, J. M., Reiss, D., Pedersen, N. L., Lichtenstein, P., Spotts, E. L., & Hansson, K.

(2004). Genetic and environmental influences on mothering of adolescents: A comparison of two samples. *Developmental Psychology, 40*(3), 335–351. doi:10.1037/0012-1649.40.3.335

Neiss, M. B., Stevenson, J., Legrand, L. N., Iacono, W. G., & Sedikides, C. (2009). Self-esteem, negative emotionality, and depression as a common temperamental core: A study of mid-adolescent twin girls. *Journal of Personality, 77*(2), 327–346. doi:10.1111/j.1467-6494.2008.00549.x

Neisser, U., Boodoo, G., Bouchard, T. J., Jr., Boykin, A. W., Brody, N., Ceci, S. J., . . . Urbina, S. (1996). Intelligence: Knowns and unknowns. *American Psychologist, 51*, 77–101.

Neitz, J., & Neitz, M. (2011). The genetics of normal and defective color vision. *Vision Research, 51*(7), 633–651. doi:http://dx.doi.org/10.1016/j.visres.2010.12.002

Neubauer, A. C., & Fink, A. (2009). Intelligence and neural efficiency. *Neuroscience and Biobehavioral Reviews, 33*(7), 1004–1023. doi:10.1016/j.neubiorev.2009.04.001

Neubauer, A. C., Spinath, F. M., Riemann, R., Borkenau, P., & Angleitner, A. (2000). Genetic (and environmental) influence on two measures of speed of information processing and their relation to psychometric intelligence: Evidence from the German Observational Study of Adult Twins. *Intelligence, 28*(4), 267–289.

Neul, J. L., Kaufmann, W. E., Glaze, D. G., Christodoulou, J., Clarke, A. J., Bahi-Buisson, N., . . . RettSearch Consortium. (2010). Rett syndrome: Revised diagnostic criteria and nomenclature. *Annals of Neurology, 68*(6), 944–950. doi:10.1002/ana.22124

Newbury, D. F., Bonora, E., Lamb, J. A., Fisher, S. E., Lai, C. S. L., Baird, G., . . . and the International Molecular Genetic Study of Autism Consortium. (2002). FOXP2 is not a major susceptibility gene for autism or specific language impairment. *American Journal of Human Genetics, 70*(5), 1318–1327.

Newbury, D. F., Monaco, A. P., & Paracchini, S. (2014). Reading and language disorders: The importance of both quantity and quality. *Genes, 5*(2), 285–309.

Newcomer, J. W., & Krystal, J. H. (2001). NMDA receptor regulation of memory and behavior in humans. *Hippocampus, 11*(5), 529–542.

Newson, A., & Williamson, R. (1999). Should we undertake genetic research on intelligence? *Bioethics, 13*(3-4), 327–342.

Nichols, P. L. (1984). Familial mental retardation. *Behavior Genetics, 14*, 161–170.

Nichols, R. C. (1978). Twin studies of ability, personality, and interests. *Homo, 29*, 158–173.

Nicolson, R., Brookner, F. B., Lenane, M., Gochman, P., Ingraham, L. J., Egan, M. F., . . . Rapoport, J. L. (2003). Parental schizophrenia spectrum disorders in childhood-onset and adult-onset schizophrenia. *American Journal of Psychiatry, 160*(3), 490–495.

Nicolson, R., & Rapoport, J. L. (1999). Childhood-onset schizophrenia: Rare but worth studying. *Biological Psychiatry, 46*(10), 1418–1428.

Nigg, J. T., & Goldsmith, H. H. (1994). Genetics of personality disorders: Perspectives from personality and psychopathology research. *Psychological Bulletin, 115*, 346–380.

Nikolas, M. A., & Burt, S. A. (2010). Genetic and environmental influences on ADHD symptom dimensions of inattention and hyperactivity: A meta-analysis. *Journal of Abnormal Psychology, 119*(1), 1–17. doi:10.1037/a0018010

Nilsson, S. E., Read, S., Berg, S., & Johansson, B. (2009). Heritabilities for fifteen routine biochemical values: Findings in 215 Swedish twin pairs 82 years of age or older. *Scandinavian Journal of Clinical and Laboratory Investigation, 69*(5), 562–569.

Nimptsch, K., & Pischon, T. (2015). Body fatness, related biomarkers and cancer risk: An epidemiological perspective. *Hormone Molecular Biology and Clinical Investigation, 22*(2), 39–51. doi:10.1515/hmbci-2014-0043

Nishizawa, D., Fukuda, K., Kasai, S., Hasegawa, J., Aoki, Y., Nishi, A., . . . Katoh, R. (2014). Genome-wide association study identifies a potent locus associated with human opioid sensitivity. *Molecular Psychiatry, 19*(1), 55–62.

Nivard, M. G., Dolan, C. V., Kendler, K. S., Kan, K. J., Willemsen, G., van Beijsterveldt, C. E., . . . Bartels, M. (2015). Stability in symptoms of anxiety and depression as a function of genotype and environment: A longitudinal twin study from ages 3 to 63 years. *Psychological Medicine, 4*, 1–11.

Novelli, V., Anselmi, C. V., Roncarati, R., Guffanti, G., Malovini, A., Piluso, G., & Puca, A. A. (2008). Lack of replication of genetic associations with human longevity. *Biogerontology, 9*(2), 85–92. doi:10.1007/s10522-007-9116-4

Nudel, R., Simpson, N. H., Baird, G., O'Hare, A., Conti-Ramsden, G., Bolton, P. F., . . . Francks, C. (2014). Genome-wide association analyses of child genotype effects and parent-of-origin effects in specific language impairment. *Genes, Brain and Behavior, 13*(4), 418–429.

Nuffield Council on Bioethics. (2002). *Genetics and human behaviour: The ethical context.* Retrieved from http://nuffieldbioethics.org/project/genetics-behaviour/

Numata, S., Ye, T., Hyde, Thomas M., Guitart-Navarro, X., Tao, R., Wininger, M., . . . Lipska,

Barbara K. (2012). DNA methylation signatures in development and aging of the human prefrontal cortex. *American Journal of Human Genetics, 90*(2), 260–272. doi:10.1016/j.ajhg.2011.12.020

Nurnberger, J. I., Koller, D. L., Jung, J., Edenberg, H. J., Foroud, T., Guella, I., ... Kelsoe, J. R. (2014). Identification of pathways for bipolar disorder: A meta-analysis. *JAMA Psychiatry, 71*(6), 657–664.

Nurnberger, J. I., Wiegand, R., Bucholz, K., O'Connor, S., Meyer, E. T., Reich, T., ... Porjesz, B. (2004). A family study of alcohol dependence: Coaggregation of multiple disorders in relatives of alcohol-dependent probands. *Archives of General Psychiatry, 61*(12), 1246–1256. doi:10.1001/archpsyc.61.12.1246

O'Connor, T. G., & Croft, C. M. (2001). A twin study of attachment in preschool children. *Child Development, 72*(5), 1501–1511.

O'Connor, T. G., Neiderhiser, J. M., Reiss, D., Hetherington, E. M., & Plomin, R. (1998). Genetic contributions to continuity, change, and co-occurrence of antisocial and depressive symptoms in adolescence. *Journal of Child Psychology and Psychiatry, 39*(3), 323–336.

Ogden, C. L., Carroll, M. D., Kit, B. K., & Flegal, K. M. (2014). Prevalence of childhood and adult obesity in the United States, 2011–2012. *JAMA, 311*(8), 806–814. doi:10.1001/jama.2014.732

Ogdie, M. N., Fisher, S. E., Yang, M., Ishii, J., Francks, C., Loo, S. K., ... Nelson, S. F. (2004). Attention deficit hyperactivity disorder: Fine mapping supports linkage to 5p13, 6q12, 16p13, and 17p11. *American Journal of Human Genetics, 75*(4), 661–668.

Ogliari, A., Spatola, C. A., Pesenti-Gritti, P., Medda, E., Penna, L., Stazi, M. A., ... Fagnani, C. (2010). The role of genes and environment in shaping co-occurrence of DSM-IV defined anxiety dimensions among Italian twins aged 8–17. *Journal of Anxiety Disorders, 24*(4), 433–439. doi:10.1016/j.janxdis.2010.02.008

Okbay, A., Beauchamp, J. P., Fontana, M. A. , Lee, J. J. Pers, T. H., Rietveld, C. A., ... Benjamin, D. J. (2016). Genome-wide association study identifies 74 loci associated with educational attainment. *Nature, 533,* 539–542.

Okbay, A., Baselmans, B. M., De Neve, J. E., Turley, P., Nivard, M. G., Fontana, M. A., ... Cesarini, D. (2016). Genetic variants associated with subjective well-being, depressive symptoms, and neuroticism identified through genome-wide analyses. *Nature Genetics, 48*(6):624–633. doi: 10.1038/ng.3552.

Olfson, E., & Bierut, L. J. (2012). Convergence of genome-wide association and candidate gene studies for alcoholism. *Alcoholism: Clinical and Experimental Research, 36*(12), 2086–2094.

Oliver, B. R., Harlaar, N., Hayiou-Thomas, M. E., Kovas, Y., Walker, S. O., Petrill, S. A., ... Plomin, R. (2004). A twin study of teacher-reported mathematics performance and low performance in 7-year-olds. *Journal of Educational Psychology, 96*(3), 504–517. doi:10.1037/0022-0663.96.3.504

Olson, R. K. (2007). Introduction to the special issue on genes, environment and reading. *Reading and Writing, 20*(1-2), 1–11.

Öncel, S. Y., Dick, D. M., Maes, H. H., & Aliev, F. (2014). Risk factors influencing smoking behavior: A Turkish twin study. *Twin Research and Human Genetics, 17*(06), 563–573.

Ooki, S. (2005). Genetic and environmental influences on stuttering and tics in Japanese twin children. *Twin Research and Human Genetics, 8*(1), 69–75.

Ortega-Alonso, A., Pietilainen, K. H., Silventoinen, K., Saarni, S. E., & Kaprio, J. (2012). Genetic and environmental factors influencing BMI development from adolescence to young adulthood. *Behavior Genetics, 42*(1), 73–85. doi:10.1007/s10519-011-9492-z

Ortman, J. M., Velkoff, V. A., & Hogan, H. (2014). An aging nation: The older population in the United States. Washington, DC: U. S. Census Bureau, 25-1140.

Ostrer, H. (2011). Changing the game with whole exome sequencing. *Clinical Genetics, 80*(2), 101–103. doi:10.1111/j.1399-0004.2011.01712.x

Otowa, T., Hek, K., Lee, M., Byrne, E. M., Mirza, S. S., Nivard, M. G., ... Hettema, J. M. (2016). Meta-analysis of genome-wide association studies of anxiety disorders. *Molecular Psychiatry.* doi:10.1038/mp.2015.197

Ott, J., Kamatani, Y., & Lathrop, M. (2011). Family-based designs for genome-wide association studies. *Nature Reviews Genetics, 12*(7), 465–474. doi:10.1038/nrg2989

Owen, M. J., Liddle, M. B., & McGuffin, P. (1994). Alzheimer's disease: An association with apolipoprotein e4 may help unlock the puzzle. *British Medical Journal, 308,* 672–673.

Pagan, J. L., Rose, R. J., Viken, R. J., Pulkkinen, L., Kaprio, J., & Dick, D. M. (2006). Genetic and environmental influences on stages of alcohol use across adolescence and into young adulthood. *Behavior Genetics, 36*(4), 483–497.

Palmer, R. H., Button, T. M., Rhee, S. H., Corley, R. P., Young, S. E., Stallings, M. C., ... Hewitt, J. K. (2012). Genetic etiology of the common liability to drug dependence: Evidence of common and specific mechanisms for DSM-IV dependence symptoms. *Drug and Alcohol Dependence, 123 Suppl 1,* S24–S32. doi:10.1016/j.drugalcdep.2011.12.015

Palmer, R. H. C., Beevers, C., McGeary, J. E., Brick, L. A., & Knopik, V. S. (in press). A preliminary study of genetic variation in the dopaminergic and serotonergic systems and genome-wide additive genetic effects on depression severity and treatment response. *Clinical Psychological Science.*

Palmer, R. H. C., Brick, L., Nugent, N. R., Bidwell, L., McGeary, J. E., Knopik, V. S., & Keller, M. C. (2015a). Examining the role of common genetic variants on alcohol, tobacco, cannabis and illicit drug dependence: Genetics of vulnerability to drug dependence. *Addiction, 110*(3), 530–537.

Palmer, R. H. C., Knopik, V. S., Rhee, S. H., Hopfer, C. J., Corley, R. C., Young, S. E., ... Hewitt, J. K. (2013). Prospective effects of adolescent indicators of behavioral disinhibition on DSM-IV alcohol, tobacco, and illicit drug dependence in young adulthood. *Addictive Behaviors, 38*(9), 2415–2421.

Palmer, R. H. C., McGeary, J. E., Heath, A. C., Keller, M. C., Brick, L. A., & Knopik, V. S. (2015b). Shared additive genetic influences on DSM-IV criteria for alcohol dependence in subjects of European ancestry. *Addiction, 110*(12), 1922–1931.

Panizzon, M. S., Lyons, M. J., Jacobson, K. C., Franz, C. E., Grant, M. D., Eisen, S. A., ... Kremen, W. S. (2011). Genetic architecture of learning and delayed recall: A twin study of episodic memory. *Neuropsychology, 25*(4), 488–498. doi:10.1037/a0022569

Panizzon, M. S., Vuoksimaa, E., Spoon, K. M., Jacobson, K. C., Lyons, M. J., Franz, C. E., ... Kremen, W. S. (2014). Genetic and environmental influences on general cognitive ability: Is g a valid latent construct? *Intelligence, 43*, 65–76.

Papassotiropoulos, A., Stephan, D. A., Huentelman, M. J., Hoerndli, F. J., Craig, D. W., Pearson, J. V., ... de Quervain, D. J. (2006). Common Kibra alleles are associated with human memory performance. *Science, 314*(5798), 475–478.

Pappa, I., Fedko, I. O., Mileva-Seitz, V. R., Hottenga, J. J., Bakermans-Kranenburg, M. J., ... & Rivadeneira, F. (2015). Single nucleotide polymorphism heritability of behavior problems in childhood: Genome-wide complex trait analysis. *Journal of the American Academy of Child & Adolescent Psychiatry, 54*(9), 737–744.

Paris, J. (1999). *Genetics and psychopathology: Predisposition-stress interactions.* Washington, DC: American Psychiatric Press.

Park, B. L., Kim, J. W., Cheong, H. S., Kim, L. H., Lee, B. C., Seo, C. H., ... Shin, H. D. (2013). Extended genetic effects of ADH cluster genes on the risk of alcohol dependence: From GWAS to replication. *Human Genetics, 132*(6), 657–668.

Park, J., Shedden, K., & Polk, T. A. (2012). Correlation and heritability in neuroimaging datasets: A spatial decomposition approach with application to an fMRI study of twins. *Neuroimage, 59*(2), 1132–1142. doi:10.1016/j.neuroimage.2011.06.066

Park, J. H., Wacholder, S., Gail, M. H., Peters, U., Jacobs, K. B., Chanock, S. J., & Chatterjee, N. (2010). Estimation of effect size distribution from genome-wide association studies and implications for future discoveries. *Nature Genetics, 42*(7), 570–575.

Parker, H. G., Kim, L. V., Sutter, N. B., Carlson, S., Lorentzen, T. D., Malek, T. B., ... Kruglyak, L. (2004). Genetic structure of the purebred domestic dog. *Science, 304*(5674), 1160–1164.

Parnas, J., Cannon, T. D., Jacobsen, B., Schulsinger, H., Schulsinger, F., & Mednick, S. A. (1993). Lifetime DSM-II-R diagnostic outcomes in the offspring of schizophrenic mothers: Results from the Copenhagen high-risk study. *Archives of General Psychiatry, 50*, 707–714.

Pashler, H., & Wagenmakers, E. J. (2012). Editors' introduction to the special section on replicability in psychological science: A crisis of confidence? *Perspectives on Psychological Science, 7*(6), 528–530.

Patel, S. (2012). Role of proteomics in biomarker discovery and psychiatric disorders: Current status, potentials, limitations and future challenges. *Expert Review of Proteomics, 9*(3), 249–265.

Patterson, D., & Costa, A. C. (2005). Down syndrome and genetics—a case of linked histories. *Nature Reviews Genetics, 6*(2), 137–147.

Pauls, D. L. (1990). Genetic influences on child psychiatric conditions. In M. Lewis (Ed.), *Child and adolescent psychiatry: A comprehensive textbook* (pp. 351–353). Baltimore: Williams & Wilkins.

Pauls, D. L., Leckman, J. F., & Cohen, D. J. (1993). Familial relationship between Gilles de la Tourette's syndrome, attention deficit disorder, learning difficulties, speech disorders, and stuttering. *Journal of the American Academy of Child and Adolescent Psychiatry, 32*, 1044–1050.

Pauls, D. L., Towbin, K. E., Leckman, J. F., Zahner, G. E. P., & Cohen, D. J. (1986). Gilles de la Tourette's syndrome and obsessive compulsive disorder. *Archives of General Psychiatry, 43*, 1180–1182.

Paunio, T., Korhonen, T., Hublin, C., Partinen, M., Kivimäki, M., Koskenvuo, M., & Kaprio, J. (2009). Longitudinal study on poor sleep and life dissatisfaction in a nationwide cohort of twins. *American Journal of Epidemiology, 169*(2), 206–213. doi:10.1093/aje/kwn305

Pavuluri, M. N., Birmaher, B., & Naylor, M. W. (2005). Pediatric bipolar disorder: A review of the past 10 years. *Journal of the American Academy of Child & Adolescent Psychiatry, 44*(9), 846–871.

Payton, A. (2009). The impact of genetic research on our understanding of normal cognitive ageing: 1995 to 2009. *Neuropsychological Review, 19*(4), 451–477. doi:10.1007/s11065-009-9116-z

Pearson, R., Palmer, R. H. C., Brick, L. A., McGeary, J. E., Knopik, V. S., & Beevers, C. (2016).

Additive genetic contribution to symptom dimensions in major depressive disorder. *Journal of Abnormal Psychology, 125*(4), 495–501.

Pedersen, N. L. (1996). Gerontological behavioral genetics. In J. E. Birren & K. W. Schaie (Eds.), *Handbook of the psychology of aging* (4th Ed., pp. 59–77). San Diego: Academic Press.

Pedersen, N. L., Gatz, M., Plomin, R., Nesselroade, J. R., & McClearn, G. E. (1989a). Individual differences in locus of control during the second half of the life span for identical and fraternal twins reared apart and reared together. *Journal of Gerontology, 44*(4), 100–105. doi:10.1093/geronj/44.4.P100

Pedersen, N. L., Lichtenstein, P., Plomin, R., deFaire, U., McClearn, G. E., & Matthews, K. A. (1989b). Genetic and environmental influences for type A-like measures and related traits: A study of twins reared apart and twins reared together. *Psychosomatic Medicine, 51*(4), 428–440.

Pedersen, N. L., McClearn, G. E., Plomin, R., & Nesselroade, J. R. (1992). Effects of early rearing environment on twin similarity in the last half of the life span. *British Journal of Developmental Psychology, 10*, 255–267.

Pedersen, N. L., Plomin, R., & McClearn, G. E. (1994). Is there G beyond g? (Is there genetic influence on specific cognitive abilities independent of genetic influence on general cognitive ability?). *Intelligence, 18*, 133–143. doi:10.1016/0160-2896(94)90024-8

Peerbooms, O. L., van Os, J., Drukker, M., Kenis, G., Hoogveld, L., de Hert, M., . . . Rutten, B. P. (2011). Meta-analysis of MTHFR gene variants in schizophrenia, bipolar disorder and unipolar depressive disorder: Evidence for a common genetic vulnerability? *Brain, Behavior, and Immunity, 25*(8), 1530–1543. doi:10.1016/j.bbi.2010.12.006

Peirce, J. L., Li, H., Wang, J., Manly, K. F., Hitzemann, R. J., Belknap, J. K., . . . Lu, L. (2006). How replicable are mRNA expression QTL? *Mammalian Genome, 17*(6), 643–656.

Pemberton, C. K., Neiderhiser, J. M., Leve, L. D., Natsuaki, M. N., Shaw, D. S., Reiss, D., & Ge, X. (2010). Influence of parental depressive symptoms on adopted toddler behaviors: An emerging developmental cascade of genetic and environmental effects. *Development and Psychopathology, 22*(4), 803–818. doi:10.1017/s0954579410000477

Pennington, B. F., & Bishop, D. V. M. (2009). Relations among speech, language, and reading disorders. *Annual Review of Psychology, 60*, 283–306.

Pennington, B. F., Filipek, P. A., Lefly, D., Chhabildas, N., Kennedy, D. N., Simon, J. H., . . . DeFries, J. C. (2000). A twin MRI study of size variations in the human brain. *Journal of Cognitive Neuroscience, 12*(1), 223–232.

Peper, J. S., Brouwer, R. M., Boomsma, D. I., Kahn, R. S., & Hulshoff Pol, H. E. (2007). Genetic influences on human brain structure: A review of brain imaging studies in twins. *Human Brain Mapping, 28*(6), 464–473. doi:10.1002/hbm.20398

Perdry, H., Müller-Myhsok, B., & Clerget-Darpoux, F. (2012). Using affected sib-pairs to uncover rare disease variants. *Human Heredity, 74*(3–4), 129–141.

Pergadia, M. L., Agrawal, A., Heath, A. C., Martin, N. G., Bucholz, K. K., & Madden, P. A. F. (2010). Nicotine withdrawal symptoms in adolescent and adult twins. *Twin Research and Human Genetics, 13*(4), 359–369.

Pergadia, M. L., Glowinski, A. L., Wray, N. R., Agrawal, A., Saccone, S. F., Loukola, A., . . . Madden, P. A. F. (2011). A 3p26-3p25 genetic linkage finding for DSM-IV major depression in heavy smoking families. *American Journal of Psychiatry, 168*(8), 848–852. doi:10.1176/appi.ajp.2011.10091319

Pergadia, M. L., Heath, A. C., Martin, N. G., & Madden, P. A. (2006a). Genetic analyses of DSM-IV nicotine withdrawal in adult twins. *Psychological Medicine, 36*(7), 963–972.

Pergadia, M. L., Madden, P. A., Lessov, C. N., Todorov, A. A., Bucholz, K. K., Martin, N. G., & Heath, A. C. (2006b). Genetic and environmental influences on extreme personality dispositions in adolescent female twins. *Journal of Child Psychology & Psychiatry, 47*(9), 902–909.

Pergament, D., & Ilijic, K. (2014). The legal past, present and future of prenatal genetic testing: Professional liability and other legal challenges affecting patient access to services. *Journal of Clinical Medicine, 3*(4), 1437–1465.

Persson, M. E., Roth, L. S. V., Johnsson, M., Wright, D., & Jensen, P. (2015). Human-directed social behaviour in dogs shows significant heritability. *Genes, Brain and Behavior, 14*(4), 337–344.

Petrill, S., Logan, J., Hart, S., Vincent, P., Thompson, L., Kovas, Y., & Plomin, R. (2012). Math fluency is etiologically distinct from untimed math performance, decoding fluency, and untimed reading performance: Evidence from a twin study. *Journal of Learning Disabilities, 45*(4), 371–381. doi:10.1177/0022219411407926

Petrill, S. A., Deater-Deckard, K., Thompson, L. A., Schatschneider, C., DeThorne, L. S., & Vandenbergh, D. J. (2007). Longitudinal genetic analysis of early reading: The Western Reserve Reading Project. *Reading & Writing, 20*, 127–146.

Petrill, S. A., Luo, D., Thompson, L. A., & Detterman, D. K. (1996). The independent prediction of general intelligence by elementary cognitive tasks: Genetic and environmental influences. *Behavior Genetics, 26*, 135–147.

Petrill, S. A., Plomin, R., Berg, S., Johansson, B., Pedersen, N. L., Ahern, F., & McClearn, G. E. (1998). The genetic and environmental relationship between general and specific cognitive abilities in twins age 80 and older. *Psychological Science, 9*(3), 183–189. doi:10.1111/1467-9280.00035

Petrill, S. A., Plomin, R., DeFries, J. C., & Hewitt, J. K. (2003). *Nature, nurture, and the transition to early adolescence.* Oxford: Oxford University Press.

Petrill, S. A., Thompson, L. A., & Detterman, D. K. (1995). The genetic and environmental variance underlying elementary cognitive tasks. *Behavior Genetics, 25*, 199–209.

Petronis, A. (2006). Epigenetics and twins: Three variations on the theme. *Trends in Genetics, 22*(7), 347–350.

Pharoah, P. D. P., Antoniou, A., Bobrow, M., Zimmern, R. L., Easton, D. F., & Ponder, B. A. J. (2002). Polygenic susceptibility to breast cancer and implications for prevention. *Nature Genetics, 31*(1), 33–36.

Phillips, D. I. W. (1993). Twin studies in medical research: Can they tell us whether diseases are genetically determined? *The Lancet, 341*, 1008–1009.

Phillips, K., & Matheny, A. P., Jr. (1995). Quantitative genetic analysis of injury liability in infants and toddlers. *American Journal of Medical Genetics (Neuropsychiatric Genetics), 60*, 64–71.

Phillips, K., & Matheny, A. P., Jr. (1997). Evidence for genetic influence on both cross-situation and situation-specific components of behavior. *Journal of Personality and Social Psychology, 73*, 129–138.

Phillips, T. J., Belknap, J. K., Buck, K. J., & Cunningham, C. L. (1998). Genes on mouse chromosomes 2 and 9 determine variation in ethanol consumption. *Mammalian Genome, 9*, 936–941.

Picchioni, M. M., Walshe, M., Toulopoulou, T., McDonald, C., Taylor, M., Waters-Metenier, S., ... Rijsdijk, F. (2010). Genetic modelling of childhood social development and personality in twins and siblings with schizophrenia. *Psychological Medicine, 40*(8), 1305–1316. doi:10.1017/s0033291709991425

Pietilainen, K. H., Kaprio, J., Rissanen, A., Winter, T., Rimpela, A., Viken, R. J., & Rose, R. J. (1999). Distribution and heritability of BMI in Finnish adolescents aged 16y and 17y: A study of 4884 twins and 2509 singletons. *International Journal of Obesity & Related Metabolic Disorders: Journal of the International Association for the Study of Obesity, 23*(2), 107–115.

Pike, A., McGuire, S., Hetherington, E. M., Reiss, D., & Plomin, R. (1996a). Family environment and adolescent depressive symptoms and antisocial behavior: A multivariate genetic analysis. *Developmental Psychology, 32*(4), 590–603. doi:10.1037/0012-1649.32.4.590

Pike, A., Reiss, D., Hetherington, E. M., & Plomin, R. (1996b). Using MZ differences in the search for nonshared environmental effects. *Journal of Child Psychology and Psychiatry, 37*, 695–704. doi:10.1111/j.1469-7610.1996.tb01461.x

Pillard, R. C., & Bailey, J. M. (1998). Human sexual orientation has a heritable component. *Human Biology, 70*(2), 347–365.

Pilling, L. C., Atikins, J. L., Bowman, K., Jones, S. E., Tyrrell, J., Beaumont, R. N., ... Melzer, D. (2016). Human longevity is influenced by many genetic variants: Evidence from 75,000 UK Biobank participants. *Aging, 8*(3), 547–563.

Pingault, J. B., Viding, E., Galera, C., Greven, C. U., Zheng, Y., Plomin, R., & Rijsdijk, F. (2015). Genetic and environmental influences on the developmental course of attention-deficit/hyperactivity disorder symptoms from childhood to adolescence. *JAMA Psychiatry, 72*(7), 651–658. doi:10.1001/jamapsychiatry.2015.0469

Pinker, S. (2002). *The blank slate: The modern denial of human nature.* New York: Penguin.

Pinto, D., Delaby, E., Merico, D., Barbosa, M., Merikangas, A., Klei, L., ... Scherer, Stephen W. (2014). Convergence of genes and cellular pathways dysregulated in autism spectrum disorders. *American Journal of Human Genetics, 94*(5), 677–694. doi:10.1016/j.ajhg.2014.03.018

Plassman, B. L., & Breitner, J. C. S. (1997). The genetics of dementia in late life. *Psychiatric Clinics of North America, 20*(1), 59–76.

Plomin, R. (1986). *Development, genetics, and psychology.* Hillsdale, NJ: Erlbaum.

Plomin, R. (1987). Developmental behavioral genetics and infancy. In J. Osofsky (Ed.), *Handbook of infant development* (2nd ed., pp. 363–417). New York: Interscience.

Plomin, R. (1988). The nature and nurture of cognitive abilities. In R. J. Sternberg (Ed.), *Advances in the psychology of human intelligence. Vol. 4* (pp. 1–33). Hillsdale, NJ: Lawrence Erlbaum Associates.

Plomin, R. (1994). *Genetics and experience: The interplay between nature and nurture.* Thousand Oaks, CA: Sage Publications Inc.

Plomin, R. (1999). Genetics and general cognitive ability. *Nature, 402*, C25–C29. doi:10.1038/35011520

Plomin, R. (2011). Commentary: Why are children in the same family so different? Non-shared environment three decades later. *International Journal of Epidemiology, 40*(3), 582–592. doi:10.1093/ije/dyq144

Plomin, R. (2014). Genotype-environment correlation in the era of DNA. *Behavior Genetics, 44*(6), 629–638. doi:10.1007/s10519-014-9673-7

Plomin, R., Asbury, K., & Dunn, J. (2001). Why are children in the same family so different? Nonshared environment a decade later. *Canadian Journal of Psychiatry, 46*(3), 225–233.

Plomin, R., & Bergeman, C. S. (1991). The nature of nurture: Genetic influence on "environmental" measures (with open peer commentary). *Behavioral and Brain Sciences, 14*(3), 373–414.

Plomin, R., & Caspi, A. (1999). Behavioral genetics and personality. In L. A. Pervin & O. P. John (Eds.), *Handbook of personality: Theory and research (2nd Edition)* (pp. 251–276). New York: Guildford Press.

Plomin, R., Chipuer, H. M., & Loehlin, J. C. (1990a). Behavioral genetics and personality. In L. A. Pervin (Ed.), *Handbook of personality theory and research* (Vol. 1, pp. 225–243). New York: Guilford.

Plomin, R., Coon, H., Carey, G., DeFries, J. C., & Fulker, D. W. (1991). Parent-offspring and sibling adoption analyses of parental ratings of temperament in infancy and childhood. *Journal of Personality, 59*(4), 705–732. doi:10.1111/j.1467-6494.1991.tb00928.x

Plomin, R., Corley, R., Caspi, A., Fulker, D. W., & DeFries, J. C. (1998). Adoption results for self-reported personality: Evidence for nonadditive genetic effects? *Journal of Personality and Social Psychology, 75*, 211–218. doi:10.1037/0022-3514.75.1.211

Plomin, R., & Crabbe, J. C. (2000). DNA. *Psychological Bulletin, 126*(6), 806–828. doi:10.1037/0033-2909.126.6.806

Plomin, R., & Craig, I. W. (1997). Human behavioral genetics of cognitive abilities and disabilities. *Bioessays, 19*, 1117–1124. doi:10.1002/bies.950191211

Plomin, R., & Daniels, D. (1987). Why are children in the same family so different from each other? *Behavioral and Brain Sciences, 10*, 1–16. doi:10.1017/S0140525X00055941

Plomin, R., & DeFries, J. C. (1985). A parent-offspring adoption study of cognitive abilities in early childhood. *Intelligence, 9*, 341–356. doi:10.1016/0160-2896(85)90019-4

Plomin, R., & DeFries, J. C. (1998). The genetics of cognitive abilities and disabilities. *Scientific American, May*, 62–69. doi:10.1038/scientificamerican0598-62

Plomin, R., DeFries, J. C., & Fulker, D. W. (1988). *Nature and nurture during infancy and early childhood*. Cambridge, U.K.: Cambridge University Press.

Plomin, R., DeFries, J. C., Knopik, V. S., & Neiderhiser, J. M. (2016). Top 10 replicated findings from behavioral genetics. *Perspectives on Psychological Science, 11*(1), 3–23. doi:10.1177/17456915617439

Plomin, R., DeFries, J. C., & Loehlin, J. C. (1977a). Assortative mating by unwed biological parents of adopted children. *Science, 196*, 499–450. doi:10.1126/science.850790

Plomin, R., DeFries, J. C., & Loehlin, J. C. (1977b). Genotype-environment interaction and correlation in the analysis of human behavior. *Psychological Bulletin, 84*, 309–322. doi:10.1037/0033-2909.84.2.309

Plomin, R., Emde, R. N., Braungart, J. M., Campos, J., Corley, R., Fulker, D. W., . . . DeFries, J. C. (1993). Genetic change and continuity from fourteen to twenty months: The MacArthur Longitudinal Twin Study. *Child Development, 64*, 1354–1376. doi:10.2307/1131539

Plomin, R., & Foch, T. T. (1980). A twin study of objectively assessed personality in childhood. *Journal of Personality and Social Psychology, 38*, 680–688. doi:10.1037/0022-3514.39.4.680

Plomin, R., Foch, T. T., & Rowe, D. C. (1981). Bobo clown aggression in childhood: Environment not genes. *Journal of Research in Personality, 14*, 331–342. doi:10.1016/0092-6566(81)90031-3

Plomin, R., Fulker, D. W., Corley, R., & DeFries, J. C. (1997). Nature, nurture and cognitive development from 1 to 16 years: A parent-offspring adoption study. *Psychological Science, 8*, 442–447. doi:10.1111/j.1467-9280.1997.tb00458.x

Plomin, R., Haworth, C. M. A., & Davis, O. S. P. (2009). Common disorders are quantitative traits. *Nature Reviews Genetics, 10*(12), 872–878. doi:10.1038/nrg2670

Plomin, R., Haworth, C. M. A., Meaburn, E. L., Price, T. S., Wellcome Trust Case Control Consortium 2, & Davis, O. S. P. (2013). Common DNA markers can account for more than half of the genetic influence on cognitive abilities. *Psychological Science, 24*(4), 562–568.

Plomin, R., & Kovas, Y. (2005). Generalist genes and learning disabilities. *Psychological Bulletin, 131*, 592–617. doi:10.1037/0033-2909.131.4.592

Plomin, R., Lichtenstein, P., Pedersen, N. L., McClearn, G. E., & Nesselroade, J. R. (1990b). Genetic influence on life events during the last half of the life span. *Psychology and Aging, 5*(1), 25–30. doi:10.1037/0882-7974.5.1.25

Plomin, R., Loehlin, J. C., & DeFries, J. C. (1985). Genetic and environmental components of "environmental" influences. *Developmental Psychology, 21*, 391–402. doi:10.1037/0012-1649.21.3.391

Plomin, R., & McClearn, G. E. (1993). Quantitative trait loci (QTL) analyses and alcohol-related behaviors. *Behavior Genetics, 23*(2), 197–211. doi:10.1007/BF01067425

Plomin, R., Reiss, D., Hetherington, E. M., & Howe, G. W. (1994). Nature and nurture:

Genetic contributions to measures of the family environment. *Developmental Psychology, 30*, 32–43. doi:10.1037/0012-1649.30.1.32

Plomin, R., & Schalkwyk, L. C. (2007). Microarrays. *Developmental Science, 10*, 19–23. doi:10.1111/j.1467-7687.2007.00558.x

Plomin, R., & Simpson, M. A. (2013). The future of genomics for developmentalists. *Development and Psychopathology, 25*(4pt2), 1263–1278.

Plomin, R., & Spinath, F. M. (2002). Genetics and general cognitive ability (g). *Trends in Cognitive Science, 6*(4), 169–176. doi:10.1016 /S1364-6613(00)01853-2

Pluess, M. (2015). *Genetics of psychological wellbeing: The role of heritability and genetics in positive psychology.* OUP Oxford.

Poelmans, G., Buitelaar, J. K., Pauls, D. L., & Franke, B. (2011). A theoretical molecular network for dyslexia: Integrating available genetic findings. *Molecular Psychiatry, 16*(4), 365–382. doi:10.1038 /mp.2010.105

Pol, H. E. H., van Baal, G. C. M., Schnack, H. G., Brans, R. G. H., van der Schot, A. C., Brouwer, R. M., ... Evans, A. C. (2012). Overlapping and segregating structural brain abnormalities in twins with schizophrenia or bipolar disorder. *Archives of General Psychiatry, 69*(4), 349–359.

Polanczyk, G., de Lima, M. S., Horta, B. L., Biederman, J., & Rohde, L. A. (2007). The worldwide prevalence of ADHD: A systematic review and metaregression analysis. *American Journal of Psychiatry, 164*(6), 942–948. doi:10.1176/appi .ajp.164.6.942

Polanczyk, G. V., Willcutt, E. G., Salum, G. A., Kieling, C., & Rohde, L. A. (2014). ADHD prevalence estimates across three decades: An updated systematic review and meta-regression analysis. *International Journal of Epidemiology, 43*(2), 434–442.

Polderman, T. J. C., Benyamin, B., de Leeuw, C. A., Sullivan, P. F., van Bochoven, A., Visscher, P. M., & Posthuma, D. (2015). Meta-analysis of the heritability of human traits based on fifty years of twin studies. *Nature Genetics, 47*(7), 702– 709.

Pollak, D. D., John, J., Hoeger, H., & Lubec, G. (2006a). An integrated map of the murine hippocampal proteome based upon five mouse strains. *Electrophoresis, 27*(13), 2787–2798.

Pollak, D. D., John, J., Schneider, A., Hoeger, H., & Lubec, G. (2006b). Strain-dependent expression of signaling proteins in the mouse hippocampus. *Neuroscience, 138*(1), 149–158.

Poorthuis, R. B., Goriounova, N. A., Couey, J. J., & Mansvelder, H. D. (2009). Nicotinic actions on neuronal networks for cognition: General principles and long-term consequences. *Biochemical Pharmacology, 78*(7), 668–676. doi:10.1016/j.bcp .2009.04.031

Posthuma, D., de Geus, E. J. C., Baare, W. F., Pol, H. E. H., Kahn, R. S., & Boomsma, D. I. (2002). The association between brain volume and intelligence is of genetic origin. *Nature Neuroscience, 5*(2), 83–84.

Posthuma, D., de Geus, E. J. C., Mulder, E. J., Smit, D. J., Boomsma, D. I., & Stam, C. J. (2005). Genetic components of functional connectivity in the brain: The heritability of synchronization likelihood. *Human Brain Mapping, 26*, 191–198.

Posthuma, D., Neale, M. C., Boomsma, D. I., & de Geus, E. J. (2001). Are smarter brains running faster? Heritability of alpha peak frequency, IQ, and their interrelation. *Behavior Genetics, 31*(6), 567–579.

Powell, J. E., Henders, A. K., McRae, A. F., Kim, J., Hemani, G., Martin, N. G., ... Visscher, P. M. (2013). Congruence of additive and non-additive effects on gene expression estimated from pedigree and SNP data. *PLoS Genetics, 9*(5), e1003502.

Power, R. A., Keers, R., Ng, M. Y., Butler, A. W., Uher, R., Cohen-Woods, S., ... Lewis, C. M. (2012). Dissecting the genetic heterogeneity of depression through age at onset. *American Journal of Medical Genetics Part B: Neuropsychiatric Genetics, 159B*(7), 859–868.

Power, R. A., & Pluess, M. (2015). Heritability estimates of the Big Five personality traits based on common genetic variants. *Translational Psychiatry, 5*(7), e604.

Prescott, C. A. (2002). Sex differences in the genetic risk for alcoholism. *Alcohol Research & Health, 26*(4), 264–273.

Prescott, C. A., Sullivan, P. F., Kuo, P. H., Webb, B. T., Vittum, J., Patterson, D. G., ... Kendler, K. S. (2006). Genomewide linkage study in the Irish affected sib pair study of alcohol dependence: Evidence for a susceptibility region for symptoms of alcohol dependence on chromosome 4. *Molecular Psychiatry, 11*(6), 603–611.

Price, R. A., Kidd, K. K., Cohen, D. J., Pauls, D. L., & Leckman, J. F. (1985). A twin study of Tourette syndrome. *Archives of General Psychiatry, 42*, 815–820.

Prince, M., Bryce, R., Albanese, E., Wimo, A., Ribeiro, W., & Ferri, C. P. (2013). The global prevalence of dementia: A systematic review and meta-analysis. *Alzheimer's & Dementia, 9*(1), 63–75.

Purcell, S. (2002). Variance components models for gene-environment interaction in twin analysis. *Twin Research, 5*(6), 554–571.

Purcell, S., & Koenen, K. C. (2005). Environmental mediation and the twin design.

Behavior Genetics, 35(4), 491–498. doi:10.1007/s10519-004-1484-9

Purcell, S. M., Moran, J. L., Fromer, M., Ruderfer, D., Solovieff, N., Roussos, P., . . . Kähler, A. (2014). A polygenic burden of rare disruptive mutations in schizophrenia. *Nature, 506*(7487), 185–190.

Purcell, S. M., Wray, N. R., Stone, J. L., Visscher, P. M., O'Donovan, M. C., Sullivan, P. F., . . . Moran, J. L. (2009). Common polygenic variation contributes to risk of schizophrenia and bipolar disorder. *Nature, 460*(7256), 748–752.

Qi, L., Kraft, P., Hunter, D. J., & Hu, F. B. (2008). The common obesity variant near MC4R gene is associated with higher intakes of total energy and dietary fat, weight change and diabetes risk in women. *Human Molecular Genetics, 17*(22), 3502–3508. doi:10.1093/hmg/ddn242

Quillen, E. E., Chen, X. D., Almasy, L., Yang, F., He, H., Li, X., . . . Deng, H. W. (2014). ALDH2 is associated to alcohol dependence and is the major genetic determinant of "daily maximum drinks" in a GWAS study of an isolated rural Chinese sample. *American Journal of Medical Genetics Part B: Neuropsychiatric Genetics, 165*(2), 103–110.

Rabbani, B., Mahdieh, N., Hosomichi, K., Nakaoka, H., & Inoue, I. (2012). Next-generation sequencing: Impact of exome sequencing in characterizing Mendelian disorders. *Journal of Human Genetics, 57*(10), 621. doi:10.1038/jhg.2012.91

Räihä, I., Kapiro, J., Koskenvuo, M., Rajala, T., & Sourander, L. (1996). Alzheimer's disease in Finnish twins. *The Lancet, 347*, 573–578.

Raine, A. (1993). *The psychopathology of crime: Criminal behavior as a clinical disorder*. San Diego: Academic Press.

Ramachandrappa, S., & Farooqi, I. S. (2011). Genetic approaches to understanding human obesity. *Journal of Clinical Investigation, 121*(6), 2080–2086. doi:10.1172/jci46044

Rankin, C. H. (2002). From gene to identified neuron to behaviour in *Caenorhabditis elegans*. *Nature Reviews Genetics, 3*(8), 622–630.

Rankinen, T., Zuberi, A., Chagnon, Y. C., Weisnagel, S. J., Argyropoulos, G., Walts, B., . . . Bouchard, C. (2006). The human obesity gene map: The 2005 update. *Obesity (Silver Spring). 14*(4), 529–644.

Rasetti, R., & Weinberger, D. R. (2011). Intermediate phenotypes in psychiatric disorders. *Current Opinion in Genetics and Development, 21*(3), 340–348. doi:10.1016/j.gde.2011.02.003

Rasmussen, S. A., & Tsuang, M. T. (1984). The epidemiology of obsessive compulsive disorder. *Journal of Clinical Psychiatry, 45*, 450–457.

Raymond, F. L. (2010). Monogenic causes of mental retardation. In S. J. L. Knight (Ed.), *Genetics of mental retardation: An overview encompassing learning disability and intellectual disability* (Vol. 18, pp. 89–100).

Read, S., Vogler, G. P., Pedersen, N. L., & Johansson, B. (2006). Stability and change in genetic and environmental components of personality in old age. *Personality and Individual Differences, 40*(8), 1637–1647.

Redon, R., Ishikawa, S., Fitch, K. R., Feuk, L., Perry, G. H., Andrews, T. D., . . . Hurles, M. E. (2006). Global variation in copy number in the human genome. *Nature, 444*(7118), 444–454.

Reed, E. W., & Reed, S. C. (1965). *Mental retardation: A family study*. Philadelphia: Saunders.

Reich, T., Edenberg, H. J., Goate, A., Williams, J., Rice, J., Van Eerdewegh, P., . . . Begleiter, H. (1998). Genome-wide search for genes affecting the risk for alcohol dependence. *American Journal of Medical Genetics, 81*, 207–215.

Reichenberg, A., Cederlöf, M., McMillan, A., Trzaskowski, M., Kapara, O., Fruchter, E., . . . Lichtenstein, P. (2016). Discontinuity in the genetic and environmental causes of the intellectual disability spectrum. *Proceedings of the National Academy of Sciences, 113*(4), 1098–1103.

Reiss, D., Leve, L. D., & Neiderhiser, J. M. (2013). How genes and the social environment moderate each other. *American Journal of Public Health, 103*(Suppl 1), S111–S121. doi:10.2105/AJPH.2013.301408

Reiss, D., Neiderhiser, J. M., Hetherington, E. M., & Plomin, R. (2000). *The relationship code: Deciphering genetic and social patterns in adolescent development*. Cambridge, MA: Harvard University Press.

Rende, R. D., Plomin, R., & Vandenberg, S. G. (1990). Who discovered the twin method? *Behavior Genetics, 20*(2), 277–285.

Reyes, A., Haynes, M., Hanson, N., Angly, F. E., Heath, A. C., Rohwer, F., & Gordon, J. I. (2010). Viruses in the faecal microbiota of monozygotic twins and their mothers. *Nature, 466*(7304), 334–338. doi:10.1038/nature09199

Reynolds, C. A., & Finkel, D. (2014). Cognitive and physical aging: Genetic influences and gene-environment interplay. In K. W. Schaie & S. L. Willis (Eds.), *Handbook of the psychology of aging* (8 ed.). Oxford: Elsevier.

Reynolds, C. A., & Finkel, D. (2015). A meta-analysis of heritability of cognitive aging: Minding the "missing heritability" gap. *Neuropsychology Review, 25*(1), 97–112.

Reynolds, C. A., Finkel, D., McArdle, J. J., Gatz, M., Berg, S., & Pedersen, N. L. (2005). Quantitative genetic analysis of latent growth curve models of cognitive abilities in adulthood. *Developmental Psychology, 41*(1), 3.

Reynolds, C. A., Finkel, D., & Zavala, C. (2014). Gene by environment interplay in cognitive aging. In D. Finkel & C. A. Reynolds (Eds.), *Behavior genetics of cognition across the lifespan* (pp. 169–199). New York: Springer.

Reynolds, C. A., Zavala, C., Gatz, M., Vie, L., Johansson, B., Malmberg, B., ... Pedersen, N. L. (2013). Sortilin receptor 1 predicts longitudinal cognitive change. *Neurobiological Aging, 34*(6), 1710-e1711.

Rhea, S.-A., Bricker, J. B., Wadsworth, S. J., & Corley, R. P. (2013). The Colorado Adoption Project. *Twin Research and Human Genetics, 16*(1), 10.1017/thg.2012.1109. doi:10.1017/thg.2012.109

Rhee, S. H., Hewitt, J. K., Young, S. E., Corley, R. P., Crowley, T. J., & Stallings, M. C. (2003). Genetic and environmental influences on substance initiation, use, and problem use in adolescents. *Archives of General Psychiatry, 60*(12), 1256–1264.

Rhee, S. H., & Ronald, A. (2014). *Behavior genetics of psychopathology.* New York: Springer-Verlag.

Rhee, S. H., & Waldman, I. D. (2002). Genetic and environmental influences on antisocial behavior: A meta-analysis of twin and adoption studies. *Psychological Bulletin, 128*(3), 490–529.

Rice, G., Anderson, C., Risch, N., & Ebers, G. (1999). Male homosexuality: Absence of linkage to microsatellite markers at Xq28. *Science, 284,* 665–667.

Rice, L. J., & Einfeld, S. L. (2015). Cognitive and behavioural aspects of Prader–Willi syndrome. *Current Opinion in Psychiatry, 28*(2), 102-106.

Richards, E. J. (2006). Inherited epigenetic variation—revisiting soft inheritance. *Nature Reviews Genetics, 7*(5), 395–401.

Ridaura, V. K., Faith, J. J., Rey, F. E., Cheng, J., Duncan, A. E., Kau, A. L., ... Gordon, J. I. (2013). Gut microbiota from twins discordant for obesity modulate metabolism in mice. *Science, 341*(6150).

Ridge, P. G., Mukherjee, S., Crane, P. K., Kauwe, J. S. K., & Alzheimer's Disease Genetics Consortium. (2013). Alzheimer's disease: Analyzing the missing heritability. *PLoS One, 8*(11): e79771. doi:10.1371/journal.pone.0079771

Riemann, R., Angleitner, A., & Strelau, J. (1997). Genetic and environmental influences on personality: A study of twins reared together using the self- and peer report NEO-FFI scales. *Journal of Personality, 65,* 449–476.

Riese, M. L. (1990). Neonatal temperament in monozygotic and dizygotic twin pairs. *Child Development, 61*(4), 1230–1237.

Rietschel, M., & Treutlein, J. (2013). The genetics of alcohol dependence. *Annals of the New York Academy of Sciences, 1282*(1), 39–70.

Rietveld, C. A., Cesarini, D., Benjamin, D. J., Koellinger, P. D., De Neve, J.-E., Tiemeier, H., ... Bartels, M. (2013a). Molecular genetics and subjective well-being. *Proceedings of the National Academy of Sciences, 110*(24), 9692–9697.

Rietveld, C. A., Conley, D., Eriksson, N., Esko, T., Medland, S. E., Vinkhuyzen, A. A. E., ... Dawes, C. T. (2014a). Replicability and robustness of genome-wide-association studies for behavioral traits. *Psychological Science, 25*(11), 1975–1986.

Rietveld, C. A., Esko, T., Davies, G., Pers, T. H., Turley, P., Benyamin, B., ... Lee, J. J. (2014b). Common genetic variants associated with cognitive performance identified using the proxy-phenotype method. *Proceedings of the National Academy of Sciences, 111*(38), 13790–13794.

Rietveld, C. A., Medland, S. E., Derringer, J., Yang, J., Esko, T., Martin, N. W., ... Agrawal, A. (2013b). GWAS of 126,559 individuals identifies genetic variants associated with educational attainment. *Science, 340*(6139), 1467–1471.

Rijsdijk, F. V., & Boomsma, D. I. (1997). Genetic mediation of the correlation between peripheral nerve conduction velocity and IQ. *Behavior Genetics, 27,* 87–98.

Rijsdijk, F. V., Vernon, P. A., & Boomsma, D. I. (2002). Application of hierarchical genetic models to Raven and WAIS subtests: A Dutch twin study. *Behavior Genetics, 32*(3), 199–210.

Rijsdijsk, F. V., Viding, E., De Brito, S., Forgiarini, M., Mechelli, A., Jones, A. P., & McCrory, E. (2010). Heritable variations in gray matter concentration as a potential endophenotype for psychopathic traits. *Archives of General Psychiatry, 67*(4), 406–413.

Riley, B., & Kendler, K. S. (2006). Molecular genetic studies of schizophrenia. *European Journal of Human Genetics, 14*(6), 669–680.

Rimfeld, K., Kovas, Y., Dale, P. S., & Plomin, R. (2016). True grit and genetics: Predicting academic achievement from personality. *Journal of Personality and Social Psychology* [Epub ahead of print].

Rimol, L. M., Panizzon, M. S., Fennema-Notestine, C., Eyler, L. T., Fischl, B., Franz, C. E., ... Dale, A. M. (2010). Cortical thickness is influenced by regionally specific genetic factors. *Biological Psychiatry, 67*(5), 493–499. doi:10.1016/j.biopsych.2009.09.032

Ripke, S., Sanders, A. R., Kendler, K. S., Levinson, D. F., Sklar, P., Holmans, P. A., ... The Schizophrenia Psychiatric Genome-Wide Association Study (GWAS) Consortium. (2011). Genome-wide association study identifies five new schizophrenia loci. *Nature Genetics, 43*(10), 969–976. doi:10.1038/ng.940

Risch, N., Herrell, R., Lehner, T., Liang, K. Y., Eaves, L., Hoh, J., . . . Merikangas, K. R. (2009). Interaction between the serotonin transporter gene (5-HTTLPR), stressful life events, and risk of depression: A meta-analysis. *Journal of the American Medical Association, 301*(23), 2462–2471.

Risch, N., Hoffmann, T. J., Anderson, M., Croen, L. A., Grether, J. K., & Windham, G. C. (2014). Familial recurrence of autism spectrum disorder: Evaluating genetic and environmental contributions. *American Journal of Psychiatry, 171*(11), 1206–1213.

Risch, N., & Merikangas, K. R. (1996). The future of genetic studies of complex human diseases. *Science, 273*, 1516–1517.

Risch, N. J. (2000). Searching for genetic determinants in the new millennium. *Nature, 405*(6788), 847–856.

Ritsner, M. S. (2009). *The handbook of neuropsychiatric biomarkers, endophenotypes and genes. Vol. 1. Neuropsychological endophenotypes and biomarkers.* New York: Springer.

Ritsner, M. S., & Gottesman, I. I. (2011). The schizophrenia construct after 100 years of challenges. In M. S. Ritsner (Ed.), *Handbook of schizophrenia spectrum disorders, volume I* (pp. 1–44). New York: Springer

Rivera, C., & Ren, B. (2013). Mapping human epigenomes. *Cell, 155*(1), 39–55. doi:http://dx.doi.org/10.1016/j.cell.2013.09.011

Robbers, S. C. C., van Oort, F. V. A., Polderman, T. J. C., Bartels, M., Boomsma, D. I., Verhulst, F. C., . . . Huizink, A. C. (2011). Trajectories of CBCL attention problems in childhood. *European Child and Adolescent Psychiatry, 20*(8), 419–427. doi:10.1007/s00787-011-0194-0

Roberts, C. A., & Johansson, C. B. (1974). The inheritance of cognitive interest styles among twins. *Journal of Vocational Behavior, 4*, 237–243.

Robins, L. N. (1978). Sturdy childhood predictors of adult antisocial behaviour: Replications from longitudinal analyses. *Psychological Medicine, 8*, 611–622.

Robins, L. N., & Price, R. K. (1991). Adult disorders predicted by childhood conduct problems: Results from the NIMH epidemiologic catchment area project. *Psychiatry, 54*, 116–132.

Robins, L. N., & Regier, D. A. (1991). *Psychiatric disorders in America.* New York: Free Press.

Robinson, D. G., Woerner, M. G., McMeniman, M., Mendelowitz, A., & Bilder, R. M. (2004). Symptomatic and functional recovery from a first episode of schizophrenia or schizoaffective disorder. *American Journal of Psychiatry, 161*(3), 473–479.

Robinson, E. B., Koenen, K. C., McCormick, M. C., Munir, K., Hallett, V., Happe, F., . . . Ronald, A. (2011). Evidence that autistic traits show the same etiology in the general population and at the quantitative extremes (5%, 2.5%, and 1%). *Archives of General Psychiatry, 68*(11), 1113–1121. doi:10.1001/archgenpsychiatry.2011.119

Robinson, J. L., Kagan, J., Reznick, J. S., & Corley, R. (1992). The heritability of inhibited and uninhibited behavior: A twin study. *Developmental Psychology, 28*, 1030–1037.

Robinson, S. W., Herzyk, P., Dow, J. A. T., & Leader, D. P. (2013). FlyAtlas: Database of gene expression in the tissues of *Drosophila melanogaster. Nucleic Acids Research, 41*(D1), D744–D750.

Rockman, M. V., & Kruglyak, L. (2006). Genetics of global gene expression. *Nature Reviews Genetics, 7*(11), 862–872.

Roisman, G. I., & Fraley, R. C. (2006). The limits of genetic influence: A behavior-genetic analysis of infant-caregiver relationship quality and temperament. *Child Development, 77*(6), 1656–1667.

Roizen, N. J., & Patterson, D. (2003). Down syndrome. *The Lancet, 361*(9365), 1281–1289.

Ronald, A., Happé, F., Price, T. S., Baron-Cohen, S., & Plomin, R. (2006). Phenotypic and genetic overlap between autistic traits at the extremes of the general population. *Journal of the American Academy of Child and Adolescent Psychiatry, 45*(10), 1206–1214. doi:10.1097/01.chi.0000230165.54117.41

Ronald, A., & Hoekstra, R. A. (2011). Autism spectrum disorders and autistic traits: A decade of new twin studies. *American Journal of Medical Genetics Part B-Neuropsychiatric Genetics, 156B*(3), 255–274. doi:10.1002/ajmg.b.31159

Ronalds, G. A., De Stavola, B. L., & Leon, D. A. (2005). The cognitive cost of being a twin: Evidence from comparisons within families in the Aberdeen children of the 1950s cohort study. *British Medical Journal, 331*(7528), 1306.

Rooms, L., & Kooy, R. F. (2011). Advances in understanding fragile X syndrome and related disorders. *Current Opinion in Pediatrics, 23*(6), 601–606. doi:10.1097/MOP.0b013e32834c7f1a

Rose, R. J., Broms, U., Korhonen, T., Dick, D. M., & Kaprio, J. (2009). Genetics of smoking behavior. In Y.-K. Kim (Ed.), *Handbook of behavior genetics* (1st ed., pp. 411–432). New York: Springer.

Rose, R. J., Dick, D. M., Viken, R. J., Pulkkinen, L., & Kaprio, J. (2004). Genetic and environmental effects on conduct disorder and alcohol dependence symptoms and their covariation at age 14. *Alcoholism: Clinical and Experimental Research, 28*(10), 1541–1548. doi:10.1097/01.alc.0000141822.36776.55

Rosenthal, D., Wender, P. H., Kety, S. S., & Schulsinger, F. (1971). The adopted-away offspring of schizophrenics. *American Journal of Psychiatry, 128*, 307-311.

Rosenthal, D., Wender, P. H., Kety, S. S., Schulsinger, F., Welner, J., & Ostergaard, L. (1968). Schizophrenics' offspring reared in adoptive homes. *Journal of Psychiatric Research, 6*, 377-391.

Rosenthal, N. E., Sack, D. A., Gillin, J. C., Lewy, A. J., Goodwin, F. K., Davenport, Y., . . . Wehr, T. A. (1984). Seasonal affective disorder. A description of the syndrome and preliminary findings with light therapy. *Archives of General Psychiatry, 41*(1), 72-80.

Roses, A. D. (2000). Pharmacogenetics and the practice of medicine. *Nature, 405*(6788), 857-865.

Ross, C. A., Aylward, E. H., Wild, E. J., Langbehn, D. R., Long, J. D., Warner, J. H., . . . Tabrizi, S. J. (2014). Huntington disease: Natural history, biomarkers and prospects for therapeutics. *Nature Reviews Neurology, 10*(4), 204-216. doi:10.1038/nrneurol.2014.24

Ross, M. T., Grafham, D. V., Coffey, A. J., Scherer, S., McLay, K., Muzny, D., . . . Yen, J. (2005). The DNA sequence of the human X chromosome. *Nature, 434*(7031), 325-337.

Rothe, C., Koszycki, D., Bradwejn, J., King, N., Deluca, V., Tharmalingam, S., . . . Kennedy, J. L. (2006). Association of the Val158Met catechol O-methyltransferase genetic polymorphism with panic disorder. *Neuropsychopharmacology., 31*(10), 2237-2242.

Roussos, P., Giakoumaki, S. G., Georgakopoulos, A., Robakis, N. K., & Bitsios, P. (2011). The CACNA1C and ANK3 risk alleles impact on affective personality traits and startle reactivity but not on cognition or gating in healthy males. *Bipolar Disorders, 13*(3), 250-259.

Rowe, D. C. (1981). Environmental and genetic influences on dimensions of perceived parenting: A twin study. *Developmental Psychology, 17*, 203-208.

Rowe, D. C. (1983). A biometrical analysis of perceptions of family environment: A study of twin and singleton sibling relationships. *Child Development, 54*, 416-423.

Rowe, D. C. (1987). Resolving the person-situation debate: Invitation to an interdisciplinary dialogue. *American Psychologist, 42*, 218-227.

Rowe, D. C. (1994). *The limits of family influence: Genes, experience, and behaviour*. New York: Guilford Press.

Rowe, D. C., Jacobson, K. C., & van den Oord, E. J. (1999). Genetic and environmental influences on vocabulary IQ: Parental education level as moderator. *Child Development, 70*(5), 1151-1162.

Roy, M. A., Neale, M. C., & Kendler, K. S. (1995). The genetic epidemiology of self-esteem. *British Journal of Psychiatry, 166*(6), 813-820.

Roysamb, E., Tambs, K., Reichborn-Kjennerud, T., Neale, M. C., & Harris, J. R. (2003). Happiness and health: Environmental and genetic contributions to the relationship between subjective well-being, perceived health, and somatic illness. *Journal of Personality and Social Psychology, 85*(6), 1136-1146. doi:10.1037/0022-3514.85.6.1136

Rubinstein, M., Phillips, T. J., Bunzow, J. R., Falzone, T. L., Dziewczapolski, G., Zhang, G., . . . Grandy, D. K. (1997). Mice lacking dopamine D4 receptors are supersensitive to ethanol, cocaine, and methamphetamine. *Cell, 90*(6), 991-1001. doi:10.1016/s0092-8674(00)80365-7

Rush, A. J., & Weissenburger, J. E. (1994). Melancholic symptom features and DSM-IV. *American Journal of Psychiatry, 151*, 489-498.

Rushton, J. P. (2002). New evidence on Sir Cyril Burt: His 1964 speech to the association of educational psychologists. *Intelligence, 30*(6), 555-567.

Rushton, J. P., & Bons, T. A. (2005). Mate choice and friendship in twins: Evidence for genetic similarity. *Psychological Science, 16*(7), 555-559.

Rutherford, J., McGuffin, P., Katz, R. J., & Murray, R. M. (1993). Genetic influences on eating attitudes in a normal female twin population. *Psychological Medicine, 23*(2), 425-436.

Rutter, M. (1996). Introduction: Concepts of antisocial behavior, of cause, and of genetic influences. In G. R. Bock & J. A. Goode (Eds.), *Genetics of criminal and antisocial behaviour* (pp. 1-15). Chichester: Wiley.

Rutter, M. (2006). *Genes and behavior: Nature-nurture interplay explained*. Oxford: Blackwell Publishing.

Rutter, M., Maughan, B., Meyer, J., Pickles, A., Silberg, J., Simonoff, E., & Taylor, E. (1997). Heterogeneity of antisocial behavior: Causes, continuities, and consequences. In D. W. Osgood (Ed.), *Nebraska Symposium on Motivation: Vol. 44: Motivation and delinquency* (pp. 45-118). Lincoln, NE: University of Nebraska Press.

Rutter, M., Moffitt, T. E., & Caspi, A. (2006). Gene-environment interplay and psychopathology: Multiple varieties but real effects. *Journal of Child Psychology & Psychiatry, 47*(3-4), 226-261.

Rutter, M., & Redshaw, J. (1991). Annotation: Growing up as a twin: Twin-singleton differences in psychological development. *Journal of Child Psychology and Psychiatry, 32*(6), 885-895.

Rutter, M., Silberg, J., O'Connor, T. G., & Simonoff, E. (1999). Genetics and child psychiatry: II. Empirical research findings. *Journal of Child Psychology and Psychiatry, 40*, 19-55.

Saba, L. M., Bennett, B., Hoffman, P. L., Barcomb, K., Ishii, T., Kechris, K., & Tabakoff, B. (2011). A systems genetic analysis of alcohol drinking by mice, rats and men: Influence of brain GABAergic transmission. *Neuropharmacology, 60*(7), 1269–1280.

Saccone, N. L., Culverhouse, R. C., Schwantes-An, T.-H., Cannon, D. S., Chen, X., Cichon, S., . . . Bierut, L. J. (2010). Multiple independent loci at chromosome 15q25.1 affect smoking quantity: A meta-analysis and comparison with lung cancer and COPD. *PLoS Genetics, 6*(8), e1001053. doi:10.1371/journal.pgen.1001053

Sadava, D. E., Hillis, D. M., Heller, H. C., & Berenbaum, M. (2010). High-throughput sequencing. In D. E. Savada et al., *Life: The science of biology.* (9th ed.). Sinauer Associates, Inc. and Sumanas, Inc.

Sadler, M. E., Miller, C. J., Christensen, K., & McGue, M. (2011). Subjective wellbeing and longevity: A co-twin control study. *Twin Research and Human Genetics, 14*(3), 249–256. doi:10.1375/twin.14.3.249

Saha, S., Chant, D., Welham, J., & McGrath, J. (2005). A systematic review of the prevalence of schizophrenia. *PLoS Med, 2*(5), e141. doi:10.1371/journal.pmed.0020141

Salahpour, A., Medvedev, I. O., Beaulieu, J. M., Gainetdinov, R. R., & Caron, M. G. (2007). Local knockdown of genes in the brain using small interfering RNA: A phenotypic comparison with knockout animals. *Biological Psychiatry, 61*(1), 65–69.

Sambandan, D., Yamamoto, A., Fanara, J. J., Mackay, T. F., & Anholt, R. R. (2006). Dynamic genetic interactions determine odor-guided behavior in *Drosophila melanogaster. Genetics, 174*(3), 1349–1363.

Samek, D. R., Hicks, B. M., Keyes, M. A., Bailey, J., McGue, M., & Iacono, W. G. (2015). Gene–environment interplay between parent–child relationship problems and externalizing disorders in adolescence and young adulthood. *Psychological Medicine, 45*(02), 333–344.

Samuelsson, S., Byrne, B., Olson, R. K., Hulslander, J., Wadsworth, S., Corley, R., . . . DeFries, J. C. (2008). Response to early literacy instruction in the United States, Australia, and Scandinavia: A behavioral-genetic analysis. *Learning and Individual Differences, 18*(3), 289–295. doi:10.1016/j.lindif.2008.03.004

Samuelsson, S., Olson, R., Wadsworth, S., Corley, R., DeFries, J. C., Willcutt, E., . . . Byrne, B. (2007). Genetic and environmental influences on prereading skills and early reading and spelling development in the United States, Australia, and Scandinavia. *Reading and Writing, 20*(1–2), 51–75.

Sanders, A. R., Martin, E. R., Beecham, G. W., Guo, S., Dawood, K., Rieger, G., . . . Kolundzija,

A. B. (2015). Genome-wide scan demonstrates significant linkage for male sexual orientation. *Psychological Medicine, 45*(07), 1379–1388.

Sandin, S., Lichtenstein, P., Kuja-Halkola, R., Larsson, H., Hultman, C. M., & Reichenberg, A. (2014). The familial risk of autism. *Journal of the American Medical Association, 311*(17), 1770–1777.

Sartor, C. E., McCutcheon, V. V., Pommer, N. E., Nelson, E. C., Grant, J. D., Duncan, A. E., . . . Heath, A. C. (2011). Common genetic and environmental contributions to post-traumatic stress disorder and alcohol dependence in young women. *Psychological Medicine, 41*(07), 1497–1505.

Saudino, K. J. (2012). Sources of continuity and change in activity level in early childhood. *Child Development, 83*(1), 266–281. doi:10.1111/j.1467-8624.2011.01680.x

Saudino, K. J., & Eaton, W. O. (1991). Infant temperament and genetics: An objective twin study of motor activity level. *Child Development, 62,* 1167–1174.

Saudino, K. J., McGuire, S., Reiss, D., Hetherington, E. M., & Plomin, R. (1995). Parent ratings of EAS temperaments in twins, full siblings, half siblings, and step siblings. *Journal of Personality and Social Psychology, 68,* 723–733. doi:10.1037/0022-3514.68.4.723

Saudino, K. J., & Micalizzi, L. (2015). Emerging trends in behavioral genetic studies of child temperament. *Child Development Perspectives, 9*(3), 144–148.

Saudino, K. J., Pedersen, N. L., Lichtenstein, P., McClearn, G. E., & Plomin, R. (1997). Can personality explain genetic influences on life events? *Journal of Personality and Social Psychology, 72,* 196–206. doi:10.1037/0022-3514.72.1.196

Saudino, K. J., & Plomin, R. (1997). Cognitive and temperamental mediators of genetic contributions to the home environment during infancy. *Merrill-Palmer Quarterly, 43,* 1–23.

Saudino, K. J., Plomin, R., & DeFries, J. C. (1996). Tester-rated temperament at 14, 20, and 24 months: Environmental change and genetic continuity. *British Journal of Developmental Psychology, 14,* 129–144. doi:10.1111/j.2044-835X.1996.tb00697.x

Saudino, K. J., Ronald, A., & Plomin, R. (2005). The etiology of behavior problems in 7-year-old twins: Substantial genetic influence and negligible shared environmental influence for parent ratings and ratings by same and different teachers. *Journal of Abnormal Child Psychology, 33,* 113–130. doi:10.1007/s10802-005-0939-7

Saudino, K. J., Wertz, A. E., Gagne, J. R., & Chawla, S. (2004). Night and day: Are siblings as different in temperament as parents say they are? *Journal of Personality and Social Psychology, 87*(5), 698–706.

Savelieva, K. V., Caudle, W. M., Findlay, G. S., Caron, M. G., & Miller, G. W. (2002). Decreased ethanol preference and consumption in dopamine transporter female knock-out mice. *Alcoholism: Clinical and Experimental Research, 26*(6), 758–764. doi:10.1111/j.1530-0277.2002.tb02602.x

Scarr, S., & Carter-Saltzman, L. (1979). Twin method: Defense of a critical assumption. *Behavior Genetics, 9,* 527–542.

Scarr, S., & Weinberg, R. A. (1978a). Attitudes, interests, and IQ. *Human Nature, April,* 29–36.

Scarr, S., & Weinberg, R. A. (1978b). The influence of "family background" on intellectual attainment. *American Sociological Review, 43,* 674–692.

Scarr, S., & Weinberg, R. A. (1981). The transmission of authoritarianism in families: Genetic resemblance in social-political attitudes? In S. Scarr (Ed.), *Race, social class, and individual differences in IQ* (pp. 399–427). Hillsdale, NJ: Erlbaum.

Schadt, E. E. (2006). Novel integrative genomics strategies to identify genes for complex traits. *Animal Genetics, 37*(Suppl. 1), 18–23.

Schafer, W. R. (2005). Deciphering the neural and molecular mechanisms of *C. elegans* behavior. *Current Biology, 15*(17), R723–R729.

Schermerhorn, A. C., D'Onofrio, B. M., Turkheimer, E., Ganiban, J. M., Spotts, E. L., Lichtenstein, P., ... Neiderhiser, J. M. (2011). A genetically informed study of associations between family functioning and child psychosocial adjustment. *Developmental Psychology, 47*(3), 707–725. doi:10.1037/a0021362

Scherrer, J. F., True, W. R., Xian, H., Lyons, M. J., Eisen, S. A., Goldberg, J., ... Tsuang, M. T. (2000). Evidence for genetic influences common and specific to symptoms of generalized anxiety and panic. *Journal of Affective Disorders, 57*(1–3), 25–35.

Schizophrenia Working Group of the Psychiatric Genomics Consortium. (2014). Biological insights from 108 schizophrenia-associated genetic loci. *Nature, 511*(7510), 421–427.

Schmitt, J. E., Prescott, C. A., Gardner, C. O., Neale, M. C., & Kendler, K. S. (2005). The differential heritability of regular tobacco use based on method of administration. *Twin Research and Human Genetics, 8*(1), 60–62.

Schmitt, J. E., Wallace, G. L., Lenroot, R. K., Ordaz, S. E., Greenstein, D., Clasen, L., ... Giedd, J. N. (2010). A twin study of intracerebral volumetric relationships. *Behavior Genetics, 40*(2), 114–124. doi:10.1007/s10519-010-9332-6

Schmitz, S. (1994). Personality and temperament. In J. C. DeFries & R. Plomin (Eds.), *Nature and nurture during middle childhood* (pp. 120–140). Cambridge, MA: Blackwell.

Scholz, H., Ramond, J., Singh, C. M., & Heberlein, U. (2000). Functional ethanol tolerance in *Drosophila. Neuron, 28*(1), 261–271. doi:10.1016/s0896-6273(00)00101-x

Schousboe, K., Willemsen, G., Kyvik, K. O., Mortensen, J., Boomsma, D. I., Cornes, B. K., ... Harris, J. R. (2003). Sex differences in heritability of BMI: A comparative study of results from twin studies in eight countries. *Twin Research, 6*(5), 409–421.

Schulsinger, F. (1972). Psychopathy: Heredity and environment. *International Journal of Mental Health, 1,* 190–206.

Schulze, T. G., Akula, N., Breuer, R., Steele, J., Nalls, M. A., Singleton, A. B., ... Rietschel, M. (2014). Molecular genetic overlap in bipolar disorder, schizophrenia, and major depressive disorder. *The World Journal of Biological Psychiatry, 15*(3), 200–208.

Schulze, T. G., Hedeker, D., Zandi, P., Rietschel, M., & McMahon, F. J. (2006). What is familial about familial bipolar disorder? Resemblance among relatives across a broad spectrum of phenotypic characteristics. *Archives of General Psychiatry, 63*(12), 1368–1376.

Schumann, G., Loth, E., Banaschewski, T., Barbot, A., Barker, G., Buchel, C., ... IMAGEN Consortium. (2010). The IMAGEN study: Reinforcement-related behaviour in normal brain function and psychopathology. *Molecular Psychiatry, 15*(12), 1128–1139. doi:10.1038/mp.2010.4

Schur, E., Afari, N., Goldberg, J., Buchwald, D., & Sullivan, P. F. (2007). Twin analyses of fatigue. *Twin Research and Human Genetics, 10*(5), 729–733. doi:10.1375/twin.10.5.729

Schutzer, S. E. (2014). Rapidly maturing field of proteomics: A gateway to studying diseases. *Proteomics, 14*(9), 991–993.

Schwab, N. (2014). Social influence constrained by the heritability of attitudes. *Personality and Individual Differences, 66,* 54–57.

Schwartzer, J. J., Koenig, C. M., & Berman, R. F. (2013). Using mouse models of autism spectrum disorders to study the neurotoxicology of gene–environment interactions. *Neurotoxicology and Teratology, 36,* 17–35.

Scott, J. P., & Fuller, J. L. (1965). *Genetics and the social behavior of the dog.* Chicago: University of Chicago Press.

Scriver, C. R. (2007). The PAH gene, phenylketonuria, and a paradigm shift. *Human Mutation, 28*(9), 831–845. doi:10.1002/humu.20526

Scriver, C. R., & Waters, P. J. (1999). Monogenetic traits are not simple: Lessons from phenylketonuria. *Trends in Genetics, 15,* 267–272.

Seale, T. W. (1991). Genetic differences in response to cocaine and stimulant drugs. In

J. C. Crabbe & R. A. Harris (Eds.), *The genetic basis of alcohol and drug actions* (pp. 279–321). New York: Plenum.

Segal, N. L. (1999). *Entwined lives: Twins and what they tell us about human behavior.* New York: Dutton.

Seidman, L. J., Hellemann, G., Nuechterlein, K. H., Greenwood, T. A., Braff, D. L., Cadenhead, K. S., ... Gur, R. C. (2015). Factor structure and heritability of endophenotypes in schizophrenia: Findings from the Consortium on the Genetics of Schizophrenia (COGS-1). *Schizophrenia Research, 163*(1), 73–79.

Sesardic, N. (2005). *Making sense of heritability.* Cambridge: Cambridge University Press.

Shakeshaft, N. G., Trzaskowski, M., McMillan, A., Rimfeld, K., Krapohl, E., Haworth, C. M. A., ... Plomin, R. (2013). Strong genetic influence on a UK nationwide test of educational achievement at the end of compulsory education at age 16. *PLoS ONE, 8*(12), e80341. doi:10.1371/journal .pone.0080341

Sham, P. C., Cherny, S. S., Purcell, S., & Hewitt, J. (2000). Power of linkage versus association analysis of quantitative traits, by use of variance-components models, for sibship data. *American Journal of Human Genetics, 66*, 1616–1630.

Shapira, N. A., Lessig, M. C., He, A. G., James, G. A., Driscoll, D. J., & Liu, Y. (2005). Satiety dysfunction in Prader-Willi syndrome demonstrated by fMRI. *Journal of Neurology Neurosurgery and Psychiatry, 76*(2), 260–262. doi:10.1136 /jnnp.2004.039024

Sharma, A., Sharma, V. K., Horn-Saban, S., Lancet, D., Ramachandran, S., & Brahmachari, S. K. (2005). Assessing natural variations in gene expression in humans by comparing with monozygotic twins using microarrays. *Physiological Genomics, 21*(1), 117–123.

Sharp, S. I., McQuillin, A., & Gurling, H. M. D. (2009). Genetics of attention-deficit hyperactivity disorder (ADHD). *Neuropharmacology, 57*(7–8), 590–600. doi:10.1016/j.neuropharm.2009.08.011

Sharpley, C. F., Palanisamy, S. K. A., Glyde, N. S., Dillingham, P. W., & Agnew, L. L. (2014). An update on the interaction between the serotonin transporter promoter variant (5-HTTLPR), stress and depression, plus an exploration of non-confirming findings. *Behavioural Brain Research, 273*, 89–105.

Shaw, P., Greenstein, D., Lerch, J., Clasen, L., Lenroot, R., Gogtay, N., ... Giedd, J. (2006). Intellectual ability and cortical development in children and adolescents. *Nature, 440*(7084), 676–679. doi:10.1038/nature04513

Sher, L., Goldman, D., Ozaki, N., & Rosenthal, N. E. (1999). The role of genetic factors in the etiology of seasonal affective disorder and seasonality. *Journal of Affective Disorders, 53*(3), 203–210.

Sherrington, R., Brynjolfsson, J., Petursson, H., Potter, M., Dudleston, K., Barraclough, B., ... Gurling, H. (1988). Localisation of susceptibility locus for schizophrenia on chromosome 5. *Nature, 336*, 164–167.

Sherva, R., Wang, Q., Kranzler, H., Zhao, H., Koesterer, R., Herman, A., ... Gelernter, J. (2016). Genome-wide association study of cannabis dependence severity, novel risk variants, and shared genetic risks. *JAMA Psychiatry, 73*(5):472–480. doi:10.1001/jamapsychiatry.2016.0036

Shih, R. A., Belmonte, P. L., & Zandi, P. P. (2004). A review of the evidence from family, twin and adoption studies for a genetic contribution to adult psychiatric disorders. *International Review of Psychiatry, 16*(4), 260–283.

Shilyansky, C., Lee, Y. S., & Silva, A. J. (2010). Molecular and cellular mechanisms of learning disabilities: A focus on NF1. In S. E. Hyman (Ed.), *Annual Review of Neuroscience* (Vol. 33, pp. 221–243). Palo Alto: Annual Reviews.

Shimada-Sugimoto, M., Otowa, T., & Hettema, J. M. (2015). Genetics of anxiety disorders: Genetic epidemiological and molecular studies in humans. *Psychiatry and Clinical Neurosciences, 69*(7), 388–401.

Shimoyama, M., De Pons, J., Hayman, G. T., Laulederkind, S. J. F., Liu, W., Nigam, R., ... Wang, S.-J. (2015). The Rat Genome Database 2015: Genomic, phenotypic and environmental variations and disease. *Nucleic Acids Research, 43*(Database Issue), D743–D750. doi:10.1093/nar/gku1026

Shinozaki, G., & Potash, J. B. (2014). New developments in the genetics of bipolar disorder. *Current Psychiatry Reports, 16*(11), 1–10.

Shorter, J., Couch, C., Huang, W., Carbone, M. A., Peiffer, J., Anholt, R. R. H., & Mackay, T. F. C. (2015). Genetic architecture of natural variation in *Drosophila melanogaster* aggressive behavior. *Proceedings of the National Academy of Sciences, 112*(27), E3555–E3563.

Siever, L. J., Silverman, J. M., Horvath, T. B., Klar, H., Coccaro, E., Keefe, R. S. E., ... Davis, K. L. (1990). Increased morbid risk for schizophrenia related disorders in relatives of schizotypal personality disordered patients. *Archives of General Psychiatry, 47*(7), 634–640.

Sigvardsson, S., Bohman, M., & Cloninger, C. R. (1996). Replication of Stockholm adoption study of alcoholism. *Archives of General Psychiatry, 53*, 681–687.

Silberg, J. L., Gillespie, N., Moore, A. A., Eaves, L. J., Bates, J., Aggen, S., ... Canino, G. (2015). Shared genetic and environmental influences on early temperament and preschool psychiatric disorders in Hispanic twins. *Twin Research and Human Genetics, 18*(02), 171–178.

Silberg, J. L., Maes, H., & Eaves, L. J. (2010). Genetic and environmental influences on the transmission of parental depression to children's depression and conduct disturbance: An extended children of twins study. *Journal of Child Psychology and Psychiatry, 51*(6), 734–744. doi:10.1111/j.1469-7610.2010.02205.x

Silberg, J. L., Rutter, M., & Eaves, L. (2001). Genetic and environmental influences on the temporal association between earlier anxiety and later depression in girls. [erratum appears in *Biological Psychiatry* 2001 Sep 1;50(5):393.]. *Biological Psychiatry, 49*(12), 1040–1049.

Silva, A. J., Kogan, J. H., Frankland, P. W., & Kida, S. (1998). CREB and memory. *Annual Review of Neuroscience, 21,* 127–148.

Silva, A. J., Paylor, R., Wehner, J. M., & Tonegawa, S. (1992). Impaired spatial learning in à-calcium-calmodulin kinase mutant mice. *Science, 257,* 206–211.

Silventoinen, K., Hasselbalch, A. L., Lallukka, T., Bogl, L., Pietilainen, K. H., Heitmann, B. L., ... Kaprio, J. (2009). Modification effects of physical activity and protein intake on heritability of body size and composition. *American Journal of Clinical Nutrition, 90*(4), 1096–1103. doi:10.3945/ajcn.2009.27689

Silventoinen, K., & Kaprio, J. (2009). Genetics of tracking of body mass index from birth to late middle age: Evidence from twin and family studies. *Obesity Facts, 2*(3), 196–202. doi:10.1159/000219675

Silventoinen, K., Rokholm, B., Kaprio, J., & Sorensen, T. I. A. (2010). The genetic and environmental influences on childhood obesity: A systematic review of twin and adoption studies. *International Journal of Obesity, 34*(1), 29–40. doi:10.1038/ijo.2009.177

Singer, J. B., Hill, A. E., Burrage, L. C., Olszens, K. R., Song, J., Justice, M., ... Lander, E. S. (2004). Genetic dissection of complex traits with chromosome substitution strains of mice. *Science, 304*(5669), 445–448.

Singer, J. J., MacGregor, J. J., Cherkas, L. F., & Spector, T. D. (2006). Genetic influences on cognitive function using the Cambridge neuropsychological test automated battery. *Intelligence, 34*(5), 421–428.

Singh, A. L., D'Onofrio, B. M., Slutske, W. S., Turkheimer, E., Emery, R. E., Harden, K. P., ... Martin, N. G. (2011). Parental depression and offspring psychopathology: A children of twins study. *Psychological Medicine, 41*(7), 1385–1395. doi:10.1017/s0033291710002059

Siontis, K. C. M., Patsopoulos, N. A., & Ioannidis, J. P. A. (2010). Replication of past candidate loci for common diseases and phenotypes in 100 genome-wide association studies. *European Journal of Human Genetics, 18*(7), 832–837.

Sison, M., & Gerlai, R. (2010). Associative learning in zebrafish (*Danio rerio*) in the plus maze. *Behavioural Brain Research, 207*(1), 99–104. doi:10.1016/j.bbr.2009.09.043

Skelly, D. A., Ronald, J., & Akey, J. M. (2009). Inherited variation in gene expression. In *Annual review of genomics and human genetics* (Vol. 10, pp. 313–332). Palo Alto: Annual Reviews.

Skelton, J. A., Irby, M. B., Grzywacz, J. G., & Miller, G. (2011). Etiologies of obesity in children: Nature and nurture. *Pediatric Clinics of North America, 58*(6), 1333–1354. doi:10.1016/j.pcl.2011.09.006

Skinner, A., & Skelton, J. A. (2014). Prevalence and trends in obesity and severe obesity among children in the United States, 1999–2012. *JAMA Pediatrics, 168*(6), 561–566. doi:10.1001/jamapediatrics.2014.21

Skodak, M., & Skeels, H. M. (1949). A final follow-up on one hundred adopted children. *Journal of Genetic Psychology, 75,* 84–125.

Skoulakis, E. M., & Grammenoudi, S. (2006). Dunces and da Vincis: The genetics of learning and memory in *Drosophila*. *Cellular and Molecular Life Sciences, 63*(9), 975–988.

Slater, E., & Cowie, V. (1971). *The genetics of mental disorders.* London: Oxford University Press.

Slof-Op 't Landt, M. C., van Furth, E. F., Meulenbelt, I., Slagboom, P. E., Bartels, M., Boomsma, D. I., & Bulik, C. M. (2005). Eating disorders: From twin studies to candidate genes and beyond. *Twin Research and Human Genetics, 8*(5), 467–482.

Smalley, S. L., Asarnow, R. F., & Spence, M. A. (1988). Autism and genetics: A decade of research. *Archives of General Psychiatry, 45,* 953–961.

Smith, C. (1974). Concordance in twins: Methods and interpretation. *American Journal of Human Genetics, 26,* 454–466.

Smith, C. F., Williamson, D. A., Bray, G. A., & Ryan, D. H. (1999). Flexible vs. rigid dieting strategies: Relationship with adverse behavioral outcomes. *Appetite, 32*(3), 295–305. doi:http://dx.doi.org/10.1006/appe.1998.0204

Smith, C. J., & Ryckman, K. K. (2015). Epigenetic and developmental influences on the risk of obesity, diabetes, and metabolic syndrome. *Diabetes, Metabolic Syndrome and Obesity: Targets and Therapy, 8,* 295–302. doi:10.2147/DMSO.S61296

Smith, E. M., North, C. S., McColl, R. E., & Shea, J. M. (1990). Acute postdisaster psychiatric disorders: Identification of persons at risk. *American Journal of Psychiatry, 147*, 202–206.

Smith, J., Cianflone, K., Biron, S., Hould, F. S., Lebel, S., Marceau, S., . . . Marceau, P. (2009). Effects of maternal surgical weight loss in mothers on intergenerational transmission of obesity. *Journal of Clinical Endocrinology and Metabolism, 94*(11), 4275–4283. doi:10.1210/jc.2009-0709

Smith, S. D., Grigorenko, E., Willcutt, E., Pennington, B. F., Olson, R. K., & DeFries, J. C. (2010). Etiologies and molecular mechanisms of communication disorders. *Journal of Developmental and Behavioral Pediatrics, 31*(7), 555–563. doi:10.1097/DBP.0b013e3181ee3d9e

Smith, T. F. (2010). Meta-analysis of the heterogeneity in association of DRD4 7-repeat allele and AD/HD: Stronger association with AD/HD combined type. *American Journal of Medical Genetics Part B-Neuropsychiatric Genetics, 153B*(6), 1189–1199. doi:10.1002/ajmg.b.31090

Smits, B. M., & Cuppen, E. (2006). Rat genetics: The next episode. *Trends in Genetics, 22*(4), 232–240.

Smoller, J. W., Block, S. R., & Young, M. M. (2009). Genetics of anxiety disorders: The complex road from DSM to DNA. *Depression and Anxiety, 26*(11), 965–975. doi:10.1002/da.20623

Smoller, J. W., & Finn, C. T. (2003). Family, twin, and adoption studies of bipolar disorder. *American Journal of Medical Genetics Part C-Seminars in Medical Genetics, 123*(1), 48–58.

Snyderman, M., & Rothman, S. (1988). *The IQ controversy, the media and publication.* New Brunswick, NJ: Transaction.

Sokolowski, M. B. (2001). Drosophila: Genetics meets behaviour. *Nature Reviews Genetics, 2*(11), 879–890.

Soler Artigas, M., Loth, D. W., Wain, L. V., Gharib, S. A., Obeidat, M. e., Tang, W., . . . Huffman, J. E. (2011). Genome-wide association and large-scale follow up identifies 16 new loci influencing lung function. *Nature Genetics, 43*(11), 1082–1090.

Sora, I., Li, B., Igari, M., Hall, F. S., & Ikeda, K. (2010). Transgenic mice in the study of drug addiction and the effects of psychostimulant drugs. *Annals of the New York Academy of Science, 1187*, 218–246. doi:10.1111/j.1749-6632.2009.05276.x

Spain, S. L., Pedroso, I., Kadeva, N., Miller, M. B., Iacono, W. G., McGue, M., . . . Lubinski, D. (2015). A genome-wide analysis of putative functional and exonic variation associated with extremely high intelligence. *Molecular Psychiatry*.

Spearman, C. (1904). "General intelligence," objectively determined and measured. *American Journal of Psychology, 15*, 201–292.

Speliotes, E. K., Willer, C. J., Berndt, S. I., Monda, K. L., Thorleifsson, G., Jackson,

A. U., . . . Loos, R. J. (2010). Association analyses of 249,796 individuals reveal 18 new loci associated with body mass index. *Nature Genetics, 42*(11), 937–948. doi:10.1038/ng.686

Spence, J. P., Liang, T., Liu, L., Johnson, P. L., Foroud, T., Carr, L. G., & Shekhar, A. (2009). From QTL to candidate gene: A genetic approach to alcoholism research. *Current Drug Abuse Reviews, 2*(2), 127–134.

Spotts, E. L., Neiderhiser, J. M., Towers, H., Hansson, K., Lichtenstein, P., Cederblad, M., . . . Reiss, D. (2004). Genetic and environmental influences on marital relationships. *Journal of Family Psychology, 18*(1), 107–119. doi:10.1037/0893-3200.18.1.107

Spotts, E. L., Pederson, N. L., Neiderhiser, J. M., Reiss, D., Lichtenstein, P., Hansson, K., & Cederblad, M. (2005). Genetic effects on women's positive mental health: Do marital relationships and social support matter? *Journal of Family Psychology, 19*(3), 339–349.

Spotts, E. L., Prescott, C., & Kendler, K. (2006). Examining the origins of gender differences in marital quality: A behavior genetic analysis. *Journal of Family Psychology, 20*(4), 605–613.

Sprott, R. L., & Staats, J. (1975). Behavioral studies using genetically defined mice — a bibliography. *Behavior Genetics, 5*, 27–82.

Stallings, M. C., Hewitt, J. K., Cloninger, C. R., Heath, A. C., & Eaves, L. J. (1996). Genetic and environmental structure of the Tridimensional Personality Questionnaire: Three or four temperament dimensions? *Journal of Personality and Social Psychology, 70*(1), 127–140.

Steel, Z., Marnane, C., Iranpour, C., Chey, T., Jackson, J. W., Patel, V., & Silove, D. (2014). The global prevalence of common mental disorders: A systematic review and meta-analysis 1980–2013. *International Journal of Epidemiology, 43*(2), 476–493. doi:10.1093/ije/dyu038

Stefansson, H., Sigurdsson, E., Steinthorsdottir, V., Bjornsdottir, S., Sigmundsson, T., Ghosh, S., . . . Stefansson, K. (2002). Neuregulin 1 and susceptibility to schizophrenia. *American Journal of Human Genetics, 71*(4), 877–892.

Stein, J. L., Medland, S. E., Vasquez, A. A., Hibar, D. P., Senstad, R. E., Winkler, A. M., . . . Enhancing Neuro Imaging Genetics through Meta-Analysis Consortium (2012). Identification of common variants associated with human hippocampal and intracranial volumes. *Nature Genetics, 44*(5), 552–561. doi:10.1038/ng.2250

Stein, M. B., Chartier, M. J., Hazen, A. L., Kozak, M. V., Tancer, M. E., Lander, S., . . . Walker, J. R. (1998). A direct-interview family study of generalized social phobia. *American Journal of Psychiatry, 155*(1), 90–97.

Stent, G. S. (1963). *Molecular biology of bacterial viruses*. New York: Freeman.

Stephens, S. H., Hartz, S. M., Hoft, N. R., Saccone, N. L., Corley, R. C., Hewitt, J. K.,... Chen, X. (2013). Distinct loci in the CHRNA5/CHRNA3/CHRNB4 gene cluster are associated with onset of regular smoking. *Genetic Epidemiology, 37*(8), 846–859.

Steptoe, A., Deaton, A., & Stone, A. A. (2015). Subjective wellbeing, health, and ageing. *The Lancet, 385*(9968), 640–648. doi:10.1016/S0140-6736(13)61489-0

Stergiakouli, E., Hamshere, M., Holmans, P., Langley, K., Zaharieva, I., Hawi, Z.,... Thapar, A. (2012). Investigating the contribution of common genetic variants to the risk and pathogenesis of ADHD. *American Journal of Psychiatry, 169*(2), 186–194. doi:10.1176/appi.ajp.2011.11040551

Sterling, M. E., Karatayev, O., Chang, G. Q., Algava, D. B., & Leibowitz, S. F. (2015). Model of voluntary ethanol intake in zebrafish: Effect on behavior and hypothalamic orexigenic peptides. *Behavioural Brain Research, 278*, 29–39.

Stessman, J., Jacobs, J. M., Stessman-Lande, I., Gilon, D., & Leibowitz, D. (2013). Aging, resting pulse rate, and longevity. *Journal of the American Geriatrics Society, 61*(1), 40–45.

Stewart, S. E., Platko, J., Fagerness, J., Birns, J., Jenike, E., Smoller, J. W.,... Pauls, D. L. (2007). A genetic family-based association study of OLIG2 in obsessive-compulsive disorder. *Archives of General Psychiatry, 64*(2), 209–214.

Stewart, S. E., Yu, D., Scharf, J. M., Neale, B. M., Fagerness, J. A., Mathews, C. A.,... Osiecki, L. (2013). Genome-wide association study of obsessive-compulsive disorder. *Molecular Psychiatry, 18*(7), 788–798.

Stoolmiller, M. (1999). Implications of the restricted range of family environments for estimates of heritability and nonshared environment in behavior-genetic adoption studies. *Psychological Bulletin, 125*, 392–409.

Stratakis, C. A., & Rennert, O. M. (2005). Turner syndrome: An update. *Endocrinologist, 15*(1), 27–36.

Straub, R. E., Jiang, Y., MacLean, C. J., Ma, Y., Webb, B. T., Myakishev, M. V.,... Kendler, K. S. (2002). Genetic variation in the 6p22.3 gene DTNBP1, the human ortholog of the mouse dysbindin gene, is associated with schizophrenia. *American Journal of Human Genetics, 71*(2), 337–348.

Strenze, T. (2007). Intelligence and socioeconomic success: A meta-analytic review of longitudinal research. *Intelligence, 35*(5), 401–426.

Strine, T. W., Chapman, D. P., Balluz, L. S., Moriarty, D. G., & Mokdad, A. H. (2008). The associations between life satisfaction and health-related quality of life, chronic illness, and health behaviors among U.S. community-dwelling adults. *Journal of Community Health, 33*(1), 40–50. doi:10.1007/s10900-007-9066-4

Stromswold, K. (2001). The heritability of language: A review and metaanalysis of twin, adoption and linkage studies. *Language, 77*(4), 647–723.

Sturtevant, A. H. (1915). Experiments on sex recognition and the problem of sexual selection in *Drosophila. Journal of Animal Behavior, 5*, 351–366.

Sullivan, P. F., Evengard, B., Jacks, A., & Pedersen, N. L. (2005). Twin analyses of chronic fatigue in a Swedish national sample. *Psychological Medicine, 35*(9), 1327–1336.

Sullivan, P. F., Kendler, K. S., & Neale, M. C. (2003a). Schizophrenia as a complex trait: Evidence from a meta-analysis of twin studies. *Archives of General Psychiatry, 60*(12), 1187–1192.

Sullivan, P. F., Kovalenko, P., York, T. P., Prescott, C. A., & Kendler, K. S. (2003b). Fatigue in a community sample of twins. *Psychological Medicine, 33*(2), 263–281.

Sullivan, P. F., Neale, M. C., & Kendler, K. S. (2000). Genetic epidemiology of major depression: Review and meta-analysis. *American Journal of Psychiatry, 157*(10), 1552–1562.

Svedberg, P., Blom, V., Narusyte, J., Bodin, L., Bergström, G., & Hallsten, L. (2014). Genetic and environmental influences on performance-based self-esteem in a population-based cohort of Swedish twins. *Self and Identity, 13*(2), 243–256.

Svedberg, P., Gatz, M., & Pedersen, N. L. (2009). Genetic and environmental mediation of the associations between self-rated health and cognitive abilities. *Experimental Aging Research, 35*(2), 178–201.

Svedberg, P., Lichtenstein, P., & Pedersen, N. L. (2001). Age and sex differences in genetic and environmental factors for self-rated health: A twin study. *The Journals of Gerontology Series B: Psychological Sciences and Social Sciences, 56*(3), S171–S178.

Svenson, K. L., Gatti, D. M., Valdar, W., Welsh, C. E., Cheng, R., Chesler, E. J.,... Churchill, G. A. (2012). High-resolution genetic mapping using the mouse Diversity Outbred population. *Genetics, 190*(2), 437–447.

Swan, G. E., Benowitz, N. L., Lessov, C. N., Jacob, P., Tyndale, R. F., & Wilhelmsen, K. (2005). Nicotine metabolism: The impact of CYP2A6 on estimates of additive genetic influence. *Pharmacogenetics and Genomics, 15*(2), 115–125. doi:10.1097/01213011-200502000-00007

Swerdlow, N. R., Gur, R. E., & Braff, D. L. (2015). Consortium on the Genetics of Schizophrenia (COGS) assessment of endophenotypes for schizophrenia: An introduction to this special issue of schizophrenia research. *Schizophrenia Research, 163*(1), 9–16.

Szatmari, P., Paterson, A. D., Zwaigenbaum, L., Roberts, W., Brian, J., Liu, X. Q., . . . Shih, A. (2007). Mapping autism risk loci using genetic linkage and chromosomal rearrangements. *Nature Genetics, 39*(3), 319–328.

Tabakoff, B., Saba, L., Kechris, K., Hu, W., Bhave, S. V., Finn, D. A., . . . Hoffman, P. L. (2008). The genomic determinants of alcohol preference in mice. *Mammalian Genome, 19*(5), 352–365. doi:10.1007/s00335-008-9115-z

Tabakoff, B., Saba, L., Printz, M., Flodman, P., Hodgkinson, C., Goldman, D., . . . Hoffman, P. L. (2009). Genetical genomic determinants of alcohol consumption in rats and humans. *BMC Biology, 7*, 70. doi:10.1186/1741-7007-7-70

Tabor, H. K., Risch, N. J., & Myers, R. M. (2002). Candidate-gene approaches for studying complex genetic traits: Practical considerations. *Nature Reviews Genetics, 3*(5), 391–397.

Tacutu, R., Craig, T., Budovsky, A., Wuttke, D., Lehmann, G., Taranukha, D., . . . de Magalhães, J. P. (2012). Human ageing genomic resources: Integrated databases and tools for the biology and genetics of ageing. *Nucleic Acids Research, 41*(Database Issue), D1027–D1033. doi:10.1093/nar/gks1155

Talbot, C. J., Nicod, A., Cherny, S. S., Fulker, D. W., Collins, A. C., & Flint, J. (1999). High-resolution mapping of quantitative trait loci in outbred mice. *Nature Genetics, 21*, 305–308.

Tambs, K., Czajkowsky, N., Roysamb, E., Neale, M. C., Reichborn-Kjennerud, T., Aggen, S. H., . . . Kendler, K. S. (2009). Structure of genetic and environmental risk factors for dimensional representations of DSM-IV anxiety disorders. *British Journal of Psychiatry, 195*(4), 301–307. doi:10.1192/bjp.bp.108.059485

Tambs, K., Sundet, J. M., & Magnus, P. (1986). Genetic and environmental contribution to the covariation between the Wechsler Adult Intelligence Scale (WAIS) subtests: A study of twins. *Behavior Genetics, 16*, 475–491.

Tang, W. W. C., Dietmann, S., Irie, N., Leitch, H. G., Floros, V. I., Bradshaw, C. R., . . . Surani, M. A. (2015). A unique gene regulatory network resets the human germline epigenome for development. *Cell, 161*(6), 1453–1467.

Tang, Y. P., Shimizu, E., Dube, G. R., Rampon, C., Kerchner, G. A., Zhuo, M., . . . Tsien, J. Z. (1999). Genetic enhancement of learning and memory in mice. *Nature, 401*, 63–69.

Tansey, K. E., Guipponi, M., Hu, X., Domenici, E., Lewis, G., Malafosse, A., . . . Uher, R. (2013). Contribution of common genetic variants to antidepressant response. *Biological Psychiatry, 73*(7), 679–682.

Tanzi, R. E., & Bertram, L. (2005). Twenty years of the Alzheimer's disease amyloid hypothesis: A genetic perspective. *Cell, 120*(4), 545–555.

Tartaglia, N. R., Howell, S., Sutherland, A., Wilson, R., & Wilson, L. (2010). A review of trisomy X (47, XXX). *Orphanet Journal of Rare Diseases, 5*, 8. doi:10.1186/1750-1172-5-8

Taylor, E. (1995). Dysfunctions of attention. In D. Cicchetti & D. J. Cohen (Eds.), *Developmental psychopathology. Volume 2. Risk, disorder, and adaptation* (pp. 243–273). New York: Wiley.

Taylor, J., Roehrig, A. D., Hensler, B. S., Connor, C. M., & Schatschneider, C. (2010a). Teacher quality moderates the genetic effects on early reading. *Science, 328*(5977), 512–514. doi:10.1126/science.1186149

Taylor, J., & Schatschneider, C. (2010b). Genetic influence on literacy constructs in kindergarten and first grade: Evidence from a diverse twin sample. *Behavior Genetics, 40*(5), 591–602. doi:10.1007/s10519-010-9368-7

Taylor, J. Y., & Wu, C. Y. (2009). Effects of genetic counseling for hypertension on changes in lifestyle behaviors among African-American women. *Journal of National Black Nurses Association, 20*(1), 1–10.

Taylor, L. E., Swerdfeger, A. L., & Eslick, G. D. (2014a). Vaccines are not associated with autism: An evidence-based meta-analysis of case-control and cohort studies. *Vaccine, 32*(29), 3623–3629.

Taylor, M. J., Charman, T., Robinson, E. B., Hayiou-Thomas, M. E., Happé, F., Dale, P. S., & Ronald, A. (2014b). Language and traits of autism spectrum conditions: Evidence of limited phenotypic and etiological overlap. *American Journal of Medical Genetics Part B: Neuropsychiatric Genetics, 165*(7), 587–595.

Taylor, S. (2011). Etiology of obsessions and compulsions: A meta-analysis and narrative review of twin studies. *Clinical Psychological Review, 31*(8), 1361–1372. doi:10.1016/j.cpr.2011.09.008

Taylor, S. (2013). Molecular genetics of obsessive-compulsive disorder: A comprehensive meta-analysis of genetic association studies. *Molecular Psychiatry, 18*(7), 799–805.

Taylor, S., Asmundson, G. J. G., & Jang, K. L. (2011). Etiology of obsessive-compulsive symptoms and obsessive-compulsive personality traits: Common genes, mostly different environments. *Depression and Anxiety, 28*(10), 863–869. doi:10.1002/da.20859

Teslovich, T. M., Musunuru, K., Smith, A. V., Edmondson, A. C., Stylianou, I. M., Koseki, M., . . .

Willer, C. J. (2010). Biological, clinical and population relevance of 95 loci for blood lipids. *Nature, 466*(7307), 707–713.

Tesser, A. (1993). On the importance of heritability in psychological research: The case of attitudes. *Psychological Review, 100*, 129–142.

Tesser, A., Whitaker, D., Martin, L., & Ward, D. (1998). Attitude heritability, attitude change and physiological responsivity. *Personality and Individual Differences, 24*(1), 89–96.

Thakker, D. R., Hoyer, D., & Cryan, J. F. (2006). Interfering with the brain: Use of RNA interference for understanding the pathophysiology of psychiatric and neurological disorders. *Pharmacology & Therapeutics, 109*(3), 413–438.

Thapar, A., Langley, K., O'Donovan, M., & Owen, M. (2006). Refining the attention deficit hyperactivity disorder phenotype for molecular genetic studies. *Molecular Psychiatry, 11*(8), 714–720.

Thapar, A., & McGuffin, P. (1996). Genetic influences on life events in childhood. *Psychological Medicine, 26*(4), 813–820.

Thapar, A., & Rice, F. (2006). Twin studies in pediatric depression. *Child and Adolescent Psychiatric Clinics of North America, 15*(4), 869–881.

Thapar, A., & Scourfield, J. (2002). Childhood disorders. In P. McGuffin, M. J. Owen, & I. I. Gottesman (Eds.), *Psychiatric genetics and genomics* (pp. 147–180). Oxford University Press.

Tobacco and Genetics Consortium. (2010). Genome-wide meta-analyses identify multiple loci associated with smoking behavior. *Nature Genetics, 42*(5), 441–447.

The Tourette Syndrome Association International Consortium for Genetics. (2007). Genome scan for Tourette disorder in affected-sibling-pair and multigenerational families. *American Journal of Human Genetics, 80*(2), 265–272.

Theis, S. V. S. (1924). *How foster children turn out.* New York: State Charities Aid Association.

Thielen, A., Klus, H., & Mueller, L. (2008). Tobacco smoke: Unraveling a controversial subject. *Experimental and Toxicologic Pathology, 60*(2-3), 141–156. doi:10.1016/j.etp.2008.01.014

Tholin, S., Rasmussen, F., Tynelius, P., & Karlsson, J. (2005). Genetic and environmental influences on eating behavior: The Swedish Young Male Twins Study. *American Journal of Clinical Nutrition, 81*(3), 564–569.

Thomas, D. (2010). Gene-environment-wide association studies: Emerging approaches. *Nature Reviews Genetics, 11*(4), 259–272. doi:10.1038/nrg2764

Thomas, D. C., Lewinger, J. P., Murcray, C. E., & Gauderman, W. J. (2012). Invited commentary: GE-Whiz! Ratcheting gene-environment studies up to the whole genome and the whole exposome. *American Journal of Epidemiology, 175*(3), 203–207.

Thompson, L. A., Detterman, D. K., & Plomin, R. (1991). Associations between cognitive abilities and scholastic achievement: Genetic overlap but environmental differences. *Psychological Science, 2*, 158–165. doi:10.1111/j.1467-9280.1991.tb00124.x

Thompson, P. M., Cannon, T. D., Narr, K. L., van Erp, T., Poutanen, V. P., Huttunen, M., . . . Toga, A. W. (2001). Genetic influences on brain structure. *Nature Neuroscience, 4*(12), 1253–1258.

Thompson, P. M., Martin, N. G., & Wright, M. J. (2010). Imaging genomics. *Current Opinion in Neurology, 23*(4), 368–373. doi:10.1097/WCO.0b013e32833b764c

Thorgeirsson, T. E., Gudbjartsson, D. F., Surakka, I., Vink, J. M., Amin, N., Geller, F., . . . Stefansson, K. (2010). Sequence variants at CHRNB3-CHRNA6 and CYP2A6 affect smoking behavior. *Nature Genetics, 42*(5), 448–453. doi:10.1038/ng.573

Tiainen, K., Sipilä, S., Alen, M., Heikkinen, E., Kaprio, J., Koskenvuo, M., . . . Rantanen, T. (2004). Heritability of maximal isometric muscle strength in older female twins. *Journal of Applied Physiology, 96*(1), 173-180.

Tiainen, K., Sipilä, S., Alén, M., Heikkinen, E., Kaprio, J., Koskenvuo, M., . . . Rantanen, T. (2005). Shared genetic and environmental effects on strength and power in older female twins. *Medicine and Science in Sports and Exercise, 37*(1), 72.

Tian, Z., Palmer, N., Schmid, P., Yao, H., Galdzicki, M., Berger, B., . . . Kohane, I. S. (2009). A practical platform for blood biomarker study by using global gene expression profiling of peripheral whole blood. *PLoS ONE, 4*(4), e5157. doi:10.1371/journal.pone.0005157

Tielbeek, J. J., Medland, S. E., Benyamin, B., Byrne, E. M., Heath, A. C., Madden, P. A. F., . . . Verweij, K. J. H. (2012). Unraveling the genetic etiology of adult antisocial behavior: A genome-wide association study. *PLoS ONE, 7*(10), e45086. doi:10.1371/journal.pone.0045086

Tienari, P., Wynne, L. C., Sorri, A., Lahti, I., Laksy, K., Moring, J., . . . Wahlberg, K. E. (2004). Genotype-environment interaction in schizophrenia-spectrum disorder. Long-term follow-up study of Finnish adoptees. *British Journal of Psychiatry, 184*, 216–222.

Timberlake, D. S., Rhee, S. H., Haberstick, B. C., Hopfer, C., Ehringer, M., Lessem, J. M., . . . Hewitt, J. K. (2006). The moderating effects of religiosity on the genetic and environmental determinants of smoking initiation. *Nicotine & Tobacco Research, 8*(1), 123–133. doi:10.1080/14622200500432054

Tissenbaum, H. A. (2012). Genetics, life span, health span, and the aging process in *Caenorhabditis elegans. The Journals of Gerontology Series A: Biological Sciences and Medical Sciences, 67*(5), 503–510.

Topper, S., Ober, C., & Das, S. (2011). Exome sequencing and the genetics of intellectual disability. *Clinical Genetics, 80*(2), 117–126. doi:10.1111/j.1399-0004.2011.01720.x

Torgersen, S. (1980). The oral, obsessive, and hysterical personality syndromes: A study of hereditary and environmental factors by means of the twin method. *Archives of General Psychiatry, 37,* 1272–1277.

Torgersen, S. (1983). Genetic factors in anxiety disorders. *Archives of General Psychiatry, 40,* 1085–1089.

Torgersen, S. (2009). The nature (and nurture) of personality disorders. *Scandinavian Journal of Psychology, 50*(6), 624–632. doi:10.1111/j.1467-9450.2009.00788.x

Torgersen, S., Edvardsen, J., Oien, P. A., Onstad, S., Skre, I., Lygren, S., & Kringlen, E. (2002). Schizotypal personality disorder inside and outside the schizophrenic spectrum. *Schizophrenia Research, 54*(1–2), 33–38.

Torgersen, S., Lygren, S., Oien, P. A., Skre, I., Onstad, S., Edvardsen, J., . . . Kringlen, E. (2000). A twin study of personality disorders. *Comprehensive Psychiatry, 41*(6), 416–425.

Torkamani, A., Dean, B., Schork, N. J., & Thomas, E. A. (2010). Coexpression network analysis of neural tissue reveals perturbations in developmental processes in schizophrenia. *Genome Research, 20*(4), 403–412. doi:10.1101/gr.101956.109

Torrey, E. F., Bowler, A. E., Taylor, E. H., & Gottesman, I. I. (1994). *Schizophrenia and manic-depressive disorder.* New York: Basic Books.

Trace, S. E., Baker, J. H., Peñas-Lledó, E., & Bulik, C. M. (2013). The genetics of eating disorders. *Annual Review of Clinical Psychology, 9,* 589–620.

Trikalinos, T. A., Karvouni, A., Zintzaras, E., Ylisaukko-Oja, T., Peltonen, L., Jarvela, I., & Ioannidis, J. P. (2006). A heterogeneity-based genome search meta-analysis for autism-spectrum disorders. *Molecular Psychiatry, 11*(1), 29–36.

True, W. R., Rice, J., Eisen, S. A., Heath, A. C., Goldberg, J., Lyons, M. J., & Nowak, J. (1993). A twin study of genetic and environmental contributions to liability for posttraumatic stress symptoms. *Archives of General Psychiatry, 50,* 257–264.

Trut, L., Oskina, I., & Kharlamova, A. (2009). Animal evolution during domestication: The domesticated fox as a model. *Bioessays, 31*(3), 349–360. doi:10.1002/bies.200800070

Trut, L. N. (1999). Early canid domestication: The fox farm experiment. *American Scientist, 87,* 160–169.

Trzaskowski, M., Davis, O. S. P., DeFries, J. C., Yang, J., Visscher, P. M., & Plomin, R. (2013). DNA evidence for strong genome-wide pleiotropy of cognitive and learning abilities. *Behavior Genetics, 43*(4), 267–273.

Trzaskowski, M., Zavos, H. M. S., Haworth, C. M. A., Plomin, R., & Eley, T. C. (2012). Stable genetic influence on anxiety-related behaviours across middle childhood. *Journal of Abnormal Child Psychology, 40*(1), 85–94. doi:10.1007/s10802-011-9545-z

Tsuang, M., & Faraone, S. D. (1990). *The genetics of mood disorders.* Baltimore: John Hopkins University Press.

Tsuang, M. T., Bar, J. L., Harley, R. M., & Lyons, M. J. (2001). The Harvard Twin Study of Substance Abuse: What we have learned. *Harvard Review of Psychiatry, 9*(6), 267–279.

Tsuang, M. T., Lyons, M. J., Eisen, S. A., True, W. T., Goldberg, J., & Henderson, W. (1992). A twin study of drug exposure and initiation of use. *Behavior Genetics, 22,* 756.

Tucker-Drob, E. M., & Bates, T. C. (2016). Large cross-national differences in gene × socioeconomic status interaction on intelligence. *Psychological Science, 27*(2), 138–149.

Tucker-Drob, E. M., & Briley, D. A. (2014). Continuity of genetic and environmental influences on cognition across the life span: A meta-analysis of longitudinal twin and adoption studies. *Psychological Bulletin, 140*(4), 949.

Tucker-Drob, E. M., Reynolds, C. A., Finkel, D., & Pedersen, N. L. (2014). Shared and unique genetic and environmental influences on aging-related changes in multiple cognitive abilities. *Developmental Psychology, 50*(1), 152.

Turkheimer, E., Pettersson, E., & Horn, E. E. (2014). A phenotypic null hypothesis for the genetics of personality. *Annual Review of Psychology, 65*(1), 515–540. doi:10.1146/annurev-psych-113011-143752

Turkheimer, E., & Waldron, M. (2000). Nonshared environment: A theoretical, methodological, and quantitative review. *Psychological Bulletin, 126,* 78–108.

Turnbaugh, P. J., & Gordon, J. I. (2009). The core gut microbiome, energy balance and obesity. *Journal of Physiology-London, 587*(17), 4153–4158. doi:10.1113/jphysiol.2009.174136

Turnbaugh, P. J., Hamady, M., Yatsunenko, T., Cantarel, B. L., Duncan, A., Ley, R. E., . . . Gordon, J. I. (2009). A core gut microbiome in obese and lean twins. *Nature, 457*(7228), 480–484. doi:10.1038/nature07540

Turner, J. R., Cardon, L. R., & Hewitt, J. K. (1995). *Behavior genetic approaches in behavioral medicine.* New York: Plenum.

Turri, M. G., Henderson, N. D., DeFries, J. C., & Flint, J. (2001). Quantitative trait locus mapping in laboratory mice derived from a replicated selection experiment for open-field activity. *Genetics, 158*(3), 1217–1226.

Tuttelmann, F., & Gromoll, J. (2010). Novel genetic aspects of Klinefelter's syndrome. *Molecular Human Reproduction, 16*(6), 386–395. doi:10.1093/molehr/gaq019

Tuvblad, C., Grann, M., & Lichtenstein, P. (2006). Heritability for adolescent antisocial behavior differs with socioeconomic status: Gene-environment interaction. *Journal of Child Psychology & Psychiatry, 47*(7), 734–743.

U.S. Department of Health and Human Services. (2014). *The health consequences of smoking—50 years of progress: A report of the Surgeon General.* Atlanta, GA: U.S. Department of Health and Human Services, Centers for Disease Control and Prevention, National Center for Chronic Disease Prevention and Health Promotion, Office on Smoking and Health, 17.

Uhl, G. R., Drgonova, J., & Hall, F. S. (2014). Curious cases: Altered dose–response relationships in addiction genetics. *Pharmacology & Therapeutics, 141*(3), 335–346.

United Nations, Department of Economic and Social Affairs, Population Division. (2013). World population ageing 2013.

Üstün, T. B., Rehm, J., Chatterji, S., Saxena, S., Trotter, R., Room, R., & Bickenbach, J. (1999). Multiple-informant ranking of the disabling effects of different health conditions in 14 countries. WHO/NIH Joint Project CAR Study Group. *The Lancet, 354*(9173), 111–115.

Uusitalo, A. L. T., Vanninen, E., Levälahti, E., Battie, M. C., Videman, T., & Kaprio, J. (2007). Role of genetic and environmental influences on heart rate variability in middle-aged men. *American Journal of Physiology-Heart and Circulatory Physiology, 293*(2), H1013–H1022.

Vaisse, C., Clement, K., Guy-Grand, B., & Froguel, P. (1998). A frameshift mutation in human MC4R is associated with a dominant form of obesity. *Nature Genetics, 20*(2), 113–114. doi:10.1038/2407

Valdar, W., Solberg, L. C., Gauguier, D., Burnett, S., Klenerman, P., Cookson, W. O., ... Flint, J. (2006a). Genome-wide genetic association of complex traits in heterogeneous stock mice. *Nature Genetics, 38*(8), 879–887.

Valdar, W., Solberg, L. C., Gauguier, D., Cookson, W. O., Rawlins, J. N. P., Mott, R., & Flint, J. (2006b). Genetic and environmental effects on complex traits in mice. *Genetics, 174*(2), 959–984. doi:10.1534/genetics.106.060004

van Baal, G. C., Boomsma, D. I., & de Geus, E. J. (2001). Longitudinal genetic analysis of EEG coherence in young twins. *Behavior Genetics, 31*(6), 637–651.

Van den Oord, J. C. G., & Rowe, D. C. (1997). Continuity and change in children's social maladjustment: A developmental behavior genetic study. *Developmental Psychology, 33*, 319–332.

van der Klaauw, A. A., & Farooqi, I. S. (2015). The hunger genes: Pathways to obesity. *Cell, 161*(1), 119–132. doi:http://dx.doi.org/10.1016/j.cell.2015.03.008

Van der Loos, M., Rietveld, C. A., Eklund, N., Koellinger, P. D., Rivadeneira, F., Abecasis, G. R., ... Biffar, R. (2013). The molecular genetic architecture of self-employment. *PLoS ONE, 8*(4), e60542.

van der Sluis, S., Dolan, C. V., Neale, M. C., Boomsma, D. I., & Posthuma, D. (2006). Detecting genotype-environment interaction in monozygotic twin data: Comparing the Jinks and Fulker test and a new test based on marginal maximum likelihood estimation. *Twin Research and Human Genetics, 9*(3), 377–392. doi:10.1375/183242706777591218

van der Sluis, S., Posthuma, D., & Dolan, C. V. (2012). A note on false positives and power in G × E modelling of twin data. *Behavior Genetics, 42*(1), 170–186. doi:10.1007/s10519-011-9480-3

van der Zwaluw, C. S., Engels, R. C. M. E., Buitelaar, J., Verkes, R. J., Franke, B., & Scholte, R. H. J. (2009). Polymorphisms in the dopamine transporter gene (SLC6A3/DAT1) and alcohol dependence in humans: A systematic review. *Pharmacogenomics, 10*(5), 853–866. doi:10.2217/pgs.09.24

Van Houtem, C., Laine, M. L., Boomsma, D. I., Ligthart, L., Van Wijk, A. J., & De Jongh, A. (2013). A review and meta-analysis of the heritability of specific phobia subtypes and corresponding fears. *Journal of Anxiety Disorders, 27*(4), 379–388.

van IJzendoorn, M. H., Bakermans-Kranenburg, M. J., Belsky, J., Beach, S., Brody, G., Dodge, K. A., ... Scott, S. (2011). Gene-by-environment experiments: A new approach to finding the missing heritability. *Nature Reviews Genetics, 12*(12), 881. doi:10.1038/nrg2764-c1

van IJzendoorn, M. H., Moran, G., Belsky, J., Pederson, D., Bakermans-Kranenburg, M. J., & Fisher, K. (2000). The similarity of siblings' attachments to their mother. *Child Development, 71*, 1086–1098.

van Jaarsveld, C. M., Boniface, D., Llewellyn, C. H., & Wardle, J. (2014). Appetite and growth: A longitudinal sibling analysis. *JAMA Pediatrics, 168*(4), 345–350. doi:10.1001/jamapediatrics.2013.4951

Van Ryzin, M. J., Leve, L. D., Neiderhiser, J. M., Shaw, D. S., Natsuaki, M. N., & Reiss, D. (2015). Genetic influences can protect against unresponsive parenting in the prediction of child social competence. *Child Development, 86*(3), 667–680. doi:10.1111/cdev.12335

van Soelen, I. L. C., Brouwer, R. M., van Baal, G. C. M., Schnack, H. G., Peper, J. S., Collins, D. L., . . . Hulshoff Pol, H. E. (2012). Genetic influences on thinning of the cerebral cortex during development. *Neuroimage, 59*(4), 3871–3880.

Vandenberg, S. G. (1972). Assortative mating, or who marries whom? *Behavior Genetics, 2*, 127–157.

Vanyukov, M. M., Tarter, R. E., Kirillova, G. P., Kirisci, L., Reynolds, M. D., Kreek, M. J., . . . Bierut, L. (2012). Common liability to addiction and "gateway hypothesis": Theoretical, empirical and evolutionary perspective. *Drug and Alcohol Dependence, 123*, S3–S17.

Venter, J. C., Adams, M. D., Myers, E. W., Li, P. W., Mural, R. J., Sutton, G. G., . . . Nodell, M. (2001). The sequence of the human genome. *Science, 291*(5507), 1304–1351.

Verkerk, A. J., Cath, D. C., van der Linde, H. C., Both, J., Heutink, P., Breedveld, G., . . . Oostra, B. A. (2006). Genetic and clinical analysis of a large Dutch Gilles de la Tourette family. *Molecular Psychiatry, 11*(10), 954–964.

Verkerk, A. J. M. H., Pieretti, M., Sutcliffe, J. S., Fu, Y. H., Kuhl, D. P. A., Pizzuti, A., . . . Warren, S. T. (1991). Identification of a gene (FMR-1) containing a CGG repeat coincident with a breakpoint cluster region exhibiting length variation in Fragile X syndrome. *Cell, 65*, 905–914.

Vernon, P. A., Jang, K. L., Harris, J. A., & McCarthy, J. M. (1997). Environmental predictors of personality differences: A twin and sibling study. *Journal of Personality and Social Psychology, 72*, 177–183.

Verweij, K. J. H., Vinkhuyzen, A. A. E., Benyamin, B., Lynskey, M. T., Quaye, L., Agrawal, A., . . . Heath, A. C. (2013). The genetic aetiology of cannabis use initiation: A meta-analysis of genome-wide association studies and a SNP-based heritability estimation. *Addiction Biology, 18*(5), 846–850.

Verweij, K. J. H., Yang, J., Lahti, J., Veijola, J., Hintsanen, M., Pulkki-Råback, L., . . . Widen, E. (2012). Maintenance of genetic variation in human personality: Testing evolutionary models by estimating heritability due to common causal variants and investigating the effect of distant inbreeding. *Evolution, 66*(10), 3238–3251.

Verweij, K. J. H., Zietsch, B. P., Lynskey, M. T., Medland, S. E., Neale, M. C., Martin, N. G., . . . Vink, J. M. (2010). Genetic and environmental influences on cannabis use initiation and problematic use: A meta-analysis of twin studies. *Addiction, 105*(3), 417–430. doi:10.1111/j.1360-0443.2009.02831.x

Viding, E. (2004). Annotation: Understanding the development of psychopathy. *Journal of Child Psychology and Psychiatry, 45*, 1329–1337.

Viding, E., Blair, R. J. R., Moffitt, T. E., & Plomin, R. (2005). Evidence for substantial genetic risk for psychopathy in 7-year-olds. *Journal of Child Psychology and Psychiatry, 46*(6), 592–597. doi:10.1111/j.1469-7610.2004.00393.x

Viding, E., Fontaine, N., Oliver, B., & Plomin, R. (2009). Negative parental discipline, conduct problems and callous-unemotional traits: A monozygotic twin differences study. *British Journal of Psychiatry, 195*, 414–419. doi:10.1192/bjp.bp.108.061192

Viding, E., & McCrory, E. J. (2012). Genetic and neurocognitive contributions to the development of psychopathy. *Development and Psychopathology, 124*(Special Issue 3), 969–983.

Villafuerte, S., & Burmeister, M. (2003). Untangling genetic networks of panic, phobia, fear and anxiety. *Genome Biology, 4*(8), 224.

Vinck, W. J., Fagard, R. H., Loos, R., & Vlietinck, R. (2001). The impact of genetic and environmental influences on blood pressure variance across age-groups. *Journal of Hypertension, 19*(6), 1007–1013.

Vink, J., Willemsen, G., & Boomsma, D. (2005). Heritability of smoking initiation and nicotine dependence. *Behavior Genetics, 35*(4), 397–406. doi:10.1007/s10519-004-1327-8

Vink, J. M., & Boomsma, D. I. (2011). Interplay between heritability of smoking and environmental conditions? A comparison of two birth cohorts. *BMC Public Health, 11*(1), 316.

Vinkhuyzen, A. A. E., Pedersen, N. L., Yang, J., Lee, S. H., Magnusson, P. K. E., Iacono, W. G., . . . Wray, N. R. (2012a). Common SNPs explain some of the variation in the personality dimensions of neuroticism and extraversion. *Translational Psychiatry, 2*, e102. doi:10.1038/tp.2012.27

Vinkhuyzen, A. A. E., van der Sluis, S., Boomsma, D. I., de Geus, E. J. C., & Posthuma, D. (2010). Individual differences in processing speed and working memory speed as assessed with the Sternberg Memory Scanning Task. *Behavior Genetics, 40*(3), 315–326. doi:10.1007/s10519-009-9315-7

Vinkhuyzen, A. A. E., van der Sluis, S., Maes, H. H. M., & Posthuma, D. (2012b). Reconsidering the heritability of intelligence in adulthood: Taking assortative mating and cultural transmission into account. *Behavior Genetics, 42*(2), 187–198.

Visser, S. N., Danielson, M. L., Bitsko, R. H., Holbrook, J. R., Kogan, M. D., Ghandour, R. M., ... Blumberg, S. J. (2014). Trends in the parent-report of health care provider-diagnosed and medicated attention-deficit/hyperactivity disorder: United States, 2003–2011. *Journal of the American Academy of Child & Adolescent Psychiatry, 53*(1), 34–46.

Vitaro, F., Brendgen, M., Boivin, M., Cantin, S., Dionne, G., Tremblay, R. E., ... Perusse, D. (2011). A monozygotic twin difference study of friends' aggression and children's adjustment problems. *Child Development, 82*(2), 617–632. doi:10.1111/j.1467-8624.2010.01570.x

von Gontard, A., Heron, J., & Joinson, C. (2011). Family history of nocturnal enuresis and urinary incontinence: Results from a large epidemiological study. *Journal of Urology, 185*(6), 2303–2306. doi:10.1016/j.juro.2011.02.040

von Gontard, A., Schaumburg, H., Hollmann, E., Eiberg, H., & Rittig, S. (2001). The genetics of enuresis: A review. *Journal of Urology, 166*(6), 2438–2443.

von Knorring, A. L., Cloninger, C. R., Bohman, M., & Sigvardsson, S. (1983). An adoption study of depressive disorders and substance abuse. *Archives of General Psychiatry, 40*, 943–950.

von Linne, K. (1735). Systema naturae. *Regnum Animale, L. Salvii, Holminae.*

vonHoldt, B. M., Pollinger, J. P., Lohmueller, K. E., Han, E., Parker, H. G., Quignon, P., ... Wayne, R. K. (2010). Genome-wide SNP and haplotype analyses reveal a rich history underlying dog domestication. *Nature, 464*(7290), 898–902. doi:10.1038/nature08837

Vrieze, S. I., Feng, S., Miller, M. B., Hicks, B. M., Pankratz, N., Abecasis, G. R., ... McGue, M. (2014). Rare nonsynonymous exonic variants in addiction and behavioral disinhibition. *Biological Psychiatry, 75*(10), 783–789.

Vrieze, S. I., McGue, M., Miller, M. B., Hicks, B. M., & Iacono, W. G. (2013). Three mutually informative ways to understand the genetic relationships among behavioral disinhibition, alcohol use, drug use, nicotine use/dependence, and their co-occurrence: Twin biometry, GCTA, and genome-wide scoring. *Behavior Genetics, 43*(2), 97–107.

Vrshek-Schallhorn, S., Mineka, S., Zinbarg, R. E., Craske, M. G., Griffith, J. W., Sutton, J., ... Adam, E. K. (2013). Refining the candidate environment interpersonal stress, the serotonin transporter polymorphism, and gene-environment interactions in major depression. *Clinical Psychological Science, 2*(3), 235–248. doi:10.1177/2167702613499329

Vukasović, T., & Bratko, D. (2015). Heritability of personality: A meta-analysis of behavior genetic studies. *Psychological Bulletin, 141*(4), 769–785.

Waddell, S., & Quinn, W. G. (2001). What can we teach *Drosophila?* What can they teach us? *Trends in Genetics, 17*(12), 719–726.

Wade, C. H., & Wilfond, B. S. (2006). Ethical and clinical practice considerations for genetic counselors related to direct-to-consumer marketing of genetic tests. *American Journal of Medical Genetics. Part C, Seminars in Medical Genetics, 142*(4), 284–292.

Wade, T. D., Treloar, S. A., Heath, A. C., & Martin, N. G. (2009). An examination of the overlap between genetic and environmental risk factors for intentional weight loss and overeating. *International Journal of Eating Disorders, 42*(6), 492–497. doi:10.1002/eat.20668

Wagner, A. J., Mitchell, M. E., & Tomita-Mitchell, A. (2014). Use of cell-free fetal DNA in maternal plasma for noninvasive prenatal screening. *Clinics in Perinatology, 41*(4), 957–966.

Wahlsten, D. (1999). Single-gene influences on brain and behavior. *Annual Review of Psychology, 50*, 599–624.

Wahlsten, D., Bachmanov, A., Finn, D. A., & Crabbe, J. C. (2006). Stability of inbred mouse strain differences in behavior and brain size between laboratories and across decades. *Proceedings of the National Academy of Sciences of the United States of America, 103*(44), 16364–16369.

Wahlsten, D., Metten, P., Phillips, T. J., Boehm, S. L., Burkhart-Kasch, S., Dorow, J., ... Crabbe, J. C. (2003). Different data from different labs: Lessons from studies of gene-environment interaction. *Journal of Neurobiology, 54*(1), 283–311.

Wainwright, M. A., Wright, M. J., Luciano, M., Geffen, G. M., & Martin, N. G. (2005). Multivariate genetic analysis of academic skills of the Queensland core skills test and IQ highlight the importance of genetic g. *Twin Research and Human Genetics, 8*(6), 602–608.

Walker, F. O. (2007). Huntington's disease. *The Lancet, 369*(9557), 218–228. doi:http://dx.doi.org/10.1016/S0140-6736(07)60111-1

Walker, S., & Plomin, R. (2005). The nature–nurture question: Teachers' perceptions of how genes and the environment influence educationally relevant behaviour. *Educational Psychology, 25*(5), 509–516. doi:10.1080/01443410500046697

Walker, S. O., & Plomin, R. (2006). Nature, nurture, and perceptions of the classroom environment as they relate to teacher assessed academic achievement: A twin study of 9-year-olds. *Educational Psychology, 26*, 541–561. doi:10.1080/01443410500342500

Wallace, G. L., Eric, S. J., Lenroot, R., Viding, E., Ordaz, S., Rosenthal, M. A., . . . Giedd, J. N. (2006). A pediatric twin study of brain morphometry. *Journal of Child Psychology and Psychiatry, 47*(10), 987–993.

Wallace, J. G., Larsson, S. J., & Buckler, E. S. (2014). Entering the second century of maize quantitative genetics. *Heredity, 112*(1), 30–38.

Waller, K., Kujala, U. M., Kaprio, J., Koskenvuo, M., & Rantanen, T. (2010). Effect of physical activity on health in twins: A 30-yr longitudinal study. *Medicine and Science in Sports and Exercise, 42*(4), 658–664. doi:10.1249/MSS.0b013e3181bdeea3

Waller, N. G., & Shaver, P. R. (1994). The importance of nongenetic influence on romantic love styles: A twin-family study. *Psychological Science, 5,* 268–274.

Walsh, C. M., Zainal, N. Z., Middleton, S. J., & Paykel, E. S. (2001). A family history study of chronic fatigue syndrome. *Psychiatric Genetics, 11*(3), 123–128.

Wang, Z., Gerstein, M., & Snyder, M. (2009). RNA-Seq: A revolutionary tool for transcriptomics. *Nature Reviews Genetics, 10*(1), 57–63. doi:10.1038/nrg2484

Ward, M. E., McMahon, G., St Pourcain, B., Evans, D. M., Rietveld, C. A., Benjamin, D. J., . . . Timpson, N. J. (2014). Genetic variation associated with differential educational attainment in adults has anticipated associations with school performance in children. *PLoS ONE, 9*(7), e100248.

Ward, M. J., Vaughn, B. E., & Robb, M. D. (1988). Social-emotional adaptation and infant-mother attachment in siblings: Role of the mother in cross-sibling consistency. *Child Development, 59,* 643–651.

Wardle, J., Carnell, S., Haworth, C. M. A., Farooqi, I. S., O'Rahilly, S., & Plomin, R. (2008a). Obesity associated genetic variation in FTO is associated with diminished satiety. *The Journal of Clinical Endocrinology & Metabolism, 93*(9), 3640–3643. doi:10.1210/jc.2008-0472

Wardle, J., Carnell, S., Haworth, C. M. A., & Plomin, R. (2008b). Evidence for a strong genetic influence on childhood adiposity despite the force of the obesogenic environment. *American Journal of Clinical Nutrition, 87*(2), 398–404.

Wardle, J., Llewellyn, C., Sanderson, S., & Plomin, R. (2009). The FTO gene and measured food intake in children. *International Journal of Obesity, 33*(1), 42–45.

Waszczuk, M. A., Zavos, H. M. S., Gregory, A. M., & Eley, T. C. (2014). The phenotypic and genetic structure of depression and anxiety disorder symptoms in childhood, adolescence, and young adulthood. *JAMA Psychiatry, 71*(8), 905–916.

Watson, J. B. (1930). *Behaviorism.* New York: Norton.

Watson, J. D., & Crick, F. H. C. (1953). Genetical implications of the structure of deoxyribonucleic acid. *Nature, 171*(4361), 964–967. doi:10.1038/171964b0

Wayne, R., & vonHoldt, B. (2012). Evolutionary genomics of dog domestication. *Mammalian Genome, 23.*

Weiner, J. (1994). *The beak of the finch.* New York: Vintage Books.

Weiner, J. (1999). *Time, love and memory: A great biologist and his quest for the origins of behavior.* New York: Alfred A. Knopf.

Weir, B. S., Anderson, A. D., & Hepler, A. B. (2006). Genetic relatedness analysis: Modern data and new challenges. *Nature Reviews Genetics, 7*(10), 771–780.

Weiss, D. S., Marmar, C. R., Schlenger, W. E., Fairbank, J. A., Jordan, B. K., Hough, R. L., & Kulka, R. A. (1992). The prevalence of lifetime and partial posttraumatic stress disorder in Vietnam theater veterans. *Journal of Traumatic Stress, 5,* 365–376.

Weiss, P. (1982). *Psychogenetik: Humangenetik in psychologie and psychiatrie.* Jena: Gustav Fisher.

Welter, D., MacArthur, J., Morales, J., Burdett, T., Hall, P., Junkins, H., . . . Hindorff, L. (2014). The NHGRI GWAS Catalog, a curated resource of SNP-trait associations. *Nucleic Acids Research, 42*(D1), D1001–D1006.

Wender, P. H., Kety, S. S., Rosenthal, D., Schulsinger, F., Ortmann, J., & Lunde, I. (1986). Psychiatric disorders in the biological and adoptive families of adopted individuals with affective disorders. *Archives of General Psychiatry, 43,* 923–929.

Wender, P. H., Rosenthal, D., Kety, S. S., Schulsinger, F., & Welner, J. (1974). Crossfostering: A research strategy for clarifying the role of genetic and experimental factors in the etiology of schizophrenia. *Archives of General Psychiatry, 30,* 121–128

Wesseling, H., Chan, M. K., Tsang, T. M., Ernst, A., Peters, F., Guest, P. C., . . . Bahn, S. (2013). A combined metabonomic and proteomic approach identifies frontal cortex changes in a chronic phencyclidine rat model in relation to human schizophrenia brain pathology. *Neuropsychopharmacology, 38*(12), 2532–2544. doi:10.1038/npp.2013.160

Westerfield, L., Darilek, S., & van den Veyver, I. B. (2014). Counseling challenges with variants of uncertain significance and incidental findings in prenatal genetic screening and diagnosis. *Journal of Clinical Medicine, 3*(3), 1018–1032.

Wheeler, H. E., & Kim, S. K. (2011). Genetics and genomics of human ageing. *Philosophical Transactions, The Royal Society of London, B,*

Biological Science, 366(1561), 43–50. doi:10.1098/rstb.2010.0259

Whitaker, K. L., Jarvis, M. J., Beeken, R. J., Boniface, D., & Wardle, J. (2010). Comparing maternal and paternal intergenerational transmission of obesity risk in a large population-based sample. *The American Journal of Clinical Nutrition, 91*(6), 1560–1567.

White, J. K., Gerdin, A.-K., Karp, N. A., Ryder, E., Buljan, M., Bussell, J. N., . . . Podrini, C. (2013). Genome-wide generation and systematic phenotyping of knockout mice reveals new roles for many genes. *Cell, 154*(2), 452–464.

Widiker, S., Kaerst, S., Wagener, A., & Brockmann, G. A. (2010). High-fat diet leads to a decreased methylation of the Mc4r gene in the obese BFMI and the lean B6 mouse lines. *Journal of Applied Genetics, 51*(2), 193–197. doi:10.1007/bf03195727

Wilhelm, M., Schlegl, J., Hahne, H., Gholami, A. M., Lieberenz, M., Savitski, M. M., . . . Kuster, B. (2014). Mass-spectrometry-based draft of the human proteome. *Nature, 509*(7502), 582–587. doi:10.1038/nature13319

Wilicox, B. J., Donlon, T. A., He, Q., Chen, R., Grove, J. S., Yano, K., . . . Curb, J. D. (2008). FOXO3A genotype is strongly associated with human longevity. *Proceedings of the National Academy of Sciences of the United States of America, 105*(37), 13987–13992. doi:10.1073/pnas.0801030105

Willcutt, E. G., Pennington, B. F., Duncan, L., Smith, S. D., Keenan, J. M., Wadsworth, S., . . . Olson, R. K. (2010). Understanding the complex etiologies of developmental disorders: Behavioral and molecular genetic approaches. *Journal of Developmental and Behavioral Pediatrics, 31*(7), 533–544. doi:10.1097/DBP.0b013e3181ef42a1

Willemsen, M. H., & Kleefstra, T. (2014). Making headway with genetic diagnostics of intellectual disabilities. *Clinical Genetics, 85*(2), 101–110.

Willemsen, R., Levenga, J., & Oostra, B. A. (2011). CGG repeat in the FMR1 gene: Size matters. *Clinical Genetics, 80*(3), 214–225. doi:10.1111/j.1399-0004.2011.01723.x

Williams, C. A., Driscoll, D. J., & Dagli, A. I. (2010). Clinical and genetic aspects of Angelman syndrome. *Genetics in Medicine, 12*(7), 385–395. doi:10.1097/GIM.0b013e3181def138

Williams, N. M., Franke, B., Mick, E., Anney, R. J. L., Freitag, C. M., Gill, M., . . . Faraone, S. V. (2012). Genome-wide analysis of copy number variants in attention deficit hyperactivity disorder: The role of rare variants and duplications at 15q13.3. *American Journal of Psychiatry, 169*(2), 195–204. doi:10.1176/appi.ajp.2011.11060822

Williams, R. W. (2006). Expression genetics and the phenotype revolution. *Mammalian Genome, 17*(6), 496–502.

Wilson, R. K. (1999). How the worm was won: The *C.elegans* genome sequencing project. *Trends in Genetics, 15*, 51–58.

Wilson, R. S. (1983). The Louisville Twin Study: Developmental synchronies in behavior. *Child Development, 54*, 298–316.

Wilson, R. S., & Matheny, A. P., Jr. (1986). Behavior genetics research in infant temperament: The Louisiville Twin Study. In R. Plomin & J. F. Dunn (Eds.), *The study of temperament: Changes, continuities, and challenges* (pp. 81–97). Hillsdale, NJ: Erlbaum.

Winterer, G., & Goldman, D. (2003). Genetics of human prefrontal function. *Brain Research Reviews, 43*(1), 134–163.

Wolf, A. P., & Durham, W. H. (2005). *Inbreeding, incest, and the incest taboo: The state of knowledge at the turn of the century.* Stanford University Press.

Wooldridge, A. (1994). *Measuring the mind: Education and psychology in England, c. 1860–c. 1990.* Cambridge: Cambridge University Press.

World Health Organization. (2011). *WHO report on the global tobacco epidemic, 2011: Warning about the dangers of tobacco.* Geneva: World Health Organization.

WormBase. Retrieved from http://www.wormbase.org/

Wray, N. R., Lee, S. H., Mehta, D., Vinkhuyzen, A. A. E., Dudbridge, F., & Middeldorp, C. M. (2014). Research review: Polygenic methods and their application to psychiatric traits. *Journal of Child Psychology and Psychiatry, 55*(10), 1068–1087. doi:10.1111/jcpp.12295

Wright, S. (1921). Systems of mating. *Genetics, 6*, 111–178.

Wright, W. (1998). *Born that way: Genes, behavior, personality.* New York: Alfred A. Knopf.

Wu, T., Snieder, H., & de Geus, E. (2010). Genetic influences on cardiovascular stress reactivity. *Neuroscience and Biobehavioral Reviews, 35*(1), 58–68. doi:10.1016/j.neubiorev.2009.12.001

Xu, L.-M., Li, J.-R., Huang, Y., Zhao, M., Tang, X., & Wei, L. (2012). AutismKB: An evidence-based knowledgebase of autism genetics. *Nucleic Acids Research, 40*(D1), D1016–D1022. doi:10.1093/nar/gkr1145

Yalcin, B., Nicod, J., Bhomra, A., Davidson, S., Cleak, J., Farinelli, L., . . . Flint, J. (2010). Commercially available outbred mice for genome-wide association studies. *PLoS Genetics, 6*(9), e1001085. doi:10.1371/journal.pgen.1001085

Yalcin, B., Willis-Owen, S. A., Fullerton, J., Meesaq, A., Deacon, R. M., Rawlins, J. N., ... Mott, R. (2004). Genetic dissection of a behavioral quantitative trait locus shows that Rgs2 modulates anxiety in mice. *Nature Genetics, 36*(11), 1197–1202.

Yamasaki, C., Koyanagi, K. O., Fujii, Y., Itoh, T., Barrero, R., Tamura, T., ... Gojobori, T. (2005). Investigation of protein functions through datamining on integrated human transcriptome database, H-Invitational database (H-InvDB). *Gene, 364*, 99–107.

Yang, C., Li, C., Kranzler, H. R., Farrer, L. A., Zhao, H., & Gelernter, J. (2014). Exploring the genetic architecture of alcohol dependence in African-Americans via analysis of a genomewide set of common variants. *Human Genetics, 133*(5), 617–624.

Yang, I. V., & Schwartz, D. A. (2012). Epigenetic mechanisms and the development of asthma. *Journal of Allergy and Clinical Immunology, 130*(6), 1243–1255. doi:http://dx.doi.org/10.1016/j.jaci.2012.07.052

Yang, J., Lee, S. H., Goddard, M. E., & Visscher, P. M. (2011a). GCTA: A tool for genome-wide complex trait analysis. *American Journal of Human Genetics, 88*(1), 76–82. doi:10.1016/j.ajhg.2010.11.011

Yang, J., Manolio, T. A., Pasquale, L. R., Boerwinkle, E., Caporaso, N., Cunningham, J. M., ... Visscher, P. M. (2011b). Genome partitioning of genetic variation for complex traits using common SNPs. *Nature Genetics, 43*(6), 519–525. doi:10.1038/ng.823

Yang, L., Neale, B. M., Liu, L., Lee, S. H., Wray, N. R., Ji, N., ... & Faraone, S. V. (2013). Polygenic transmission and complex neuro developmental network for attention deficit hyperactivity disorder: Genome-wide association study of both common and rare variants. *American Journal of Medical Genetics Part B: Neuropsychiatric Genetics, 162*(5), 419–430.

Yeo, G. S. H., Farooqi, I. S., Aminian, S., Halsall, D. J., Stanhope, R. C., & O'Rahilly, S. (1998). A frameshift mutation in MC4R associated with dominantly inherited human obesity. *Nature Genetics, 20*(2), 111–112. doi:10.1038/2404

Yin, H., Kanasty, R. L., Eltoukhy, A. A., Vegas, A. J., Dorkin, J. R., & Anderson, D. G. (2014). Non-viral vectors for gene-based therapy. *Nature Reviews Genetics, 15*(8), 541–555.

Yin, J. C. P., Del Vecchio, M., Zhou, H., & Tully, T. (1995). CRAB as a memory modulator: Induced expression of a dCREB2 activator isoform enhances long-term memory in *Drosophila. Cell, 8*, 107–115.

Young, J. P. R., Fenton, G. W., & Lader, M. H. (1971). The inheritance of neurotic traits: A twin study of the Middlesex Hospital Questionnaire. *British Journal of Psychiatry, 119*, 393–398.

Young, S. E., Friedman, N. P., Miyake, A., Willcutt, E. G., Corley, R. P., Haberstick, B. C., & Hewitt, J. K. (2009). Behavioral disinhibition: Liability for externalizing spectrum disorders and its genetic and environmental relation to response inhibition across adolescence. *Journal of Abnormal Psychology, 118*(1), 117–130. doi:10.1037/a0014657

Young, S. E., Rhee, S. H., Stallings, M. C., Corley, R. P., & Hewitt, J. K. (2006). Genetic and environmental vulnerabilities underlying adolescent substance use and problem use: General or specific? *Behavior Genetics, 36*(4), 603–615.

Young-Wolff, K. C., Enoch, M.-A., & Prescott, C. A. (2011). The influence of gene-environment interactions on alcohol consumption and alcohol use disorders: A comprehensive review. *Clinical Psychological Review, 31*(5), 800–816. doi:10.1016/j.cpr.2011.03.005

Yuferov, V., Levran, O., Proudnikov, D., Nielsen, D. A., & Kreek, M. J. (2010). Search for genetic markers and functional variants involved in the development of opiate and cocaine addiction and treatment. In G. R. Uhl (Ed.), *Addiction reviews 2* (Vol. 1187, pp. 184–207).

Zachar, P., & First, M. B. (2015). Transitioning to a dimensional model of personality disorder in DSM 5.1 and beyond. *Current Opinion in Psychiatry, 28*(1), 66–72.

Zammit, S., Hamshere, M., Dwyer, S., Georgiva, L., Timpson, N., Moskvina, V., ... Jones, P. (2014). A population-based study of genetic variation and psychotic experiences in adolescents. *Schizophrenia Bulletin, 40*(6), 1254–1262.

Zarrei, M., MacDonald, J. R., Merico, D., & Scherer, S. W. (2015). A copy number variation map of the human genome. *Nature Reviews Genetics, 16*(3), 172–183. doi:10.1038/nrg3871

Zavos, H. M. S., Freeman, D., Haworth, C. M. A., McGuire, P., Plomin, R., Cardno, A. G., & Ronald, A. (2014). Consistent etiology of severe, frequent psychotic experiences and milder, less frequent manifestations: A twin study of specific psychotic experiences in adolescence. *JAMA Psychiatry, 71*(9), 1049–1057.

Zeggini, E., Weedon, M. N., Lindgren, C. M., Frayling, T. M., Elliott, K. S., Lango, H., ... Hattersley, A. T. (2007). Replication of genome-wide association signals in UK samples reveals risk loci for type 2 diabetes. *Science, 316*(5829), 1336–1341. doi:10.1126/science.1142364

Zhang, C., & Pierce, B. L. (2014). Genetic susceptibility to accelerated cognitive decline in the US Health and Retirement Study. *Neurobiological Aging, 35*(6), 1512–e1511.

Zhang, L., Chang, S., Li, Z., Zhang, K., Du, Y., Ott, J., & Wang, J. (2012). ADHDgene: A genetic database for attention deficit hyperactivity disorder. *Nucleic Acids Research, 40*(D1), D1003–D1009. doi:10.1093/nar/gkr992

Zhang, T. Y., & Meaney, M. J. (2010). Epigenetics and the environmental regulation of the genome and its function. *Annual Review of Psychology, 61,* 439–466.

Zhang, X. (2014). Exome sequencing greatly expedites the progressive research of Mendelian diseases. *Frontiers of Medicine, 8*(1), 42–57. doi:10.1007/s11684-014-0303-9

Zhang, Y., Brownstein, A. J., Buonora, M., Niikura, K., Ho, A., Correa da Rosa, J., . . . Ott, J. (2015). Self administration of oxycodone alters synaptic plasticity gene expression in the hippocampus differentially in male adolescent and adult mice. *Neuroscience, 285,* 34–46. doi:http://dx.doi.org/10.1016/j.neuroscience.2014.11.013

Zhang, Y., Proenca, R., Maffei, M., Barone, M., Leopold, L., & Friedman, J. M. (1994). Positional cloning of the mouse obese gene and its human homologue. *Nature, 372,* 425–432.

Zheng, J., Xiao, X., Zhang, Q., & Yu, M. (2014). DNA methylation: The pivotal interaction between early-life nutrition and glucose metabolism in later life. *British Journal of Nutrition, 112*(11), 1850-1857.

Zhong, S., Chew, S. H., Set, E., Zhang, J., Xue, H., Sham, P. C., . . . Israel, S. (2009). The heritability of attitude toward economic risk. *Twin Research and Human Genetics, 12*(1), 103–107.

Zhou, K., Dempfle, A., Arcos-Burgos, M., Bakker, S. C., Banaschewski, T., Biederman, J., . . . Asherson, P. (2008). Meta-analysis of genome-wide linkage scans of attention deficit hyperactivity disorder. *American Journal of Medical Genetics Part B-Neuropsychiatric Genetics, 147B*(8), 1392–1398. doi:10.1002/ajmg.b.30878

Zhou, Z., Enoch, M.-A., & Goldman, D. (2014). Gene expression in the addicted brain. In H. Robert & M. Shannon (Eds.), *International review of neurobiology* (Vol. 116, pp. 251–273). New York: Academic Press.

Zigman, W. B. (2013). Atypical aging in Down syndrome. *Developmental Disabilities Research Reviews, 18*(1), 51–67.

Zombeck, J. A., DeYoung, E. K., Brzezinska, W. J., & Rhodes, J. S. (2011). Selective breeding for increased home cage physical activity in collaborative Cross and Hsd:ICR mice. *Behavior Genetics, 41*(4), 571–582. doi:10.1007/s10519-010-9425-2

Zucker, R. A. (2006). The developmental behavior genetics of drug involvement: Overview and comments. *Behavior Genetics, 36*(4), 616–625.

Zucker, R. A., Heitzeg, M. M., & Nigg, J. T. (2011). Parsing the undercontrol-disinhibition pathway to substance use disorders: A Multilevel developmental problem. *Child Development Perspectives, 5*(4), 248–255. doi:10.1111/j.1750-8606.2011.00172.x

Zwijnenburg, P. J. G., Meijers-Heijboer, H., & Boomsma, D. I. (2010). Identical but not the same: The value of discordant monozygotic twins in genetic research. *American Journal of Medical Genetics Part B: Neuropsychiatric Genetics, 153B*(6), 1134–1149. doi:10.1002/ajmg.b.31091

Zyphur, M. J., Narayanan, J., Arvey, R. D., & Alexander, G. J. (2009). The genetics of economic risk preferences. *Journal of Behavioral Decision Making, 22*(4), 367–377. doi:10.1002/bdm.643

Name Index

Subject Index

Note: Page numbers followed by f, t, and b indicate figures, tables, and boxes, respectively.